Disrupting Dark Networks

This is the first book in which counterinsurgency theory and social network analysis are coupled. *Disrupting Dark Networks* focuses on how social network analysis can be used to craft strategies to track, destabilize, and disrupt covert and illegal networks. The book begins with an overview of the key terms and assumptions of social network analysis and various counterinsurgency strategies. The next several chapters introduce readers to algorithms and metrics commonly used by social network analysts. These chapters include worked examples from four different social network analysis software packages (UCINET, NetDraw, Pajek, and ORA) using standard network datasets. Moreover, data from an actual terrorist network serves as a running example throughout the book. *Disrupting Dark Networks* concludes by considering the ethics of and various ways that social network analysis can inform counterinsurgency strategizing. By contextualizing these methods in a larger counterinsurgency framework, this book offers scholars and analysts an array of approaches for disrupting dark networks.

Sean F. Everton is Assistant Professor in the Department of Defense Analysis, as well as the Co-Director of the CORE Lab, at the Naval Postgraduate School.

Structural Analysis in the Social Sciences

Mark Granovetter, editor

The series Structural Analysis in the Social Sciences presents studies that analyze social behavior and institutions by reference to relations among such concrete social entities as persons, organizations, and nations. Relational analysis contrasts on the one hand with reductionist methodological individualism and on the other with macro-level determinism, whether based on technology, material conditions, economic conflict, adaptive evolution, or functional imperatives. In this more intellectually flexible structural middle ground, analysts situate actors and their relations in a variety of contexts. Since the series began in 1987, its authors have variously focused on small groups, history, culture, politics, kinship, aesthetics, economics, and complex organizations, creatively theorizing how these shape and in turn are shaped by social relations. Their style and methods have ranged widely, from intense, long-term ethnographic observation to highly abstract mathematical models. Their disciplinary affiliations have included history, anthropology, sociology, political science, business, economics, mathematics, and computer science. Some have made explicit use of social network analysis, including many of the cutting-edge and standard works of that approach, whereas others have kept formal analysis in the background and used "networks" as a fruitful orienting metaphor. All have in common a sophisticated and revealing approach that forcefully illuminates our complex social world.

Other Books in the Series

1. Mark S. Mizruchi and Michael Schwartz, eds., *Intercorporate Relations: The Structural Analysis of Business*
2. Barry Wellman and S. D. Berkowitz, eds., *Social Structures: A Network Approach*
3. Ronald L. Brieger, ed., *Social Mobility and Social Structure*
4. David Knoke, *Political Networks: The Structural Perspective*
5. John L. Campbell, J. Rogers Hollingsworth, and Leon N. Lindberg, eds., *Governance of the American Economy*
6. Kyriakos Kontopoulos, *The Logics of Social Structure*
7. Philippa Pattison, *Algebraic Models for Social Structure*
8. Stanley Wasserman and Katherine Faust, *Social Network Analysis: Methods and Applications*
9. Gary Herrigel, *Industrial Constructions: The Sources of German Industrial Power*
10. Philippe Bourgois, *In Search of Respect: Selling Crack in El Barrio*
11. Per Hage and Frank Harary, *Island Networks: Communication, Kinship, and Classification Structures in Oceana*
12. Thomas Schweitzer and Douglas R. White, eds., *Kinship, Networks, and Exchange*
13. Noah E. Friedkin, *A Structural Theory of Social Influence*
14. David Wank, *Commodifying Communism: Business, Trust, and Politics in a Chinese City*
15. Rebecca Adams and Graham Allan, *Placing Friendship in Context*

(*continued after the Index*)

Disrupting Dark Networks

SEAN F. EVERTON

U.S. Naval Postgraduate School, Monterey, CA

CAMBRIDGE
UNIVERSITY PRESS

CAMBRIDGE UNIVERSITY PRESS
Cambridge, New York, Melbourne, Madrid, Cape Town,
Singapore, São Paulo, Delhi, Mexico City

Cambridge University Press
32 Avenue of the Americas, New York, NY 10013-2473, USA

www.cambridge.org
Information on this title: www.cambridge.org/9781107606685

First published 2012

Printed in the United States of America

A catalog record for this publication is available from the British Library.

Library of Congress Cataloging in Publication data

Everton, Sean F.
Disrupting dark networks / Sean F. Everton.
   p.   cm. – (Structural analysis in the social sciences)
Includes bibliographical references and index.
ISBN 978-1-107-02259-1 (hardback) – ISBN 978-1-107-60668-5 (pbk.)
1. Social networks – Research.   2. Social sciences – Network analysis.   I. Title.
HM711.E94   2012
302.30285–dc23   2012016085

ISBN 978-1-107-02259-1 Hardback
ISBN 978-1-107-60668-5 Paperback

Additional resources for this publication at https://sites.google.com/site/sfeverton

To Deanne, Brendan, and Tara

Contents

Figures   *page* xiii
Tables   xxiii
Preface   xxv
Acknowledgments   xxxv

PART I. INTRODUCTION

1 Social Network Analysis: An Introduction   3
   1.1 Introduction   3
   1.2 Misconceptions and Differences   6
   1.3 Basic Terms and Concepts   8
   1.4 Assumptions   14
   1.5 Social Networks, Human Agency, and Culture   29
   1.6 Summary and Conclusion   31

2 Strategic Options for Disrupting Dark Networks   32
   2.1 Introduction   32
   2.2 Strategic Options for Disrupting Dark Networks   33
   2.3 Crafting Strategies with Social Network Analysis   38
   2.4 Summary and Conclusion   44

PART II. SOCIAL NETWORK ANALYSIS: TECHNIQUES

3 Getting Started with UCINET, NetDraw, Pajek, and ORA   49
   3.1 Introduction   49
   3.2 UCINET   49
   3.3 NetDraw   55
   3.4 Pajek   62
   3.5 ORA (Organizational Risk Analyzer)   69
   3.6 Summary and Conclusion   74

4 Gathering, Recording, and Manipulating Social Networks   76
   4.1 Introduction   76

4.2   Boundary Specification   77
4.3   Ego Networks and Complete Networks   80
4.4   Types of Social Network Data   82
4.5   Collecting Social Network Data   87
4.6   Recording Social Network Data   91
4.7   Deriving One-Mode Networks from Two-Mode
      Networks   102
4.8   Combining, Aggregating, and Parsing Networks   107
4.9   Extracting and Simplifying Networks   122
4.10 Summary and Conclusion   132

PART III. SOCIAL NETWORK ANALYSIS: METRICS

5 Network Topography   135
   5.1 Introduction   135
   5.2 Some Basic Topographical Metrics   137
   5.3 The Provincial-Cosmopolitan Dimension   138
   5.4 The Hierarchical-Heterarchical Dimension   141
   5.5 Estimating Network Topographical Metrics   143
   5.6 Summary and Conclusion   166

6 Cohesion and Clustering   170
   6.1 Introduction   170
   6.2 Components   171
   6.3 Cores   182
   6.4 Factions   187
   6.5 Newman Groups   194
   6.6 Summary and Conclusion   204

7 Centrality, Power, and Prestige   206
   7.1 Introduction   206
   7.2 Centrality and Power   211
   7.3 Centrality and Prestige   240
   7.4 Summary and Conclusion   251

8 Brokers, Bridges, and Structural Holes   253
   8.1 Introduction   253
   8.2 Structural Holes   254
   8.3 Bridges, Bi-Component, and Cutpoints   264
   8.4 Key Players   271
   8.5 Affiliations and Brokerage   277
   8.6 Bridges and Network Flow   282
   8.7 Summary and Conclusion   284

9 Positions, Roles, and Blockmodels   286
   9.1 Introduction   286
   9.2 Structural Equivalence   287

9.3   Automorphic Equivalence   289
9.4   Regular Equivalence   292
9.5   Blockmodeling in UCINET, Pajek, and ORA   295
9.6   Summary and Conclusion   315

PART IV. SOCIAL NETWORK ANALYSIS: ADVANCES

10 Dynamic Analyses of Dark Networks   319
    10.1   Introduction   319
    10.2   The Longitudinal Analysis of Dark Networks   319
    10.3   Fusing Geospatial and Social Network Data   333
    10.4   Summary and Conclusion   341

11 Statistical Models for Dark Networks   343
    11.1   Introduction   343
    11.2   Statistical Models for Social Network Data   348
    11.3   Statistical Models in UCINET and ORA   349
    11.4   Summary and Conclusion   360

PART V. CONCLUSION

12 The Promise and Limits of Social Network Analysis   365
    12.1   Introduction   365
    12.2   The Promise and Limits of Social Network Analysis   366
    12.3   Disrupting Dark Networks Justly   367
    12.4   Summary and Conclusion   383

    Appendix 1: The Noordin Top Terrorist Network   385
    Appendix 2: Glossary of Terms   397
    Appendix 3: Multidimensional Scaling with UCINET   404
    Appendix 4: The Just War Tradition   417

    References   421
    Index   445

Figures

1.1	Illustrative Link Analysis Diagram	*page* 6
1.2	Illustrative SNA Diagrams	7
1.3	Hypothetical Social Network	9
1.4	Solomon Asch's Conformity Experiment	16
1.5	Strong and Weak Ties	20
1.6	Granovetter's Forbidden Triad	20
2.1	Marriage Ties among Renaissance Florentine Families	41
3.1	UCINET Interface	51
3.2	UCINET Display Dialog Box	52
3.3	UCINET Output Log	53
3.4	UCINET Helper Application Dialog Box	55
3.5	NetDraw Home Screen	56
3.6	NetDraw Display of Krackhardt High-Tech Data	57
3.7	Node Size Dialog Box	61
3.8	NetDraw Map of Krackhardt Data Size Reflecting Tenure	62
3.9	Pajek Net File (Edge List)	63
3.10	Pajek Main Screen	64
3.11	Pajek Draw Screen	66
3.12	Pajek's Main Screen	68
3.13	Krackhardt Advice Network with Varying Node Size and Color (Pajek)	68
3.14	ORA Main Screen	71
3.15	Accessing ORA's Visualizer from ORA's Main Screen	72
3.16	ORA Visualizer	72
3.17	ORA Editor	73
3.18	Krackhardt Advice Network with Varying Node Size and Color (ORA)	74
4.1	Hypothetical Ego Network	81
4.2	Subset of Padgett and Ansell's Marriage Data	83
4.3	Sociogram of Padgett and Ansell's Marriage Data	84

4.4	Krackhardt Advice Network Data	85
4.5	Sociogram of Krackhardt's Advice Network	85
4.6	Davis's Southern Women Network Data	86
4.7	Sociogram of Davis's Southern Women	88
4.8	Padgett and Ansell's Marriage Network (UCINET)	91
4.9	ORA's New Meta-Network Dialog Box (Krackhardt High-Tech)	93
4.10	Krackhardt's Advice Network Matrix (ORA)	93
4.11	Davis's Southern Women Matrix (UCINET Spreadsheet Editor)	94
4.12	ORA's Create New Meta-Network Dialog Box (Davis's Southern Women)	95
4.13	Davis's Southern Women Matrix (ORA)	96
4.14	Krackhardt High-Tech Attribute Data (UCINET)	97
4.15	Krackhardt High-Tech Attribute Data (ORA)	97
4.16	UCINET Export to Pajek Dialog Box	98
4.17	UCINET DL Export Dialog Box	99
4.18	ORA's Data Import Wizard	101
4.19	ORA's Data Import Dialog Box	102
4.20	Importing Attribute Data in ORA	103
4.21	Importing Attribute Data in ORA Dialog Box	103
4.22	Southern Club Women: Co-Membership Network	104
4.23	Southern Club Women: Event Overlap Network	104
4.24	UCINET Affiliations Dialog Box	105
4.25	Pajek Display of Davis's Southern Women Co-Membership Network	106
4.26	Transforming Two-Mode Network into One-Mode Network in ORA	107
4.27	ORA's Fold Network Dialog Box	107
4.28	Sampson Monastery Data (UCINET Log)	109
4.29	Sampson Monastery Data (UCINET Spreadsheet Editor)	110
4.30	UCINET Unpack Dialog Box	110
4.31	NetDraw Drawing of Sampson's Monastery Data	111
4.32	UCINET's Join/Merge Datasets Function	113
4.33	UCINET within Dataset Aggregations Dialog Box	113
4.34	UCINET between Dataset Statistical Summaries Dialog Box	114
4.35	UCINET Boolean Combination Dialog Box	114
4.36	Pajek Edgelist of Padgett Marriage and Business Network Data	115
4.37	Pajek Network Map of Padgett Multirelational Data	116
4.38	Two Networks Highlighted in Pajek's Network Drop-Down Menus	117

4.39	UCINET within Dataset Cellwise Transformations Dialog Box	118
4.40	UCINET between Dataset Statistical Summaries Dialog Box	119
4.41	UCINET between Dataset Aggregations Output Log	120
4.42	Pajek Drawing of Sampson Monastery Liking and Disliking Data	120
4.43	Noordin's Trust Network Loaded in ORA	121
4.44	ORA Visualization of Noordin's Trust Network	122
4.45	Transform Meta-Network Dialog Box (ORA)	123
4.46	UCINET Subgraphs from Partition Dialog Box	123
4.47	NetDraw Graph of Noordin Top's Alive and Free Operational Network	124
4.48	NetDraw Collapse Nodes by Attribute Dialog Box	125
4.49	NetDraw Graph of Noordin's Operational Network Collapsed by Role	126
4.50	Pajek Drawing of Noordin Top's Alive Operational Network	127
4.51	Pajek Drawing of Noordin's Operational Network Collapsed by Role	129
4.52	ORA Attribute Partition Tool	130
4.53	ORA Drawing of Noordin's Incarcerated Trust Network	130
4.54	ORA's Meta-Node Manager	131
4.55	ORA's Meta-Node Network Map	132
5.1	Strong and Weak Ties	139
5.2	UCINET's Matrix Browser	144
5.3	UCINET's Old Geodesic Distance Output	144
5.4	UCINET's Dichotomize Dialog Box	147
5.5	UCINET's Density Dialog Box	148
5.6	UCINET's Density and Average Degree Output	148
5.7	UCINET's Clustering Coefficient Output	150
5.8	UCINET's Degree Centrality Dialog Box	154
5.9	UCINET's Eigenvector Centrality Dialog Box	154
5.10	UCINET's Closeness Centrality Dialog Box	155
5.11	UCINET's Degree Centrality Output	156
5.12	UCINET's Betweenness Centrality Output	156
5.13	Noordin Trust and Communication Networks (NetDraw)	159
5.14	Pajek's Info>Network>General Report	160
5.15	Pajek's Main Screen	160
5.16	Pajek's Distribution of Distances Report	161
5.17	Pajek's Info>Network>General Report	162
5.18	Pajek's Clustering Coefficient Report (Communication Network)	162
5.19	Pajek's Degree Centralization Report	163

5.20   ORA's Main Screen with Network Statistics   164
5.21   ORA's Standard Network Analysis Report Dialog Box   165
5.22   Noordin School Network (Isolates Removed)   168
6.1   Simple Unconnected Directed Network (from de Nooy
       et al. 2005:66)   171
6.2   UCINET Components Dialog Box   172
6.3   UCINET (Strong) Components Output Log   173
6.4   UCINET (Weak) Components Output Log   174
6.5   NetDraw Visualization of the Drug-User Network's Main
       Component   175
6.6   NetDraw Visualization of the Drug-User Network's
       Weak Components   176
6.7   Pajek Visualization of the Drug-User Network's Weak
       Components   177
6.8   Pajek Report of Partition Information   178
6.9   Noordin's Combined Network Components (Pajek)   179
6.10   Components of Noordin's Alive Trust Network (Pajek)   179
6.11   Components of Noordin's Alive Combined Network
       (ORA)   180
6.12   *k*-Cores of Drug-User Network (NetDraw)   183
6.13   UCINET *k*-Core Output File (Noordin's Alive Trust
       Network)   184
6.14   *k*-Cores of Noordin's Alive Trust Network (NetDraw)   185
6.15   Pajek Report of General Network Information   186
6.16   Pajek Drawing of Noordin's Alive Operational Network
       k-Cores   187
6.17   A Perfectly Factionalized Network (NetDraw)   188
6.18   UCINET Factional Analysis Output   189
6.19   An Almost–Perfectly Factionalized Network (NetDraw)   189
6.20   UCINET Faction Analysis Output   190
6.21   UCINET Faction Dialog Box   191
6.22   Three-Block (top) and Four-Block (bottom) Faction
       Analyses: Noordin Alive and Free Combined Network
       (NetDraw)   193
6.23   NetDraw Factions Dialog Box   194
6.24   UCINET Girvan-Newman Dialog Box   196
6.25   UCINET Girvan-Newman Output   197
6.26   UCINET Cluster Adequacy Function   198
6.27   UCINET Cluster Adequacy Output   199
6.28   Two-Cluster (top) and Three-Cluster (bottom)
       Girvan-Newman: Alive and Free Combined Network
       (NetDraw)   199
6.29   NetDraw Girvan-Newman Dialog Box   200
6.30   ORA Locate Subgroups Dialog Box   201

6.31	ORA Locate Subgroups Dialog Box	202
6.32	ORA Locate Subgroups Report (Text File)	203
6.33	ORA's Visualization of Newman Groups	203
7.1	UCINET's Centrality and Power Menu	207
7.2	UCINET's Degree Centrality Dialog Box	212
7.3	UCINET's Degree Centrality Output Log (Padgett Data)	213
7.4	UCINET's Degree Centrality Output (Noordin Alive Combined Network)	214
7.5	Noordin Alive Combined Network (Node Size = Degree) (Pajek)	215
7.6	UCINET's Extract Main Component Dialog Box	217
7.7	UCINET's Freeman Closeness Centrality Output	218
7.8	UCINET's Closeness Centrality Dialog Box	220
7.9	UCINET's Closeness (ARD) Centrality Output	220
7.10	Noordin Alive Combined Network (Node Size = ARD) (Pajek)	221
7.11	UCINET's Betweenness Centrality Output Log	223
7.12	Noordin Alive Combined Network (Node Size = Betweenness) (Pajek)	225
7.13	UCINET Eigenvector Centrality Dialog Box	226
7.14	Noordin Alive Combined Network (Node Size = Eigenvector) (Pajek)	227
7.15	UCINET Eigenvector Centrality Output	229
7.16	UCINET Multiple Centrality Measures Dialog Box	229
7.17	UCINET Regression Dialog Box	230
7.18	UCINET Regression Output Log	230
7.19	NetDraw Size of Nodes Dialog Box	231
7.20	NetDraw Centrality Measures Dialog Box	232
7.21	Pajek Info Partition/Vector Dialog Box	233
7.22	Pajek Drawing of Alive Trust Network, Layered by Degree Centrality	234
7.23	Alive Trust Network, Top-Ten Hubs/Authorities Highlighted (Pajek)	236
7.24	Pajek Main Screen	236
7.25	ORA's Generate Reports Dialog Box	237
7.26	ORA's Generate Reports Dialog Box	238
7.27	ORA Network Map with Node Size Varying by Eigenvector Centrality	239
7.28	UCINET's Unpack Dialog Box	240
7.29	UCINET's Indegree (and Outdegree) Centrality Output	241
7.30	UCINET's Hubs and Authorities Output	243
7.31	UCINET's Reach Centrality Output	244
7.32	Pajek's Partition Information Report (Indegree Centrality Scores)	245

7.33   Pajek's Partition Information Report (Authority Scores)   246
7.34   Pajek's Partition Information Report (Input Domain)   247
7.35   Pajek's Partition Information Report (Restricted Input
        Domain)   248
7.36   Pajek's Main Screen   249
7.37   Pajek's Vector Information Report (Proximity Prestige)   249
7.38   ORA's Standard Network Analysis Report (Indegree
        Centrality)   250
7.39   Advice Network with Node Size by Indegree and
        Authority Centrality (ORA)   251
8.1   Four Types of Triads   255
8.2   Victor's Ego Network (from de Nooy et al. 2005:146)   256
8.3   UCINET's Structural Holes Dialog Box   256
8.4   UCINET's Structural Holes Output   257
8.5   NetDraw's Size of Nodes Dialog Box   259
8.6   NetDraw Map of the Strike Network's Structural Holes
        (rConstraint)   259
8.7   Alive Communication Network (Pajek): Original and
        Dyadic Constraint   261
8.8   Pajek Network Map of Communication Network's
        Structural Holes   262
8.9   ORA Network Map of Communication Network's
        Structural Holes   263
8.10   Scatter Plot Comparison of Constraint and Betweenness
        (ORA)   264
8.11   Alive and Free Operational Network: Bi-Component
        Analysis   265
8.12   UCINET Bi-Component Output Log   267
8.13   NetDraw Color of Nodes Dialog Box   267
8.14   Pajek Bi-Component Hierarchy   268
8.15   Alive and Free Operational Network with Cutpoints
        Highlighted (Pajek)   269
8.16   ORA All Measures Report Identifying Boundary Spanners
        (Cutpoints)   270
8.17   ORA Measure Charts Function Identifying Boundary
        Spanners   270
8.18   Boundary Spanners Identified in ORA's Visualizer   271
8.19   Key Player Program   273
8.20   Key Players in the Alive Combined Network   275
8.21   ORA Critical Set Dialog Box   276
8.22   ORA Visualization of Critical Set in Combined Alive
        Network   277
8.23   Brokerage Roles of "John"   278
8.24   UCINET Brokerage Role Dialog Box   279

8.25	UCINET Brokerage Role Output Log	280
8.26	NetDraw Drawing of Gatekeeper Roles in Combined Alive Network	282
8.27	Pajek Drawing of Gatekeeper Roles in Combined Alive Network	283
8.28	Combined Alive Network, Tie-Width Equals Edge Betweenness (NetDraw)	284
9.1	Structural Equivalence of Wasserman and Faust Network	288
9.2	Automorphic Equivalence of Wasserman and Faust Network	290
9.3	UCINET MaxSim Output of Wasserman and Faust Network	292
9.4	Regular Equivalence of Wasserman and Faust Network	293
9.5	Wasserman and Faust (1994) Structural Equivalence Network	296
9.6	UCINET Structural Equivalence Profile Similarity Dialog Box	296
9.7	UCINET Structural Equivalence Matrix	297
9.8	UCINET Structural Equivalence Partition	297
9.9	UCINET Block Image Dialog Box	298
9.10	UCINET Permuted and Partitioned Matrix	298
9.11	Image Matrix Graph (NetDraw)	299
9.12	UCINET CONCOR Dialog Box	300
9.13	UCINET CONCOR Density Matrix	301
9.14	Final Image Matrix (Blockmodel), Zero-Block Method (UCINET)	302
9.15	UCINET Block Image Dialog Box	303
9.16	UCINET Dichotomize Dialog Box	303
9.17	Final Image Matrix, Threshold Method (UCINET)	304
9.18	Sociogram of Final Image Matrix (NetDraw)	304
9.19	UCINET Interactive CONCOR Dialog Box	305
9.20	UCINET Optimization Structural Equivalence Dialog Box	305
9.21	Final Image Matrix, Optimization Method (UCINET)	307
9.22	Alive Operational Network with CONCOR Partition (NetDraw)	307
9.23	Alive Operational Network with Optimization Partition (NetDraw)	308
9.24	Pajek Blockmodeling Dialog Box	309
9.25	Pajek Blockmodeling Report	309
9.26	Blockmodel of Alive Operational Network (Pajek)	310
9.27	Pajek-Generated Permuted Matrix	311
9.28	Pajek Blockmodeling Dialog Box with User-Defined Option	312

9.29   ORA's Locate Subgroups Dialog Box with CONCOR
       Option   313
9.30   ORA Visualization of CONCOR Groups   314
9.31   ORA Visualization of CONCOR Grouping (from
       Visualizer)   314
10.1   Partial Listing of Sampson.net   321
10.2   Sampson Liking Network at Times 2, 3, and 4 (Pajek)   324
10.3   Partial Listing of Noordin's Alive and Free Operational
       Network   325
10.4   ORA's Data Import Wizard (Pajek Option Selected)   327
10.5   UCINET Pajek Import Dialog Box   327
10.6   ORA's Main Screen with Networks Highlighted   328
10.7   Measures over Time of Alive and Free Operational
       Network   329
10.8   Measures over Time of Alive Operational Network   331
10.9   Change Detection Noordin Alive Operational Network   332
10.10 Node Class Editor   333
10.11 ORA Create Attributes Dialog Box   334
10.12 Node Class Editor with Latitude, Longitude, and
       MGRS Attributes   335
10.13 Configure Locations Dialog Box   335
10.14 ORA's GIS Visualization of Noordin Alive Operational
       Network   336
10.15 Google Earth Maps of Alive and Free Operational
       Network   337
10.16 ORA's Create Node Class Dialog Box   338
10.17 ORA's Create Network Dialog Box   338
11.1   UCINET's Attribute Regression Dialog Box   350
11.2   UCINET's Attribute Multivariate Regression Output   351
11.3   UCINET's QAP Correlation Dialog Box   352
11.4   UCINET's QAP Correlation Report   353
11.5   UCINET's MRQAP Network Regression Dialog Box   354
11.6   UCINET's Network Regression Output   355
11.7   ORA's Attribute Regression (Overall Statistics)   356
11.8   ORA's Attribute Regression (Coefficients)   357
11.9   ORA's Network Regression Dialog Box   358
11.10 ORA's Network Regression Dialog Box   359
11.11 ORA's Network Correlation and Regression Report   360
A3.1   UCINET's Metric MDS Dialog Box   406
A3.2   UCINET's Metric MDS Output (2-D)   406
A3.3   UCINET's Metric MDS Output (3-D)   407
A3.4   UCINET's Nonmetric MDS Scaling Dialog Box   408
A3.5   UCINET's Nonmetric MDS Output (2-D)   408
A3.6   UCINET's Nonmetric MDS Output (3-D)   409

A3.7   Nonmetric MDS Map of Padgett Marriage Network
       (NetDraw)   410
A3.8   UCINET's Export to Mage Dialog Box   410
A3.9   UCINET's Launch Mage Program Dialog Box   411
A3.10 Mage's Visualization of Padgett Marriage Data   411
A3.11 UCINET's Structural Equivalence Profile Dialog Box   412
A3.12 NetDraw's Nonmetric MDS Graph of Krackhardt Advice
       Network (2-D)   413
A3.13 Mage's Nonmetric MDS Graph of Krackhardt Advice
       Network (3-D)   413
A3.14 Bipartite Graph of Davis's Southern Women   414
A3.15 UCINET's Bipartite Dialog Box   415
A3.16 UCINET's Geodesic Distance Dialog Box   415
A3.17 NetDraw's Geodesic MDS Graph of Davis's Southern
       Women (2-D)   416
A3.18 Mage's Geodesic MDS Graph of Davis's Southern
       Women (3-D)   416

Tables

2.1	Strategic Options of Social Network Analysis	*page* 38
3.1	Meta-Matrix Representation of Meta-Network	69
4.1	Boundary Specification Typology	80
4.2	Aggregation of Noordin Top's Terrorist Network Ties	112
5.1	Diameter, Average Distance, and Fragmentation of Noordin's Network	145
5.2	Density, Average Degree, Clustering Coefficient, and Small World Q	151
5.3	Centralization Scores	157
5.4	Standard Deviation	158
6.1	Components of Noordin's Alive Network	181
6.2	Faction Analysis of Noordin's Alive and Free Combined Network (Fit)	192
7.1	Normalized Degree Centrality of Noordin Alive Networks	216
7.2	Normalized Closeness (ARD) Centrality of Noordin Alive Networks	222
7.3	Normalized Betweenness Centrality of Noordin Alive Networks	224
7.4	Normalized Eigenvector Centrality of Noordin Alive Networks	228
8.1	Correlation of Constraint and Betweenness Scores	258
8.2	Key Players in Alive Combined Network	274
8.3	Gould and Fernandez Brokerage Scores for Alive Combined Network	281
10.1	Comparison of Various Metrics over Time	323
10.2	Comparison of Standard and Geospatially Weighted Centrality Metrics	340
11.1	Crosstab of Key Players and College Education	344
11.2a	Crosstab of Key Players and College Education (Indonesians)	344

11.2b Crosstab of Key Players and College Education
     (Non-Indonesians)   344
11.3a Crosstab of Key Players and College Education
     (Afghan Vet)   345
11.3b Crosstab of Key Players and College Education
     (Non–Afghan Vet)   345
11.4   Regression of Key Player on Variables of Interest   346
12.1   Summary of Strategies Identified for Disrupting Noordin's
     Network   368

Preface

The Problematic Nature of Dark Networks

This book is concerned with the use of social network analysis (SNA) for tracking, destabilizing, and disrupting dark networks. Following Jörg Raab and Brint Milward, dark networks are defined here as covert and illegal networks (Milward and Raab 2006; Raab and Milward 2003), namely, any group that seeks to conceal itself and its activities from authorities. While the term is typically used to refer to groups such as terrorists, gangs, drug cartels, arms traffickers, and so on, it can refer to benign groups as well. For instance, Żegota, the predominantly Roman Catholic underground organization that addressed the social welfare needs of Jews in German-occupied Poland from 1942 to 1945 (Tomaszewski and Webowski 1999), would be considered a dark network because it was covert and, at least from the perspective of the Nazis, illegal. That said, this book implicitly assumes that the theories and methods it discusses will be used for the disruption of dark networks that seek to harm innocent civilians and the societies in which they live.[1]

Social network analysts have long considered the nature of dark networks. Georg Simmel (1906, 1950b), for example, was one of the first to explore their structure in his essay on secret societies, a study that Bonnie Erickson (1981) later expanded and modified. A decade later Malcolm Sparrow (1991) considered the usefulness of SNA for tracking criminal networks, and Wayne Baker and Richard Faulkner (1993) used SNA to examine three price-fixing conspiracy networks in the heavy electrical equipment industry. Since 9/11, analysts have become increasingly drawn to the use of SNA as a tool for understanding dark networks (Reed 2007;

---

[1] Of course, that does not prevent individuals, groups, organizations, or states from using the techniques discussed herein for ill rather than good. This is a genuine concern and a topic that the book's final chapter addresses.

Ressler 2006), largely because of Valdis Krebs's (2001) analysis of the 9/11 hijacker network. For instance, Sageman (2004) analyzed the network of 172 Islamic terrorist operatives affiliated with the global salafi jihad; José Rodriguez (2005) mapped the March 11, 2004, Madrid bombings; and Ami Pedahzur and Arie Perliger (2006) examined the nature of suicide attack networks. These, of course, are just a few examples; several other notable studies exist (see, e.g., Asal and Rethemeyer 2006; Carley 2003a; Koschade 2006; Magouirk, Atran, and Sageman 2008; Moody 2005; Tsvetovat and Carley 2005; van Meter 2001), many of which we will consider later in the book.

An overriding concern of many of these analysts has been the structure of dark networks. Simmel (1906, 1950b), for instance, argued that since secret societies are organized to conceal themselves and protect their members from detection, they adopt practices and organizational structures that help protect them and their members. He believed that the ideal organizational structure for dark networks was a hierarchy, but Erickson (1981) later showed that while some are, many are not, and that their structure is a function of risk and the group's desire to maximize security. Baker and Faulkner (1993) uncovered similar dynamics in their analysis of price-fixing conspiracies. Using reconstructed communication networks, they found that the conspiracies' structure was driven more by the need to maximize concealment than efficiency, so they adopted decentralized structures. Their findings fit nicely with other studies that have found that because of their adaptability, decentralized networks are generally better suited for solving nonroutine, complex, and/or rapidly changing "problems" or challenges (Arquilla and Ronfeldt 2001; Bakker, Raab, and Milward 2011; Klerks 2001; Krebs 2001; Milward and Raab 2006; Powell 1985, 1990; Raab and Milward 2003; Ronfeldt and Arquilla 2001; Saxenian 1994, 1996). Such structures create problems for those seeking to disrupt dark networks because the networks can adapt quickly to changing environmental pressures. As a case in point, prior to the September 11th attacks, Al Qaeda was a somewhat vertically integrated organization, at least at the command and control level, but since the U.S. invasion of Afghanistan, available evidence indicates that it has become far more decentralized (Raab and Milward 2003:425; Sageman 2008).

In practical terms what all this means is that dark networks are constantly evolving, which suggests that gathering timely and accurate data is always difficult. This difficulty is exasperated by the fact that dark networks actively try to remain hidden, which often renders data on them incomplete (Borgatti, Carley, and Krackhardt 2006; Krebs 2001; Sparrow 1991). That said, there is a surprising amount of detailed information on dark networks, much of it in the open-source literature. The challenge that many analysts have is not finding data but sorting through it. Moreover, the notion that open-sourced information is somehow "second class" is misguided (Flynn, Pottinger, and Batchelor 2010:23). As former director of the Defense Intelligence Agency, Lieutenant General Samuel V. Wilson has noted (cited in Flynn, Pottinger, and Batchelor 2010:23): "Ninety percent of intelligence comes from open sources. The other 10 percent, the clandestine work, is just the more dramatic. The real intelligence hero is Sherlock Holmes, not James Bond"; this means that analysts need to "embrace open-source, population-centric information as the lifeblood of their analytical work" (Flynn, Pottinger, and Batchelor 2010:23).

In recent years the quality and timeliness of social network data have increased due in large part to the improvement of link-analysis programs such as Analyst's Notebook[2] and Palantir,[3] which facilitate the collection of structured and unstructured data. While these programs are not SNA programs per se (see discussion of the difference in Chapter 1), they do include functionality that allows users to export data in formats that dedicated SNA programs can use. For example, Palantir currently exports social network data in formats that can be read by SNA programs such as UCINET,[4] NetDraw,[5] Pajek,[6] and Organizational Risk Analyzer (ORA),[7] and ORA imports Analyst's Notebook files.

Another advance in the collection of social network data is the development of smart-phone-based systems. For example, the smart-phone application Lighthouse[8] uses menu-driven forms to guide the collection of all types of data, including social network data, which then flow from the collection point to analysts in near real time, regardless of location or physical proximity. The system then exports the data into formats ready for geospatial, link, social network, and other types of analysis. In 2010, Lighthouse was used to collect relational, geospatial, and other ethnographic data in the Khakrez District (located in northern Kandahar Province) as part of the village stability operations in Afghanistan.[9] The resulting dataset included up-to-date and accurate relational data

---

[2] http://www.i2group.com/us/products-services/analysis-product-line/analysts-notebook.

[3] http://www.palantirtech.com/government.

[4] UCINET 6.0 (Borgatti, Everett, and Freeman 2011) is available at www.analytictech.com.

[5] NetDraw (Borgatti 2002–2005) comes as part of the UCINET 6.0 package but can also be downloaded separately at the Analytic Technologies website: www.analytictech.com.

[6] Pajek (Batagelj and Mrvar 2012) is a network analysis and graph drawing program designed to handle extremely large data sets that can be downloaded for free for noncommercial use from the Pajek Wiki website: http://pajek.imfm.si/doku.php?id=download.

[7] ORA (Carley 2001–2011) can be downloaded for free for noncommercial use from the ORA website: http://www.casos.cs.cmu.edu/projects/ora/.

[8] Lighthouse was developed by Captain Carrick Longley with the help of Chief Warrant Officer Chad Machiela: http://lhproject.info/.

[9] *Village stability operations* refers to the program of putting special forces units (e.g., civil affairs units) in rural villages to make it harder for Taliban and other insurgent groups to find safe haven. The villages receive assistance to improve infrastructure development, governance, and security that they can take back to their village.

on several hundred individuals and organizations (i.e., business, kinship, organizational, personal, elder, and tribal affiliations). For example, in three weeks collection efforts identified the community's most central actor as a Taliban sympathizer (his son was in the Taliban) who was (not surprisingly) resistant to efforts by the United States to reduce the Taliban's influence in the area. While this individual's centrality was not "news" to the local forces, analysts not only identified this individual within a shorter period of time than the local forces did, but they also provided the local forces with an array of noncoercive strategies that could decrease this individual's influence by elevating the centrality of others who were more sympathetic to the village stability operations.

Another aspect of dark networks that can create problems for analysts is that they do not necessarily operate independently from one another but instead are often connected through actors who function as brokers between these networks:

> A truism of the network approach is that, at some level, everything is connected to everything else. This is no less true of dark networks. There is increasing evidence of a close connection between Al Qaeda and the failed states of Liberia, Sierra Leone, and Burkina Faso in West Africa. The connection appears based on Al Qaeda's need to exchange cash for diamonds. This is fueled by the pressure from the United States and Western Europe to clamp down on Al Qaeda's use of legitimate banks for international monetary transactions. Diamonds provide a ready currency for Al Qaeda, and the failed states of the region have perhaps provided a safe haven for Al Qaeda's operatives in the wake of 11 September in exchange for arms and money for the warlords of the region. (Raab and Milward 2003:425)

Consequently, accurately specifying a network's boundaries is of the utmost importance, a topic we take up in Chapter 4. Misspecification can lead to the incorrect estimation of metrics and the development of inappropriate strategies and recommendations.

The Social Network Analysis of Dark Networks

To be sure, these three problems – dynamic and evolving networks, the potential incompleteness of data, and fuzzy boundaries (Krebs 2001; Sparrow 1991) – are not unique to dark networks. They arise with light networks as well. It is just that with dark networks, they can be more acute. Does that mean we should abandon the social network approach for disrupting dark networks? No, I do not think so. In recent years SNA has enhanced our understanding of how dark networks organize themselves (Milward and Raab 2006; Raab and Milward 2003) and has offered potential strategies for their disruption (see, e.g., Krebs 2001; Pedahzur and Perliger 2006; Roberts and Everton 2011; Rodriguez 2005; Sageman 2003, 2004), some of which have been successful. Perhaps the best-known success story is the capture of Saddam Hussein (Wilson 2010), but it has been successfully used to destabilize improvised explosive devices (IED) network (Gjelten 2010) as well as to roll up an insurgency in Iraq (Anonymous 2009).

Nevertheless, there seems to be far too much emphasis on using centrality and brokerage measures (or variations on them) to identify high-value targets within dark networks (Jordan, Mañas, and Horsburgh 2008; Krebs 2001; Pedahzur and Perliger 2006; Roberts and Everton 2011; Sageman 2004; for a similar critique, see Tsvetovat and Carley 2005). While targeting key players is intuitively appealing and might provide short-term satisfaction, it can be misplaced and may make tracking and destabilizing dark networks more difficult than it already is (Arquilla 2008; Schmitt and Perlez 2009; Yasin 2010). As Brafman and Beckstrom (2006) have noted, removing high-value targets in decentralized organizations, which as we previously noted dark networks often are, does not always shut them down but sometimes drives them to become more decentralized, making them even harder to disrupt. This is not to suggest that analysts should abandon the use of metrics that identify key players, but rather that they view them as one set of algorithms among many that can be used to help flesh out a range of strategic options. Indeed, a whole host of nonkinetic (i.e., noncoercive) strategies exist such as institution building, psychological operations (PsyOp),[10] information operations (IO), and rehabilitation and reintegration efforts,[11] many of which have already proved successful. For example, intelligence officers in northern Iraq used SNA to craft a PsyOp campaign that caused an insurgent network in Iraq to turn on itself (Anonymous 2009), and rehabilitation and reintegration programs in Singapore appear to be meeting with some success[12] (Yasin 2010). To be sure, nonkinetic strategies take patience and are often for the long haul, but as Tilly (2005) notes, while the integration of dark networks (not a term he uses) into civil society is necessary, it often takes time. Nonkinetic strategies are hardly new, of course; they have been used successfully in the past (see, e.g., Galula [1964] 2006; Kilcullen 2009, 2010; Nagl 2005), but what SNA brings

---

[10] The Department of Defense recently dropped the term Psychological Operations (PsyOp) in favor of Military Information Support Operations (MISO) (Maurer 2010). This book uses the former term because of its familiarity.

[11] These strategies are discussed in more detail in Chapter 2.

[12] See, e.g., http://www.singaporeunited.sg/cep/index.php/web/layout/set/print/content/view/full/3037, http://www.rrg.sg/subindex.asp?id=A266_07, and http://www.asiancrime.org/pdfdocs/Singapore_CT_Efforts_Corsi.doc.

to the table are methods for more accurately identifying those institutions, groups, and/or individuals that would be receptive to noncoercive approaches. Unfortunately, there appears to be a lack of awareness of the various nonkinetic strategies available. Thus, this book seeks to fill this vacuum by placing the SNA of dark networks into a larger strategic framework that considers both kinetic and nonkinetic approaches to dark network disruption.

In particular, this book has in mind four primary audiences: (1) scholars who study terrorist and other dark networks but have little or no background in SNA, (2) social network analysts who want to move beyond simple employment of social network metrics in order to see how such metrics can be placed within a strategic framework, (3) students who are looking for a text that not only introduces them to SNA but also applies it to a specific phenomenon, and (4) policy makers who often operate in arenas where terms such as "social network analysis" are bandied about with little genuine knowledge of what the terms actually mean and who would like to expand their understanding of the topic.

Organization of the Book

The book is structured in such a way that it not only introduces researchers to basic social network theories and techniques, but also embeds these theories and techniques in the larger strategic framework that is crucial for tracking, destabilizing, and/or disrupting dark networks. Unlike a number of monographs on social network analysis that focus on a particular phenomenon (see, e.g., Friedkin 1998; Jackson 2008; Kilduff and Tsai 2003; Kontopoulos 1993; Lewis 2009), this book not only explores the theoretical aspects of dark networks, but, following the lead of others (de Nooy, Mrvar, and Batagelj 2005, 2011; Hanneman and Riddle 2005), also illustrates how to use social network software (i.e., UCINET, NetDraw, Pajek, and ORA) to estimate the various metrics illustrated and discussed in the text. To facilitate this, a particular dark network – the Noordin Top terrorist network – serves as a running example throughout the book, from the initial collection of social network data to estimating various SNA metrics to strategies for disrupting dark networks in general (see Appendix 1 for a description of the data).[13]

---

[13] Prior to his death in September 2009, Top was Indonesia's most wanted terrorist (International Crisis Group 2006, 2009a, 2009b). He began as one of Jemaah Islamiyah's (JI) key bomb makers and financiers before striking off on his own to set up a more violent group that is believed to be responsible for the August 2003 Marriot Bombing in Jakarta, Australian embassy bombing in Jakarta in September 2004, the second Bali bombing of October 2005 (Bali II – JI was responsible for the first Bali bombing in October 2002), and the Jakarta bombings of the Marriott and the Ritz-Carlton in July 2009.

The book demonstrates how to examine the topography of Noordin's network, identify its central actors, uncover any cohesive subgroups, pinpoint its key brokers and bridges, detect classes of structurally equivalent actors, and examine it both over time and geospatially.[14] Drawing on a typology suggested by Krebs (2001:51), four aspects of Noordin's network will be analyzed: his trust, operational, communication, and business and finance networks, as well as the combination of these networks into a single network. Moreover, we will often extract and analyze subnetworks from these four types of networks (five if you count the combined network) based on whether network members are alive, dead, or in jail. In other words, in addition to analyzing Noordin's "Trust," "Operational," "Communication," "Business and Finance," and "Combined" networks, we will explore the "Alive and Free," "Alive," and "Incarcerated" subnetworks of these larger networks, giving us a total of twenty Noordin networks available for analysis. For what should be obvious reasons, we will not analyze all twenty networks in every chapter. To do so would be needlessly repetitive. Instead, in each chapter networks are chosen that, in part, help illustrate the algorithms under consideration.[15]

The book's first two chapters serve as an introduction to the use of social network analysis for the disruption of dark networks. The first chapter provides an overview of the basic terms, concepts, and assumptions of social network theories and methods, while the second outlines the various strategies with which SNA can be combined and a process for doing so. Some may wonder whether these theoretical and strategic discussions, however brief, are necessary. Obviously, I think they are. And that is because they attempt to show that SNA should not be used for disrupting dark networks apart from a basic knowledge of the theories and assumptions lying behind the various methods, as well as the array of strategies available to analysts.

The next two chapters introduce readers to some SNA basics. Chapter 3 seeks to help users become comfortable with the four SNA software packages illustrated in this guide: UCINET, the "granddaddy" of SNA software programs; NetDraw, a program for visualizing social network data developed by the same people who created UCINET; Pajek, a SNA package that integrates metrics and visualization; and ORA (Organizational Risk Analyzer), a relatively new software package that allows analysts to analyze more than social networks. Chapter 4 builds on this chapter and introduces the basics of collecting, recording, manipulating, and visualizing social network data using these software programs.

---

[14] Other social networks are used to illustrate various aspects of social network analysis as well, but only the Noordin Top network is used throughout the book.

[15] In the real world, of course, analysts will want to examine as many permutations of the dark networks they are analyzing as possible before they sit down to craft strategies for disruption.

The next five chapters examine some of the more common SNA methodologies as well as consider how they can inform crafting strategies for dark network disruption: Chapter 5 looks at a variety of metrics for getting a sense of how the network is structured as a whole (i.e., its topography); Chapter 6 explores a variety of methods for detecting clusters and subgroups within the larger network; Chapter 7 examines how various measures of centrality can be used to detect a network's key and peripheral players; Chapter 8 explores methods for locating actors and ties that broker the flow of information and other resources within and through the network; and Chapter 9 looks at algorithms for identifying actors who are located in similar positions in the social network.

The next two chapters introduce readers to some of the recent advances in SNA that can be of use to dark network analysts. Chapter 10 introduces readers to the dynamic analysis of social networks, a burgeoning and varied field in social network analysis. Here we only brush the surface of this type of the various approaches that fall under this nomenclature. Specifically, we examine approaches for analyzing longitudinal networks and fusing social network and geospatial data. Chapter 11 examines some of the statistical models available for social network analysts – in particular, those that help analysts disentangle genuine from spurious effects.

While, for the most part, Chapters 5 through 11 stand on their own, in many ways they build on one another (especially from a strategic perspective). Thus, it is probably wise to work your way through the book sequentially.

The book's final chapter considers the promises and limitations of social network analysis. SNA should not be seen as a silver bullet in the fight against terrorist and criminal networks but rather one tool among many that can be used for crafting potential strategies. This chapter also addresses the concern that the theories and methods outlined in this book will be used for ill rather than good. While we have little or no control over how such knowledge will be consumed by others, we can still provide guidelines on how we believe such knowledge can be used. Thus, the final chapter explores the ethics of using SNA to disrupt dark networks. It considers a variety of ethical traditions before arguing that the use of SNA for the disruption of dark networks should be guided by the goal of encouraging those practices that allow human beings to flourish.

The book is, for the most part, decidedly nontechnical. The focus is placed on the assumptions lying behind the metrics that are explored. Consequently, mathematical equations are kept to a minimum and only included when I believe they either facilitate comparisons between various metrics or illuminate the metric being considered. For those interested in exploring SNA's mathematical and graph theoretical foundations, there are plenty of resources available (see, e.g., Brandes and Erlebach 2005; Jackson 2008; Lewis 2009; Wasserman and Faust 1994). The book also does not attempt to provide a comprehensive introduction to all the various theories and techniques associated with SNA. There are a number of available monographs that do just that.[16] Instead, it seeks to bridge the gap between theory and practice by demonstrating how to apply various theories and methods to specific examples. Finally, it adopts the approach used by Everton (2004); de Nooy, Mrvar, and Batagelj (2005, 2011); and Hanneman and Riddle (2005) in that it not only discusses various social network techniques and metrics, it illustrates how to estimate them with worked examples, in this case using UCINET, NetDraw, Pajek, and ORA.[17] The example datasets used in the book, except for the Noordin dataset, are publicly available, and most are provided with the UCINET software package. Nevertheless, all have been gathered and made available at a single website (https://sites.google.com/site/sfeverton18/). Because these programs are regularly updated, it is likely that the various dialog boxes, command menus, and report windows illustrated here will not always match what readers encounter when working with these programs. It is also likely that I will make statements about what the programs can and cannot do that will no longer be true because of updates that occurred after this manuscript was submitted. Nevertheless, most changes should be minor and should not cause the readers too much difficulty. That said, Pajek was significantly updated shortly after this manuscript was completed, so I strongly recommend using the "Book Edition 2" (version 2.05), which can be downloaded at the Pajek website (http://pajek.imfm.si/doku.php?id=download), while using this book and then updating to a newer version afterward.

---

[16] Readers who are interested in general introductions to social network analysis should consult Degenne and Forsé (1999), Kadushin (2012), Knoke and Yang (2007), Prell (2011), Scott (2000), and Scott and Carrington (2011). Wasserman and Faust (1994) offer a more comprehensive (and mathematical) introduction. Easley and Kleinberg (2010) introduce the topic from the perspective of an economist and network scientist. Robert Hanneman and Mark Riddle (2005) have written a helpful introduction to social network analysis methods using UCINET, while Walter de Nooy, Andrej Mrvar, and Vladimir Batagelj (2005, 2011) have done the same for those interested in Pajek.

[17] Following de Nooy, Mrvar, and Batagelj (2005, 2011) these commands are placed in the margin next to the text discussing the technique/metric in order to make them easier to follow and locate.

Acknowledgments

Formally, this book traces its roots to a manual I wrote for the Disrupting Dark Networks class I began teaching in the Fall of 2007. Professors Nancy Roberts and Doug Borer, who at the time were co-directors of the CORE Lab, which is housed in the Defense Analysis Department at the Naval Postgraduate School in Monterey, California, used funding from the Pentagon's Rapid Reaction Technology Office (RRTO) to hire me as a postdoc in order to write the manual's first iteration and teach classes in SNA. The initial manual simply brought together notes and labs from the Dark Networks course. It then underwent several iterations based on feedback from students and advances in the SNA field. The manual forms the basis of the book's first eight chapters, although each one has been substantially rewritten because the original manual did not include worked examples using ORA. Moreover, the datasets have been updated, requiring that all of the tables and figures be redone. Chapters 9 through 11 grew out of labs and lectures I prepared for another class, Dynamic Network Analysis, the title of which was borrowed from the type of analysis advocated and incorporated in ORA.

Informally, this book can be traced back to a time when one of my fellow graduate students, Jen van Stelle, invited me to join Mark Granovetter's Networks of Silicon Valley working group at Stanford University. Within a couple of weeks of joining, I was assigned the task of using existing software packages (i.e., UCINET and Pajek – NetDraw and ORA were not around at the time) to visualize social networks, a task that not only resulted in the writing of a visualization manual for the working group (Everton 2004) but helped further my own interest in SNA, which was initially piqued by the work of social scientists who highlighted the important role that social ties play in the recruitment of individuals to various groups (see, e.g., Lofland and Stark 1965; McAdam 1986; McAdam and Paulsen 1993; Snow, Zurcher, and Ekland-Olson 1980; Stark and Bainbridge 1980). Mark ultimately became my advisor on a dissertation that examined (from a social network perspective) the causes and consequences of status within the venture capital industry (Everton 2007). To say that Mark's influence on my own work has been profound would be an understatement, as is evidenced by the numerous times I draw on his work in the pages that follow. That said, he should not be held responsible for any of the conclusions I draw here.

The book has benefited from the suggestions of, conversations with, and encouragement from several individuals, in particular John Arquilla, Nancy Ann Budden, Deak Childress, Ian Davis, Dorothy Denning, Karen Flaherty, Carrick Longley, Chad Machiela, Gordon McCormick, Ian McCulloh, Brint Milward, Phil Murphy, Carlos Padilla, Jörg Raab, Ben Riley, Rob Schroeder, John Taylor, Kristen Tsolis, David Tucker, Nathan Whitfield, Greg Wilson, Carrie Worth, and Doug Zimmerman. Doug Borer and Nancy Roberts deserve special mention because they helped me to think through the strategic use of social network analysis for the disruption of dark networks. Indeed, the article that I wrote with Nancy Roberts (Roberts and Everton 2011) on the topic helped to solidify my thinking on these matters. It forms the basis of the first part of Chapter 2 as well as some of the earlier comments in the preface and in other parts of the book. Dan Cunningham, one of the CORE Lab's research associates, Don Steiny, and editors from Cambridge University Press and Aptara, Inc., carefully read and commented on several of the chapters and helped me catch mistakes and make the book more readable. Ron Breiger provided helpful comments on what eventually became Chapter 9 and the section on ethics in Chapter 12. And James Moody's comments on the article that Nancy Roberts and I wrote on the strategic use of SNA were extremely helpful. I also benefited from the comments of two anonymous reviewers who made valuable suggestions as to how the manuscript could be improved.

Finally, I would not have been able to write this book without the patience and support of my mom (Mary Ellen), dad (Harold), wife (Deanne), and children (Brendan and Tara). In particular, Deanne, Brendan, and Tara put up with the endless hours I spent writing and rewriting with amazing patience, and it is to them that I dedicate this book.

Part I

Introduction

1

Social Network Analysis: An Introduction

1.1 Introduction

While notions of social structure can be found in the writings of classical social theorists such as Auguste Comte, Emile Durkheim, Karl Marx, Herbert Spencer, and Max Weber, Georg Simmel is generally seen as the intellectual forbearer of social network analysis (SNA). Simmel ([1908] 1955, [1908] 1971) argued that to understand social behavior we must study patterns of interaction, and he offered penetrating insights into the nature of secret societies (1950b), the differing dynamics of dyads and triads (Simmel 1950a, c),[1] how increasing social complexity has led to concomitant rise in individualism ([1908] 1955), as well as others. While Simmel's theoretical contributions continue to influence the discipline today, SNA's early formal development can be traced to two major strands (Prell 2011; Scott 2000): the work of (1) social psychologists, such as Fritz Heider, Kurt Lewin, and Jacob Moreno (Heider 1977; Lewin 1951; Moreno 1953), who emphasized how organized patterns shape how we see and interpret the world; and (2) social anthropologists, such as Siegfried Nadel (1957) and Alfred Radcliffe-Brown (1940), who focused on the relationship between social patterns and social structure and who, in turn, influenced the research of social scientists such as Elton Mayo (1933, 1945; see also Roethlisberger and Dickson 1939), W. Lloyd Warner (Warner and Lunt 1941), John Barnes (1954), Elizabeth Bott (1957), and J. Clyde Mitchell (1969). These individuals did not create a distinct SNA paradigm, but their efforts laid the groundwork for its development at Harvard in the 1960s and 1970s, in an effort led by sociologist Harrison White and his students, including Ronald Breiger, Ivan Chase, Bonnie Erickson, Mark Granovetter, Michael Schwartz, and

---

[1] A dyad is a pair of actors with a tie between them. A triad is a set of three actors that may or may not have ties among them.

Barry Wellman (Freeman 2004; Prell 2011; Scott 2000). White, who also earned a Ph.D. in theoretical physics, emphasized the need for an empirically based social science that unapologetically focused on social phenomena. He argued that sociology, in spite of its claims to study social phenomena, was beholden to individualistic forms of analysis that drew conclusions based on the aggregated characteristics of individuals, often aided by statistical analysis of survey data. This, he believed, was a mistake. Thus, along with his students, he developed an approach that drew on case studies to focus on social relations and the patterns that emerge from them. The result is what we now know as social network analysis, and the discipline has blossomed ever since (Freeman 2004; Prell 2011). Social network analysts have created their own organization (International Network for Social Network Analysis), launched their own journals (*Connections, Social Networks,* and the *Journal of Social Structure*), gathered annually in either North America or Europe (Sunbelt meetings), and produced a number of monographs on SNA (de Nooy, Mrvar, and Batagelj 2005, 2011; Degenne and Forsé 1999; Knoke and Yang 2007; Scott 2000; Wasserman and Faust 1994).[2]

In recent years physicists and other scientists have entered the field, which has helped lead to an increased interest in SNA, attracting researchers from a wide array of disciplines and generating a number of highly creative studies (see, e.g., Barabási 2002; Barabási and Albert 1999; Buchanan 2001, 2002; Girvan and Newman 2002; Kleinberg 1999, 2000; Onnela et al. 2007; Watts 1999a, b, 2003). Unfortunately, many of these network scientists have been unaware of SNA's rich theoretical history (Scott 2011), which has led to a split in the field and the unnecessary replication of previous research:

> The physicists Barabási and Albert, for example, reported a "new" result having to do with the tendency of nodes in a network to display gross inequalities in the number of others to which they are linked. And they went on to develop a model designed to explain that tendency. But Paul Lazarsfeld had described the same tendency in 1938 (Moreno and Jennings 1938),

---

[2] The story, of course, is more complex than this brief account. For example, faculty and students at University of California, Irvine, made significant contributions (Freeman 2004:155–158). In fact, one faculty member, Linton Freeman, developed the first version of UCINET, probably the most widely used social network software in the world, and one of his students, Stephen Borgatti, along with Martin Everett, has since taken over its development. Other traditions that have informed SNA include graph theory (Harary 1953, 1969; Harary and Norman 1953; Lewis 2009), exchange theory (Cook and Whitmeyer 1992; Emerson 1972a, b, 1976), and research into the recruitment of individuals to religious and social movements (Gould 1991, 1993a; Lofland 1977; Lofland and Stark 1965; McAdam 1986, 1988b; Snow and Phillips 1980; Snow, Zurcher and Ekland-Olson 1980).

and Derek de Solla Price had developed essentially the same model as early as 1976. (Freeman 2004:166)

Nevertheless, there are signs that the two communities are bridging the gap. Duncan Watts, for example, took a position in the sociology department at Columbia University, and network scientists routinely attend the annual Sunbelt meetings (Freeman 2004). Thus, the long-term prospect for collaboration between the two groups looks promising, which will undoubtedly lead to further advances in the field.

What exactly is SNA? Briefly, it is a collection of theories and methods that assumes that the behavior of actors (whether individuals, groups, or organizations) is profoundly affected by their ties to others and the networks in which they are embedded. Rather than viewing individuals (and groups and organizations) as unaffected by those around them, SNA assumes that we are social beings whose interaction patterns affect what we do, say, and believe. Interaction patterns are anything but random, of course. Actors tend to interact with similar others, and repeated interaction can lead (among other things) to the emergence of social formation at the micro (e.g., individual), meso (e.g., group), and macro (e.g., institutions, nations) levels that can be the object of SNA in their own right. Intense social interaction can generate feelings of group solidarity, norms of behavior, symbols of group belonging (e.g., team mascots, gang colors, national flags, sacred religious symbols such as the Christian cross and the Jewish star, etc.), and a sense of identity (Collins 2004; White 1992, 2008). All of this is just a fancy way of saying that social networks not only enable and constrain behavior but that they are also chock-full of meaning (White 1992, 2008),[3] and as such help us make sense of our world, shape our preferences, and influence the choices we make (Passy 2003:23). Consequently, a primary goal of SNA has been to develop metrics that help analysts gain a better understanding of a particular network's structural features. And although organizational theorists tend to explore such questions with the goal of identifying factors that will help strengthen organizations, those who study dark networks are generally more interested in identifying those aspects that will undermine them.

The remainder of this chapter introduces the basic terms, concepts, and assumptions of SNA as well as considers certain issues germane to this approach. It begins with a discussion of common misconceptions of what SNA is and how it differs from other analytic approaches. It then briefly discusses SNA's basic terms and concepts before moving to an extended exploration of the assumptions that underlie it. The chapter's final section considers the roles that human agency and culture play within SNA.

---

[3] Technically, in White's view meaning comes from switching between networks (Steiny 2007).

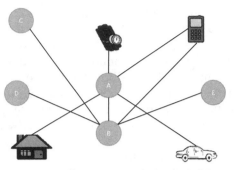

Figure 1.1. Illustrative Link Analysis Diagram

1.2   Misconceptions and Differences

SNA differs from other analytic methods and is often mistaken for other theoretical traditions. For example, the term *network* is used in different ways. Within some circles networks are seen as decentralized, informal, and/or organic types of organizations, and hierarchies are seen as centralized, formal, and/or bureaucratic types (Arquilla and Ronfeldt 2001; Burns and Stalker 1961; Podolny and Page 1998; Powell 1990; Powell and Smith-Doerr 1994; Ronfeldt and Arquilla 2001). This distinction is useful (and appropriate) in some theoretical contexts, but within the world of SNA all organizations are seen as networks. Some may be more hierarchical than others, but they are nevertheless networks (Nohria 1992). Indeed, algorithms have been developed that measure the degree to which a particular network is hierarchical (see, e.g., Davis 1979; de Nooy et al. 2005:205–212; Krackhardt 1994). This is not to say that there is a right or wrong way to use the term network. Rather, the term means different things in different contexts, and within SNA everything is considered a network.

SNA is also sometimes confused with link analysis, a related but distinct analytic approach that also examines the relational patterns of various objects. The basic difference between the two approaches is that although link analysis diagrams often include different types of objects (e.g., individuals, cars, cell phones) and the ties between them, social network diagrams only include ties between similar types of objects. Take, for example, a link analysis diagram where two individuals (A and B) each have links to five other objects, but the objects to which they have ties differ from one another (Figure 1.1). In this example, person A is linked to person B as well as a bomb, a cell phone, a house, and a car, whereas person B is linked to four individuals (A, C, D, and E) and a cell phone. Although both have five ties (which is the definition of *degree centrality* – see

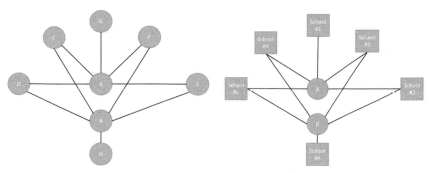

Figure 1.2. Illustrative SNA Diagrams

discussion in Section 7.1), we cannot meaningfully compare the number of ties of these two individuals because the ties are to different types of objects. It would be like comparing apples and oranges.

By contrast, in an SNA diagram actors have ties to similar objects, making direct comparison of numbers of ties meaningful. This is illustrated in Figure 1.2 where in the left panel individuals A and B each have five ties to five other individuals, and in the right panel they have five ties to five different schools. In both cases, A's ties are comparable to B's because they are to the same type of object. Of course, social network analysts are interested in more than the count of an actor's ties (although degree centrality is one of the oldest and most common metrics used by social network analysts), but other SNA algorithms generally assume that ties are between similar types of objects as well.

Finally, SNA differs from more traditional approaches (i.e., variable-based) in that although the latter focus on actors' attributes (e.g., gender, race, education) and ignore the broader social interaction patterns in which they are embedded (e.g., at home, work, and place of worship), SNA focuses on how these interaction patterns affect behavior, noting that although many attributes remain the same across social contexts, most interaction patterns do not, suggesting that interaction patterns are just as (or perhaps more) important for predicting and understanding behavior than are attributes:

> A woman who holds a menial job requiring little initiative in an office may be a dynamic leader of a neighborhood association and an assertive PTA participant. Such behavioral differences are difficult to reconcile with unchanging gender, age, and status attributes, but comprehensible on recognizing that people's structural relations can vary markedly across social contexts. (Knoke and Yang 2007:5)

SNA, then, is a collection of theories and techniques that provide empirical content to social context. It has been used successfully to explain varieties of behavior because it forces researchers "to think in terms of constraints and options that are inherent in the way social relations are organized" (Raab and Milward 2003). For example, Padgett and Ansell (1993) found that whether or not certain elite families in fifteenth-century Florence supported the Medicis or one of their rival political factions depended more on the pattern of economic, patronage, and marital ties than on the various families' class and status attributes (Knoke and Yang 2007:5).

1.3   Basic Terms and Concepts

Actor

In SNA the term *actor* refers to discrete individuals, subgroups, organizations, collectivities, communities, nation-states, and so on that are involved in social relations. In other words, SNA does not always focus on individuals, a fact that is often ignored by analysts using SNA in their attempts to disrupt dark networks. Within SNA, actors are sometimes referred to as *nodes* and *vertices*.

Tie

Actors are linked together by *ties*. Ties can vary in terms of type, strength, and direction. Examples of types of ties include (adapted from Wasserman and Faust 1994:18):

- Ties of sentiment (friendship, liking, respect)
- Resource ties (business transactions, financial flows)
- Ties of association or affiliation (members of the same church, club, etc.)
- Behavioral ties (communication ties)
- Ties based on geographic movement (migration, physical mobility)
- Ties based on status movement (social mobility)
- Ties based on physical connection (road, river, or bridge connecting two points)
- Formal ties (organizational hierarchy)
- Biological ties (kinship)

Ties can be said to vary on a continuum from strong to weak (Granovetter 1973, 1974). At the individual level, we can think of strong ties as those where actors have repeated and relatively intense interactions with one another, whereas we can think of weak ties as those where actors see one another occasionally or rarely. Nevertheless, it is not always self-evident where the cutoff between a strong and weak tie exists (Krackhardt

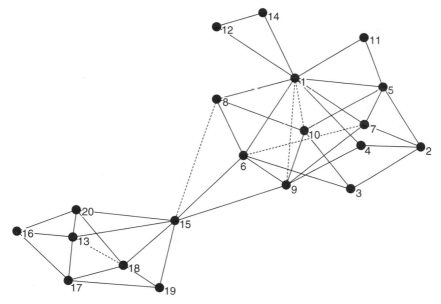

Figure 1.3. Hypothetical Social Network

1992). Moreover, what distinguishes a weak tie from the numerous, random, and usually unrepeated encounters actors experience daily is not always clear (Azarian 2005:37). Determining a threshold or cutoff value for identifying what constitutes a tie is (or at least should be) a difficult task. It is helpful to think of a social tie as "a theoretical construction, abstracted by the analyst from the bulk of largely erratic streams of affections, encounters, and interactions between a pair of actors, be they human beings, informal groups, formal organizations, or others" (Azarian 2005:37). A tie that has directionality (e.g., the flow of resources from one actor to another, where one actor communicates with another actor) is sometimes referred to as an arc. A tie that does not have directionality (e.g., spouse, kin) is sometimes referred to as an edge.

Social Network (and Social Network Analysis)

A social network is "a finite set or sets of actors" that share ties with one another (Wasserman and Faust 1994:20), and social network analysis involves "detecting and interpretating patterns of social ties among actors" (de Nooy et al. 2005:5). Figure 1.3 depicts a hypothetical social network where the circles represent actors and the lines (solid and broken) represent ties or relations. As this network illustrates, seldom are actors located randomly in networks; instead, they typically cluster within relatively distinct subgroups. Moreover, some actors are embedded deeply within a subgroup, while others sit more on the periphery, sometimes serving as bridges between subgroups.

Path (and Path Distance)

Notions of *path* and *path distance* are probably easier to illustrate than define, so here we do both. A *path* is defined as a *walk* (i.e., a sequence of actors and ties) in which no actor between the first and last actor of the walk occurs more than once, whereas the *path distance* between two actors is the number of steps between the two actors (Wasserman and Faust 1994:107).[4] Looking at Figure 1.3 you can trace a path from actor 9 to actor 19 through actor 15, and a path from actor 6 to actor 11 through actor 1. In both cases the distance between the actors is two (i.e., two steps). It is quite common for there to be numerous paths between actors, with some paths longer and shorter than others. The shortest path between two actors is known as a *geodesic*.

Topography

Networks differ from one another in terms of their overall structure or *topography*, and evidence suggests that a network's topography has a strong impact on the behavior of its members and is related to its performance and/or efficiency. For example, researchers have found that network density is positively related to the likelihood that actors within the network will follow accepted norms and behavior, which is why a primary basis for moral order is highly connected social networks. Why? One reason is that in dense networks it is easier for people to monitor the behavior of others and prevent them from engaging in deviant behavior (Granovetter 1992, 2005). Another is that most people are more likely to conform to social norms when they run the risk of losing their relationships to others if they do not (Finke and Stark 2005), and in dense networks we are more likely to have ties (relationships) that we are unwilling to lose, whereas in sparse networks we often lack the social ties that would otherwise prevent us from misbehaving. Take frontier areas like the Wild West, for instance. People are constantly passing through, which makes it hard for social ties to form, so social networks tend to be sparse. Sparse networks also make it difficult for institutions

---

[4] When discussing traveling from one actor to another, social network analysts distinguish between three types of connections: walks, trails, and paths. A *walk* is a sequence of actors and ties that begins and ends with actors and can involve the same actor more than once. A *trail* is also a walk but a particular tie can only be traversed (i.e., used) once. Thus, while all trails are walks, not all walks are trails. Finally, a *path* is a walk where, with one exception, each actor and each tie can only be used once. The exception is that the beginning and ending actor can be the same. See Wasserman and Faust 1994:105–108.

(like churches) to form, which is why frontiers tend to be short on piety and long on deviance (Finke and Stark 2005).

Another phenomenon related to network density is what some call the law of group polarization (Sunstein 2003:111–144), which "predicts that when like-minded people deliberate as an organized group, the general opinion shifts toward extreme versions of their common beliefs. In a product-liability trial, for instance, if nine jurors believe the manufacturer is somewhat guilty and three believe it is entirely guilty, the latter will draw the former toward a larger award than the nine would allow on their own. Or, if people who object in varying degrees to the war in Iraq convene to debate methods of protest, all will emerge from the discussion more resolved against the war" (Bauerlein 2004:B8). Sageman's (2004) study of the global Salafi jihad (GSJ) uncovered similar group dynamics.[5] He found that people who joined the GSJ were often homesick young men who drifted to familiar settings, such as mosques, looking for companionship. There, small clusters of friends formed. They often moved into apartments together where they underwent a long period of intense social interaction in their apartments and developed strong mutual intimacy (i.e., formation of dense networks). As they became closer, they progressively adopted the beliefs of the group's most extreme members. This distanced them further from their childhood friends and family, leading to increased isolation and loyalty to the group, which in turn intensified their faith, and they were then ready to join the jihad.

A network's topography can vary along several dimensions, and there are a number of measures available to social network analysts:

- *Density* is probably the most common metric; it captures the interconnectedness of a network and is equal to the ratio of actual ties to possible ties. As we will see, however, its formal measure has its limitations, and this has led researchers to suggest the use of alternative measures.
- *Centralization* is perhaps the next most common and (as the name suggests) measures the extent to which a network is centralized around a few actors; like density it has its limitations, and it varies depending on which centrality measure is used.

---

[5] By global Salafi jihad, Sageman means those Muslims who believe that in order for Islam to recapture the economic, cultural, and military preeminence that it once enjoyed, not only do Muslims need to return to the practices of their devout ancestors (*salaf* in Arabic), but also that it is permissible to use violence against both the near enemy (Muslim states that have fallen away from the true faith) and the far enemy (the West, in particular the United States and Israel). When speaking of the global Salafi jihad, he generally is referring to terrorists who focus their efforts on the West.

- Another useful measure is *fragmentation*, which is the proportion of all pairs of actors that are not tied with one another.

Other topographical measures include *network size* (the number of actors in a network), *average distance* (the average length of the geodesics between all actors in a network), and *diameter* (the length of a network's longest geodesic). We consider these and other measures in depth in Chapter 5.

Cohesive Subgroups (Subnetworks)

A major focus of SNA is to identify dense clusters of actors "among whom there are relatively strong, direct, intense, and/or positive ties" (Wasserman and Faust 1994:249). Social network analysts often refer to these clusters of actors as *cohesive subgroups* or *subnetworks* and generally assume that "social interaction is the basis for solidarity, shared norms, identity, and collective behavior, so people who interact intensively are likely to consider themselves a social group" (de Nooy et al. 2005: 61). If we lived in an ideal world, there would be one method that analysts could use to identify cohesive subgroups, but since we do not, it should not be a surprise that social network analysts have developed a variety of methods for identifying clusters of actors (Scott 2000). Chapter 6 explores some of the various approaches for using patterns of ties for identifying cohesive subgroups within social networks.

Centrality

The notion that certain actors within a network are more central than others goes back at least as far as Jacob Moreno's (1953) conception of sociometric stars and isolates (de Nooy et al. 2005; Scott 2000). Alex Bavelas (1950) was the first to formally investigate the properties of centrality as he looked at how a network influences the flow of communication in experimental groups (Scott 2000). Most social networks contain people or organizations that are more central than others and because of this they enjoy better access to resources and are in better positions to spread information. Social network analysts have identified several measures of centrality, each based on different assumptions of what it means to be more central (these are discussed in further detail in Chapter 7). The most commonly used measures are degree, closeness, betweenness, and eigenvector:

- *Degree centrality* is the count of the number of an actor's ties.
- *Closeness centrality* measures (based on path distance) how close, on average, each actor is to all other actors in a network; as we

will see, there are some limitations to the traditional closeness measure, but alternative measures are available.

- *Betweenness centrality* measures the extent to which each actor lies on the shortest path between all other actors in a network.
- *Eigenvector centrality* assumes that ties to highly central actors are more important than ties to peripheral actors, so it weights an actor's summed ties to other actors by their centrality scores.

Brokers and Bridges

Bridges are ties that span gaps in a social network, whereas *brokers* are those actors who sit aside a bridge. Both can be seen as being in a position to control the flow of resources through a network. In terms of Figure 1.3, the edges between actor 15 and actors 6, 8, and 9 would all be considered bridges, while the four actors would be considered brokers. That said, because actor 15 sits aside all three bridges, whereas the other three actors sit aside only one, actor 15 is clearly in more of a position of brokerage than are 6, 8, and 9. In other words, brokerage potential is not something that actors have or don't have, but rather is more a matter of degree. The same can be said of bridges. As we will see in our analysis of brokers and bridges in Chapter 8, some bridges are more crucial than are others.

Roles and Positions

Social network analysts typically analyze network data in one of two ways: (1) a relational, or (2) a positional approach (Emirbayer and Goodwin 1994). The former focuses on the direct and indirect ties between actors and seeks to explain behavior and social processes in light of those ties (Emirbayer and Goodwin 1994:1419). It highlights the importance of the topography of networks, the centrality of actors, the cohesiveness of subgroups, and the brokers and bridges between such groups. By contrast, the positional approach differs in that rather than focusing on the ties between actors, it seeks to identify structurally equivalent actors, that is, actors who may or may not have ties to one another but hold a similar position within a particular social network (e.g., the chief surgeons of different hospitals, the chairs of sociology departments in different academic institutions, the detachment commanders of a special forces operational detachment). It assumes (among other things) that structurally equivalent actors are likely to behave in similar ways regardless of whether a tie exists between them or not. Structurally equivalent positions can be observed by looking at the actors to whom a particular actor is connected (e.g., a chief surgeon interacts with surgical nurses and other surgeons; the chair of a sociology department interacts with graduate students, other professors, chairs of other departments, and university administrators; a detachment commander interacts with other officers and those under his or her command). "The relevant issue from this point of view is the specific 'position' or 'role' that a set of actors occupies within the system as a whole. Any such set is termed a 'block'" (Emirbayer and Goodwin 1994:1422), and the process by which such blocks are identified is referred to as *blockmodeling* (White, Boorman, and Breiger 1976). Analysts have developed a number of different types of algorithms for identifying structural equivalent actors (e.g., structural equivalence, automorphic equivalence, regular equivalence) and multiple algorithms within each of these types. We consider blockmodeling in Chapter 9.

Attributes

While SNA focuses primarily on the pattern of ties between actors, most social network analysts do not completely ignore attribute data (although some do – see the discussion of social networks, human agency, and culture in Section 1.5), which are characteristics of individual actors. If the actors in a network are individuals, then attribute data include things such as gender, race, ethnicity, years of education, income level, age, and so on. If the actors are corporations, then attribute variables can be those that measure total sales, net income, age of the corporation, number of employees, and so on. And if the actors are countries, then attribute variables would include measures such as GDP per capita or population size. As we will see later, centrality measures (once calculated) become attributes of actors as well. Sometimes the boundary between attributes and affiliations can be somewhat fuzzy. As a general rule, something is an affiliation if two actors' participation in that affiliation indicates a relationship, but it is also possible for an affiliation to function as an attribute as well.

1.4   Assumptions

While some have noted that SNA is more a collection of methods than a coherent theory (see, e.g., Granovetter 1979), most SNA methods are built on a common set of assumptions (Azarian 2005; Christakis and Fowler 2009; Knoke and Yang 2007; Wasserman and Faust 1994):

- Actors and their related actions are interdependent, rather than independent, with other actors.
- Ties between actors are conduits for the transfer or flow of various types of material and/or nonmaterial goods or resources (e.g., funds, supplies, information, trust, enmity).

- Social structures are seen in terms of enduring patterns of ties between actors (i.e., social networks).
- Repeated interactions between actors give rise to social formations that take on a life of their own, follow their own logic, and cannot be reduced to their constituent parts even though they remain dependent on those parts.
- An actor's position in the social structure (i.e., its structural location) impacts its beliefs, norms, and observed behavior.
- Social networks are dynamic entities that change as actors, subgroups, and ties between actors enter, form, leave, or are removed from the network.

Each of these assumptions is discussed in turn and illustrated with examples from various studies not only to make them more intelligible but also to draw out possible implications for applying SNA to the study of dark networks.[6]

Interdependence of Actors

SNA assumes that actors do not make decisions as autonomous units but instead are strongly influenced by the behavior and choices of other actors. At the individual level this can be illustrated by Solomon Asch's (1955) conformity experiments and Stanley Milgram's (1974) obedience to authority experiments.

Solomon Asch: Social Conformity. In his social conformity experiment, Solomon Asch sorted college students into groups of eight to ten subjects and told them that they were participating in a study about visual perception. The experiment entailed eighteen trials in which two cards, similar to those in Figure 1.4, were projected on a screen. Asch instructed the students that they were to choose the bar on the right card that was the same length as the bar on the left card. Moreover, they were to state their answers out loud so that all the other participants could hear their answer.

Of course, the experiment was rigged. Only one of the students was a real subject – the rest were Asch's confederates, who gave incorrect answers on twelve of the eighteen trials. Asch made sure that the real subjects were next-to-last to announce their answers so that they would hear most of the confederates' incorrect responses before they gave their own. He was curious to see whether the subjects would feel any pressure

---

[6] One could argue that some of these assumptions can be derived from others and thus should not be considered an assumption. For instance, the third assumption can be derived from the fourth, and the fifth can be derived from the first and third. Nevertheless, in getting at the essence of SNA, it is easier to simply list and discuss them separately.

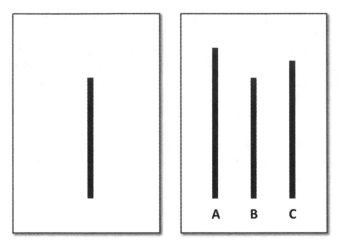

Figure 1.4. Solomon Asch's Conformity Experiment

to give the same answers as the confederate majority, even when the latter clearly answered incorrectly. Asch found that thirty-seven of the fifty subjects conformed to the majority at least once, while fourteen conformed on more than six of the twelve trials. The average conformity rate was one-third (four out of twelve trials). Asch varied the number of confederates from one to fifteen and found that subjects conformed to a group of three or four as readily as they did to larger groups. He did discover, however, that subjects were less likely to conform if they had an ally. If one of Asch's confederates gave the correct answer, subjects conformed only one-fourth as often as they did in the original experiment.

Stanley Milgram: Obedience to Authority. Subjects who participated in Stanley Milgram's "Obedience to Authority" experiments were told that the experiment was designed to test the effect of punishment on learning. Upon arriving they were sorted into "teachers" and "learners" by the drawing of slips. Unbeknownst to them, the drawing of slips was set up in such a way that the true subjects always ended up as teachers and Milgram's confederates always ended up as learners. Milgram (or one of his experimenters) told the teachers (i.e., the subjects) that their job was to teach a series of word pairs to the learners; their specific task was to administer a shock to the learners each time they made a mistake recalling a word. The teachers watched as the learners were strapped into an electric chair with an electrode taped to their wrist that the teachers were told was attached to a shock generator. The teachers were then taken to an adjacent room and seated in front of the shock generator. The generator had thirty switches, indicating the number of volts that could be administered, ranging from 15 to 450 volts, accompanied by labels ranging from "Slight Shock" to "Very Strong Shock" to "Danger: Severe Shock" to "XXX" (evidently indicating a lethal level of shock). The experimenter then told the teachers that they were to increase the shock level by 15 volts each time the learners gave a wrong answer.

The learners (i.e., the confederates) did not really receive any shocks, but the teachers (i.e., the subjects) did not know this. Initially, the learners only voiced verbal protests about the painfulness of the shocks, but once the shock level reached 300 volts, they began pounding the wall and, from that point on, did not answer. Eventually, they even stopped pounding. Throughout the experiment, the experimenter would restate the teachers' duties. If the teachers looked to the experimenter for guidance, the experimenter would say, "Please continue." If they protested that the learners were not answering, the experimenter would state that the learners' failure to answer should be treated as a wrong answer. If the teachers expressed reluctance to continue or suggested that the learners' condition should be checked, the experimenter would insist that "the experiment requires that you continue." If the teachers became really insistent, the experimenter would say, "You have no choice; you must go on."

In the end, every single teacher (i.e., subject) went beyond the 300-volt level and more than half – 65 percent – obeyed to the 450-volt end. These results shocked a great number of people, and not just those involved in the experiment. Up until this point many people believed that the Holocaust was a product of German culture or psyche, but these experiments suggested that in certain social contexts, ordinary individuals could do horrible things to their fellow human beings (Saltzman 2000). This is especially true when people are asked to obey people they perceive to be authorities or experts in their field (Sunstein 2003:35). Interestingly, in a variation on the experiment where it was conducted at an office in a rundown commercial building, only 47.5 percent of the subjects obeyed to the end (Milgram 1974:66–70), highlighting the important role that social context can play in human behavior.

Implications. These studies and others (Zimbardo, Maslasch, and Haney 2000) suggest that far from acting independently of those around them, people do just the opposite. In the face of peer pressure, Asch's student subjects chose to go along with the crowd even when the correct answer was obvious. How much more likely are people to go along with the crowd when they are presented with much more ambiguous information? Milgram's subjects demonstrate how perceived expertise or authority can lead people to make choices that one would hope they would otherwise not make. How are we to effectively combat the global Salafi jihad (Sageman 2003, 2004) when members of terrorist networks look to "respected" authorities such as Osama bin Laden and Ayman al-Zawahiri for inspiration (even after they are no longer living)? Put simply, these studies suggest that when analyzing the behavior of actors, if we do not take into account the social context in which they are embedded, we could arrive at a serious misunderstanding of their actions.

Following the crowd is not limited to individuals. As Paul DiMaggio, John Meyer, and Woody Powell (and their numerous colleagues) have repeatedly pointed out (see, e.g., DiMaggio and Powell 1983; Frank, Hironaka, and Schofer 2000; Meyer et al. 1997; Meyer and Rowan 1977; Powell and DiMaggio 1991), groups, corporations, and nation-states are no more likely to act autonomously than are individuals. For example, organizations that interact with one another tend to become more like one another over time. This tendency is not driven primarily by concerns over the bottom line, but rather by the concern that these organizations maintain their legitimacy in the eyes of other similar organizations (DiMaggio and Powell 1983).

> When an organizational practice or structure becomes commonly understood as a defining feature of a "legitimate" organization of a certain type, organizational elites feel pressure to institute that practice or structure. If there is a cultural norm that says, "In order for an organization to be a good organization, it must have characteristic X," organizations feel pressure to institute characteristic X. (Chaves 1997:32–33)

Ties as Conduits

Another SNA assumption is that ties (i.e., relations) between actors can function as conduits for the diffusion of various types of material and nonmaterial "goods," such as information, feelings, financial resources, norms, diseases, opinions, and trust. The Columbia University Drug Study, which documented the adoption by medical doctors of a new drug (Coleman, Katz, and Menzel 1957), illustrates this. Researchers gained access to local pharmacy prescription records and recorded when physicians first prescribed the drug. They also collected friendship and communication ties between the doctors, asking each to name three doctors whom they considered to be personal friends and three doctors with whom they would discuss medical matters. What they found was that the use of the new drug diffused quicker through social ties than apart from them. Subsequent studies found that other factors were important (Burt 1987), but they still affirmed the channeling effect of social ties (Strang and Tuma 1993).

The Strength of Weak Ties. Perhaps the best-known example of how ties can function as conduits for information is Mark Granovetter's (1973,

1974) study of how people got their present jobs. He found that they were far more likely to have used occasional personal contacts in finding their present job than by other means, suggesting that a particular type of tie, what he called "weak ties," plays an important role in the diffusion of information, such as job information. Granovetter collected data on how people found their current jobs and although approximately 19 percent used formal means[7] and another 19 percent directly applied for their job,[8] approximately 56 percent found their jobs through personal ties, of which most were weak ties (i.e., acquaintances, not close friends). Only 16.7 percent said that they saw their contact regularly at the time they heard about the job, while 55.6 percent said they saw their contact occasionally, and 27.8 percent said rarely (Granovetter 1973:1371). Moreover, workers who were not job hunting when they found their present jobs were more likely to have heard about them through weak ties.

All this led Granovetter to argue that when it comes to finding jobs, our weak ties – that is, our acquaintances – are more useful than our strong ties. Why? Because our acquaintances (i.e., our weak ties) are less likely to be socially involved with one another than are our close friends (i.e., our strong ties). Imagine the pattern of social ties suggested by this argument (Figure 1.5) and take any individual in the network. He or she will most likely have a collection of close friends, most of whom know one another. This same individual will also probably have a collection of acquaintances, few of whom know one another. But these acquaintances, in turn, are likely to be embedded in tightly knit networks of their own although different from our original individual. According to Granovetter, weak ties are important in terms of the overall structure of a network because they form the crucial bridges that tie these densely knit clusters of people together. In fact, if it were not for these weak ties, these clusters would not be connected at all.

Granovetter (1973:1363) also concluded that while not all weak ties are bridges, all bridges are weak ties. This is because of a process captured by what he referred to as the forbidden triad (Figure 1.6). Imagine that the ties between A and B and A and C are strong, and that initially B and C have no relationship with one another. In the short run the strong ties that run from C to B through A will function as a bridge between C and B. However, in the long run a tie will form between C and B (this is known as triadic closure) because A regularly interacts with B and C and odds

---

[7] Formal means is where the job seekers used the services of impersonal intermediaries such as advertisements, public and private employment agencies, interviews, and placements sponsored by universities or professional associations.

[8] Direct application is where the job seekers went or wrote directly to a firm, did not use a formal or personal intermediary, and had not heard about a specific opening from a personal contact.

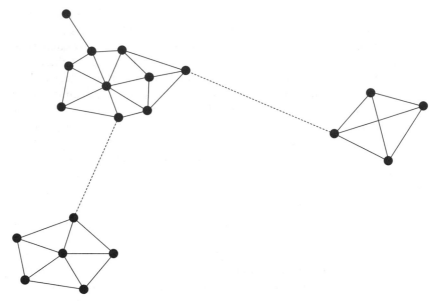

Figure 1.5. Strong and Weak Ties

are that in the long run B and C will meet and a tie will form between them. The resulting tie may be strong or weak, but the end result is that the ties running between C and B through A will no longer function as a bridge between C and B. Put differently, our close friends' close friends are likely to at least become acquaintances and possibly even friends (Rapoport 1953a, b; Rapoport and Horvath 1961). While Granovetter conceded that his argument was something of an exaggeration, he noted that research suggests that it holds true most of the time (Holland and

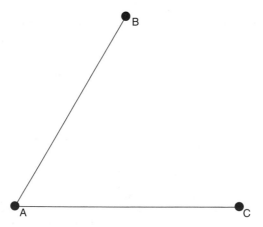

Figure 1.6. Granovetter's Forbidden Triad

Leinhardt 1971, 1972), meaning that weak ties are much more likely to form bridges than are strong ties (Onnela et al. 2007).

Granovetter's argument suggests that whatever good is to be diffused – whether it is job information, influence, resources, or trust – it will reach more people and travel a greater social distance if it passes through weak rather than strong ties (Granovetter 1973:1366). It also implies that actors with few weak ties are more likely to be "deprived of information from distant parts of the social system and will be confined to the provincial news and views of their close friends" (Granovetter 1983:202). Their lack of weak ties "will not only insulate them from the latest ideas and fashions, but it may also put them at a disadvantage in the labor market, where . . . knowing about appropriate job openings at just the right time" is paramount (Granovetter 1983:202).

Implications. Does this have any other implications for dark networks? Yes. In his analysis of the March 11, 2004, Madrid bombings, Rodriguez (2005) concludes that weak ties were a key feature of the terrorist network in that they enabled its cells to maintain operative ties with the larger network from which they were able to draw material supplies and ideological support. Rodriguez also believes that weak ties provide benefits to dark networks in other ways. He argues, for instance, that weak ties provide them with (1) relative stability when members are arrested or missions fail, (2) more flexibility that allows them to rapidly adapt to a changing environment, and (3) higher levels of security because weak ties are harder to detect than strong ones.

This is not to argue that strong ties are of no value. Indeed, "there is a mountain of research showing that people with strong ties are happier and even healthier because in such networks members provide one another with strong emotional and material support in times of grief or trouble and someone with whom to share life's joys and triumphs" (Stark 2007:37). Thus, feelings of trust and solidarity are more likely to be shared across strong ties than weak ones. This suggests that in order for dark networks to operate effectively they require an optimal mix, or what Aristotle called the "golden mean," of weak and strong ties. It also suggests that if we want to disrupt a dark network, altering this mix may prove to be a viable strategy. We will return to this topic in Chapter 5.

Social Structure in Terms of Social Networks

Social scientists frequently refer to the concept of *social structure*. By this term they usually have in mind the enduring patterns of behavior and relationships within social systems (e.g., roles) or the social institutions and norms that have become embedded in social systems in such a way that they shape behavior (Wikipedia 2007). Take, for example, this passage from an introductory sociology textbook:

> If you stand on the sidelines and watch the world pass you by, what you see is people moving about and somehow avoiding each other, people talking, people going in and out of buildings, people sitting on benches, people driving cars, people congregating, and in general you see just a maze of activity as individuals move about in physical space. There is fluidity to social life when examined this way, but there is also order, at least most of the time. People are not randomly moving about, talking, driving, entering and exiting buildings, or sitting around; they have purposes and goals as they move in space and talk to each other. But there is more than just purpose; there is structure to what you see as you look at the ebb and flow of human activity. Part of this structure inheres in the organization of symbols into culture, as it directs and guides individuals to act in certain ways. But for culture to be really effective in regulating conduct, it must be attached to something that orders social life. This extra "something" is social structure. *Social structures constrain who is present, where they stand, what they can do, and how they are related to each other. This structure is as real as the buildings that people occupy.* (Turner 2006:88, emphasis added)

However, while social structure may be as real as the buildings that people occupy, it is notoriously difficult to measure. It is easy to talk about social structure in the abstract but much harder to quantify. Within SNA social structures are seen in terms of enduring patterns of ties between actors (i.e., social networks). Thus, what SNA does is provide a method for systematically and empirically studying the causes and consequences of social structure (Degenne and Forsé 1999). It is an approach designed to explore and empirically capture the patterns of ties between people, groups of people, organizations, and countries.

Emergent Social Formations

Implicit but often unstated in the previous assumption is the belief that repeated interactions between actors (e.g., individuals) can give rise to social formations (e.g., groups, formal organizations) that take on a life of their own, follow their own logic, and cannot be reduced to or explained by their constituent parts even though they remain dependent on those parts (Clayton and Davies 2006; White 2008). While this may seem like an extraordinary claim, examples of emergence are quite common in the physical world, such as the combination of hydrogen (H) and oxygen (O) into water (H_2O):

> Water cannot exist apart from the hydrogen and oxygen that compose it . . . However, in their combination, the hydrogen and oxygen give rise to a truly new thing that is quite unlike either H or O, whether taken alone or as a sum of the separate parts H and O. Water, for example, has the characteristic of wetness, while hydrogen and oxygen do not. Water, furthermore, has the capacity to extinguish fires, while H and O feed fires. Water is the emergent reality brought about by a particular combination of hydrogen and oxygen. Water is very real and unique in its existence. It is composed of definite substances. But it is irreducible to that of which it is composed. Literally and truly something new has come into existence that is more than the sum of its parts. (Smith 2010:27)

Much like water cannot be reduced to or explained entirely by its underlying atoms but is still dependent on them, emergent social formations such as groups and organizations are products of interactions between actors that cannot be entirely explained by looking solely at the characteristics of those actors. Instead, they take on a life of their own and follow their own logic, which means that actors of all types and levels – whether they are individuals, groups, organizations, or nations – can be examined using SNA without needing to reduce them to the lower-level actors of which they are comprised.[9] For example, we can examine the social networks of Sudanese tribes (Colloton, Maitre, and Stoner 2007) and social movement organizations (Osa 2003) apart from the individuals who populate such tribes and organizations.

Implications. As we will see in the next chapter, this has important implications for the crafting of strategies because it means that SNA can be used for analyzing dark networks at the micro (e.g., individual), meso (e.g., group), and macro (e.g., institutional) levels. One last aspect of emergence worth noting is that emergent social formations can exert what is referred to as *downward causation* on lower-level entities, by which is meant that the former influences the actions of the latter. This fact serves as a nice segue to the next assumption of SNA: namely, the idea that an actor's structural location profoundly impacts its beliefs, behavior, and identity.

---

[9] It is important to note that the language of lower and higher does not imply an evaluative judgment of better or worse (Smith 2010:33).

Structural Location: Beliefs, Norms, Intentions, Behavior, and Identity

SNA assumes that actors' attitudes, beliefs, intentions, behavior, and even their identities are largely determined by their location in the social structure. Such an assumption is at odds with what many moderns believe to be true:

> Humans come to believe in a world full of continuous, neatly bounded, self-propelling individuals whose intentions interact with accidents and natural limits to produce all of social life... Closely observed, however, these same humans turn out to be interacting repeatedly with others, renegotiating who they are, adjusting the boundaries they occupy, modifying their actions in rapid response to other peoples' reactions, selecting among and altering available scripts, improvising new forms of joint action, speaking sentences no one has ever uttered before, yet responding predictably to their locations within webs of social relations they themselves cannot map in detail... They actually live in deeply relational worlds. (McAdam, Tarrow, and Tilly 2001:131)

The impact of social structure on actor behavior can be illustrated by examining what social scientists have learned about the process of conversion (recruitment) to religious and social movements. These studies show that people who are structurally (i.e., socially) close to a particular movement, religious or otherwise, are much more likely to join that movement than are those who are not.[10]

Conversion and Recruitment: Moonies, Mormons, and Movements. For years deprivation theory was the reigning theory of conversion. It argued that people join particular groups because they suffer from some sort of deprivation that the group's ideology (or theology) addresses. Thus, religious groups were seen as meeting particular needs – whether they were economic, social, or political. Consequently, researchers would look at a group's ideology to see what kinds of deprivation it addressed, and then conclude that people who joined that group must have been suffering from that sort of deprivation. For instance, because Christian Science promises to restore health, social scientists might conclude that Christian Science draws disproportionately from people suffering from chronic health problems or hypochondria (Glock 1964, cited in Stark 1996a:15). Of course, you could also argue the opposite that only people with good health would join and stay with a faith that believes that illness is only a

---

[10] To be clear, this is not the only way that the behavior of actors is affected by their structural location. It is just one among many.

state of the mind (Stark 1996a:15). Although it makes perfect sense that some people will find a particular ideology or theology more appealing than others, this does not explain why only some of these ideologically or theologically suited people actually join. That is where social network theory comes in. The basic insight of social network theory is that people will choose one religious group over another (or none at all) based on their patterns of ties. People are much more likely to join groups where they know people than where they do not.

Take, for instance, John Lofland and Rodney Stark's (1965; see also, Stark 1996a:13–21) study of people converting to the Unification Church, more commonly known as the Moonies. A woman named Young Oon Kim, who had come to California from Korea where she had been a university professor, started the local Moonies group. When she first arrived, she spoke at a number of public events, but these did not yield a single convert. Instead, her first three converts were close friends of hers whom she first got to know after she became a lodger with one of them. Next, some of the friends' husbands joined, and these were then followed by friends from work. The next converts were old friends, relatives, or people who first formed close friendships with one or more members in the group. As Stark notes, when he and Lofland first began watching the group, it "had never succeeded in attracting a stranger" (Stark 1996a:16). Moreover, Stark and Lofland witnessed a number of people who were sympathetic with the group's doctrines, but in the end did not join because they had numerous ties with people who disapproved of the Moonies. This led them to conclude that the people who ultimately joined the Moonies tended to be those whose ties to group members exceeded their ties to nonmembers (Stark 1996a:16).

In another study, Rodney Stark and Bill Bainbridge (1980) looked at the role that social ties play in recruiting people to the Mormon Church. Mormons tend to keep very good records of their missionary efforts and which methods work better than others, and Stark and Bainbridge were provided with data for all missionaries in the state of Washington during 1976–1977 (Stark and Bainbridge 1980:1386). Mormons recruit through a variety of means: They go door to door, they follow up on referrals, and they meet potential recruits in the home of a relative or friend of the potential recruits. Interestingly, when missionaries went door to door, their success rate was only 0.1 percent. Referrals provided a somewhat higher rate of success (7 percent for covert referrals and 8 percent for overt referrals). Their highest rates of success, however, occurred when Mormons invited non-Mormon friends and relatives into their homes to meet Mormon missionaries. In those instances, they enjoyed a success rate close to 50 percent. This suggests that the best strategy for conversion is not cold-calling but forming friendships with non-Mormons.

Stark and Bainbridge noted that an article in the Mormon Church's official magazine provided detailed instructions on how to recruit new members, and a recurring theme was the importance of building close personal ties with non-Mormons. It also explicitly instructed its readers that they should downplay or avoid discussing religion while forming these ties. Only later were they to bring up that they were Mormons (Stark 2005:79–80). "Another way of looking at these findings is that missionaries do not serve as the primary instrument of recruitment to the Mormon faith. Instead, recruitment is accomplished primarily by the rank and file of the church as they construct intimate interpersonal ties with non-Mormons and thus link them into a group network" (Stark and Bainbridge 1980:1387–1388).

Shortly after the Stark and Bainbridge study appeared, a study by David Snow and his colleagues (Snow, Zurcher, and Ekland-Olson 1980) highlighted essentially the same dynamic: Successful social movements, religious or otherwise, recruit primarily through social networks of friends and families. All of the groups they studied, except the Hare Krishna, recruited more than 50 percent of their members through either kinship or friendship networks with several recruiting more than 90 percent of their members through such networks. The lone exception was the Hare Krishnas. Why? Because the Hare Krishnas demand exclusive participation from their members and require them to sever all extramovement ties. Thus, they have no social networks outside of the group through which they can recruit, and this forces them to recruit from public places. That is why they are so small. Successful social movements must maintain open social networks in order to grow.

Implications. What these studies tell us is that people do not join groups randomly. Instead, individuals who are located socially proximate to a group are far more likely to join that group than are those who are socially distant. Put differently, the structural location of actors is a large factor in determining which groups they will join and which ones they will not. That is why it is not surprising that Sageman (2003, 2004) discovered that recruitment to the GSJ occurs primarily through social ties. He found that 65 percent of the terrorist group's members had preexisting friendship ties with someone in the group, whereas another 15 percent had kinship ties. After eliminating overlaps between the two types of ties, 75 percent of the terrorists Sageman studied joined through friendship and kinship ties. He found that another 8 percent had ties to teachers who had links to the jihad, meaning that 83 percent of the individuals who joined the GSJ joined through some sort of social ties. This led him to conclude that although factors such as anger at U.S. policies may increase the pool of potential recruits to the GSJ, only those who have a link to the group actually join.

Dynamic Social Networks

Finally, SNA assumes that networks are always changing as actors enter and leave the network and as ties form and dissolve. For example, the removal of key actors can disrupt the flow of information through the network, whereas the departure of a network's peripheral players could lead the network to become more isolated. Similarly, an actor's entrance into a network could temporarily destabilize the network as new lines of communication and trust are negotiated among network members. What this means in practical terms is that network structures are constantly in flux. Over time they become more or less fragmented, more or less dense, as well as grow or shrink in size. Additionally, groups of actors that cluster together at one point in time and that were central today may become less so next week (and vice versa). To make matters even more complicated, actors often move from one geographic location to another, which can potentially affect the impact they have on their network's operations. For example, if a dark network's one and only bomb maker is forced to move hundreds of miles away from where it carries out its operations, then the network's efficiency will almost certainly suffer.

Although social network analysts have always known this, historically, longitudinal network data have been difficult to come by and methods for their analysis were undeveloped. Indeed, Stanley Wasserman and Katherine Faust's classic SNA text makes little mention of longitudinal networks. Only in the book's final chapter does it note the importance of developing good and easy-to-use methods for examining longitudinal network data (Wasserman and Faust 1994:730–731).

This situation is beginning to change. Longitudinal network data and their analysis are becoming more common. Much of this analysis is largely descriptive in nature, but the development of model-based approaches are allowing analysts to uncover the underlying processes that may be at work in particular networks (Breiger, Carley, and Pattison 2003; de Nooy 2011; Doreian and Stockman 1997; McCulloh and Carley 2011; Snijders 2005; Snijders, Bunt, and Steglich 2010; Steglich, Snijders, and Pearson 2010). As appealing and promising as these models are, however, as of yet most do not fall into Wasserman and Faust's "easy-to-use" category, and their implementation often requires specialized software. Moreover, a lot can be said for techniques that allow analysts to track changes in a network's topographical characteristics, the degree of clustering among its members, and the emergence and decline of various actors. These more descriptive approaches can also be used to test hypotheses and are capable of uncovering many of a network's underlying dynamics (see, e.g., de Nooy et al. 2005:84–96). Although this book relies primarily on more descriptive approaches, it does explore some of the newer models, such as those that seek to detect significant changes in a network's structure, those that take into account the geographic location of actors, and those that allow researchers to sort between genuine and spurious correlations.

Implications. All this suggests that not only do researchers need to closely monitor changes in dark networks but also that careful analyses will often suggest ways to disrupt or destabilize them. For example, Marc Sageman (2003, 2004) drew on the work of Albert-László Barabási and his colleagues (Barabási 2002; Barabási and Albert 1999; Barabási, Albert, and Jeong 1999; Barabási and Bonabeau 2003) to offer suggestions as to how to disrupt the GSJ. According to Barabási, the world is "small" because it exhibits the characteristics of a "scale-free network," which is a network where a handful of actors have many connections (i.e., hubs), but most actors have very few. Because most actors in a scale-free network have very few ties, scale-free networks are relatively immune to random failures but are vulnerable to targeted attacks. Research suggests that the removal of 10 to 15 percent of the hubs in a scale-free network will generally disconnect the network (Barabási 2002; Barabási and Bonabeau 2003). In his research, Sageman discovered that the GSJ also exhibits the characteristics of a scale-free network, which led him to argue that the United States should focus its efforts on destroying hubs rather than randomly stopping terrorists at its borders. "[The latter] may stop terrorists from coming here, but will leave the network undisturbed. However . . . if the hubs are destroyed, the system breaks down into isolated nodes. The jihad will be incapable of mounting sophisticated large scale operations like the 9/11 attacks and be reduced to small attacks by singletons" (Sageman 2003). To be sure, the simultaneous removal of 10 to 15 percent of a dark network's hubs is easier said than done, and research suggests that hubs are often quickly replaced by other highly central and/or structurally equivalent actors (Pedahzur and Perliger 2006; Tsvetovat and Carley 2005). Nevertheless, Sageman's approach illustrates how the removal of a few key nodes could significantly alter the dynamics of a dark network.

More recently, Ian McCulloh and Kathleen Carley (2011) applied social network change detection (SNCD) techniques to a number of longitudinal networks, including the Al Qaeda communication network from 1988 to 2004 (Carley 2006). SNCD is an analytic method for monitoring social networks that alerts analysts whether and when statistically significant changes have occurred in a network (either at the topographical or actor level), which allows them to potentially detect causes for the change and predict significant events or behaviors (McCulloh and Carley 2011:6, 10). For example, using SNCD to analyze yearly snapshots of the Al Qaeda communication network in terms of three social network measures – density, average closeness centrality, and average betweenness centrality – McCulloh and Carley detected that a statistically significant change occurred in the network in 1997, which they then traced back to a series of events that helped unite Islamic militants and organize Al Qaeda for terrorist attacks aimed at the United States (McCulloh and Carley 2011:21). One can only wonder what might have been if these data and techniques had been available prior to September 2001.

1.5 Social Networks, Human Agency, and Culture

The priority that SNA places on relations between actors over individual attributes in explaining behavior and processes inevitably leads to questions of human agency and culture. Put simply, does SNA leave room for free will and the effects of culture? The answer is yes and no. Some versions of it do; some don't. Mustafa Emirbayer and Jeff Goodwin (1994:1424–1436) identified three social network paradigms to which most social network analysts adhere: structural determinism, structural instrumentalism, and structural constructionism. According to Emirbayer and Goodwin, *structural determinism* leaves no room for human agency or culture. It entirely ignores (or dismisses) the possible causal role that actors' beliefs, values, and commitments play in terms of social processes and historical change. The early writings of Harrison White (Boorman and White 1976; White, Boorman, and Breiger 1976) reflect this view as do those of the early network theorist, Bruce Mayhew:

> Structuralists do not attribute social or psychological characteristics to individual humans. Rather, structuralists view individual human beings as biological organisms. Hence, individual characteristics might include pulse rate, blood pressure, height, metabolic rate, and so on. But there are no social characteristics of individuals. To structuralists, social phenomena are properties of social networks (properties of organizations); they are never characteristics of biological individuals. Furthermore, for structuralists, psychological phenomena do not exist (they are not defined). (Mayhew 1980:346)

For Mayhew, individuals are no more than biological machines and human consciousness is irrelevant to understanding the social world (Smith 2010:242). Free will, in other words, does not exist in Mayhew's world.

By contrast *structural instrumentalism* does allow room for human agency, but social network analysts who adopt this approach tend to view it solely in terms of rational choice, instrumental action, and utility maximization. "Many, if not most, such network analysts assume unproblematically that actors – individuals and even groups or organizations – are utility maximizers who pursue their material interests in money, status, and power in precisely the ways predicted by theorists of rational choice" (Emirbayer and Goodwin 1994:1428). Roger Gould's masterful network analyses of the Paris Commune (1991, 1993b) are examples of this because they assume that instrumental motivation lies behind the political mobilization they attempt to explain. The numerous studies of religious phenomena by Rodney Stark and his colleagues (see, e.g., Lofland and Stark 1965; Stark 1991, 1996a, b; Stark and Bainbridge 1980) fit into this paradigm as well. Given that ample evidence exists supporting the premise that actors do respond to incentives (see, e.g., Becker 1976; Berman 2009; Iannaccone 1995; Levitt and Dubner 2005), this approach clearly improves on the previous one. As Granovetter puts it, "while the assumption of rational action must always be problematic, it is a good working hypothesis that should not easily be abandoned" (Granovetter 1985:506). Nevertheless, as the structural constructionist approach discussed in the following paragraph highlights, it is not without its shortcomings.

Structural constructionism, like structural instrumentalism, takes seriously the role of human agency in attempting to account for social change, but unlike structural instrumentalism, it sees actors as motivated by additional concerns, such as norms, values, cultural commitments, and collective and individual identities. In short, adherents to this perspective hold that culture plays a role as well. Emirbayer and Goodwin hold up Doug McAdam's (1986, 1988a) analysis of Freedom Summer as an example of this approach (see also McAdam et al. 2001), whereas Christian Smith (2010) points to David Knoke, who argues that

> a sophisticated understanding of . . . action requires blending cultural, rational, and structural constraints in complex specifications for given substantive problems. The structural perspective should be seen as an enriching, rather than a competing, paradigm. (Knoke 1990:19, quoted in Smith 2010:228)

The later writings of Harrison White (1992, 2008), with his emphasis on the importance of narratives, stories, and networks of meaning, can also be located here.

While the methodologies detailed in this book tend to be agnostic on issues of structure, culture, and agency, the use of SNA to craft strategies for tracking and disrupting dark networks cannot be. The constraints and opportunities afforded to actors by the networks in which they are embedded cannot be considered apart from the cultural influences, normative commitments, and instrumental concerns of the actors involved. For example, consider the issues surrounding the collection of kinship network data. What constitutes a kinship network in the West can differ considerably from what constitutes one in some Middle Eastern and Asian cultures. Or take, for instance, the FARC (Fuerzas Armadas

Revolucionarias de Colombia – Revolutionary Armed Forces of Colombia), the Colombian guerrilla group that is believed to be the oldest and, at its height, the largest guerrilla group in the world. It began as a Marxist-inspired movement in 1964 in order to protect rural peasants against the harsh policies and practices of large landowners; it also provided them with education in exchange for food and supplies (Metelits 2010). As it grew and sought additional funding sources for its activities, however, it turned to first the "taxing" and eventually the running of a substantial portion of the Colombian drug trade (Safford and Palacios 2002). Consequently, while it is likely that some of its members are ideologically motivated (i.e., Marxist), a substantial portion is probably only in it for the (drug) money. Thus, analysts may want to separately map the ideological and instrumental networks prior to crafting strategies to disrupt it.

1.6   Summary and Conclusion

This chapter has provided an overview of social network analysis, how it differs from other analytic approaches, the basic terms and concepts that it employs, and the key assumptions that underlie much, if not all, of what social network analysts do. These assumptions are often more implicit than explicit in the work of social network analysts, but nevertheless they are there (or at least one hopes they are). They provide the foundation on what we cover in later chapters. For instance, the various centrality metrics that we will examine provide analysts with a sense of actors' structural locations. Similarly, measures of density and centralization attempt to capture the overall structure of a social network. We will not always draw explicit ties between these assumptions and specific metrics, but we hope they become more obvious as you immerse yourself in this field. This chapter also took up the related issues of culture and human agency and what role these play in social network analysis. As we saw, not all social network analysts include human agency and culture into their causal models, but when it comes to crafting strategies for disrupting dark networks, such factors cannot be ignored. The crafting of strategies is the topic of the next chapter, to which we now turn.

2

Strategic Options for Disrupting Dark Networks

2.1 Introduction

Given the time and energy that has been devoted to the collection of data on dark networks (see, e.g., Koschade 2006; Krebs 2001; Rodriguez 2005; Sageman 2004, 2008; van Meter 2001), it is surprising that little attention has been paid to exploring strategies for their disruption (Roberts and Everton 2011). Strategies for combating them are poorly documented in the literature, and with one exception (Lempert et al. 2008), little or no research compares alternative strategies with a view of balancing potential gains and costs. Moreover, it appears to be almost an article of faith that once a dark network's structure has been mapped and its key members identified, one is supposed to capture and eliminate designated high-value targets. However, as noted in the preface, while targeting key players is one option to consider (Walzer 2009:274), other options exist that may offer better alternatives when taking into account costs, human lives, and the consequences for affected communities (see Chapter 12).

This chapter argues that various strategies for countering dark networks need to be considered prior to the use of formal social network analysis. It begins by distinguishing between two general approaches to countering dark networks: kinetic and nonkinetic.[1] The former involves aggressive and offensive measures designed to eliminate or capture network members and their supporters, while the latter involves the use of subtle, noncoercive means designed to reduce a network's effectiveness and impair a combatant's will to fight. This chapter then moves to an overview of the process through which analysts can generate strategies

---

[1] There is little agreement in the literature on how to describe the alternative approaches to countering terrorism. Some authors use different characterizations such as direct and indirect strategies (Arreguin-Toft 2001, 2005; Fridovich and Krawchuck 2007; Krawchuck ND). Here the focus is on combatant behavior and the level of the coercion involved in their strategies; hence, the terms "kinetic" and "nonkinetic" are used.

for disrupting networks, a process that involves the drafting of working hypotheses, the identification of relations of interest, the aggregation and/or parsing of these networks, the exploratory analysis and interpretation of the networks, and a revisiting of the original hypotheses. The chapter then concludes with a brief reflection on the proper uses of SNA for the disruption of covert and illegal networks.

2.2   Strategic Options for Disrupting Dark Networks[2]

Of the two approaches to combating dark networks, the kinetic approach tends to receive more attention because the capture or elimination of high-value targets attracts headlines and engenders popular support. One only has to recall the media attention (and spontaneous celebrations across the United States) that Osama bin Laden's assassination engendered to know that this is true. The nonkinetic approach, which typically requires patience and skill, tends to attract far less attention, probably because of its subtlety and lack of newsworthiness. Nevertheless, the former U.S. Special Operations Commander, Admiral Eric T. Olson, has tried to shift the emphasis away from kinetic, high-profile raids and toward the use of more nonkinetic approaches. He acknowledges that while kinetic action may be "urgent and necessary" in the short term, he believes that it is merely "a holding action that buys time for non-kinetic approaches to have their effects" (quoted in Roberts and Everton 2011:4). Because of the importance that these two approaches play in counter-insurgency operations, both are explored in greater depth in the following sections.

Kinetic Approach

Kinetic operations target enemy combatants and their supporters in order to neutralize, capture, or eliminate them. They are typically referred to as *targeting strategies* and can be pursued at the individual, group, and organizational (i.e., institutional) levels. Regardless of the level of analysis, they involve the removal of key actors (i.e., individuals, groups, or organizations) or the severing of ties between such actors. When individuals are the target, such as the capture or elimination of Saddam Hussein, Abu Musab al-Zarqawi, or Osama bin Laden, the U.S. military describes such operations as man-hunting (Marks, Meer, and Nilson 2005). When

---

[2] This section has been adapted from Nancy Roberts and Sean F. Everton. 2011. "Strategies for Combating Dark Networks." *Journal of Social Structure* 12(2):1–32. Accessed at http://www.cmu.edu/joss/content/articles/volume12//RobertsEverton .pdf. Used with permission. Nancy, of course, should not be held responsible for my adaptations.

groups or organizations are the target, they are referred to as group or organizational targeting. Examples of the former include the roundup of specific groups fashioning improvised explosion devices (IEDs) in Iraq (Peter 2008), the disruption of the Syrian recruitment network bringing jihadists into Iraq (Felter and Fishman 2007), and the shutdown of the financial network supporting the Indonesia-based Jemaah Islamiyah (JI) (Abuza 2003); examples of the latter include Malaysia's successful effort to close down Luqmanul Hakiem, a jihadist religious boarding school (Rabasa 2005) and the Al Qaeda–linked Islamic NGO, Pertubuhan al Ehasan, in 2002 (Abuza 2003).

Sometimes military forces function in a consulting role and work "through, by, and with" indigenous forces to build their capacity to conduct effective targeting operations against common enemies (Fridovich and Krawchuck 2007). An example of this approach is when U.S. Special Operation Command forces deployed to Basilan to advise and train the Armed Forces of the Philippines in their fight against the Abu Sayyaf Group (ASG) (Fridovich and Krawchuck 2007; Krawchuck ND; Wilson 2006).

Nonkinetic Approach

The nonkinetic approach is a less aggressive means for countering insurgencies. It involves a more subtle and patient application of power by seeking to undermine insurgencies "more through cooperation and collaboration with partners than through unilateral...action, more with the diplomatic and economic tools of national power than with the military, stressing inspiration rather than prescription" (Brimley and Singh 2008:313). Its goal is to secure the population's safety and support while undermining the enemy's influence and control (Galula [1964] 2006; Kilcullen 2008, 2009; McCormick 2005; Wendt 2005) and employs numerous ways to accomplish this goal: institution-building, psychological operations (PsyOp), information operations (IO), rehabilitation and reintegration programs, and the tracking and monitoring of key network actors. Like the kinetic approach, it can target individuals, groups, or organizations.

Institution-Building. This strategy promotes reconstruction in war-torn communities and requires the active involvement of civil affairs forces that provide humanitarian and civic assistance and work in tandem with intergovernmental and interagency partners in the reconstruction process. The emphasis is on building healthy host-government institutions of governance, rule of law, economic development, and transportation infrastructure (Fridovich and Krawchuck 2007; Kilcullen 2009). As we will see in the final chapter, contemporary "just war" theorizing sees institution-building as a necessary criterion of what it means to fight a "just war" (Allman and Winright 2010).

Psychological Operations (PsyOp). Psychological operations involve the dissemination of information for the purpose of influencing the emotions, perceptions, attitudes, objective reasoning, and ultimately the behavior of foreign nationals (individuals, groups, organizations, governments) so that they are more aligned with one's goals and objectives during times of conflict and peace (U.S. Special Operations Command 2003). They are also employed to counter adversary propaganda and to sow disaffection and mistrust among network members to reduce their will to fight and ultimately induce their surrender. This strategy also includes tactics that attempt to set network members and/or subgroups against each other. One example is the British plan to split the Taliban from within by securing the defection of its senior members and a large number of their supporters. It follows from former British Prime Minister Gordon Brown's decision to focus on courting "moderate" Taliban leaders and "tier-two" foot soldiers who fight more for money and a sense of tribal loyalty than for the Taliban's ideology as well as from the United States' consideration of a divide-and-conquer strategy to peel away some lower-level members of the Taliban and win back the population (Cooper 2009; Rubin 2011).

Information Operations (IO). This strategy uses integrated employment of electronic warfare and computer network operations to combat terrorism.[3] Examples include the disruption of fund transfers, the monitoring of charitable donations, and the detection of money laundering, black market activity, and the drug trade. Activities also include interventions to compromise terrorists' cell phone and online connections and the use of these platforms to locate leaders and their followers.

Rehabilitation and Reintegration. Charles Tilly (2004, 2005) has noted that throughout history trust networks (e.g., insurgencies, trade diasporas, clandestine religious groups, terrorist groups) have often segregated themselves from what they perceive to be hostile or predatory regimes.[4] In so doing they "hoard" various resources (material and nonmaterial) for

---

[3] In contrast to military doctrine (U.S. Director of Operations 2006), in this book psychological operations are separated from information operations because the latter puts a strong emphasis on technology-centric interventions that involve computer and other sophisticated electronic systems, whereas the former puts a strong emphasis on human factors.

[4] Tilly defines trust networks as "ramified interpersonal connections, consisting mainly of strong ties, within which people set valued, consequential long-term resources and enterprises at risk to the malfeasance, mistakes, or failures of others" (Tilly 2005:41).

themselves. Tilly argues, however, that regimes, in particular democratic ones, cannot survive without the partial integration of trust networks (and their resources) into civil society. The rehabilitation and reintegration strategy seeks to do just that. An example is Singapore's counter-ideological program founded by Muslim scholars who seek to "correct" the thinking of its detainees (Ramakrishna 2005). This program also seeks to extend its influence into the wider Muslim community by giving talks, disseminating publications, and hosting a website in order to "immunize" the minds of Singaporean Muslims against violent radical Islamist ideologies. In addition, the Singapore government is attempting to forge closer ties between Muslims and non-Muslims through the Community Engagement Program, using Inter-Racial and Religious Confidence Circles in neighborhoods, workplaces, and schools. Similar rehabilitation programs also have been introduced to other countries such as Indonesia, Saudi Arabia, and Yemen.[5] While these efforts are encouraging, if recent research on the effectiveness of U.S. faith-based prison programs that seek to reduce recidivism is of any relevance here, then efforts at redirecting or reframing the extremist ideologies of detainees (Juergensmeyer 2001) may not be enough to bring about their lasting transformation. What may also be necessary are "after care" programs that steer former detainees away from the networks that gave rise to their extremism in the first place and toward networks that support their new theological outlook (Johnson 2011).[6]

One reason this strategy is so attractive is because dark networks often suffer considerable damage if one of their members defects. Studies of insurgent groups have found that groups that keep defection to a minimum tend to be more successful than those that do not because, as political scientist Samuel Popkin discovered when he returned to Vietnam in the 2000s in order to ask former Viet Cong insurgents questions he couldn't ask when he was a graduate student in the 1960s, defection can shut an insurgency down for months (Popkin 2007, cited in Berman 2009:29):

> *Popkin*: "If one of your members was killed, how long did it take for the organization to recover?"
> *Former Viet Cong Rebel*: "A few days."
> *Popkin*: "And if a member defected?"
> *Former Viet Cong Rebel*: "Between a week and two months."

[5] For a review of Saudi Arabia's program, see Boucek (2008a, b). The report by Fink and Hearne (2008) on deradicalization and disengagement from violent extremism provides a general overview of topic. See also Horgan (2009) and Jones and Libicki (2008).

[6] The connection between Johnson's work and rehabilitation programs such as these was first suggested to me by a student of mine, Major Justin Duvall.

Why? Because an insurgency's leaders do not know what information has been passed to the authorities, so drop points need to be changed, members have to lie low, and plans have to be altered because they may have been compromised (Berman 2009:29).

Tracking and Monitoring. While it may seem counterintuitive, sometimes the best strategy may be to do nothing. Well, not exactly nothing, but because information on a particular dark network is often incomplete, rather than taking immediate action, it is sometimes better in the short run to track and monitor certain actors with the hope of improving knowledge of the network, which will in turn improve the selection of strategies adopted down the road (Arquilla 2008). As John Arquilla notes

> In the successful strikes against al Qaeda affiliates in Singapore, Morocco, and Saharan Africa, the key doctrinal approach was to wait and watch for a considerable period, then to swarm the targets simultaneously at their moment of maximum illumination. This strategic patience grew out of the understanding that striking at nodes *as* they were identified might actually reduce the ability to detect and track other cells in the networks in question. It is a curious doctrinal point about netwar: the more that is disrupted, the less may be known. (Arquilla 2009:34)

When using this approach, then, analysts will want to draw on those SNA metrics that help identify the individuals, subgroups, organizations, and so on that appear to be worth tracking.

Summary

This section has distinguished between two general approaches to countering dark networks: kinetic and nonkinetic. The kinetic approach pursues aggressive measures designed to eliminate or capture network members and their supporters. By contrast, the nonkinetic approach employs neither bombs nor bullets but instead uses noncoercive means to counter networks and impair a combatant's will to fight. It includes activities such as the reconstruction of war-torn areas, the disruption of electronic fund transfer networks, information campaigns to win over the "hearts and minds" of local populations, efforts at the rehabilitation and reintegration of dark network members into civil society, and the tracking of certain members in order to improve our knowledge and understanding of the network. Table 2.1 summarizes these options.

Of course, a single approach will seldom suffice. Often, multiple strategies will need to be adopted, some focused on the short term, some on the long term. Moreover, analysts need to take into account unanticipated second- (and third- and fourth-) order effects. For example, implementing

Table 2.1. *Strategic options of social network analysis*

	Kinetic			Nonkinetic		
Strategies	Targeting	Institution Building	PsyOp	Information Operations	Rehabilitate/ Reintegrate	Track, Monitor
Level			Individual, Group, and Institutional			

a raid to capture an insurgent in an otherwise friendly neighborhood is its first-order effect, but the raid's second-order effect may be to decrease support for the host-nation government and increase support for the insurgents if done incorrectly. If the second-order effects of a successful but unpopular raid begin to outweigh the first-order benefits, the secondary effects should take precedence in the planning cycle. Simply put, commanders and policy officials must consider kinetic and non-kinetic actions, approaches, and most importantly effects together as a net positive or net negative in order to most effectively craft strategies for disrupting dark networks.[7]

2.3   Crafting Strategies with Social Network Analysis

In practice, using social network analysis (SNA) to craft strategies for the disruption of dark networks is an iterative process that involves both exploratory analysis and confirmatory analysis (i.e., hypothesis testing). Exploratory SNA "involves visualization and manipulation of concrete networks, whereas hypothesis testing boils down to numbers representing abstract parameters and probabilities" (de Nooy et al. 2005:xxv). The general process for doing this is as follows:

- Develop working hypotheses
- Identify and record relationships of interest
- Aggregate (i.e., combine) and/or parse networks of interest
- Analysis and interpretation
- Craft strategies for the disruption of the network

While we focus on each of these steps in more depth later in this book, it is appropriate to discuss each of them briefly before proceeding.

Developing Working Hypotheses

Before attempting to use SNA, researchers need to first develop working (i.e., tentative) hypotheses as to how best to disrupt the dark network

[7]   I thank LCDR Kristian Kearton, CW3 Chad Machiela, and LT Bobby Ramirez for pointing this out to me.

they are analyzing. First, they have to decide whether they intend to use kinetic or nonkinetic approaches or a combination of both and then determine which relationships of interest best lend themselves to their chosen strategies. Some, for example, may decide that the best approach is to focus on the network's financial ties, believing that by shutting down or disrupting the flow of funds, it will be difficult for the network to finance operations. Others may conclude that targeting a network's operational ties offers the best opportunity for disruption, assuming that without its key operatives, a network will not have the personnel necessary to carry out operations. Still others may seek to breed distrust among network members in order that it implodes from within (Anonymous 2009). Some may choose not to focus on a network's individual actors at all but instead on its formal and informal organizations, arguing that the network can more effectively be disrupted by focusing on the groups and organizations that helped give rise to and currently sustain the insurgency (Smith 1996). For example, in the fight against radical forms of Islam, analysts could identify central jihadi schools and build alternative schools nearby, ones that promote moderate forms of Islam and instruct students in subjects other than the memorization of the Qur'an (e.g., reading, writing, and arithmetic; Roberts and Everton 2011). This would clearly constitute a long-term strategy, one that aims not so much at disrupting the current contours of a network but one that aims to deprive it of a key resource (McAdam 1982; McCarthy and Zald 1977; Wiktorowicz 2004). In short, there are multiple ways of disrupting dark networks, of which these are only a few examples. The broader point is that before beginning to collect data on a dark network, researchers need to first develop working hypotheses as to how they plan to disrupt the network.

Identifying, Collecting, and Recording Social Network Data

Working hypotheses guide the types of relationships researchers will eventually collect and record. At the individual level these can be friendship ties, school ties, operational ties, religious ties, and so on. At the group level, they can be ties between two institutions because they share a common member.[8] That said, collecting social network data can be a tedious and complicated process. Not only do we have to determine which ties are important, we have to determine a network's boundaries – that is, where it begins and ends. We may decide to analyze a particular network, but identifying which actors are members of the network and which ones

---

[8] For example, if someone teaches at a particular school and attends a local community of faith, one could argue that a tie exists between the school and the community of faith.

are not is generally easier said than done. "Networks naturally spread out, so no boundary is ever perfect," but we hope "to find a set of actors with relatively good separateness from the rest of the world" from which we can draw reasonable conclusions (Erickson 2001:317). We take up this topic in more depth in the Chapter 4.

Although new tools are being developed to ease the collection of social network data, analysts have typically recorded relational data in matrix form (see Chapter 4). Take, for instance, the following subset of marital ties between Renaissance Florentine families collected and recorded by John Padgett and Christopher Ansell (1993) and used by Breiger and Pattison (1986) (Figure 2.1). A tie was determined to exist if a member of one family married a member of another family. The data are recorded in a square matrix with a row and column for each family. If a marriage occurred between two families, then a "1" appears in the families' common cells (e.g., Acciaiuol and Medici).[9] If not, a "0" appears. As we will see, there are instances where ties are not reciprocal and are recorded accordingly.

As one can imagine, when working with very large networks, recording network data in matrix form can prove challenging and is why social network analysts often turn to other methods when working with large networks. For our purposes here, however, we focus on recording data in matrix form.

Aggregating (Combining) and/or Parsing Networks

Actors are typically involved in more than one type of relation (Hanneman and Riddle 2005). For example, most individuals are embedded in a number of different types of ties, such as friendship, kinship, and economic. Business organizations are no different. They engage in financial and informational exchanges and sometimes form alliances with one another (Saxenian 1994). The same is true with countries. They are explicitly linked through numerous cultural, economic, military, and political ties, and implicitly linked through ties created by transnational corporations, nongovernmental organizations, and international agencies (Meyer et al. 1997). Such multiplexity is important because ties often pull actors in different directions (Simmel [1908, 1922] 1955). For example, our work ties may push us in the direction of making one choice, while our friendship and kinship ties may pull us in another. This suggests that if we want a more accurate picture of a network's dynamics, we often need to combine a number of different relationships before we analyze them. "Indeed it is a basic assumption of those subscribing to the network approach that

---

[9]   Because marriage ties are reciprocal, a "1" not only appears in the Acciaiuol-Medici cell, but also in the Medici-Acciaiuol cell.

		1	2	3	4	5	6	7	8	9	10	11	12	13	14	15	16
		ACCIAIUOL	ALBIZZI	BARBADORI	BISCHERI	CASTELLAN	GINORI	GUADAGNI	LAMBERTES	MEDICI	PAZZI	PERUZZI	PUCCI	RIDOLFI	SALVIATI	STROZZI	TORNABUON
1	ACCIAIUOL	0	0	0	0	0	0	0	0	1	0	0	0	0	0	0	0
2	ALBIZZI	0	0	0	0	0	1	1	0	1	0	0	0	0	0	0	0
3	BARBADORI	0	0	0	0	1	0	0	0	1	0	0	0	0	0	0	0
4	BISCHERI	0	0	0	0	0	0	1	0	0	0	1	0	0	0	1	0
5	CASTELLAN	0	0	1	0	0	0	0	0	0	0	1	0	0	0	1	0
6	GINORI	0	1	0	0	0	0	0	0	0	0	0	0	0	0	0	0
7	GUADAGNI	0	1	0	1	0	0	0	1	0	0	0	0	0	0	0	1
8	LAMBERTES	0	0	0	0	0	0	1	0	0	0	0	0	0	0	0	0
9	MEDICI	1	1	1	0	0	0	0	0	0	0	0	0	1	1	0	1
10	PAZZI	0	0	0	0	0	0	0	0	0	0	0	0	0	1	0	0
11	PERUZZI	0	0	0	1	1	0	0	0	0	0	0	0	0	0	1	0
12	PUCCI	0	0	0	0	0	0	0	0	0	0	0	0	0	0	0	0
13	RIDOLFI	0	0	0	0	0	0	0	0	1	0	0	0	0	0	1	1
14	SALVIATI	0	0	0	0	0	0	0	0	1	1	0	0	0	0	0	0
15	STROZZI	0	0	0	1	1	0	0	0	0	0	1	0	1	0	0	0
16	TORNABUON	0	0	0	0	0	0	1	0	1	0	0	0	1	0	0	0

Figure 2.1. Marriage Ties among Renaissance Florentine Families

behavior cannot be explained in terms of any one single activity" (Breiger 1975, cited in Azarian 2005:39).

This, of course, raises questions of strategy and the manipulation of social network data. For example, if we want to disrupt a dark network's financial operations, we may choose to aggregate actors' financial ties (e.g., ties of financial flows between actors) and their affiliations with institutions that provide financial support to the dark network (e.g., businesses, criminal activities, and/or charities and foundations acting as a financial front to the network). But what if a network's financial operations rely heavily on ties of trust between actors? Then we may want to combine these ties with friendship, kinship, and religious ties, or we may want to first analyze only the network's financial ties and then add the friendship and kinship ties for additional analysis. The aggregation of networks is not the only option open to us, however. Sometimes we may want to parse them, seeking to identify actors who participate in two or more networks of interest (or actors who are active in a particular network and share one or more common attributes). For example, we may be interested in mapping the network of individuals who are involved in both the financing and operations of a particular dark network but not just one or the other. Obviously, there are no clear-cut answers as to how and which networks to aggregate or parse. Such decisions have to be made on a case-by-case basis.

Analysis and Interpretation

Social network metrics play an important role in analyzing a social network's dynamics. Analysts generally use a variety of metrics (rather than just one or two) in their attempts to gain an overall understanding of a network. Metrics are not the only tool available to social network analysts, however. Network visualization is another helpful tool that can help us see patterns that may not be readily apparent by simply looking at tables of metrics (Brandes, Raab, and Wagner 2001; Castilla et al. 2000; Freeman 2000). For example, a visualization that highlights the centrality of actors in a network may better illuminate the degree of variation among actors than a corresponding table of centrality metrics. Little variation could lead analysts to conclude that it makes little sense to pursue a kinetic targeting strategy because there are several high-value targets. Or, sometimes, clustering algorithms provide multiple "solutions" as to the identity of different subgroups within a network, and often the only way to decide between the various alternatives is through network visualization. In short, metrics and visualization are complementary parts of the SNA toolbox. Most SNA programs either come with network mapping algorithms (e.g., Pajek, ORA) or integrate with network visualization programs that do (e.g., UCINET and NetDraw).

Part of our analysis involves interpreting what we have found. We need to ask questions such as:

- What is the network's overall structure? Does it exhibit any characteristics (e.g., density, centralization, cohesion, fragmentation) that might suggest whether it is more or less effective than other networks?
- Are there some relations that appear to be more constitutive to the network as a whole than others (e.g., school ties)? If so, is it possible and desirable to exploit the network at a different level (e.g., the school network)?
- Are there any subnetworks within the larger network? Do some appear more critical or central than others? If so, can they be exploited (e.g., set them at odds with one another)? Can other more peripheral subgroups be targeted for rehabilitation campaigns or infiltration?
- Are there key actors or ties between actors whose removal or isolation (e.g., by being discredited) will render the network less effective? If so, is it feasible to remove or isolate them? Could there be any second-order effects (e.g., causing the network to become more violent, generating hostility among the surrounding community) in pursuing such a policy?
- Do some actors hold structurally equivalent positions in the network with other actors? Since such actors are essentially substitutable for one another, this could indicate potential emergent leaders. That is, when a particular actor is removed, there is a strong probability that they will be replaced with a structurally equivalent actor. This could help identify a particular strategy's second-order effects.
- Are there key actors who could be targeted for the diffusion of misinformation (i.e., a deception campaign) or monitored in order to improve our knowledge of the network?
- Are there peripheral actors that could possibly be enticed to leave the network, making it more vulnerable to disruption or isolation?
- Are there organizations within the network (e.g., schools, businesses, faith communities) that are attractive targets for infiltration or removal?
- How has the network changed over time? What have previous research and case studies told us about how dark networks adapt to exogenous and endogenous shocks?
- Does a spatial analysis of the network yield different insights as to which actors are central and how the network has adapted over time?

- Have we adequately separated genuine from spurious correlations?

Needless to say, the answers we give to these questions and others inform the strategies we craft and the policies we recommend.

Crafting Strategies

At this point it is time to reevaluate our original hypotheses to see whether they need amending in light of what the exploratory analysis and interpretation of the network yielded. Following Admiral Olson's observation that kinetic action is merely "a holding action that buys time for" nonkinetic approaches to have their effects" (quoted in Roberts and Everton 2011:4), we may seek to implement a combination of kinetic and nonkinetic strategies. Or, if General Flynn is correct that kinetic attacks sometimes multiply enemies rather than decrease them (Flynn, Pottinger, and Batchelor 2010:8), we may only consider nonkinetic strategies that will take longer to implement but may yield better results. The broader point is that SNA provides various ways of teasing out the nature of dark networks, which in turn provides us with valuable information as to what strategies may best disrupt them.

2.4   Summary and Conclusion

This chapter has focused on the role that social network analysis should play in the crafting of strategies for the disruption of dark networks. It began with a discussion of the various strategic approaches and then moved to a brief overview of how to use SNA in conjunction with the crafting of strategies. Its goal was to illustrate how SNA can be useful for the crafting of strategic options within the kinetic and nonkinetic approaches.

That said, it recognizes that the use of SNA for such a purpose has its challenges. Three are worth mentioning. As noted in the preface, data on insurgencies and terrorists can be difficult to collect and are often incomplete (Borgatti, Carley, and Krackhardt 2006; Krebs 2001; Sparrow 1991), meaning that analysts have to use caution when crafting strategies. Another is that critics have challenged the use of SNA for military purposes, in particular the use of SNA for targeting purposes (Gjelten 2010). This book shares these concerns and addresses them in more depth in Chapter 12. For now it is sufficient to acknowledge that, as previously noted, not only may lethal targeting increase, rather than reduce, the level of violence, an emphasis on kinetic operations often neglects or minimizes the use of SNA for rebuilding and rehabilitating purposes. Finally, the use of SNA to generate strategic options should not be confounded with its use for decision making. The latter depends on a whole host of issues – knowledge of context and local culture, and the assessment of risks, costs, and potential for unintended consequences, just to name a few (Moody 2005). SNA should not be seen as a silver bullet or substitute for other critical elements in the decision process. It certainly can inform decisions, but it should not determine them. That is why this book emphasizes the use of SNA for the *crafting* of alternative strategies for countering dark networks, not their selection.

Part II

Social Network Analysis: Techniques

3

Getting Started with UCINET, NetDraw, Pajek, and ORA

3.1 Introduction

The advent of the personal computer has played a large role in the growth of social network analysis (SNA). Indeed, it is unlikely that SNA could have developed like it has without it (Freeman 2004:139–141; Wolfe 1978) because SNA relies on complex mathematical and graphical algorithms (Freeman 2004:3, 135–136). Over the years, a number of SNA software packages have been developed, all of which have their own strengths and weaknesses – see Huisman and van Duijn (2011) for a comprehensive review of the available packages. In this book we focus on UCINET (along with its integrated visualization program, NetDraw), Pajek, and ORA, not because they are necessarily the best programs (although they are quite good), but because they are readily available, widely used, and relatively inexpensive (all but UCINET are free). Indeed, in Huisman and van Duijn's (2011:585–590) review of general stand-alone SNA software packages, these three were among the five packages that were discussed at length.[1] Moreover, users who gain a familiarity with the logic and features of these programs should be able to migrate to other SNA packages with relative ease. This chapter provides a basic introduction to these programs – their interfaces, features, visualization capabilities, strengths, weaknesses, and so on – whereas Chapter 4 discusses the collection, recording, and manipulation of network data.

3.2 UCINET

UCINET was initially developed by Linton Freeman at the University of California, Irvine (hence, the "UCI" in "UCINET"), and was later

[1] Multinet (Richards and Seary 2009) and Netminer (Cyram 2009) were the other two.

refined by others, in particular, Steve Borgatti and Martin Everett (Scott 2000:178–179). It is the best-known and most widely used social network software, primarily because it has been around for a long time and it contains a large number of SNA metrics and data management tools (Huisman and van Duijn 2005:275–280, 2011:585–586). Not only does it implement most of the routines needed for estimating measures of network topography (e.g., density, centralization, fragmentation), calculating actor centrality (e.g., degree, betweenness, closeness, eigenvector), identifying subgroups (e.g., cliques, components, factions, Newman groups), and estimating various measures of structural equivalence (e.g., structural, automorphic, regular), but it also includes tools for selecting subsets of files, merging and stacking datasets, transposing and/or recoding data, and importing and exporting of data in a variety of formats (Huisman and van Duijn 2005, 2011). UCINET is menu driven. Its commands call up dialog boxes that specify the inputs needed for it to run its various routines; results are displayed using Window's Notepad program and subsequently saved in log files.

UCINET's comprehensiveness is what makes it so valuable. Not only can you find and estimate most of the metrics you will need for SNA, if you can record social network data in UCINET format, but you can also get it into just about any other format you may need for analyzing with other software programs (e.g., Pajek, ORA, R, Excel, and SPSS). Moreover, UCINET is constantly being updated by its developers, who are adding new routines and fixing any bugs that come to light.

In UCINET, social network data are recorded in matrix format. Users can enter data using either UCINET's internal spreadsheet function or a commercial spreadsheet program, such as Microsoft Excel, which can then be imported (or pasted) into UCINET. UCINET also reads edge and node lists, which are quite useful when working with large datasets or when data are stored in database programs such as Microsoft Access. In storing data, UCINET uses a dual file system: one containing the actual data (extension .##d) and one containing information about the data (extension .##h). Because you need both files in order to analyze social network data in UCINET, this dual file system can occasionally lead to problems. For example, when estimating routines that create new data files, UCINET will sometimes store one of the two newly created files in separate folders, making it impossible to open or analyze the data until the two files are reunited. Because UCINET's creators regularly provide updates to the program in order to fix bugs and glitches, problems such as this are generally corrected relatively quickly. Nevertheless, they can be frustrating when they do happen. A related problem occurs when analysts share social network data with one another and send only one of the two files to the other. All this is to highlight how important it is to be aware of UCINET's dual file system.

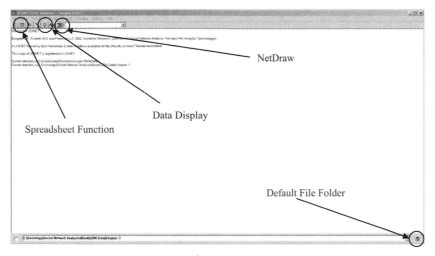

Figure 3.1. UCINET Interface

Getting Started with UCINET

When you open UCINET you encounter an interface similar to the one displayed in Figure 3.1. Across the top of the screen are a series of menus (i.e., *File*, *Data*, *Transform*, *Tools*, *Network*, *Visualize*, *Options*, and *Help*). We will explore some of the commands found under these menus that are useful to know before trying to do too much with UCINET. For now, we will postpone discussing other commands (e.g., commands for estimating various centrality measures). Just below the menus are a handful of speed buttons. Moving from left to right, the first closes UCINET, the second opens UCINET's internal spreadsheet program, the third opens Microsoft's Notepad program (useful for editing some data files), the fourth allows users to display a social network file in matrix format, and the fifth opens NetDraw, a social network drawing program that reads and displays UCINET files (see discussion of NetDraw in Section 3.2). Let's now turn to a discussion of some of the commands found under UCINET's various menus.

The *File* menu contains several useful functions, two of which we will discuss here. One is the *File>Change Default Folder* command, which *File>Change* tells UCINET where to look for social network data (its companion *Default Folder* speed button is circled in Figure 3.1). When you open UCINET for the first time, the default folder will be C:\Program Files\Analytic Technologies\Ucinet6\datafiles or C:\Program Files (x86)\Analytic Technologies\Ucinet6\datafiles (note that UCINET lists the default folder at the bottom of its interface – see Figure 3.1), which is where all of the standard social network datasets that come with UCINET are stored. Issuing this command brings up a dialog

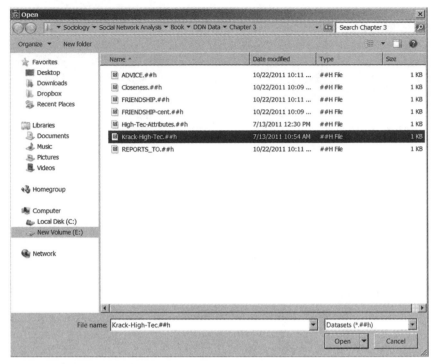

Figure 3.2. UCINET Display Dialog Box

box that allows you to navigate through your computer's folders in order to pick the default folder of your choice. It is probably a good idea to change the default folder to where you are storing the data that are used with this book. Later, when working with your own data, you will want to change it to the folder where your data are stored. Another useful *File>Text* command worth noting is the *File>Text Editor* command; it opens *Editor* Microsoft's Notepad program, which can be used for editing data files.

Data>Data   The *Data* menu includes several helpful functions. The *Data>Data*
Editors>Matrix *Editors>Matrix Editor* command accesses UCINET's internal spread-
Editor sheet function, which you can use for creating and editing social networks
Data>Display (its companion speed button is circled in Figure 3.1). The *Data>Display* command (its companion speed button is circled) displays UCINET social network files. To get a sense of what this latter command does, use it to open a dialog box similar to that in Figure 3.2. Select the Krack-High-Tec.##h file and click "Open." (Note that although you cannot see the Krack-High-Tec. ##d file, it is there – if it was not, you would not be able to display the data file.)

This generates a UCINET output log (see Figure 3.3), which is gener-ally how UCINET displays results and/or information. Note that in the

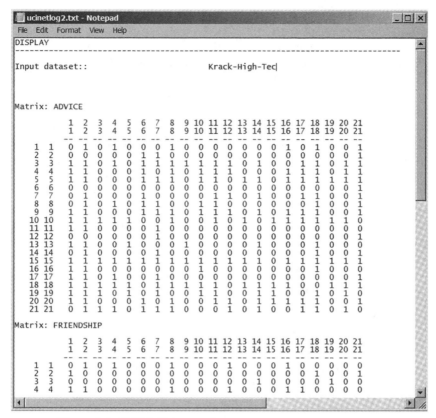

Figure 3.3. UCINET Output Log

upper-left corner of the output log is the label "Matrix #1: ADVICE." If you scroll down the log, you will discover that the file contains two more networks: FRIENDSHIP and REPORTS_TO. We will postpone discussing how you can (and why you might want to) "stack" networks in this way (see Chapter 4). For now, all you need to know is that David Krackhardt (1987a, 1992) collected data on twenty-one managers in a Silicon Valley company that manufactured high-tech equipment. He asked each manager whom they went to for advice and whom they considered their friends. He also determined to whom each manager reported from company documents. A "1" recorded in the cell of the advice network indicates that the manager listed on the far left seeks advice from the manager listed across the top. For instance, you can see in Figure 3.3 that manager #1 seeks advice from manager #2, but manager #2 does not seek advice from manager #1. Similarly, a "1" recorded in the cell of the friendship network indicates that the manager listed on the left considers the manager listed across the top to be a friend, and a "1" recorded in the cell of the reports to network indicates that the manager listed on the left reports to the manager listed across the top. Krackhardt also collected attribute data on the managers: age (in years), length of service or tenure (in years), their level in the corporate hierarchy (1 = CEO, 2 = Vice President, 3 = Manager), and the department to which they belong (coded 1, 2, 3, and 4, with the CEO in department 0). These data, however, are stored in a different file.

Presently, we will not explore any of the commands found under the *Transform*, *Tools*, or *Network* menus. A quick glance at the *Transform* and *Tools* menus indicates that UCINET includes a number of routines for transforming and analyzing social network data. We will not utilize all of these commands, but we will use a few. The commands that will occupy most of our time are found under the *Network* menu. Here you will find routines for estimating measures of network topography, calculating actor centrality, detecting subgroups, and locating structurally equivalent actors.

Help>Help Topics Jumping over to the *Help* menu, the *Help>Help Topics* command leads users to its "Overview of Help" function. The "Introduction Section" link provides access to a series of help topics that covers most (but not all) of UCINET's functions (when new functions are added to UCINET, it sometimes takes a while before they are covered). The "Overview of Help" function also provides a "Standard Datasets" link that provides users with a brief discussion of all the social network datasets that come *Help>Hanneman Tutorial* with UCINET. Finally, the *Help>Hanneman Tutorial* command links users to the very helpful UCINET guide written by Hanneman and Riddle (2005).

The *Visualize* menu provides users with access to three visualization programs: NetDraw, Pajek, and Mage. We will focus primarily on NetDraw and Pajek in this book, although it is worth mentioning that before the advent of Pajek and NetDraw, Mage was the program of choice for many social network analysts (Freeman 1999, 2000; Freeman, Webster, and Kirke 1998), which is why this book includes an appendix on its use (see Appendix 3). Mage was initially developed as a device to be used in molecular modeling (Richardson and Richardson 1992), but social network analysts found it attractive because it produces elegant three-dimensional interactive images. In Mage, researchers can rotate images, turn parts of the display off and on, use the computer mouse to select and identify various parts of the network, and animate changes between different arrangements of objects.

Generally, you will want to leave the default settings included under *Options>Helper Applications* the *Options* menu untouched. The one exception is the *Options>Helper Applications* command. Clicking on this command brings up a dialog box (see Figure 3.4). As you can see this allows users to change the folders where the four helper applications are currently incorporated

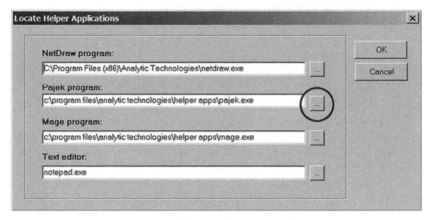

Figure 3.4. UCINET Helper Application Dialog Box

by UCINET (NetDraw, Pajek, Mage, and Notepad). Chances are you will never need to tell UCINET to look for NetDraw and Notepad in a different folder than the default folders set by UCINET. However, you will probably want to change where UCINET looks for Pajek because the version of Pajek distributed by UCINET is typically not the most recent. You will want to download and install Pajek in its default location. So before doing anything else, click on the radio button to the right of the Pajek program location (circled in Figure 3.4) and change Pajek's default location to C:\pajek\Pajek\. Doing this will ensure that each time you open Pajek from within UCINET you will open the most recent version (assuming, of course, that you update Pajek on a regular basis).

It is now time to turn our attention to NetDraw, a network visualization program that integrates nicely with UCINET. Because we can open NetDraw from within UCINET, there is no need to close UCINET at this time.[2]

3.3 NetDraw

In recent years, social network analysts have begun using a series of mathematical techniques to locate a social network's actors in such a way that the distances between them are meaningful. These algorithms use the concepts of space and distance in order to represent a network's internal structure, which they hope will reveal, among other things, which actors are "close" to one another and whether potential cleavages exist between sets of actors. NetDraw is a program developed by one of UCINET's

---

[2] If NetDraw does not open automatically from within UCINET, it is probably because UCINET is looking for it in the wrong place. Using UCINET's Helper Application dialog box (Figure 3.4), you can insert the correct path for finding NetDraw.

Figure 3.5. NetDraw Home Screen

creators (Steve Borgatti) that is designed to draw networks using some of these algorithms. Network maps created by NetDraw can be rotated, flipped, resized, and stored in several different formats (Huisman and van Duijn 2005:306). In addition to its mapping algorithms, NetDraw also includes a handful of other algorithms for calculating centrality, detecting subgroups, identifying sets of key players, and so on.

Although technically a stand-alone program, NetDraw essentially functions as an extension of UCINET: It is distributed with UCINET, it can be opened from within UCINET, and it reads UCINET files without the need for using any importing and/or exporting functions (Huisman and van Duijn 2005:306). Whereas NetDraw's initial iterations did not handle large networks very well, more recent versions seem to do just fine. Moreover, if you save network data in NetDraw's native *.vna format, it can handle very large network files. Like UCINET, NetDraw's creators continually update the program with new procedures, routines, and bug fixes.

Getting Started with NetDraw

[UCINET]
Visualize>
NetDraw

To open NetDraw from UCINET, either use the *Visualize>NetDraw* command or click on the NetDraw speed button located just under the *Network* menu in UCINET (see Figure 3.1). This will open NetDraw's home screen, which should look similar to Figure 3.5. Like UCINET, NetDraw has a full set of menus as well as a series of speed buttons across the top of its interface. We will consider of a few of these here.

To get a sense of how NetDraw visualizes networks, open the Krackhardt dataset (Krack-High-Tec.##h) using NetDraw's

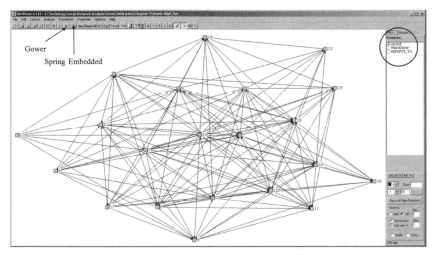

Figure 3.6. NetDraw Display of Krackhardt High-Tech Data

File>Open>Ucinet dataset>Network command. This should yield a network map that looks similar to the one displayed in Figure 3.6. A couple of features are worth noting before proceeding. First, along the upper right side of NetDraw's homepage (circled in Figure 3.6) note the tab entitled Rels, below which is located a list of the three networks (i.e., advice, friendship, reports to) included in the Krackhardt file. Chances are only the box next to the advice network is checked. This indicates that only those ties are currently shown in the graph. If you check the boxes next to "friendship" and "reports to networks," NetDraw will show those ties, as well. Second, NetDraw allows you to assign different colors to the various relations by using the dialog box (not shown) called up by the *Properties>Lines>Color>Relation* command. Note that NetDraw automatically assigns colors to the different types of ties. You can change these defaults by clicking on the color box. Generally, however, NetDraw's defaults tend to provide a nice contrast between the types of ties, so it is advisable to at least begin with the default colors. You can always change them later. Note also that when two actors share more than one tie, NetDraw colors these relationships gray. You can change this default as you do the others by clicking on the color box. Once you click "Apply," NetDraw assigns the different colors to the different types of ties.

[NetDraw]
File>Open>
Ucinet dataset>
Network

Properties>Lines>
Color>Relation

Mapping Algorithms in NetDraw

Social network analysts have long used network maps (i.e., sociograms, graphs) to visualize social networks. The goal of graphing networks is to place actors and the ties between them, such that those who share a similar pattern of ties (and often have ties with one another) are located close to one another in the graph and those who do not are located far from one another. It may be helpful to think of network maps as attempts to locate actors in *social space* as opposed to geographic space. That is, actors who are socially close (i.e., they share similar patterns of ties) are placed near one another in a network map, whereas those who are socially distant are placed far from one another.

A common technique in the early days of SNA was to construct the data around the circumference of a circle. NetDraw includes a command that *Layout>Circle* creates this type of network map: *Layout>Circle*. Unfortunately, while this approach is useful, the relations between the graph's points do not reflect any specific mathematical properties. The points are arranged arbitrarily, and the distances between them are meaningless, which, depending on how they were arranged, can lead to varying interpretations of the data (McGrath, Blythe, and Krackhardt 1997). NetDraw also includes an *Layout>Random* algorithm that randomly allocates a network's nodes (*Layout>Random*), but this type of layout suffers from the same weaknesses as a circular layout; that is, the distances between the graph's nodes mean nothing.

In recent years, analysts have begun using a series of mathematical algorithms to locate the points of a network in such a way that the distances between them are meaningful. Multidimensional scaling (MDS) is one such technique. MDS uses the concepts of space and distance to represent a network's structure, which, in turn, can help reveal, among other things, which actors are "close" to one another, as well as potential divisions between them (Wasserman and Faust 1994). The typical input to MDS is a one-mode symmetric matrix (see Chapter 4) that contains measures of similarity or dissimilarity between pairs of actors. The output generally consists of a set of estimated distances among pairs of actors that can be then represented in one-, two-, three-, or higher-dimensional space (Kruskal and Wish 1978; Wasserman and Faust 1994). Distance here differs from distance in graph theory. In graph theory, the distance between two points is measured in terms of path length. With MDS it "is a distance that follows a route 'as the crow flies,' and that may be across 'open space' and need not – indeed, it normally will not – follow a graph theoretical path" (Scott 2000:148–149).

There are different types of multidimensional scaling: metric and nonmetric MDS. Metric MDS takes a given matrix of similarities or dissimilarities among actors and calculates a set of points in k-dimensional space, such that the distances between them correspond as closely as possible to the input. There are some limitations to using metric MDS for visualizing social networks. Many networks are binary (i.e., dichotomous) in that they only indicate either the presence or absence of a tie. Unfortunately, we cannot use binary data to directly estimate proximities.

Instead, we need to first convert it into other measures, such as correlation coefficients, before calculating distances between actors. However, such data conversion can lead researchers to draw unjustifiable conclusions about the data. For example, although it is reasonable to assume that an actor with four ties is more central than one with only two, we cannot be certain that the former is twice as central as the latter (Scott 2000:157). Even when the data are valued, metric assumptions may be inappropriate. Imagine two actors with four ties between them and two other actors with only one. Although the first set of actors is almost certainly more closely tied than the second set, it is difficult to know how much more closely tied together they are (Scott 2000:157). Nonmetric MDS procedures offer a solution to this problem. Like metric MDS procedures, they use symmetrical adjacency (one-mode) matrices in which the cells reflect the similarities or dissimilarities among actors, but unlike metric MDS procedures, they treat the data as ordinal, seeking "a solution in which the rank ordering of the distances is the same as the rank ordering of the original values" (Scott 2000:157). Moreover, nonmetric MDS is often preferred because it tends to provide a better "goodness-of-fit" (stress) statistic.[3]

Currently, NetDraw only includes metric MDS algorithms although plans for nonmetric MDS algorithms are in the works.[4] Implementing NetDraw's metric MDS routine is relatively straightforward with its *Layout>Graph Theoretic layout>MDS* command. Nodes that are "socially" close to one another (because there is a tie between them or they are tied to a common friend) should be located close to one another in the graph, whereas nodes that are socially distant from one another (i.e., they are not tied to one another nor do they share a common tie) should be located far from one another in the graph. It is important to note that there is no single correct way to graph the data (i.e., there is not a single "solution"), which is why analysts will generally want to implement an algorithm (or various algorithms) multiple times. Another metric MDS algorithm included in NetDraw is the *Layout>Graph Theoretic layout>Gower* command (or click on the "G" speed button – see Figure 3.6). Note that all of these routines provide a slightly different network map from one another, which makes it difficult to choose which network map fits the data best. An alternative is to calculate the coordinates in UCINET and import them into NetDraw (see Appendix 3).

Layout>Graph Theoretic layout>MDS

Layout>Graph Theoretic layout>Gower

---

[3] The lower the stress (0 = perfect fit), the better. Generally, stress levels below "0.1" are considered excellent while levels above "0.2" are considered unacceptable.

[4] See the options found under the *Layout>Scaling/Ordination* submenu – only the Iterative metric MDS algorithm has been implemented and produces a very different solution than the other MDS routines found in NetDraw. Users can calculate metric and nonmetric MDS coordinates in UCINET and then use these coordinates in NetDraw, however. See Appendix 3 for details.

The advantage of doing this is that UCINET's MDS routines provide users with stress statistics that indicate how well the coordinates fit the data.

Another common set of routines for graphing social networks are spring-embedded algorithms. Pajek, in fact, currently (i.e., through version 2.04) uses only spring-embedded algorithms. These algorithms treat the nodes as pushing and pulling on one another and seek to find an optimum solution wherein there is a minimum amount of stress on the springs connecting the whole set of nodes (Freeman 2000). Generally, ties between nodes are treated as an attractive force (a "spring" pulling them together), whereas nodes that do not share a tie are pushed apart (Moody 2001). The spring-embedding algorithm in NetDraw can be implemented *Layout>Graph* using the *Layout>Graph Theoretic layout>Spring embedding* command. *Theoretic* This calls up a dialog box (not shown) that provides a variety of options *layout>Spring* for using the spring-embedding layout. It is a good idea to use NetDraw's *embedding* defaults, although varying the options tends not to change the graph's layout too dramatically. The "lightning bolt" speed button is another way to implement this routine.

Freeman (2005:251) refers to MDS and spring-embedded algorithms as search algorithms because they all involve a search for the optimal location for nodes. He contrasts these with determinate approaches, which are based on the singular value decomposition (SVD) algebraic procedure:

> SVD transforms the N original variables into N new variables, or dimensions. These new dimensions are ordered from largest to smallest in terms of how much of the variance, or patterning, in the original data is associated with each. The most variance is always associated with the first dimension. Each succeeding dimension is, in turn, associated with progressively less of the variance. If a one-, two-, or three-dimensional visual image is going to be useful, the hope is that the first or the first two or three of these new dimensions will be associated with virtually all the variance contained in the original data (Weller and Romney 1990). If, in contrast, the first few dimensions are associated with very little of the original variance, SVD will not yield useful results. (Freeman 2005)

Layout>Graph NetDraw includes a mapping algorithm that uses SVD, principal com- *Theoretic* ponents, which is accessible through the *Layout>Graph Theoretic* *layout>Principal* *layout>Principal Component* command and typically produces network *Components* maps that look considerably different from the others.

Visualizing Attribute Data in NetDraw

A nice feature of NetDraw is that it allows analysts to incorporate attribute data into its network graphs. Open the attribute file

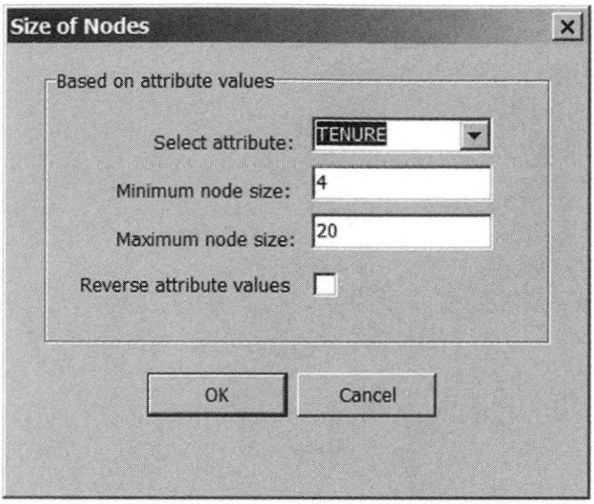

Figure 3.7. Node Size Dialog Box

(High-Tec-Attributes.##h) associated with the Krackhardt data (which should still be loaded into memory), using the *File>Open>Ucinet dataset>Attribute data* command. You can use attributes (i.e., variables) to vary the size, shape, and color of the nodes. In general, you will want to visualize nominal attributes, that is, variables with two or more categories but where there is no intrinsic ordering to the categories (e.g., gender, ethnicity, country of origin), by varying either the shape or size of the node. By contrast, when visualizing ordered or continuous variables (e.g., age, income, education level), it is better to vary the size of the node.

File>Open> Ucinet dataset> Attribute data

Let's begin by adjusting the size of the nodes based on tenure using the *Properties>Nodes>Symbols>Size>Attribute-based* command. This should call up a dialog box similar to Figure 3.7. Using the drop-down menu choose the attribute you wish to use to vary the size of the node (in this case *TENURE*). Next, adjust the shape of the node using the *Properties>Nodes>Symbols>Shape>Attribute-based* command to reflect the department to which each manager belongs and you should get a network map similar to Figure 3.8. Typically, varying node color rather than shape is more effective for visualizing nominal attributes, but because this book cannot display color, we will leave it for readers to experiment with NetDraw's *Properties>Nodes>Symbols>Color>Attribute-based* command.

Properties> Nodes> Symbols>Size> Attribute-based

Properties> Nodes> Symbols>Shape> Attribute-based

Properties> Nodes>Symbols> Color> Attribute-based

There are a number of other functions available within NetDraw, most of which we will consider further on, but three worth mentioning now. Note that there are three sets of speed buttons included in NetDraw: "Z z," "A ᴀ," and "S s." The first increases or decreases the size of the graph,

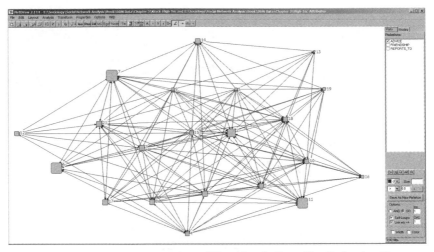

Figure 3.8. NetDraw Map of Krackhardt Data Size Reflecting Tenure

the second increases or decreases the size of the labels in the graph, and the third increases or decreases the size of the nodes in the graph.

File>Save Data   Before turning to our exploration of Pajek, save the Krackhardt data
As>Vna in NetDraw's native format (**.vna) using its *File>Save Data As>Vna* command. A helpful feature of the VNA format is that it saves both relations *and* attributes in a single file, which is useful when working with the same data over and over again. It also avoids the potential problems that UCINET's dual file system may cause.

3.4   Pajek

Pajek – which means "spider" in Slovenian – was created by Vladimir Batagelj and Andrej Mrvar in 1996 and is designed to handle very large datasets (Scott 2000:179–180). Although Pajek does not include as many algorithms as UCINET, it still offers many of those that analysts use. In particular, it includes routines that lend themselves to the visualization and simplification of large networks while allowing users to visualize networks in two or three dimensions (Huisman and van Duijn 2005:280, 2011:587). It runs on Windows-compatible computers, can be downloaded for free, and is routinely updated by its developers. Pajek uses six different types of data objects, or structures:

- Networks (nodes/actors and ties)
- Partitions (discrete classification of actors where each actor is assigned to one *and only one* class – for example, a dark network partition might assign each actor to a specific role – it is here that actors' nominal attributes are stored)

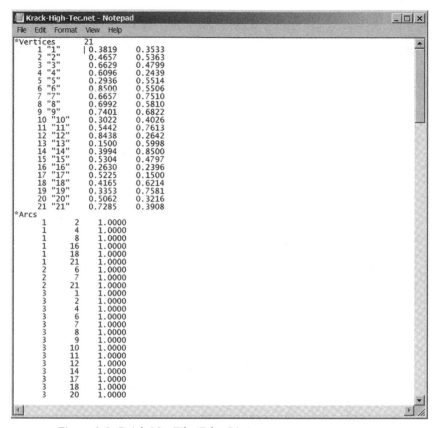

Figure 3.9. Pajek Net File (Edge List)

- Vectors (continuous properties of actors, that is, ordered attributes – for example, an actor's age, level of education, centrality score, etc. – are stored here)
- Permutations (reordering of nodes)
- Clusters (subsets of nodes)
- Hierarchies (hierarchically ordered clusters and nodes)

We will not explore all of these data objects – indeed, we will utilize primarily the first three – networks, partitions, and vectors – but it is helpful to at least be aware of them.

Pajek stores network data as an edge list, which is simply a list of vertices (i.e., actors/nodes) and edges/arcs (i.e., ties). Figure 3.9 displays a portion of the Pajek Krackhardt High-Tech network data file. It begins by specifying the number of vertices (i.e., actors); then each vertex is identified on a separate line by a serial number, a label (enclosed in quotation marks), and two numbers between 0 and 1, which are simply two sets of coordinates for visualizing the network data in two-dimensional space.

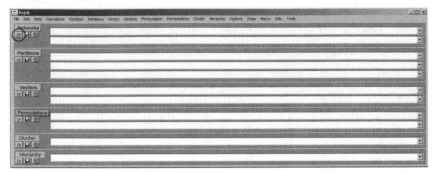

Figure 3.10. Pajek Main Screen

The list of vertices is then followed by a list of arcs (or edges). Each line identifies the number of the sending and receiving actors and the value of the tie between them. Thus, you can see that the first manager (vertex 1) sought advice from managers 2, 4, 8, 16, 18, and 21. An advantage of edge lists is that they tend to be smaller in size because you do not have to code nonties (i.e., 0s), which means that they can handle very large social networks.

Like NetDraw, Pajek allows users to load and keep multiple networks and other data objects (e.g., partitions) in memory at the same time. This is quite helpful because, like other social network software programs, most of Pajek's routines generate new networks or other data objects. All of these can then be stored in what Pajek calls a "project file," which means that after analyzing one or more social networks, users can save all of their work in a single file. This decreases the likelihood that users will have to "recreate the wheel" in doing their analysis.

Pajek's primary drawback is that it contains fewer algorithms than UCINET (although it does include a few that UCINET does not have), and its network manipulation features are somewhat limited. Thus, many analysts sometimes use UCINET for data manipulation and then Pajek for visualization. To Pajek's credit, however, it now allows users to call up the statistical packages R and SPSS to perform procedures not available in Pajek.

Getting Started with Pajek

The Pajek main screen looks very different from that of UCINET and NetDraw (see Figure 3.10). As you can see, it is organized by the type of data object or structure. Network data are loaded into the Network drop-down menu, partition data into the Partition drop-down menu, vector data into the Vector drop-down menu, and so on. In order to make working with more than one network, partition, vector, or permutation at the same time easier, beginning with version 1.21, Pajek's main screen can display two or three drop-down menus for each of the data objects. You can change the number of visible drop-down menus by clicking on the buttons labeled "Networks," "Partitions," "Vectors," or "Permutations" (see Figure 3.10). As we will see, this is a very helpful feature. However, users need to be careful when working with various objects in Pajek. For example, if you are seeking to obtain information on a particular network using Pajek's *Info>Network>General* command, you have to make sure that *Network* appears in the first or top Network drop-down menu. The same holds true if you are getting information on a partition, vector, or hierarchy using the *Info>Partition, Info>Vector,* and *Info>Hierarchy* commands, respectively, because in most cases, Pajek looks to the object that is listed first.

*Info>Network>
General*

Info>Partition
Info>Vector
Info>Hierarchy

   To open a network file into Pajek, we use Pajek's *File>Network>Read* command or click on the folder icon located under the "Networks" button (circled in Figure 3.10). Here, however, we are going to open a Pajek project file, which like NetDraw's *.vna file format, allows users to store network and attribute data in a single file. To open the Krackhardt project file, use Pajek's *File>Pajek Project File>Read* command (or press the F1 key) and select the `Krackhardt High Tech.paj` file.[5] Note that Pajek loads all three networks in the Network drop-down menu; the department attribute in the Partition drop-down menu; and the age, level, and tenure attributes in the Vector drop-down menu (not shown). You can open any of these drop-down menus and see the list of networks, partitions, and vectors stored in the project file by left-clicking on the triangle on the right.

[Main Screen]
*File>Network>
Read*

*File>Pajek
Project
File>Read*

   The functions available in Pajek are vast, and probably only Pajek's developers along with their colleague Wouter de Nooy know all that Pajek can do (de Nooy, Mrvar, and Batagelj 2005, 2011). Pajek's functions are organized based on the task analysts plan to use. For example, if you are working with an individual network, then you will primarily use the functions found under the *Net* menu. If you are manipulating two networks, then the algorithms located under the *Nets* menu will probably be useful. Similarly, if you are working with a single partition (or vector), then you will most likely turn to those found under the *Partition* (or *Vector*) menu, whereas if you are working with two or more partitions (or vectors), then you will look to those functions found under the *Partitions* (or *Vectors*) menu. A similar logic holds true if you are manipulating or analyzing permutations, clusters, or hierarchies. Often you will work with a network in conjunction with a vector and/or partition. If you are

---

[5] Pajek does not currently read UCINET files. However, UCINET allows you to export network and attribute data in formats that Pajek can read. We will explore these features in subsequent chapters.

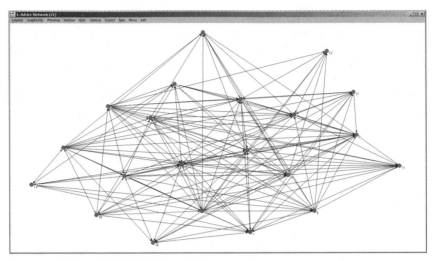

Figure 3.11. Pajek Draw Screen

seeking to manipulate network data, then it is likely that you will use one or more of the algorithms located under the *Operations* menu. If you plan to visualize them, then the *Draw* menu will be where you turn.

Mapping Algorithms in Pajek

To view Krackhardt's network, make sure that the Advice network is showing in the first or top Network drop-down menu and then issue *Pajek>Draw>Draw* command. This will open Pajek's Draw screen, which will look similar, but probably not identical, to Figure 3.11. Before exploring Pajek's drawing capabilities, we should choose a couple of options. To change the background use the *Options>Color>Background* command located in Pajek's Draw screen (not Main screen). This brings up a dialog box showing a number of colors from which to choose. Select the background of your choice. Light backgrounds are generally a good choice if you plan to print network screenshots. You will generally want to tell Pajek that a tie between two actors indicates a similarity or closeness between them. This is done with the *Options>Values of Lines>Similarities* command. Next, select the *Layout>Energy>Starting Positions>Given xy* (i.e., horizontal and vertical dimensions) option; this indicates that with each new drawing Pajek begins with the nodes/actors where they are (as opposed to randomly placing them before drawing the network map); this assumes that repeated drawings of networks yield increasingly better solutions. Finally, choose the node size you prefer with Pajek's *Options>Size>of Vertices* command. This brings up a dialog box where you enter the desired size (note that the size of the nodes in

[Main Screen]
Pajek>Draw>
Draw

[Draw Screen]
Options>Color>
Background

Options>Values
of Lines>
Similarities

Layout>
Energy>
Starting
Positions>
Given xy

Options>Size>
of Vertices

Figure 3.11 is set to 8). Pajek includes an "auto-size" option (type a "0" in the dialog box), which is quite useful when you are varying the size of a node based on an attribute that contains considerable variation (e.g., betweenness centrality).

As noted previously, through version 2.04 Pajek has only implemented spring-embedding algorithms for its layouts. In particular, it uses two: Fruchterman Reingold (1991) and Kamada-Kawai (1989). The Kamada-Kawai algorithm assumes attraction between actors that are tied with one another and repulsion between actors that are not. The Fruchterman Reingold algorithm is similar, except that instead of assuming attraction or repulsion between actors, it attempts to simulate a system of mass particles where the vertices simulate mass points repelling each other while the edges simulate springs with attracting forces. It then tries to minimize the "energy" of this physical system.

To implement the Fruchterman Reingold layout algorithm, use Pajek's *Layout>Energy>Fruchterman Reingold>2D, 3D* command; to implement Kamada-Kawai, use its *Layout>Energy>Kamada-Kawai>Free* command. Which one should you choose? On the one hand, the Kamada-Kawai algorithm works well with small, connected networks but is not recommended for networks with more than 500 actors (de Nooy et al. 2011:17). It draws layouts similar to nonmetric MDS and tends to be better than Fruchterman Reingold at mapping sparse networks. Unfortunately, it places isolated nodes randomly on the graph, so they can sometimes appear to be in the center of a network when in reality they are not. The Fruchterman Reingold algorithm is faster than Kamada-Kawai and works well with large networks. It also is able to map networks in both two-dimensional and three-dimensional space (whereas Kamada-Kawai only maps networks in two-dimensional space). As long as the network is not too large, it is often helpful to first visualize the network using Fruchterman Reingold, and then (after making sure that the *Layout>Energy>Starting Positions>Given xy* option has been selected) use Kamada-Kawai.

Pajek does not provide goodness-of-fit statistics for network maps, which makes it more difficult for analysts to objectively evaluate the accuracy of a network map. It does, however, evaluate the aesthetic properties of a network drawing with the series of commands found under the *Draw>Info* submenu. For example, some argue that the number of crossing lines in a graph should be kept to a minimum and that unconnected vertices should not be drawn too closely to one another (de Nooy et al. 2011:18). And, if you select the *Draw>Info>Closest Vertices* command, Pajek identifies the nodes that perform the worst in this regard and assigns them a different color, making them easy to identify. You can then use the mouse to drag the two vertices farther apart.

[Draw Screen]
Layout>Energy>
Fruchterman
Reingold>2D,
3D

Layout>Energy>
Kamada-
Kawai>Free

Layout>Energy>
Starting
Positions>
Given xy

[Draw Screen]
Draw>Info

[Main Screen]
Draw>Info>
Closest Vertices

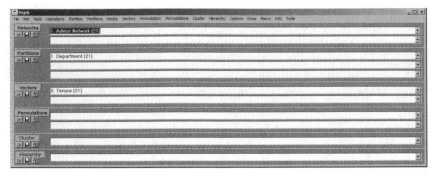

Figure 3.12. Pajek's Main Screen

Visualizing Attribute Data in Pajek

We will now look at how to work with attribute data in Pajek. Return to Pajek's main screen. With the Krackhardt advice network highlighted in the first Network drop-down menu, the *Department* partition highlighted in the first Partition drop-down menu and the *Tenure* vector highlighted in the first Vector drop-down menu (see Figure 3.12), select Pajek's *Draw>Draw-Partition-Vector* command and energize it using one or both of the visualization algorithms. This should produce a drawing similar (but again, not identical) to the one in Figure 3.13, where the color of the nodes indicates the department to which each manager belongs and the size of the nodes indicates each manager's tenure. In

Draw>Draw-Partition-Vector

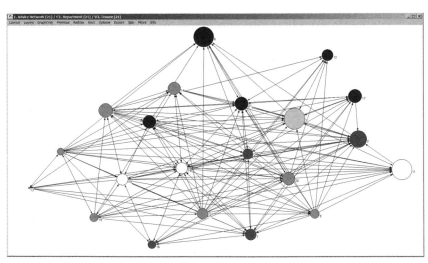

Figure 3.13. Krackhardt Advice Network with Varying Node Size and Color (Pajek)

Table 3.1. *Meta-matrix representation of a meta-network*

	Agents	Knowledge	Tasks	Organizations
Agents	Social Network	Knowledge Network	Assignment Network	Membership Network
Knowledge		Information Network	Needs Network	Organizational Capability
Tasks			Precedence Network	Institutional Support Network
Organizations				Interorganizational Network

Figure 3.13, the layout was obtained using the Fruchterman Reingold two-dimensional algorithm, and the node color has been set using one of Pajek's greyscale options. The latter option is accessed with the *[Draw Screen] Options>Colors>Partition Colors>for Vertices* command, which calls up a dialog box (not shown) where you can select specific colors for various partition classes or use one of Pajek's preset options. Here, the preset "GreyScale 1" option was chosen. As you can see, there is some clustering based on department, and tenure does not appear to determine the centrality of managers in the network. We would, of course, want to test this latter observation by correlating tenure with various centrality measures – but we are getting ahead of ourselves. It is now time to turn our attention to ORA.

[Draw Screen] Options> Colors>Partition Colors>for Vertices

3.5 ORA (Organizational Risk Analyzer)

Organizational Risk Analyzer (ORA; Carley 2001–2011) is a recent entry in the SNA arena that has gained a wide following in a very short time. For instance, in Huisman and Duijn's (2005) original review of available social network packages, ORA was not even mentioned. By 2011, it was one of the five general-purpose packages the authors explored in depth (Huisman and van Duijn 2011). ORA was developed by Kathleen Carley, who is a former student of Harrison White and currently teaches at Carnegie Mellon University. ORA is user-friendly and designed to find those actors, types of skills or knowledge, and tasks that are critical to a network's performance. Lying at the heart of ORA's approach is the notion of a meta-matrix of networks (Carley 2001–2011; Carley, Lee, and Krackhardt 2002) that includes not only social networks but also knowledge networks (who knows what), information networks (what ideas are related to what), assignment networks (who is doing what), need networks (what knowledge is needed to do the task), and so on. Table 3.1 illustrates (but does not entirely capture) ORA's meta-network approach (adapted from Carley 2003b).

Unlike UCINET, NetDraw, and Pajek, ORA is report based; that is, when analyzing networks, you typically do not request a single metric from ORA, but rather a report containing a series of related metrics. For example, if you wish to identify central actors using ORA, you would probably ask for ORA's "Standard Network Analysis" report, which provides the estimated scores of the most commonly used centrality measures. Like Pajek, ORA includes both a main screen, where you can analyze networks using a variety of algorithms, and a draw screen, where you can visualize networks using different mapping algorithms in either two or three dimensions. A helpful feature of ORA's draw screen is that it includes its own analytical capabilities; that is, it implements several algorithms and metrics (in this respect, it is similar to NetDraw), which is an advantage it has over Pajek. ORA also includes features for simulating various scenarios (e.g., the effect of removing or isolating various actors from a network at different points of time), geospatially analyzing and mapping social networks that can then be plotted in various geospatial programs, creating different types of charts (e.g., histograms, bar charts, and scatter plots) that can be quite useful for analysis and presenting results, and analyzing changes over time with its "view measures overtime" feature.

Like the other programs, ORA has its weaknesses. For example, although its report-based approach is quite handy, its reports will sometimes include metrics that are inappropriate for a particular network, such as estimating closeness centrality (Freeman 1979) when analyzing a disconnected network, or calculating Krackhardt's (1994) measure of hierarchy when examining an undirected (i.e., symmetric) network. This could lead analysts to conclude that certain actors are more important than they really are, which of course could lead to using mistaken assumptions when crafting strategies. And although its visualization capabilities are adequate and offer some useful options, the network maps it produces tend not to be as robust as Pajek's, at least when visualizing valued networks (i.e., where ties between actors are ordered rather than just "0s" and "1s"). Nevertheless, ORA is a powerful tool. Moreover, because it has been funded in part by Department of Defense dollars,[6] it is quite popular among those in the intelligence community.

Getting Started with ORA

Like Pajek, ORA has both a main screen and a draw screen (the ORA visualizer). Figure 3.14 presents ORA's main screen. As you can see it is broken down into three sections or panels: the (1) Meta-Network Manager, (2) Network Information/Editor, and (3) Report panels. The

---

[6] See http://www.casos.cs.cmu.edu/projects/ora/sponsors.php.

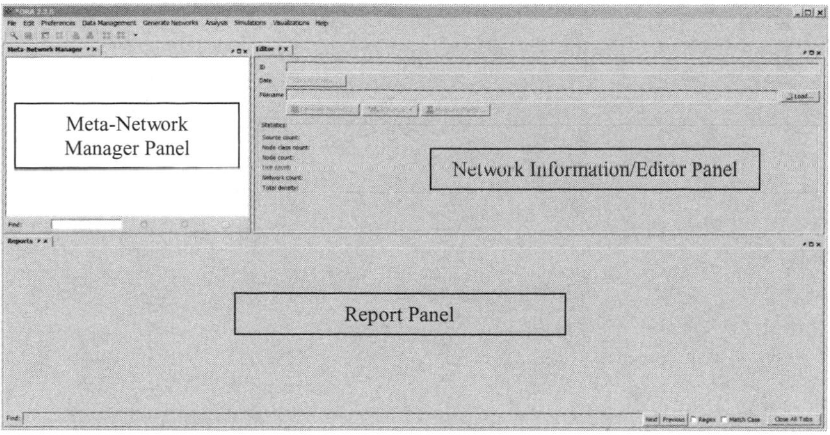

Figure 3.14. ORA Main Screen

first displays a list of the meta-networks that are currently loaded into ORA. In this case, all three of the Krackhardt networks have been loaded into ORA. We can view information about a particular network by single-clicking and highlighting it. Here, the advice network has been selected, causing its basic statistics to appear in the Network Information/Editor panel. If you selected the Editor tab, you could examine (and modify, if you so choose) the ties between the actors in the network. Finally, the Report panel is where ORA displays the results of any analyses that have been run on a network or set of networks.

ORA's menus follow a logical pattern. We will spend most of our time utilizing the tools found under the *Analysis* and *Visualizations* menus, although functions found under other menus will be of use to us as well. For example, under the *File* menu you will find commands for reading, importing, saving, and exporting data, and under the *Edit* menu there are tools for copying and pasting data. The *Preferences* menu includes features for preferred displays and fonts. Using, for instance, the *Preferences>Other>General>Select* command, I changed ORA's default color (blue) to gray. The *Data Management* menu has a series of tools for manipulating data, a few of which we will use throughout the course of this book. We will not utilize too many of the features found under the *Simulations* or *Generate Networks* menus, although in the next chapter we will see how to record network data in ORA.

[Main Screen] Preferences> Other>General> Select

Mapping Algorithms in ORA

To read network data into ORA, use ORA's *File>Open Meta-Network* command and select the `Krackhardt High Tech.xml` file that accompanies this book. ORA's visualizer can be accessed by clicking "Visualize" on the Network Information/Editor panel or by accessing the

[Main Screen] File>Open Meta-Network

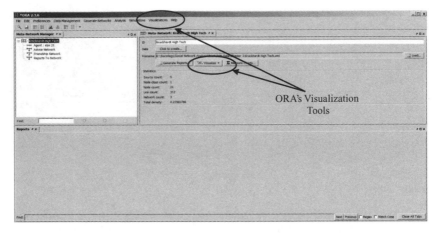

Figure 3.15. Accessing ORA's Visualizer from Ora's Main Screen

Visualizations>   *Visualizations>View Networks* command (see Figure 3.15). Both features
View Networks   allow you to visualize the network in either two or three dimensions. To
do so, either hold down the "Visualize" button and select the "Network
Visualizer" option or choose one of the two dimensions from the menu
command. Because the analytical capabilities of ORA's two-dimensional
visualizer are more robust, we will focus more on it. After selecting the
two-dimensional option for viewing the Krackhardt data, you should get
a network drawing that looks similar to Figure 3.16 (Here I've selected
[Visualizer]   ORA's *Display>Grayscale* option). By default, ORA visualizes all of the
Display>   networks (i.e., advice, friendship, reports to) in the Krackhardt dataset.
Grayscale   If you want to visualize only one, as Figure 3.16 does, then uncheck the
boxes of the networks you do not want to visualize.

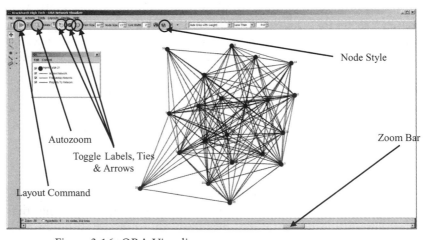

Figure 3.16. ORA Visualizer

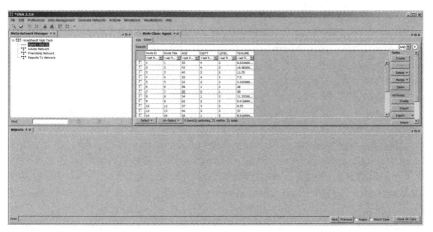

Figure 3.17. ORA Editor

ORA's visualizer includes a number of features that are useful in displaying and analyzing social networks. We will not explore all of these, but a few are worth mentioning now. Circled in the upper-left corner, is the layout command. ORA's default is a spring-embedded algorithm, but it can be changed to an alternative spring-embedded algorithm designed for large network data using the *Layouts>Spring Embedded (with enhancements for large data)* command. Another option is to use ORA's MDS routine, which is accessed with its *Layouts>Run MDS Layout* command. This calls up a dialog box (not shown) that asks you to indicate how many iterations you wish to run. A minimum of 100 generally produces good results. Note that there are a number of other visualization options, some of which you can try out on your own. Sometimes after visualizing a network, it becomes too large or too small for the screen. ORA's Autozoom feature, which is just to the right of the layout button (see Figure 3.16), both centers and fits the network in the visualizer. Working from left to right across the menu, you can see that ORA includes a number of additional features that allow you to rotate the network; toggle on and off labels, ties, and arrows; vary the size of fonts, nodes, and ties; change the node style; and hide ties of a particular strength. In addition, at the base of the visualizer, you can vary the size of the network by dragging the zoom bar to the left or right.

Layouts>Spring Embedded (with enhancements for large data)

Layouts>Run MDS Layout

Visualizing Attribute Data in ORA

To visualize attribute data in ORA, first return to ORA's main screen to see where they are stored. Select the node class icon in the Meta-Network Manager panel and click on the Editor tab in the Network Information/Editor panel (see Figure 3.17). ORA uses "node classes" to store characteristics (e.g., attributes) about nodes/actors. Note that in the Editor tab we can (among other things) create and delete nodes as well as create, import, export, and delete attributes. Because the attribute data are already loaded and stored within the Krackhardt data file, we do not need to explore these features here.

[Visualizer] Node Appearance> Node Color> Color Nodes by Attribute or Measure

Display> Grayscale

Display>Node Appearance>Size Nodes by Attribute or Measure

Return to ORA's visualizer. To change the color of the nodes based on the department attribute, under the *Display* menu, choose the *Node Appearance>Node Color>Color Nodes by Attribute or Measure* command. At the resulting dialog box (not shown), use the *Select an Attribute* drop-down menu and choose the "DEPT" attribute. Click "Apply Changes" and close the dialog box. I have chosen ORA's grayscale option, which you can select with the *Display>Grayscale* command. To change the size of the node, choose the *Display>Node Appearance>Size Nodes by Attribute or Measure* command. Select "LEVEL," click "Apply Changes," and close the dialog box. The nodes in your network map should now vary in color and size and look similar to Figure 3.18.

3.6   Summary and Conclusion

In this chapter we have briefly examined some of the basic features of UCINET, NetDraw, Pajek, and ORA. All four programs are widely used within the SNA community. All four have their strengths and weaknesses. Generally, analysts use UCINET for estimating metrics and manipulating data, NetDraw for the basic drawing of social networks, and Pajek for

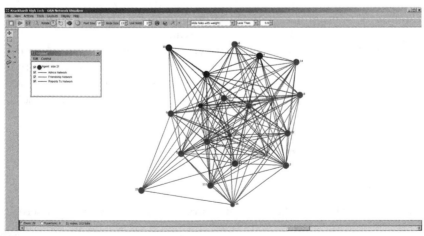

Figure 3.18. Krackhardt Advice Network with Varying Node Size and Color (ORA)

analyzing large networks and robust visualizations of social networks. ORA is the newcomer on the block and offers several useful features, such as the calculation of numerous metrics (some that are unique to ORA), the ability to handle relatively large datasets, and visualization features that lend themselves to presentations and analysis.

4

Gathering, Recording, and Manipulating Social Networks

4.1 Introduction

Social network analysis software packages such as UCINET, NetDraw, Pajek, and ORA often come with ready-to-use data. In the real world, however, we have to collect and record it on our own. Knowing how to do this is an important first step in SNA. We can gather and prepare social network data in a variety of ways, but most social network analysts record social network data in matrix form. For small datasets it usually makes sense to enter the data directly into UCINET or ORA, using their internal spreadsheet functions. When working with large networks, however, it is generally preferable to initially enter social network data into a standard spreadsheet program, such as Microsoft Excel, and then import (or paste) it into UCINET, Net-Draw, Pajek, or ORA. One of Excel's attractions is its "auto-complete" feature that compares the text you are typing into a cell with text already entered into the same column, which increases accuracy (e.g., consistently spelling the same name the same way each time) and input time.[1]

This chapter focuses on collecting, recording, and manipulating network data. Before turning to the nuts and bolts of how to do this, however, we need to first consider how social network analysts specify a network's boundaries, the difference between personal (ego) and complete networks, the various types of social network data, and the variety of ways that researchers collect social network data. Only then will we be ready to collect, record, and manipulate actual social network data.

---

[1] If the same word has been used before, it completes typing the entry for you.

4.2 Boundary Specification

An important concern in social network study is which actors to include in the network and which ones not to include. Sometimes it is relatively clear. Sometimes it is not. The goal should be "to find a set of actors with relatively good separateness from the rest of the world" from which we can draw reasonable conclusions (Erickson 2001:317). Laumann, Marsden, and Prensky (1983, 1989) note that researchers adopt various approaches for determining the boundaries of their networks. Generally, their approaches cut across two dimensions: one that leads them to choose between realist or nominalist strategies, and another that causes them to focus on one of three aspects of a network such as actor attributes, relations, or participation in activities/events. We consider these in turn.

Realist vs. Nominalist Strategies

The *realist* approach is a more subjective strategy for identifying the boundaries of a network. It allows actors to define the boundary of the network. It seeks to adopt the "vantage point of the actors themselves... [and] the network is treated as a social fact only in that it is consciously experienced... by the actors composing it" (Laumann et al. 1983:20). It assumes that the network exists as a social entity for most (or perhaps all) actors of the network (Laumann, Marsden, and Presnsky 1983). Thus, actors and their ties are only included to the extent that other actors consider them to be part of the network (Knoke and Yang 2007:15). This approach implicitly assumes that natural boundaries actually exist for the network. Knoke and Laumann (1982) adopted this approach when identifying core U.S. energy and health national policy organizations for analysis; they only included those organizations that energy and health policy insiders considered to be influential players in setting energy and health policies in the United States (Knoke and Yang 2007:15–16).

> The key aspect of the realist approach is identifying, early on, who are the key informants [in the] target population. You need to be confident that the informants you speak with are ones who have a good understanding of the network in question and can offer an accurate picture of the members of the network. Thus, locating who is a "key informant" might be a tricky process in itself. (Prell 2011:66)

By contrast, the *nominalist* approach is a more objective strategy in that rather than looking to the perceptions of network members, it imposes an a priori framework based on the analyst's theoretical concerns

(Knoke and Yang 2007; Wasserman and Faust 1994). "For example, a researcher might be interested in studying the flow of computer messages among researchers in a scientific specialty. In such a study, the list of actors might be the collection of people who published papers on the topic in previous years. The list is constructed for the analytical purposes of the researcher, even though the scientists themselves might not perceive the list as constituting a distinctive social entity" (Wasserman and Faust 1994:32). In essence it imposes somewhat arbitrary boundaries on a network based on the needs of the researcher. For example, researchers might choose to only examine the social networks of second-grade children at a particular school; even though these second-graders have ties outside of that group, they are ignored for the purposes of the study. However, if we define a network's boundary in this way, we need to be aware that we could "be potentially ignoring important ties that influence the behaviours of each participant in [our] study . . . Thus [we] need to be able to fully justify [our] reasons for drawing a boundary . . . based on this approach" (Prell 2011:67).

Although it is analytically useful to draw a distinction between these two approaches, it is probably better to think of them as two poles of a continuum where it is possible to imagine a strategy that adopts a little of both approaches in defining a network's boundary. For example, you might begin with a nominalist approach in studying a dark network by drawing on court proceedings and newspaper accounts to initially define the network. But then you could supplement your research through interviews of network members, asking them to identify any other individuals and organizations that should be included in the network.

Definitional Focus: Attributes, Relations, or Events

This approach to drawing boundaries leads researchers to focus on certain features of a network, namely, the attributes of actors, types of relations, or participation in events, while leaving the remaining features free to vary (Laumann et al. 1983:22). Social network analysts who focus on the *attributes* of actors generally do so in one of two ways: either in terms of position (i.e., where a membership test refers to the presence or absence of some attribute, such as holding a position in a formal group) or reputation (e.g., one that draws on the judgments of knowledgeable informants for identifying participant actors). Examples would include tracing the network of individuals who are members of a terrorist group (International Crisis Group 2006, 2009b) or of organizations that are involved in a particular social movement (Osa 2003).

When social network analysts use a relational focus to determining network boundaries, they focus on a specific type of tie (or set of ties) between actors (e.g., friendship, kinship, business, school, faith community). For example, researchers may be interested in studying the friendship and acquaintance ties of a particular high school or elementary school (Mc-Farland 2004). If so, then they could (theoretically) obtain a roster of the students and then ask them to identify whom they consider to be their close friends, acquaintances, and so on. Krackhardt's (1987a, 1992) examination of the advice and friendship networks of a Silicon Valley high-technology firm is also an example of this approach. In the case of dark networks, analysts may be interested in mapping the trust network of a particular dark network and consequently focus on those types of ties that are indicative of trust (e.g., friendship, kinship, religious, school).

Finally, some researchers use participation in a particular event or activity to select actors and the social relationships among them into a network. The Southern Club Women network, which was constructed based on the attendance of eighteen women at fourteen different social events (Davis, Gardner, and Gardner 1941), is one of the more widely known examples of this approach. It is a favorite among social theorists (Breiger 1974; Homans 1950), and one of the standard datasets included with UCINET. Other examples of networks delineated based on this approach include the network of individuals who participated in the Madrid bombing (Rodriguez 2005), the first Bali bombing (Koschade 2006), and the network of nations active in the global economy (Smith and White 1992).

It is important to stress that these foci are not necessarily mutually exclusive, so we will sometimes want to use them in conjunction with one another. Indeed, it may be more common for researchers to use multiple foci rather than only one. For example, we may examine the friendship ties of members of a particular community of faith as well as ties formed through participation on various boards and committees.

Summary

Table 4.1 combines these two dimensions into a single matrix in order to illustrate the array of possible approaches that researchers can use to specify the boundaries of the network they are studying. What should be clear is that analysts are not limited to a single type of approach (i.e., types I through VI in the table) but rather can adopt approaches that combine two or more foci and land somewhere on the continuum between nominalist and realist strategies. What is ultimately important is not the approach taken but rather that the boundary of the network being analyzed is correctly specified. As with any empirical approach to studying social phenomena, misspecification can lead to erroneous conclusions, something we do not want to do when we are trying to track, disrupt, and/or destabilize a dark network.

Table 4.1. *Boundary specification typology*

	Definitional focus			
	Actor attributes	Type of relation	Event or activity	Multiple foci
Strategy	I	II	III	
Realist (Subjective)	• Actors included are members of a socially defined group that group members recognize • Example: Members of a self-identified high school group (e.g., jocks, stoners)	• Focus on members' degree or type of relation • Example: A primary (face-to-face) group or clique	• Actors included are those who attend or participate in a series of events or activities • Example: Davis et al.'s (1941) study of 18 women who attended 14 social events	• Combination of types I, II, and III
	IV	V	VI	
Nominalist (Objective)	• Focus on attributes objectively defined • Example: Business elite defined as members of Forbes 500 corporation boards	• Actors' inclusion based on their presence in a type of relation • Example: Krackhardt's (1987, 1992) Advice and Friendship Networks	• Difficult to define as participation in event is self-conscious activity • Example: Citation networks, "invisible" college of academics – membership determined by areas of interest (e.g., SNA)	• Combination of types IV, V, and VI

Note: Adapted from Laumann, Marsden, and Prensky (1983).

4.3   Ego Networks and Complete Networks

A difficulty facing social network analysts is that it is next to impossible to study very large social networks – for example, the United States, California, Silicon Valley, and San Jose. It would be wonderful if social network analysts could use sampling to collect social network data because then we could generalize our findings to entire populations. Unfortunately, sampling does not work for most forms of SNA, and it is easy to see why. Imagine if we drew a sample of 1,200 individuals

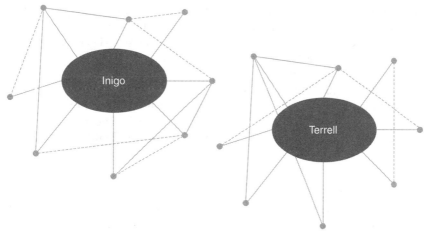

Figure 4.1. Hypothetical Ego Network

and asked them to name their friends and identify the ties between them. Chances are that their friends would not be part of the original sample, which means that we would not have enough relational data to analyze because most of the people surveyed would not know one another. Social network researchers have responded to this fact in two different ways. One approach actually uses sampling but focuses only on what social network analysts refer to as ego networks; the other, which is more common, analyzes what social network analysts call complete social networks. We briefly consider each of these.

Ego Networks

An ego-centered approach focuses on the person surveyed – typically termed *ego* – and the set of contacts (i.e., *alters*) who have ties to the person and measurements on the ties among these alters. Each person surveyed is generally asked for a set of contacts (Burt 1984, 1985), using questions such as "Looking back over the last six months, who are the people with whom you discussed matters important to you?" After providing a list of contacts, they are then asked about the ties (if any) between their contacts (e.g., if they know one another, attend the same church, are friends, and so on). Needless to say, ties between an ego and his or her alters with different egos and their alters are not (and generally cannot be) recorded. This yields a data structure similar to that displayed in Figure 4.1. As one can see, only those ties within the ego network of the people sampled (i.e., Inigo and Terrel) are recorded, whereas ties between ego networks are not.

A common use of ego network data is to estimate the size of peoples' core networks to see whether it has changed over time or is correlated with certain types of behavior (Marsden 1987). For example, Miller McPherson, Lynn Smith-Lovin, and Matthew Brashears (2006), using data gathered with the 2004 General Social Survey (GSS), concluded that from 1985 to 2004 the average size of individuals' core discussion networks dropped from 2.94 to 2.08, whereas the modal size dropped from 3.00 to 0.00. According to their study, almost one quarter of the population now reports that they do not discuss important matters with anyone! Their conclusions have been challenged by sociologist Claude Fischer who believes the research team's findings are highly implausible. He contends

> that the question used in the 2004 survey to measure the size of respondents' networks yielded results that were so inconsistent with other data, and so internally anomalous and implausible, that they are almost surely the product of an artifact. These data do not provide a reliable estimate of what happened to Americans' networks between the 1980s and 2004. (Fischer 2009: 657)

This led him to conclude that we should not infer from the 2004 GSS that Americans' social networks have changed substantially between 1985 and 2004. His conclusions also highlight the difficulty of generalizing ego network data gathered in surveys to the wider population.

Complete Networks

A more common approach to SNA collects relational data on an entire network (assuming that we know the boundaries of that network – see Section 4.2). Most social network methodologies are built on the assumption that the network being studied is a complete network that not only includes all relevant actors but also all relevant ties between actors. Because the complete network approach places limits on the size of the networks that can be studied, social network analysts focus primarily on case studies, which is what we will do in this book.

4.4   Types of Social Network Data

Social network analysts work with three types of data: one-mode social network data (symmetric and asymmetric), two-mode social network data, and attribute data. We discussed the nature of attribute data in Chapter 1, so here we limit our discussion to one- and two-mode network data.

	1	2	3	4	5	6	7	8	9	10	11	12	13	14	15	16
	AC	AL	BA	BI	CA	GI	GU	LA	ME	PA	PE	PU	RI	SA	ST	TO
	CI	BI	RB	SC	ST	NO	AD	MB	DI	ZZ	RU	CC	DO	LV	RO	RN
	AI	ZZ	AD	HE	EL	RI	AG	ER	CI	I	ZZ	I	LF	IA	ZZ	AB
	UO	I	OR	RI	LA		NI	TE		I			I	TI	I	UO
	L		I	N			S							I		N
1 ACCIAIUOL	0	0	0	0	0	0	0	0	1	0	0	0	0	0	0	0
2 ALBIZZI	0	0	0	0	0	1	1	0	1	0	0	0	0	0	0	0
3 BARBADORI	0	0	0	0	1	0	0	0	1	0	0	0	0	0	0	0
4 BISCHERI	0	0	0	0	0	0	1	0	0	0	1	0	0	0	1	0
5 CASTELLAN	0	0	1	0	0	0	0	0	0	0	1	0	0	0	1	0
6 GINORI	0	1	0	0	0	0	0	0	0	0	0	0	0	0	0	0
7 GUADAGNI	0	1	0	1	0	0	0	1	0	0	0	0	0	0	0	1
8 LAMBERTES	0	0	0	0	0	0	1	0	0	0	0	0	0	0	0	0
9 MEDICI	1	1	1	0	0	0	0	0	0	0	0	0	1	1	0	1
10 PAZZI	0	0	0	0	0	0	0	0	0	0	0	0	0	1	0	0
11 PERUZZI	0	0	0	1	1	0	0	0	0	0	0	0	0	0	1	0
12 PUCCI	0	0	0	0	0	0	0	0	0	0	0	0	0	0	0	0
13 RIDOLFI	0	0	0	0	0	0	0	0	1	0	0	0	0	0	1	1
14 SALVIATI	0	0	0	0	0	0	0	0	1	1	0	0	0	0	0	0
15 STROZZI	0	0	0	1	1	0	0	0	0	0	1	0	1	0	0	0
16 TORNABUON	0	0	0	0	0	0	1	0	1	0	0	0	1	0	0	0

Figure 4.2. Subset of Padgett and Ansell's Marriage Data

Symmetric One-Mode Networks

One-mode networks, sometimes referred to as adjacency matrices, consist of a single set of actors, which can be people, groups, families, tribes, organizations, corporations, nation-states, etc. The ties between actors can be friendship or kinship ties; material transactions such as business transactions including the import or export of goods; communication networks involving the sending or receiving of messages; and so on. An example of a one-mode network, which we briefly examined in the Chapter 2, is Padgett and Ansell's (1993) Florentine families network. Padgett and Ansell collected nine types of relational data on ninety-two prominent fifteenth-century Florentine families in order to explain Cosimo de' Medici's rise to power. Included with UCINET is a subset of this data that delineates the business and marriage ties between sixteen of the ninety-two families (Breiger and Pattison 1986). A marital tie was determined to exist if a member of one family married a member of another family, while a business tie was determined to exist if a member of one family granted credits, made a loan, or entered into a joint partnership with a member of another family (Wasserman and Faust 1994). Figure 4.2 presents a UCINET display (i.e., *Data>Display*) of the Padgett and *Data>Display* Ansell's marriage data.

One-mode networks always result in square matrices because each actor (in this case, each family) appears as both a row and a column. For example, the Acciaiuol family's ties are recorded in both the first row and first column, the Albizzi family's ties are recorded in the second row and second column, the Barbadori family's ties in the third row and third column, and so on. In this case, the ties are *dichotomous* because they only take the values of "0" or "1," with "1" indicating the presence

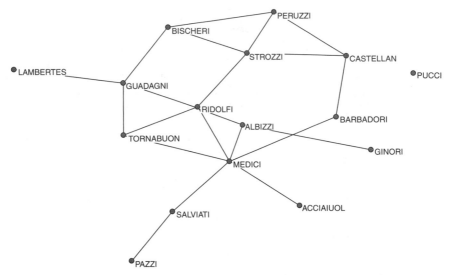

Figure 4.3. Sociogram of Padgett and Ansell's Marriage Data

of a marriage tie and "0" indicating the absence of one.[2] Also, the ties between families are necessarily reciprocal; they go both ways. In other words, not only does the Albizzi family have a marriage tie with the Ginori family (note the "1" in row 2, column 6), but the Ginori family has a marriage tie with the Albizzi family (note the "1" in row 6, column 2). From this matrix, you can see that the Medici family had ties to six families (Acciaiuol, Albizzi, Barbadori, Ridolfi, Salviati, and Tornabuon), the Strozzi family had ties to four families (Bishcheri, Castellan, Peruzzi, and Salviati), while the Pucci family has ties to no other family. Figure 4.3 displays a sociogram (i.e., network map) created in Pajek of the network. As you can see, the Pucci family is the only family that shares no marriage ties with any of the other families. The Medicis are also relatively central to the network although they do not appear to be any more central than some of the other families. Of course, this is just a subset of the data, so it may not be indicative of the actual Florentine families network.

Asymmetric One-Mode Networks

Ties are not always reciprocal, of course. Take, for example, the social network data we explored earlier, the data collected by David Krackhardt (1987a, 1992) on twenty-one managers in a Silicon Valley high-technology company. You will recall that Krackhardt asked each manager to whom they went to for advice and whom they considered a friend. He

---

[2] Cell values can also be "valued," indicating some sort of numerical relationship between two actors. For example, a cell may indicate the amount of imports between two countries.

		1	2	3	4	5	6	7	8	9	10	11	12	13	14	15	16	17	18	19	20	21
		1	2	3	4	5	6	7	8	9	10	11	12	13	14	15	16	17	18	19	20	21
1	1	0	1	0	1	0	0	0	1	0	0	0	0	0	0	0	0	1	0	1	0	1
2	2	0	0	0	0	0	1	1	0	0	0	0	0	0	0	0	0	0	0	0	0	1
3	3	1	1	0	1	0	1	1	1	1	1	1	1	0	1	0	0	1	1	0	1	1
4	4	1	1	0	0	0	1	0	1	0	1	1	1	0	0	0	1	1	1	0	1	1
5	5	1	1	0	0	0	1	1	1	0	1	0	1	1	0	1	0	1	1	1	1	1
6	6	0	0	0	0	0	0	0	0	0	0	0	0	0	0	0	0	0	0	0	0	1
7	7	0	1	0	0	0	1	0	0	0	0	1	1	0	1	0	0	1	1	0	0	1
8	8	0	1	0	1	0	1	1	0	0	0	1	1	0	0	0	0	1	0	0	0	1
9	9	1	1	0	0	0	1	1	1	0	1	1	1	0	1	0	1	1	1	0	0	1
10	10	1	1	1	1	1	0	0	1	0	0	1	0	1	0	1	1	1	1	1	1	0
11	11	1	1	0	0	0	0	1	0	0	0	0	0	0	0	0	0	0	0	0	0	0
12	12	0	0	0	0	0	0	1	0	0	0	0	0	0	0	0	0	0	0	0	0	1
13	13	1	1	0	0	1	0	0	0	1	0	0	0	0	1	0	0	0	1	0	0	0
14	14	0	1	0	0	0	0	1	0	0	0	0	0	0	0	0	0	0	1	0	0	1
15	15	1	1	1	1	1	1	1	1	1	1	1	1	1	1	0	1	1	1	1	1	1
16	16	1	1	0	0	0	0	0	0	0	0	1	0	0	0	0	0	1	0	0	0	0
17	17	1	1	0	1	0	0	1	0	0	0	0	0	0	0	0	0	0	0	0	0	1
18	18	1	1	1	1	1	0	1	1	1	0	1	1	1	1	1	0	0	1	1	1	1
19	19	1	1	1	0	1	0	1	0	0	1	1	0	0	1	1	0	0	1	1	0	0
20	20	1	1	0	0	0	1	0	1	0	0	1	1	0	1	1	1	1	1	0	0	1
21	21	0	1	1	1	0	1	1	1	0	0	0	1	0	1	0	0	1	1	0	1	0

Figure 4.4. Krackhardt Advice Network Data

also determined from company documents to which manager each manager reported. Figure 4.4 presents the advice network data in matrix form, which indicates that although virtually every manager seeks advice from managers #2 and #21, managers #2 and #21 do not always reciprocate. For example, while manager #1 seeks advice from manager #21, manager #21 does not seek advice from manager #1 in return. By contrast, manager #15 is not too popular in terms of giving advice, but he is not shy in asking for it himself. While only four managers (10, 18, 19, and 20) seek his advice, he seeks advice from every other manager in the company.

Figure 4.5 presents a Pajek-generated sociogram of the network. While no major patterns jump out, at first glance some managers appear more

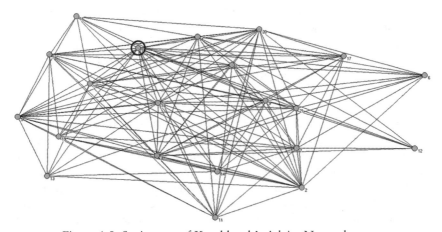

Figure 4.5. Sociogram of Krackhardt's Advice Network

		1 E1	2 E2	3 E3	4 E4	5 E5	6 E6	7 E7	8 E8	9 E9	10 E10	11 E11	12 E12	13 E13	14 E14
1	EVELYN	1	1	1	1	1	1	0	1	1	0	0	0	0	0
2	LAURA	1	1	1	0	1	1	1	1	0	0	0	0	0	0
3	THERESA	0	1	1	1	1	1	1	1	1	0	0	0	0	0
4	BRENDA	1	0	1	1	1	1	1	0	0	0	0	0	0	0
5	CHARLOTTE	0	0	1	1	1	0	1	0	0	0	0	0	0	0
6	FRANCES	0	0	1	0	1	1	0	1	0	0	0	0	0	0
7	ELEANOR	0	0	0	0	1	1	1	1	0	0	0	0	0	0
8	PEARL	0	0	0	0	0	1	0	1	1	0	0	0	0	0
9	RUTH	0	0	0	0	1	0	1	1	1	0	0	0	0	0
10	VERNE	0	0	0	0	0	0	1	1	1	0	0	1	0	0
11	MYRNA	0	0	0	0	0	0	0	1	1	1	0	1	0	0
12	KATHERINE	0	0	0	0	0	0	0	1	1	1	0	1	1	1
13	SYLVIA	0	0	0	0	0	0	1	1	1	1	0	1	1	1
14	NORA	0	0	0	0	0	1	1	0	1	1	1	1	1	1
15	HELEN	0	0	0	0	0	0	1	1	0	1	1	1	0	0
16	DOROTHY	0	0	0	0	0	0	0	1	1	0	0	0	0	0
17	OLIVIA	0	0	0	0	0	0	0	0	1	0	1	0	0	0
18	FLORA	0	0	0	0	0	0	0	0	1	0	1	0	0	0

Figure 4.6. Davis's Southern Women Network Data

central than others. The centrality of some may be misleading, however. Take manager #15, for example (circled in Figure 4.5). He is relatively central in the sociogram, but the reason is because, as we discussed previously, he indicated that he sought advice from every other manager in the company, which means that he has ties to every other manager, why he appears to be a central player in the network, and why we cannot rely on network visualizations alone.

Two-Mode Networks

Two-mode networks differ from one-mode networks in that rather than consisting of a single set of actors, they either consist of two sets of different actors, or one set of actors and one set of events or affiliations. Researchers often refer to two-mode networks as *affiliation matrices* or *networks*, but they sometimes call them *membership networks*, *dual networks*, and *hypernetworks*. Examples of two-mode networks include membership in various organizations, attendance at particular events, employees at a particular company, and so on. An example of a two-mode network is Davis's Southern Women, which we discussed in Section 4.2 (Breiger 1974; Davis, Gardner, and Gardner 1941) and records the observed attendance of eighteen southern women at fourteen social events. The women are listed by row; the events by column. As Figure 4.6 indicates, Evelyn attended eight events (1, 2, 3, 4, 5, 6, 8, and 9), while Olivia, Dorothy, and Flora attended only two (9 and 11).

A key assumption underlying the use of two-mode networks by social network analysts is that membership in an organization or participation in an event is a source of social ties. Why? Because people who join or participate in a common organization and/or event often share similar tasks and/or interests, and they are much more likely to interact with one another than two randomly selected people. That said, we need to be careful when using two-mode data. Just because two people participate in a common event or are members of the same faith community does not necessarily mean that a tie exists between them.

A Pajek-generated sociogram of Davis's Southern Women appears in Figure 4.7. Note the difference between this one and the previous two. Here, both sets of actors, the women and events, appear together and are assigned different colors (or, in this case, shades of gray). The graph suggests that there are three clusters of events (E1–E5, E6–E9, and E10–E14) and two primary sets of women (Laura through Ruth; Silvia through Verne), plus a few women who appear less involved than the rest (Dorothy, Olivia, and Flora). As we will see, there are ways of converting two-mode networks to one-mode networks, which is another way of exploring which actors are central and which ones are not.

4.5 Collecting Social Network Data

Social network analysts collect social network data in a variety of ways. The most common are questionnaires, interviews, direct observation, and written records (Wasserman and Faust 1994:45–54). Not all of these are useful for collecting data on dark networks, but it is still useful to briefly consider the various approaches for collecting social network data.[3]

Questionnaires

Questionnaires are a common method for collecting social network data, especially when actors are individuals, although they are probably the least common method when it comes to collecting relational data on dark networks. They contain questions such as whom people consider to be their friends, to whom do they go to for advice, with whom do they regularly communicate (e.g., talk face-to-face, e-mail, telephone), and so on. Such data can be recorded either symmetrically or asymmetrically. Say, for instance, actor "A" considers actor "B" to be a friend, but "B" does not consider "A" to be a friend. In such a case, researchers can either record the data as Krackhardt did (i.e., asymmetrically) by placing a "1" in the "A-B" cell of the matrix but a "0" in the "B-A" cell of the matrix, or they can record it symmetrically by placing a "0" in both cells under the assumption that a friendship tie only exists if both actors indicate that they consider the other to be a friend. Analysts use various formats for collecting social network data using questionnaires; they fall under three broad categories: (1) Roster vs. Free Recall, (2) Free vs. Fixed Choice, and (3) Ratings vs. Complete Rankings (Wasserman and Faust 1994:45).

Roster vs. Free Recall. Sometimes analysts present each respondent filling out a questionnaire with a complete roster of the actors in the network

---

[3] For a more in-depth but relatively brief summary of various methods for collecting social network data, see Prell (2011:68–74).

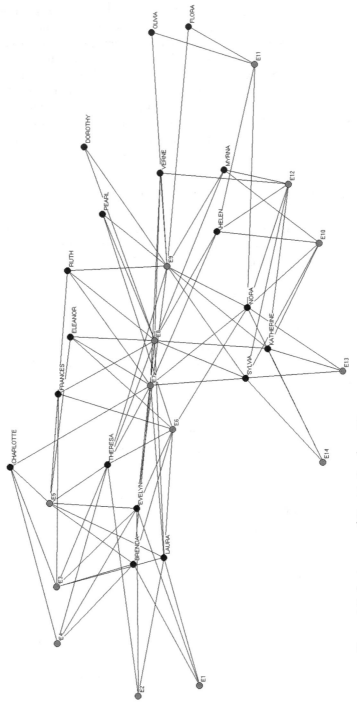

Figure 4.7. Sociogram of Davis's Southern Women

or allow the respondents to generate a list of names. Rosters can only be used when researchers know the members in the network prior to gathering data (Wasserman and Faust 1994:46). This, of course, raises the network boundary issue discussed earlier: How do researchers know a priori which actors belong to a network and which ones do not? When working with a self-contained organization (e.g., a small high-technology start-up), this is sometimes relatively obvious (at least for the purposes of the study), but it is not always so clear-cut. In the latter case, it is usually advisable to use the free-recall approach.

Free vs. Fixed Choice. In some network designs analysts tell respondents how many other actors they are to nominate on a questionnaire (e.g., "Name five people with whom you have regular contact"); at other times they are not presented with any such constraints as to how many nominations they can make (e.g., "Name everyone with whom you have regular contact"). The former (fixed choice) can underestimate the size or density of a network and produce misleading results.

Ratings vs. Complete Rankings. Finally, sometimes analysts ask each respondent to rate or rank the ties in terms of strength between all actors in the network (Wasserman and Faust 1994:48). Ratings can be either dichotomous (e.g., ties are either present or absent) or valued (e.g., respondents choose one of a few possible categories for the strength of each tie). Rankings differ in that each actor is asked to rank their ties to every other actor in the network. This latter approach becomes increasingly difficult as the size of the network increases.

Interviews

Social network analysts sometimes use interviews (either face to face or over the phone; Wasserman and Faust 1994:48). Interviews with captured members of dark networks may prove useful for mapping the networks, but these should probably be supplemented with other methods (e.g., direct observation, written records).

Direct Observation

Another way to record data is to have an observer record all interactions that take place among actors in the network (Wasserman and Faust 1994:49). Dan McFarland (2004) used this approach to record student interaction patterns at two different high schools. An obvious drawback to this approach is that in some situations interactions can be so numerous and occur so closely together that it becomes next to impossible to record all interactions. Moreover, those being observed often alter their behavior when they are aware that their interactions are being recorded (Roethlisberger and Dickson 1939). Nevertheless, analysts of dark networks might find this approach useful when recording affiliation (i.e., two-mode) network data. For example, they can record which members of a particular dark network visit specific sites or attend specific events in connection with their participation with the network.

Written Records

Written records can be valuable sources of relational data. E-mails, memos, phone calls (if available), historical marriage records, and court proceedings are just a few examples of sources from which one can determine ties between individual actors. At the corporate level, written records indicating joint ventures, interlocking directorates (i.e., where the same individual sits on the boards of two different companies), and membership in the same trade association may indicate ties, while records indicating the trade manufactured goods or the exchange of diplomats may indicate ties between countries. In terms of collecting relational data on dark networks, Sageman (2004, 2008:26–27) drew on captured documents, trial transcripts, intercepted conversations, legal documents, and testimony notes in order to determine some of the ties among members of the global salafi jihad. And throughout this book we draw on a narrative about Noordin's terrorist network that, in turn, drew in part on court records (International Crisis Group 2006).

Other Approaches

These are not the only approaches to collecting social network data. They are simply the most common. Other forms of data collection include cognitive social structure data, experiments, diaries, and small worlds (Wasserman and Faust 1994:51–54). When collecting cognitive social structure data, researchers ask respondents for their perception of other actors' network ties (e.g., "Who is friends with whom?"; Krackhardt 1987a). Social network analysts sometimes use experiments to observe the behavior of a set of actors in experimentally controlled environments (Bavelas 1950; Emerson 1962). Diaries are used by social network analysts to ask respondents to keep a continuous record of people with whom they interact (Wasserman and Faust 1994:54). And finally, researchers will use variations on small world network design (Milgram 1967; Travers and Milgram 1969) to estimate how many steps (i.e., degrees of separation) a respondent is removed from a randomly chosen target (Watts, Dodds, and Newman 2003).

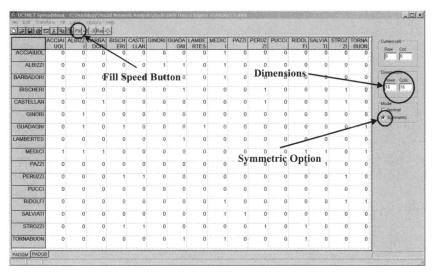

Figure 4.8. Padgett and Ansell's Marriage Network (UCINET)

4.6   Recording Social Network Data

In this section we illustrate how to record social network data in both UCINET and ORA and then export these data in formats readable by Pajek.[4] We begin by demonstrating the process for recording symmetric and asymmetric one-mode networks before moving to demonstrating it for a two-mode social network. Because so many network datasets often come in UCINET format, we also show how to read such datasets in Pajek and ORA. This section also shows (and briefly discusses) the recording of attribute data. The next section takes up how to aggregate and parse multiple networks.

Recording One-Mode Social Network Data

UCINET: Recording One-Mode Social Network Data. In UCINET, social network data can easily be recorded in matrix form using its internal spreadsheet editor. For example, if we wanted to enter Padgett marriage data discussed previously, we would first open the spreadsheet editor (Figure 4.8) using either the *Data>Data editors>Matrix Editor* command or the "Matrix" speed button located just under the *Data* menu (see Figure 3.1 in Chapter 3).

Next, because we are entering symmetric network data, we should select the "symmetric" option located on the right panel of the spreadsheet

[UCINET] Data>Data editors >Matrix Editor

---

[4]   Although you can record network data using Pajek, it is generally easier to record the data in either UCINET or ORA and then export the data in a form that Pajek can read.

editor (circled in Figure 4.8). This option ensures that each entry we make is replicated in the corresponding cell. In other words, if we enter a "1" in the cell located in the third row and the first column, UCINET automatically enters a "1" in the cell located in the first row and third column. Before entering values into cells, however, enter the names of the families in the rows (UCINET's symmetric option will automatically place them in the corresponding column). Then enter "1s" wherever a tie between two families exists (see Figure 4.8). UCINET's "Fill" feature means that we do not have to enter "0s." Instead, after indicating the dimensions of the matrix (i.e., the number of rows and columns) on the right side of the spreadsheet editor, use either the *Fill>Blanks w/0s* command or click the "Fill" speed button to fill all the empty cells with "0s." Your completed spreadsheet should look similar to Figure 4.8.

[Spreadsheet] Fill>Blanks w/0s

Of course, if we are entering asymmetric network data, we would not want to select the symmetric option. There is no point in illustrating this here, because, except for selecting the symmetric option, the process of entering asymmetric network data is identical to that of symmetric data. Instead, we will discuss how to enter social network data in ORA using an asymmetric network.

ORA: Recording One-Mode Social Network Data. We will use Krackhardt's advice network to illustrate how to record one-mode social network data in ORA. The first step in the process is to access ORA's "Create New Meta-Network" dialog box with the *Generate Networks>Create New Meta-Network* command. Next, specify the name of the meta-network and then indicate the various types of actors (i.e., node classes) in the network. This is a one-mode network, by definition there is only one type of actor, and in this instance they are individuals, so we should indicate that both types of nodes are agents. We also need to tell ORA that the size of the network (i.e., node class) is 21 (i.e., 21 managers).

[ORA] Generate Networks >Create New Meta-Network

Finally, we have to identify the various types of networks that will be included in the meta-network – advice, friendship, and reports to – and that they are all one-mode networks (i.e., source and target actor/node type are the same). After all this is entered (Figure 4.9), click "Create" and a new meta-network (without the ties) will be created.

The next step involves recording the ties between actors. Select the advice network in the Meta-Network Manager and then click on the Editor tab in the Network Information/Editor panel. Because this is a binary (i.e., dichotomous) network, we simply check the cells where a tie exists between two actors. In ORA we do not need to record "0s" because ORA assumes that a cell value is "0" unless it is checked. When you are finished, it should look similar to Figure 4.10. If we want to record valued data (as opposed to just "1s" and "0s"), then we would click and

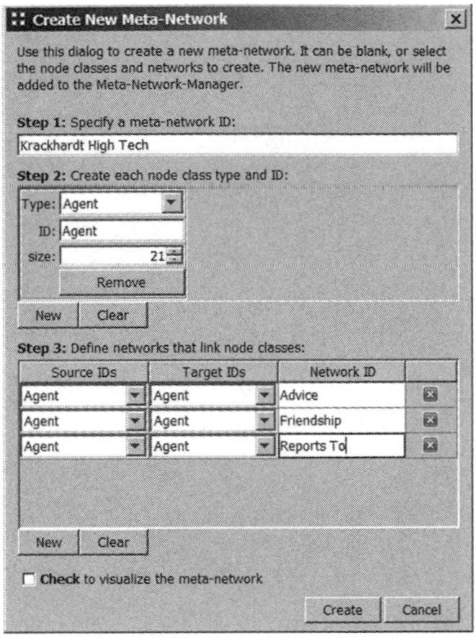

Figure 4.9. ORA's New Meta-Network Dialog Box (Krackhardt High-Tech)

hold down the "Display Options" button in the lower-right portion of the editor and select the "Numeric Link Values" option.

Recording Two-Mode Social Network Data

UCINET: Recording Two-Mode Social Network Data. We enter two-mode data into UCINET's spreadsheet function similar to the way we did

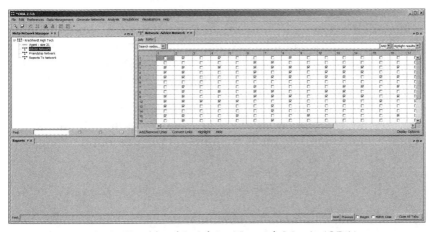

Figure 4.10. Krackhardt's Advice Network Matrix (ORA)

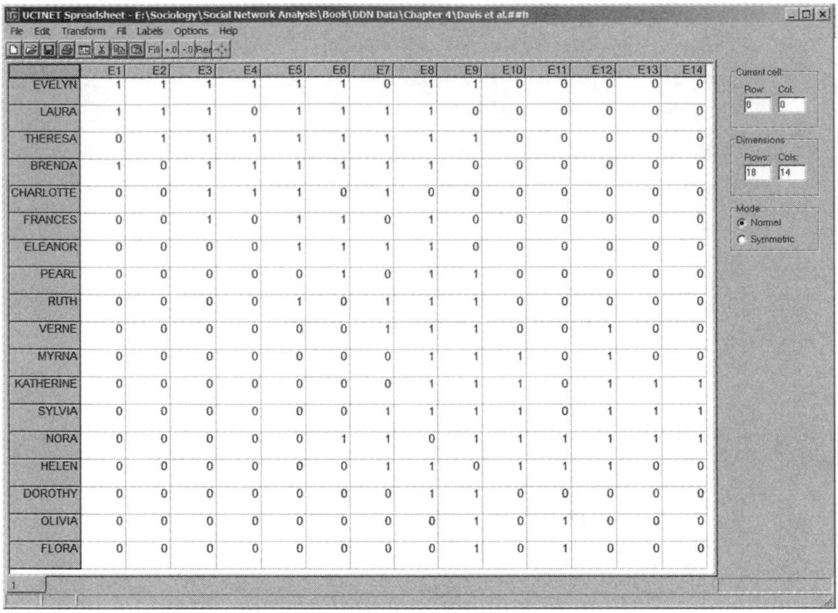

UCINET Spreadsheet - E:\Sociology\Social Network Analysis\Book\DDN Data\Chapter 4\Davis et al.##h

File Edit Transform Fill Labels Options Help

	E1	E2	E3	E4	E5	E6	E7	E8	E9	E10	E11	E12	E13	E14
EVELYN	1	1	1	1	1	1	0	1	1	0	0	0	0	0
LAURA	1	1	1	0	1	1	1	1	0	0	0	0	0	0
THERESA	0	1	1	1	1	1	1	1	1	0	0	0	0	0
BRENDA	1	0	1	1	1	1	1	1	0	0	0	0	0	0
CHARLOTTE	0	0	1	1	1	0	1	0	0	0	0	0	0	0
FRANCES	0	0	1	0	1	1	0	1	0	0	0	0	0	0
ELEANOR	0	0	0	0	1	1	1	1	0	0	0	0	0	0
PEARL	0	0	0	0	0	1	0	1	1	0	0	0	0	0
RUTH	0	0	0	0	1	0	1	1	1	0	0	0	0	0
VERNE	0	0	0	0	0	0	1	1	1	0	0	1	0	0
MYRNA	0	0	0	0	0	0	0	1	1	1	0	1	0	0
KATHERINE	0	0	0	0	0	0	0	1	1	1	0	1	1	1
SYLVIA	0	0	0	0	0	0	1	1	1	1	0	1	1	1
NORA	0	0	0	0	0	1	1	0	1	1	1	1	1	1
HELEN	0	0	0	0	0	0	1	1	0	1	1	1	0	0
DOROTHY	0	0	0	0	0	0	0	1	1	0	0	0	0	0
OLIVIA	0	0	0	0	0	0	0	0	1	0	1	0	0	0
FLORA	0	0	0	0	0	0	0	0	1	0	1	0	0	0

Current cell: Row 0 Col 0

Dimensions: Rows 18 Cols 14

Mode: Normal / Symmetric

Figure 4.11. Davis's Southern Women Matrix (UCINET Spreadsheet Editor)

with one-mode data, except that we do not select the symmetric option and the form of data entry differs because rather than consisting of a single set of actors, two-mode networks either consist of two sets of different actors, or one set of actors and one set of events or affiliations. Taking Davis's Southern Women as an example: The names of the women appear in rows, whereas the columns list the various events that the women attended (Figure 4.11). This could easily be reversed where the names of the events appear in rows, and the names of the women appear in the columns. However, social network analysts often work with an implicit "left to right" logic. Thus, because the women are more "logically" seen as attending various events (rather than the events attracting the women – although this is true as well), the women appear first (in rows), and the events appear second (in columns). Here, we can see that Evelyn attended events E1 through E6, E8, and E9, while Laura attended events E1 through E3 and E5 through E7. The same logic holds when recording actors' membership in various institutions. For instance, if a series of actors attended one (or more) faith-based organizations (e.g., churches, synagogues, temples, mosques), then we would typically list the actors first (i.e., in the rows) and the organizations second (i.e., in the columns).

ORA: Recording Two-Mode Social Network Data. Entering two-mode social network data in ORA is quite similar to entering one-mode data,

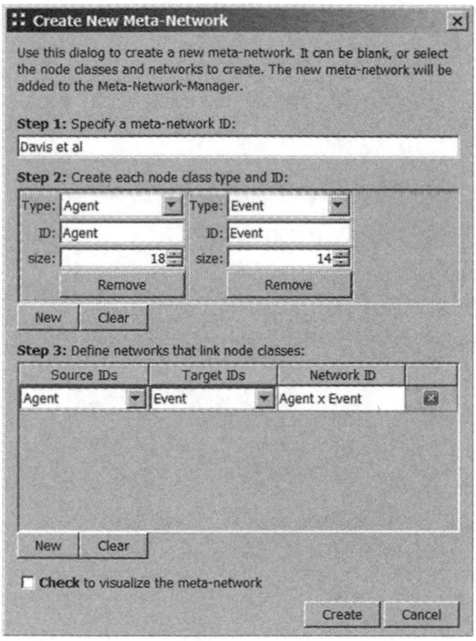

Figure 4.12. ORA's Create New Meta-Network Dialog Box (Davis's Southern Women)

although there are differences. We begin as we did before with ORA's *Generate Networks>Create New Meta-Network* command. Next, we specify the name of the meta-network and delineate the various types of actors/nodes (i.e., node classes) in the network. Since this is a two-mode network, we need to indicate as such in the dialog box. As you can see in Figure 4.12, two types of node classes have been identified: agent and event; the first has 18 nodes/actors and the second has 14 nodes/actors. And, as before, we need to tell ORA the types of networks that will be in the meta-network; in this case, just one. Because this is two-mode network, the source and target node/actor types differ. The source type is an agent (i.e., the women); the target type is an event (i.e., the social events). After this information is entered, click "Create" and a new meta-network matrix is created into which we can enter the ties indicating which women attended which events. The process of entering these ties is identical to that of one-mode networks. Since they are binary, all we need to do is check the cells where ties exist between the women and the various events. The final matrix should look similar (but probably not identical) to Figure 4.13.

[ORA] Generate Networks >Create New Meta-Network

Recording Attribute Data

As we discussed earlier, although SNA focuses primarily on the pattern of ties between actors, it does not ignore actors' attribute data. We can

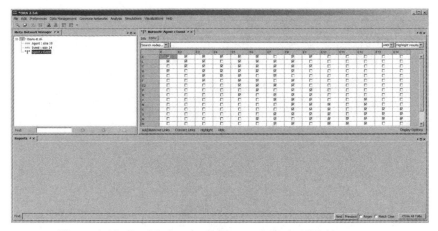

Figure 4.13. Davis's Southern Women Matrix (ORA)

use attribute data in various ways, some of which we will explore further on in this book. For now, it is only necessary to demonstrate how it is recorded in UCINET and ORA. As with social network data, if you want to use attribute data in Pajek, it is generally easier to record attribute data in either ORA or UCINET and then export it in formats that Pajek can read.

UCINET: Recording Attribute Data. Recording attribute data in UCINET is relatively straightforward. Figure 4.14 displays attribute data associated with Krackhardt's High-Tech network data. As you can see, the names of actors appear in rows, whereas the various types of attributes appear in columns. These data differ from social network data in that each column is self-contained. For example, the first column indicates the age of the managers while the fourth indicates the department to which each manager belongs. Obviously, without a code book, there is no way to know to what department each number refers.

ORA: Recording Attribute Data. In ORA, attribute data is recorded and stored in conjunction with a particular node class. To record attribute data in ORA, first select the "Agent" node class in the Meta-Network Manager panel and then click on the Editor tab in the Network Information/Editor panel (see Figure 4.15). On the far right of the screen, under the Attributes heading, note that there are a series of speed buttons for creating, importing, exporting, and deleting attribute data (we will consider the "Measures" option at a later time). To record attribute data, click on the "Create" button, which brings up a dialog box that asks you to provide a name for the attribute and to indicate what type it is. If you are entering nonordered data, then you will want to use either

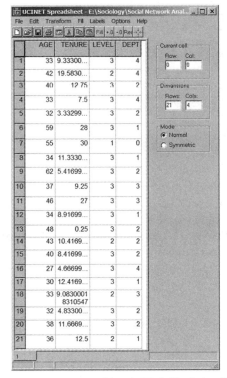

Figure 4.14. Krackhardt High-Tech Attribute Data (UCINET)

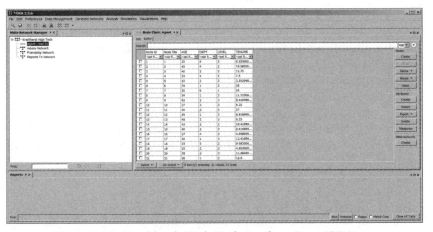

Figure 4.15. Krackhardt High-Tech Attribute Data (ORA)

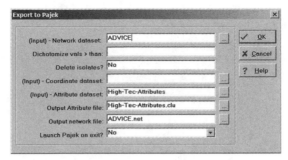

Figure 4.16. UCINET Export to Pajek Dialog Box

the "Text Category" or "Number Category" options; if you are entering ordered or continuous data, then you will want to use either the "Text" or "Number" options. Since the Krackhardt data are generally recorded as numbers, here we would select the "Number" option for entering the age, level, and tenure data, and the "Number Category" option for entering the department data.

Exporting Social Network Data to Pajek

UCINET: Exporting One-Mode Social Network Data. There are multiple methods for exporting one-mode social network data from UCINET to Pajek. The easiest way to export one-mode data is by using the

[UCINET] *Data>Export>Pajek>Network* command (note that UCINET provides
Data a choice of exporting the data in a number of formats: DL, Krack-
>Export plot, Mage, Pajek, Metis, Raw, and Excel). This brings a dialog box
>Pajek (Figure 4.16). UCINET provides a series of options although most of the
>Network time you will want to accept UCINET's default settings. A good rule of thumb is that if you do not know what the option is asking, then accept UCINET's defaults (note that you can click on the dialog box's "Help" button for a detailed discussion of each of the options).

The one possible exception to this rule concerns the final option, which allows you to launch Pajek from within UCINET once the data are exported. You only want to use this option if (1) you do not already have Pajek open and (2) you have set UCINET's options so that it will open the most recent version of Pajek. Otherwise, it will launch the version of Pajek that comes with UCINET, which is often somewhat dated. If you choose yes, another dialog box will appear asking you (again) whether you want to launch Pajek. If all goes well, UCINET launches Pajek when you click "OK." If not, you can open Pajek and import the newly created Pajek network file manually.

Note that here, rather than exporting the entire Krackhardt HighTech file, we have only loaded the advice network to be exported. This is

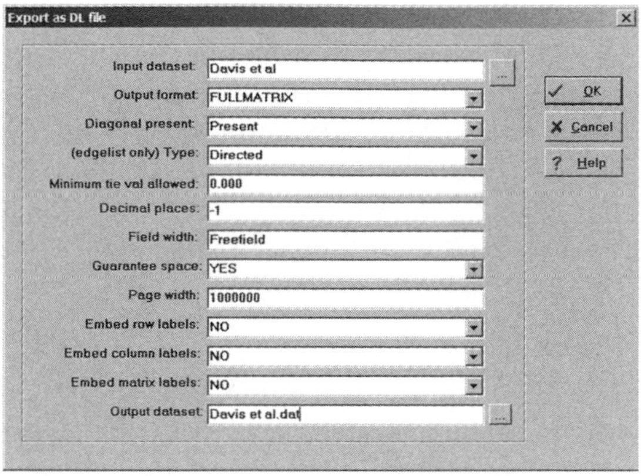

Figure 4.17. UCINET DL Export Dialog Box

because currently this command only exports single, one-mode networks and not datasets that include more than one one-mode network. If we wanted to export the entire Krackhardt file, we would need to use the same function we use to export two-mode networks from UCINET to Pajek: namely, UCINET's *Data>Export>DL* command (see the next section). *Data >Export >DL*

Also note that UCINET allows us to export attribute data as well. Here, you can see that the attribute file associated with the Krackhardt data have been loaded for export. The one drawback to this function is that it exports all of the attributes as Pajek partition files, which if you recall, are designed for nonordered attribute data. Thus, if UCINET attribute files include continuous or ordered data (as these do), then we should export them as Pajek vector files. Luckily, UCINET includes commands for this. To export attribute data as Pajek partition files, use the *Data>Export>Pajek>Categorical Attribute* command; for Pajek vector files, use the *Data>Export>Pajek>Quantitative Attribute* command. *Data >Export >Pajek >Categorical Attribute, Quantitative Attribute*

UCINET: Exporting Two-Mode Social Network Data. Because UCINET does not currently export two-mode networks in Pajek format, we have to export using its *Data>Export>DL* command. This calls up a dialog box (see Figure 4.17) where, once again, several options are offered but you will generally want to accept UCINET's defaults except the last one: Manually change the extension of the output dataset to "*.dat" (rather than "*.txt") because Pajek looks for DL files with *.dat extensions not *.txt ones. *Data >Export >DL*

ORA: Exporting Social Network Data. Exporting network data from ORA to other programs is straightforward using ORA's *File>Data>Export* command. This brings up a dialog box (not shown) where you *[ORA] File>Data >Export* first use a drop-down menu to indicate which network you intend to export, then using a second drop-down menu you identify what type of format you wish to export the data. ORA offers several options: UCINET (typically, you will want to use the binary option), NetDraw, Pajek, and others. After selecting the type, click on the "Browse" button to either type in or locate the name of the file you are exporting. Then, select "Export." If things work as they should, your data will be waiting for you in the file format of your choice.

Importing/Reading UCINET Data into Pajek and ORA

Because so many network datasets often come in UCINET format, it is also helpful to demonstrate how to read or import such datasets into Pajek and ORA. We begin with Pajek before moving on to ORA.[5]

Pajek: Importing UCINET Data. As noted previously, in order to move social network data from UCINET to Pajek, we first need to export the data from UCINET in either Pajek or DL formats, the former for single, one-mode networks, the latter for multiple one-mode networks or single two-mode networks. To read either type of file into Pajek, we use Pajek's *File>Network>Read* command, which brings up a dialog box (not shown) that usually defaults to looking for Pajek-formatted files (i.e., network files with a *.net extension). Thus, we should not have to change any defaults if we are looking for Krackhardt's advice network, which we previously exported as a Pajek-formatted file. However, if we are looking for Davis's Southern Women file, which we exported as a DL-formatted file, then in the type of file drop-down menu, we need to indicate that we are looking for UCINET DL files (*.dat). Either way, select the file you want to import and click "Open."

[Pajek] File>Network >Read

One thing to keep in mind when importing data that originated as a UCINET file, regardless of whether you exported the data using UCINET's *Data>Export>Pajek>Network* command or its *Data> Export>DL* command, when Pajek reads the file into memory, it reads the ties as arcs (not edges). This is acceptable when you are working with directional data (i.e., asymmetric networks and two-mode networks), but if you are working with nondirectional data (i.e., symmetric networks), you will want to transform the arcs into edges using Pajek's *Net>Transform>Arcs→Edges>All* command. This command calls up a dialog box (not shown) that asks if you want to create a new network. This is a good idea since you typically do not overwrite the original. Clicking "OK" brings up another dialog box (not shown), asking if you want to remove multiple lines. Select option five (single line) and click "OK."

Net >Transform >Arcs →Edges >All

---

[5] As we saw in the Chapter 3, NetDraw reads UCINET files.

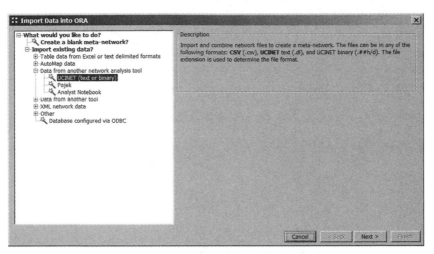

Figure 4.18. ORA's Data Import Wizard

You should now have a network that consists only of edges, not arcs. Importing attribute data originally created in UCINET is simple as well. To read nonordered attribute data, use Pajek's *File>Partition>Read* command. To read ordered or continuous attribute data, use Pajek's *File>Vector>Read* command.

File >Partition >Read

File>Vector >Read

ORA: Importing UCINET Data. To import network data into ORA created in another social network tool such as UCINET, we use the *File>Data Import Wizard*, which calls up a dialog box similar to Figure 4.18. Here, we have selected the "Data from another network analysis tool" option and highlighted "UCINET" as the type of network data we are importing (note that Pajek and Analyst Notebook are the other options). Clicking on the "Next" button brings up second dialog box (not shown) where you assign the network a name; clicking on "Next" calls up a third "Import Data into ORA" dialog box similar to Figure 4.19.

[ORA] File >Data Import Wizard

Using the "Browse" radio buttons (see Figure 4.19), locate the UCINET files you intend to import (in this case, it is the Krackhardt advice, friendship, and reports to networks–ADVICE.##h, FRIEND-SHIP.##h, REPORTS_TO.##h), indicate that both its source and target type is "Agent," provide it with a name (i.e., Network ID), and click on the "Click to import another file" button. Repeat this process for each file you intend to import into the current meta-network. Here, we have also included the friendship and reports-to networks. Click "Finish," and you should be returned to ORA's main screen where the imported network is shown in the Meta-Network Manager panel.

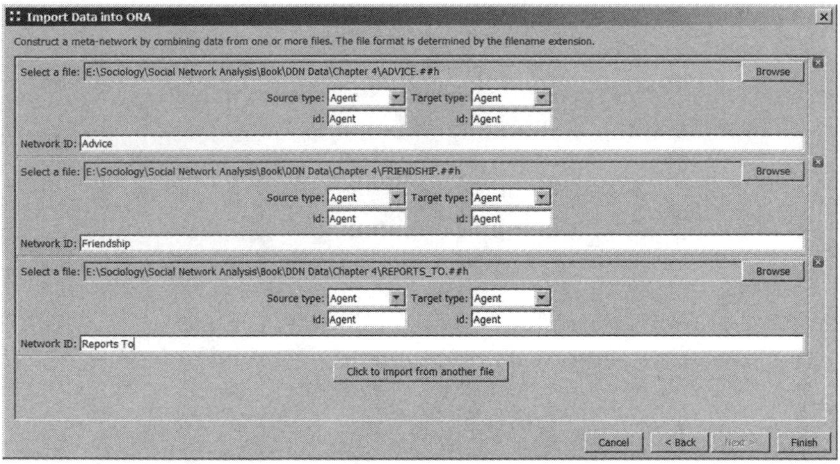

Figure 4.19. ORA's Data Import Dialog Box

To import attribute data into ORA, select the "Agent" node class in the Meta-Network Manager panel and click on the Editor tab in the Network Information/Editor panel (Figure 4.20). As we saw before, on the far right of the Editor tab, there are a series of speed buttons related to attribute data. Clicking on the "Import" button calls up a dialog box similar to Figure 4.21.

Currently, ORA's attribute import function reads `*.csv` files more reliably than `*.xls` files, so if your data are stored in an Excel file, you may need to first save your data as a `*.csv` file.[6] In this case, we have already done that for you. Use the "Browse" button to locate and select the attribute file you want to import. *It is imperative that it relates to the network file already loaded into ORA's memory.* Here, we are importing the `High Tech Attribute.csv`. Next, indicate that the rows are in the same order as are the network data. Then, uncheck the first box and then tell ORA that age, tenure, and level are "number" types of data, while department is either a text or number category type of data (see Figure 4.21). Finally, click on the "Import" button and the attribute data should be loaded into ORA.

4.7   Deriving One-Mode Networks from Two-Mode Networks

We can derive two one-mode networks (i.e., an actor-by-actor – "Co-membership" – network and an event-by-event – "event overlap" – network) from a two-mode network by multiplying the original affiliation

---

[6] You can also import attribute data in ORA using the *File> Data Import Wizard* function and assigning it to the appropriate node class during the process.

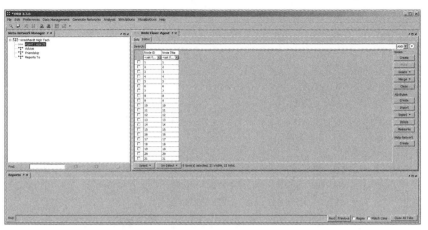

Figure 4.20. Importing Attribute Data in ORA

matrix by its transpose. Thankfully, UCINET, Pajek, and ORA have made this process relatively simple for users. Before turning to how to do this, we will first look at some of the interesting properties that such derived networks possess (Breiger 1974). Figure 4.22 displays co-membership network of Davis's Southern Women, and like all one-mode networks, the rows and columns refer to the same actors (in this case, the women who attended the social events). If two women attended the same event, then there will be a tie in the corresponding matrix cells (one-mode networks derived from two-mode networks are necessarily symmetric). If they attended more than one event together, then the value in the cell indicates the number. For example, Evelyn and Laura attended six of the same events, while Evelyn and Flora attended only one. Moreover, Evelyn

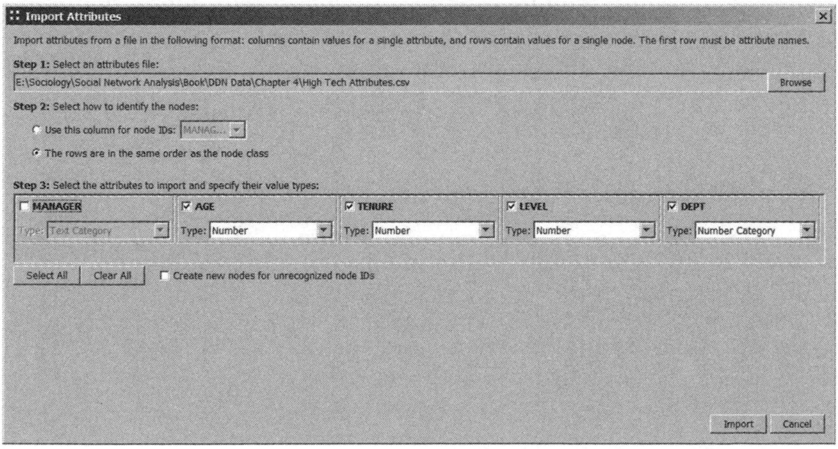

Figure 4.21. Importing Attribute Data in ORA Dialog Box

```
                             1 1 1 1 1 1 1 1 1
           1 2 3 4 5 6 7 8 9 0 1 2 3 4 5 6 7 8
           E L T B C F E P R V M K S N H D O F
           ---------------------------------
 1    EVELYN  8 6 7 6 3 4 3 3 3 2 2 2 2 2 1 2 1 1
 2     LAURA  6 7 6 6 3 4 4 2 3 2 1 1 2 2 2 1 0 0
 3   THERESA  7 6 8 6 4 4 4 3 4 3 2 2 3 3 2 2 1 1
 4    BRENDA  6 6 6 7 4 4 4 2 3 2 1 1 2 2 2 1 0 0
 5 CHARLOTTE  3 3 4 4 4 2 2 0 2 1 0 0 1 1 1 0 0 0
 6   FRANCES  4 4 4 4 2 4 3 2 2 1 1 1 1 1 1 1 0 0
 7   ELEANOR  3 4 4 4 2 3 4 2 3 2 1 1 2 2 2 1 0 0
 8     PEARL  3 2 3 2 0 2 2 3 2 2 2 2 2 2 1 2 1 1
 9      RUTH  3 3 4 3 2 2 3 2 4 3 2 2 3 2 2 2 1 1
10     VERNE  2 2 3 2 1 1 2 2 3 4 3 3 4 3 3 2 1 1
11     MYRNA  2 1 2 1 0 1 1 2 2 3 4 4 4 3 3 2 1 1
12 KATHERINE  2 1 2 1 0 1 1 2 2 3 4 6 6 5 3 2 1 1
13    SYLVIA  2 2 3 2 1 1 2 2 3 4 4 6 7 6 4 2 1 1
14      NORA  2 2 3 2 1 1 2 2 2 3 3 5 6 8 4 1 2 2
15     HELEN  1 2 2 2 1 1 2 1 2 3 3 3 4 4 5 1 1 1
16   DOROTHY  2 1 2 1 0 1 1 2 2 2 2 2 2 1 1 2 1 1
17    OLIVIA  1 0 1 0 0 0 0 1 1 1 1 1 1 2 1 1 2 2
18     FLORA  1 0 1 0 0 0 0 1 1 1 1 1 1 2 1 1 2 2
```

Figure 4.22. Southern Club Women: Co-Membership Network

attended at least one event with every other woman in the network, while Olivia and Flora attended none of the same events as Laura, Brenda, Charlotte, Frances, and Eleanor. The cell values along the diagonal have their own unique properties. They tell us how many total events each of the women attended. As you can see, Evelyn attended eight, Laura seven, Theresa eight, and Brenda seven, while Dorothy, Olivia, and Flora attended the fewest (two).

The event-overlap network (Figure 4.23) provides useful information as well. Here, the diagonal tells us how many women attended each event, while the off-diagonal cells tell us how many women each event "shared." In other words, three women attended events E1, E2, E13, and E14, while events E7 (ten women), E8 (fourteen women), and E9 (twelve women) were by far the most popular. And, events E1 and E2 shared two women (i.e., two women attended both E1 and E2), whereas events E8 and E9 shared nine women. In other words, by simply transforming a two-mode network into a one-mode network, we create helpful information about

```
         1  2  3  4  5  6  7  8  9 10 11 12 13 14
        E1 E2 E3 E4 E5 E6 E7 E8 E9 E1 E1 E1 E1 E1
        -- -- -- -- -- -- -- -- -- -- -- -- -- --
 1 E1    3  2  3  2  3  3  2  3  1  0  0  0  0  0
 2 E2    2  3  3  2  3  3  2  3  2  0  0  0  0  0
 3 E3    3  3  6  4  6  5  4  5  2  0  0  0  0  0
 4 E4    2  2  4  4  4  3  3  3  2  0  0  0  0  0
 5 E5    3  3  6  4  8  6  6  7  3  0  0  0  0  0
 6 E6    3  3  5  3  6  8  5  7  4  1  1  1  1  1
 7 E7    2  2  4  3  6  5 10  8  5  3  2  4  2  2
 8 E8    3  3  5  3  7  7  8 14  9  4  1  5  2  2
 9 E9    1  2  2  2  3  4  5  9 12  4  3  5  3  3
10 E10   0  0  0  0  0  1  3  4  4  5  2  5  3  3
11 E11   0  0  0  0  0  1  2  1  3  2  4  2  1  1
12 E12   0  0  0  0  0  1  4  5  5  5  2  6  3  3
13 E13   0  0  0  0  0  1  2  2  3  3  1  3  3  3
14 E14   0  0  0  0  0  1  2  2  3  3  1  3  3  3
```

Figure 4.23. Southern Club Women: Event Overlap Network

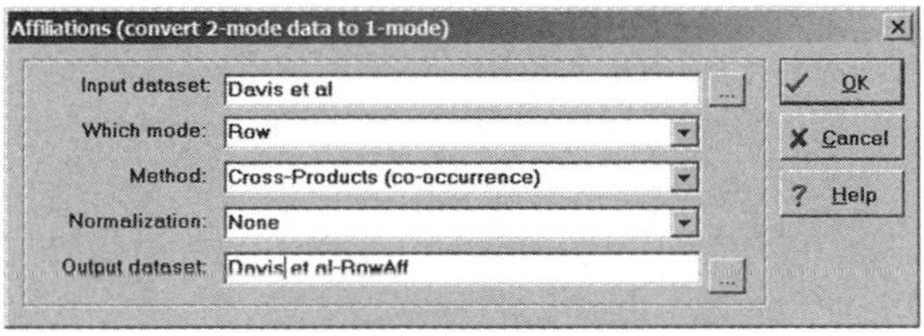

Figure 4.24. UCINET Affiliations Dialog Box

the network we are examining, long before we estimate more complicated metrics.

UCINET: One-Mode Networks from Two-Mode Networks. In UCINET you derive one-mode networks from two-mode networks (in this case, Davis et al.##h) using the *Data>Affiliations (2-mode to 1-mode)* command. This brings up a dialog box like the one illustrated in Figure 4.24. For an actor-by-actor matrix, choose "Row" in the "Which mode" drop-down menu since actors are generally listed in rows; for an event-by-event matrix, choose "Column" in the "Which mode" option since events (affiliations) are generally listed in columns.

[UCINET] Data >Affiliations (2-mode to 1-mode)

Be sure to save the files ("Output dataset") under different file names, otherwise if you derive both an actor-by-actor matrix and an event-by-event matrix, whichever one you derive last may overwrite any ones you derived earlier. Unfortunately, a warning box does not appear in UCINET when you are about to overwrite an already existing file. You can display the two newly created networks by either choosing the "Display" option found under the *Data* menu or by clicking on "D" icon located just below UCINET's menu bar. They should look similar to Figures 4.22 and 4.23.

Data>Display

Pajek: One-Mode Networks from Two-Mode Networks. Deriving one-mode networks from two-mode networks in Pajek is simple, but (like in UCINET) you need to know which actors/events are assigned to the rows and columns. First, we need to read the network data (Davis et al.net) into Pajek using the *File>Network>Read* command or click on the folder icon located under the "Networks" button (circled in Figure 3.10). To create an actor-by-actor (co-membership) matrix choose the "Rows" option under the *Net>Transform>2-Mode to 1-Mode* submenu (assuming that that actors appear are listed in rows). After issuing the command, the Report window will appear. Close this and you will see that a new network appears in the Network drop-down menu. Repeat the procedure, except choose the "Columns" option. If you want to display the co-membership network in matrix format, make sure that it is highlighted in the first or top Network drop-down menu, and then

[Pajek] File >Network >Read

Net >Transform >2-Mode to 1-Mode>Rows, Columns

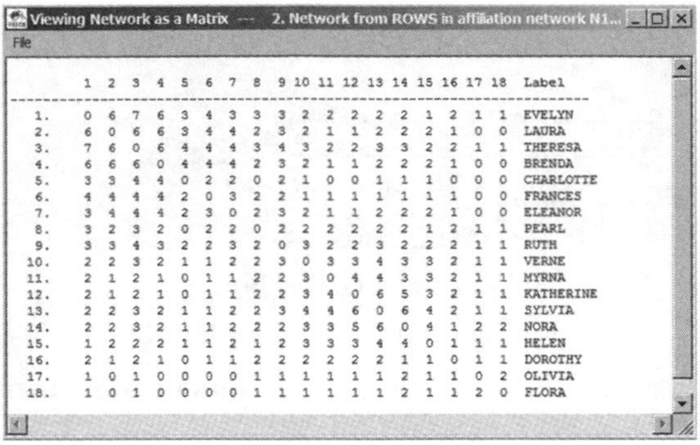

```
Viewing Network as a Matrix  ---  2. Network from ROWS in affiliation network N1...   _ □ ×
File

        1  2  3  4  5  6  7  8  9 10 11 12 13 14 15 16 17 18  Label
-------------------------------------------------------------------------
 1.     0  6  7  6  3  4  3  3  3  2  2  2  2  1  2  1  1  1  EVELYN
 2.     6  0  6  6  3  4  4  2  3  2  1  1  2  2  2  1  0  0  LAURA
 3.     7  6  0  6  4  4  4  3  4  3  2  2  3  3  2  2  1  1  THERESA
 4.     6  6  6  0  4  4  4  2  3  2  1  1  2  2  2  1  0  0  BRENDA
 5.     3  3  4  4  0  2  2  0  2  1  0  0  1  1  1  0  0  0  CHARLOTTE
 6.     4  4  4  4  2  0  3  2  2  1  1  1  1  1  1  1  0  0  FRANCES
 7.     3  4  4  4  2  3  0  2  3  2  1  1  2  2  2  1  0  0  ELEANOR
 8.     3  2  3  2  0  2  2  0  2  2  2  2  2  2  1  2  1  1  PEARL
 9.     3  3  4  3  2  2  3  2  0  3  2  2  3  2  2  1  1  1  RUTH
10.     2  2  3  2  1  1  2  2  3  0  3  3  4  3  2  1  1  1  VERNE
11.     2  1  2  1  0  1  1  2  2  3  0  4  4  3  2  1  1  1  MYRNA
12.     2  1  2  1  0  1  1  2  2  3  4  0  6  5  3  2  1  1  KATHERINE
13.     2  2  3  2  1  1  2  2  3  4  4  6  0  6  4  2  1  1  SYLVIA
14.     2  2  3  2  1  1  2  2  3  3  5  6  0  4  1  2  2  2  NORA
15.     1  2  2  1  1  2  2  3  3  3  4  4  0  1  1  1  1  1  HELEN
16.     2  1  2  1  0  1  1  2  2  2  2  2  1  1  0  1  1  1  DOROTHY
17.     1  0  1  0  0  0  0  1  1  1  1  1  1  2  1  1  0  2  OLIVIA
18.     1  0  1  0  0  0  0  1  1  1  1  1  1  2  1  1  2  0  FLORA
```

Figure 4.25. Pajek Display of Davis's Southern Women Co-Membership Network

double-click anywhere on the Network drop-down menu. This will call up a dialog box (not shown) that asks what type of presentation you want: binary, valued, or lists. Generally, you will want to accept Pajek's default, which in this case is *valued*. Click "OK" and you should get an output similar to Figure 4.25.

Note that in Pajek, the diagonal cell values all equal zero. If we want Pajek to include diagonal values when we transform two-mode networks to one-mode networks, then prior to doing so, we need to first select Pajek's *Net>Transform>2-Mode to 1-Mode>Include Loops* option ("loops" is another term for diagonal cell values because they refer to ties that actors have to themselves). Be careful when doing this, however, because the inclusion of loops will alter centrality calculations in Pajek.

ORA: One-Mode Networks from Two-Mode Networks. To derive one-mode networks from two-mode networks in ORA, in the Meta-Network Manager panel highlight and right-click on the two-mode network (Davis et al.xml) you wish to transform. This brings up a set of options. From these, choose the "Fold" option (Figure 4.26), which is ORA's term for transforming a two-mode network into a one-mode network.

This brings up a dialog box (Figure 4.27), which asks the type of "folding" method you want to use, whether you want rows or columns, and the name that you want to call the new network. In terms of method, you will typically want to keep the "Shared Links" default. Here, we have chosen to look at the co-membership network (i.e., rows) and accepted ORA's default name for the new file. Clicking on the "Fold" button creates a new network in the meta-network that you can examine under the Editor tab or visualize with ORA's visualizer.

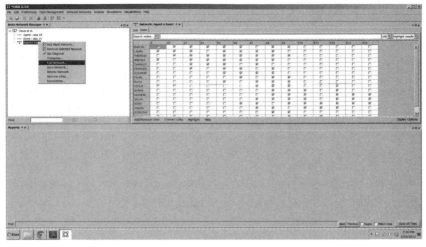

Figure 4.26. Transforming Two-Mode Network into One-Mode Network In ORA

4.8   Combining, Aggregating, and Parsing Networks

Up to this point we have focused on single types of relationships among actors: friendship, advice, attendance at a particular event, and so on. In the real world, however, actors are typically involved in more than one type of relation (Hanneman and Riddle 2005). As we have already seen, most individuals are embedded in several types of ties (e.g., friendship, kinship, and economic), and corporate and state actors are no different. Businesses engage in financial and informational exchanges and some-times form alliances with one another (Saxenian 1994), while countries are linked through numerous cultural, economic, military, and politi-cal ties, not to mention transnational corporations, nongovernmental

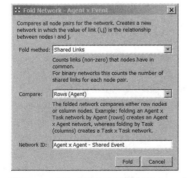

Figure 4.27. ORA's Fold Network Dialog Box

organizations, and international agencies (Meyer et al. 1997). More important, different types of ties can pressure actors to make conflicting choices (Simmel [1908, 1922] 1955). Thus, being able to combine, aggregate, and parse multiple relations is highly important and something we explore in this section. We first examine UCINET because its tools for manipulating network data are excellent. We then consider NetDraw's capabilities for visualizing multiple networks that work quite nicely with UCINET datasets. Next, comes Pajek, which is not as user-friendly as UCINET when it comes to manipulating data but has powerful visualization tools. Finally, we consider ORA, which provides a number of helpful functions for manipulating and visualizing networks.

In this section we also introduce the Noordin Top Terrorist Network data, combining, aggregating, and parsing it into the networks we will explore throughout the book. The data are discussed in detail in Appendix 1. Before turning our attention to these data, however, we will first examine a somewhat simpler network dataset: the Sampson Monastery dataset, which was recorded by Samuel Sampson (1968) who, for his Ph.D. dissertation, spent a year in a Roman Catholic monastery in the late 1960s observing the social interactions among a group of monks. During his stay, a "crisis in the cloister" developed in reaction to the changes introduced by Vatican II that resulted in the expulsion of four monks and the voluntary departure of several others.[7] In the end, only four monks remained (Bonaventure, Berthold, Ambrose, and Louis). While he was there, Sampson coded four types of relational data that he further subdivided into positive and negative ties. He had each monk rank his top three choices for each type of relation, although some offered tied ranks for their top four choices. The relations he recorded were esteem (SAMPES) and disesteem (SAMPDES), liking (SAMPLK – three different time periods were recorded) and disliking (SAMPDLK – only one time period), positive (SAMPIN) and negative influence (SAMPNIN), and praise (SAMPPR) and blame (SAMPNPR). In each network, a "3" indicates the monk's highest or first choice and a "1" indicates his last choice.

Multirelational Data in UCINET and NetDraw

UCINET includes a variety of tools for analyzing multiplex data. Some allow you to extract an individual network from a multiple network file, while others allow you to combine separate data files. One of the most common ways of storing multiple network data is by "stacking" a set of *[UCINEL]* actor-by-actor networks, one for each type of relation. Figure 4.28 dis-
Data>Display plays part of the output from a *Data>Display* command for the Sampson

---

[7] Vatican II was a conference of all the bishops and cardinals of the Roman Catholic Church who met from 1962 to 1965 in which numerous changes were introduced in order to modernize the Church (Finke and Stark 2005; Stark and Finke 2000).

```
ucinetlog2.txt - Notepad
File  Edit  Format  View  Help
DISPLAY
-------------------------------------------------------------------
Input dataset::                        sampson|


Matrix: SAMPLK1

                 1  2  3  4  5  6  7  8  9 10 11 12 13 14 15 16 17 18
                RO BO AM BE PE LO VI WI JO GR HU BO MA AL AM BA EL SI
                MU NA BR RT TE UI CT NF HN EG GH NI RK BE AN SI IA MP
                L_ VE OS H_ R_ S_ OR _1 _1 _2 _1 _1 _7 RT D_ L_ S_ _1
                10 N_ E_  6  4 11 _8  2        4  5     _1 13 _3 17 _8
                    5  9                        6
                -- -- -- -- -- -- -- -- -- -- -- -- -- -- -- -- -- --
    1  ROMUL_10   0  0  0  0  3  0  1  0  0  0  2  0  0  0  0  0  0  0
    2 BONAVEN_5   0  0  0  0  3  2  0  0  0  0  0  0  0  0  1  0  0  0
    3 AMBROSE_9   0  2  0  0  0  3  0  0  0  0  0  0  1  0  0  0  0  0
    4   BERTH_6   0  0  2  0  3  0  0  0  1  0  0  0  0  0  0  0  0  0
    5   PETER_4   2  3  0  1  0  0  0  0  0  0  0  0  0  0  0  0  0  0
    6  LOUIS_11   0  3  0  0  0  0  1  0  0  0  2  0  0  0  0  0  0  0
    7  VICTOR_8   0  0  1  0  0  0  0  0  0  0  0  0  0  0  0  0  0  0
    8   WINF_12   0  0  0  0  0  0  0  0  3  2  1  0  0  0  0  0  0  0
    9    JOHN_1   0  3  0  0  0  0  0  0  0  1  0  0  0  0  2  0  0  0
   10    GREG_2   0  0  0  0  0  0  0  0  3  0  1  0  2  0  0  0  0  0
   11   HUGH_14   0  0  0  0  1  0  2  3  0  2  0  0  0  0  0  0  0  0
   12   BONI_15   0  0  0  0  0  0  0  3  2  1  0  0  0  0  0  0  0  0
   13   MARK_7    0  0  0  0  0  1  0  0  2  0  0  0  3  0  0  0  0  0
   14 ALBERT_16   0  0  0  0  0  0  0  1  2  0  0  3  0  0  0  0  0  0
   15  AMAND_13   0  2  0  0  0  0  0  0  0  0  0  1  0  0  0  0  0  3
   16   BASIL_3   0  0  0  0  0  0  0  0  2  3  0  0  0  0  0  0  1  0
   17  ELIAS_17   0  0  0  0  0  0  0  0  0  0  0  0  2  3  0  1
   18   SIMP_18   0  0  0  0  0  0  0  0  2  3  0  0  1  0  0  0  0  0

Matrix: SAMPLK2

                 1  2  3  4  5  6  7  8  9 10 11 12 13 14 15 16 17 18
                RO BO AM BE PE LO VI WI JO GR HU BO MA AL AM BA EL SI
                MU NA BR RT TE UI CT NF HN EG GH NI RK BE AN SI IA MP
                L_ VE OS H_ R_ S_ OR _1 _1 _2 _1 _1 _7 RT D_ L_ S_ _1
                10 N_ E_  6  4 11 _8  2        4  5     _1 13 _3 17 _8
                    5  9                        6
                -- -- -- -- -- -- -- -- -- -- -- -- -- -- -- -- -- --
    1  ROMUL_10   0  1  0  0  3  0  0  0  0  0  0  0  0  0  2  0  0  0
    2 BONAVEN_5   0  0  0  0  3  1  0  0  2  0  0  0  0  0  0  0  0  0
    3 AMBROSE_9   0  1  0  0  0  0  3  2  0  0  0  0  0  0  0  0  0  0
    4   BERTH_6   0  0  2  0  3  0  0  0  1  0  0  0  0  0  0  0  0  0
```

Figure 4.28. Sampson Monastery Data (UCINET Log)

Monastery dataset (`sampson.##h`). At the top of the log/output, you can see the entire "Liking, Time One" dataset, and just below you can see a portion of the "Liking, Time Two" dataset. Scrolling down through UCINET's output displays the other networks that are included in the dataset.

You can also examine stacked network datasets using UCINET's spreadsheet function, which if you recall, is accessed with UCINET's *Data>Data Editors>Matrix Editor* command. Once this is called up, you can open any UCINET file using the *File>Open* command, which brings up a dialog box (not shown) that enables you to identify the network data you wish to open. The Sampson data are displayed in Figure 4.29. As you can see, UCINET's spreadsheet function is similar to commercial spreadsheet programs. Each type of relation appears under a different tab that you can click on and examine. In this case, the "Liking, Time One" data are displayed.

Next, let us examine at how to unpack stacked network data in UCINET. To do this, select the *Data>Unpack* command. This brings up an "Unpack" dialog box (Figure 4.30) that asks you for the input dataset and which relations to unpack. You can choose to unpack all of the relations or just some. UCINET's default is "All," but if you wanted to only unpack some, click on the "L" radio button, which brings up an additional dialog box that lets you pick the matrices of your choice. In this

*Data
>Data Editors
>Matrix Editor*

*[Spread Sheet]
File>open*

Data>Unpack

UCINET Spreadsheet - E:\Sociology\Social Network Analysis\Book\DDN Data\Chapter 4\sampson.##h

File Edit Transform Fill Labels Options Help

	ROMUL_10	BONAVEN_5	AMBROSE_9	BERTH_6	PETER_4	LOUIS_11	VICTOR_8	WINF_12	JOHN_1	GREG_2	HUGH_14
ROMUL_10	0	0	0	0	3	0	1	0	0	0	2
BONAVEN_5	0	0	0	0	3	2	0	0	0	0	0
AMBROSE_9	0	2	0	0	0	0	3	0	0	0	0
BERTH_6	0	0	2	0	3	0	0	0	1	0	0
PETER_4	2	3	0	1	0	0	0	0	0	0	0
LOUIS_11	0	3	0	0	0	0	1	0	0	0	2
VICTOR_8	0	0	1	0	0	0	0	0	3	2	0
WINF_12	0	0	0	0	0	0	0	0	3	2	1
JOHN_1	0	3	0	0	0	0	0	0	0	0	1
GREG_2	0	0	0	0	0	0	0	0	3	0	1
HUGH_14	0	0	0	0	0	1	0	2	3	0	0
BONI_15	0	0	0	0	0	0	0	0	3	2	1
MARK_7	0	0	0	0	0	0	1	0	0	2	0
ALBERT_16	0	0	0	0	0	0	0	0	1	2	0

Current cell: Row / Col
Dimensions: Rows: 18 Cols: 18
Mode: Normal / Symmetric

SAMPLK1 | SAMPLK2 | SAMPLK3 | SAMPDLK | SAMPES | SAMPDES | SAMPIN | SAMPNIN | SAMPPR | SAMNPR

Figure 4.29. Sampson Monastery Data (UCINET Spreadsheet Editor)

case, we have kept UCINET's default, which means that clicking "OK" will unpack ten separate matrices/networks. You can examine each of the new networks using either UCINET's display or spreadsheet functions. UCINET also allows you to join separate datasets into a single stacked dataset; we will see how to do this when we examine the Noordin Top network data.

Now, let's see how we can visualize the Sampson data using NetDraw, which allows users to view stacked networks with different colored lines. Open the sampson.##h dataset, using the *File>Open>Ucinet dataset>Network* command. Recall that the Rels tab (see Figure 4.31) allows you to select which network to view, which can be useful for combining and switching back and forth between relations. In this case, four relations have been selected. You can assign different colors to the various relations by using the dialog box (not shown) that the *Properties>Lines>Color>Relation* command calls up. Here, because we cannot display colors, the relations appear in gray scale, but typically it is easiest to accept NetDraw's default colors. Note that when two actors share more than one relation (e.g., liking and esteem), NetDraw assigns a

[NetDraw]
File>Open
>Ucinet dataset
>Network

Properties
>Lines
>Color
>Relation

Unpack

Input dataset:

Which relations to unpack: All

✓ OK
✗ Cancel
? Help

Figure 4.30. UCINET Unpack Dialog Box

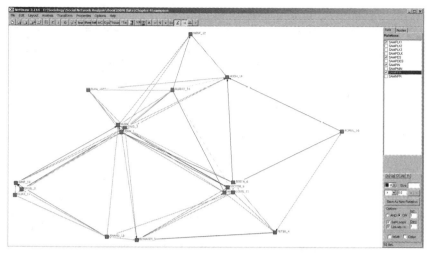

Figure 4.31. NetDraw Drawing of Sampson's Monastery Data

separate color to that tie. In Figure 4.31 multiple relations ties are black, but NetDraw's default is usually gray.

Combining Networks in UCINET. It is easy in UCINET to combine separate networks into a stacked dataset, which we will illustrate using the Noordin Top Terrorist Network data, which were drawn primarily from *Terrorism in Indonesia: Noordin's Networks*, a publication of the International Crisis Group (2006; see Appendix 1). We will begin by aggregating and analyzing the following relations into four types of "networks," which are adapted from a typology suggested by Krebs (2001:51) and summarized in Table 4.2.[8]

The classmate, friendship, kinship, soulmate, and internal communication networks were originally coded as one-mode networks, while the meeting, operations, training, and business and finance networks were derived from two-mode networks. The logistics network was parsed from two two-mode networks – logistical place and logistical function – that

---

[8] As noted in the preface, the Noordin network serves as a running example throughout this book. In subsequent chapters these trust, operational, communication, and business and finance networks will sometimes be combined into a single network. Moreover, subnetworks of these four networks (five if you count the combined network) will be extracted based on whether particular actors are dead, alive, or in jail (see Appendix 1). In other words, the four original networks plus the combined network can each be examined as a whole, as well as parsed into and analyzed as separate subnetworks. We will not analyze each of the twenty possible variations on Noordin's network in every chapter because to do so would be needlessly repetitive. Instead, in each chapter, networks are chosen that help illustrate the algorithm under consideration. When analyzing dark networks in the real world, analysts will want to consider (within reason) all possible permutations of a network before they begin to craft strategies for its disruption.

Table 4.2. *Aggregation of Noordin Top's terrorist network ties*

	Network			
	Trust	Operational	Communications	Finance
Relations	• Classmates • Friendship • Kinship • Soulmates	• Logistics • Meetings • Operations • Training	• Communications	• Business and Finance

were converted to two one-mode networks. In order for there to be a tie between two individuals in the logistics network, they had to share a tie in both the logistical place and logistical function networks.[9] Of course, one could argue that this sorting of relations could have been done differently. Perhaps ties made at school (i.e., classmates) should not be considered ties of trust, or that business and finance ties should be included in the operational network. But that would be missing the point. As we saw in the second chapter, which networks are chosen to be combined, aggregated, or parsed is part of the process for crafting strategies. The important thing is to be clear with what you do so that others may follow (and sometimes disagree) with your analysis.

[UCINET]
Data>Join
Figure 4.32 illustrates the use of the *Data>Join* command for creating the Noordin trust network. As you can see the classmates (Classmates.##h), friendship (Friendship.##h), kinship (Kinship.##h), and soulmates (Soulmates.##h) networks have been selected for aggregation, and that the name of the new network is "Trust Network" (UCINET's default name is "Join"). Note also that the "Matrices" option under the Dimensions to Join panel has been selected because we are combining matrices. You can also combine the rows of two or more matrices (keeping the columns the same) or the columns of two or more matrices (keeping the rows the same). This latter option is useful for combining and analyzing series of two-mode networks (e.g., schools and faith communities).

Aggregating Networks in UCINET. Sometimes, you may want to create a single-valued network from a series of stacked networks. To
Transform
>Matrix
Operations
>Within dataset
> Aggregations
do this we need to use the *Transform>Matrix Operations>Within dataset>Aggregations* command, which calls up a dialog box similar to Figure 4.33. In this case, the operational network has been selected, which if you recall, is a stacked network consisting of the logistics

---

[9] How to parse two (or more) networks in such a way is discussed further on in the chapter.

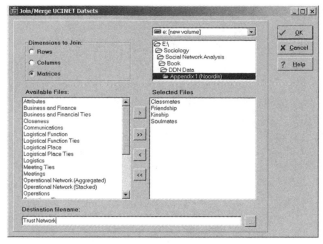

Figure 4.32. UCINET's Join/Merge Datasets Function

(Logistics.##h), meetings (Meetings.##h), operations (Operations.##h), and training (Training.##h) networks (see Table 4.2). This function provides several different arithmetic operation options – you can sum, average, and get the maximum, minimum, or standard deviation of the corresponding cells in each network. Here, we are asking UCINET to sum the networks, which means that UCINET will aggregate the number of times each pair of actors share a tie. In other words, if two actors share logistic and operations ties, then the value of their tie in the aggregated network will equal two. If they share logistic, operations, and training ties, then the value of their tie will equal three.

You can also aggregate networks of the same size that have not been combined into a stacked network using the *Transform>Matrix Operations>Between datasets>Statistical Summaries* command, which brings up a dialog box (Figure 4.34). Here, the networks that were previously combined into the operational network have been selected. Clicking "OK" combines the matrices into a single-valued matrix that should be identical to the one we created previously using the within dataset aggregations command.

Transform >Matrix Operations >Between datasets >Statistical Summaries

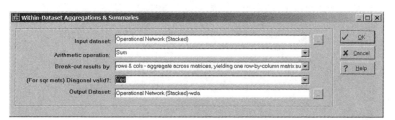

Figure 4.33. UCINET within Dataset Aggregations Dialog Box

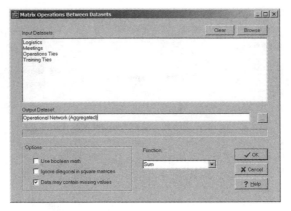

Figure 4.34. UCINET between Dataset Statistical Summaries Dialog Box

Parsing Networks in UCINET. Just because two people are members of the same organization or attend the same event does not mean that they necessarily are friends or even know each other. Thus, we may want to use some sort of threshold before concluding that a tie actually exists between two actors. Taking the Noordin logistical place and logistical function networks as an example, let us assume that a tie only exists between two actors if they shared *both* the same logistical location and logistical function. For example, if they are both located in Ambon and handle transportation functions, then we will assume a tie exists between the two actors. However, if they are both located in Ambon but do not share the same functional responsibilities, or if they share the same functional responsibilities but are located in different cities, then we will assume that a tie does not exist between them.

Transform >Matrix Operations >Between datasets >Boolean Combinations   To do this, we take the co-membership networks of the logistical place (`Logistical Place.##h`) and logistical function (`Logistical Function.##h`) two-mode networks and use UCINET's *Transform>Matrix Operations>Between datasets>Boolean Combinations* command. The resulting dialog box (Figure 4.35) is nothing more than a means for testing if/then statements. As you can see, we have

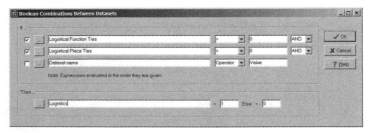

Figure 4.35. UCINET Boolean Combination Dialog Box

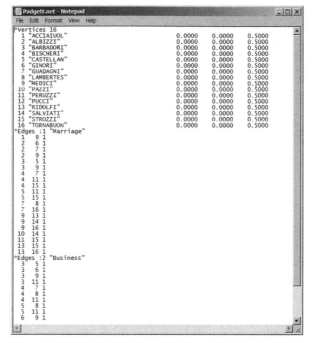

Figure 4.36. Pajek Edgelist of Padgett Marriage and Business Network Data

selected the one-mode network derived from the logistical function network in the first network file box and the one-mode network derived from the logistical place network in the second. To the right of both of these boxes, we have chosen the "$>$" sign in both operator boxes and a "0" in the value boxes; these tell UCINET to look for every instance where the tie between each pair of actors is greater than zero. When this is true, UCINET will assign a value of one for each tie because in the last (bottom) network file box we have indicated the value for each tie, which if both statements are true, should be one. In this final box, we have also assigned a name for the new file that will be created (i.e., "Logistics") when we click "OK."

Multirelational Data in Pajek

How does Pajek store multirelational network data? It does so by assigning relation numbers to a set of ties (i.e., arcs, edges), as Figure 4.36 illustrates with the Padgett marriage and business networks (Padgett.net). The figure shows that, after a list of the vertices (i.e., actors) in the network, Pajek includes a separate edge (or arc) list for each relation, each of which is preceded by a number and name.

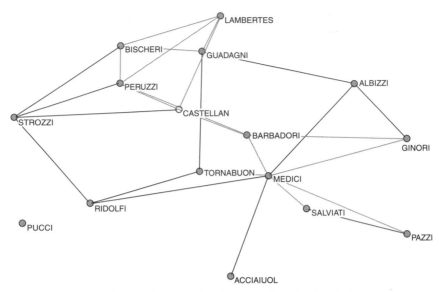

Figure 4.37. Pajek Network Map of Padgett Multirelational Data

[Pajek – Draw
Screen]
Data
>Export
>DL

Data
>Export
>Pajek

Options
>Colors>Edges
>Relation
Number

Options
>Colors>Arcs
>Relation
Number

Options>Colors
>Relation
Colors

Options
>Lines
>Draw Lines
>Relations Ins

Looking at Figure 4.36 you can see that the list of the sixteen families in the network is followed first by the marriage edge list then the business edge list (only a portion of the latter edge list appears in the figure).[10] By and large you will use multirelational data that have been recorded in and exported from UCINET using the latter's *Data>Export>DL* command (rather than the *Data>Export>Pajek* command), which is the same command we used earlier to export two-mode networks into Pajek-readable formats.

As with NetDraw in Pajek we can represent the relation number of a line-by-line color; this is accomplished in Pajek's Draw screen with the *Options>Colors>Edges>Relation Number* (for edges) and *Options>Colors>Arcs>Relation Number* (for arcs) commands. We can choose the color of each relation number in the *Options>Colors> Relation Colors* dialog screen. Figure 4.37 presents a network map of the Padgett data where marriage ties are colored black and the business ties are colored gray. When two actors share a tie (e.g., Bischeri and Peruzzi), Pajek colors the ties by the last relation in the file (in this case, business = gray). This differs from NetDraw, which you will recall colors multiple relations gray. We can also choose to display some but not all of the relations with the *Options>Lines>Draw Lines>Relations Ins*

---

10 The first line of the marriage edge list indicates that vertex 1 (the Acciaiuols) shares a tie with vertex 9 (the Medicis) of strength one; the first line of the business edge list indicates that vertex 3 (the Barbadoris) shares a tie with vertex 5 (the Castellans).

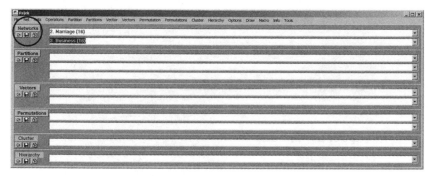

Figure 4.38. Two Networks Highlighted in Pajek's Network Drop-Down Menus

command, which calls up a dialog box where you indicate which relations (numbers) you want to view.

Pajek also allows users to extract one or more relations from a multiple relations network with its *Net>Transform>Multiple Relations>Extract Relation(s)* command (accessed at Pajek's main screen). When we issue this command, Pajek generates a new network for each of the selected relation numbers, preserving the relation number and name. We can also recode relation number and change relation labels with the *Net>Transform>Multiple Relations>Change Relation Number-Label* command. We can also change the label name of a relation by opening and editing the Pajek file in a text editor such as Notepad. That is how the labels were added to Figure 4.37.

[Main Screen]
Net>Transform >Multiple Relations >Extract Relation(s)

Net>Transform >Multiple Relations >Change Relation Number-Label

Aggregating Networks in Pajek. In Pajek we can only combine two networks at a time, which is why when you are working with more than two, you will probably want to combine and aggregate in UCINET. Nevertheless, we briefly illustrate how to aggregate files in Pajek using the Padgett network data. First open the Padgett project file (`Padgett.paj`) using Pajek's *File>Pajek Project File>Read* command (or you can use the "F1" button). Next, click on the "Network" radio button (circled in Figure 4.38) in order to display two Network drop-down menus (Figure 4.38). In the first, display either the marriage or business network, and in the second, display the other. Then, select the *Nets>Union of Lines* command. This will create a new network that Pajek labels *Fusion of 2 and 3*, which you can rename using the *File>Network>Change Label* command. When Pajek combines networks using the *Union of Lines* command, it treats them as a single relation with multiple lines. If you want to combine the two networks into a single-valued network, make sure that the newly created (i.e., fused) network is highlighted in the first network drop list, then select the *Sum Values* command under the *Net>Transform>Remove>Multiple lines* submenu.

Pajek's File>Pajek Project File>Read

Nets>Union of Lines

File>Network >Change Label

Net>Transform >Remove >Multiple lines

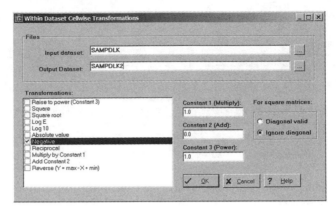

Figure 4.39. UCINET within Dataset Cellwise Transformations Dialog Box

Excursus: Positive and Negative Relations in UCINET and Pajek

Before examining how to work with multirelational data in ORA, we will first explore one way of simultaneously working with positive and negative ties. Here we will use the Sampson network data because it contains both positive (e.g., like) and negative (e.g., dislike) ties; however, the techniques that are illustrated can be applied to any dark network data that contain positive (e.g., friend) and negative (e.g., enemy) ties. In this section, we will multiply one of the negative networks ("dislike") by "–1" in order to transform the values into "negative" values and then add this transformed network to a positive network ("like" at time 3), which will give us a network that contains both positive and negative ties. We will then export this network to Pajek in order to visualize it.

[UCINET]
Transform>
Matrix
Operations>
Within
dataset>Cellwise
Transformations

UCINET. Let's begin by transforming these positive values into negative ones using the *Transform>Matrix Operations>Within dataset>Cellwise Transformations* command. In the resulting dialog box (Figure 4.39) note that we selected SAMPDLK.##h as our input dataset, named the transformed dataset SAMPDLK2.##h, and have checked the "Negative" box among the "Transformation" options. Click "OK" and UCINET should produce an output log (not shown) that indicates that the values in the new network are negative.

Transform>
Matrix
Operations>
Between
datasets>
Statistical
Summaries

The next step is to add this newly created network to the SAMPLK3.##h network with UCINET's *Transform>Matrix Operations> Between datasets>Statistical Summaries* command. This brings up a dialog box (Figure 4.40) where we use the "Browse" button to locate the files we intend to aggregate (SAMPDLK2.##h and SAMPLK3.##h) and assign a name to the output file (SAMPLKDLK.##h).

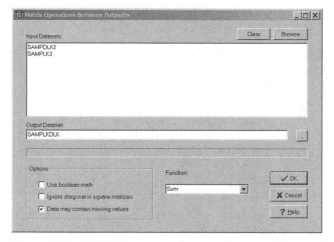

Figure 4.40. UCINET between Dataset Statistical Summaries Dialog Box

After clicking "OK," UCINET generates a new file and produces an output log that shows an aggregated network containing both positive and negative numbers (Figure 4.41).

The next step is to export this newly created aggregated network using the *Data>Export>DL* command (not shown) so that it is readable in Pajek. As before, we need to change the extension of the exported file to *.dat. The reason for using this command to export the data rather than the *Data>Export>Pajek>Network* command is because (at least currently) the latter command exports negative ties as positive ties.

*Data>Export
>DL*

*Data>Export
>Pajek>Network*

Pajek. Open Pajek and read in the network data you just exported from UCINET using the *File>Network>Read* command (remember that the network file you are trying to read has a *.dat extension not a *.net. one). Next, visualize the network using the *Draw>Draw* command and energize it using either the Kamada-Kawai or Fruchterman Reingold layout algorithms (or both; Figure 4.41). Note that there are both solid lines and negative lines between the nodes. In Pajek, solid lines indicate positive connections while dotted lines indicate negative connections. Moreover, as long as the *Options>Values of Lines>Similarities* option has been selected, the positive lines will pull nodes closer together while the negative lines will push them farther apart. This should, in theory, provide us with a better picture of the social closeness and distance between the monks.

*[Pajek – Main
Screen]
File>Network
>Read
Draw>Draw
[Draw Screen]
Layout>Energy
>Kamada-
Kawai
>Free*

*Options
>Values of
Lines
>Similarities*

If the nodes are hard to distinguish with all of the lines, you can increase the size of the node using the *Options>Size>of Vertices* command in Pajek's Draw screen. Figure 4.41 uses a vertex size of "10." Generally,

*Options
>Size>of
Vertices*

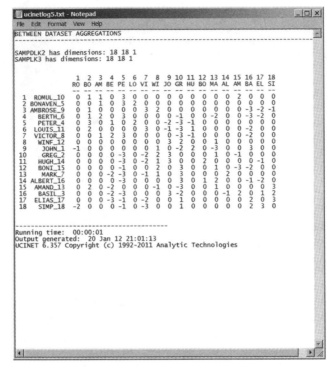

Figure 4.41. UCINET between Dataset Aggregations Output Log

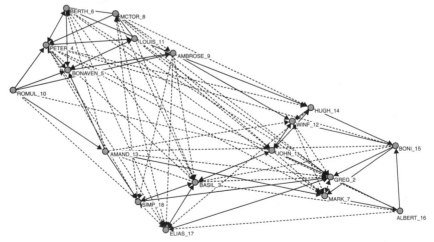

Figure 4.42. Pajek Drawing of Sampson Monastery Liking and Disliking Data

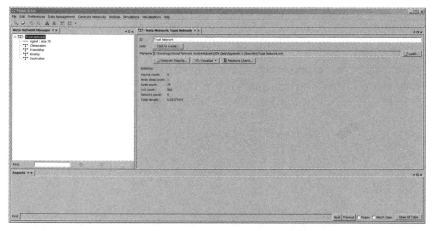

Figure 4.43. Noordin's Trust Network Loaded in ORA

however, it is wise to use the default setting ("0"), which tells Pajek to automatically set the size of the vertices. This is an especially useful option when node size reflects an attribute that varies considerably (e.g., age, centrality, etc.).

Multirelational Data in ORA

We have already seen in Section 4.5 how ORA stores relational data using its meta-network approach (see Figure 4.20). Network data can be entered directly using ORA's editor function (see Figures 4.9 and 4.10) or imported with its data import wizard (see Figures 4.18 and 4.19). One of ORA's more helpful features is that it imports network data that have been "stacked" in UCINET as a multirelational network. For example, using *UCINET's File>Data Import Wizard*, Noordin's multirelational trust network (Trust Network (Stacked).##h) was imported into ORA (Figure 4.43). As we will see later, ORA's analysis reports allow users to acquire metrics on one or all of the networks included in a meta-network.

[ORA] File>Data Import Wizard

To visualize this network, simply click on the "Visualize" speed button located in the Network Information/Editor panel or use the *Visualizations>View Networks>2D Visualization* command (Figure 4.44). As we discussed earlier, you can visualize all of the different types of relations at the same time, or (as we do in NetDraw) check the boxes of the relations you want to visualize or uncheck the boxes of the relations you do not. You can also alter the color of the ties by clicking on the name of the relation in the Legend box, which brings up an edge color dialog box (not shown) that allows you to choose an edge color for each type of tie. In Figure 4.43 each of the ties is colored a different scale of

Visualizations >View Networks>2D Visualization

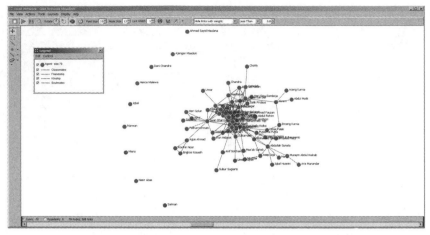

Figure 4.44. ORA Visualization of Noordin's Trust Network

gray. For most purposes, however (e.g., presentations), you will want to choose actual colors since they are more easily distinguishable.

Aggregating Networks in ORA. Like UCINET and Pajek, ORA allows users to aggregate individual networks into a single-valued network. To do so, first highlight the meta-network you intend to aggregate in the Meta-Network Manager panel. Then, select the *Data Management> Meta-Network Transform* command, which calls up a dialog box similar to Figure 4.45. Next, select the "Create a new meta-network and then apply the transform" and "Combine into meta-network with one node class and one network" options. The former option is selected so that ORA does not overwrite the original network; the latter option is chosen in order to aggregate all of the networks in the meta-network into a single network. Finally, click on the "Transform" button, and a new meta-network will be generated that aggregates all of the networks contained in the meta-network you originally selected for aggregation.

Data Management >Meta- Network Transform

4.9   Extracting and Simplifying Networks

Finally, let us consider a few techniques for simplifying networks and extracting subnetworks from the larger network. When working with large social networks, it is sometimes hard to make sense of the pattern of ties. In such situations, being able to shrink a network or extract a subset of a network can aid the analysis process. In particular, these techniques can be useful when you want to examine a subset of a network or to see whether there are patterns among the data that are not immediately observable when the network is looked at in its entirety.

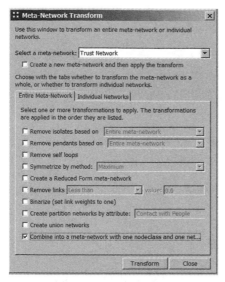

Figure 4.45. Transform Meta-Network Dialog Box (ORA)

Extracting Networks in UCINET

UCINET includes a tool for extracting subnetworks from larger networks: the *Data>Subgraphs from partitions* command. As its name suggests, you use a partition in order to identify the set or class of actors you want to extract from the network. This command brings up a dialog box similar to Figure 4.46. Note that we have to supply UCINET with both a network (`Operational Network (Aggregated).##h`) and a partition (`Attributes.##h`). In this particular case, we are extracting three subnetworks based on the current status attribute, which is located

[UCINET]
Data
>Subgraphs
from partitions

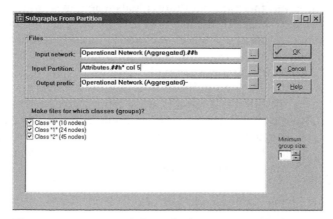

Figure 4.46. UCINET Subgraphs from Partition Dialog Box

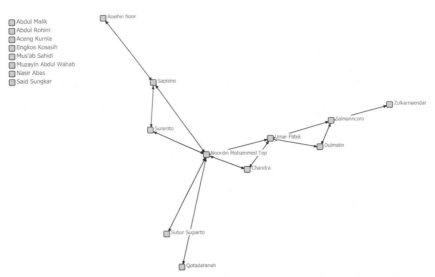

Abdul Malik
Abdul Rohim
Aceng Kurnia
Engkos Kosasih
Mus'ab Sahidi
Muzayin Abdul Wahab
Nasir Abas
Said Sungkar

Figure 4.47. NetDraw Graph of Noordin Top's Alive and Free Operational Network

in the fifth column of the attribute partition (note that the fifth column is designated in the "Input Partition" box) and identifies which actors are dead (Class "0," 10 actors), which ones are alive and free (Class "1," 24 actors), and which ones are alive but in jail (Class "2," 45 actors; see Appendix 1). If we were only interested in obtaining the alive and free network, then we would have unchecked the "0" and "2" boxes. Clicking "OK" produces the three separate networks.

Figure 4.47 displays a NetDraw generated graph of Noordin's alive and free operational network. It indicates that Noordin sits at the center of this network and that several of its members have no ties with one another. Moreover, there are eight individuals who appear to be isolated from the network (located in the upper left of the graph), suggesting that they may no longer play a role in its operations. Interestingly, Nasir Abas, who was once the head of one of the local affiliates of Jemaah Islamiyah, the terrorist group from which Noordin's network emerged, now works with Indonesian authorities to get other terrorists to leave their violent pasts behind and rejoin Indonesian society (Mydans 2008). Unfortunately, in UCINET (and ORA) we cannot currently extract more than one type of actor into a single subnetwork (e.g., a network that includes everyone who was alive, regardless of whether they were free or not). We can do this in Pajek, however.

Simplifying (Collapsing) Networks in NetDraw

NetDraw does not include a tool for extracting subnetworks, but it does have one that allows users to collapse (i.e., shrink) networks based on

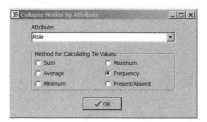

Figure 4.48. NetDraw Collapse Nodes by Attribute Dialog Box

a particular attribute (e.g., nationality, role, group membership). When collapsing a network, we shrink all of the actors that share a particular characteristic to a single new node. This type of analysis is something we might choose to do when we are interested in examining the pattern of ties between types of actors rather than the pattern of ties between the actors themselves. This is what some call a "global view" of the network (de Nooy et al. 2005:39–41), and it might illuminate patterns that were not detectable at the "street-level view," so to speak.

To collapse a network in NetDraw, first read the aggregated Noordin operational network file (`Operational Network (Aggregated.##h`) into NetDraw either with the *File>Open>Ucinet dataset>Network* command or by clicking on the open folder icon. Next, open the related attribute file (`Attributes.##h`) using the *File>Open>Ucinet dataset>Attribute data* command. If the attribute data do not match up with the network data (i.e., they have a different number of nodes), then you will receive a warning from NetDraw to that effect. If the data do match up correctly, you will receive no notice at all. If you want to examine the attribute data, you can access NetDraw's attribute editor (not shown) with its *Transform>Node attribute editor* command. Next, select the *Transform>Collapse Nodes by attribute* command, which brings up a dialog box similar to Figure 4.48. Here, we have selected "Role" as the characteristic/attribute on which to collapse the network. As you can see, NetDraw provides several options for calculating tie values between the collapsed nodes. In this case, we have selected "Frequency." Clicking "OK" completes the process and yields a network drawing similar to Figure 4.49.

NetDraw (and Pajek and ORA) does not know the meaning of the various types of roles within the role attribute file, so it cannot assign meaningful labels to collapsed nodes. Instead, it places the letter "G" in front of all of the types of roles along with the number corresponding to that particular role. In Figure 4.49 the labels have been changed using NetDraw's *Properties>Nodes>Labels>Text* command. Under the label column at the bottom of the resulting dialog box (not shown), the various labels assigned to each role by NetDraw can be found. There, the nodes

File>Open >Ucinet dataset >Network

[NetDraw] File>Open >UCINET dataset >Network

Transform >Node attribute editor

Transform >Collapse Nodes by attribute

Properties >Nodes>Labels >Text

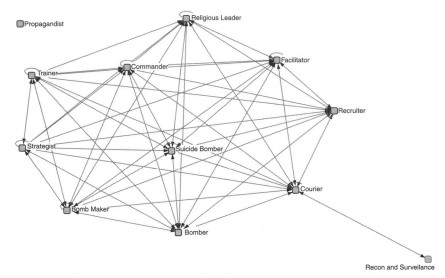

Figure 4.49. NetDraw Graph of Noordin's Operational Network Collapsed by Role

were relabeled using the codebook (see Appendix 1), which indicates which number is assigned to which role.

Extraction and Simplification in Pajek

Extracting Networks in Pajek. First, let's see how to extract a multiclass subnetwork in Pajek. Specifically, we will extract those actors within the operational network who are alive and either free or in jail. To do this we first have to load the Noordin network project file (`Noordin Network.paj`) using the *File>Pajek Project File>Read* command. Then, we need to ensure that the "Operational Network (Aggregated)" is showing in the Network drop-down menu and the "Current Status (ICG Report)" partition is showing in the Partition drop-down menu. Next, under the *Operations* menu, select the *Extract Network>Partition* command. A dialog box will appear that asks you which clusters (i.e., which classes) to select. Because we want those who are alive, choose clusters "1" and "2." When you click "OK," Pajek produces a new network and a new partition both of which contain sixty-nine actors.

Now, let's create an education-level vector that matches the size of this new "alive" network. Make sure that the education-level vector is showing in the Vector drop-down menu. This vector contains the education level of the seventy-nine individuals included in the Noordin network. Next, make sure the current status partition is displayed in the Partition drop-down menu. Then, under the *Vector* menu, select

Margin notes:

[Pajek]
[Main Screen]
File>Pajek
Project
File>Read

Operations
Extract
Network
>Partition

Vector
>Extract
Subvector

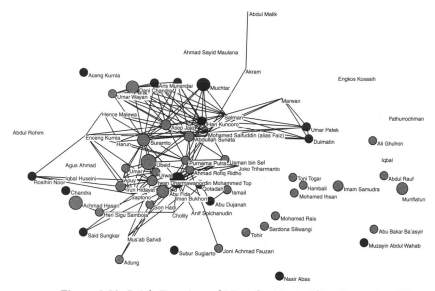

Figure 4.50. Pajek Drawing of Noordin Top's Alive Operational Network

the *Extract Subvector* command. A dialog box will appear, and like before, choose clusters "1" and "2" and click "OK." Pajek will create a new education vector with only sixty-nine actors. Finally, after making sure that the "Alive" Network, the new current status Partition, and the new Education Vector are all showing in their respective drop-down menus, select the *Draw-Partition-Vector* command under the *Draw* menu. Energize the drawing, and you should see a drawing similar to Figure 4.50 where the node colors indicate whether they are alive and free (black) or in alive and in jail (gray), and the node size indicates each individual's education level. Note that the nodes of some individuals are nonexistent. This is because they have an education level of "0." Note also that higher education level appears to be somewhat associated with the centrality of an individual in the network. In Chapter 7, we will see how to test to see if this is, in fact, true.

Draw>Draw-Partition-Vector

You can change Pajek's default colors with the *Options>Colors> Partition Colors* command. This calls up a dialog box (not shown) that contains forty squares that are colored and contain the partition's class numbers with which they are associated. For Figure 4.50, the "Default GreyScale 1" option has been chosen. If you click on the "Default Partition Colors" button, Pajek resets the original colors. If you want to change the color of a particular class, click on the square that contains the desired color and type in the number of the class with which you want to associate this color, and Pajek will swap the colors.

[Draw Screen] Options >Colors >Partition Colors

Simplifying Networks In Pajek. Shrinking (i.e., collapsing) networks in Pajek is straightforward. To illustrate how it is done, let's replicate what we did previously using NetDraw. That is, let's collapse Noordin's operational network by role. At Pajek's main screen, make sure that the "Operational Network (Aggregated)" is showing in the Network drop-down menu and the roles partition is showing in the Partition drop-down menu. Then, under the *Operations* menu, select the *Shrink Network>Partition* command. The first dialog box to appear asks you for the minimum number of connections between clusters. This refers to the minimum number of ties that must exist between pairs of shrunk nodes in order for there to be a tie between them. Generally, you will want to choose "1," which is the default. In the second dialog box, you can choose a class of actors not to be shrunk if that is what you want to do. In most cases, however, you will probably want to shrink all of the classes, so you need to choose a partition number that is not used in the partition you are using to shrink the network. In this instance, you will not want to choose "0" (Pajek's default) because "0" is a potential class in the current partition (see Appendix 1). Instead, choose "999." When you click "OK," Pajek shrinks all classes except the selected class and adds the shrunk network and a corresponding partition to the Network and Partition drop-down menus, respectively.

[Main Screen]
*Operations
>Shrink
Network
>Partition*

Like NetDraw, Pajek does not know the labels of the shrunken nodes, so it chooses the label of the first actor of a particular shrunken class that is shrunk and adds a "#" sign. If there is only one actor associated with a particular class (e.g., propagandist), it lists the actor's name without a "#" sign. In Pajek you can change the labels by manually editing the shrunk partition using the *File>Partition>Edit* command (of course, the shrunken partition has to be showing in the Partition drop-down menu before you select this command). One additional edit has been done to produce Figure 4.51. Because the "propagandist" and "recon and surveillance" roles each include only one actor, they appear as outliers when the network is visualized (see Figure 4.49). Thus, they were removed using the *Operations>Extract Network>Partition* command, where in the "Select Clusters" dialog box (not shown) the numbers "1–5,7–8, 10–12" were entered (the "recon and surveillance" cluster was "6," while the propagandist cluster was "9"). This graph appears to show that three roles are more central to Noordin's network (bomber, strategist, and trainer) than are the others (Noordin is classified as a strategist). This suggests that if Noordin were to be killed or captured,[11] then there is a strong probability that the network's future leadership would come from one of these more central roles.

*File
>Partition
>Edit*

*Operations
>Extract
Network
>Partition*

---

[11] Noordin actually was killed in September 2009 by Indonesian authorities (International Crisis Group 2010).

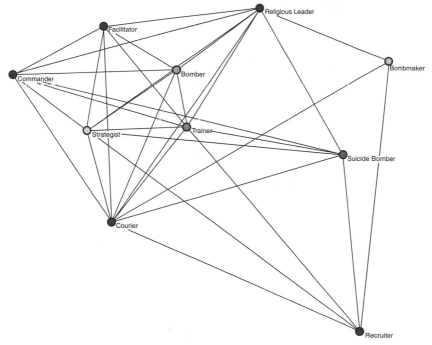

Figure 4.51. Pajek Drawing of Noordin's Operational Network Collapsed by Role

Extraction and Simplification in ORA

Extracting Networks in ORA. In ORA, open Noordin's trust network (Trust Network.xml) with its *File>Open Meta-Network* command. This meta-network contains the classmates, friendship, kinship, soulmates networks along with the associated attributes. To extract subnetworks in ORA, we use the *Attribute Partition Tool*, which is found under the *Data Management* menu. This calls up a dialog box similar to Figure 4.52. Here, we will extract only those members of the trust network who are incarcerated. To do this, we first have to select the trust network, then the current status attribute, and finally the attribute number (i.e., "2") that indicates whether someone is in jail or not. Clicking on the "Partition" button produces a new meta-network of those individuals who are alive but in jail (Figure 4.53). The isolates have been hidden using the *Actions>Isolates>Hide Isolate Nodes* command.

Figure 4.53 indicates that some members of Noordin's incarcerated trust network are more central than are others. And we know from previous research that individuals on the periphery of a network are more likely to defect than are those at its center (Popielarz and McPherson 1995; Stark and Bainbridge 1980). This suggests that strategies that seek

[ORA – Main Screen]
File
>Open Meta-Network

Data Management
>Attribute Partition Tool

[Draw Screen]
Actions
>Isolates
>Hide Isolate Nodes

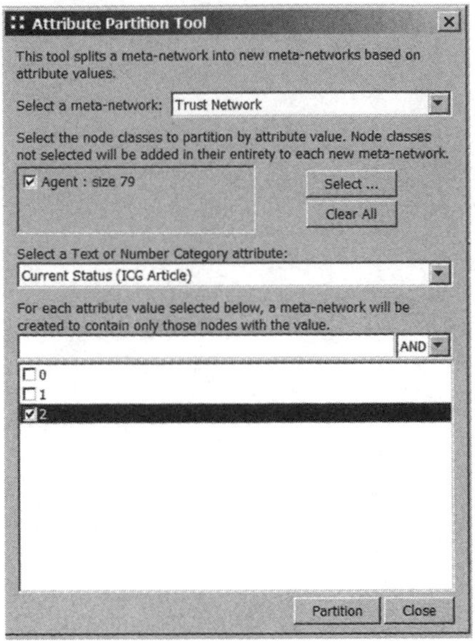

Figure 4.52. ORA Attribute Partition Tool

to rehabilitate captured terrorists (Mydans 2008) will probably be more effective if they focus their efforts on those on the periphery of the network than on those at the center.

Simplifying Networks in ORA. To shrink/collapse a network in ORA, highlight it in ORA's main screen Meta-Network Manager panel and then click the "Visualize" button or select the *Visualizations>View*

Visualizations >View Networks >2D Visualization

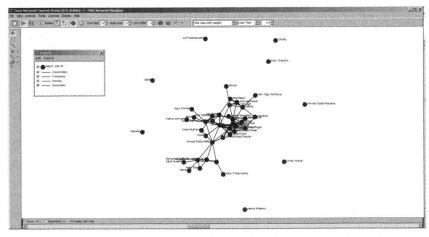

Figure 4.53. ORA Drawing of Noordin's Incarcerated Trust Network

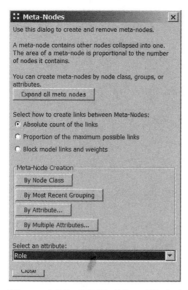

Figure 4.54. ORA's Meta-Node Manager

Networks>2D Visualization command. At the draw screen, choose the
Tools>Meta-Nodes command, which calls up the Meta-Node dialog box   *Tools>Meta-*
(Figure 4.54). Select the "Absolute count of the links" options, and in the   *Nodes*
Select an attribute drop-down menu, indicate the attribute by which you
want to collapse/shrink the network. Click on "Close" and ORA gener-
ates a collapsed network.

Like Pajek and NetDraw, ORA does not know what to call the collapsed nodes, but it does allow us to rename the labels of the "metanodes," although it takes a few steps. First, we need to add the collapsed
network to the meta-network using the draw screen's *File>Add Meta-*   *File>Add*
Nodes to Current Meta-Network command. This command creates a   *MetaNodes to*
new node class (probably called "Meta Node 1: size 12") and two new   *Current*
networks in the Meta-Network Manager in the main screen. Select the   *Meta-Network*
new node class and click on the Editor tab located in the Network Infor-
mation/Editor panel of the main screen. Two columns should be visible,
one labeled "Node ID," the other labeled "Node Title." Under the latter,
change the label names in the individual cells similar to the way we did
it in NetDraw and Pajek. After doing this, select the "Meta Node 1 X
Meta Node 1" network and click the "Visualize Only This Network"
button, which will generate a new network map that should look similar
to Figure 4.55. In the case of Noordin's trust network, strategists are
the most central, which is not surprising considering that Noordin is a
strategist. Nevertheless, other roles appear to be important in terms of
Noordin's trust network, indicating that they may be crucial in terms of

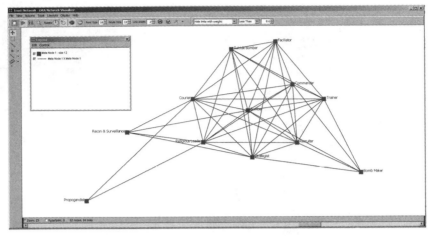

Figure 4.55. ORA's Meta-Node Network Map

the network's longevity (e.g., recruiting new members, preventing defections, etc.).

Finally, it is worth noting that like Pajek, ORA lets you save all the files you have imported or created into a single "project file," which ORA calls a Meta-Network, with its *File>Save Meta-Network As...* command.

File>Save Meta-Network As...

4.10   Summary and Conclusion

This chapter has focused on methods for collecting and recording social network data. It began with a brief discussion on how social network analysts define the boundaries of the networks they are examining. It then examined the difference between ego and complete networks, noting that social network analysts generally use complete networks when applying social network methods. Next, we considered the different types of data social network analysts use: one-mode, two-mode, and attribute data. We then discussed the various ways that social network analysts collect network data before looking at how social network data are recorded in matrix form. We then examined various methods for manipulating network data: deriving one-mode networks from two-mode networks; combining, aggregating, and parsing networks; and extracting and simplifying networks. It is now time to turn our attention to the various families of metrics that analysts use to examine social networks. We begin with methods for tapping into the various aspects of network topography.

Part III

Social Network Analysis: Metrics

5

Network Topography[1]

5.1 Introduction

As noted in the second chapter, although social network analysis appears to have wide appeal as a methodological tool for targeting members of dark networks (see, e.g., Gjelten 2010), it can be applied far more broadly than it has been thus far. Furthermore, strategy should drive the choice of metrics rather than the other way around. Unfortunately, just the opposite often occurs. The tail (i.e., the choice of metrics) is often found wagging the dog (i.e., the strategic choices) rather than the other way around. Indeed, the most common application of SNA to the study of dark networks has focused on targeting central actors within the network for elimination or capture (aka the "whack a mole" strategy). Although this focus is intuitively appealing and can provide short-term results, it may be misplaced and, in fact, make tracking, disrupting, and destabilizing terrorist networks more difficult. As Brafman and Beckstrom (2006) have noted, targeting key players in decentralized organizations seldom shuts them down. Instead, it only drives them to become more decentralized, making them harder to target. In terms of terrorist networks, such a strategy may in fact exacerbate what Sageman (2008) refers to as the "leaderless jihad," by which he means the numerous independent and local groups that have branded themselves with the Al Qaeda name and are attempting to emulate bin Laden and his followers by conceiving and executing terrorist operations from the bottom up.[2]

This chapter argues that analysts need to first explore a terrorist network's overall topography (i.e., its level of density, centralization, degree

---

[1] Portions of this chapter have been adapted from Sean Everton. 2012. "Network Topography, Key Players and Terrorist Networks." *Connections* 31(2):1–8. Used with permission.

[2] For critiques of Sageman's notion of leaderless jihad, see Hoffman (2008) and Tucker (2010).

of fragmentation, etc.) before identifying subgroups and estimating centrality, brokerage, and other types of metrics. This is not to say analysts have completely neglected the topographical dimensions of terrorist networks. There have been exceptions. Pedahzur and Perliger (2006), for example, noted that terrorist networks with a large number of cliques (see Chapter 6) appear to be more effective than those with few, and the most recent U.S. Army and Marine counterinsurgency manual (U.S. Army 2007) argues that network density is positively associated with network efficiency and, as such, should guide tactics. Perhaps the best-known example is Sageman's (2004) initial study of what he calls the global Salafi jihad (GSJ) in which he found that it exhibits the characteristics of a scale-free network. This led him to argue that the United States should focus its efforts on taking out hubs (i.e., nodes that have many connections) rather than randomly stopping terrorists at borders. "[The latter] may stop terrorists from coming here, but will leave the network undisturbed. However... if the hubs are destroyed, the system breaks down into isolated nodes or subgroups. The jihad will be incapable of mounting sophisticated large scale operations like the 9/11 attacks and be reduced to small attacks by singletons" (Sageman 2003). The simultaneous removal of 10 to 15 percent of a terrorist network's hubs is easier said than done, and subsequent research has found that hubs are often quickly replaced by other highly central and/or structurally equivalent actors (Pedahzur and Perliger 2006; Tsvetovat and Carley 2005), but it does not change the fact that Sageman's approach illustrates how the exploration of a network's overall topography can inform strategic decision making.

In this chapter we examine a series of metrics that capture various aspects of network topography. We begin by exploring a few basic metrics: network size, average distance, diameter, and network fragmentation. We then turn to two interrelated but analytically distinct dimensions of network topography: what I call the (1) provincial-cosmopolitan and (2) hierarchical-heterarchical (or decentralized) dimensions. With regards to the former, we consider "light network" research that suggest that networks that are too provincial (e.g., dense, high levels of clustering, an overabundance of strong ties) or too cosmopolitan (e.g., sparse, low levels of clustering, an overabundance of weak ties) tend to perform more poorly than do networks that maintain a balance between the two. With regards to the latter, we explore a series of studies that suggest that a similar dynamic is at work in terms of network hierarchy: Networks that are too hierarchical (e.g., centralized, high levels of variance) or too heterarchical (e.g., decentralized, low levels of variance) tend to underperform those that lie between the two extremes. We then consider the implications of these findings if similar dynamics hold true for dark networks. If so, then while targeting central actors may be an appropriate strategy in some instances, it may not be in others, all of which suggests that analysts need to take into account a network's overall topography before crafting strategies for its disruption. Finally, we turn to the techniques to calculating these metrics in UCINET, Pajek, and ORA.

5.2 Some Basic Topographical Metrics

In this section we consider a few basic network metrics – network size, average distance, diameter, and network fragmentation. Network size refers to the number of actors in a network. Average distance refers to the average length of all the shortest paths (i.e., geodesics) between all actors in a network and may be indicative of the speed that information spreads through a network. In other words, information should diffuse faster through networks with lower average distance than those with higher average distance. This could have implications for the success and failure of deception campaigns that seek to spread disinformation through criminal or terrorist networks. Obviously, one would suspect that such a campaign is more likely to be successful in dark networks with lower average distances; however, because networks constantly change (i.e., they are dynamic), their average distance will almost certainly vary over time, suggesting that deception campaigns may be more attractive options at particular points of time than at others. For now, we need to put this aside until we take up the topic of longitudinal network in Chapter 10.

Network diameter refers to a network's longest geodesic and could indicate how dispersed a network is. As we will see, because decentralized networks are better suited for solving nonroutine, complex, and/or rapidly changing problems or challenges because of their adaptability, dark networks are probably more likely to be decentralized than they are hierarchical. A network's diameter could possibly be used as a supplementary measure to the centralization measures we will discuss in more detail. That is, networks with large diameters may be more decentralized than those with small diameters. Because, however, network diameter is, in part, a function of network size (all else being equal, the diameters of larger networks – i.e., networks with more actors – are longer than those of smaller networks), diameter should be used carefully when comparing networks of different size. It may be more useful when examining the same network over time, but even then the network size will almost certainly vary as well.

Finally, network fragmentation, as its name implies, measures the degree to which a network is fragmented. The standard fragmentation measure is equal to the proportion of all pairs of actors that cannot either directly or indirectly reach one another. UCINET, however, calculates both the standard measure as well as a weighted one that takes into account the (path) distance between actors.[3] It also calculates measures of cohesion (or compactness), which are simply one minus the respective fragmentation scores. Network fragmentation could prove useful in the crafting of strategies. For instance, if analysts were interested in determining which scenarios would fragment a network more, one could take measure fragmentation before and after the various (hypothetical) scenarios. In fact, UCINET reports a series of scores for each actor in the network that indicates the degree of network fragmentation, the degree of distance-weighted network fragmentation, the change in network fragmentation, the change in distance-weighted network fragmentation, the percent of change in fragmentation, and the percent of change in distance-weighted fragmentation if a particular actor is removed from the network.

5.3 The Provincial-Cosmopolitan Dimension

Previously we saw how Mark Granovetter (1973, 1974) discovered that when it came to finding jobs, people were far more likely to use personal contacts than other means. Moreover, of those who found their jobs through personal contacts, most of those contacts were weak (i.e., acquaintances) rather than strong ties (i.e., close friends). This was because not only do we tend to have more weak ties than strong ties (because weak ties demand less of our time), but also because our weak ties are more likely to form the crucial bridges that tie together densely knit clusters of people (see Figure 5.1). In fact, if it were not for these weak ties, Granovetter argues, these clusters would not be connected at all. Thus, whatever is to be spread (e.g., information, influence, and other types of resources) will reach a greater number of people when it passes through weak ties rather than strong ones. Because of this, actors with few weak ties are more likely to "confined to the provincial news and views of their close friends" (Granovetter 1983:202).

Granovetter does not believe that strong ties are of no use, however. He notes that although weak ties provide individuals with access to information and resources beyond those available in their immediate social circles, strong ties have greater motivation to be sources of support in times of uncertainty. Others have noted this as well (see, e.g., Krackhardt 1992; Stark 2007). "There is a mountain of research showing that people with strong ties are happier and even healthier, because in such networks members provide one another with strong emotional and material support in times of grief or trouble and someone with whom to share life's joys and

---

[3]   Distance-weighted fragmentation is one less the average reciprocal distance between all pairs of nodes.

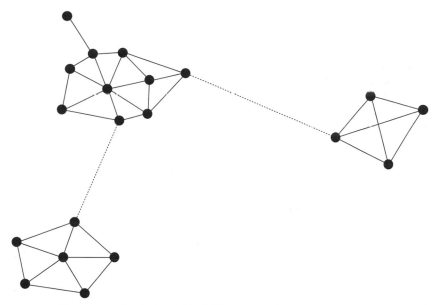

Figure 5.1. Strong and Weak Ties

triumphs" (Stark 2007:37). This suggests that people's networks differ in terms of their mix of weak and strong ties. Individuals' networks range from local or provincial ones, consisting primarily of strong, redundant ties and very few weak ties, to worldly or cosmopolitan ones, consisting of numerous weak ties and very few strong ties (Stark 2007:37–38). It also suggests that peoples' networks should ideally consist of a mix of weak and strong ties. Their networks should be neither too provincial nor too cosmopolitan but rather should land somewhere between the two extremes, not necessarily at the arithmetic mean, but rather at a "golden mean" of sorts (Aristotle 1998:36–43).

Pescosolido and Georgianna's (1989) study of suicide illustrates this dynamic. It found that the density of actors' social networks has a curvilinear (or inverted U) relationship to suicide. Individuals whose social networks are very sparse (i.e., cosmopolitan) or very dense (i.e., provincial) are far more likely to commit suicide than are those whose networks lie between the two extremes. Why? People located in sparse social networks often lack the social and emotional ties that provide them with the support they need during times of crisis. They also typically lack ties to others who might otherwise prevent them from engaging in self-destructive (i.e., deviant) behavior (Finke and Stark 2005; Granovetter 2005). On the other hand, individuals embedded in dense networks are often cut off from people outside of their immediate social group, which increases the likelihood that they will lack the ties to others who would otherwise prevent them from taking the final, fatal step.

An ideal mix of weak and strong ties appears to provide benefits not only at the individual level but also at the organizational level. In his study of the New York apparel industry, Brian Uzzi (1996) found that a mix of weak and strong ties proved beneficial to the long-term survival of apparel firms.[4] The firms he studied tended to divide their market interactions into two types: "market" or "arms-length" relationships (i.e., weak ties) and "special" or "close" relationships (i.e., strong ties), which Uzzi refers to as "embedded" ties. He found that, although market relationships were more common than embedded ties, they tended to be less important. Embedded ties were especially important in situations where fine-grained information had to be passed to the other party, and when certain types of joint problem solving were on the agenda (Uzzi 1996:677). According to Uzzi, embeddedness increases economic effectiveness along a number of dimensions crucial to competitiveness in the global economy: organizational learning, risk-sharing, and speed-to-market. He also found, however, that firms that are too embedded suffer because they lack access to information from distant parts of the social structure, rendering them vulnerable to rapidly changing situations. This led him to argue that firms should seek to maintain a balance of embedded and market ties. In support of this, he found that the topography of interfirm networks (i.e., in terms of embedded and market ties) varied and that a U-shaped association exists between the degree of embeddedness and the probability of firm failure (Uzzi 1996:675–676). Firms with high levels of embedded ties (i.e., provincial networks) or high levels of market ties (i.e., cosmopolitan networks) were much more likely to fail than were those that maintained a balance between the two.

Interestingly, Uzzi and Spiro (2005) found that an inverted U relationship also existed between the extent to which the networks of creative teams that produced Broadway musicals from 1945 to 1989 exhibited "small-worldness" (measured by what they called "small world Q") and the probability that a musical would be a critical and financial success. Building on the research of Stanley Milgram (Milgram 1967; Travers and Milgram 1969) and Duncan Watts and Steven Strogatz (1998), Uzzi and Spiro argue that this relationship existed because up to a point, connectivity and cohesion facilitated the flow of diverse and innovative material across the network. Moreover, connectivity and cohesion made risk-taking among the teams more likely because they were embedded in networks of trust:

> As the level of Q increases, separate clusters become more interlinked and linked by persons who know each other. The processes distribute creative material among teams and help to build

---

[4] Uzzi does not use the weak and strong tie terminology in the article.

> a cohesive social organization within teams that support risky collaboration around good ideas. (Uzzi and Spiro 2005:464)

However, as connectivity and cohesion increase, homogenization and imitation set in and returns become negative:

> Increased structural connectivity reduces some of the creative distinctiveness of clusters, which can homogenize the pool of creative material. At the same time, problems of excessive cohesion can creep in. The ideas most likely to flow can be conventional rather than fresh ideas because of the common information effect and because newcomers find it harder to land "slots" on productions. (Uzzi and Spiro 2005:464)

In other words, connectivity and cohesion initially increase a network's overall creativity by encouraging human innovation, but beyond a certain point, they can stifle it.

Although it may be difficult to conceive of criminal and terrorist networks as varying in their ability to encourage innovative thinking and creative risk-taking, these studies should give us pause. They suggest that in order to be successful, dark networks can be neither too provincial nor too cosmopolitan. What constitutes a particular dark network's optimum balance will likely vary depending on the environment in which it operates (e.g., the IRA can operate more openly in Ireland than Al Qaeda can in the United States). However, because the survival of dark networks depends largely on their recruiting members whom they can trust (Berman 2009; Tilly 2004, 2005), they tend to recruit through strong (rather than weak) ties, and networks formed primarily by strong ties become increasingly dense as ties form between previously unlinked actors (Granovetter 1973; Holland and Leinhardt 1971; Rapoport 1953a, b; Rapoport and Horvath 1961). Thus, we should expect that dark networks will be denser than light networks, all else being equal.

5.4 The Hierarchical-Heterarchical Dimension

Another well-developed body of research has explored how the degree to which an organization is hierarchically structured impacts its performance (see, e.g., Nohria and Eccles 1992; Podolny and Page 1998; Powell 1985, 1990; Powell and Smith-Doerr 1994). This literature typically identifies two ideal types of organizational form: networks and hierarchies. The former are seen as decentralized, informal, and/or organic, while the latter are seen as centralized, formal, and/or bureaucratic (see, e.g., Burns and Stalker 1961; Powell 1990; Ronfeldt and Arquilla 2001). As we have noted, however, although this distinction can be useful (see, e.g., Arquilla and Ronfeldt 2001; Castells 1996; Podolny and Page 1998; Powell and Smith-Doerr 1994; Ronfeldt and Arquilla 2001) within the world of SNA, all organizations are seen as networks, regardless of whether they are hierarchical or decentralized. Thus, it is better to think of these two ideal types as poles on either end of a continuum, running from highly decentralized forms on one end to highly centralized ones on the other.

More importantly, at least for our purposes here, research suggests that the hierarchical-heterarchical dimension impacts network performance much like the provincial-cosmopolitan one: That is, an optimal level of centralization or hierarchy appears to exist. For example, Rodney Stark (1987, 1996b), in his analysis of why some new religious movements succeed, identified centralized authority as an important factor. Nevertheless, he notes that too much centralization can be a bad thing and successful religious movements, such as the Mormon (Latter-day Saints; LDS) Church, balance centralized authority structures with decentralized ones:

> But it would be wrong to stress only the hierarchical nature of LDS authority and its authoritarian aspects, for the Latter-day Saints display an amazing degree of amateur participation at all levels of their formal structure. Moreover, this highly authoritarian body also displays extraordinary levels of participatory democracy – to a considerable extent the rank-and-file Saints are the church. A central aspect of this is that among the Latter-day Saints to be a priest is an unpaid, part-time role that all committed males are expected to fulfill. (Stark 2005:125)

Like the provincial-cosmopolitan dimension, the optimal level almost certainly varies depending on environmental context. As David Tucker (2008) notes:

> The most important issue is how well an organization's structure is adapted to its environment, which includes what its enemies are doing, given what the organization wants to achieve and the resources available to it. No one organizational structure is always inherently superior to another. Some are better for some things, some for others. These principles apply to al Qaeda as well as the governmental network (the federal, state, and local governments) in the United States. (Tucker 2008:2)

Because decentralized networks are better suited for solving nonroutine, complex, and/or rapidly changing problems or challenges because of their adaptability (Saxenian 1994, 1996), and because available evidence suggests that highly centralized networks are vulnerable to the removal of central, well-connected nodes (Albert, Jeong, and Barabási 2000; Bakker, Raab, and Milward 2011; Barabási 2002; Barabási and Bonabeau 2003), it is likely that, all else being equal, successful dark networks tend fall on the decentralized end of the continuum (Arquilla and Ronfeldt 2001; Ronfeldt and Arquilla 2001). Even here, though, dark networks that are too decentralized may find it difficult to mobilize resources, leading them to underperform, once again suggesting that analysts need to take into account this dimension of a network when crafting strategies to disrupt it.

5.5   Estimating Network Topographical Metrics

We now turn to the techniques for estimating the topographical metrics discussed previously. We will illustrate them using the four Noordin networks outlined in the previous chapter: namely, the trust, operational, communications, and business and finance networks.[5] We begin with UCINET before turning to Pajek and ORA.

Network Topography in UCINET

There are various ways to discover a network's size in UCINET. One way is by using UCINET's Matrix Browser, which is accessed with the *Data>Browse* command, which brings up a dialog box similar (but not identical) to Figure 5.2. Using the browser's *File>Open* command, open the stacked trust network file – Trust Network (Stacked).##h – each network visible, and on the right panel are statistics that indicate the size of the network. Here, we can see that this stacked network includes four networks (Mats), each of which includes seventy-nine actors, as indicated by the number of rows and columns. Of course, if we had opened a two-mode network in the browser, the number of rows and columns would most likely differ but would indicate the number of the two types of actors in the network. *[UCINET] Data>Browse [Matrix Browser] File>Open*

Average distance and diameter are calculated in UCINET using the *Network> Cohesion>Geodesic Distance (old)* command. Unfortunately, this command only works with individual rather than stacked networks, so in order to examine individual networks embedded in a stacked trust network, we need to first unpack them using UCINET's *Data>Unpack* command. Once this is done, use the *Geodesic Distance (old)* command, select the friendship network, accept UCINET's defaults, and click "OK." The output (Figure 5.3) first indicates the average (path) distance among reachable pairs (since not all actors can reach one another). This is followed by (path) distance-weighted measures of fragmentation and cohesiveness (remember, cohesion is simply 1.0 minus the fragmentation *Network >Cohesion >Geodesic Distance (old)* *Data>Unpack*

---

[5]   Here, we will use the one-mode individual network derived from the business and finance affiliation network.

UCINET Spreadsheet - E:\Sociology\Social Network Analysis\Book\DDN Data\Chapter 5\Trust Network (Stacked).##h

File Edit Transform Fill Labels Options Help

	Abdul Malik	Abdul Rauf	Abdul Rohim	Abdullah Sunata	Abdullah Sungkar	Abu Bakar Ba'asyir	Abu Dujanah	Abu Fida	Aceng Kurnia	Achmad Hasan	Adung	Agu Ahma
Abdul Malik	0	0	0	0	0	0	0	0	0	0	0	
Abdul Rauf	0	0	0	0	1	1	0	0	0	0	0	
Abdul Rohim	0	0	0	0	0	0	0	0	0	0	0	
Abdullah Sunata	0	0	0	0	0	0	0	0	0	0	0	
Abdullah Sungkar	0	1	0	0	0	1	1	0	0	0	1	
Abu Bakar Ba'asyir	0	1	0	0	1	0	0	0	0	0	1	
Abu Dujanah	0	0	0	0	1	0	0	0	0	0	0	
Abu Fida	0	0	0	0	0	0	0	0	0	0	0	
Aceng Kurnia	0	0	0	0	0	0	0	0	0	0	0	
Achmad Hasan	0	0	0	0	0	0	0	0	0	0	0	
Adung	0	0	0	0	1	1	0	0	0	0	0	
Agus Ahmad	0	0	0	0	0	0	0	0	0	0	0	
Ahmad Rofiq Ridho	0	0	0	0	1	1	0	0	0	0	0	
Ahmad Sayid Maulana	0	0	0	0	0	0	0	0	0	0	0	
Ajengan Masduki	0	0	0	0	0	0	0	0	0	0	0	
Akram	0	0	0	0	0	0	0	0	0	0	0	
Ali Ghufron	0	0	0	0	1	0	1	0	0	0	0	
Anif Solchanudin	0	0	0	0	0	0	0	0	0	0	0	
Apuy	0	0	0	0	0	0	0	0	0	0	0	
Aris Munandar	0	0	0	0	0	0	0	0	0	0	0	
Asep Jaja	0	0	0	1	0	0	0	0	0	0	0	
Asmar Latin Sani	0	1	0	0	1	1	0	0	0	0	0	
Azhari Husin	0	0	0	0	1	0	1	0	0	0	0	
Baharudin Soleh	0	1	0	0	1	1	0	0	0	0	0	

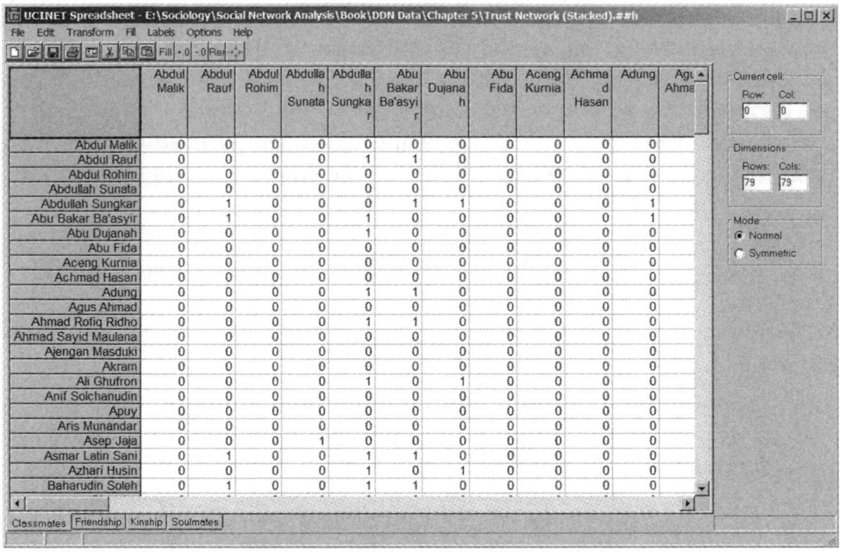

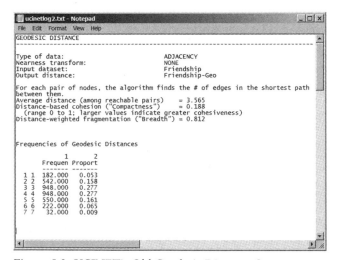

Figure 5.2. UCINET's Matrix Browser

score). These measures are, in turn, followed by the number of geodesics at various distance levels (from shorter to longer). The largest level equals the network's diameter. Below these metrics (not shown in Figure 5.3) is geodesic distance matrix, which indicates the path distance between all pairs of actors. If a geodesic matrix is all you are interested in obtaining, you can use the *Network>Cohesion>Geodesic Distance* command,

ucinetlog2.txt - Notepad

File Edit Format View Help

```
GEODESIC DISTANCE
--------------------------------------------------------------------------------

Type of data:                                   ADJACENCY
Nearness transform:                             NONE
Input dataset:                                  Friendship
Output distance:                                Friendship-Geo

For each pair of nodes, the algorithm finds the # of edges in the shortest path
between them.
Average distance (among reachable pairs)       = 3.565
Distance-based cohesion ("Compactness")        = 0.188
  (range 0 to 1; larger values indicate greater cohesiveness)
Distance-weighted fragmentation ("Breadth") = 0.812


Frequencies of Geodesic Distances

              1       2
        Frequen Proport
        ------- -------
  1 1   182.000   0.053
  2 2   542.000   0.158
  3 3   948.000   0.277
  4 4   948.000   0.277
  5 5   550.000   0.161
  6 6   222.000   0.065
  7 7    32.000   0.009
```

Figure 5.3. UCINET's Old Geodesic Distance Output

Table 5.1. *Diameter, average distance, and fragmentation of Noordin's network*

Relation	Diameter	Average distance	Fragmentation	Distance-weighted fragmentation
Trust Network				
Classmates	7.000	2.213	0.784	0.877
Friendship	7.000	3.565	0.444	0.812
Kinship	2.000	1.158	0.994	0.994
Soulmates	2.000	1.313	0.995	0.996
Aggregated	7.000	2.834	0.216	0.664
Operational Network				
Logistics	4.000	1.913	0.970	0.981
Meetings	4.000	2.068	0.895	0.941
Operations	3.000	1.667	0.759	0.837
Training	4.000	1.870	0.863	0.912
Aggregated	5.000	2.109	0.261	0.595
Communications	6.000	2.703	0.123	0.623
Business & Finance	2.000	1.167	0.994	0.995
Combined Network	4.000	1.990	0.025	0.443

which can handle stacked networks but does not provide information on a network's average distance, fragmentation, or cohesion.

You can also estimate fragmentation scores using UCINET's *Network>Centrality and Power>Fragmentation* command. This command also reports an unweighted score, which is the same score reported by ORA. As noted previously, a helpful feature of this command is that it reports a series of scores (not shown) for each actor that indicates whether that actor is removed from the network: (1) what the network fragmentation will be ("Frag"); (2) what the distance-weighted network fragmentation will be ("DwFrag"); (3) what the change in fragmentation will be ("FragDiff"); (4) what the change in distance-weighted fragmentation will be ("DwFragDiff"); (5) what the percent change in fragmentation will be ("PctFragChg"); and (6) what the percent change in distance-weighted fragmentation will be ("PctFragChg"). *Network >Centrality and Power >Fragmentation*

Table 5.1 summarizes the diameter, average distance, fragmentation, and distance-weighted fragmentation for each of the four Noordin networks, as well as the aggregated trust, operational, and combined[6] networks. The size of each network is not listed because it is the same across all seventy-nine networks and, for our purposes here, uninteresting. Note the considerable variation across the networks. Their diameter ranges from as low as 2.0 to 7.0, and average distance ranges from 1.158 to

---

[6] The combined network is the aggregation of the trust, operational, communications, and business and finance networks.

3.565. It is helpful to recall that the latter score is the average distance between actors that are connected to one another (either directly or indirectly), so it is not unusual in highly fragmented networks (i.e., where there is a high proportion of pairs of actors that cannot directly or indirectly reach one another) for the average path distance to be quite small. The kinship and soulmates networks are examples of this. Both are highly fragmented, and the average distance (and diameter) of both are among the lowest of the networks. Note also how the distance-weighted fragmentation measure differs from the traditional fragmentation measure. When average path distance is not taken into account, the trust network is less fragmented than the operational network. However, when the average distance between connected actors is taken into account, the operational network is less fragmented. The trust network also appears to be more spread out than the operational network because both its diameter and average distance are larger than those of the operational network. Of course, although these and other comparisons can be interesting and provide insights into a network, it is by looking at them longitudinally that we can gain a sense of how they are changing over time and reacting to exogenous and endogenous factors. We will postpone taking up this task until Chapter 10.

Provincial-Cosmopolitan Dimension, Part I: Network Density and Average Degree. Two measures that help analysts tap into the provincial-cosmopolitan dimension of networks are network density and average degree. Network density (d) is formally defined as the total number of ties divided by the total possible number of ties:

$$d = \frac{L}{\frac{n(n-1)}{2}} \tag{5.1}$$

where L refers to the actual number of ties (or lines) in a network and n to the number of actors (or nodes) in the network. Because each actor can potentially be connected to all other actors in the network (except to himself), in an undirected network (i.e., where ties are reciprocal), the total possible number of ties equals $\frac{n(n-1)}{2}$. Calculating density with a directed graph is similar except that with a directed graph you do not have to divide the denominator by two:

$$d = \frac{L}{n(n-1)} \tag{5.2}$$

In practical terms what both of these equations mean is that network density scores range from 0.0 to 1.0. In networks with a density of 0.0 (or 0.0 percent), no ties exist between actors, whereas in networks with a density of 1.0 (or 100.0 percent), all possible ties exist between actors.

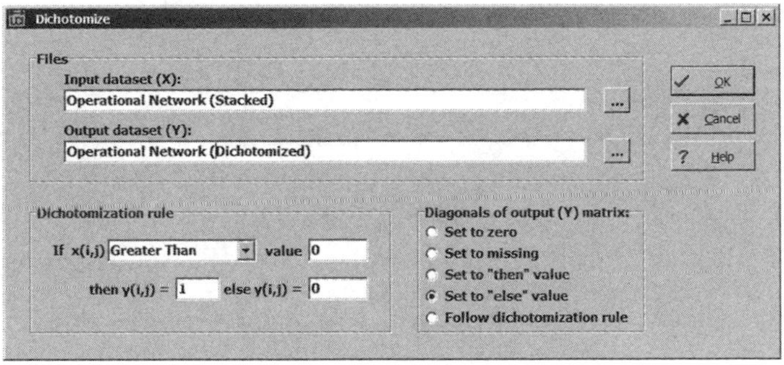

Figure 5.4. UCINET's Dichotomize Dialog Box

Unfortunately, the formal measure of density is inversely related to network size (i.e., all else being equal the larger the network, the lower the density) because the number of possible lines increases exponentially as actors are added to the network, while the number of ties that each actor can maintain tends to be limited. That is why social network analysts often turn to average degree, which is simply the average number of ties that each actor in the network has, in order to measure how "dense" a network is (de Nooy et al. 2005; Scott 2000).[7]

In UCINET you calculate network density using the *(new)Density Overall* command found under the *Network>Cohesion>Density* submenu. Before doing this, however, first dichotomize (binarize) the stacked operational network because some of the networks included therein are valued networks (e.g., the tie between some pairs of individuals are greater than one because they participated in more than one operation together, or attended two or more training events together), and typically you do not want to take into account tie values when calculating density. To dichotomize networks in UCINET, we use the *Transform>Dichotomize* command, which calls up a dialog box (Figure 5.4), which asks you to indicate your input dataset. The example uses the `Operational Network (Stacked)` file. UCINET provides a few "dichotomization rule" options that allow you to indicate what you want your cutoff value for dichotomizing the network to be. Here, we have chosen to accept UCINET's default because we want every tie that is currently greater than 0 to equal 1. UCINET also provides a default output file name, but here we have chosen our own: `Operational Network (Dichotomized)`.

UCINET's overall density command calls up a dialog box (see Figure 5.5) where you indicate your input network (`Operational Network (Dichotomized)`). Click "OK."

The resulting output log (Figure 5.6) lists both the density and average degree for each network in the stacked network. As you can see, the

[*UCINET*]
Network >Cohesion >Density (new)Density Overall

Transform >Dichotomize

---

[7] See Chapter 7 for the equation used for calculating degree centrality.

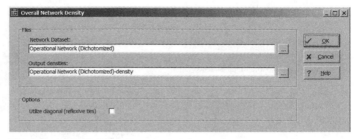

Figure 5.5. UCINET's Density Dialog Box

operations network is the densest (and has the highest average degree) of the four networks.

Transform
>Matrix
Operations
>Within
datasets
>Aggregations

We may also be interested in aggregating the stacked trust (Trust Network (Stacked.##h)) and operational (Operational Network (Stacked.##h)) networks and calculating their density and average degree. To do this we use UCINET's *Transform>Matrix Operations>Within datasets>Aggregations* command, which we discussed at length in Chapter 4. After aggregating the networks, we then

Transform
>Dichotomize

need to dichotomize the network (because some cells have values of greater than 1) using UCINET's *Transform>Dichotomize* command.

Network
>Cohesion
>Density
>(new) Density
Overall

After the aggregated networks are dichotomized, then we calculate the density of the overall network just as we did before, using the *Network>Cohesion>Density>(new) Density Overall* command.

Provincial-Cosmopolitan Dimension, Part II: Clustering Coefficient and Small World Q. Two other measures that are sometimes used to capture the provincial-cosmopolitan dimension are the clustering coefficient and the small world quotient (*SWQ*). The former is estimated directly, although as we will see, there are different methods for doing so. The latter is typically calculated by first estimating both the clustering coefficient (*CC*) and average path distance (*AP*). These are then normalized by calculating the ratio of each to the respective clustering coefficient

```
ucinetlog2.txt - Notepad                                    _□×
File  Edit  Format  View  Help
DENSITY / AVERAGE MATRIX VALUE
--------------------------------------------------------------
Input dataset:                    Operational Network (Dichotomized)
Output dataset:                   Operational Network (Dichotomized)-density |

                    Density    No. of Ties      Avg Degree
                   ---------  -------------   -------------
         Logistics   0.0094       58.0000          0.7342
          Meetings   0.0204      126.0000          1.5949
        Operations   0.0867      534.0000          6.7595
   Training Events   0.0477      294.0000          3.7215

--------------------------------------------------------------
Running time:  00:00:01
```

Figure 5.6. UCINET's Density and Average Degree Output

and average path distance of a random network of the same size and density:

$$CC_{Ratio} = \frac{CC_{Actual}}{CC_{Random}} \tag{5.3}$$

$$AP_{Ratio} = \frac{AP_{Actual}}{AP_{Random}} \tag{5.4}$$

The small world quotient is simply the ratio of the CC_{Ratio} to the AP_{Ratio}:

$$SWQ = \frac{CC_{Ratio}}{AP_{Ratio}} \tag{5.5}$$

Because the CC and density of a random network are approximately equal to one another and the latter is, by definition, equal to the density of the original small world network, dividing the original network's CC by its density is typically sufficient for calculating the CC_{Ratio}. Moreover, in a later analysis of the Broadway musical data, Uzzi (2008) found that the AP_{Ratio} almost always equaled one, and a subsequent analysis of simulated and real-world networks discovered that Uzzi's discovery applied to a larger range of networks than Broadway musicals (Everton 2012; Everton and Lieberman 2009). What this means is that a network's small world quotient can be estimated by simply dividing the original network's CC by its density.

The clustering coefficient is estimated by first taking the ego network of each actor (i.e., each actor's ties to other actors – aka an actor's "alters" – and the ties between them), then calculating the density of each ego network (but not including ego or ego's ties in the calculation – i.e., only the ties between ego's alters are used) and taking the average of these scores. Luckily, UCINET (and Pajek and ORA) has automated all of this for us. To obtain the clustering coefficient, select UCINET's *Network>Cohesion>Clustering Coefficient* command. In the resulting dialog box (not shown), select the dichotomized networks you wish to analyze as your input dataset, and click "OK." The resulting output (Figure 5.7 – here we have estimated the clustering coefficients for the trust network (`Trust Network (Stacked.##h)`) provides the clustering coefficient scores for each network in a file. And as we just noted, to estimate a network's small world quotient, we simply divide the clustering coefficient by network density. Note that UCINET provides two scores: an overall graph clustering coefficient and a weighted overall graph clustering coefficient. It is the former metric that interests us here. *Network >Cohesion >Clustering Coefficient*

Table 5.2 summarizes the density, average degree, clustering coefficient, and small world quotient for each of the Noordin networks. Notice the variation in scores across the various networks. In terms of density and

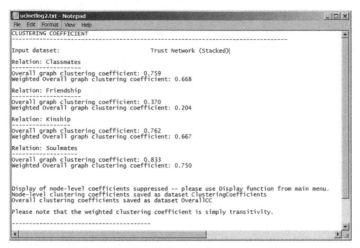

Figure 5.7. UCINET's Clustering Coefficient Output

average degree, the operational network is the densest of the four networks and the business and finance network is the sparsest.[8] Within the trust and operational networks, certain types of relations appear to play a more central role. For example, within the trust network, the classmate network is by far the densest, with the friendship network coming a somewhat distant second; by contrast, the kinship and religious networks are relatively sparse and contribute few ties at all to the network as a whole. This is somewhat in contrast to Sageman's (2004) finding that the global Salafi jihad has primarily been formed through friendship and kinship ties. Moreover, the prominence of classmate ties suggests that analysts may want to consider exploring potential vulnerabilities in Noordin's school network (where a tie between two schools indicates that at least one individual is affiliated with both). For example, they might want to develop a kinetic strategy that shuts down schools from which Noordin has recruited a number of followers; in fact, that is what the Indonesian authorities did with the Luqmanul Hakeim School. Or, they might consider a nonkinetic strategy of building alternative schools nearby, schools that promote moderate forms of Islam and instruct students in subjects other than the memorization of the Qur'an (Roberts and Everton 2011).

The clustering coefficient and small world quotient scores highlight one of the peculiarities of how the overall clustering coefficient is calculated. As one might guess, it equals the mean of the sum of the actors' clustering coefficient scores. However, UCINET, Pajek, and ORA only calculate the clustering coefficients for actors who have two or more alters, and when calculating the average, they divide the sum by the number of actors

[8] Because the networks are the same size, comparing their density levels is permissible.

Table 5.2. *Density, average degree, clustering coefficient, and small world Q*

Relation	Density	Average degree	Clustering coefficient WS/alternate	Small world quotient WS/alternate
Trust Network				
Classmates	0.057	4.430	0.759/0.308	13.32/5.40
Friendship	0.030	2.304	0.370/0.173	12.33/5.77
Kinship	0.005	0.405	0.762/0.068	152.40/13.60
Soulmates	0.004	0.278	0.833/0.074	208.25/18.50
Aggregated	0.084	6.557	0.528/0.381	6.29/4.54
Operational Network				
Logistics	0.009	0.734	0.749/0.104	83.22/11.56
Meetings	0.020	1.595	0.768/0.223	38.40/11.15
Operations	0.087	6.760	0.923/0.444	10.61/5.10
Training	0.048	3.722	0.833/0.401	17.35/8.35
Aggregated	0.142	11.063	0.791/0.661	5.57/4.66
Communications	0.065	5.063	0.562/0.441	8.65/6.79
Business & Finance	0.005	0.380	0.938/0.095	187.60/19.00
Combined Network	0.202	15.772	0.692/0.648	3.43/3.21

who have clustering coefficient scores (not by the number of actors in the network). This is the well-known Watts-Strogatz (WS) clustering co-efficient (Watts and Strogatz 1998), but in sparse networks with a few well-connected actors, it can mislead one into thinking that a network is more clustered than it actually is. Interestingly, until recently, Pajek calculated an alternative clustering coefficient that divided the sum of the clustering coefficient scores by the number of actors in the network. Both scores are reported in Table 5.2. The Watts-Strogatz scores appear to the left of the slash mark; the alternative scores appear to the right. When comparing these scores to the density and average degree scores, the alternative scores appear more reasonable. Note, for example, that in terms of network density and average degree, the classmate and friendship networks are more provincial than the kinship and soulmate networks, but in terms of the WS clustering coefficient, the latter appear more provincial. That is not the case with the alternative scores, however, suggesting they more accurately reflect the overall clustering of the network. Note, however, that when working with a well-connected network (e.g., the combined network), the difference between the two scores is minimal.

The small world quotient scores calculated using the alternative clustering coefficient scores also appear to be more reasonable. There is less variation because the alternative clustering coefficients scores do not over-state a sparse network's clustering level. Still, the small world quotients for the kinship, soulmate, and business and finance networks are larger than the scores of the other networks (unlike their respective density, average degree, and clustering coefficient scores), which at first glance may seem incorrect. However, because the small world quotient is the ratio of the clustering coefficient to density, networks that are extremely sparse but have small and highly dense clusters should score quite high. They are also the type of network that will probably find it difficult to mobilize effectively, and as we saw, that is exactly what Uzzi and Spiro (2005) discovered. Networks that score too high (and too low) in terms of the small world quotient are less likely to succeed than are those whose scores land somewhere in between.

Hierarchical-Heterarchical Dimension: Centralization and Variance. Network centralization, variance, and standard deviation are measures that help researchers determine how hierarchical (or nonhierarchical) a network is. Centralization uses the variation in actor centrality within the network to measure the level of centralization. More variation yields higher network centralization scores, while less variation yields lower scores. Formally, centralization equals

$$C = \frac{\sum [Cmax - C(n_i)]}{\max \sum [Cmax - C(n_i)]} \qquad (5.6)$$

where *Cmax* equals the largest centrality score for all actors and $C(n_i)$ is the centrality score for actor n_i, and $\max \sum [Cmax - C(n_i)]$ is the theoretical maximum possible sum of differences in actor centrality. In other words, network centralization is the ratio of the actual sum of differences in actor centrality over the theoretical maximum, yielding (like density) a score somewhere between 0.0 and 1.0. In general, the larger a centralization index is, the more likely it is that a single actor is very central, whereas the other actors are not (Wasserman and Faust 1994:176); thus, they can be seen as measuring how unequal the distribution of individual actor values are. Finally, because network centralization scores are based on the type of centrality estimated (e.g., degree, betweenness, closeness, and eigenvector), we need to interpret them in light of the centrality metric estimated. For example, degree centrality counts the number of ties each individual actor has; thus, we would expect that a centralization metric based on it would capture the extent to which one or a handful of actors possess a lot of ties, whereas other actors in the network do not. By contrast, a centralization measure based on betweenness centrality, which measures the extent to which actors lie between other actors in the network, could be interpreted as indicating the degree to which a handful of a network's actors are in a position of brokerage. Put differently, the higher the score, the more likely it is that only a few actors score high in terms of betweenness centrality.

An alternative measure to centralization that has been recommended by Coleman (1964), Hoivik and Gleditsch (1975), and Snijders (1981) is the variance (*V*) of actor centrality scores found in a network (see also Wasserman and Faust 1994:177, 180–181), although the standard deviation (*SD*) is preferable, as it brings us back to the original unit of measure (Hamilton 1996:72–73).

$$V = \frac{\left[\sum_{i=1}^{n} (C(n_i) - \overline{C})^z\right]}{n} \tag{5.7}$$

$$SD = \sqrt{\frac{\left[\sum_{i=1}^{n} (C(n_i) - \overline{C})^z\right]}{n}} \tag{5.8}$$

Those familiar with standard statistics will recognize these equations as standard measures of variance and standard deviation. The variance (5.7) equals the sum of the squared differences between each actor's centrality score ($C(n_i)$) and the average centrality score ($\overline{C}$), whereas the standard deviation (see equation 5.8) is simply the square root of the variance.[9] Comparing equations 5.6 and 5.7, one can see that they differ in that, whereas centralization (5.6) uses the difference between the network's largest centrality score and each actor's centrality score to estimate variance in actor centrality, the traditional variance (5.7) and standard deviation (5.8) measures use the difference between the network's mean centrality score and each actor's centrality score. Thus, although both attempt to capture the level of variance in centrality scores, they look to different baseline measures (i.e., largest centrality score vs. average centrality score) for doing this.[10]

To calculate these measures in UCINET, we use its various centrality commands. In other words, to calculate degree centrality, we use the *Network>Centrality and Power>Degree* command; for betweenness centralization, *Network>Centrality and Power>Freeman Betweenness*; for closeness, *Network> Centrality and Power>Closeness*, and for eigenvector, *Network>Centrality and Power>Eigenvector*. Within each of these commands, there are a few options that should be noted. For instance, when you issue the degree centrality command, the dialog box (Figure 5.8) that is called up asks whether the network data are symmetric.

Network >Centrality and Power >Degree Freeman Betweenness, Closeness, Eigenvector

---

[9] Because the sum of the differences always equals zero, we first square the differences. Squaring the differences eliminates negative values and gives us a measure that can be used to measure variation. However, because the variance is measured in unnatural squared units (e.g., centrality^2), taking the square root of the variance (i.e., the standard deviation) returns us to a more understandable unit of measure (e.g., centrality).

[10] One last set of measures worth noting are Krackhardt's (1994) graph theoretical measures of hierarchy. These can be quite informative, but they are intended for directed data, and to date, most SNA data collected on dark networks have been undirected, which is why we do not consider Krackhardt's measures at any length in this book.

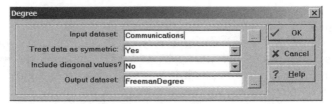

Figure 5.8. UCINET's Degree Centrality Dialog Box

Although UCINET's default is "Yes," it sometimes defaults to "No," so if you are analyzing symmetric data, you will want to make sure that this option is selected correctly (in Chapter 7 we will see how we use this option to analyze asymmetric data).

Network >Centrality and Power >Freeman Betweenness >Node Betweenness — In terms of betweenness centrality, we generally want to select the *Node Betweenness* menu option. This is the most common betweenness centrality measure and the one we will use here. At the resulting dialog box (not shown), accept UCINET's defaults and click "OK." With eigenvector centrality, you will typically accept UCINET's default options *except* make sure you check the box that "forces the majority of scores to be positive" (Figure 5.9).

As we have noted, closeness centrality measures how close, in terms of path distance, each actor is, on average, to every other actor in the network. Unfortunately, the standard closeness measure, which we will discuss in more detail in Chapter 7, cannot be calculated when some actors or clusters of actors are disconnected from others because the path distance between some actors is infinite.

One way to work around this problem is to extract the network's largest component (see Chapter 6), calculate closeness for the actors that are a part of it, and assign scores of "0.00" to those that that are not. An alternative approach, the one that is used here (but currently can only be calculated in UCINET), is to sum (and average) the reciprocal distance between all actors; this approach works with disconnected networks because the reciprocal of infinity is typically regarded as equaling

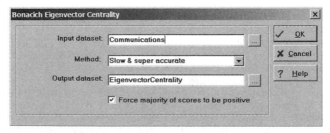

Figure 5.9. UCINET's Eigenvector Centrality Dialog Box

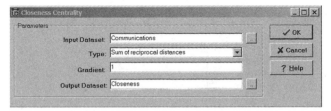

Figure 5.10. UCINET's Closeness Centrality Dialog Box

zero (Borgatti 2006).[11] To use this measure of closeness, after issuing the closeness centrality command, select the "Sum of reciprocal distances" option in the resulting dialog box (Figure 5.10) and click "OK."

Figure 5.11 presents a portion of the output from using UCINET's degree centrality command with the communication network (Communications.##h). At the bottom it displays the descriptive statistics for the network; just above these are some of the individual actor centrality scores. The descriptive statistics are what interest us here. We will consider actor centrality scores in Chapter 7. As you can see from Figure 5.11, the descriptive statistics section of the output provides users with a lot of information, more than most analysts will need. Moreover, most of the metrics are presented in terms of their raw, normalized, and share scores.[12] Two metrics that we considered previously, network size (N of Obs) and average (mean) degree, are also included in this report.[13] More pertinent to the current discussion is that this report includes the variance, standard deviation, and centralization scores.[14] A number of other measures not discussed in this book are also included in the report; readers who are interested in learning more about these should see UCINET's Help function, as well as consult Hanneman and Riddle (2005).

Figure 5.12 presents the output generated by UCINET's betweenness centrality command. As you can see, although the output is not identical to the degree centrality output, it is similar. This is true of the output generated by the other centrality commands as well. Looking at both figures, you will note that the network centralization score appears just below the descriptive statistics, whereas the average degree, variance, and standard deviation scores are "buried" in the descriptive statistics themselves. When you analyze dichotomized data, centralization scores

---

[11] It is this measure of closeness that is used for calculating distance-weighted fragmentation.

[12] Normalized scores have been adjusted for network size, whereas individual share scores have been adjusted so that they sum to 1.00.

[13] Close observers may have noted that normalized average degree equals network density.

[14] Note, however, that the centralization score appears separately at the bottom of the output. This is because it is the same whether the raw, normalized, or share scores are used to calculate it.

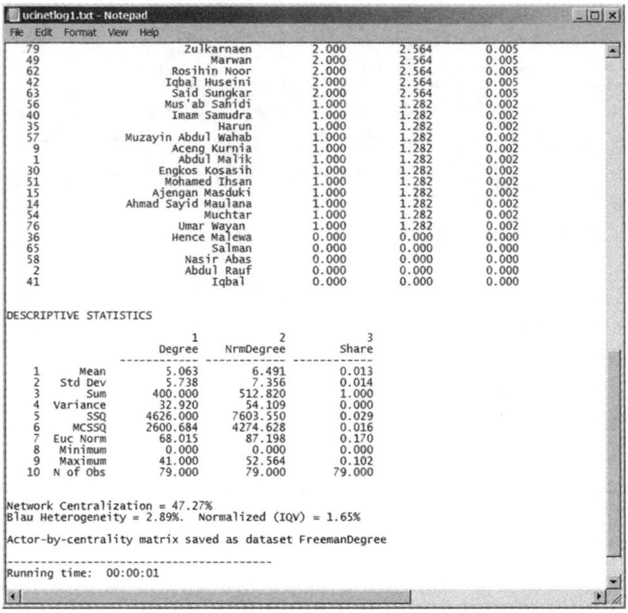

ucinetlog1.txt - Notepad

File Edit Format View Help

```
 79                 Zulkarnaen     2.000     2.564     0.005
 49                     Marwan     2.000     2.564     0.005
 62               Rosihin Noor     2.000     2.564     0.005
 42              Iqbal Huseini     2.000     2.564     0.005
 63               Said Sungkar     2.000     2.564     0.005
 56              Mus'ab Sahidi     1.000     1.282     0.002
 40               Imam Samudra     1.000     1.282     0.002
 35                      Harun     1.000     1.282     0.002
 57        Muzayin Abdul Wahab     1.000     1.282     0.002
  9               Aceng Kurnia     1.000     1.282     0.002
  1                Abdul Malik     1.000     1.282     0.002
 30             Engkos Kosasih     1.000     1.282     0.002
 51             Mohamed Ihsan      1.000     1.282     0.002
 15            Ajengan Masduki     1.000     1.282     0.002
 14        Ahmad Sayid Maulana     1.000     1.282     0.002
 54                    Muchtar     1.000     1.282     0.002
 76                 Umar Wayan     1.000     1.282     0.002
 36               Hence Malewa     0.000     0.000     0.000
 65                     Salman     0.000     0.000     0.000
 58                 Nasir Abas     0.000     0.000     0.000
  2                Abdul Rauf      0.000     0.000     0.000
 41                      Iqbal     0.000     0.000     0.000

DESCRIPTIVE STATISTICS

                           1            2            3
                      Degree    NrmDegree        Share
                ------------ ------------ ------------
  1       Mean         5.063        6.491        0.013
  2    Std Dev         5.738        7.356        0.014
  3        Sum       400.000      512.820        1.000
  4   Variance        32.920       54.109        0.000
  5        SSQ      4626.000     7603.550        0.029
  6      MCSSQ      2600.684     4274.628        0.016
  7   Euc Norm        68.015       87.198        0.170
  8    Minimum         0.000        0.000        0.000
  9    Maximum        41.000       52.564        0.102
 10   N of Obs        79.000       79.000       79.000

Network Centralization = 47.27%
Blau Heterogeneity = 2.89%.  Normalized (IQV) = 1.65%

Actor-by-centrality matrix saved as dataset FreemanDegree

----------------------------------------
Running time:  00:00:01
```

Figure 5.11. UCINET's Degree Centrality Output

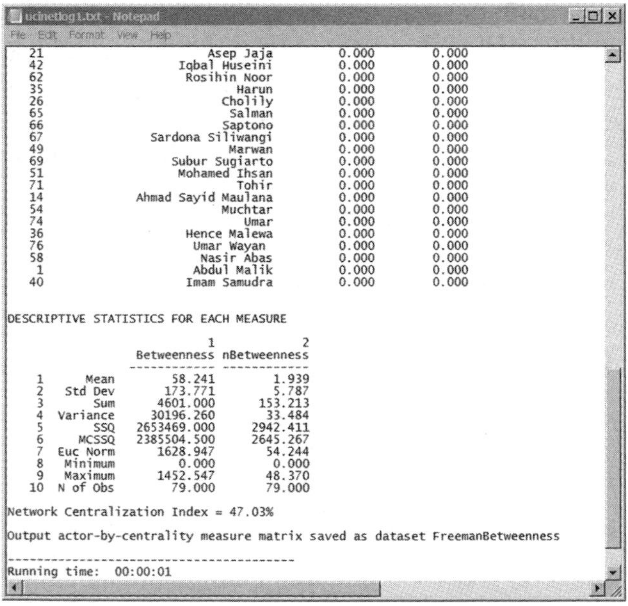

ucinetlog1.txt - Notepad

File Edit Format View Help

```
 21                  Asep Jaja        0.000          0.000
 42              Iqbal Huseini        0.000          0.000
 62               Rosihin Noor        0.000          0.000
 35                      Harun        0.000          0.000
 26                    Cholily        0.000          0.000
 65                     Salman        0.000          0.000
 66                    Saptono        0.000          0.000
 67          Sardona Siliwangi        0.000          0.000
 49                     Marwan        0.000          0.000
 69             Subur Sugiarto        0.000          0.000
 51              Mohamed Ihsan        0.000          0.000
 71                      Tohir        0.000          0.000
 14        Ahmad Sayid Maulana        0.000          0.000
 54                    Muchtar        0.000          0.000
 74                       Umar        0.000          0.000
 36               Hence Malewa        0.000          0.000
 76                Umar Wayan         0.000          0.000
 58                 Nasir Abas        0.000          0.000
  1                Abdul Malik        0.000          0.000
 40               Imam Samudra        0.000          0.000

DESCRIPTIVE STATISTICS FOR EACH MEASURE

                           1            2
                 Betweenness nBetweenness
                 ----------- ------------
  1       Mean        58.241        1.939
  2    Std Dev       173.771        5.787
  3        Sum      4601.000      153.213
  4   Variance     30196.260       33.484
  5        SSQ   2653469.000     2942.411
  6      MCSSQ   2385504.500     2645.267
  7   Euc Norm      1628.947       54.244
  8    Minimum         0.000        0.000
  9    Maximum      1452.547       48.370
 10   N of Obs        79.000       79.000

Network Centralization Index = 47.03%

Output actor-by-centrality measure matrix saved as dataset FreemanBetweenness

----------------------------------------
Running time:  00:00:01
```

Figure 5.12. UCINET's Betweenness Centrality Output

Table 5.3. *Centralization scores*

Relation	Degree centralization	Closeness centralization	Betweenness centralization	Eigenvector centralization
Trust Network				
Classmates	29.69%	55.75%	5.77%	43.33%
Friendship	18.02%	46.52%	24.84%	75.25%
Kinship	3.41%	6.68%	0.07%	94.83%
Soulmates	4.90%	9.56%	0.10%	4.37%
Aggregated	28.21%	48.96%	14.73%	39.68%
Operational Network				
Logistics	12.19%	25.83%	1.18%	6.50%
Meetings	24.21%	46.88%	5.58%	72.82%
Operations	39.78%	64.89%	9.24%	34.39%
Training	17.47%	39.63%	3.66%	42.87%
Aggregated	42.01%	58.10%	15.67%	31.60%
Communications	47.27%	69.96%	47.03%	65.21%
Business & Finance	4.76%	9.36%	0.10%	80.19%
Combined Network	51.60%	58.96%	20.25%	29.43%

will range from 0 to 1 (or 0–100 percent), but if you analyze valued data, they will sometimes be larger than 1 (or 100 percent). As a general rule, you will want to dichotomize your data before estimating network centralization (the closeness and betweenness commands automatically do this if valued data are used).

Table 5.3 presents the centralization scores for each of the various networks, whereas Table 5.4 presents the corresponding standard deviation scores. The scores are somewhat consistent across types of centrality and between the two measures of centralization (i.e., centralization and standard deviation). Networks that are highly centralized in terms of degree centrality are often highly centralized in terms of closeness, betweenness, and eigenvector centrality. Likewise, networks that are identified as more centralized in terms of centralization tend to be similarly identified in terms of the standard deviation. There are, of course, a few exceptions. For instance, in terms of betweenness centrality, the communication network is far more centralized relative to the other networks than it is in terms of the other centrality measures. And, although in terms of degree, closeness, and betweenness centralization the kinship and business and finance networks are not in the least bit centralized, in terms of eigenvector centrality, they are. Or again, according to the degree and closeness centralization metrics, the communication network is more centralized than the operational network, but according to the corresponding standard deviation scores, the opposite is true. These are not the only exceptions, of course, but they illustrate that different metrics based on different

Table 5.4. *Standard deviation*

Relation	Degree standard deviation	Closeness standard deviation	Betweenness standard deviation	Eigenvector standard deviation
Trust Network				
Classmates	6.358	10.688	26.476	0.093
Friendship	2.587	9.203	121.902	0.092
Kinship	0.685	0.750	0.249	0.110
Soulmates	0.841	0.976	0.401	0.109
Aggregated	6.612	11.458	103.574	0.088
Operational Network				
Logistics	1.874	3.144	5.352	0.105
Meetings	3.188	6.696	20.415	0.098
Operations	8.315	13.084	33.945	0.092
Training	4.818	8.072	15.090	0.097
Aggregated	8.728	13.881	84.815	0.080
Communications	5.738	9.963	173.771	0.079
Business & Finance	0.959	1.039	0.335	0.109
Combined Network	10.260	8.581	84.884	0.064

centrality measures will sometimes provide different answers as to how centralized a particular network is.

Caution should be in order when interpreting centralization measures (both centralization and standard deviation). Networks that differ substantially in terms of centralization may look quite similar. Take, for instance, Noordin's trust and communication networks (Figure 5.13). They are almost mirror images of one another, but as we can see in Table 5.3, the communications network is far more centralized than the trust network, whereas according to Table 5.4, the trust network is more centralized. This illustrates the importance of using network metrics and visualization in conjunction with one another.

Network Topography in Pajek

Let's begin by checking to see if Pajek gives us the same scores in terms of network size, average distance, and diameter. Dichotomized versions of the four sets of networks are included in the project file, Noordin's Network (Dichotomized).paj, having been exported from UCINET *[Pajek-Main Screen]* using the techniques discussed in Chapter 4. Read this file into Pajek using *File* the *File>Pajek Project File>Read* command. Before making any calcu- *>Pajek Project* lations, we need to convert all arcs to edges (because Pajek reads ties in *File* networks exported from UCINET as arcs rather than edges), remove any *>Read* loops (i.e., ties along the diagonal) from the networks, and then extract

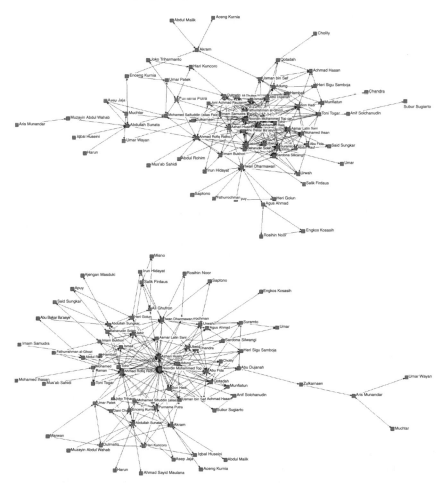

Figure 5.13. Noordin Trust and Communication Networks (NetDraw)

the individual relations from all of the multirelational (i.e., stacked) networks (i.e., trust and operational). The first of these steps is accomplished using Pajek's *Net>Transform>Arcs→Edges> All* command for *each of the four networks*. This brings up a dialog box asking whether you want to create a new network. Select "Yes." Pajek will then ask whether you want to remove multiple lines. Most of the time you will want to choose the "Single" option (#5). Pajek will assign the new networks with names such as "Symmetrizing (Single) of N1," which means that the new network was symmetrized (i.e., arcs-to-edges) using the "Single" option from the first network (N1) listed in the Network drop-down menu. You can rename them with the *File>Network>Change Label* command.

*Net>Transform
>Arcs→Edges
>All*

*File>Network
>Change Label*

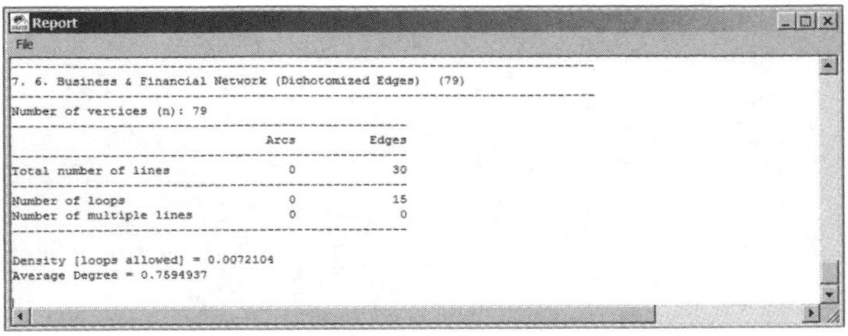

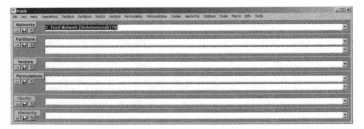

Figure 5.14. Pajek's Info>Network>General Report

Next, we need to remove any loops that are in the networks so that Pajek does not take them into account when calculating density and average degree. Not all networks have loops, however. To determine *Info>Network* whether they do, we use the *Info>Network>General* command for each *>General* network (note that the network for which we are seeking information needs to be highlighted in the first or top Network drop-down menu). Accept Pajek's defaults in the dialog box and click "OK." This calls up Pajek's report window with output similar to Figure 5.14, which indicates that the business and finance network has fifteen loops. To *Net>Transform* remove these, we select the *Net>Transform>Remove Loops* command. *>Remove* Once again, you will be asked to create a new network; select "Yes" *Loops* and give the new network a name. Finally, for the (symmetrized) trust and operational networks, we need to extract each relation. To do this, *Net>Transform* we use Pajek's *Net>Transform>Multiple Relations>Extract Relation(s)* *>Multiple* command. In the resulting dialog box tell Pajek that you want to extract *Relations* relations 1 through 4 (because there are four relations in both the trust *>Extract* and operational networks). *Relation(s)*

The size of each network is indicated by the number in parentheses *Net>Paths* next to the network's name. As you can see in Figure 5.15, the trust *between* network (as expected) contains seventy-nine actors. To obtain the aver- *2 vertices* age distance and diameter of a network in Pajek, we use the *Net>Paths* *>Distribution of Distances >From All Vertices*

Figure 5.15. Pajek's Main Screen

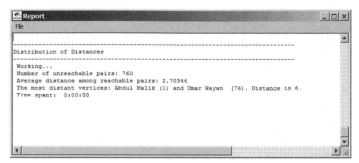

Figure 5.16. Pajek's Distribution of Distances Report

between 2 vertices>Distribution of Distances>From All Vertices command. The output contained in Pajek's report window provides the number of unreachable pairs, the average distance, and the most distant vertices (i.e., the network's diameter).

Figure 5.16 presents the output generated by Pajek for the (symmetrized) communications network. As you can see it indicates that the diameter of the network is 6.0 and the average distance between reachable pairs is 2.703. These scores agree with those listed in Table 5.1. Note that Pajek reports the names of the actors who are most distant as well as the number of unreachable pairs.

Unfortunately, Pajek does not currently provide a fragmentation score. However, you can calculate it by dividing the number of unreachable pairs (760) by the total number of possible pairs in the network, which is equal to network size multiplied by network size minus one, that is, $79*(79 − 1) = 6,162$, and $760/6,162 = .123$, which agrees to the standard fragmentation score listed in Table 5.1.

Network Density and Average Degree. Whereas estimating density and average degree is very simple with Pajek when working with individual networks, it is somewhat more complex when working with multirelational (i.e., stacked) networks. This is why when working with the latter, most of the time you will probably want to estimate them in UCINET. Nevertheless, it is helpful to see how it is done in Pajek so you do not need to switch back and forth between programs unnecessarily. To obtain the density and average degree of the network appearing in the top or first Network drop-down menu, select the *Info>Network>General* command. This generates the same report (Figure 5.17) that we saw previously, at the bottom of which you will find the network's density and average degree.

Unlike UCINET, in Pajek you can only estimate network density and average degree one network at a time. Here, we have requested information on the business and finance network. Note that the report indicates

Info>Network >General

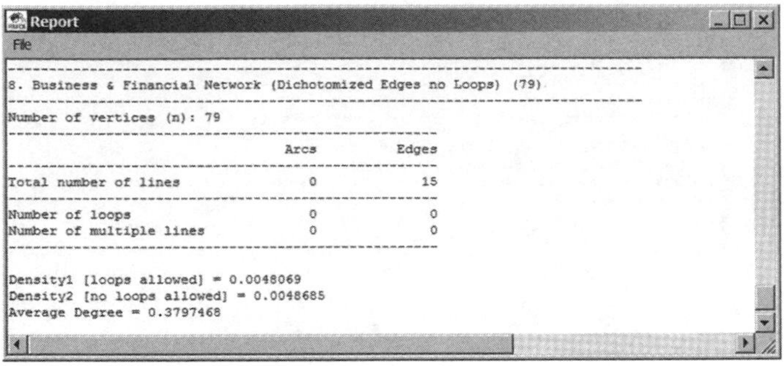

Figure 5.17. Pajek's Info>Network>General Report

network density with and without loops (i.e., including and not including the cells along the diagonal into the calculation). Looking at Figure 5.17, we can see that the density of the communications network is .005, while the average degree is .380, which agrees with UCINET's calculations (see Table 5.1).

Clustering Coefficient and Small World Q. The clustering coefficient is
Net>Vector
>Clustering
Coefficient
>CC1 calculated with the *Net>Vector>Clustering Coefficient>CC1* command. This creates one partition, two vectors, and a report (Figure 5.18) containing the Watts-Strogatz clustering coefficient (compare to Table 5.2 communication network score).

Net>Partitions
>Degree
Net>Vector
>Centrality
>Closeness *Centralization.* Like UCINET, Pajek generates centralization scores when it calculates centrality. Degree centralization is obtained with the *Net>Partitions>Degree>All, Input, Output* command; closeness centralization with the *Net>Vector>Centrality>Closeness>All, Input,*

Figure 5.18. Pajek's Clustering Coefficient Report (Communication Network)

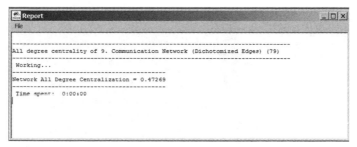

Figure 5.19. Pajek's Degree Centralization Report

Output command;[15] betweenness centralization with the *Net>Vector> Centrality>Betweenness* command; and eigenvector centralization with the *Net>Vector>Important Vertices>1-Mode: Hubs-Authorities* command. Figure 5.19 presents the report generated using Pajek's degree centrality command with the communication network. Note that it agrees with the score calculated by UCINET (Table 5.3). Unfortunately, Pajek does not calculate standard deviation. As we will see in the following section, ORA does.

*Net>Vector
>Centrality
>Betweenness*

*Net>Vector
>Important
Vertices
>1-Mode:
Hubs-Authorities*

Network Topography in ORA

To see how to calculate topographical metrics using ORA, we need to first load the four sets of networks (Trust Network.xml, Operational Network.xml, Communications.xml, and Business and Finance Ties.xml) using ORA's *File>Open Meta-Network* command. ORA automatically provides users with a count of the number of actors and the density of networks that are loaded into the program's Meta-Network Manager. Simply select a particular network and the number of actors (i.e., the count) and density appear in the "Statistics" portion of the Network Information/Editor panel. For example, in Figure 5.20 we selected the classmates subnetwork. We have also "deselected" the "Allow self-loops" box (this is similar to examining the "no loops allowed" density calculation in Pajek). Looking at the Network Information/Editor panel (admittedly quite small in the screen shot), we can see that the size of the network is seventy-nine and the density is .0568 (both are circled in Figure 5.20), both of which agree with our previous calculations.

*[ORA]
File>Open
Meta-Network*

Of course, we are typically interested in learning more than just the count and density of a particular network. To acquire the topographical characteristics discussed in this chapter we can use ORA's Standard

---

[15] Pajek calculates the traditional measure of closeness centrality, so it will not estimate closeness centralization with a disconnected network.

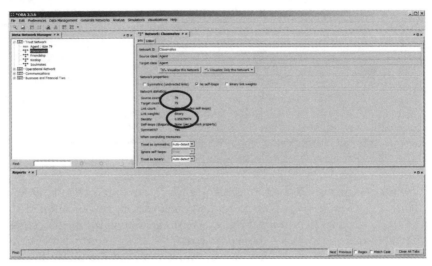

Figure 5.20. ORA's Main Screen with Network Statistics

Analysis >Generate Reports >Locate Key Entities >Standard Network Analysis

Network Analysis report, which is accessed with the *Analysis>Generate Reports>Locate Key Entities>Standard Network Analysis* command. At the first dialog box (not shown), make sure that the meta-network you are analyzing is selected (e.g., the trust network) and click "Next." This brings up a second dialog box (Figure 5.21) where you want to select all of the subnetworks you intend to analyze. Typically, you will want to select all of the subnetworks as we have here (i.e., classmates, friendship, kinship, and soulmates) although there may be occasions when you will only want to analyze a subset. After making your selection, click "Next."

At the next dialog box (not shown) accept ORA's defaults and click "Next." The next dialog box (not shown) will ask what type of output you want. For now, select "Text" (we will explore the other types of output further on), indicate where (i.e., in what folder) you want the report to be stored, and give the report a name (e.g., trust network). Click "Finish" and in relatively short order, a separate report for each network will appear under the Reports panel (each under its own tab). Click on one of the tabs, scroll down, and you will find ORA's calculations of *Network Level* measures, including count, density, characteristic path length (i.e., average distance), clustering coefficient, network levels (i.e., diameter), fragmentation, degree centralization, betweenness centralization, and closeness centralization. Scroll down a bit further, and you will discover a series of *Node Level* measures, including the average (and standard deviation) degree, eigenvector, closeness, and betweenness centrality – both normalized (scaled) and raw (unscaled). The unscaled scores should agree with what we calculated previously. Note that ORA

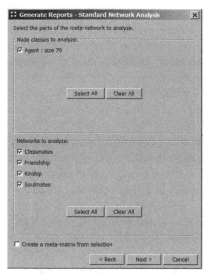

Figure 5.21. ORA's Standard Network Analysis Report Dialog Box

calculates total degree, indegree, and outdegree centrality. Although we will postpone our discussion of the difference between total indegree and outdegree until the Chapter 7, note that average total degree centrality is twice that of average degree in UCINET and Pajek, while average indegree and outdegree centrality equals average degree in UCINET and Pajek.

In other words, in this single report, ORA has given us all of the topographical metrics that we have been exploring in this chapter. This illustrates one of ORA's greatest strengths. Rather than issuing a different command for each set of metrics, ORA provides them all in a single report. You can even create your own custom reports with ORA's *Preferences>Other* command. That said, you need to be careful when using ORA's standard reports. They sometimes include metrics that are inapplicable for the network under analysis. For example, ORA Standard Network Analysis reports closeness centralization scores for disconnected networks, which it should not, and Krackhardt's measure of hierarchy for symmetric networks when the algorithm is only designed for asymmetric networks. This illustrates why it is important for you to have a working understanding of SNA. Otherwise, you could end up using an inappropriate metric when crafting strategies for the disruption of a particular dark network.

Preferences >Other

A Cautionary Note

This chapter's discussion has essentially treated the various dimensions as conceptually distinct from one another, but the formal measures of these dimensions are anything but independent from one another. For example, sensitive to network size but also affected by the degree of network centralization. "Because density is based on how many ties are present in the network, one or two individuals having a disproportionately high number of ties to others in the network might raise the density score" (Prell 2011:168). Thus, the two measures may often want to be used in conjunction:

> Using degree centralization alongside density is somewhat similar to what statisticians do when they make use of a mean and standard deviation. The mean is a measure of central tendency and the standard deviation is a measure of spread or variance. Similarly, centralization measures the extent to which ties hover around one actor, and density measures the extent to which all the ties are actually present. (Prell 2011:170)

To this we could also add that it would make sense to compare density with the variance and standard deviation scores discussed in previous sections.

As Noah Friedkin (1981) has noted, density is also sensitive to the number of cohesive groups within a network. It can be "a misleading indicator of cohesion in cases where the network in question has many cohesive subgroups... low densities in large networks may reflect more structural cohesion than higher densities in smaller networks, as such large networks have fewer cohesive subgroups, and hence, less amount of 'fragmentation'" (Prell 2011:171). Thus, in addition to considering density, average degree, the clustering coefficient, and the small world quotient as measures of network cohesiveness, we would be well advised to examine fragmentation as well. The broader point, of course, is that many network measures are interdependent with one another, and that they should not be examined in isolation but rather together.

5.6   Summary and Conclusion

In this chapter we explored how to use UCINET, Pajek, and ORA to calculate several different sets of network topography metrics: size, diameter, average distance, fragmentation, density, and centralization. UCINET is able to estimate all the metrics covered in this chapter, while Pajek and ORA are able to estimate most. ORA's report-based approach probably makes it the easiest of the programs to use, but as we saw, it will report metrics even when they do not apply to the network being analyzed. As mentioned in Chapter 3, Pajek's strength lies in its ability to calculate these (and other) metrics with very large networks. This ability did not come into play in this chapter because the Noordin network is relatively small, but not all dark networks are small (e.g., the FARC).

We also briefly considered a series of studies of "light" networks that suggest that effective networks can be neither too dense nor too sparse, neither too centralized nor too decentralized. Instead, they must land somewhere on a continuum between the two sets of extremes. If these same dynamics are at work in dark networks, then analysts need to take into account network topography in the crafting of strategies to disrupt them. For example, imagine a scenario where the dark network we are seeking to disrupt is located toward the dense or provincial side of the cosmopolitan-provincial continuum. Moreover, let's assume that the network has crossed the tipping point and has become too dense and is no longer as effective as it used to be. If, in such a situation, we targeted a central actor for capture or elimination, that could have the unintended effect of making the network less dense and (consequently) more effective. Instead, we may want to adopt a strategy (or an array of strategies) that pushes the network in the opposite direction (e.g., peeling off peripheral members through rehabilitation and reintegration programs), causing it to become even more dense and hopefully less effective. Of course, the crafting of strategies is seldom so simple. We often need to take into consideration second-order effects. As we saw in the first chapter, for example, research has found that extremely dense networks that are effectively cut off from the wider society, tend to become more extreme (Sunstein 2003, 2009), and, in fact, this is what appears to have happened with the Hamburg cell whose members participated in the 9/11 attacks. Sageman (2004) found that they had met at a local mosque, moved into the same apartment where they underwent a long period of intense social interaction, progressively adopted the beliefs and faith of their most extreme members, and then eventually joined the global salafi jihad. Thus, if we do attempt to force a network to become more dense, then we need to be prepared (at least in the short term) for the effects that such a strategy could have.

With regards to Noordin's network, we have drawn a few tentative conclusions and suggested possible strategies for disruption. For example, we saw that the classmates network is relatively dense (Table 5.2) and somewhat centralized (Tables 5.3 and 5.4). This suggests that strategists may want to target the schools that contributed most to the forming of these ties. Figure 5.22 presents the school network, which was derived from the two-mode school network (see Appendix 1). Here, a tie between two schools indicates that at least one individual is associated with both schools. For example, if a person attended one school and teaches at another, then a tie has been drawn between the two schools.

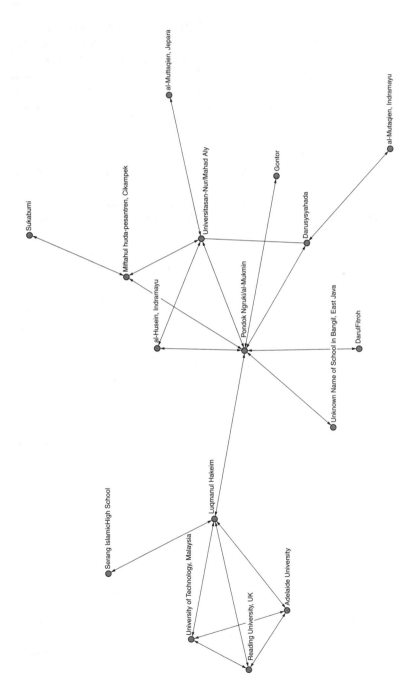

Figure 5.22. Noordin School Network (Isolates Removed)

Although it will not be until Chapter 7 that we examine various measures of centrality, clearly certain schools are more central in Noordin's network than are others: namely, the Universitas an-Nur, Pondok Ngruki, and Luqmanul Hakeim schools. As noted previously, a kinetic strategy might seek to close down one of these schools, which is exactly what the Indonesian authorities did to the Luqmanul Hakeim school; it is unclear whether this had a noticeable effect on the functioning of Noordin's network (or, for that matter, Jemaah Islamiyah) because it is relatively easy to set up another school somewhere else. A nonkinetic strategy of building alternative schools that teach traditional subjects (e.g., reading, writing, arithmetic, and moderate forms of Islam) near the more central schools in Noordin's network might prove to be a more effective strategy in the long run, because it would most likely facilitate the integration of Indonesians into civil society (Roberts and Everton 2011; Tilly 2005).

Of course, the School network is not the only network analysts would want to consider. For example, the communication network is relatively dense and highly centralized, suggesting that it might be vulnerable to the removal of a few actors (i.e., a kinetic action) or the diffusion of disinformation through the network (i.e., a nonkinetic action). In both cases, centrality measures might prove useful in identifying key actors as could Borgatti's (2006) key player algorithms. We take up the former in Chapter 7 and the latter in Chapter 8.

Finally, in this chapter we have only considered these metrics in terms of a single snapshot in time. In reality, as we noted in the first chapter, dark networks are in a constant state of flux, with actors entering and leaving almost continuously. In other words, the density, centralization, and fragmentation of a network will almost certainly change from one time period to the next. Thus, we also need to monitor these networks over time to see whether they are becoming more or less dense or more or less centralized. Such information will (or at least should) inform the crafting of strategies as well. We will explore how to do this in Chapter 10. For now, we turn to examining how to use SNA to identify the subgroups of particular networks and how this information might be used in the disruption of dark networks.

6

Cohesion and Clustering

6.1 Introduction

A major focus of social network analysis is to identify dense clusters of
actors "among whom there are relatively strong, direct, intense, and/or
positive ties" (Wasserman and Faust 1994:249). Social network analysts
often refer to these clusters of actors as cohesive subgroups and generally assume that "social interaction is the basis for solidarity, shared
norms, identity, and collective behavior, so people who interact intensively are likely to consider themselves a social group" (de Nooy, Mrvar,
and Batagelj 2005:61). Social network analysts use several approaches
for identifying cohesive subgroups. One way is to cluster actors based on
attributes (e.g., race, gender), but the more common approach is to focus
on the pattern of ties (i.e., relations) among actors. Perhaps not surprisingly, social network analysts have developed a variety of algorithms for
identifying subgroups:

> Once analysts began to try to formalize the idea of the clique and
> to devise mathematical measures of the number and cohesion of
> cliques, it was . . . recognized that there were a number of differ-
> ent ways of operationalizing the apparently simple idea of the
> "clique": for example, cliques could be seen as groups of mutu-
> ally connected individuals or as pockets of high density. Thus, a
> number of different theoretical models of subgroups emerged,
> variously described as "cliques," "clusters," "components,"
> "cores," and "circles." Apart from beginning with the letter "c,"
> these concepts have very little in common with one another.
> (Scott 2000:100)

This chapter explores some (but not all) of the various approaches for
using patterns of ties for identifying cohesive subgroups within social

170

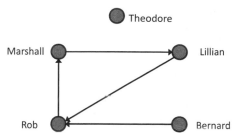

Figure 6.1. Simple Unconnected Directed Network (from De Nooy et al. 2005:66)

networks.[1] Specifically, it examines components, cores, factions, and Newman groups. It does not consider perhaps the strictest algorithm for identifying subnetworks, namely, "cliques," which are defined as a subset of actors wherein each actor is directly connected to all other actors (in other words, the density of a clique is 100 percent). Cliques are not considered for two reasons: One is because the assumption that each member of a subgroup has a tie to every other member is probably unreasonable. The second is that actors in a network can belong to more than one clique, which makes identifying distinct subgroups often impossible. We briefly mention the algorithm here, though, because as we will see further on, ORA uses a count of the number of cliques to which an actor belongs as a proxy of that actor's centrality.

6.2 Components

Probably the simplest forms of subgroups are components, which are subnetworks in which members are connected (either directly or indirectly) to one another but are not to members of other subnetworks (Hanneman and Riddle 2005). In directed networks, you can identify two types of components: strong and weak. Strong components take into consideration the direction of ties, whereas weak components do not. In a strong component each pair of actors is connected by a (directed) path and no other actor can be added without destroying its connectedness. By contrast, in a weak component each pair of actors is connected by an undirected path (i.e., a semipath) and no other actor can be added without destroying its connectedness.[2] Take, for example, the network in Figure 6.1 (adapted from de Nooy et al. 2005:66). The network contains three

---

[1] See Hanneman and Riddle (2005, 2011) for an exhaustive review of the various cohesive subgroup algorithms available in UCINET.
[2] Recall that a path is a walk (i.e., a sequence of actors and ties) in which no actor between the first and last actor of the walk occurs more than once (see Chapter 1).

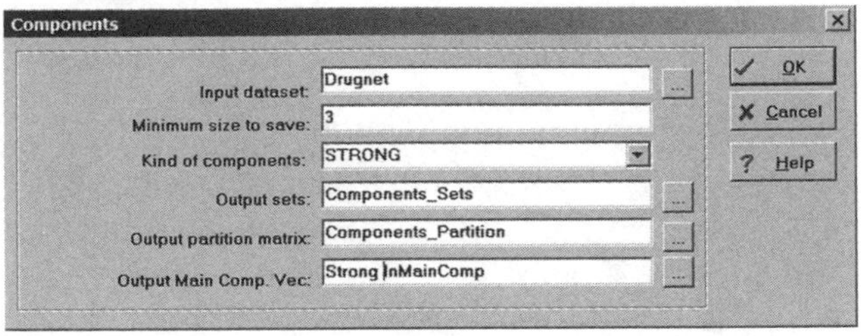

Figure 6.2. UCINET Components Dialog Box

strong components – (1) Bernard; (2) Theodore; and (3) Rob, Lillian, and Marshall – and two weak components – (1) Theodore and (2) Bernard, Rob, Lillian, and Marshall. Bernard, Rob, Lillian, and Marshall do not constitute a strong component because if you follow the directions of the arrows, you cannot "walk" from Rob, Lillian, or Marshall to Bernard. They do, however, constitute a weak component because anyone can walk to anyone else if the direction of the arrows is ignored. (Theodore, of course, cannot reach any of the other actors and is not part of the weak component.) In short, then, strong connectedness is more restrictive than weak connectedness. Thus, although each strongly connected network is also weakly connected, a weakly connected network is not necessarily strongly connected. Figure 6.1 also illustrates that weak components within a given network are (by definition) isolated from one another (unless, of course, there is only one), which suggests that attempting to identify components in a well-connected and undirected network may not prove to be a good use of one's time. Instead, a quick glance at a network map will do the trick. However, as we will see in the next chapter, when faced with a disconnected network, one approach to estimating closeness centrality is to first extract a network's main component (i.e., its largest weak component), calculate closeness centrality for actors included in the main component, and then assign scores of 0.00 to all other actors in the network.

Identifying Components in UCINET

We will begin by examining a directed (i.e., asymmetric), dichotomous network (Drugnet.##h) that comes with UCINET and is from a study of the needle-sharing habits of 293 drug users that were recruited through street outreach and a personal drug-user network referral in Hartford, Connecticut (Weeks et al. 2002). To detect components in UCINET we use the *Network>Regions>Components>Simple graphs* command, which brings up a dialog box (Figure 6.2). Because the drug-user network is directed, under the *Kind of components* drop-down menu, we have selected the "Strong" option and changed the name of three of the

[UCINET]
Network
 >Regions
 >Components
 >Simple graphs

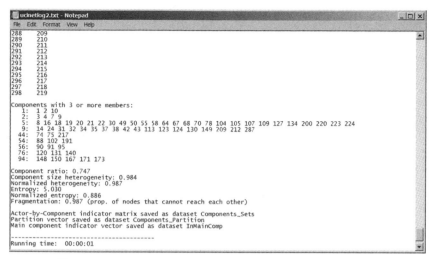

Figure 6.3. UCINET (Strong) Components Output Log

output files. Otherwise, UCINET's defaults have been accepted, including the option to only detect components of size 3 or greater because components of less than three actors are relatively uninteresting. Note that the dialog box indicates that UCINET produces four different output files,[3] two of which will concern us here: (1) the partition matrix and (2) the main component vector. The "partition matrix" indicates the component of which each actor is a part (if at all – remember we accepted UCINET's default of setting the minimum component size to 3). We will use this file for visualization purposes in NetDraw. The main component vector is another partition that we can use to identify which actors belong to the largest (i.e., main) component, which we can use for visualization purposes as well.

Clicking "OK" yields an output log that first lists the various components and their sizes (including components with sizes less than the minimum size indicated in the dialog box). It then lists the components to which each of the actors (i.e., nodes) belongs (again including components with sizes less than the indicated minimum size). Finally, it lists the components that are the minimum size (in this case three) or larger. This portion of the output log is shown in Figure 6.3. Note that the output indicates that there are nine strong components of size three or greater, with the largest having twenty-seven members (#5) and the second largest having eighteen members (#9). Notice that the output also includes a measure of fragmentation, which, as you will recall, we discussed in Chapter 5.

---

[3] Interestingly, the output log indicates that the output only includes three files. It does not appear that UCINET currently outputs the fourth file indicated by the dialog box.

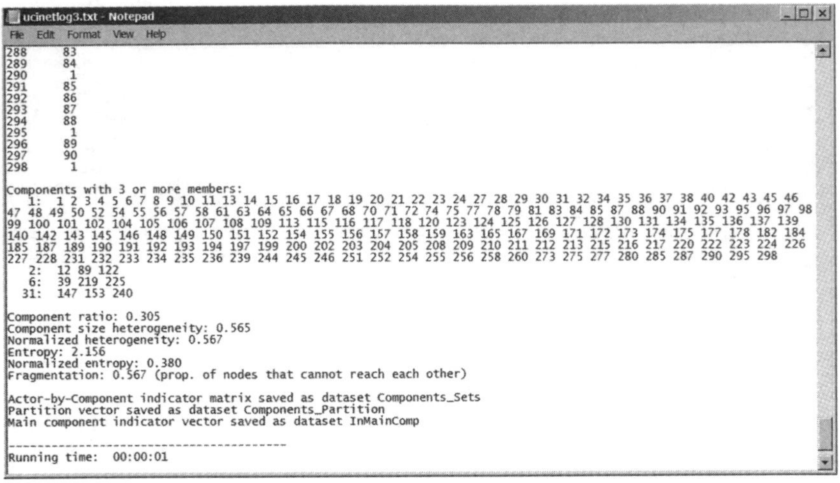

```
ucinetlog3.txt - Notepad
File Edit Format View Help
288      83
289      84
290       1
291      85
292      86
293      87
294      88
295       1
296      89
297      90
298       1

Components with 3 or more members:
   1:  1 2 3 4 5 6 7 8 9 10 11 13 14 15 16 17 18 19 20 21 22 23 24 27 28 29 30 31 32 34 35 36 37 38 40 42 43 45 46
47 48 49 50 52 54 55 56 57 58 61 63 64 65 66 67 68 70 71 72 74 75 77 78 79 81 83 84 85 87 88 90 91 92 93 95 96 97 98
99 100 101 102 104 105 106 107 108 109 113 115 116 117 118 120 123 124 125 126 127 128 130 131 134 135 136 137 139
140 142 143 145 146 148 149 150 151 152 154 155 156 157 158 159 163 165 167 169 171 172 173 174 175 177 178 182 184
185 187 189 190 191 192 193 194 197 199 200 202 203 204 205 208 209 210 211 212 213 215 216 217 220 222 223 224 226
227 228 231 232 233 234 235 236 239 244 245 246 251 252 254 255 256 258 260 273 275 277 280 285 287 290 295 298
   2:  12 89 122
   6:  39 219 225
  31:  147 153 240

Component ratio: 0.305
Component size heterogeneity: 0.565
Normalized heterogeneity: 0.567
Entropy: 2.156
Normalized entropy: 0.380
Fragmentation: 0.567 (prop. of nodes that cannot reach each other)

Actor-by-Component indicator matrix saved as dataset Components_Sets
Partition vector saved as dataset Components_Partition
Main component indicator vector saved as dataset InMainComp

------------------------------------
Running time:  00:00:01
```

Figure 6.4. UCINET (Weak) Components Output Log

What happens if we treat the network as an undirected network by indicating that we want weak components rather than strong? Figure 6.4 displays the answer. When the direction of the network is ignored, UCINET detects only four components of size 3 or more. Note also that the fragmentation score is much lower. That is because the direction of the ties is not taken into account when the score is being calculated, so more pairs of actors can reach one another when they do not have to pay attention to the direction of the arrows.

Network >Regions >Components >Simple graphs

These two examples help illustrate the fact that the components routine is much better at identifying subgroups when it works with directed rather than undirected data. You can see this for yourself with the Noordin data. Try the *Network>Regions>Components>Simple graphs* command with the `Combined Network (Dichotomized).##h` Noordin data file. You will discover that there is only one component of size 3 or greater, regardless of whether you use the "Strong" or "Weak" option. This illustrates the value of collecting directed data whenever possible (e.g., e-mail and phone communication, the flow of financial and other types of resources).

Visualizing Components in NetDraw

[NetDraw] File>Open >Ucinet dataset >Network

Now let us see how NetDraw can help us visualize components. In NetDraw first open the `Drugnet.##h` network file using NetDraw's *File>Open>Ucinet dataset>Network* command. Next, open the `Drugnet Strong Components_Partition.##h, Drugnet Strong InMainComp.##h, Drugnet Weak Components Partition.`

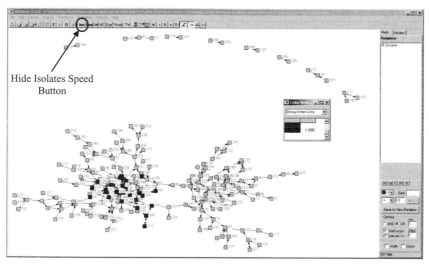

Hide Isolates Speed
Button

Figure 6.5. NetDraw Visualization of the Drug-User Network's Main
Component

##h, and Drugnet Weak InMainComp.##h files using NetDraw's *File>Open* *File>Open>Ucinet dataset>Attribute data* command. Finally, use the *Properties>Nodes>Symbols>Color>Attribute-based* command so that NetDraw assigns each actor a different color based on the component to which it belongs (i.e., choose the "Strong Components" attribute). This should yield a very colorful picture (not shown) that may not be all that helpful. You can improve the picture somewhat by hiding the isolates by clicking on the "Hide isolates" speed button (see Figure 6.5). Note that the strong components partition generated by UCINET includes more than the nine components of size 3 or greater. It includes all of the components identified by UCINET. Thus, it is hard to visually distinguish the nine largest components in the network. We can, however, identify the largest (i.e., the main) component quite easily by assigning colors to actors using the "Strong InMain Component" attribute (after issuing the *Properties>Nodes>Symbols>Color>Attribute-based* command). This will yield a picture similar to Figure 6.5 where the black-colored actors belong to the main component.

Next, assign colors to the nodes using the "Weak Components" attribute. It should yield a network map similar (here, we have converted the colors to gray scale) to Figure 6.6, where the lower portion of the network is the same color because it is a single (weak) component. Every actor can "travel" to every other actor as long as the direction of the ties is ignored. If you were to select the "Weak InMain Component" attribute, you should not be surprised to discover that this is also the main component when tie direction is ignored. Note that the network's

File>Open
>Ucinet dataset
>Attribute data

Properties>Nodes
>Symbols>Color
>Attribute-based

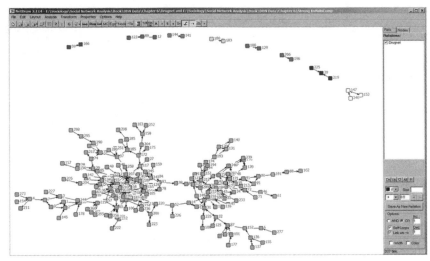

Figure 6.6. NetDraw Visualization of the Drug-User Network's Weak Components

other (and smaller) weak components are assigned their own colors as well.

Analysis > Components

Finally, NetDraw can identify weak components with its *Analysis> Components* command and will produce a network map similar to Figure 6.6. It is helpful to remember, though, that if you are working with directed data and want to identify strong components, then you need to do this in UCINET (or Pajek or ORA) and not NetDraw.

Identifying Components in Pajek

[Pajek's] File > Pajek Project File > Read

Net>Components >Strong, Strong-Periodic, Weak, Bi-Components

Read the Hartford drug network project file (Drugnet.paj) into Pajek. Under Pajek's *Net>Components* submenu, you will discover that Pajek includes functions for identifying four types of components: strong, strong-periodic, weak, and bi-components. In this chapter, we will only consider strong and weak components; however, in Chapter 8, in conjunction with examining how to identify brokers and bridges, we will explore bi-components. When you execute the *Strong* or *Weak* command, a dialog box appears that asks for the minimum size of components. As we noted previously, small components are generally uninteresting, so you typically will want to increase the minimum size to three or higher to eliminate isolated actors, which are counted as separate components, and dyads (components of size 2).

The command creates a partition in which each class of actors represents a component (actors that do not belong to a component are assigned to class "0"). You can examine the new partition using the "Edit

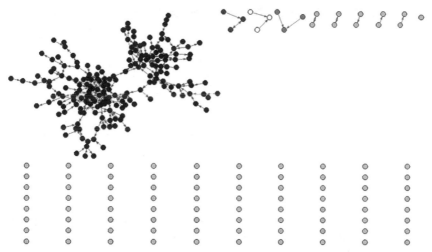

Figure 6.7. Pajek Visualization of the Drug-User Network's Weak Components

Partition" button (located just to the left of the Partition drop-down menu) or the *File>Partition>Edit* command. If you draw the network and partition using the *Draw>Draw-Partition* command, make sure the network and strong components partition are highlighted in the first Network and Partition drop-down menus, respectively. The *Draw>Draw-Partition* command was used to generate Figure 6.7, which is a network map of the drug-user network's weak components. Node color was selected with Pajek's *Options>Colors>Partition Colors>For Vertices* command and then choosing the "Default GreyScale 1" option. The size of the nodes was changed from the default size 4 to 7 using the *Options>Size>of Vertices* command. The components were separated from one another using the *Layout>Energy>Kamada-Kawai>Separate Components* command (you can also use Ctrl-K), which is very useful drawing option in this respect. Finally, the labels were hidden using the *Options>Mark Vertices Using>No Labels* command (you can also use Ctrl-D; Ctrl-L turns the labels back on).

Say you were interested in examining only those users who were a member of the largest weak component. First, with the weak component partition highlighted in the first Partition drop-down menu, use Pajek's *Info>Partition* command (accepting Pajek's defaults), which generates a report similar to the one displayed in Figure 6.8, where you can see that the largest weak component contains 193 actors and has been assigned to class "1" (91 actors have been assigned to class "0," which includes all actors who were members of components of size 2 or smaller). Next, with the drug-user network and weak components partition highlighted

*File>Partition
>Edit*

*Draw>Draw-
Partition*

*[Draw Screen]
Options>Colors
>Partition
Colors
>For Vertices*

*Options>Size
>of Vertices*

*Layout>Energy
>Kamada-
Kawai>Separate
Components*

*Options
>Mark Vertices
Using
>No Labels*

Info>Partition

Report

File

Frequency distribution of cluster values:

Cluster	Freq	Freq%	CumFreq	CumFreq%	Representative
0	91	31.0580	91	31.0580	25
1	193	65.8703	284	96.9283	1
2	3	1.0239	287	97.9522	12
3	3	1.0239	290	98.9761	39
4	3	1.0239	293	100.0000	147
Sum	293	100.0000			

Figure 6.8. Pajek Report of Partition Information

Operations >Extract from Network >Partition

Draw>Draw

in their respective drop-down menus, use the *Operations>Extract from Network>Partition* command. Tell Pajek to extract all actors in class one by typing "1" in the resulting dialog box. Click "OK" and Pajek will generate a new network and partition of size 193. You can then use the *Draw>Draw* command to visualize the largest weak component (not shown).

Net >Components >Strong, Weak

Draw>Draw-Partition

Noordin's Network. As we discussed in Chapter 2, one approach to disrupting dark networks involves the use of deception tactics (i.e., PsyOps) that attempt to set network members and/or subgroups against each other. Because trust is such an important resource for dark networks (Carrington 2011; van der Huist 2011), undermining that trust might prove to be an effective strategy. With this in mind, let's examine Noordin's aggregated trust network, which is included in the dichotomized Noordin project file (`Noordin's Network (Dichotomized Edges).paj`). Because it is so well connected, all of the actors, save nine isolates, belong to the same large component. You can see this for yourself by first issuing Pajek's *Net>Components>Strong* or *Weak* command (it does not matter, as the network is undirected), using three as the cutoff size for the smallest component, and then visualizing it with the resulting partition using the *Draw>Draw-Partition* command (Figure 6.9).

Operations >Extract from Network >Partition

This suggests that we may want to drill down and examine a smaller aspect of the network. For example, we might be able to identify meaningful components focusing on Noordin's alive trust network. To do this, we can use the "Current Status (ICG Article)" attribute to extract those network members who were alive (either free or in jail) at the time that the ICG article was published. First, make sure that Noordin's trust network is highlighted in the first or top Network drop-down menu and the current status partition is highlighted in the first or top Partition drop-down menu. Next, extract the alive network using Pajek's *Operations>Extract from Network>Partition* command. Be sure to select clusters (i.e., class) "1–2," because "0" = dead,

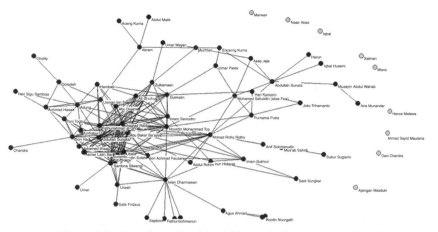

Figure 6.9. Noordin's Combined Network Components (Pajek)

"1" = alive, and "2" = alive but in jail (see Appendix 1). Next, use Pajek's *Net>Components>Strong* or *Weak* command (again using three as the cutoff value) and Pajek will create a new partition. Then visualize the alive network with the new component partition using Pajek's *Draw>Draw-Partition* command. It should look similar to Figure 6.10. Here again, component analysis is not much help. We could continue to drill down to the alive and free trust network, but at that level the network contains very few ties, which makes it difficult to exploit. This is a good example of how social network routines for identifying cohesive subgroups are not always successful, which is why we often have to employ a number of algorithms in our analyses. For now, save your work as a project file, and we will return to it when examining cores.

Net>Components >Weak

Draw>Draw-Partition

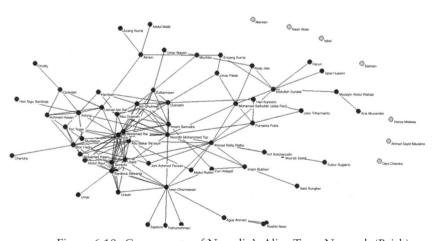

Figure 6.10. Components of Noordin's Alive Trust Network (Pajek)

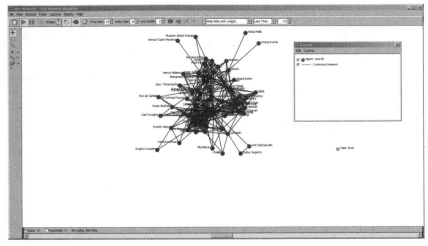

Figure 6.11. Components of Noordin's Alive Combined Network (ORA)

Identifying Components in ORA

There are two ways in ORA to identify components. One is by using ORA's "Local Groups" report that is accessible from ORA's main screen. The other is through the components command found in ORA's visualizer. Because the local groups report not only identifies components but also Newman groups, cliques, and an array of other cluster types, we will postpone our examination of the local groups report until the final section in this chapter. For now, we will examine how to identify components in the ORA visualizer.

[ORA-Main Screen] File>Open Meta-Network

To begin, open the alive Noordin meta-network (Alive Network.xml) using ORA's *File>Open Meta-Network* command. Click on the visualize button in the Information/Editor panel. This will open up ORA's visualizer screen. In the Legend box, deselect the combined network ties because these simply repeat the other four types of ties. Next,

Display> Node Color>Color Nodes by Component

select the *Display>Node Color>Color Nodes by Component* command, and you should get a network map similar to Figure 6.11 (Note: Grayscale coloring was obtained using the *Display>Grayscale* option). Once again, we see that in this case using the components algorithm is relatively unhelpful in detecting subgroups in the Noordin network.

Display> Grayscale

Table 6.1 summarizes component analysis of each of the four networks plus the combined network in terms of all seventy-nine actors in the dataset, those who are alive (sixty-nine actors), those who are incarcerated (forty-five actors), and those who are alive and free (twenty-four actors). It lists the number of components, the range in size of each component (note that the table includes components of size two), as well as the

Table 6.1. *Components of Noordin's alive network*

Relation	Number of components[4]	Smallest	Largest	Isolates
Trust Network				
Whole (79)	1	70	70	9
Alive (69)	1	62	62	7
Incarcerated (45)	1	37	37	8
Alive and Free (24)	3	2	10	10
Operational Network				
Whole (79)	1	68	68	11
Alive (69)	1	61	61	8
Incarcerated (45)	2	12	29	4
Alive and Free (24)	1	16	16	8
Communications				
Whole (79)	1	74	74	5
Alive (69)	1	63	63	6
Incarcerated (45)	1	33	33	12
Alive and Free (24)	1	14	14	10
Business & Finance				
Whole (79)	4	5	2	64
Alive (69)	4	2	5	57
Incarcerated (45)	3	2	3	36
Alive and Free (24)	0	0	0	24
Combined Network				
Whole (79)	1	78	78	5
Alive (69)	1	68	68	1
Incarcerated (45)	1	44	44	1
Alive and Free (24)	1	19	19	5

number of isolates. In general, component analysis does not do a very good job at identifying distinct subgroups in the various networks. In virtually every case, only one or two components are present, and they are generally visible to the naked eye. That is, they are detectable simply by looking at a network map. The one exception appears to be the business and finance network. This is misleading, however, because the size of each of the components is quite small (2 to 5), which reflects the fact that the network is relatively sparse and disconnected (note how many isolates there are in the network). Thus, in this case, component analysis is relatively unhelpful. Nevertheless, if you were interested in drilling down to (i.e., extracting) a particular subsection of the network (e.g., the largest/main component of the incarcerated portion of the operational network), then component analysis could be a useful first step. Moreover, as we have noted in this chapter and will see in the Chapter 7, extracting the main component is one approach to estimating closeness centrality

---

[4] The number of components does not include isolates but does include components of size 2 or greater.

when working with a disconnected graph. It is now time to turn our attention to the analysis of cores.

6.3   Cores

As we saw in the previous chapter, degree centrality counts the number of ties of each individual actor and can serve as an alternative measure for the network. We can also use it to identify clusters of actors that are tightly connected through what is known as the k-core approach. Formally, a k-core is a maximal[5] group of actors, all of whom are connected to some number (k) of other group members (de Nooy et al. 2005:70; Hanneman and Riddle 2005, 2011:352; Wasserman and Faust 1994:266–267). In other words, all actors in a 2-core have two or more ties to other actors in the 2-core, all actors in a 3-core have three or more ties to other actors in the 3-core, and so on. This means that higher k-cores are nested within lower k-cores. Actors in a 4-core are also members of a 3-core, actors in a 3-core are also members of a 2-core, and so on. The reverse is not necessarily true, however. Not all actors in a 2-core are members of a 3-core, and not all members of a 3-core are members of a 4-core. In fact, one way that we use k-core analysis to detect cohesive subgroups is by removing the lowest k-cores (or extracting the highest k-cores) until the network begins to fragment. That said, because higher k-cores are nested in lower ones, we generally do not want to use k-core analysis to identify actors who are in a position of brokerage between the two groups. Faction analysis (Section 6.3) and Newman's community-detection algorithms (Section 6.4) are better suited for that purpose.

It is important to note that the highest k-core in a network does not necessarily correspond to the highest centrality score obtained by an actor in the network. A simple example illustrates this. Take a network in which one actor has a degree centrality of ten but no one else has a degree centrality higher than four. The highest k-core will not be a 10-core because every actor in a 10-core would need to be tied to ten other actors, and in this example that is not the case.

Another characteristic about k-core analysis is that, although it can identify relatively dense subnetworks, a particular k-core is not necessarily a cohesive subgroup in and of itself (de Nooy et al. 2005:71). This is illustrated in Figure 6.12 (created in NetDraw) where the 3-core (black nodes) is composed of two distinct groups, and the 1-core (white nodes) is composed of several different subgroups. Only the 2-core (gray nodes)

---

[5]   The term *maximal* means that no other actor can be added to the cluster without destroying its defining characteristic, which in this case is the minimum number of ties that each actor must have in order to belong to a particular k-core.

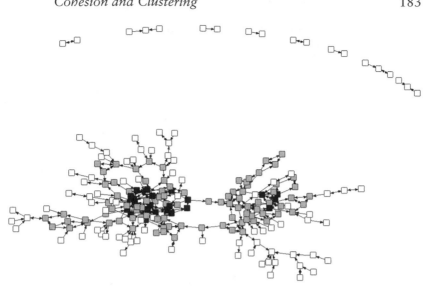

Figure 6.12. *k*-Cores of Drug-User Network (NetDraw)

appears to be connected. This is not necessarily a limitation of *k*-core analysis, however. For example, if we were to extract the 3-core (i.e., remove the 1- and 2-cores), we would be left with two distinct groups, one of size 4 and one of size 19, both of which might lend themselves to further analysis.

Because ORA does not currently include a function for identifying cores, this portion of our analysis is limited to UCINET, NetDraw, and Pajek. Also, to keep things manageable, we will not examine *k*-cores for all of the various networks; instead, we will focus our efforts on the "alive" portions of the trust and operational networks.

Identifying Cores in UCINET and NetDraw

In UCINET, *k*-cores are detected using the *K-Cores* command found under the *Network>Regions* submenu, which brings up a dialog box (not shown) that asks you to identify the network you wish to analyze. Unfortunately, UCINET only allows us to change the file name of one of the two output files (in this case the default is K-Cores) but not the file we will later import into NetDraw for visualization, which is automatically assigned the name K-Coreness. In practice what this means is that we cannot give the file a meaningful name, and (more importantly) it makes it easy to overwrite the file when conducting multiple *k*-core analyses.

[UCINET] Network >Regions >K-Cores

Let's use this command to examine Noordin's alive trust network (Alive Trust Network.##h). After selecting OK, UCINET produces an output file similar to the one displayed in Figure 6.13. There are several

Network >Regions >K-Cores

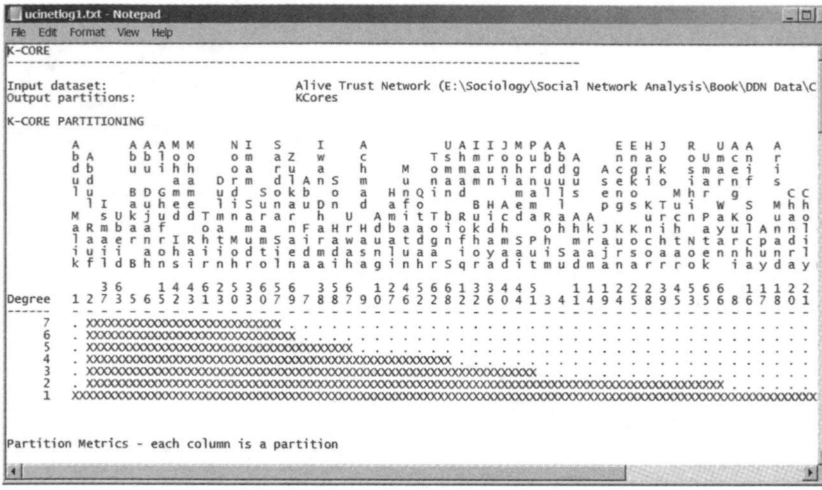

Figure 6.13. UCINET *k*-Core Output File (Noordin's Alive Trust Network)

important things to note about the output. First, if the network is asymmetric, UCINET issues a warning that it has symmetrized the network (i.e., it transformed it from a directed to undirected network) and then for each pair of cells assigned cell values based on the maximum value found in the two cells. That is not the case here, but you should be aware of this feature. Next, UCINET's output includes a *k*-core partitioning dendogram that indicates the *k*-core layers to which each actor belongs. Across the top are the names of the actors and down the side is a legend indicating the various *k*-core layers (under the heading, "Degree"). As you can see in Figure 6.13, the largest *k*-core is a 7-core and the smallest is a 1-core. Most actors belong to the 1-core (indicated by the "x" under their name in the bottom row – those that do not belong have a "." under their name), and as the *k*-core level increases, fewer and fewer actors are members. The dendogram also clearly illustrates how members of higher cores are nested in lower cores. Next, if you scroll down the output file, UCINET provides some metrics (not shown) that indicate the proportion of actors per *k*-core; below this you will find a partition that assigns each actor to the highest *k*-core to which it belongs.

[NetDraw] File >Open>Ucinet dataset>Network

If we open the Noordin's alive trust network (`Alive Trust Network. ##h`) and its related *k*-core partition (`K-Coreness. ##h`) – the latter of which is an attribute (not a network) file – in NetDraw using its *File>Open>Ucinet dataset>Network* and *File>Open>Ucinet dataset>Attribute data* commands, respectively, we can then assign node colors based on the *k*-core partition using NetDraw's *Properties>Nodes>Symbols>Colors>Attribute-based* command. This should

File>Open >Ucinet dataset >Attribute data

Properties >Nodes>Symbols >Colors> Attribute-based

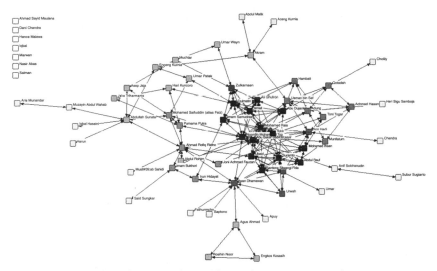

Figure 6.14. *k*-Cores of Noordin's Alive Trust Network (NetDraw)

result in a network map similar to the one shown in Figure 6.14, where the higher the *k*-core layer, the darker the node color. Although with the grayscale coloring it is somewhat hard to distinguish between the cores, what the analysis shows is that there is a well-connected central subgroup (7-core) surrounded by four slightly less connected subgroups (2-core through 5-core – the 6-core consists of one person, who has ties with most of the members of the 7-core).

What might this tell us in terms of strategy? Well, a rehabilitation and reintegration strategy (e.g., a counter-ideology program) would probably not succeed if it targeted 6- and 7-core members because central and well-connected actors are less likely to defect than are peripheral and poorly connected actors (Stark and Bainbridge 1980). Instead, if that is the strategy analysts have chosen to pursue, then they should probably concentrate their efforts on members of the *k*-cores surrounding the 6- and 7-cores. Better yet, because this network includes actors who are both free and in jail, a rehabilitation program that focused on incarcerated actors lying on the network's periphery might be the most cost-effective approach (Mydans 2008). It will be interesting to see if the alive operational network displays similar dynamics. We will examine the *k*-cores of that network using Pajek.[6]

---

[6] Keep in mind the caveat raised in Chapter 2 concerning rehabilitation programs that seek to reprogram or redirect actors' extremist ideologies: The probability that the reprogramming will "take" in the long run will be increased if the former detainees are prevented from returning to the extremist networks of which they used to be a part, and are instead embedded in networks that support their new ideological orientation (Johnson 2011).

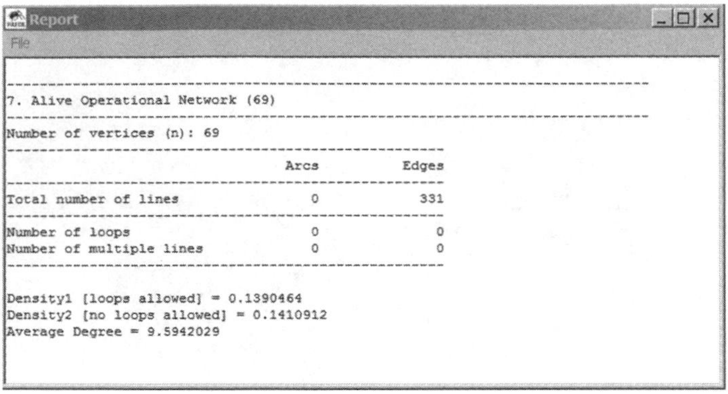

Figure 6.15. Pajek Report of General Network Information

Identifying Cores in Pajek

File>Pajak Project File>Read

Noordin's alive operational network is included in the Noordin network project file (`Noordin's Network (Dichotomized Edges).paj`), so the first step is to read this project file into Pajek. After ensuring that the alive operational network is listed in the first Network drop-down menu, we need to check to see whether the network is directed or

Info>Network >General

undirected using the *Info>Network>General* command. This provides a brief output (see Figure 6.15) that indicates the number of vertices (actors), lines, loops, and multiple lines in the network. It also indicates whether the lines are arcs, edges, or a combination of both. As the report indicates, all of the lines in the network consist of edges, which means that it is a symmetric (i.e., undirected) network. If the network included arcs, we would want to convert them to edges using its *Net>Transform>Arc*

Net>Transform >Arc →
Edges>All

→ *Edges>All* command because we generally do not take into account tie direction when identifying *k*-cores.

In Pajek, *k*-cores are detected with the *Core* command found in the

Net>Partitions >Cores

Net>Partitions submenu. The *Input, Output,* and *All* commands distinguish between input cores (based on the number of lines pointing to an actor), output cores (based on the number of lines pointing away from an actor), and cores that ignore the direction of lines. Most of the time we will want to use the *All* command and only to apply it to simple undirected networks. The command creates an "All core partition" that assigns each

Info>Partition

actor to the highest *k*-core in which it appears. Use the *Info>Partition* command to call up a report on the partition (not shown). The report indicates that largest *k*-core is a 14-core that includes fifteen members (if you think about this, this means that every member of the 14-core is connected to every other member of the core).

Draw>Draw-Partition

If you visualize the network with the *k*-core partition using the *Draw>Draw-Partition* command, you should get a drawing similar to

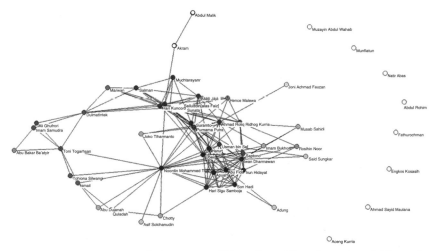

Figure 6.16. Pajek Drawing of Noordin's Alive Operational Network *k*-Cores

the one in Figure 6.16. As the figure illustrates, the alive operational network is structured very differently than the alive trust network. Whereas the *k*-core analysis of the latter found a well-connected core at the center of the network, this analysis detects a series of clusters that appear to center around a single individual: Noordin Mohammed Top. This is perhaps not terribly surprising as it is, after all, Top's network, but it does suggest that the network could be vulnerable to Top's removal or isolation. Of course, the 14-core, of which Noordin is a part, would be unreceptive to most, if not all, rehabilitation and reintegration programs, just like the 7-core of the alive trust network. What analysts could consider is exploring which individuals are on the periphery of both the alive trust and operational networks, and of those, which ones are in jail.

What is clear is that, at least with regards to Noordin's networks, a *k*-core analysis has proved to be more fruitful than the components analysis. That will not always be the case, of course, which again points to the need for analysts to explore networks in a variety of ways in their attempts to get a handle on their underlying structure. Now let us turn to a somewhat different approach to identifying subgroups: faction analysis.

6.4 Factions

Recall that when we looked for components we imagined a "world" where each actor is connected to all other actors in their own subnetwork but have no connections with actors in other subnetworks. What we discovered was that the real-world social networks seldom divide

Figure 6.17. A Perfectly Factionalized Network (NetDraw)

themselves as neatly as this. Nevertheless, imagining such a world serves as a useful benchmark for gauging the extent to which a network is "factionalized." That is the approach of faction analysis: It compares an actual network with an idealized one, and then assesses the extent to which the actual network "fits" the idealized one. It is perhaps easiest to illustrate this approach with a couple of simple examples. The above network (Figure 6.17) represents a completely factionalized network. All ties between actors are within their respective subgroups, and there are no ties between actors in different subgroups.

Factional analysis of this network in UCINET yields the output presented in Figure 6.18, of which there are several things worth noting. First, it provides a "badness of fit" score where a lower score is better than a higher score. In this case the score is "0," which means that it is a perfect fit: No ties are absent that should be present, and no ties are present that should be absent. Each time a tie is absent or present when it should not be, it is counted as an error, and the badness-of-fit score is simply a count of such errors. The next measure, "final proportion correct," is a different way of expressing the same thing. Here, the higher the score the better. A grouped adjacency matrix is presented next. Grouped adjacency matrices rearrange the rows and columns so that members of each group are next to one another, and a dashed line indicates the border between the groups. As you can see in this perfectly factionalized network, all possible ties are present within the blocks (i.e., groups) along the diagonal and no ties are present in the off-diagonal blocks. The density table at the bottom of the output is another way of assessing how well the actual network compares to the idealized one. Here, you can see that the density of each block along the diagonal is 100 percent, whereas the density of

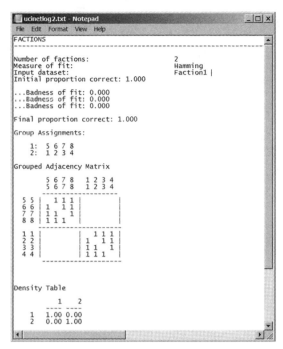

Figure 6.18. UCINET Factional Analysis Output

the off-diagonal blocks is 0 percent, which is what we would expect with a perfectly factionalized network.

Now consider the network in Figure 6.19 where two distinct groups clearly exist but one tie is present between the groups and one tie is absent within each of the two groups.

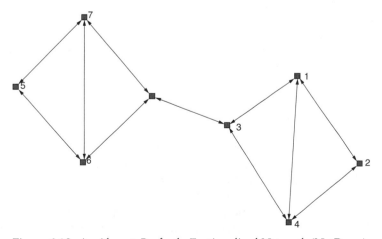

Figure 6.19. An Almost–Perfectly Factionalized Network (NetDraw)

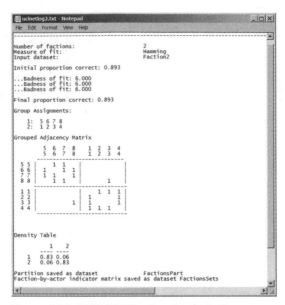

Figure 6.20. UCINET Faction Analysis Output

The analysis (Figure 6.20) paints a slightly different picture. The badness-of-fit score is 6 because two ties between actors of different groups are present (i.e., the tie between 3 and 8 is counted twice – see the grouped adjacency matrix in the output) and four ties that should be present within the groups are not (ties between 5 and 8, and 3 and 2 – again counted twice). The presence of these errors lowers the proportion correct to 89.3 percent (50/56) and is illustrated in the grouped adjacency matrix. A quick glance at the density table also tells us that the network is not perfectly factionalized. The density of the blocks along the diagonal is less than 100 percent (.83), whereas the density of the off-diagonal blocks is greater than 0 percent (.06).

How is factional analysis used to detect subgroups? Generally, we use it in an exploratory way, examining the results from several runs where we allow the number of factions to vary in order to see what number yields the best fit (i.e., badness of fit, proportion correct, etc.). Both UCINET and NetDraw implement "faction" algorithms that find the optimal arrangement of actors and measure how well the data actually fit the ideal type. At the time of this writing, ORA does not include one in its toolbox. Pajek does, but we do not cover it here because it is part of its blockmodeling routines, as factions are a special type of block model (Wasserman and Faust 1994:422–423). We will briefly examine Pajek's approach in Chapter 9, however.

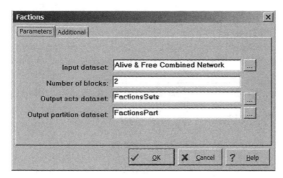

Figure 6.21. UCINET Faction Dialog Box

Identifying Factions in UCINET and NetDraw

To illustrate factional analysis in UCINET and NetDraw, we will use the combined Noordin alive and free network (`Alive & Free Combined Network.##h`) because faction analysis is easier to illustrate with smaller networks. Also, experience has found that faction analysis appears to work better with smaller networks. We use UCINET's *Network>Subgroups>Factions* command to identify the ideal number of factions in a network. Because we only want UCINET to count the number of errors and not take into account values in each cell of the network matrix, we will want to dichotomize valued networks with the *Transform>Dichotomize* command before proceeding. This is not necessary here because the network has already been dichotomized, but you will want to keep this in mind in the future. If the network contains isolates, which is the case here, we will want to remove them with the *Data>Remove>Remove Isolates* command before running the faction algorithm because UCINET has trouble dealing with isolates. By contrast, NetDraw groups all isolates into a single "faction," and then computes its measures of fit basically ignoring the isolates.

Network
>Subgroups
>Factions

Transform
>Dichotomize

Data>Remove
>Remove
Isolates

When we issue the *Factions* command in UCINET, it brings up a dialog box similar to the one displayed in Figure 6.21. Note that in addition to asking for the input file, UCINET also asks us to indicate how many "blocks" (i.e., groups) we wish to identify. Here we may be guided by an a priori hunch as to how many subgroups exist (e.g., based on prior analysis), or we may simply engage in an exploratory analysis of the network, varying the number of subgroups and looking for a result that produces the best fit.

Under the Additional tab you will find three "measure-of-fit" options: Hamming, Phi, and Modularity. *Hamming* is the conventional measure of fit and the one illustrated previously in Figures 6.18 and 6.20. *Phi* measures the correlation between the actual data matrix and an idealized one where the density of the diagonal blocks is 100 percent and the density

Table 6.2. *Faction analysis of Noordin's alive and free combined network (fit)*

Number of factions	Hamming (proportion correct)	Phi (final correlation)	Modularity (final modularity)
2	0.690	0.411	0.285
3	0.807	0.528	0.319
4	0.842	0.585	0.312
5	0.860	0.602	0.300
6	0.871	0.629	0.284
7	0.877	0.648	0.265
8	0.883	0.669	0.240
9	0.883	0.673	0.219
10	0.883	0.656	0.207
11	0.865	0.620	0.171

of the off-diagonal is 0 percent. *Modularity* is a measure developed by Mark Newman (2006) that compares the ties within and across blocks to what one would expect in a random graph of the same size and having the same number of ties. Formally, it is the fraction of internal ties in each block less the expected fraction, if they were distributed at random but with the same frequency of ties. It is the same measure used to evaluate the fit of Newman groups. All three "measure-of-fit" options produce a similar output, the only difference being the measure of fit that appears at the top of the output.

The results of an analysis of the combined alive network appear in Table 6.2. As you can see, the three measures of fit provide different answers as to what is the optimal number of blocks. According to the conventional Hamming measure, the optimal number of blocks is 8 through 10. Generally, we prefer fewer groups over more, so if we relied solely on this measure, we would probably choose 8 blocks as the optimal number. However, given that the Phi measure identifies 9 blocks as optimal, we may want to consider the latter. When we turn to Newman's modularity score, however, we are presented with a completely different picture. It identifies 3 (possibly 4) blocks as the ideal number.

What should we choose? This is an example of where we should combine metric analysis with visualization. In other words, what number of blocks looks visually correct? While it is impractical to display all ten different options here, Figure 6.22 visually compares what the network looks like broken down into three blocks (i.e., factions, groups) with what it looks like broken down into four. Higher numbers of blocks were also visualized, but the clustering deteriorated as the number of blocks climbed higher than five, suggesting that Newman's modularity score may be the best measure of fit for faction analysis. The difference between the

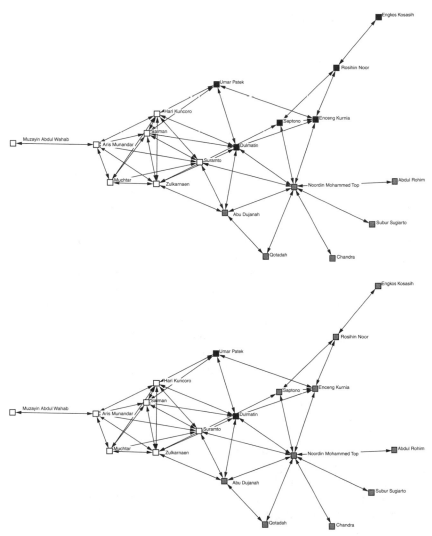

Figure 6.22. Three-Block (top) and Four-Block (bottom) Faction Analyses: Noordin Alive and Free Combined Network (NetDraw)

three-block and four-block network maps is minimal. In the four-block analysis, Dulmatin and Umar Patek are separated from Saptono, Enceng Kurnia, Rosihin Noor, and Engkos Kosasih, whereas in the three-block analysis they are all grouped together. Although one could probably make a good argument for either blocking scheme, at this point the three-block scheme appears to provide a better fit. As always, of course, we would want to check such a conclusion with other forms of intelligence.

Figure 6.23. NetDraw Factions Dialog Box

[NetDraw]
File>Open
>Ucinet
dataset
>Network

Analysis
>Subgroups
>Factions

At this point it is probably best to see whether NetDraw yields similar or completely different results. Open the network (`Alive & Free Combined Network.##h`) with NetDraw's *File>Open>Ucinet dataset>Network* command. To conduct faction analysis in NetDraw, we use its *Analysis>Subgroups>Factions* command, which calls up a dialog box similar to Figure 6.23. Note that you are prompted to indicate the number of groups or blocks you desire to break the network down into, as well as two options for estimating the degree of fit: "Speed" and "Quality." In this case I have chosen the former (although the latter identifies a similar number of ideal blocks) and have estimated measures of fit for a two (44.00), three (32.00), four (30.00), and five (32.00) blocks. Here you can see that NetDraw identifies four factions as the ideal number of groups although the difference between its score and the three and five block scores does not differ substantially. A nice feature of NetDraw is that each time you use it to identify factions it automatically colors the nodes according to their block membership, which facilitates the visual comparison of different blocking schemes. Once again, we are caught between choosing three or four as the ideal number of blocks. The question appears to be whether we should treat Dulmatin and Umar Patek as a separate group or lump them together with Saptono, Enceng Kurnia, Rosihin Noor, and Engkos Kosasih. Let us turn to our next set of clustering algorithms, Newman groups, to see whether it helps us resolve this dilemma.

6.5   Newman Groups

Perhaps the greatest advance in recent years for detecting subgroups are the community-detecting algorithms developed by Mark Newman and his colleagues (Clauset, Newman, and Moore 2004; Girvan and Newman 2002; Newman 2006). Newman's approach is similar to faction analysis in that subgroups are defined as having more ties within and fewer ties between groups than would be expected in a random graph of the same size with the same number of ties. He has developed several algorithms, two of which have found their way into ORA and one (which is one of the two implemented in ORA) that has been implemented in UCINET/NetDraw. Pajek has yet to include any Newman group algorithms, so here we only explore how they are implemented in NetDraw and ORA.

Girvan-Newman (2002) is probably the best-known and most widely implemented Newman group algorithm and is found in UCINET, NetDraw, and ORA. It begins with a connected network and then strategically removes ties, a process that partitions the network into an increasing number of clusters. Each time a new cluster forms (i.e., breaks apart from a larger cluster), the algorithm estimates the network's modularity (discussed previously), and the partition with the highest modularity score is generally considered to represent the optimal partitioning of the network.

Key to the Girvan-Newman algorithm is the notion of edge betweenness. Edge betweenness is similar to (node) betweenness centrality, which we introduced in the first chapter and will take up in more depth in the next. The difference is that edge betweenness estimates the betweenness centrality of edges (i.e., ties) in the network, whereas node betweenness estimates the betweenness centrality of nodes (i.e., actors). Like node betweenness, edge betweenness measures the extent to which each edge in a network lies on the shortest path linking all pairs of actors (i.e., geodesic) in the network. Thus, the more geodesics on which an edge lies, the higher its betweenness score. The fewer geodesics, the lower its betweenness score. In fact, if an edge does not lie on any geodesics, then its betweenness score is zero.

In the Girvan-Newman algorithm, edge betweenness is used to determine the order that edges are removed. "Girvan and Newman reasoned that since there should be relatively few edges linking individuals in different groups, those linking edges should display a high degree of betweenness" (Freeman 2011:32). The algorithm begins by calculating edge betweenness for all ties in the network. It then removes the edge (or edges) with the highest edge betweenness score. After they are removed, the edge betweenness of all the ties is recalculated, and the edge (or edges) with the highest score is removed. This process is repeated until no edges remain. Each time the removal of an edge causes the network to break into separate clusters, the algorithm calculates a modularity score, and, as noted previously, the clustering level that yields the highest score is considered to be the ideal partitioning of the group.

The development of the Girvan-Newman algorithm led to a sudden rush among physicists and computer scientists to develop community-detection algorithms (Freeman 2011:32–33) that were more efficient and quicker. One of the criticisms of the original Girvan-Newman algorithm

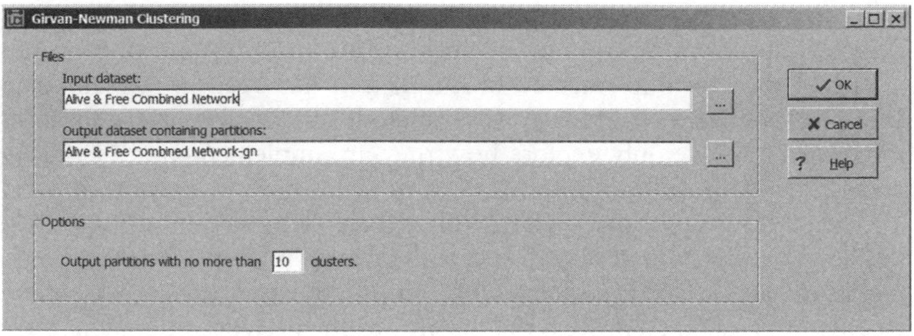

Figure 6.24. UCINET Girvan-Newman Dialog Box

was that it was somewhat slow in detecting communities in networks.[7] Newman (2004) himself agreed, and in response he proposed a "greedy" algorithm that begins by treating each actor as a cluster unto itself, and then "at each stage in the process, the pair of clusters that yields the highest modularity is merged" (Freeman 2011:33). He then teamed with Aaron Clauset and Cristopher Moore to improve its efficiency (Clauset, Newman, and Moore 2004), and it is this algorithm, along with the Girvan-Newman, that is implemented in ORA. Like the initial greedy algorithm, the Clauset, Newman, Moore algorithm begins with each actor being the member of a community of one. It then repeatedly joins together the two communities whose combination produces the largest increase in modularity. It repeats this process until all actors are joined together into a single community. And as with Girvan-Newman, the network partition that yields the highest modularity score is considered to be the optimal partition of the network.

Identifying Newman Groups in UCINET and NetDraw

Although both UCINET and NetDraw include the Girvan-Newman algorithm in their toolboxes, NetDraw's implementation is currently superior to UCINET's because it generates a modularity score and UCINET does not.[8] We begin by briefly considering how to use Girvan-Newman in UCINET before moving to NetDraw.

In UCINET the algorithm is accessed with the *Network>Subgroups> Girvan-Newman* command (still using the Alive & Free Combined Network.##h), which calls up a dialog box similar to Figure 6.24. Like most UCINET dialog boxes, it asks users to indicate the network that is

[UCINET] Network >Subgroups >Girvan-Newman

---

[7] *Slow* is a relative term here. When working with networks of the size we examine in this book, the Girvan-Newman algorithm is able to detect the optimum partition within a matter of seconds.

[8] UCINET does, however, include a "Cluster adequacy" function where you can obtain the modularity score (and four other measures of fit) for any network cluster partition.

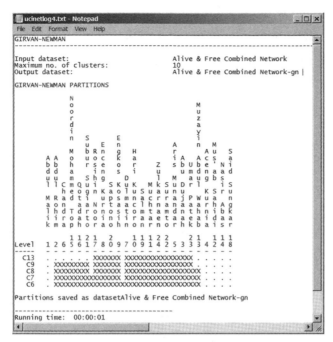

Figure 6.25. UCINET Girvan-Newman Output

to be analyzed, and it "offers" a default name for the output file, which, of course, can be changed. At the bottom of the dialog box, UCINET allows users to choose the maximum number of clusters into which the network will be partitioned.

If we click "OK," UCINET generates an output file (see Figure 6.25) and a partition that we can use to visualize the various clustering levels identified by the algorithm. You can see from the output that UCINET has identified five partitions: one with six clusters (6C), one with seven (7C), one with eight (8C), one with nine (9C), and one with thirteen (13C). But, you might be asking, Didn't we ask UCINET to give us no more than ten clusters? We did, but UCINET treats each isolate as a separate cluster and does not count those clusters as "real" clusters. In other words, the six-cluster partition is really just one cluster (i.e., six clusters less the five isolates), the seven-cluster partition is really two, the eight-cluster, three, and so on.

Although UCINET Girvan-Newman function does not calculate a modularity score for each of the partitions, UCINET's "cluster adequacy" function does. In fact, it provides users with five measures of fit for any combination of network and network partition. This is accessed with the *Tools>Cluster Analysis>Cluster adequacy* command, which calls up a dialog box similar to Figure 6.26.

Tools>Cluster Analysis>Cluster adequacy

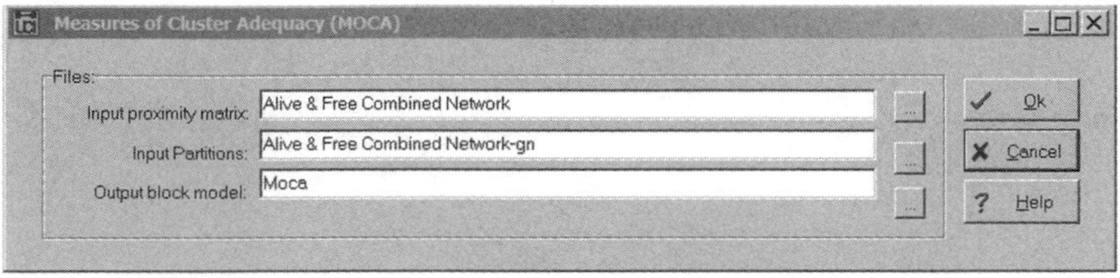

Figure 6.26. UCINET Cluster Adequacy Function

Here, you see that the network has been loaded in the *Proximity Matrix* drop-down menu, and the related Girvan-Newman partition has been loaded as the clustering partition. When we click OK, UCINET generates five measures of fit (i.e., cluster adequacy). We will not discuss all these here but simply point out that the second line ("Q") contains the modularity score.[9] As you can see, the three-cluster (8C) provides the best fit with the two-cluster (7C) not too far behind. As we will see, these measures agree with those we will obtain using NetDraw (Figure 6.27).

To visualize the network and its companion Girvan-Newman partition in NetDraw, we need to read in both Noordin's alive and free combined network (Alive & Free Combined Network) into NetDraw and the corresponding partition (Alive & Free Combined Network-gn) using the *File>Open>Ucinet dataset>Network* and *File>Open>Ucinet dataset>Attribute data* commands, respectively. Then with NetDraw's *Properties>Nodes>Symbols>Color>Attribute-based* command, we can indicate which partitions we want NetDraw to visualize. Figure 6.28 compares the two-cluster (i.e., C7) and three-cluster (i.e., C8) partitions (the isolates are hidden). The only difference is that in the nine individuals that are treated as a single group in the two-cluster (right-hand side of the graph) are divided into two groups in the three-cluster. Comparing these results with those we obtained using faction analysis (Figure 6.22), we can see that the primary difference is that Dulmatin and Umar Patek are no longer treated as a group unto themselves or grouped with Saptono, Enceng Kurnia, Rosihin Noor, and Engkos Kosasih, but instead are grouped with Hari Kuncoro, Suramto, Salman, Zulkarnaen, Muchtar, Aris Munandar, Muzayin Abdul Wahab, and Abu Dujanah. Abu Dujanah is also placed in a different group with this algorithm than with faction analysis. What are we to make of these conflicting results? One thing they suggest is that Dulmatin and Patek may be their own "group" and that together they act as brokers between the other two groups with which they are occasionally tied. Abu Dujanah may also be in a position of brokerage.

[NetDraw] File >Open>Ucinet dataset >Network

File>Open >Ucinet dataset >Attribute data

Properties >Nodes >Symbols >Color >Attribute-based

---

[9]   See UCINET's Help function for a description of the other measures of fit.

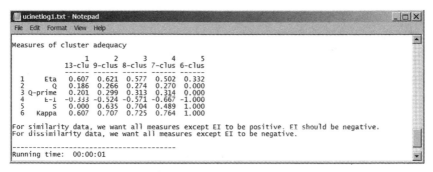

Figure 6.27. UCINET Cluster Adequacy Output

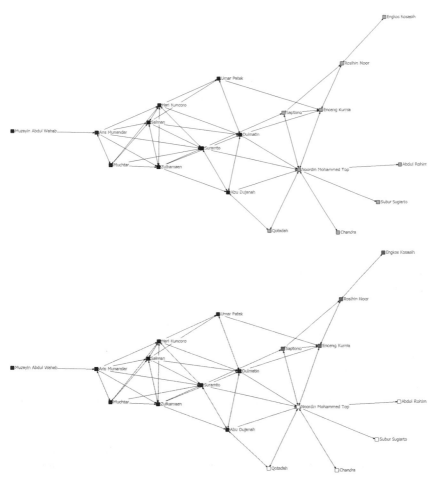

Figure 6.28. Two-Cluster (top) and Three-Cluster (bottom) Girvan-Newman: Alive and Free Combined Network (NetDraw)

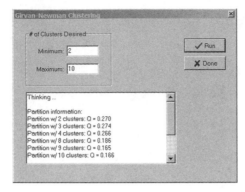

Figure 6.29. NetDraw Girvan-Newman Dialog Box

Analysis >Subgroups

We can detect Newman groups in NetDraw using its *Girvan-Newman* command, which is located under the *Analysis>Subgroups* menu. It calls up a dialog box similar to Figure 6.29. Notice that NetDraw asks you to indicate the minimum and maximum number of clusters you want to identify. The defaults are 2 and 10 (which are used here), but they are easily changed. Clicking on "Run" generates output in the open box below the cluster option boxes. As you can see, NetDraw identifies the number of clusters (not counting isolates) in each partition along with the associated modularity score ("Q"). It also automatically colors the nodes according to partition with fewest groups, but this can be changed with its *Properties>Nodes>Symbols>Color>Attribute-based* command. NetDraw's analysis agrees with UCINET and indicates that the partition with the highest modularity score is the one with three clusters. Let's see if ORA provides a similar answer.

Identifying Newman Groups in ORA

In ORA, users can identify Newman groups from either the main screen or the visualizer. First, we need to open the alive and free meta-network (`Alive and Free Network.xml`) using ORA's *File>Open Meta-Network* command. To detect Newman groups from ORA's main screen, we use the "Locate SubGroups" report, which is accessed through the *Analysis>Generate Reports>Characterize Groups and Networks>Locate SubGroups* command. After highlighting the alive and free meta-network in ORA's Meta-Network panel, issue the command and a dialog box (not shown) will appear. After ensuring that the alive and free network box is selected, click "Next," and another dialog box similar to Figure 6.30 should appear.

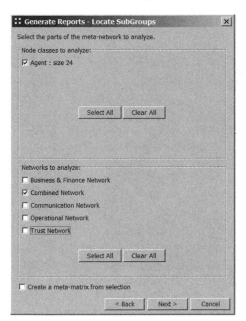

Figure 6.30. ORA Locate Subgroups Dialog Box

Note that all of the networks in the meta-network are listed. If all of them are selected, however, ORA does not detect clusters for each separate network but instead combines them and identifies clusters based on this combination. Thus, we need to identify the specific network we wish to examine. Because we are focusing on the combined alive and free network, we should deselect all of the boxes except this one (see Figure 6.30). Clicking "Next" again brings up the next dialog box in the series (Figure 6.31), and this illustrates what we noted back in Section 6:1; namely, that with its report-based approach to SNA, ORA allows users to access several different clustering algorithms at the same time and have them appear in a single report.

As you can see, ORA implements two different Newman algorithms (the first one listed is the Clauset, Newman, Moore algorithm), components, cliques (which we discussed briefly at the beginning of the chapter), CONCOR (a type of blockmodeling that we will consider in Chapter 9), and five other clustering techniques that we do not consider in this book.[10] We will typically want to select the "Remove isolates before clustering" option at the top of the dialog box. Also, both of the Newman groups clustering algorithms automatically compute the number of groups (i.e., the ideal partition based on modularity), but if you are working with an a priori theory as to what the number of groups should be or you simply

[10] See ORA's Help function for a description of the other clustering algorithms.

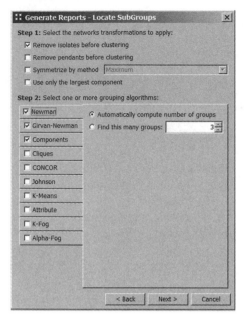

Figure 6.31. ORA Locate Subgroups Dialog Box

want to compare different partitions, you can "force" ORA to detect a particular number of groups. Finally, under the components tab, you can tell ORA to group isolates into a single cluster. Clicking "Next" brings up another dialog box (not shown); accept ORA's defaults (although at some point you may want to explore what these options do), then click "Next" and the final dialog box appears (not shown). Here, tell ORA where (i.e., which folder) you want to save a text file of the report and under what name. Click "Finish" and a report will appear in the main screen's report panel as well as an HTML page in your computer's browser.

Figure 6.32 presents a portion of the text file report generated by ORA. It shows the results of the Girvan-Newman and the Clauset, Newman, Moore (just listed as Newman) algorithms. The results are almost identical except that the algorithms disagree where to place Abu Dujanah. They assign him to different groups. Because the Clauset, Newman, Moore algorithm has a slightly higher modularity score, we would generally be inclined to follow its results. Interestingly, the latter algorithm assigns Dujanah to the same group of individuals that faction analysis did. Nevertheless, the fact that these various algorithms disagree as to where to place Dujanah lends additional support to the possibility that he may be a broker in the network. Let's now turn to see how to detect Newman groups from ORA's visualizer.

After highlighting the combined network in the Meta-Network Manager, click on the "Visualize This Network" button in the Information/ Editor panel. This will call up ORA's visualizer and only highlight

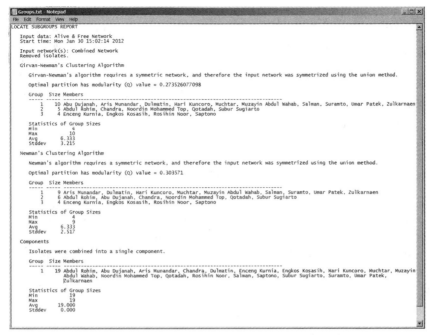

Figure 6.32. ORA Locate Subgroups Report (Text File)

the ties of the combined network. Next, issue the *Display>Node Appearance>Node Color>Color Nodes by Newman Grouping* command. This will color the actors by the Newman group to which they have been assigned as well as provide a modularity score (Figure 6.33). As you may have noticed, the visualizer has only one of the two

[ORA Visualizer] Display>Node Appearance >Node Color >Color Nodes by Newman Grouping

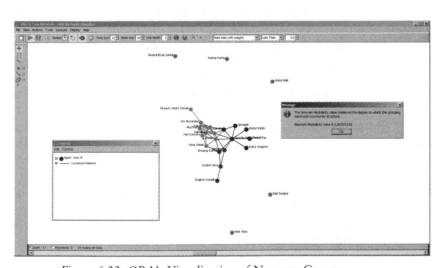

Figure 6.33. ORA's Visualization of Newman Groups

Newman group algorithms (Clauset, Newman, Moore), and it does produce the same results (i.e., the modularity score is the same, and although it is difficult to distinguish the groups with ORA's grayscale option, the individuals have been assigned to the same groups). The ease with which you can identify groups in ORA's visualizer makes it an attractive option. However, if you want a report that you can print or incorporate into a report, then you probably will want to generate ORA's "Locate Subgroups" report.

6.6   Summary and Conclusion

In this chapter we have explored four sets of algorithms for detecting cohesive subgroups: components, cores, factions, and Newman groups. There are several more we have not considered. What should be clear by now is that we may have to use multiple algorithms before we succeed in detecting cohesive subgroups. Of course, when working with small groups, we can often detect them visually; however, as groups become larger it becomes increasingly necessary to turn to algorithms in order to identifying subgroups. Once they are detected, then we can possibly use this information for constructing strategies to disrupt the larger network, such as targeting amnesty programs at peripheral members or using disinformation campaigns to sow seeds of distrust between two or more subgroups. As social movement scholars have noted, infighting can led to a decline of an insurgency or movement (McAdam 1982, 1999).

What have we learned about Noordin's network, and how might this knowledge inform our attempts to disrupt it? Components analysis did not prove terribly useful although if later we are interested in focusing on a particular subsection of the network, then it could be a useful first step. By contrast, k-core analysis was somewhat more helpful. Our k-core analysis of the alive trust and operational networks identified a series of dense clusters of individuals. Because higher k-cores are nested within lower ones, k-core analysis can be useful for identifying clusters that are deeply embedded in particular networks and those that are not. Because research has shown that individuals deeply embedded in networks are unlikely to defect (Popielarz and McPherson 1995; Stark and Bainbridge 1980), a reconciliation campaign directed at Noordin's network will most likely do better if it targets individuals in the lower k-cores of the alive trust and operational networks. Indeed, because individuals who are currently incarcerated comprise a captive audience of sorts, it would make sense to identify those individuals who are both in jail and not deeply embedded in the network. They are probably the ones most open to leaving their violent pasts behind.

The use of factional analysis and Newman groups with the alive and free combined network yielded similar but not identical subgroups. In particular, three individuals were difficult to place – Dulmatin, Umar Patek, and Abu Dujanah – suggesting that they may be in positions of brokerage within the network. One strategy would be to remove them from the network, which would cause the network to fragment and possibly become less effective. However, as we have noted previously, this is not always the case. Networks often heal quickly, and the removal of key individuals can make them harder to track (Arquilla 2009:34). Another approach is to target individuals in positions of brokerage as portals for the diffusion of disinformation through a network (Anonymous 2009). In the case of Noordin's network, a deception campaign that used Dulmatin, Patek, and Dujanah to sow seeds of distrust between the subgroups could cause the network to implode or at least cease to function. A third approach recognizes that our information is often incomplete, and that rather than removing brokers and other key actors from the network, it is sometimes better to monitor them in the short run with the idea of improving our knowledge of the network and improving the selection of strategies adopted in the future (Arquilla 2009:34). Finally, this discussion of brokerage and key actors provides a nice segue into the following two chapters: Chapter 7, which looks at metrics that help to identify central, powerful, and prestigious actors in a network, and Chapter 8, which looks specifically algorithms used for identifying a network's brokers.

7

Centrality, Power, and Prestige

7.1 Introduction

Of all the social network analysis metrics, centrality is perhaps the most intuitive, which probably explains why it is one of the oldest concepts in social network analysis. Notions that certain actors are more central than others can be traced at least as far back as Jacob Moreno's (1953) conception of sociometric stars and isolates (Wasserman and Faust 1994:169), and its formal properties were among the first to be tested experimentally (Bavelas 1948, 1950; Leavitt 1951). Exchange theorists (Cook and Emerson 1978; Cook et al. 1983; Cook et al. 1986; Cook and Whitmeyer 1992; Emerson 1962, 1972a, b, 1976) built upon these early experiments to further our understanding of the relation between centrality and power,[1] and scholars such as Linton Freeman (1977, 1979), Phillip Bonacich (1972a, 1987), Noah Friedkin (1991), and Steve Borgatti and Martin Everett (e.g., Borgatti 2005; Borgatti and Everett 2006; Everett and Borgatti 2005) have refined and expanded the measures of centrality available to analysts who have used them to explore a number of different social phenomena.

Researchers conceptualize centrality in a variety of ways (Bonacich 1987; Borgatti 2005; Borgatti and Everett 2006; Freeman 1979;

---

[1] Interestingly, while power is a central concern of social network analysts, many ignore the contributions of exchange theory, probably because of its close association with rational choice theory, which not only assumes that actors are driven by instrumental concerns but also takes issue with certain structuralist positions in sociology that hold that all important social phenomena can be explained, if not completely, at least substantially by social structure (see discussion of structure and agency in Chapter 1). However, like social network analysis, exchange theory conceptualizes social structure in terms of actors and ties. Moreover, its fundamental unit of analysis is not the individual actor but rather the relationship between actors. It does, nevertheless, depart from those forms of network analysis that only focus on social structure and do not take the interests of individual actors into consideration (Cook and Whitmeyer 1992).

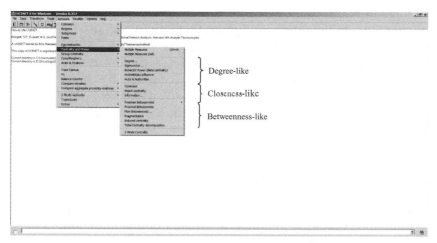

Figure 7.1. UCINET's Centrality and Power Menut

Wasserman and Faust 1994). A central actor can be seen as someone who has numerous ties to other actors (e.g., degree centrality), as someone who has numerous ties to highly central actors (e.g., eigenvector centrality, hubs, and authorities), as someone who is close (in terms of path distance) to other actors in the network (e.g., closeness centrality), or as someone who lies on the shortest path between numerous pairs of actors in a network (e.g., betweenness centrality). These, of course, are not the only centrality measures available to researchers. In fact, if one takes into account the different available options, UCINET currently implements over twenty centrality measures. Most of these are variations of the aforementioned. Freeman (1979), in fact, argues that centrality measures can be sorted into three broad families or classifications: degree-like centrality, closeness-like centrality, and betweenness-like centrality (Borgatti and Everett 2006). Indeed, close inspection of UCINET's centrality measure options (*Network > Centrality and Power*) reveals that this is how they are organized (Figure 7.1). While some may disagree with Freeman's classification, it does provide a useful starting point for our discussion of centrality. The rest of this section provides a brief overview of available centrality metrics and is organized in terms of degree-like, closeness-like, and betweenness-like centrality. The following two sections then look at how analysts can use centrality metrics to capture notions of power (Section 7.2) and prestige (Section 7.3), respectively. As with previous chapters, these two sections provide working examples using UCINET/NetDraw, Pajek, and ORA while analyzing Noordin's network. The final section (7.4) summarizes what has been covered, what we have learned about Noordin's network, and how this might inform attempts to disrupt dark networks.

[UCINET] Network > Centrality and Power

Figure 7.1 highlights several of the degree-, closeness-, and between-ness-like centrality measures available in UCINET, many of which are also available in Pajek and ORA. In what follows, we begin by considering the degree-like measures, which all assume that the number of an actor's ties is important in determining an actor's centrality. We then explore a variety of closeness-like measures where the path distance between actors is of overriding concern. Finally, we briefly examine betweenness-like measures, which assume that lying between other actors in a network should be considered important when measuring centrality.

Degree-Like Measures

The simplest and most common degree-like measure is, of course, degree centrality (Freeman 1979), which, when working with binary (i.e., dichotomized) network data, is simply a count of an actor's ties. If you are examining valued network data, then it equals the sum of the value of an actor's ties. Although researchers often prefer estimating degree centrality with binary data (i.e., they want the count of each actor's ties), it can be useful for examining valued data if, for example, the value of each tie is a measure of tie strength. In other words, if two actors, A and B, both have five ties, but most or all of A's are strong ties, whereas most or all of B's are weak ties, A will have a higher degree-centrality score than B.

Eigenvector centrality (Bonacich 1972a) is considered a degree-like measure (Borgatti and Everett 2006) because like degree centrality, it counts the number of ties of each actor. It differs in that it weights the score by the centrality of the actors to whom he or she is connected. Klein-berg's (1999) "hubs and authorities" measure, which was developed to rank pages on the World Wide Web, is based on the same assumption as eigenvector centrality and, in fact, produces identical scores. One advantage that it has over eigenvector centrality is that it can be applied to directed networks, which are often useful for measuring an actor's prestige within a network. Google's Page Rank algorithm is also a variant on eigenvector centrality (Austin 2011). The Hubbel and Katz (and Taylor) influence measures (Hubbell 1965; Katz 1953; Taylor 1969) are in many ways precursors to Bonacich's eigenvector centrality; quite early on, in fact, Bonacich noted the similarity of Hubbell's equation and the definition of an eigenvector (Bonacich 1972a; Borgatti and Everett 2006). Bonacich's power (or beta) centrality is similar to his eigenvector centrality, except that it introduces a parameter that allows researchers "to vary the degree and direction (positive or negative) of the dependence on each unit's score on the score of other units" (Bonacich 1987:1173). In other words, when the parameter is a negative value, an actor's score is higher when it is connected to actors with low power, and when the parameter is a positive value an actor's score is higher when it is connected to actors with high power.

Degree-like measures differ in many respects, but they each begin with a count of the number of an actor's ties, assuming that "count" is an important characteristic in measuring an actor's centrality. By contrast, closeness-like measures begin with the lengths of the paths in which actor is involved, assuming that how far (or close) an actor is to other actors is an important factor in determining an actor's centrality and power. We now turn to an overview of closeness-like measures.

Closeness-Like Measures

The best-known closeness centrality measure is Freeman's (1979), which calculates the average geodesic distance that each actor is from every other actor in the network. Freeman's measure is technically a distance or farness measure rather than a closeness measure, so it is generally "normalized" so that a score of 1.00 indicates that an actor is one step away from every other actor in the network, while scores nearing 0.00 are approaching the maximum distance possible from every other actor in the network.

As we have mentioned before and will explore in more detail, Freeman's measure is unusable with a disconnected network, which either requires researchers to modify the network in some way (e.g., removing isolates, extracting the largest weak component) or use an alternative measure. One such alternative measure that we will consider (and that we briefly encountered in our discussion of fragmentation) is average reciprocal distance (ARD) closeness centrality. Reach (or k-path) centrality (Sade 1989) is another closeness-like measure that counts the number of nodes each node can reach in k steps or less. When $k = 1$, the resulting score is the same as degree centrality; when it equals $n - 1$ (i.e., the size of the network less 1, which is its maximum value), the resulting score (when it is normalized) equals ARD closeness centrality plus one. One other closeness measure is Stephenson and Zelen's (1989) information centrality that attempts to estimate the information contained on all paths originating with each actor. It takes into account all paths between two actors (including but not limited to the geodesics) and assigns them weights based on their lengths. "A weighted function of this combined path is then calculated, using as weights the inverses of the lengths of the paths being combined" (Wasserman and Faust 1994:193).

Like with degree-like measures, closeness-like measures differ in their particulars but share a common characteristic: Namely, they take into account the length of the paths with which each actor is involved in calculating their centrality. Degree- and closeness-like measures also share a common characteristic: They focus on paths that begin or end with particular actors. By contrast, betweenness-like measures, which we consider next, focus on the paths that pass through actors on their way to somewhere else (Borgatti and Everett 2006), assuming that lying on the path between two actors is a structural feature that should be considered when evaluating the centrality and power of actors.

Betweenness-Like Measures

The most widely used betweenness-like measure is Freeman's (1979) node betweenness centrality, which measures the extent to which each actor in a network lies on the shortest paths (i.e., geodesics) connecting all pairs of actors in the network. We encountered a variation on this algorithm in the previous chapter, edge betweenness, which measures the degree to which each edge in a network lies on the geodesics linking all pairs of actors in the network.

A weakness of betweenness centrality is that there is no guarantee that two actors will always follow the shortest path between them. They may choose another path, even if it is longer and less efficient. Flow betweenness centrality (Freeman, Borgatti, and White 1991) takes into account this possibility. It assumes that actors will use all pathways between them in proportion to the length of the pathways. It measures the proportion of the entire flow between two actors that occurs on paths of which a particular actor is a part. In other words, each actor's flow betweenness score captures the extent to which each actor is involved in all of the flows between all other pairs of actors in the network (Hanneman and Riddle 2005, 2011:366–367).

Proximal betweenness estimates the proportion of all geodesics linking two actors (e.g., A and C) that pass through a particular actor (e.g., B) who is the second to last actor (i.e., the penultimate actor) on the geodesic. In other words, on the geodesic that runs from actor A to C and passes through B, B would be considered the penultimate actor if the tie between B and C is the last edge of the geodesic. Proximal betweenness can therefore be thought of as a measure of the number of times an actor occurs in a penultimate position on a geodesic.

One last betweenness-like centrality measure worth noting is fragmentation centrality, which we discussed somewhat at length in Chapter 5. As we noted there, this algorithm calculates a series of scores for each actor in the network that indicates (1) what the network fragmentation will be; (2) what the distance-weighted network fragmentation will be; (3) what the change in network fragmentation will be; (4) what the change in distance-weighted network fragmentation will be; (5) what the percent change in fragmentation will be; and (6) what the percent change in distance-weighted fragmentation will be if they are removed from the network.

Summary

In what follows we will not consider all these measures; instead, we will focus on those that analysts tend to use the most: in particular, degree, closeness, betweenness, and eigenvector (hubs and authorities) centrality. And unlike previous chapters, the formulas for many (not all) of these measures are included in order to illustrate the similarity between some measures (e.g., alternative closeness scores) and how we can normalize them so that they are comparable across networks. The remainder of the chapter is divided into two main sections: The first focuses on those centrality measures that researchers use to estimate power within a network; the second focuses on those that researchers use to estimate prestige. In each section we begin with how to estimate the metrics in UCINET and NetDraw before moving on to Pajek and ORA.

7.2   Centrality and Power

Centrality in UCINET

Degree Centrality in UCINET. As noted previously the most common (and oldest) measure of centrality is degree centrality, which in an undirected, binary network[2] is simply a count of the number of ties each actor has (i.e., the number of the neighbors). Because degree centrality depends on network size n (degree centrality's maximum value is $n - 1$, that is, where an actor has a tie to every other actor in the network), it is generally advisable to normalize it, which allows you to compare the measure across different-sized networks. Raw (i.e., nonnormalized) degree centrality is calculated as follows:

$$C_i^{DEG} = \sum_{j=1}^{n} x_{ij} \tag{7.1}$$

Normalized degree centrality is calculated as follows:

$$C_i^{NDEG} = \frac{\sum_{j=1}^{n} x_{ij}}{n - 1} \tag{7.2}$$

where the numerator is an actor's raw degree score (equation 7.1) and the denominator is network size minus the actor. Comparing the two formulas, one can see that normalized degree is simply the ratio of the sum of each actor's ties over total possible ties.

---

[2] An undirected, dichotomous network is one that contains only edges (not arcs) and the presence or absence of a tie is indicated by either a "1" or a "0."

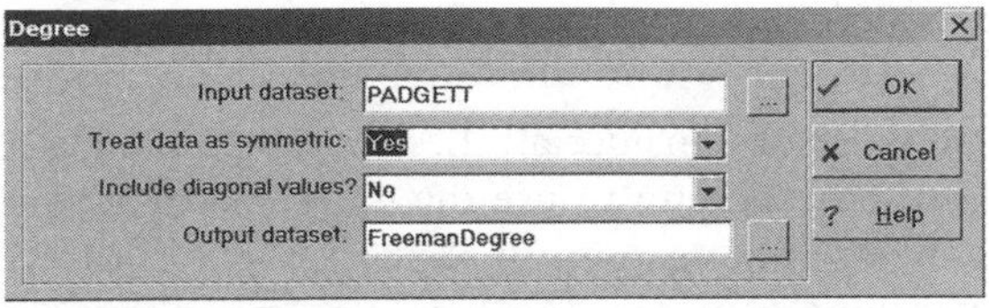

Figure 7.2. UCINET's Degree Centrality Dialog Box

In UCINET, all of the algorithms for estimating actor centrality are found in the *Network>Centrality and Power* submenu. Let us begin with a simple example: the business and marital ties between Renaissance Florentine families collected and recorded by John Padgett and Christopher Ansell (1993). Select the *Degree* centrality command found in the *Network>Centrality* submenu, which brings up a dialog box similar to Figure 7.2. Select the `Padgett.##h` file, accept UCINET's defaults[3] (unless you want to change the name of the output file) and click "OK."

[UCINET]
Network
>Centrality and
Power

Network
>Centrality
>Degree

This will call up a UCINET output log that should look similar to Figure 7.3. The first item listed is a table that itemizes the (1) degree centrality; (2) normalized degree centrality (expressed as a percentage for each actor); and (3) share of each actor in the network, which is each actor's centrality measure divided by the sum of all of the actor centralities in the network (thus, they sum to one). The output log also includes a handful of descriptive statistics (some of which we examined in Chapter 5), such as the mean/average degree centrality, standard deviation, variance, minimum value, and maximum value. Following the descriptive statistics is the degree network centralization index expressed as a percentage (which we also examined in Chapter 5) as well as two additional measures that we do not consider in this book. Because this is a stacked matrix, if you scroll down the output log, you will discover that not only does the output include centrality measures for the marriage data but also for the business data. As you can see, the Medici family is the most central in terms of both marriage and business ties. Earlier, we noted that sometimes we will be working with valued data where the value in each matrix cell may represent tie strength between actors, the sum of ties between actors, etc. In such cases degree centrality will equal the sum of the tie values. It also means that the calculations of network centralization and normalized degree centrality will sometimes yield scores greater than one, which is why with valued data, we should focus only on nonnormalized values and ignore degree centralization scores. If we are working with valued data but do not want to take into account cell values (or we want to estimate the degree centralization of a valued network),

---

3   Although UCINET's default setting for treating the data as symmetric is "Yes," sometimes it defaults to "No." For now, be sure that it is set to "Yes" as in Figure 7.2.

```
ucinetlog5.txt - Notepad
File Edit Format View Help
FREEMAN'S DEGREE CENTRALITY MEASURES:
------------------------------------------------------------------------------

Diagonal valid?                     NO
Model:                              SYMMETRIC
Input dataset:                      Padgett

Relation 1: PADGM

                              1            2            3
                         Degree    NrmDegree        Share
                   ------------ ------------ ------------
  1  ACCIAIUOL         1.000        6.667        0.025
  2    ALBIZZI         3.000       20.000        0.075
  3  BARBADORI         2.000       13.333        0.050
  4   BISCHERI         3.000       20.000        0.075
  5  CASTELLAN         3.000       20.000        0.075
  6     GINORI         1.000        6.667        0.025
  7   GUADAGNI         4.000       26.667        0.100
  8  LAMBERTES         1.000        6.667        0.025
  9     MEDICI         6.000       40.000        0.150
 10      PAZZI         1.000        6.667        0.025
 11    PERUZZI         3.000       20.000        0.075
 12      PUCCI         0.000        0.000        0.000
 13    RIDOLFI         3.000       20.000        0.075
 14   SALVIATI         2.000       13.333        0.050
 15    STROZZI         4.000       26.667        0.100
 16  TORNABUON         3.000       20.000        0.075

DESCRIPTIVE STATISTICS

                              1            2            3
                         Degree    NrmDegree        Share
                   ------------ ------------ ------------
  1       Mean         2.500       16.667        0.063
  2    Std Dev         1.458        9.718        0.036
  3        Sum        40.000      266.667        1.000
  4   Variance         2.125       94.444        0.001
  5        SSQ       134.000     5955.556        0.084
  6      MCSSQ        34.000     1511.111        0.021
  7   Euc Norm        11.576       77.172        0.289
  8    Minimum         0.000        0.000        0.000
  9    Maximum         6.000       40.000        0.150
 10   N of Obs        16.000       16.000       16.000

Network Centralization = 26.67%
Blau Heterogeneity = 8.38%.  Normalized (IQV) = 2.27%

Relation 2: PADGB
```

Figure 7.3. UCINET's Degree Centrality Output Log (Padgett Data)

we need to first dichotomize (i.e., binarize) the network with UCINET's *Transform>Dichotomize* command.

Turning to Noordin's network, select the *Degree* centrality command in the *Network>Centrality and Power* submenu and choose the `Alive Combined Network.##h` network file. Accept UCINET's defaults (change the name of the output file) and click "OK." The output log (Figure 7.4) lists the degree centrality scores of each actor; because the network is dichotomized, the scores indicate the number of each actor's "neighbors." Note that in contrast to the output log displayed in Figure 7.3, here UCINET lists the degree centrality scores of each actor in descending order. This is because in this case we are analyzing a single relation rather than a stacked (i.e., multirelational) network. When working with the latter, UCINET cannot place the actors in rank order because their ranking typically differs from network to network.

Network >Centrality and Power >Degree

Looking at Noordin's combined alive network, it is not surprising that Noordin is the most central actor. It is his network, after all. Note that although there is considerable variation in centrality scores among the first seven or eight actors, the variation among the remainder is minimal.

```
ucinetlog4.txt - Notepad                                              _|□|×|
File  Edit  Format  View  Help
FREEMAN'S DEGREE CENTRALITY MEASURES:
-----------------------------------------------------------------------------

Diagonal valid?                    NO
Model:                             SYMMETRIC
Input dataset:                     Alive Complete Network

                                        1          2          3
                                     Degree    NrmDegree     Share
                                  ---------- ---------- ----------
      50          Noordin Mohammed Top   46.000     67.647      0.052
      60                      Suramto     28.000     41.176      0.032
      63                        Ubeid     27.000     39.706      0.031
      38                Iwan Dharmawan     25.000     36.765      0.028
       4               Abdullah Sunata     25.000     36.765      0.028
      58                     Son Hadi     24.000     35.294      0.027
      23                      Dulmatin     21.000     30.882      0.024
      29                        Harun     20.000     29.412      0.023
      44   Mohamed Saifuddin (alias Faiz)  20.000     29.412      0.023
       7                     Abu Fida     20.000     29.412      0.023
      28                 Hari Kuncoro     19.000     27.941      0.022
      36                  Irun Hidayat     19.000     27.941      0.022
       9                  Achmad Hasan     19.000     27.941      0.022
      31            Heri Sigu Samboja     18.000     26.471      0.020
      43                 Mohamed Rais     17.000     25.000      0.019
      35                 Iqbal Huseini     17.000     25.000      0.019
      65                   Umar Patek     17.000     25.000      0.019
      67                        Urwah     17.000     25.000      0.019
      42                Mohamed Ihsan     17.000     25.000      0.019
      12            Ahmad Rofiq Ridho     17.000     25.000      0.019
      69                   Zulkarnaen     17.000     25.000      0.019
      27                      Hambali     16.000     23.529      0.018
       5             Abu Bakar Ba'asyir    16.000     23.529      0.018
      17                         Apuy     16.000     23.529      0.018
      64                         Umar     16.000     23.529      0.018
      11                   Agus Ahmad     16.000     23.529      0.018
      68                Usman bin Sef     16.000     23.529      0.018
      33                 Imam Samudra     16.000     23.529      0.018
      19                    Asep Jaja     15.000     22.059      0.017
      24                Enceng Kurnia     15.000     22.059      0.017
      62                   Toni Togar     15.000     22.059      0.017
      61                        Tohir     15.000     22.059      0.017
      15                  Ali Ghufron     14.000     20.588      0.016
       2                  Abdul Rauf     14.000     20.588      0.016
      57             Sardona Siliwangi     14.000     20.588      0.016
      20                      Chandra     14.000     20.588      0.016
      51               Purnama Putra     14.000     20.588      0.016
      37                       Ismail     13.000     19.118      0.015
      55                       Salman     13.000     19.118      0.015
      22                 Dani Chandra     12.000     17.647      0.014
      18                Aris Munandar     11.000     16.176      0.013
      66                   Umar Wayan     10.000     14.706      0.011
      10                        Adung     10.000     14.706      0.011|
       6                  Abu Dujanah     10.000     14.706      0.011
```

Figure 7.4. UCINET's Degree Centrality Output (Noordin Alive Combined Network)

Indeed, there is very little difference between the scores of the remaining actors. This illustrates why arbitrary cutoffs (e.g., top-ten lists) that purport to distinguish between high- and low-value targets can be misleading.

This relative lack of variation in degree centrality scores is captured by the network map presented in Figure 7.5, where node size varies in terms of actor's degree centrality. Aside from Noordin (circled), one can see that a number of actors score similar in terms of degree centrality. To be sure, actors on the periphery of the network score considerably lower than do those in the middle, but once one moves just one or two steps inward from the periphery, the variation between actors is minimal. Results such as these should give pause to analysts using social network analysis to craft disruption strategies. As noted previously, an arbitrary cutoff that attempts to distinguish between high- and low-value targets could lead one to draw unwarranted conclusions. Moreover, it suggests that the removal of key individuals, except for perhaps Noordin, may have little

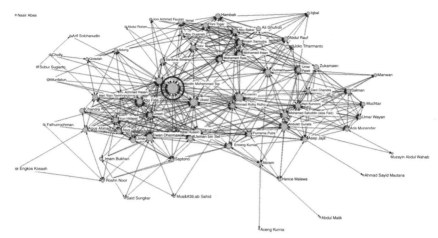

Figure 7.5. Noordin Alive Combined Network (Node Size = Degree) (Pajek)

or no disruptive effect on the network. In other words, what this example illustrates (or at least attempts to illustrate) is the importance of combining the analysis of metrics with the visual inspection of network maps. Metrics by themselves may not adequately capture the nature of network and may lead analysts to make ill-advised strategic decisions.

While we only illustrated calculating the degree centrality scores for combined alive network, Table 7.1 summarizes the normalized degree centrality scores for the top-ten actors (including ties) in all five of the alive networks. A cutoff of ten has been used here, not because it is ideal (indeed, in light of the previous paragraph's discussion and the display in Figure 7.5, it probably is not) but because it is impractical to present larger tables given the space constraints we are faced with here. Nevertheless, these results do suggest some things about the network. For example, there are several individuals (e.g., Noordin, Suramto, Son Hadi) who are central in a number of different networks (those who score in the top ten in three or more networks are in bold in the table), while others are central in only one or two (e.g., Mohamed Rais, Abu Bakar Ba'asyir, Dulmatin), suggesting that when identifying key individuals, we will want to pay close attention to which network they are affiliated with. The rankings also indicate that the business and finance network is very different from the others. Our previous topographical analysis (see Chapter 5) found that this network is much sparser than the others. Here, we can see that individuals who do not appear to play central roles in other networks do so in the business and finance network. Again, while we do not want to deduce too much from this table, the results are suggestive and probably warrant further analysis.

Table 7.1. *Normalized degree centrality of Noordin alive networks*

Trust network	Operational network	Communication network	Business & finance network	Combined network
Noordin Top (23.53)	**Noordin Top** (50.00)	**Noordin Top** (51.47)	Son Hadi (7.35)	**Noordin Top** (67.65)
Mohamed Rais (22.06)	Iwan Dharmawan (33.82)	Ahmad Rofiq Ridho (20.59)	Achmad Hasan (5.88)	Suramto (41.18)
Abu Bakar Ba'asyir (20.59)	Ubeid (30.88)	**Abdullah Sunata** (17.65)	Suramto (5.88)	Ubeid (39.71)
Tohir (20.59)	**Abdullah Sunata** (29.41)	Purnama Putra (16.18)	Usman bin Sef (5.88)	**Abdullah Sunata** (36.76)
Ubeid (19.12)	Harun (29.41)	**Abu Fida** (14.71)	Ismail (4.41)	Iwan Dharmawan (36.76)
Iwan Dharmawan (17.65)	Faiz (29.41)	**Iwan Dharmawan** (14.71)	Mohamed Rais (4.41)	Son Hadi (36.76)
Dulmatin (16.18)	**Abu Fida** (26.47)	Adung (13.24)	**Noordin Top** (4.41)	Dulmatin (30.88)
Suramto (16.18)	Suramto (26.47)	Usman bin Sef (13.24)	Agus Ahmad (2.94)	**Abu Fida** (29.41)
Ahmad Rofiq Ridho (14.71)	Hari Kuncoro (25.00)	Akram (11.76)	Asep Jaja (2.94)	Harun (29.41)
Sardona Siliwangi (14.71)	Irun Hidayat (25.00)	**Ubeid** (11.76)	Chandra (2.94)	Faiz (29.41)
Son Hadi (14.71)			Purnama Putra (2.94)	
			Rosihin Noor (2.94)	

Closeness Centrality in UCINET. As noted previously the most widely used closeness measure is Freeman's (1979), in which an actor's closeness score is based on the total distance between one actor and all other actors, where larger distances yield lower closeness centrality scores and vice versa. This measure is implemented in UCINET, NetDraw, Pajek, and ORA. UCINET actually generates two closeness scores: (1) "Farness," which is the average sum of all geodesic distances between each actor and all other actors in the network:

$$C_i^{FAR} = \sum_{j=1}^{n} d_{ij} \tag{7.3}$$

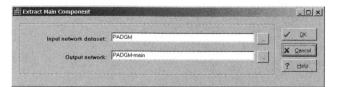

Figure 7.6. UCINET's Extract Main Component Dialog Box

where $\sum_{j=1}^{n} d_{ij}$ represents the sum of all the geodesic distances between pairs of actors i and j; (2) and "Normalized Closeness," which is the ratio of the number of other actors in a network (i.e., $n - 1$) over the sum of all geodesic distances between the actor and all other actors in the network (i.e., each actor's farness score):

$$C_i^{CLO} = \frac{1}{\sum\limits_{j=1}^{n} d_{ij}} \qquad (7.4)$$

$$C_i^{NCLO} = \frac{n - 1}{\sum\limits_{j=1}^{n} d_{ij}} \qquad (7.5)$$

As you can see, the normalized closeness is derived from a nonnormalized score (equation 7.4), which is simply the inverse of the farness score. Placing the number of actors in the network in the numerator (equation 7.5) successfully normalizes the score because $n - 1$ equals the minimum farness score actors can obtain if they are one step away (i.e., they are adjacent) from every other actor in the network. Thus, an actor's closeness score will equal 1.00 if they are one step away from all other actors in the network; it will equal 0.50 if they are, on average, two steps away, and so on.

As noted, Freeman's measure of closeness cannot be calculated when a network is disconnected because the distance between two disconnected actors is infinite. Thus, to use Freeman's measure with a disconnected network, we need to first extract the network's largest weak component (also known as its "main" component). As it turns out, the Padgett marriage and business networks are disconnected. Both contain an isolated family – the Pucci family. Thankfully, UCINET has made extracting main components a relatively easy task with its *Data>Extract>Main Component* command,[4] which calls up a dialog box (Figure 7.6) where you can select the network from which you want to extract the main component. Here, *Data>Extract >Main Component*

---

[4] When a disconnected network only contains isolates (rather than separate clusters of actors), an alternative method of extracting the main component is to use UCINET's *Data>Remove>Remove Isolates* command. *Data>Remove >Remove Isolates*

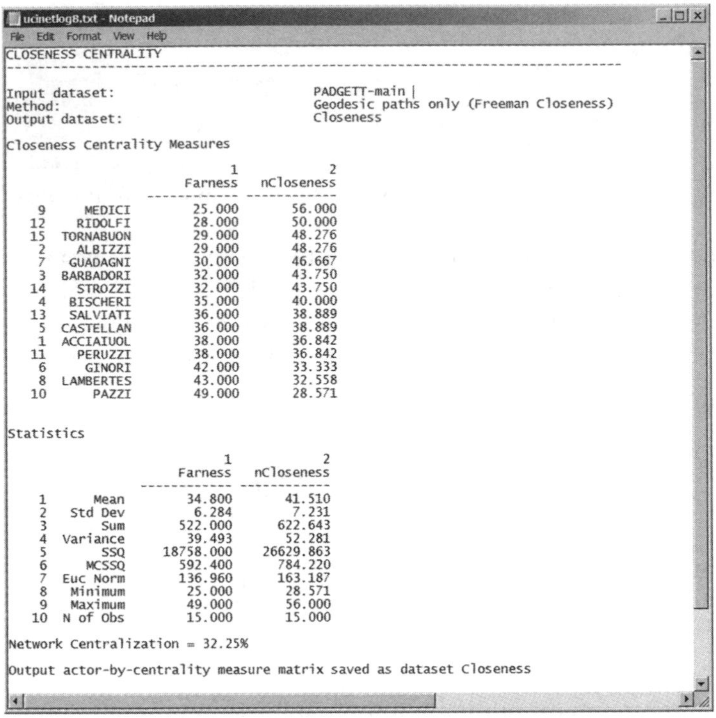

```
ucinetlog8.txt - Notepad
File Edit Format View Help
CLOSENESS CENTRALITY
--------------------------------------------------------------------------------

Input dataset:                          PADGETT-main |
Method:                                 Geodesic paths only (Freeman Closeness)
Output dataset:                         Closeness

Closeness Centrality Measures

                          1            2
                    Farness   nCloseness
               ------------ ------------
  9      MEDICI      25.000       56.000
 12    RIDOLFI      28.000       50.000
 15  TORNABUON      29.000       48.276
  2    ALBIZZI      29.000       48.276
  7   GUADAGNI      30.000       46.667
  3  BARBADORI      32.000       43.750
 14    STROZZI      32.000       43.750
  4   BISCHERI      35.000       40.000
 13   SALVIATI      36.000       38.889
  5  CASTELLAN      36.000       38.889
  1  ACCIAIUOL      38.000       36.842
 11    PERUZZI      38.000       36.842
  6     GINORI      42.000       33.333
  8  LAMBERTES      43.000       32.558
 10      PAZZI      49.000       28.571


Statistics

                          1            2
                    Farness   nCloseness
               ------------ ------------
  1       Mean       34.800       41.510
  2    Std Dev        6.284        7.231
  3        Sum      522.000      622.643
  4   Variance       39.493       52.281
  5        SSQ    18758.000    26629.863
  6      MCSSQ      592.400      784.220
  7   Euc Norm      136.960      163.187
  8    Minimum       25.000       28.571
  9    Maximum       49.000       56.000
 10   N of Obs       15.000       15.000

Network Centralization = 32.25%

Output actor-by-centrality measure matrix saved as dataset Closeness
```

Figure 7.7. UCINET's Freeman Closeness Centrality Output

we have selected the Padgett marriage data (PADGM). It is important to note that this function does not work with stacked networks. If you do select a stacked network, it will only extract the main component of the first network.

Network >Centrality Power >Closeness

To calculate closeness centrality in UCINET we use the *Network>Centrality and Power>Closeness* command and the newly generated (isolate-free) network. UCINET's closeness centrality output (Figure 7.7) is somewhat similar to its degree centrality output.[5] Note that the output lists and ranks the actors in terms of closeness/farness: The actor that is closer, on average, to all other actors in the network is listed first, whereas the actor that is farthest, on average, from all other actors is listed last. An actor's farness score is the sum of the lengths of the geodesics to every other actor, whereas an actor's closeness score ("nCloseness") is the total number of other actors (i.e., $n - 1$, which in this case equals 14) divided by the actor's farness score. As you can see the Medici family is closer (on average) to every other actor in the

[5] It is important to note, however, that unlike its degree centrality algorithm, UCINET closeness algorithm *only calculates closeness centrality for the first network in a stacked network*.

network. Because its score is larger than 50 (56.00), we know that the average path length between the Medicis and all other families is less than 2.00. Similarly, the Ginori family's closeness score (33.33) tells us that they are, on average, three steps away from every other family in the network. Like the output log for degree centrality, this one also includes descriptive statistics, such as the mean closeness centrality, standard deviation, variance, minimum value, and maximum value. Following this, the closeness network centralization index is listed.

As we noted in Chapter 5 when discussing closeness centralization, Freeman's closeness measure is not the only one available in UCINET. One alternative (that is currently can only available in UCINET) is to sum (and average) the reciprocal distance between all actors. Average reciprocal distance (ARD) is attractive because it can be used with disconnected networks (Borgatti 2006):

$$C_i^{RD} = \sum_{j=1}^{n} \frac{1}{d_{ij}} \tag{7.6}$$

Note the similarity between this measure and Freeman's nonnormalized closeness score (equation 7.4). In both cases the geodesic distance between actors is included in the denominator. However, with Freeman's measure, the distances are summed first before being placed in the denominator, but because infinite distances cannot be summed (at least in ways that provide meaningful results), the calculation becomes impossible, which is why we cannot use it with disconnected networks. With ARD, however, the reciprocal of the distances is calculated first and then summed, and since the reciprocal of infinity is conventionally set to zero, it is includable in the summation, and the measure can be used with disconnected networks. ARD is probably also a better approach than Freeman's measure when calculating the closeness centrality for actors included in the main component (and setting the scores of all others in the network to zero), because with ARD, all network actors and those that are located in clusters (but not the largest cluster/component) receive a score of greater than zero. ARD is normalized by placing the number of other actors (i.e., $n - 1$) in the denominator (rather than in the numerator as with Freeman's measure):

$$C_i^{ARD} = \frac{\sum_{j=1}^{n} \frac{1}{d_{ij}}}{n - 1} \tag{7.7}$$

This is because ARD reaches its maximum value when an actor is adjacent to all other actors in the network (i.e., when it equals $n - 1$), which means that its normalized score will equal 1.00 when it is one step away from every other actor in the network. Currently, UCINET is the only one

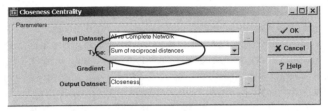

Figure 7.8. UCINET's Closeness Centrality Dialog Box

of the four SNA packages considered in this monograph that estimates ARD, but one gets the sense that it may eventually become the standard. As we will see, UCINET now includes ARD rather than the Freeman measure of closeness in its multiple centrality measure command.

Network >Centrality

Power >Closeness

ARD closeness centrality is accessed with the same closeness command used to get Freeman's measure (*Network>Centrality and Power>Closeness*), except rather than accepting UCINET's default, select the "Sum of reciprocal distances" option in the dialog box (Figure 7.8) and then click "OK." This will generate output (Figure 7.9) similar to the output obtained from Freeman's measure. However, rather than farness and closeness scores, with ARD you get raw and normalized closeness scores.

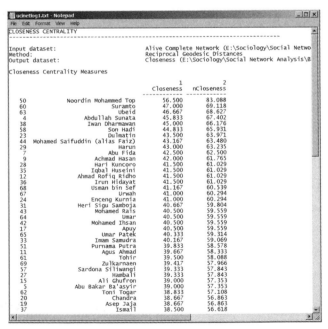

Figure 7.9. UCINET's Closeness (ARD) Centrality Output

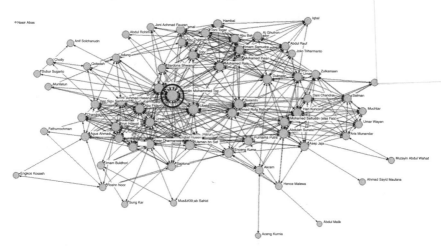

Figure 7.10. Noordin Alive Combined Network (Node Size = ARD) (Pajek)

Once again, Noordin is the most central actor. He is closer, on average, to other actors in the network than are any of the other actors in the network. Moreover, he is followed in rank by many of the same individuals who ranked closely behind him in terms of degree centrality (Figure 7.4).[6] This is not unusual, as actors who score high on one measure of centrality often score high on others (but not always), and we saw that degree and closeness centrality share certain similarities to one another.

It is notable that there is even less variation here than there was with degree centrality, which raises many of the same concerns we discussed with regard to degree centrality and again highlights the importance of the visual inspection of network maps (see Figure 7.10) before drawing conclusions about the network.

Table 7.2 summarizes the normalized ARD closeness centrality scores for the top-ten actors (including ties) in all five of the alive networks. Individuals who rank in the top ten of three or more networks are highlighted in bold type. Here again, the results are suggestive. A number of those who were central in terms of degree centrality are central in terms of closeness, and there are several individuals who are central across several networks, while there are others who are only central in one or two. The rankings also indicate that the business and finance network is very different from the others. Actors who are central here are not elsewhere. Of course, like before, we do not want to deduce too much from this table, but the results do provide food for thought.

[6] In terms of rank order, these scores are comparable (but not identical) to the closeness centrality scores estimated using Freeman's closeness algorithm (not shown) with the complete alive network with isolates removed.

Table 7.2. *Normalized closeness (ARD) centrality of Noordin alive networks*

Trust network	Operational network	Communication network	Business & finance network	Combined network
Noordin Top (52.33)	**Noordin Top** (68.87)	**Noordin Top** (70.10)	Son Hadi (5.88)	**Noordin Top** (83.09)
Mohamed Rais (49.44)	Iwan Dharmawan (58.46)	Ahmad Rofiq Ridho (53.16)	Achmad Hasan (5.15)	Suramto (69.12)
Ubeid (48.77)	Faiz (58.09)	Abdullah Sunata (50.22)	Suramto (5.15)	Ubeid (68.63)
Abu Bakar Ba'asyir (48.77)	Ubeid (57.72)	Purnama Putra (49.24)	Usman bin Sef (5.15)	Abdullah Sunata (67.40)
Tohir (47.84)	Harun (57.11)	Iwan Dharmawan (48.01)	Chandra (3.68)	Iwan Dharmawan (66.18)
Iwan Dharmawan (47.06)	**Abdullah Sunata** (55.88)	Abu Fida (47.77)	Ismail (2.94)	Son Hadi (65.93)
Ahmad Rofiq Ridho (46.32)	Suramto (55.64)	Usman bin Sef (47.03)	Mohamed Rais (2.94)	Dulmatin (63.97)
Dulmatin (45.15)	Abu Fida (54.53)	Akram (47.03)	**Noordin Top** (2.94)	Faiz (63.48)
Suramto (44.66)	Hari Kuncoro (53.43)	**Ubeid** (46.79)	Agus Ahmad (1.47)	Harun (63.24)
Abu Dujanah (43.43)	Apuy (53.06)	Adung (46.30)	Asep Jaja (1.47)	Abu Fida (62.50)
	Umar (53.06)		Purnama Putra (1.47)	
	Urwah (53.06)		Rosihin Noor (1.47)	

Betweenness Centrality in UCINET. Betweenness centrality differs from degree and closeness centrality in that it assumes that an actor is in a position of potential power over any two other actors when it lies on the shortest path (geodesic) between them in a given network of relations. "Loosely described, the betweenness centrality of a node is the number of times that any actor needs a given actor to reach any other actor" (Borgatti and Everett 2006:474). Formally, if we let g_{ij} indicate the number of geodesics from actor i to actor j and g_{ikj} indicate the number of geodesic paths from actor i to actor j that pass through actor k, then the betweenness centrality equals

$$C_i^{BET} = \sum_i \sum_j \frac{g_{ikj}}{g_{ij}} \qquad (7.8)$$

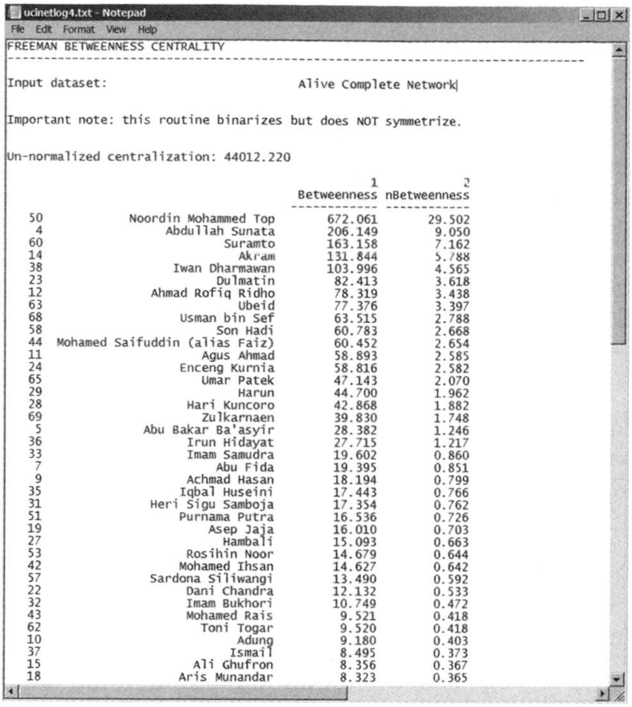

ucinetlog4.txt - Notepad

File Edit Format View Help

FREEMAN BETWEENNESS CENTRALITY

Input dataset: Alive Complete Network

Important note: this routine binarizes but does NOT symmetrize.

Un-normalized centralization: 44012.220

		1 Betweenness	2 nBetweenness
50	Noordin Mohammed Top	672.061	29.502
4	Abdullah Sunata	206.149	9.050
60	Suramto	163.158	7.162
14	Akram	131.844	5.788
38	Iwan Dharmawan	103.996	4.565
23	Dulmatin	82.413	3.618
12	Ahmad Rofiq Ridho	78.319	3.438
63	Ubeid	77.376	3.397
68	Usman bin Sef	63.515	2.788
58	Son Hadi	60.783	2.668
44	Mohamed Saifuddin (alias Faiz)	60.452	2.654
11	Agus Ahmad	58.893	2.585
24	Enceng Kurnia	58.816	2.582
65	Umar Patek	47.143	2.070
29	Harun	44.700	1.962
28	Hari Kuncoro	42.868	1.882
69	Zulkarnaen	39.830	1.748
5	Abu Bakar Ba'asyir	28.382	1.246
36	Irun Hidayat	27.715	1.217
33	Imam Samudra	19.602	0.860
7	Abu Fida	19.395	0.851
9	Achmad Hasan	18.194	0.799
35	Iqbal Huseini	17.443	0.766
31	Heri Sigu Samboja	17.354	0.762
51	Purnama Putra	16.536	0.726
19	Asep Jaja	16.010	0.703
27	Hambali	15.093	0.663
53	Rosihin Noor	14.679	0.644
42	Mohamed Ihsan	14.627	0.642
57	Sardona Siliwangi	13.490	0.592
22	Dani Chandra	12.132	0.533
32	Imam Bukhori	10.749	0.472
43	Mohamed Rais	9.521	0.418
62	Toni Togar	9.520	0.418
10	Adung	9.180	0.403
37	Ismail	8.495	0.373
15	Ali Ghufron	8.356	0.367
18	Aris Munandar	8.323	0.365

Figure 7.11. UCINET's Betweenness Centrality Output Log

In short, betweenness centrality measures actor *k*'s share of all shortest paths from actor *i* to actor *j*, summed across all choices of actors *i* and *j*:

$$C_i^{NBET} = \frac{\sum_i \sum_j \frac{g_{ikj}}{g_{ij}}}{(n-1)(n-2)/2} \tag{7.9}$$

Because an actor's betweenness centrality is a function of the number of pairs of actors in a network, we can normalize it by dividing through by the number of pairs of actors that do not include actor *k*, which equals $(n-1)\,(n-2)/2$ (equation 7.9).

To calculate betweenness centrality in UCINET, select the *Freeman Betweenness>Node Betweenness* command from the *Network>Centrality and Power* submenu (dialog box not shown). As with closeness centrality, the output generated by UCINET (Figure 7.11) differs somewhat from that the degree centrality output. For instance, like closeness centrality UCINET only calculates betweenness centrality for the first matrix in the dataset, which means that if we want betweenness scores for all of the networks in a stacked dataset, we would first have to extract

Freeman Betweenness> Node Betweenness

Network >Centrality and Power

Table 7.3. *Normalized betweenness centrality of Noordin alive networks*

Trust network	Operational network	Communication network	Business & finance network	Combined network
Noordin Top (21.93)	Noordin Top (30.40)	Noordin Top (55.74)	Son Hadi (0.13)	Noordin Top (29.50)
Iwan Dharmawan (**17.10**)	Faiz (10.69)	Abu Dujanah (10.50)		Abdullah Sunata (9.04)
Ahmad Rofiq Ridho (15.09)	Suramto (5.67)	Abdullah Sunata (10.49)		Suramto (7.16)
Abdullah Sunata (12.18)	Ahmad Rofiq Ridho (4.91)	Ahmad Rofiq Ridho (8.11)		Akram (5.79)
Usman bin Sef (8.76)	Iwan Dharmawan (**4.70**)	Zulkarnaen (7.77)		Iwan Dharmawan (4.57)
Abu Bakar Ba'asyir (7.93)	Abdullah Sunata (4.19)	Iwan Dharmawan (6.95)		Dulmatin (3.62)
Ubeid (7.78)	Harun (3.31)	Akram (6.19)		Ahmad Rofiq Ridho (3.44)
Faiz (6.07)	Hambali (3.08)	Aris Munandar (5.31)		Ubeid (3.40)
Akram (5.95)	Mohamed Ihsan (3.08)	Purnama Putra (4.89)		Usman bin Sef (2.79)
Adung (5.19)	Toni Togar (3.08)	Agus Ahmad (3.15)		Son Hadi (2.67)

each network and estimate betweenness centrality for each of them sep-arately. However, like degree centrality UCINET provides both raw and normalized betweenness scores as well as a number of descriptive statis-tics, including mean, variation, standard deviation, and network. Note also that UCINET automatically binarizes the network before making its calculation, which means that you will receive the same scores whether you are analyzing a valued or dichotomized network. Put differently, if you are examining a valued network, you do not have to dichotomize it prior to estimating betweenness centrality. UCINET does it for you.

Looking at the betweenness centrality scores for the combined alive Noordin network, we can see that, once again, Noordin is the most central and a number of the individuals we saw when calculating degree and closeness centrality appear in this output as well. What is striking, however, is that there is far more variability between the actors scores.

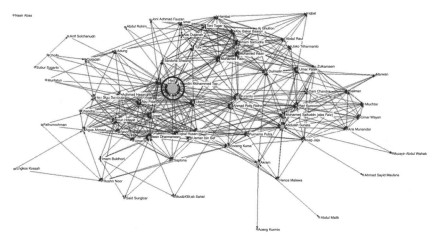

Figure 7.12. Noordin Alive Combined Network (Node Size = Betweenness) (Pajek)

Although this can be detected with a close inspection of UCINET's output (see Table 7.3), it is even more obvious in the network map where node size is allowed to vary by betweenness centrality (Figure 7.12).

Table 7.3 summarizes the normalized betweenness centrality scores for the top-ten actors for all five alive networks. Although many of the individuals listed here were listed in Tables 7.1 and 7.2, there are a number of "new" ones. What might we be able to do with this information? The variability between scores suggests that in this case at least, this measure might be delineating between high- and low-value individuals. We should be cautious because as with all social network analysis metrics, betweenness centrality only measures an actor's potential power, not necessarily their actual power. They could be complete idiots and only find themselves in the position they are in out of "luck." There is no guarantee that they recognize their structural power or have the ability to capitalize on it. That said, analysts have successfully used high betweenness centrality measures to target individuals within dark networks for the planting of misinformation in order to sow seeds of distrust and cause the network to implode (Anonymous 2009).

Eigenvector Centrality in UCINET. Eigenvector centrality assumes that ties to highly central actors are more important than are ties to peripheral actors and as such weights an actor's centrality by the centrality scores of its neighbors (i.e., the actors to which it has ties). Formally, if A is an adjacency matrix (i.e., a one-mode network), then we can allow for this

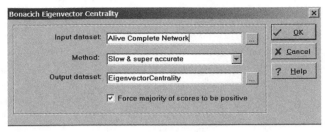

Figure 7.13. UCINET Eigenvector Centrality Dialog Box

effect by making actor *i*'s centrality proportional to the average of the centralities of *i*'s neighbors:

$$C_i^{EIG} = \frac{1}{\lambda} \sum_{j=1}^{n} A_{ij} x_j \qquad (7.10)$$

where λ is a constant and *i*'s associated eigenvalue; the largest eigenvalue is generally preferred (Bonacich 1987). The normalized eigenvector centrality is the scaled eigenvector centrality divided by the maximum difference possible, expressed as a percentage (Borgatti, Everett, and Freeman 2011):

$$C_i^{NEIG} = \frac{\frac{1}{\lambda} \sum_{j=1}^{n} A_{ij} x_j}{C_{Max}^{EIG}} \qquad (7.11)$$

Network >Centrality Eigenvector

To compute eigenvector centrality in UCINET, select the *Eigenvector* command under the *Network>Centrality and Power* submenu, which calls up a dialog box similar to Figure 7.13. A few items are worth noting here. First, as long as you are not analyzing a very large network, you will generally want to select the "Slow & super accurate" option. With a large network, you will probably be better off choosing the "Fast – for large matrices" option. Second, you will also want to check the box at the bottom of the dialog box that forces most scores to be positive. Finally, when calculating eigenvector centrality for several networks, you will want to provide your own name for the output dataset rather than accepting UCINET's default file name.

UCINET's output (Figure 7.14) first lists a series of eigenvalues before each actor's eigenvector centrality scores. Like the output for degree and closeness centrality, it provides a number of descriptive statistics, including network centralization based on closeness. However, analysts need to be careful because UCINET's output lists the actor's scores in the order they appear in the network, not in their rank order, which means that at a glance, you cannot determine which actors are more central than others.

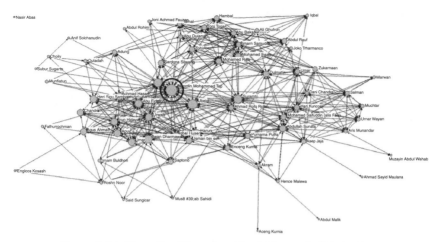

Figure 7.14. Noordin Alive Combined Network (Node Size = Eigenvector) (Pajek)

Table 7.4 summarizes the eigenvector centrality scores for all five alive networks. As before, Noordin is the most central actor in the combined network, but as with the degree and closeness centrality, there is minimal variation in the scores (see Figure 7.15). This, of course, raises the same issues that we have discussed, suggesting that at least in the case of the combined network, eigenvector centrality may not be an ideal metric for identifying central players. Interestingly, Noordin does not rank first in the trust network, as he has previously in terms of eigenvector centrality. In fact, he is not even in the top five. Instead, the top-ranked individual is Mohammed Rais, who previously ranked high (but not first) in terms of degree and closeness centrality, followed by Tohir, Abu Bakar Ba'asyir, Ubeid, and Suramto. What this may suggest is that if Noordin were to be removed from the network, these individuals, with their connections to other central members of the network, may be the most likely candidates to succeed Noordin.[7]

Multiple Centrality Measures in UCINET. UCINET includes a *Multiple Measures* command under the *Network>Centrality and Power* submenu, which calculates a number of centrality measures, including degree, closeness (ARD), betweenness, and eigenvector centrality along with Bonacich's power centrality (a degree-like measure that is a variation on eigenvector centrality), and *k*-step reach centrality (a closeness-like measure). You do not have to estimate all six metrics; the multiple measures dialog box (Figure 7.16) allows you to select which measures you

Network >Centrality and Power Multiple Measures

---

[7] Noordin was killed in a fire fight with Indonesian authorities in September 2009. Some members did attempt to join with other Indonesian terrorists, but many were caught in a raid in Aceh, Indonesia, in early 2010 (International Crisis Group 2010).

Table 7.4. *Normalized eigenvector centrality of Noordin alive networks*

Trust Network	Operational Network	Communication Network	Business & Finance Network	Combined Network
Mohamed Rais (48.65)	Noordin Top (40.01)	Noordin Top (72.67)	Son Hadi (74.05)	Noordin Top (43.53)
Tohir (45.69)	Ubeid (37.02)	Ahmad Rofiq Ridho (38.46)	Achmad Hasan (68.18)	Ubeid (34.44)
Abu Bakar Ba'asyir (37.56)	Iwan Dharmawan (35.98)	Purnama Putra (32.87)	Suramto (68.18)	Son Hadi (30.76)
Ubeid (36.52)	Harun (34.70)	Abu Fida (31.02)	Usman bin Sef (68.18)	Suramto (30.65)
Suramto (36.13)	Abu Fida (33.32)	Abdullah Sunata (28.97)	Chandra (24.00)	Iwan Dharmawan (28.99)
Noordin Top (34.38)	Apuy (32.08)	Usman bin Sef (28.27)	Ismail (1.27)	Abu Fida (27.13)
Sardona Siliwangi (33.69)	Umar (32.08)	Adung (27.25)		Harun (26.51)
Mohamed Ihsan (31.88)	Urwah (32.08)	Ubeid (26.97)		Achmad Hasan (25.77)
Dulmatin (28.95)	Irun Hidayat (31.78)	Son Hadi (23.97)		Urwah (25.03)
Ali Ghufron (28.24)	Heri Sigu Samboja (30.88)	Enceng Kurnia (23.59)		Irun Hidayat (24.79)

want. This is a handy feature when analyzing larger networks because the larger the network, the longer it takes for UCINET to calculate the scores. Note also that you can indicate whether the data are directed or undirected, or you can let UCINET detect it on its own, and you can ask for raw or normalized scores. Note also that the function is designed for binary data, so if you use it with valued data, UCINET will dichotomize the network before calculating any metrics.

Excursus: Correlating Centrality Metrics with Attributes

Finally, you may be interested in seeing how much various centrality measures correlate with ordered or continuous attributes, such as age or education. It makes no sense, of course, to estimate the correlation between centrality and a nominal attribute such as nationality, role, or gender.

Tools>Testing Hypotheses >Node-Level >Regression

To do this in UCINET, we use UCINET's *Tools>Testing Hypotheses> Node-Level>Regression* command, which calls up a dialog box

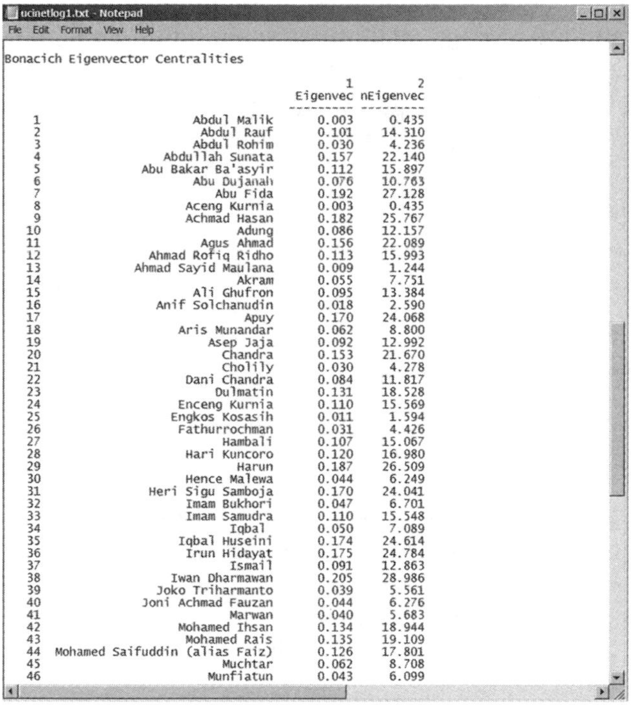
ucinetlog1.txt - Notepad

Bonacich Eigenvector Centralities

		1 Eigenvec	2 nEigenvec
1	Abdul Malik	0.003	0.435
2	Abdul Rauf	0.101	14.310
3	Abdul Rohim	0.030	4.236
4	Abdullah Sunata	0.157	22.140
5	Abu Bakar Ba'asyir	0.112	15.897
6	Abu Dujanah	0.076	10.763
7	Abu Fida	0.192	27.128
8	Aceng Kurnia	0.003	0.435
9	Achmad Hasan	0.182	25.767
10	Adung	0.086	12.157
11	Agus Ahmad	0.156	22.089
12	Ahmad Rofiq Ridho	0.113	15.993
13	Ahmad Sayid Maulana	0.009	1.244
14	Akram	0.055	7.751
15	Ali Ghufron	0.095	13.384
16	Anif Solchanudin	0.018	2.590
17	Apuy	0.170	24.068
18	Aris Munandar	0.062	8.800
19	Asep Jaja	0.092	12.992
20	Chandra	0.153	21.670
21	Cholily	0.030	4.278
22	Dani Chandra	0.084	11.817
23	Dulmatin	0.131	18.528
24	Enceng Kurnia	0.110	15.569
25	Engkos Kosasih	0.011	1.594
26	Fathurrochman	0.031	4.426
27	Hambali	0.107	15.067
28	Hari Kuncoro	0.120	16.980
29	Harun	0.187	26.509
30	Hence Malewa	0.044	6.249
31	Heri Sigu Samboja	0.170	24.041
32	Imam Bukhori	0.047	6.701
33	Imam Samudra	0.110	15.548
34	Iqbal	0.050	7.089
35	Iqbal Huseini	0.174	24.614
36	Irun Hidayat	0.175	24.784
37	Ismail	0.091	12.863
38	Iwan Dharmawan	0.205	28.986
39	Joko Triharmanto	0.039	5.561
40	Joni Achmad Fauzan	0.044	6.276
41	Marwan	0.040	5.683
42	Mohamed Ihsan	0.134	18.944
43	Mohamed Rais	0.135	19.109
44	Mohamed Saifuddin (alias Faiz)	0.126	17.801
45	Muchtar	0.062	8.708
46	Munfiatun	0.043	6.099

Figure 7.15. UCINET Eigenvector Centrality Output

(Figure 7.17) in which you indicate the "dependent" variable (i.e., education level) is the first column of the Attribute dataset. You will also need to indicate your independent variables, which in this case are all the columns from the Alive Combined Network-cent dataset, which was created with UCINET's multiple measures command. Clicking "OK" generates an output similar to Figure 7.18. For now we will only pay

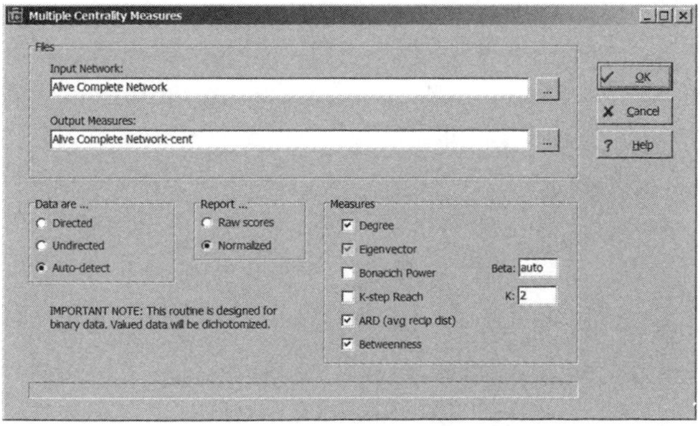

Figure 7.16. UCINET Multiple Centrality Measures Dialog Box

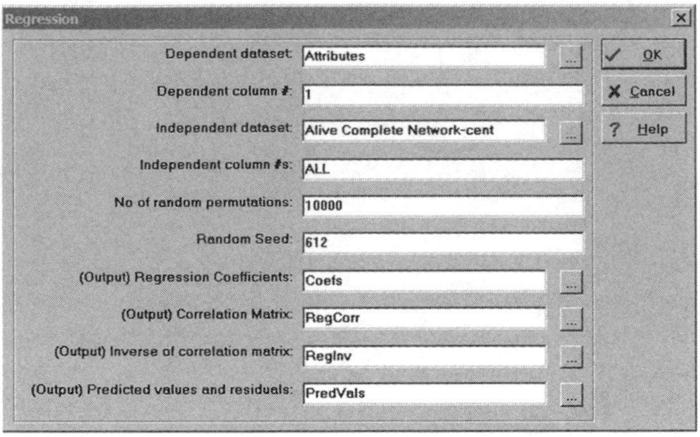

Figure 7.17. UCINET Regression Dialog Box

attention to the correlation matrix at the top of the screen because we are not estimating a formal regression model (see, however, Chapter 11). Looking at the matrix you can see that education (column 5) is positively correlated with degree, closeness (ARD), betweenness, and eigenvector centrality, all of which suggests (but does not prove) that individuals

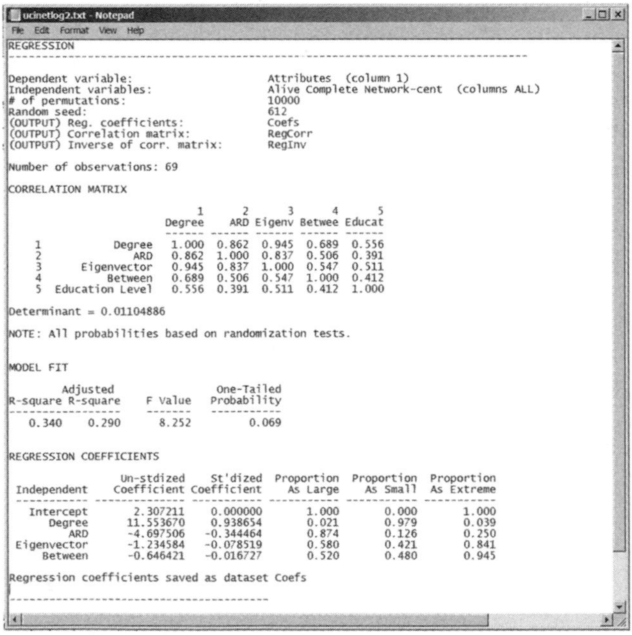
ucinetlog2.txt - Notepad

REGRESSION

Dependent variable:	Attributes (column 1)
Independent variables:	Alive Complete Network-cent (columns ALL)
# of permutations:	10000
Random seed:	612
(OUTPUT) Reg. coefficients:	Coefs
(OUTPUT) Correlation matrix:	RegCorr
(OUTPUT) Inverse of corr. matrix:	RegInv

Number of observations: 69

CORRELATION MATRIX

		1 Degree	2 ARD	3 Eigenv	4 Betwee	5 Educat
1	Degree	1.000	0.862	0.945	0.689	0.556
2	ARD	0.862	1.000	0.837	0.506	0.391
3	Eigenvector	0.945	0.837	1.000	0.547	0.511
4	Between	0.689	0.506	0.547	1.000	0.412
5	Education Level	0.556	0.391	0.511	0.412	1.000

Determinant = 0.01104886

NOTE: All probabilities based on randomization tests.

MODEL FIT

R-square	Adjusted R-square	F Value	One-Tailed Probability
0.340	0.290	8.252	0.069

REGRESSION COEFFICIENTS

Independent	Un-stdized Coefficient	St'dized Coefficient	Proportion As Large	Proportion As Small	Proportion As Extreme
Intercept	2.307211	0.000000	1.000	0.000	1.000
Degree	11.553670	0.938654	0.021	0.979	0.039
ARD	-4.697506	-0.344464	0.874	0.126	0.250
Eigenvector	-1.234584	-0.078519	0.580	0.421	0.841
Between	-0.646421	-0.016727	0.520	0.480	0.945

Regression coefficients saved as dataset Coefs

Figure 7.18. UCINET Regression Output Log

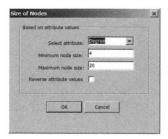

Figure 7.19. NetDraw Size of Nodes Dialog Box

with higher levels of education are more likely to be in positions of power than are those with lower levels of education.[8]

Centrality in NetDraw

Centrality scores are essentially attributes of actors, which means that we can use them to vary the size of nodes in network maps. In this section we will first examine how to use centrality scores calculated in UCINET to modify our visualization of networks in NetDraw. Then, we will see that NetDraw also includes a feature for calculating centrality scores that can then be utilized in our visualizations.

Visualizing UCINET Centrality Scores in NetDraw. In NetDraw, open the `Alive Combined Network.##h` data file, and energize it by choosing one of its layout algorithms. Next, open the multiple measures centrality attribute file associated with this data (i.e., `Alive Combined Network-cent.##h`). Then, using the *Properties> Nodes>Symbol>Size>Attribute-based* command select one or more of the centrality measures (in the Size of Nodes dialog box – see Figure 7.19) to vary the size of the nodes. If you choose degree centrality (as in Figure 7.19), then you will end up with a network map similar (but not identical) to Figure 7.5. If you choose ARD (closeness), then your network map will look similar to Figure 7.10; if you choose betweenness, then it will look like Figure 7.12; if you choose eigenvector, then it will look like Figure 7.15. You can also save your network maps as metafiles, bitmaps, and jpegs with NetDraw's *File>Save Diagram As* command.

Estimating Centrality Scores in NetDraw. NetDraw also calculates centrality measures with its *Analysis>Centrality measures* command. This calls up a dialog box (Figure 7.20) where you can choose which

[NetDraw]

*Properties
>Nodes
>Symbol>Size
>Attribute-
based*

*File>Save
Diagram As*

*Analysis
>Centrality
measures*

---

[8] See Chapter 11 for a discussion of how to determine whether a particular correlation or regression coefficient is statistically significant.

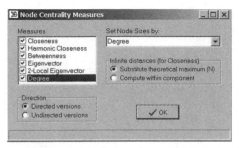

Figure 7.20. NetDraw Centrality Measures Dialog Box

centrality measures you want NetDraw to calculate. Note also that NetDraw has yet to implement ARD, but it does allow you to substitute a theoretical maximum based on network size for disconnected actors; it also allows you to compute only the closeness centrality within each component (not just the main component). You can also indicate what measure you want NetDraw to use to set the node size. Regardless of what you choose here, you can always change it later with *Properties>Nodes>Symbol>Size>Attribute-based* command. Another thing to keep in mind when estimating centrality in NetDraw is that if you load a stacked matrix into NetDraw (i.e., where multiple types of ties are listed in the relations box found on the right side of NetDraw), it will only calculate centrality on the relations that are checked. For example, if you read in the stacked Noordin trust network but only select the friendship network, NetDraw will only calculate centrality for the friendship network. If you select the kinship and friendship network, it will calculate centrality on the combined kinship and friendship network, and so on.

Properties
>Nodes
>Symbol>Size
>Attribute-
based

Centrality in Pajek

Estimating centrality in Pajek is relatively straightforward, although to date it has only implemented four centrality algorithms: degree, closeness, betweenness, and eigenvector (hubs and authorities). It is possible to visualize other measures of centrality in Pajek, but you need to estimate the scores in another program such as UCINET and then import the scores into Pajek as either a partition or vector.

[Pajek]
File>Pajek
Project
File>Read

Degree Centrality in Pajek. Begin by reading the `Noordin Alive Network.paj` project file into Pajek. Pajek treats degree centrality as a discrete, rather than as a continuous, attribute of an actor (i.e., it is always an integer), so Pajek stores it as a partition. To calculate degree centrality in Pajek, choose either the *Input*, *Output*, or *All* option found under the *Net>Partitions>Degree* submenu. *Input* counts all incoming

Net
>Partitions
>Degree>Input,
Output, All

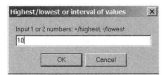

Figure 7.21. Pajek Info Partition/Vector Dialog Box

lines (indegree), *Output* counts all outgoing lines (outdegree), and *All* counts both. Note that an edge, which has no direction, is considered to be incoming as well as outgoing, so each edge is counted only once by all three commands. In other words, in an undirected network it makes no difference whether you select *Input*, *Output*, or *All*. As we will see when we are looking at measures of prestige, however, your selection does matter with directed networks. You should also be aware that when an undirected network is exported from UCINET and read into Pajek, edges become arcs, and you will need to symmetrize your data (i.e., make it symmetric) before calculating degree centrality, using the *Net>Transform>Arcs→Edges>All* command. Pajek will ask whether you want to create a new network (select Yes) and whether you want to remove multiple lines and loops (select option 5, single line). *Net >Transform >Arcs→Edges >All*

When you estimate degree centrality Pajek, it generates both a partition, which stores the raw degree centrality scores, and a vector, which stores the normalized degree centrality scores. One way to examine the raw scores is to select the *File>Partition>Edit* command (or select the "Edit" radio button). This calls up an editing box that allows you to not only scroll through each actor's scores but also edit them if you so choose. Another way is to use Pajek's *Info>Partition* command. If you accept Pajek's defaults in the resulting dialog boxes, you will be provided basic information about the degree centrality scores. If you want more information, in the first dialog box (Figure 7.21) you can indicate that you want to get the scores of actors in rank order. If you type "10," Pajek will list the top-ten ranked actors; if you type "20," Pajek will list the top twenty, and so on (if you type "–10," Pajek will list the bottom ten). You can obtain similar information on the normalized score using Pajek's *File>Vector>Edit* and *Info>Vector* commands. *File >Partition >Edit* *Info >Partition* *File>Vector >Edit* *Info>Vector*

In Pajek, partitions can be used to alter the color of nodes, whereas vectors can be used to alter the size of nodes. To illustrate this, with the alive trust network (the network which the following example used to estimate degree centrality) showing in the first Network drop-down menu, the "All Degree partition of N (69)" showing in the first Partition drop-down menu, and the "Normalized All Degree partition of N1 (69)" showing in the first Vector drop-down menu, view the network with node size adjusted for degree centrality by selecting the *Draw>Draw-Partition-Vector* command and then using one of the two-dimensional *Draw >Draw-Partition-Vector*

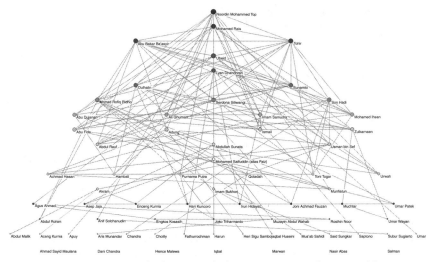

Figure 7.22. Pajek Drawing of Alive Trust Network, Layered by Degree Centrality

[Draw]
Options
>Size>of
Vertices

layout algorithms (be sure that the *Options>Value of Lines>Similarities* command is checked). If the node sizes do not seem to vary, you may need to adjust them using the *Size>of Vertices* option under the *Options* menu. Select "0" to tell Pajek to automatically adjust the size of the nodes.

Layers
>Type of
Layout>2D

Layers>In y
direction

In Pajek it is fairly easy to layer networks based on an attribute, such as degree centrality. To do this with the current network, indicate that it is a two-dimensional layout with the *Layers>Type of Layout>2D* command found in the draw screen, and then tell Pajek to layer the drawing in the "y-direction" with the *Layers>In y direction* command. This will place Noordin at the bottom of the drawing (i.e., the person with the highest degree centrality) and those with the lowest degree centrality at the top. If you hold down the "X" key, you can rotate the drawing so that Noordin is at the top. Now your drawing is layered in terms of degree centrality with everyone having the same degree centrality located at the same horizontal level (Figure 7.22).

[Main Screen]

Net
>Vector
>Centrality
>Closeness
>Input,
Output, All

Closeness Centrality in Pajek. In Pajek, the computation of closeness and betweenness centrality is similar to that of degree, except that Pajek treats both as vectors rather than partitions because they are continuous rather than discrete measures. Consequently, the centrality command for both are located in *Net>Vector>Centrality* submenu. The command to compute closeness centrality for all vertices in the network includes *Input*, *Output*, and *All* options, which with an undirected network yield the same results. If the network is disconnected (i.e., where there are isolates),

Pajek assigns isolated actors a closeness score of "0." Of course, because all the alive networks are disconnected, we should probably first identify each network's weak components with Pajek's *Net>Components>Weak* command, and then extract the largest component from each with Pajek's *Operations>Extract from Network>Partition* command before estimating closeness centrality.

You can examine the scores of individual actors by selecting the *File>Vector>Edit* command (or select the "Edit" radio button). This calls up an editing box that allows you to not only scroll through each actor's scores but also edit them if you so choose. Or, you can use Pajek's *Info>Vector* command, which functions much like its *Info>Partition* command. That is, if you accept Pajek's defaults in the resulting dialog boxes, you will be provided basic information about the closeness centrality scores. If you want more information, in the first dialog box (Figure 7.22) you can indicate that you want to get the scores of actors in rank order. In other words, if you type "10," Pajek will list the top-ten ranked actors; if you type "20," Pajek will list the top twenty, and so on.

File>Vector >Edit

Info>Vector

Betweenness Centrality in Pajek. Betweenness centrality is calculated and visualized in Pajek in essentially the same way that we estimated closeness centrality, using the *Net>Vector>Centrality>Betweenness* command. However, because betweenness centrality does not take the direction of ties into consideration, only the path length between actors, Pajek does not include *In*, *Out*, and *All* options for betweenness. When you issue this command, Pajek creates a vector that you can examine using Pajek's *File>Vector>Edit* and *Info>Vector* commands or view with the Noordin network using the *Draw>Draw-Vector* command.

Net>Vector >Centrality >Betweenness

File>Vector >Edit

Info>Vector

Draw>Draw-Vector

Eigenvector (Hubs and Authorities) Centrality in Pajek. Technically, Pajek does not estimate eigenvector centrality, but it does include an equivalent set of metrics known as "hubs and authorities" The hubs and authorities algorithm was initially designed for identifying Web pages that functioned as hubs and ones that functioned as authorities. A good *hub* is defined as one that points to many good *authorities*, and a good *authority* is one that is pointed to by many good *hubs* (Kleinberg 1999). Consequently, the algorithm is designed to work with directed networks, but when used with undirected networks, it generates identical hubs and authorities scores.

To obtain hubs and authorities scores in Pajek we use the *Net> Vector>Important Vertices>1-Mode: Hubs and Authorities* command, which calls up two dialog boxes that at first blush can be confusing. The first asks how many hubs you want; the second asks how many authorities. What Pajek is asking is how many hubs and authorities you want Pajek to identify for the hubs and authority partition it will create. The

Net>Vector >Important Vertices >1-Mode: Hubs and Authorities

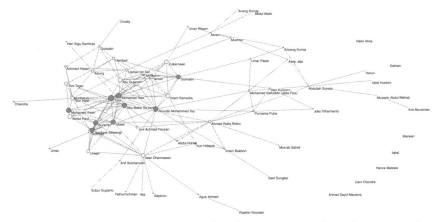

Figure 7.23. Alive Trust Network, Top-Ten Hubs/Authorities High-lighted (Pajek)

default is ten, but you can indicate however many you want. After you work your way through the dialog boxes, Pajek generates a partition and a vector that you can view in the draw screen using the same command that you used previously (Figure 7.23). In Figure 7.23 the size of the nodes varies based on eigenvector (hubs and authorities) centrality, and the actors ranked in the top ten are colored gray.

Excursus: Correlation in Pajek

To calculate the correlation between education and degree centrality in Pajek, highlight both vectors in the Vector drop-down menus (see Figure 7.24). If only one Vector drop-down menu is showing, click on the "Vector" speed button. To calculate the correlation between the two vec-

Vectors>Info   tors, issue Pajek's *Vectors>Info* command, which will generate a report (not shown) that details the correlation between the two vectors.

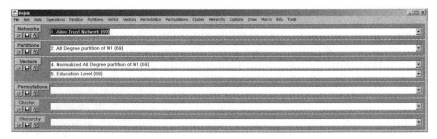

Figure 7.24. Pajek Main Screen

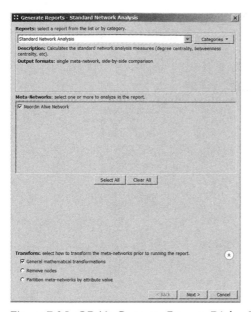

Figure 7.25. ORA's Generate Reports Dialog Box

Centrality in ORA

Begin by opening the alive Noordin meta-network (`Alive Noordin Network.xml`) using ORA's *File>Open Meta-Network* command. Once again the report that interests us here is the Standard Network Analysis report, which can be accessed using ORA's *Analysis>Generate Reports>Locate Key Entities>Standard Network Analysis* command.

This brings up a dialog box similar to Figure 7.25. Because these networks are already dichotomized, there is no need to binarize them. However, if we were working with a valued network but wanted to analyze it dichotomously, then we would want to select the "General mathematical transformations" option (see Figure 7.25), and then at the next dialog box (not shown) we could indicate that we wanted to binarize the network before estimating any metrics. In the next dialog box (Figure 7.26) make sure that all five networks are selected so that ORA will calculate metrics for all five networks.

At the top of the next dialog box (not shown) check to see that the number of ranked nodes to be displayed is at least ten. Click the "Next" button, and in what is the final dialog box, select both the "Text" and "HTML" options, choose where you want ORA's output to go, provide a name for the output file(s), and click "Finish." Once ORA finishes running, you will note that it produces a tremendous amount of output. The first HTML file (which will appear in your Internet browser) serves as a directory, of sorts, with links to pages that describe the data analyzed

[ORA]
File>Open Meta-Network

Analysis >Generate Reports >Locate Key Entities >Standard Network Analysis

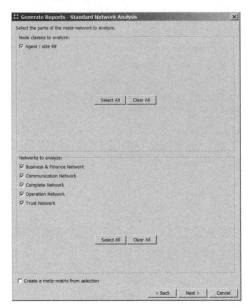

Figure 7.26. ORA's Generate Reports Dialog Box

as well as reports for each of the networks.[9] Scroll down through the HTML output and note that it generates graphics that you may want to use for presentations. You need to be careful here, though, because some of the graphs (e.g., the graph of "key nodes") are summaries of all of the measures computed in the report, even if some are effectively counted more than once (e.g., eigenvector centrality, hubs, authorities), or if some are inapplicable because of the type of data being analyzed (e.g., undirected instead of directed, closeness centrality with disconnected graphs, etc.). Each of the reports contains a tremendous amount of metrics (e.g., degree, closeness, eigenvector, hub, authority, information, betweenness, etc.) – both raw (unscaled) and normalized (value) – some of which apply to this network and some that do not. For example, because the traditional closeness centrality measure was used and this is a disconnected network, the results are incorrect. One "centrality" measure that ORA includes is a count of the number of cliques to which actors belong. As noted in the previous chapter, clique analysis is one of the oldest but most restrictive methods for identifying clusters within a network, but because individual actors can be members of more than one clique, many analysts find it unhelpful for identifying distinct clusters within a network. However, the count of the number of cliques to which actors belong tends to correlate highly with other centrality measures, so it is sometimes used as

---

[9] In order to see all of the HTML output, you may need to turn off your pop-up blocker.

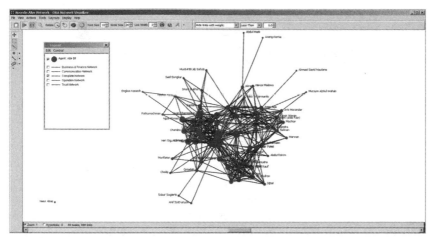

Figure 7.27. ORA Network Map with Node Size Varying by Eigenvector Centrality

a proxy for centrality. A very helpful part of the output is the "Key Nodes Table," which appears at the very end of the report. It lists the top-ten actors (because we told ORA to list the top ten) in terms of the four centrality measures that we have focused on in this chapter (although it does not display the scores).

Return to ORA's main screen and visualize the network. Next, select the *Display Node Appearance>Size Nodes by Attribute or Measure* command. This brings up the "Node Size Selector" dialog box (not shown), which allows you to vary the size of the nodes by various measures. One of the most helpful features of this dialog box is that when you place your mouse next to a measure, a pop-up box appears that explains what the measure is and what it represents. Finally, choose a measure and click on "Close." The actors in your network map should now vary in size by the measure you have selected. In the network map of the alive combined network (Figure 7.27), the nodes vary in terms of eigenvector centrality.

Display Node Appearance >Size Nodes by Attribute or Measure

Summary

Until now, we have considered measures for undirected networks. We now turn to metrics designed for analyzing directed networks and capturing the notion of prestige. The most common measure of prestige builds upon degree centrality, but there are other approaches. Because the Noordin data are undirected, we will use Krackhardt's advice and friendship networks, which are discussed in more detail in the following section.

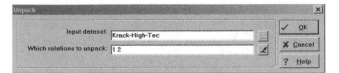

Figure 7.28. UCINET's Unpack Dialog Box

7.3   Centrality and Prestige

Social network researchers sometimes define a "prestigious actor as one who is the object of extensive ties" (Wasserman and Faust 1994:174), which is why they often use indegree centrality as a measure of prestige, which is the count of incoming ties. For example, a member of a dark network to whom people go to for advice (e.g., a mentor) could be seen as enjoying higher levels of prestige than those who only seek advice from others. Of course, if we were looking at the flow of money and other financial resources through a dark network, then outdegree might be a better measure of prestige. As we will see, there are measures of prestige, but indegree (and outdegree) centrality is typically the place where analysts start.

Because calculating indegree and outdegree centrality scores requires directional (i.e., asymmetric) network data, we will use data collected by David Krackhardt from the managers of a company that manufactured high-tech equipment on the West Coast (Krack-High-Tec.##h). According to the description of the dataset in UCINET (Borgatti, Everett, and Freeman 2011), at the time of Krackhardt's study, the firm had been in existence for ten years, produced high-tech machinery for other companies and employed approximately one hundred people, twenty-one of whom were managers (see also Krackhardt 1987a, 1992); these managers serve as the actors in the dataset. Krackhardt gave each manager a roster of the names of the other managers and asked to check the other managers to whom they would go for advice at work ("Advice") and with whom they were friends ("Friends"). He also collected data on "who reports to whom" for all twenty-one managers ("Reports to").

Estimating Prestige in UCINET

Indegree (and Outdegree) Centrality. Because the Krackhardt data are stored in three stacked 21 by 21 matrices, the first thing we need to do is *[UCINET]* unpack the advice and friendship matrices with UCINET's *Data>Unpack* *Data* command, which brings up UCINET's Unpack dialog box (Figure 7.28). *>Unpack* Next, click on the "*L*" button to the right of the *Which relations to unpack* drop-down menu. This brings up the "Select labels" dialog box. Highlight the advice and friendship networks and click "OK." The "Unpack" dialog box should look similar to Figure 7.28. Click "OK."

```
ucinetlog2.txt - Notepad
File  Edit  Format  View  Help
FREEMAN'S DEGREE CENTRALITY MEASURES
-----------------------------------------------------------

Diagonal valid?                    NO
Model:                             ASYMMETRIC
Input dataset:                     ADVICE|

                       1          2          3          4
                   OutDegree   InDegree   NrmOutDeg   NrmInDeg
                   ---------   --------   ---------   --------
    15   15          20.000      4.000     100.000     20.000
    18   18          17.000     15.000      85.000     75.000
     3    3          15.000      5.000      75.000     25.000
     5    5          15.000      5.000      75.000     25.000
    10   10          14.000      9.000      70.000     45.000
     9    9          13.000      4.000      65.000     20.000
     4    4          12.000      8.000      60.000     40.000
    20   20          12.000      8.000      60.000     40.000
    21   21          11.000     15.000      55.000     75.000
    19   19          11.000      4.000      55.000     20.000
     8    8           8.000     10.000      40.000     50.000
     7    7           8.000     13.000      40.000     65.000
     1    1           6.000     13.000      30.000     65.000
    13   13           6.000      4.000      30.000     20.000
    17   17           5.000      9.000      25.000     45.000
    16   16           4.000      8.000      20.000     40.000
    14   14           4.000     10.000      20.000     50.000
     2    2           3.000     18.000      15.000     90.000
    11   11           3.000     11.000      15.000     55.000
    12   12           2.000      7.000      10.000     35.000
     6    6           1.000     10.000       5.000     50.000


DESCRIPTIVE STATISTICS

                       1          2          3          4
                   OutDegree   InDegree   NrmOutDeg   NrmInDeg
                   ---------   --------   ---------   --------
     1    Mean        9.048      9.048      45.238     45.238
     2    Std Dev     5.323      3.970      26.613     19.849
     3    Sum       190.000    190.000     950.000    950.000
     4    Variance   28.331     15.760     708.277    393.991
     5    SSQ      2314.000   2050.000   57850.000  51250.000
     6    MCSSQ     594.952    330.952   14873.810   8273.810
     7    Euc Norm   48.104     45.277     240.520    226.385
     8    Minimum     1.000      4.000       5.000     20.000
     9    Maximum    20.000     18.000     100.000     90.000
    10    N of Obs   21.000     21.000      21.000     21.000

Network Centralization (Outdegree) = 57.500%
Network Centralization (Indegree) = 47.000%
```

Figure 7.29. UCINET's Indegree (and Outdegree) Centrality Output

An alternative method for unpacking stacked networks (and a relatively new addition to UCINET) is to read the Krackhardt data into the UCINET internal spreadsheet program (accessed by the *Data>Data Editors>Matrix Editor* command), and resave the dataset using the *File>Save as multiple files* command. Unlike the "Unpack" command, you cannot choose the networks you want to extract. Instead, it will extract all the files in the data file. Nevertheless, it is a relatively convenient and alternative way to unpack stacked network data.

Data >Data Editors >Matrix Editor

[UCINET Spreadsheet] File>Open file>Save as multiple files

To calculate indegree centrality in UCINET, first select the *Degree* option found under the *Network>Centrality and Power* submenu. This will bring up UCINET's "Degree Centrality" dialog box (not shown). Make sure that the advice network is highlighted in the "Input dataset" option box. Next, select the "No" option in the "Treat data as symmetric" option box; this tells UCINET to calculate both the indegree and outdegree centrality scores of each actor in a network. (When you select "Yes," it calculates and then selects the higher of the indegree or outdegree centrality of each actor.) Click "OK," and UCINET will generate output similar to that in Figure 7.29.

Network >Centrality and Power>Degree

The output is similar to the standard degree centrality report, except that now it distinguishes between indegree and outdegree and does not report a share score. Note that outdegree is listed first, then indegree, so if we want to use indegree as a measure of prestige, we need to look to the second (and fourth) columns. Also, UCINET lists the actors in terms of declining outdegree scores, not their indegree scores, so we simply cannot look at the top of the list to find our most prestigious actor. According to the indegree scores, the advice of manager #2 is sought out more than any other manager's advice (indegree centrality = 18), so we could conclude that in terms of the advice network, manager #2 is the most prestigious and is followed closely by managers #18 and #21, whose indegree centrality scores equal 15. If we were to make the assumption that outdegree is a measure of insecurity, then manager #15 is clearly the least secure with an outdegree score of 20, meaning he or she seeks the advice of every other manager in the company. Of course, this may not be a good assumption because manager #18 scores second highest in terms of outdegree, and as we just saw, he or she ranks second in terms of indegree. As always, we need to be careful when interpreting our results. Repeat this step using the friendship network. In terms of the friendship network, which actor enjoys the highest level of prestige?

Hubs and Authorities. Hubs and authorities scores offer another approach to estimating prestige in a network, and although we did not mention it in our previous discussion of eigenvector centrality, these scores can be estimated in UCINET with the *Network>Centrality and Power>Hubs & Authorities* command. If you recall, the hubs and authorities algorithm was initially designed for ranking web pages. A good *hub* is defined as one that points to many good *authorities*, and a good *authority* is one that is pointed to by many good *hubs* (Kleinberg 1999). Thus, in terms of prestige, it allows analysts to not only take into account the number of ties an actor receives (i.e., an authority) but also to weight those ties by whether the actor that is sending the tie (i.e., a hub) also sends ties to other prestigious actors in the network. This command generates an output similar to Figure 7.30.

Network >Centrality and Power >Hubs & Authorities

As you can see, the hubs scores, which are similar to outdegree scores, are listed first, and the authority scores, which are similar to indegree scores, are listed second. Manager #2 is still ranked the highest in terms of prestige (i.e., authority) and #18 ranks second, but #21 is no longer tied with #18. In fact, manager #21 actually ranks behind manager #1. Why? Because the managers who seek the advice of manager #18 tend to seek the advice of other managers who score high in terms of authority, more often than do the managers who seek advice from manager #21.

Reach Centrality. As de Nooy et al. (2005) have noted, indegree centrality is a somewhat limited prestige measure because it only considers direct

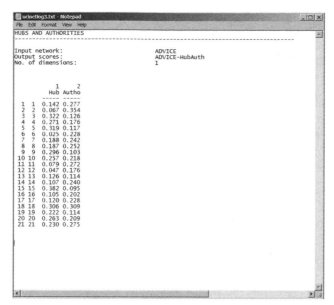

Figure 7.30. UCINET's Hubs and Authorities Output

choices (see also Wasserman and Faust 1994:203–205). Consequently, social network analysts have developed alternative measures that take into account direct and indirect choices. Reach centrality is one such measure. As discussed previously, it counts the number of nodes that each node can reach (or be reached) in k steps or less. When $k = 1$, the resulting score is the same as degree centrality, which means that if we are analyzing a directed network, the resulting scores will equal indegree and outdegree centrality. When $k = n - 1$ (i.e., the size of the network less 1, which is its maximum value), its raw score equals the total number of actors that can be reached in $n - 1$ (i.e., k) steps. Therefore, the resulting raw scores equal the total direct and indirect choices each actor receives (or sends, if we are focusing on outdegree). As we will see further on in this chapter, this is similar to what Pajek refers to as an actor's input (or output) domain.

Calculating reach centrality in UCINET is as straightforward as any of the other centrality measures. The command is located in the *Centrality and Power* submenu. The command first calculates the weighted distance reach centrality of each node, which is the sum of the number of actors that can be reached in k steps divided by k, which is the same as ARD centrality plus one. Figure 7.31 presents a portion of UCINET's reach centrality output with regard to Krackhardt's advice network. Here again, manager #2 ranks first in terms of this measure of prestige with #18 and #21 tied for second.

Network > Centrality and Power > Reach Centrality

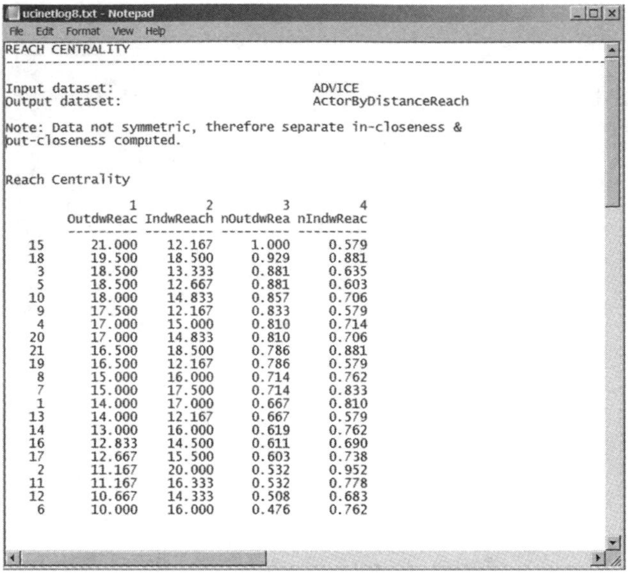

ucinetlog8.txt - Notepad

File Edit Format View Help

REACH CENTRALITY

Input dataset: ADVICE
Output dataset: ActorByDistanceReach

Note: Data not symmetric, therefore separate in-closeness & out-closeness computed.

Reach Centrality

	1 OutdwReac	2 IndwReach	3 nOutdwRea	4 nIndwReac
15	21.000	12.167	1.000	0.579
18	19.500	18.500	0.929	0.881
3	18.500	13.333	0.881	0.635
5	18.500	12.667	0.881	0.603
10	18.000	14.833	0.857	0.706
9	17.500	12.167	0.833	0.579
4	17.000	15.000	0.810	0.714
20	17.000	14.833	0.810	0.706
21	16.500	18.500	0.786	0.881
19	16.500	12.167	0.786	0.579
8	15.000	16.000	0.714	0.762
7	15.000	17.500	0.714	0.833
1	14.000	17.000	0.667	0.810
13	14.000	12.167	0.667	0.579
14	13.000	16.000	0.619	0.762
16	12.833	14.500	0.611	0.690
17	12.667	15.500	0.603	0.738
2	11.167	20.000	0.532	0.952
11	11.167	16.333	0.532	0.778
12	10.667	14.333	0.508	0.683
6	10.000	16.000	0.476	0.762

Figure 7.31. UCINET's Reach Centrality Output

Estimating Prestige in Pajek

File>Project
File>Read
Net>Partitions>Degree>Input
Info>Partition

Indegree and Outdegree Centrality. Read the Krackhardt project file (`Krack-High-Tec.paj`) into Pajek. Make sure that the advice network is listed in the first Network drop-down menu. Select the *Net>Partitions>Degree>Input* command, which creates a new partition (and a vector) based on indegree. You can use the *Info>Partition* command to obtain a ranking of the indegree scores. Be sure that the new partition is showing in the first Partition drop-down menu. In the first dialog box, type "21," which indicates that you want to see the top twenty-one scores (in this case, the scores for all the managers in the network); in the second box accept Pajek's default. This should create a report that looks something like Figure 7.32.

File>Partition>Edit

The upper part of the report ("The highest clusters values") ranks the actors in terms of indegree centrality (*Cluster* is the indegree centrality score), while the lower portion ("Frequency distribution of cluster values") indicates the number of actors in each cluster/class. Thus, manager #2 has an indegree centrality of 18 and there are four actors (19.05 percent of the network) with an indegree centrality of 4, which is the lowest score in the network, whereas only one actor has an indegree centrality of 18, which as we have already seen, is the highest score in the network. If you close the report menu and select the *File>Partition>Edit* command, a window will be called up that displays the indegree centrality measures of each actor in the network.

```
Report                                              _ | □ | x |
File

-----------------------------------------------------------------
2. Input Degree partition of N1 (21)
-----------------------------------------------------------------
Dimension: 21
The lowest value:  4
The highest value: 18

The highest clusters values:

      Rank    Vertex  Cluster     Id
-----------------------------------------
        1        2       18        2
        2       21       15       21
        3       18       15       18
        4        7       13        7
        5        1       13        1
        6       11       11       11
        7       14       10       14
        8        6       10        6
        9        8       10        8
       10       10        9       10
       11       17        9       17
       12       20        8       20
       13        4        8        4
       14       16        8       16
       15       12        7       12
       16        3        5        3
       17        5        5        5
       18       15        4       15
       19        9        4        9
       20       19        4       19
       21       13        4       13

Frequency distribution of cluster values:

    Cluster     Freq      Freq%   CumFreq  CumFreq% Representative
-------------------------------------------------------------------
        4        4     19.0476        4    19.0476 9
        5        2      9.5238        6    28.5714 3
        7        1      4.7619        7    33.3333 12
        8        3     14.2857       10    47.6190 4
        9        2      9.5238       12    57.1429 10
       10        3     14.2857       15    71.4286 6
       11        1      4.7619       16    76.1905 11
       13        2      9.5238       18    85.7143 1
       15        2      9.5238       20    95.2381 18
       18        1      4.7619       21   100.0000 2
-------------------------------------------------------------------
      Sum       21    100.0000
```

Figure 7.32. Pajek's Partition Information Report (Indegree Centrality Scores)

Hubs and Authorities. In the previous section we learned how Pajek estimates hubs and authorities centrality scores with its *Net>Vector> Important Vertices>1-Mode:Hubs-Authorities* command. Pajek's *Info> Vector* feature produces a report (Figure 7.33) that lists the authority scores for the advice network (remember to indicate in the first dialog box that you want to see the scores for all twenty-one managers). As you can see, Pajek's results are the same as UCINET's, which is what we would expect.

Net >Vector >Important Vertices >1-Mode:Hubs-Authorities

Info>Vector

Input Domain and Proximity Prestige. Indegree centrality is a somewhat restricted measure of prestige because it only considers direct choices. As a result, Pajek's developers have included routines for two additional measures that can be used to estimate actor prestige: input domain and proximity prestige (Lin 1976; Wasserman and Faust 1994:203–205). Input domain is a measure of prestige that counts all people by whom someone is chosen whether directly or indirectly. The larger a person's input

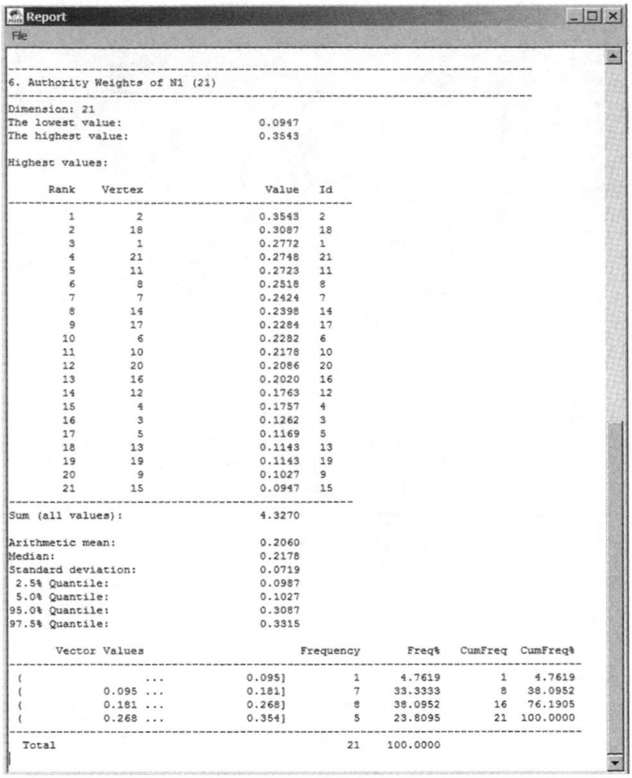

```
Report
File
------------------------------------------------------------------------------
6. Authority Weights of N1 (21)
------------------------------------------------------------------------------
Dimension: 21
The lowest value:                          0.0947
The highest value:                         0.3543

Highest values:

      Rank    Vertex                       Value   Id
-----------------------------------------------------
         1         2                      0.3543   2
         2        18                      0.3087   18
         3         1                      0.2772   1
         4        21                      0.2748   21
         5        11                      0.2723   11
         6         8                      0.2518   8
         7         7                      0.2424   7
         8        14                      0.2398   14
         9        17                      0.2284   17
        10         6                      0.2282   6
        11        10                      0.2178   10
        12        20                      0.2086   20
        13        16                      0.2020   16
        14        12                      0.1763   12
        15         4                      0.1757   4
        16         3                      0.1262   3
        17         5                      0.1169   5
        18        13                      0.1143   13
        19        19                      0.1143   19
        20         9                      0.1027   9
        21        15                      0.0947   15
-----------------------------------------------------
Sum (all values):                          4.3270

Arithmetic mean:                           0.2060
Median:                                    0.2178
Standard deviation:                        0.0719
 2.5% Quantile:                            0.0987
 5.0% Quantile:                            0.1027
95.0% Quantile:                            0.3087
97.5% Quantile:                            0.3315

      Vector Values                    Frequency      Freq%   CumFreq  CumFreq%
---------------------------------------------------------------------------------
 (                ...        0.095]          1      4.7619         1    4.7619
 (          0.095 ...        0.181]          7     33.3333         8   38.0952
 (          0.181 ...        0.268]          8     38.0952        16   76.1905
 (          0.268 ...        0.354]          5     23.8095        21  100.0000
---------------------------------------------------------------------------------
  Total                                     21    100.0000
```

Figure 7.33. Pajek's Partition Information Report (Authority Scores)

Net >Partitions >Domain >Input

domain, the higher his or her prestige. To calculate input domain, use Pajek's *Net>Partitions>Domain>Input* command. A dialog box allows you to specify a maximum distance for the input domain. To begin with, accept Pajek's default ("0," no limit). This produces one partition and two vectors. The partition specifies the number of actors in each actor's input domain. The vector labeled "Normalized Size of input domain" lists the size of each actor's input domain as a proportion of all actors (minus the actor itself), and the second vector gives the average distance to an actor from all other actors in its input domain. We will use these two vectors when calculating proximity prestige. After ensuring that the new partition is listed in the first Partition drop-down menu, use the *Info>Partition* command to obtain a ranking of the actors in terms of input domain (Figure 7.34).

Info>Partition

As Figure 7.34 illustrates, an actor's unrestricted input domain is an imperfect measure of prestige. In a well-connected network such as this one, it often contains all or almost all other actors, so it does a poor job of distinguishing between actors. Indeed, Krackhardt's advice network

```
 Report                                                    _ □ ×
 File
─────────────────────────────────────────────────────────────────
4. Size of input domain in N1 (21)
─────────────────────────────────────────────────────────────────
Dimension: 21
The lowest value:  20
The highest value: 20

The highest clusters values:

     Rank   Vertex  Cluster    Id
    ─────────────────────────────────
       1       1       20       1
       2      21       20      21
       3      20       20      20
       4      19       20      19
       5      18       20      18
       6      17       20      17
       7      16       20      16
       8      15       20      15
       9      14       20      14
      10      13       20      13
      11      12       20      12
      12      11       20      11
      13      10       20      10
      14       9       20       9
      15       8       20       8
      16       7       20       7
      17       6       20       6
      18       5       20       5
      19       4       20       4
      20       3       20       3
      21       2       20       2

Frequency distribution of cluster values:

   Cluster     Freq     Freq%   CumFreq  CumFreq%  Representative
  ───────────────────────────────────────────────────────────────
      20        21   100.0000      21   100.0000   1
  ───────────────────────────────────────────────────────────────
     Sum        21   100.0000
```

Figure 7.34. Pajek's Partition Information Report (Input Domain)

does not distinguish the actors at all. Each actor's unrestricted input domain equals twenty. One solution to this is to assume that choices by closer actors (in terms of path length) are more important than they are from distant actors and then restrict the input domain to neighbors at a prespecified maximum distance chosen by the analyst. For example, Christakis and Fowler (2009) have argued that a person's influence ceases to have a noticeable effect on others beyond three degrees of separation,[10] so they might argue that the influence that each manager has in terms of advice giving does not extend beyond a path length of three (i.e., an advisee of an advisee of an advisee); thus, we should restrict the input domain to three. In the case of the advice network, however, because each manager is within three steps of every other actor in the network, we get the same scores as before (i.e., each actor's input domain equals twenty). With a restricted input domain of two, though, we do get some differentiation in the scores (Figure 7.35), but not too much.

The choice of a maximum distance from neighbors within a restricted input domain can be somewhat arbitrary. The concept of proximity prestige overcomes this by taking into account all actors within an actor's input domain while weighting choices by closer neighbors higher than

[10] Christakis and Fowler's method for estimating this effect has been persuasively challenged on mathematical and statistical grounds (Cohen-Cole and Fletcher 2008; Lyons 2011).

```
Report                                                          _ □ ×
File
----------------------------------------------------------------
6. Size of input [2] domain in N1 (21)
----------------------------------------------------------------
Dimension: 21
The lowest value:  15
The highest value: 20

The highest clusters values:

        Rank    Vertex  Cluster     Id
----------------------------------------------------------------
           1         7       20      7
           2        14       20     14
           3         6       20      6
           4         2       20      2
           5        21       20     21
           6        17       20     17
           7         4       20      4
           8        18       20     18
           9         8       20      8
          10         3       19      3
          11        12       19     12
          12        11       19     11
          13        20       19     20
          14         1       17      1
          15        16       17     16
          16        10       16     10
          17         9       15      9
          18        19       15     19
          19         5       15      5
          20        13       15     13
          21        15       15     15

Frequency distribution of cluster values:

     Cluster     Freq      Freq%   CumFreq   CumFreq% Representative
----------------------------------------------------------------
          15        5    23.8095         5    23.8095 5
          16        1     4.7619         6    28.5714 10
          17        2     9.5238         8    38.0952 1
          19        4    19.0476        12    57.1429 3
          20        9    42.8571        21   100.0000 2
----------------------------------------------------------------
         Sum       21   100.0000
```

Figure 7.35. Pajek's Partition Information Report (Restricted Input Domain)

those of distant neighbors. In other words, a choice by a close neighbor contributes more to an actor's proximity prestige than does a choice by a distant neighbor. This helps analysts avoid the problem we ran into previously with unrestricted input domain (i.e., in a well-connected network unrestricted input domain does a poor job of distinguishing between actors). At the same time, however, because proximity prestige does take into account the choices from distant actors, they are not entirely discounted as they might be with restricted input domain. Consequently, many distant choices may contribute as much as a single close choice (de Nooy et al. 2005:197).

To calculate proximity prestige, we divide the unrestricted (and normalized) input domain size by the average distance. To do this, first be sure that the vector with the normalized size of the input domain ("Normalized Size of input domain in N1 (21)") is highlighted in the first Vector drop-down menu and the vector with average distances ("Average distance from input domain in N1 (21)") is highlighted in the second Vector drop-down menu (Figure 7.36).

Vectors >Divide First by Second

Then, choose the command *Divide First by Second* in the *Vectors* menu. This will create a new vector containing the proximity prestige

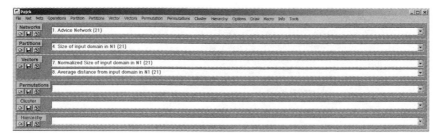

Figure 7.36. Pajek's Main Screen

scores of all vertices. If we examine them with the *Info>Vector* command   *Info>Vector*
(Figure 7.37), we can see that manager #2 is ranked highest with managers
#21 and #18, who are tied with one another and not too far behind. They
are followed by manager #7, after whom are managers #14, #6, #1, and
#11, with all the same score.

Although this set of rankings is similar to those found using the indegree
and authority algorithms, it is not identical. Which one should you use?
There is no hard-and-fast rule. In general, you will want to compare the
rankings. Here, manager #2 has consistently been ranked first with #21
and #18 always near the top. After that the rankings become a little
muddier, but managers #1, #7, #11, and #14 are always in the running.

```
Report                                                    _ □ ×
File
--------------------------------------------------------------
13. Divide V7 by V8 (21)
--------------------------------------------------------------
Dimension: 21
The lowest value:                      0.4878
The highest value:                     0.9091

Highest values:

        Rank    Vertex          Value   Id
--------------------------------------------------------------
          1        2           0.9091    2
          2       21           0.8000   21
          3       18           0.8000   18
          4        7           0.7407    7
          5       14           0.6667   14
          6        6           0.6667    6
          7        1           0.6667    1
          8       11           0.6667   11
          9        8           0.6667    8
         10       17           0.6452   17
         11        4           0.6250    4
         12       20           0.6061   20
         13       12           0.5882   12
         14       10           0.5714   10
         15       16           0.5714   16
         16        3           0.5556    3
         17        5           0.5000    5
         18       15           0.4878   15
         19       13           0.4878   13
         20       19           0.4878   19
         21        9           0.4878    9
--------------------------------------------------------------
Sum (all values):                     13.1973

Arithmetic mean:                       0.6284
Median:                                0.6250
Standard deviation:                    0.1128
  2.5% Quantile:                       0.4878
  5.0% Quantile:                       0.4878
 95.0% Quantile:                       0.8000
 97.5% Quantile:                       0.8545
```

Figure 7.37. Pajek's Vector Information Report (Proximity Prestige)

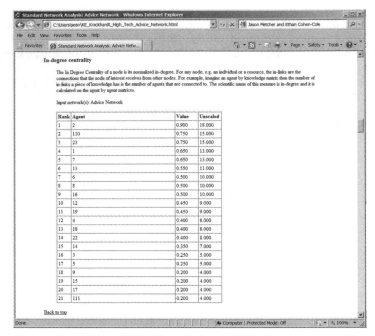

In-degree centrality

The In Degree Centrality of a node is its normalized in-degree. For any node, e.g. an individual or a resource, the in-links are the connections that the node of interest receives from other nodes. For example, imagine an agent by knowledge matrix then the number of in-links a piece of knowledge has is the number of agents that are connected to. The scientific name of this measure is in-degree and it is calculated on the agent by agent matrices.

Input network(s): Advice Network

Rank	Agent	Value	Unscaled
1	2	0.900	18.000
2	110	0.750	15.000
3	23	0.750	15.000
4	1	0.650	13.000
5	7	0.650	13.000
6	13	0.550	11.000
7	6	0.500	10.000
8	8	0.500	10.000
9	16	0.500	10.000
10	12	0.450	9.000
11	19	0.450	9.000
12	4	0.400	8.000
13	18	0.400	8.000
14	22	0.400	8.000
15	14	0.350	7.000
16	3	0.250	5.000
17	5	0.250	5.000
18	9	0.200	4.000
19	15	0.200	4.000
20	17	0.200	4.000
21	111	0.200	4.000

Back to top

Figure 7.38. ORA's Standard Network Analysis Report (Indegree Centrality)

Estimating Prestige in ORA

[ORA] File>Open Meta-Network

Indegree and outdegree scores are included in ORA's standard network analysis report. Thus, after reading the Krackhardt meta-network file (`Krackhardt High Tech.xml`) into ORA with its *File>Open Meta-Network* command, issue its *Analysis>Generate Reports>Locate Key Entities>Standard Network Analysis* command. In the second dialog box ensure that the advice network is selected and change the number of ranked nodes to be displayed to twenty-one. Click "Next" and in the dialog box select both the "Text" and "HTML" options; choose where you want ORA's output to go, provide a name for the output file(s), and click "Finish." As before, ORA will produce a lot of output, and to see all the HTML output, you may need to turn off your pop-up blocker. Because we indicated that we wanted ORA to list the top twenty-one actors (rather than the default of ten), all the tables in the report include scores for each manager in the network. Figure 7.38 displays only the indegree centrality results, but it should be noted that ORA's standard network analysis report includes hubs and authorities scores too.

[ORA-Visualizer] Display Node Appearance>Size Nodes by Attribute or Measure

Return to ORA's main screen and visualize the advice network. Next, select the *Display Node Appearance>Size Nodes by Attribute or Measure* command. This brings up the "Node Size Selector Dialog Box" (not

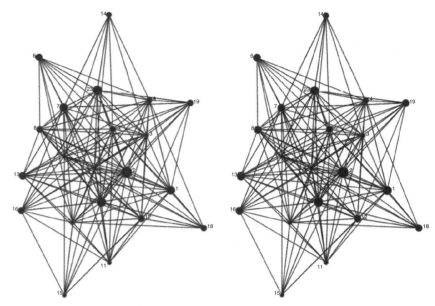

Figure 7.39. Advice Network with Node Size by Indegree and Authority Centrality (ORA)

shown), which if you recall allows you to vary the size of the node by various measures. If you choose indegree centrality and click "Close," the actors in your network map will vary in size in terms of indegree centrality. If you choose authority centrality, the actors in your network map will vary in size in terms of authority centrality. Figure 7.39 presents the advice network with the nodes varying in terms of indegree centrality (left) and authority centrality (right). Although the network maps are not identical, their difference is minimal, suggesting that both measures are tapping into the same dynamic.

7.4 Summary and Conclusion

In this chapter we have explored one of the oldest, and perhaps the most intuitive, social network analysis metrics. It has been used by social psychologists (Bavelas 1950; Moreno 1953) and exchange theorists (Cook and Emerson 1978; Cook et al. 1983; Cook et al. 1986; Cook and Whitmeyer 1992; Emerson 1962, 1972a, b, 1976), and has been formalized by others (Bonacich 1972a, b, 1987; Borgatti 2005; Borgatti and Everett 2006; Everett and Borgatti 2005; Freeman 1977, 1979; Friedkin 1991). We have seen that a central actor can be seen as someone who has numerous ties to other actors (e.g., degree centrality), as someone who has numerous ties to highly central actors (e.g., eigenvector centrality, hubs and authorities), as someone who is close (in terms of path distance) to other actors in the network (e.g., closeness centrality), or as someone who lies on the shortest path between numerous pairs of actors in a network (e.g., betweenness centrality). In addition to considering measures of centrality, we briefly explored how with directed (i.e., asymmetric) networks, "indegree and outdegree" and "hubs and authorities," centrality can potentially be used as measures of prestige. We also explored two variations on the former measures that take into account direct and indirect choices.

What did we learn about Noordin Top's network? We discovered that in addition to Noordin Top, there were a handful of individuals who repeatedly scored high in terms of various measures of centrality across the trust, operational, communication, and combined networks. The one exception was the business and finance network, which as we have seen in previous chapters differs substantially from the other networks. What should we do with this knowledge? As we noted in Chapter 2, it is tempting to use it for the kinetic targeting of high-value actors, but this is not always the best use of resources and often ignores possible second- and third-order effects. For example, anecdotal evidence suggests that direct attacks on insurgents may sometimes worsen the threat (Schmitt and Perlez 2009) by multiplying enemies instead of subtracting them (Flynn, Pottinger, and Batchelor 2010:8). One option has already been mentioned (see Chapter 6): Namely, we might want to monitor individuals who score high in terms of centrality with the hope of improving our knowledge of the network and the selection of strategies adopted (Arquilla 2009:34). Another approach might be to use what we learned about the communication network to craft information operation (IO) disruption strategies that seek to compromise the cell phone and online connections of highly central actors. Finally, we may want to consider using low centrality scores to identify peripheral actors in the network who may be open to reintegration and rehabilitation programs.

8

Brokers, Bridges, and Structural Holes

8.1 Introduction

Betweenness centrality, which we examined in the previous chapter, implicitly introduced the concept of *brokerage*, which is the idea that some actors are more likely to control the flow of resources than others. In this chapter we explore the notion of brokerage in more depth. We begin by looking at Ron Burt's (1992a, b) notion of structural holes, which builds upon Mark Granovetter's (1973, 1974) work regarding weak ties. Burt argues that actors who sit on either side of bridges (i.e., ties) that span gaps in the social structure (i.e., structural holes) are in a position to broker the flow of resources through the network. Somewhat related to Burt's approach is bi-component analysis, which identifies the bridges and actors (i.e., cutpoints) that if removed, disconnect the network (Wasserman and Faust 1994:112–115). Although the notion that the dissolution of certain ties or the isolation of particular actors will disconnect a network is intuitively appealing, in well-connected networks, it is often difficult to find such actors and bridges. Their removal may isolate one or two actors, but it may not disconnect the network in a substantive way. However, we can identify *sets of actors*, that if removed, will either disconnect a network or substantially fragment it (Borgatti 2006). This is known as the *key player* approach, and we will examine it in Section 8.4. Similarly, by measuring the degree to which a tie functions as a bridge in a network, we can ascertain which ties are more likely to disrupt the flow of resources through a network if they are removed (Freeman 2011; Girvan and Newman 2002). We take up this method in Section 8.6.

Implicit in all of these approaches is that identifying brokers and the ties that bind them reveals the cohesive subgroups of which they are (and are not) a part. Put differently, these approaches bring together aspects of the previous two chapters; Section 8.5 focuses on an algorithm that explicitly brings these two aspects together. It assumes that brokerage is a function of the different groups with which actors are affiliated; thus, not only does it require network data, but it also requires attribute data indicating the specific groups to which people belong.

8.2   Structural Holes

In order to understand Ron Burt's notion of structural holes, we need to briefly return to what Mark Granovetter discovered when exploring how people had acquired their current jobs. He found that they were far more likely to have used personal contacts in finding their present job than by other methods. Moreover, of those who found their jobs through personal contacts, most of these contacts were acquaintances (i.e., weak ties) not close friends (i.e., strong ties). Why? According to Granovetter this occurs because our acquaintances are less likely to be socially involved with one another than are our close friends. Aquaintances play an important role in terms of the overall structure of a network, because they form the crucial bridges that tie together densely knit clusters of people. In fact, if it were not for these weak ties, these clusters would not be connected at all. Granovetter went so far as to argue that, at least in the long run, although not all weak ties are bridges, all bridges are weak ties.

Burt builds on Granovetter's argument, but he takes exception to the idea that only weak ties can be bridges. He concedes that weak ties are more likely to be bridges than are strong ties, but he contends that both can function as bridges. By making this theoretical move, Burt directs attention away from the type of tie a particular bridge is (a construct that is often difficult to measure) and toward the gap in the social structure it spans. Burt refers to these gaps in the social structure as "structural holes" and argues that individuals whose ties span these gaps, regardless of whether they are weak or strong, are at a competitive advantage over those whose ties do not span these gaps, because such ties provide them with the opportunity to broker the flow of various resources through the network. In constructing his structural holes measure, Burt focuses on an actor's ego networks (i.e., the actor, their neighbors, and the ties between them), the triads in which they are embedded, and the constraint (or lack thereof) their position in these triads places on them. To get a sense of this, compare the four different types of triads pictured in Figure 8.1 (adapted from de Nooy et al. 2005:144), which consists of three actors (Ed, Jake, and Isabella) and the ties among them. According to Georg Simmel (1950c), when three people are fully connected (i.e., closed), such as in the first triad, they share norms, create trust, and manage conflicts (de Nooy et al. 2005:144). However, in the other three triads, which are open, the actors in the middle are at an advantage because they are in a position to broker between the other two actors. Moreover, in complete

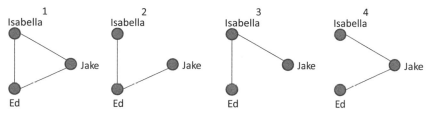

Figure 8.1. Four Types of Triads

triads actors cannot dissolve either tie without putting themselves at a disadvantage. For example, in the first triad, Ed has to maintain his ties to Isabella and Jake if he is to prevent either one from finding themselves in a position of brokerage. For instance, if he were to cut his tie to Jake (the result of which is Triad 3), then Isabella would be in a position of brokerage that she could exploit. Of course, Ed would benefit (and probably prefer) if Isabella cut her tie to Jake (resulting in Triad 2); Jake undoubtedly feels the same way about Isabella's tie to Ed.

In short, open triads provide brokerage opportunities for some actors, whereas complete triads offer only constraints. That is why Burt's structural holes measure does not identify structural holes per se but rather estimates the constraint that all actors in a network face, in light of all the triads in which they are embedded. Less constraint means more autonomy and greater brokerage potential. At this point we do not have to explore the intricacies of how Burt calculates constraint,[1] but the following example (Figure 8.2) adapted from de Nooy et al. (2005:146) should provide a basic understanding of the assumptions lying behind it. First, consider Rick's tie to Victor. It is characterized by three open triads because Guillermo, Enzo, and Renault are not directly connected to Victor. This provides Rick with the opportunity to broker between Victor and Guillermo, Victor and Enzo, and Victor and Renault. By contrast, the constraint placed on Rick because of his ties with Guillermo, Enzo, and Renault is quite high because he is embedded in three complete triads (Rick-Guillermo-Enzo, Rick-Enzo-Renault, and Rick-Guillermo-Renault). Thus, if he were to withdraw from any of these ties, he would place one of them in a position of brokerage. Nevertheless, if Guillermo, Enzo, and Renault have no other ties, they face more constraint (and less autonomy) than Rick because Rick is embedded in three open triads, while Guillermo, Enzo, and Renault are embedded only in closed ones.[2]

Basically, Burt's structural holes algorithm calculates each actor's constraint based on the types of triads in which they are involved, weights

---

[1] We will explore some of these details as we examine how UCINET and Pajek calculate actor constraint and brokerage potential.

[2] Whether Victor faces more or less constraint than Rick depends on whether he has ties to others who do not share a connection with Rick.

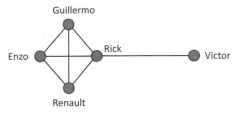

Figure 8.2. Victor's Ego Network (from de Nooy et al. 2005:146)

this by the number of ties in which an actor is involved, and then sums the resulting calculations to arrive at a measure of constraint. If you subtract an actor's constraint score from 1.125 (i.e., the maximum value of constraint – see Buskens and van de Rijt 2008), you have a measure of autonomy or brokerage potential. In keeping with the pattern of the previous chapters, we first examine how UCINET and NetDraw implement Burt's measure before turning to Pajek and ORA. All four programs calculate the aggregate constraint for each actor, but only NetDraw provides an additive inverse of the constraint measure (i.e., a measure of autonomy), which is helpful when visualizing network maps where node size varies by constraint/autonomy, as it is somewhat more intuitive to vary the node size where larger node size indicates more autonomy and less constraint. We will also see how Burt's measures assign isolates the lowest possible level of constraint (and thus high brokerage potential), which, of course, makes no sense because it is hard to imagine how an actor with no ties is in a position to broker anything. In UCINET, NetDraw, and ORA we have to adjust for this (or at least take it into account), while in Pajek we do not because it makes the adjustment on its own.

Constraint (Structural Holes) in UCINET and NetDraw

[UCINET] Network>Ego Networks >Structural Holes

Using Noordin's alive communication network (`Alive Communication Network.##h`), select UCINET's *Network>Ego Networks >Structural Holes* command. In the resulting dialog box (Figure 8.3),

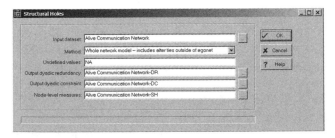

Figure 8.3. UCINET's Structural Holes Dialog Box

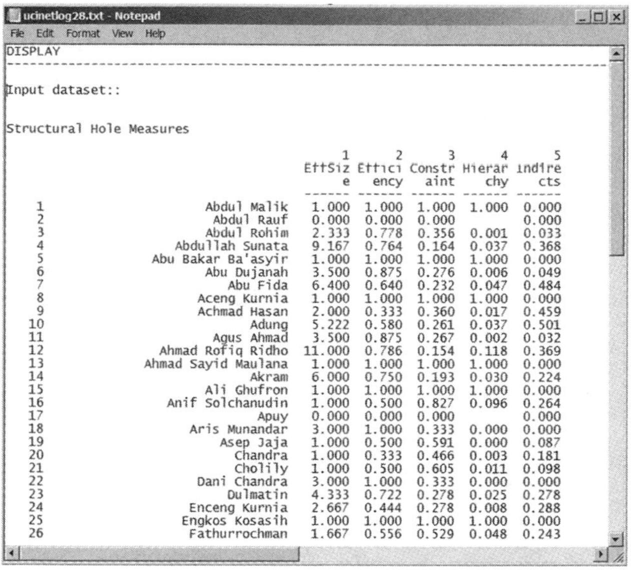

DISPLAY

Input dataset::

Structural Hole Measures

		1 EffSize	2 Efficiency	3 Constraint	4 Hierarchy	5 Indirects
1	Abdul Malik	1.000	1.000	1.000	1.000	0.000
2	Abdul Rauf	0.000	0.000	0.000		0.000
3	Abdul Rohim	2.333	0.778	0.356	0.001	0.033
4	Abdullah Sunata	9.167	0.764	0.164	0.037	0.368
5	Abu Bakar Ba'asyir	1.000	1.000	1.000	1.000	0.000
6	Abu Dujanah	3.500	0.875	0.276	0.006	0.049
7	Abu Fida	6.400	0.640	0.232	0.047	0.484
8	Aceng Kurnia	1.000	1.000	1.000	1.000	0.000
9	Achmad Hasan	2.000	0.333	0.360	0.017	0.459
10	Adung	5.222	0.580	0.261	0.037	0.501
11	Agus Ahmad	3.500	0.875	0.267	0.002	0.032
12	Ahmad Rofiq Ridho	11.000	0.786	0.154	0.118	0.369
13	Ahmad Sayid Maulana	1.000	1.000	1.000	1.000	0.000
14	Akram	6.000	0.750	0.193	0.030	0.224
15	Ali Ghufron	1.000	1.000	1.000	1.000	0.000
16	Anif Solchanudin	1.000	0.500	0.827	0.096	0.264
17	Apuy	0.000	0.000	0.000		0.000
18	Aris Munandar	3.000	1.000	0.333	0.000	0.000
19	Asep Jaja	1.000	0.500	0.591	0.000	0.087
20	Chandra	1.000	0.333	0.466	0.003	0.181
21	Cholily	1.000	0.500	0.605	0.011	0.098
22	Dani Chandra	3.000	1.000	0.333	0.000	0.000
23	Dulmatin	4.333	0.722	0.278	0.025	0.278
24	Enceng Kurnia	2.667	0.444	0.278	0.008	0.288
25	Engkos Kosasih	1.000	1.000	1.000	1.000	0.000
26	Fathurrochman	1.667	0.556	0.529	0.048	0.243

Figure 8.4. UCINET's Structural Holes Output

select the "Whole network model – includes alter ties outside of egonet" option and click "OK."

The output log, a portion of which is displayed in Figure 8.4, first lists measures of dyadic redundancy and dyadic constraint, which are used in calculating aggregate constraint, although the details of their calculation need not concern us here.[3] Next, it lists Burt's constraint measure along with several other related measures. Note that Abdul Rauf's and Apuy's constraint scores equal 0.00 even though they are isolates. They (and all other isolates) should be changed to 1.125. The easiest way to do this in UCINET (at least with a network of this size) is to open the network data in UCINET's spreadsheet editor and make the change yourself.

Data>Data Editors >Matrix Editor

What might we expect to find from an analysis of a network or series of related networks using Burt's measure? Given what we have seen in previous chapters, we might suppose that there will be a positive correlation of constraint scores across networks. We would also probably not be too surprised if a negative correlation existed between Burt's measure of constraint and betweenness centrality, as both attempt to tap into the brokerage potential of actors in a network. Table 8.1 summarizes the correlation of constraint scores with those of other networks (first five rows) and with the betweenness scores of their corresponding network (sixth row). Clearly, a correlation of constraint scores does exist

[3] Hanneman and Riddle (2005:Chapter 9) provide a nice summary of all of UCINET's output.

Table 8.1. *Correlation of constraint and betweenness scores*

	Trust network constraint	Operational network constraint	Communication network constraint	Business & finance network constraint	Combined network constraint
Trust Constraint	1.000	0.312	0.516	0.218	0.506
Operational Constraint		1.000	0.329	0.138	0.798
Communication Constraint			1.000	0.189	0.474
Business & Finance Constraint				1.000	0.149
Combined Constraint					1.000
Betweenness Centrality	−0.551	−0.287	−0.369	−0.287	−0.263

across networks although it is stronger between some than others. For example, the degree of constraint within the trust and communication networks is strongly correlated (0.516), which may indicate that those who broker the flow of communication through the network are also those who lie in positions of brokerage within the trust network. By contrast, but not surprisingly, the correlations between the constraint scores of the business and finance network and those of the other networks are far weaker, indicating once again that the business and finance network differs substantially from the other networks. Comparing the constraint scores of each network to the betweenness scores of the corresponding network, we can see that in all cases a negative correlation exists. Moreover, all of the correlations are relatively strong, which probably indicates that Burt's measure of constraint is capturing much of the same dimension of brokerage as is betweenness. That said, the correlations are not perfect (i.e., −1.00), which tells us that, whereas betweenness helped identify individuals within these networks who were in positions of brokerage, it appears that Burt's measure of constraint has identified others whom we should identify and take note of.

[NetDraw] File >Open>Ucinet dataset >Networks

Because network visualization should be a regular companion of the estimation of metrics (Brandes, Raab, and Wagner 2001), open the alive communication network (i.e., Alive Communication Network.##h) in NetDraw. Also read in (as attribute data) the data file

[NetDraw] File >Open>Ucinet dataset >Attribute data

containing the structural holes measures generated by UCINET (probably named Alive Communication Network-SH) using NetDraw's *File>Open>Ucinet dataset>Attribute data* command. Then vary the size

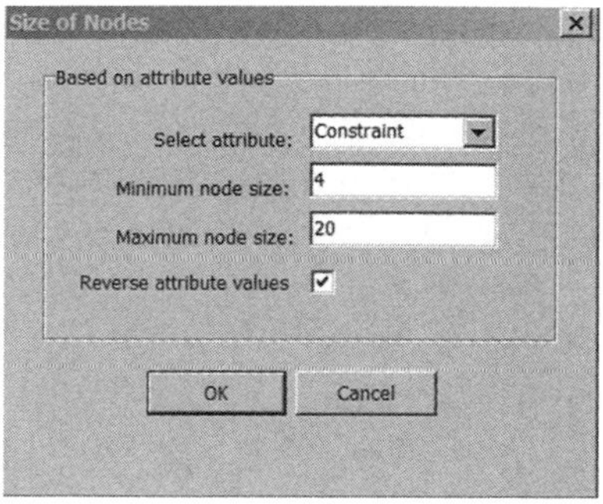

Size of Nodes   ×

Based on attribute values

    Select attribute: Constraint   ▼

    Minimum node size: 4

    Maximum node size: 20

    Reverse attribute values   ✓

            OK   Cancel

Figure 8.5. NetDraw's Size of Nodes Dialog Box

of the nodes to reflect the constraint of each actor using *Properties>* *Nodes>Symbols>Size>Attribute-based* command. In the dialog box that this command calls up, select the "Constraint" attribute and check the "Reverse attribute values" box (see Figure 8.5); this tells NetDraw to draw the size of the nodes in terms of the inverse of Burt's measure of constraint. This should produce a network map similar to Figure 8.6. Not surprisingly, Burt's measure has also found that within the communication network Noordin Top is in a position of brokerage, as are a number of the individuals identified in our previous analysis of the communication network using betweenness centrality (Table 7.3). However, the variation in Burt's measure of constraint is far less than the variation in betweenness centrality scores, which may indicate that brokerage potential is more widespread in the network than previously thought.

Properties *>Nodes* *>Symbols>Size* *>Attribute-based*

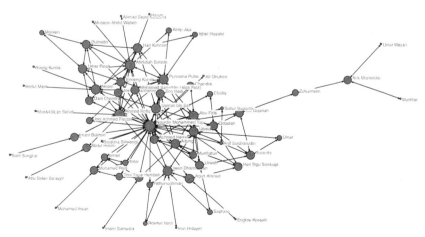

Figure 8.6. NetDraw Map of the Strike Network's Structural Holes (rConstraint)

Analysis>
Structural
Holes>Whole
Network model
NetDraw also provides for the calculation of structural holes as well with its *Analysis>Structural Holes>Whole Network model* command. It also generates an *rConstraint* attribute (i.e., the additive inverse of *Constraint*) that you can use to visualize your network without checking the "Reverse attribute values" box in the "Size of Nodes" dialog box as we did previously.

Constraint (Structural Holes) in Pajek

[Pajek Main
Screen]
Net>Vector
>Structural
Holes
Read the alive Noordin network project file (`Alive Noordin Net-work.paj`) into Pajek. In Pajek the command *Net>Vector>Structural Holes* computes the structural holes measures for all the actors in a network as well as two new networks, proportional strength and dyadic constraint, in which the line values equal the strength and constraint between actors. If you draw the dyadic constraint network, actors with relations characterized by high constraint will be drawn closer together than they would in the original network. Similarly, those with low constraint will be drawn farther apart, which, in turn, should create a space between them that looks something like a hole or gap in the social structure.[4] Figure 8.7 attempts to capture the difference between the two networks. The lower panel is the alive communication network, in which the ties between actors equal the level of dyadic constraint between them; the upper panel is the original alive communication network in which the ties are simply the communication ties between actors. Comparing the two networks you can see that in the lower panel the gap between Noordin and the rest of those to whom he has ties is much larger than in the upper panel, not surprisingly indicating that Noordin sits aside a structural hole and is in a position of brokerage. Compare also the gap between Hari Kuncoro and Dulmatin in the upper-right portion of the network maps. It is relatively small in the regular network (upper panel), but quite pronounced in the dyadic constraint network (lower panel). This suggests that Kuncoro and Dulmatin are sitting aside a structural hole and able to control some of the communication that passes through the network. Thus, dissolving the tie between them could possibly disrupt the ability of members of Noordin's network to communicate with one another. Of course, Kuncoro's and Dulmatin's peripheral positions in the network could mitigate the effect.

[Pajek Main
Screen]
Draw>Draw-
Vector
If you want the size of the actors in your drawing to represent their respective aggregate constraint, then use Pajek's *Draw>Draw-Vector* command, making sure that aggregate constraint vector is showing in the first Vector drop-down box. At the draw screen, you may want to

---

[4] UCINET also generates a dyadic constraint matrix or network that can be visualized in this way in NetDraw.

Figure 8.7. Alive Communication Network (Pajek): Original and Dyadic Constraint

select the *Autosize* option in the *Options>Size>of Vertices* submenu; otherwise, the vertices will be drawn too small. If they are still too small after choosing the auto-size option, try setting the size of the vertices to a larger size, such as "8." If you want the size of the vertex to be positively related to the inverse of the aggregate constraint (i.e., you want larger vertices to indicate better brokerage potential), select the *Vector>Transform>Add Constant* command, and in the dialog box type in the value "–1.000."[5] Then redraw the network as before, except with the newly created vector showing in the Vector drop-down menu. Pajek will inform you that it has drawn negative lines as positive lines, which is OK because all the lines are negative. You should get a network map that looks similar to Figure 8.8.

[Pajek Draw Screen] Options>Size >of Vertices

[Pajek Main Screen] Vector >Transform >Add Constant

---

5 Pajek assigns a maximum value of 1.00 when calculating constraint, so rather than adding –1.125 here, we add only –1.00.

Figure 8.8. Pajek Network Map of Communication Network's Structural Holes

As in Figure 8.6, Noordin appears to be the actor with the most brokerage potential in the network but his brokerage "advantage" is not substantial given the lack of variation in the network.

Constraint (Structural Holes) in ORA

Open the alive Noordin meta-network (`Alive Noordin Network .xml`) into ORA. Currently, in order to calculate constraint in ORA analysts have to select ORA's "All Measures" report: *Analysis>Generate Reports>Show me everything (All Measures)*. As with most of ORA's reports, you will need to work through a number of dialog boxes (not shown) before the report is generated. Typically, you can accept ORA's default settings. Interestingly, with this report ORA reports the results for all the actors in the network rather than those ranked in the top ten, which it typically reports (you can change this if you prefer in the third dialog box). If you plan on merging the results with other data, then you may want to select the CSV option in the final dialog box; this will generate a spreadsheet-like output than be easily imported into spreadsheet programs such as Excel. Finally, because this is an all measure report, it can take some time to be generated.

If you do not wish to generate a report with the structural holes measures for all the actors in a network but instead want to visualize it such that the sizes of the nodes vary in terms of Burt's measure of constraint, first visualize the communication network using ORA's *Visualizations>View Networks>2-D Visualization* command (or its companion speed button on the Editor panel). Next at ORA's visualizer, vary the size of each node by Burt's measure of constraint with ORA's

[ORA-Main Screen] Analysis >Generate Reports >Show me everything (All Measures)

Visualizations >View Networks >2-D Visualization

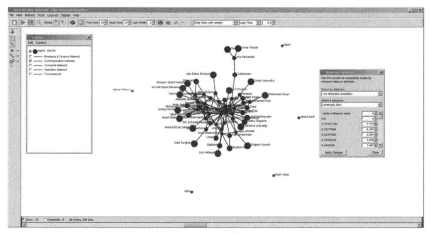

Figure 8.9. ORA Network Map of Communication Network's Structural Holes

Display>Node Appearance>Size Nodes by Attribute or Measure command. In the "Select a Measure" option in the dialog box that is called up, select "Constraint, Burt," and you should get a network map similar to Figure 8.9. Note that unlike the previous graphs we have generated, here larger nodes indicate higher levels of constraint and, concomitantly, lower brokerage potential. Note also, however, that ORA does not adjust constraint scores if an actor is an isolate. The node size of the isolates in the graph indicates low constraint and high brokerage potential, which, as we discussed previously, makes little sense.

[ORA-Visualizer] Display>Node Appearance >Size Nodes by Attribute or Measure

One feature of ORA that is quite useful for analyzing and comparing metrics is its "Measure Charts" function, which is accessed either through the *Visualizations>Measure Charts* command or the companion speed button on ORA's Editor panel. After selecting the Noordin alive network in the Meta-Network Manager and issuing the command, a dialog box appears (not shown here). Accept ORA's defaults and click "Next." This brings up ORA's measure charts interface (Figure 8.10), which most likely will default to the Bar Charts tab; although, as you can see, several options are available (scatter plots, histograms, regression). You will probably want to explore all of these at some point, but here we will focus on the scatter plot feature. Click on the Scatter Plot tab. For the X-Axis measure, indicate you want the betweenness centrality (i.e., "Centrality, Betweenness") scores of the communication network. For the Y-Axis measure, indicate you want the Burt's measure of constraint (i.e., "Constraint, Burt") scores of the communication network. This will produce a scatter plot similar to Figure 8.10. As expected, there is a negative association between the two metrics (as indicated by the downward sloping line). ORA includes a few metrics with the scatter

[ORA-Measure Charts] Visualizations >Measure Charts

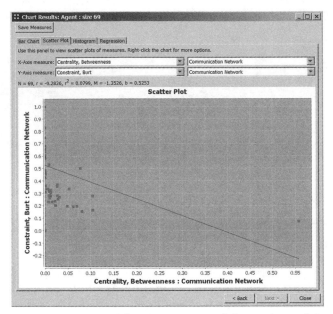

Figure 8.10. Scatter Plot Comparison of Constraint and Betweenness (ORA)

plot, including the correlation between the two measures: $r = -.2826$. However, if you compare this to the correlation we got with UCINET (Table 8.1), you will note that they are not the same. The reason is simple: We have already seen that ORA does not adjust the constraint score of isolates to reflect the inability of isolates to broker anything. If you recall, UCINET does not either (Pajek does, however), but we did adjust the scores manually before estimating the correlation between the two metrics. Thus, while this is a useful feature, it should be used with some caution.

8.3   Bridges, Bi-Components, and Cutpoints

In order to illustrate how the location of certain ties and actors can be crucial to the flow of material and nonmaterial resources through the network, let's turn to Noordin's alive and free operational network (Figure 8.11). Clearly, Noordin, Saptono, and Suramto hold crucial positions in the network because the removal of any one of them (or the dissolution of two of the three ties between them) disconnects the network into separate components. Actors whose removal disconnects the network or disconnects a component of a network are called cutpoints (UCINET and

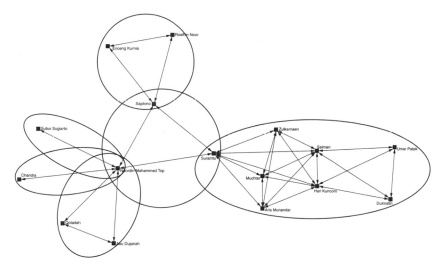

Figure 8.11. Alive and Free Operational Network: Bi-Component Analysis

NetDraw), cut-vertices (Pajek), articulation points (UCINET and Pajek), or boundary spanners (ORA).

Parts of a network that are invulnerable to the removal or isolation of a single actor are known as bi-components. Formally, *bi-components* are components without a cutpoint. They are the sections of a network in which the removal of a single actor does not create a new component. This means that in a bi-component no actor completely controls the flow of resources between two other actors because there is always an alternative path through which resources can flow. Thus, bi-components tend to be more cohesive than strong or weak components because there are at least two different paths between each pair of actors. In the alive and free operational network, there are six bi-components, all of which are circled in Figure 8.11. Often, analysts define a bi-component as a component *of minimum size 3* without a cutpoint, but bi-components of size 2 are of special interest for analysts because they represent ties in the network that if removed or dissolved will disconnect the network. In other words, a bi-component of size 2 is a bridge in the network. In the alive and free operational network there are two such ties (or bridges): the tie between Noordin and Chandra and the tie between Noordin and Sugiarto. Note also that bi-components sometimes overlap with one another. Indeed, where they overlap is where a network's cutpoints are located. Put differently, cutpoints are nodes that belong to two or more bi-components.

Bridges, Bi-Components, and Cutpoints in NetDraw and UCINET

[UCINET]
Network
>Regions
>Bi-Component

In UCINET we detect cutpoints and bi-components using UCINET's *Network>Regions>Bi-Component* command. UCINET does not provide an option for choosing a minimum size of bi-components; instead, it detects bi-components of all sizes (Figure 8.12). Applying this command to the alive and free operational network (Alive & Free Operational Network.##h), UCINET's output log first indicates the members of each block (i.e., bi-component) and then lists the articulation points (i.e., cutpoints) in the network. A quick glance indicates that it agrees with what is illustrated in Figure 8.11.

UCINET also generates a partition (Cutpoints.##h) that can be used to highlight the cutpoints in NetDraw. However, because NetDraw's bi-component routine works quite well and is superior to UCINET's in some respects, there is no need to import the partition files created in UCINET

[NetDraw]
Analysis
>Blocks &
Cutpoints

into NetDraw. Instead, use NetDraw's *Analysis>Blocks & Cutpoints* command, which not only automatically assigns the cutpoints one color and the non-cutpoints another, but also creates partitions that can be used to highlight the various bi-components in the network. Indeed, it was this combination of features that helped generate the network map in Figure 8.11.[6]

[NetDraw]
Properties
>Nodes>
Symbols>Color
>Attribute-
based

If you want to change the color of the cutpoints or color the nodes to reflect the bi-component of which they are a part, use the *Properties> Nodes>Symbols>Color>Attribute-based* command. In the resulting dialog box, select the block (i.e., bi-component) you want to highlight (Figure 8.13).

Bridges, Bi-Components, and Cutpoints in Pajek

[Pajek] Net
>Components
>Bi-Components

Read Noordin's alive and free project file (Alive and Free Noordin Network.paj) into Pajek. In Pajek, the *Bi-components* command is found under the *Net>Components* submenu. Upon selecting this command, a dialog box prompts you to specify the minimum size of the bi-components to be identified. While the default value (three) will identify the bi-components within the network, it will only report cutpoints that connect two or more bi-components of size 3. If you select a minimum size of two, it will identify all bi-components, bridges, and cutpoints, including cutpoints connecting bridges. Pajek will ask if you want to overwrite the current network with a partition of lines. Select "No" (it is unclear why "Yes" is the default), click "OK," and the *Bi-components* command will generate a new network, two partitions, and something we have not

---

[6] Whereas NetDraw identified the various bi-components in the network, the drawing tool in Microsoft Word was used to circle the bi-components in Figure 8.11.

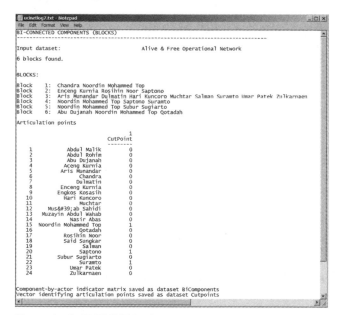

Figure 8.12. UCINET Bi-Component Output Log

encountered until now: a hierarchy. If you draw the new network and in the draw screen select the *Options>Colors>Edges>Relation Number* command, the lines will be different colors, reflecting the bi-components of which they are a part. The first partition ("Vertices belonging to exactly one bi-component") indicates the bi-component class (i.e., number) to which an actor belongs. Actors that do not belong to a bi-component (e.g., isolates) are assigned to class 0, and actors belonging to two or more bi-components (i.e., cutpoints) are assigned to class 9999998.

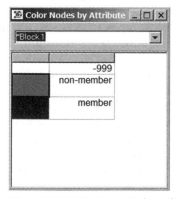

Figure 8.13. NetDraw Color of Nodes Dialog Box

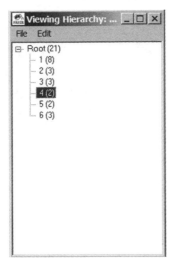

Figure 8.14. Pajek Bi-Component Hierarchy

The second partition ("Articulation points") indicates the number of bi-components to which a vertex belongs: 0 for isolates, 1 for actors that belong to exactly one bi-component, 2 for actors that belong to two bi-components, and so on. Finally, the hierarchy shows the bi-components to which each actor belongs. Pajek uses hierarchy objects to store the bi-components because cutpoints can belong to two or more bi-components.

Because bridges are components of size 2 in an undirected network without multiple lines, it is easy to find the bridges in the hierarchy of *File>Hierarchy* bi-components: Open the Edit screen with the hierarchy of bi-components *>Edit* with the command *File>Hierarchy>Edit* or with the Edit button on the left of the Hierarchy drop-down menu. Next, click on the "+" sign to the left of the word "Root." This should produce a figure similar to Figure 8.14; this lists the six bi-components in the alive and free operational network. The size of each subnetwork is reported between parentheses, as to identify the actors that are a part of the two bi-components of size 2.

Draw>Draw- Next, open the draw screen using the *Draw>Draw-Partition* option *Partition* from the main menu, making sure that the partition "Articulation points" is highlighted at the first Partition drop-down menu. Now, you should see a drawing (Figure 8.15), where the isolates are one color (e.g., white), most of the members of the operational network are another color (e.g., black), and a handful of employees are yet another color (e.g., various shades of gray). Here, the actors that are not black or white are cutpoints in the network.

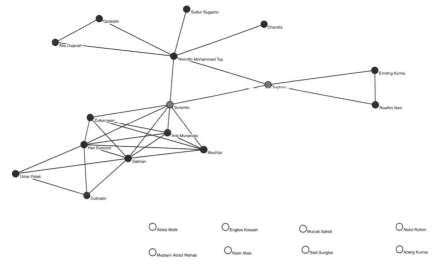

Figure 8.15. Alive and Free Operational Network with Cutpoints Highlighted (Pajek)

Cutpoints (Boundary Spanners) in ORA

Open Noordin's alive and free meta-network (`Alive and Free Noordin Network.xml`) into ORA. Currently, ORA does not detect bi-components; it does, however, identify cutpoints, which it calls *boundary spanners*. One way that you can identify cutpoints in ORA is through the "Show me everything report," which we previously referenced in the discussion of constraint and structural holes. This will generate a report, a portion of which will contain information similar to that presented in Figure 8.16. Note that cutpoints are assigned a score of 1.00, and as one would expect (and hope) these results mirror those that we found using UCINET, NetDraw, and Pajek. A related metric that may also be of interest to analysts, is generated by the same report, and immediately follows the cutpoint results is what ORA refers to as *Boundary Spanner, Potential* (Cormen et al. 2009), which is the ratio of betweenness centrality to degree centrality. It assumes that actors that score high in terms of the former but low in terms of the latter potentially act as ties between groups of entities.

[ORA-Main Screen] Analysis >General Reports>Show me everything (All Measures)

In addition to the all-measures report, analysts can identify boundary spanners using the ORA visualizer or its *Measure Charts* function. For example, Figure 8.17 presents the bar chart generated by the measure charts function. Note that ORA allows you to control the number of actors (nodes) that are displayed, how you want to sort the results (by value or name), and whether you want the names of the actors displayed.

Visualizations >View Networks >2D Visualization

Agent-level Measures

Input data: Alive & Free Network
Start time: Tue Nov 15 10:03:42 2011

	Boundary Spanner Operational Network	Boundary Spanner Potential Operational Network
Abdul Malik	0.000	0.000
Abdul Rohim	0.000	0.000
Abu Dujanah	0.000	0.000
Aceng Kurnia	0.000	0.000
Aris Munandar	0.000	0.000
Chandra	0.000	0.000
Dulmatin	0.000	0.000
Enceng Kurnia	0.000	0.000
Engkos Kosasih	0.000	0.000
Hari Kuncoro	0.000	0.066
Muchtar	0.000	0.000
Mus'ab Sahidi	0.000	0.000
Muzayin Abdul Wahab	0.000	0.000
Nasir Abas	0.000	0.000
Noordin Mohammed Top	1.0000*	0.313*
Qotadah	0.000	0.000
Rosihin Noor	0.000	0.000
Said Sungkar	0.000	0.000
Salman	0.000	0.066
Saptono	1.0000*	0.249
Subur Sugiarto	0.000	0.000
Suramto	1.0000*	0.307
Umar Patek	0.000	0.000
Zulkarnaen	0.000	0.000
MIN	0.000	0.000
MAX	1.000	0.313
AVG	0.125	0.042
STDDEV	0.331	0.096
GINI-COEFFICIENT	0.875	0.853
HERFINDAHL-INDEX	0.304	0.231
BRILLOUIN-INDEX	0.139	0.269

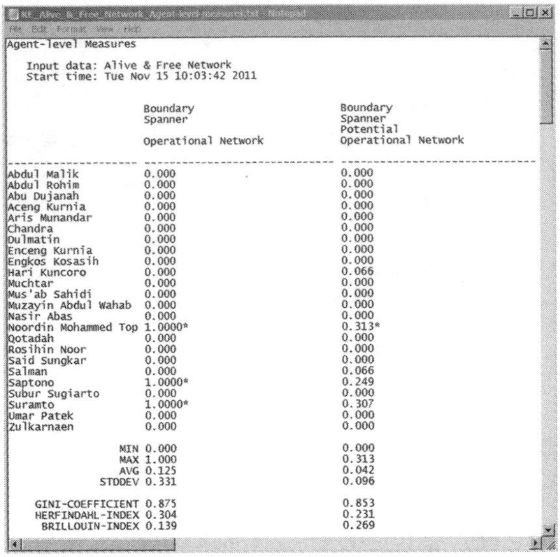

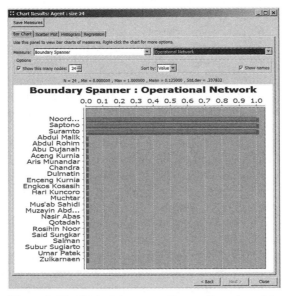

Figure 8.16. ORA All Measures Report Identifying Boundary Spanners (Cutpoints)

Figure 8.17. ORA Measure Charts Function Identifying Boundary Spanners

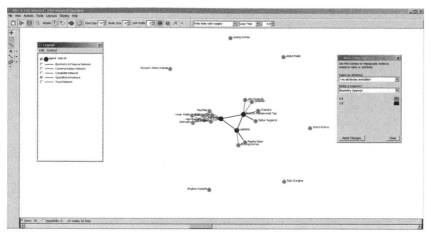

Figure 8.18. Boundary Spanners Identified in ORA's Visualizer

The default number of displayed nodes is ten, but here we have raised it to twenty-four so that results for all of the actors in the network are displayed. Obviously, displaying the results for all network members is only realistic with small networks like this one. When working with large networks, you will want to try alternative numbers of nodes until you find one that adequately captures the results. As you may have already discovered or guessed, ORA's bar chart function allows you to display the results for all of the metrics estimated by ORA (e.g., boundary spanner potential, various centrality measures, constraint, and so on). *Visualization >View Networks >Measure Charts*

Finally, probably the best approach for using ORA's visualizer to identify the cutpoints in a network is by adjusting the color (rather than the size) of the nodes. In other words, using the *Display>Node Appearance>Node Color>Color Nodes by Attribute or Measure* command, adjust the color of the nodes (see Figure 8.18) to indicate whether a particular actor is a boundary spanner or not. As you can see from the resulting network map, it has produced results similar to those displayed in Figures 8.11 and 8.15. *[ORA Visualizer] Display >Node Appearance >Node Color >Color Nodes by Attribute or Measure*

8.4   Key Players

While intuitively appealing, identifying cutpoints is somewhat limited, as there has to exist a single actor that disconnects a network. In the real world, this can be a rare occurrence because most networks are too well connected. Instead, what we need is an algorithm that can identify an optimal set of actors that either completely disconnects the network or at least fragments it to such an extent that it makes the flow of resources across the network (e.g., communication) more difficult. To complicate matters somewhat, simply removing, say, the five or ten most central actors in a network (however, one defines "central") will not necessarily do the trick either, because highly central actors often reach or connect the same actors and groups. To address this issue Borgatti (2006) developed an algorithm that seeks to identify an optimal *set of actors* whose removal either *disconnects or significantly fragments* the network. Two variations of the algorithm exist. The first ("Fragmentation") uses the standard measure of fragmentation (discussed in Chapter 5) to gauge how much various sets of actors fragment the network when they are removed from the network. That is, a fragmentation score is calculated both prior to and after the removal of each of the sets, and the set that increases the level of fragmentation the most is considered optimal. The second variation ("Distance-weighted Fragmentation") is similar to the first except that rather than using the standard fragmentation measure, it uses a distance-weighted measure (also discussed in Chapter 5), that essentially identifies the optimal set of actors whose removal lengthens the average distance (in terms of path length) between all pairs of actors in the network.

Recognizing that the removal of actors may not always be the best or desired strategy when working with dark networks, and that analysts may want to "select an efficient set of actors to surveil, to turn (as into double-agents), or to feed misinformation to," Borgatti has developed an additional algorithm that looks "for a set of network nodes that are optimally positioned to quickly diffuse information, attitudes, behaviors or goods and/or quickly receive the same (Borgatti 2006:22). Put differently, this algorithm is designed to find the optimal set of actors that reaches the highest number of other actors. Here again, Borgatti has developed two variations on this algorithm. The first ("Percent Nodes Reached") simply counts the proportion of distinct actors reached by the set of key actors, while the second ("Distance-weighted Reach") weights this calculation by the path distance between the set of key actors and all other actors in the network.[7]

While it has yet to be implemented in UCINET, it has (somewhat) been implemented in NetDraw. Better than NetDraw's version, however, is Borgatti's *Key Player* program (2011), which comes with each version of UCINET. ORA has also implemented the key player algorithms (which it calls "critical sets") although it currently does not include the distance-weighted versions of the algorithms. We begin by examining how Borgatti's Key Player program has implemented these algorithms before turning to see how ORA has done the same.

---

[7] Both distance-weighted algorithms use average reciprocal distance (ARD) in their calculations rather than the standard measure of closeness because (as we discussed in the previous chapter) the former can be used with disconnected graphs while the latter cannot.

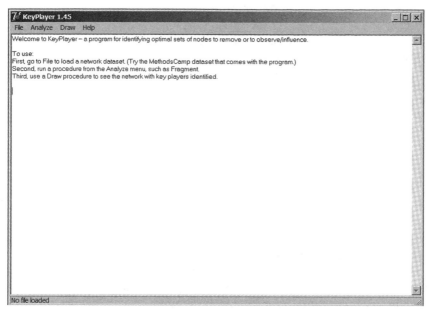

Figure 8.19. Key Player Program

Identifying Key Players with Key Player

Borgatti's Key Player program can be found in the *Analytic Technologies* >*Helper Applications*>*Key Player* folder in the *Program Files* directory. It reads UCINET files and is relatively straightforward to use. Open Key Player by double-clicking on the icon in the Key Player folder, which will open an interface that looks similar to Figure 8.19. Load the combined alive network (`Alive Combined Network.##h`) using the *File*>*Load Network Data*>*UCINET Dataset* command. To run the standard key player fragmentation algorithm, select the *Analyze*>*KPP-1 Select Nodes to Remove*>*Fragmentation Criterion* command. This calls up a dialog box that prompts you to indicate how large you want your key player "set" to be. After indicating the size, click "OK," and the program identifies a set of key players for removal and creates a corresponding partition (`fragmentvec.##h`) that can be inspected or used to visualize in NetDraw. Key Player also provides "before" and "after" fragmentation scores, which can be useful when comparing and choosing between different size sets. For example, if a set of size 6 does not increase fragmentation to any great degree over a set of size 5, then it probably makes more sense to choose the smaller set over the larger one. It is important to note that because Key Player identifies the optimal set, it does not list the actors of the set in rank order. Rather, it lists them in the order that they appear in the dataset. To obtain a set of key

*[Key Player]
File>Load
Network Data
>UCINET
Dataset*

*Analyze
>KPP-1 Select
Nodes to
Remove
>Fragmentation
Criterion*

Table 8.2. *Key players in alive combined network*

Fragmentation	Distance-weighted fragmentation	Reach	Distance-weighted reach
Abdullah Sunata Akram	Abdullah Sunata Akram	Abdullah Sunata	Abdullah Sunata Akram
			Imam Samudra
Iwan Dharmawan	Iwan Dharmawan		Iwan Dharmawan
		Mohamed Saifuddin Nasir Abas	
Noordin Top Rosihin Noor	Noordin Top	Noordin Top	Noordin Top
	Suramto		
		Usman bin Sef	

Analyze >KPP-1 Select Nodes to Remove >Distance-Weighted Fragmentation Criterion

players using the distance-weighted algorithm use the *Analyze>KPP-1 Select Nodes to Remove>Distance-Weighted Fragmentation Criterion* command. This generates a corresponding partition (`distvec.##h`) that can be inspected or used for visualization purposes in NetDraw.

[NetDraw] File>Open >UCINET Dataset >Network

File>Open >UCINET Dataset >Attribute Data

To visualize the results, first read the network that you analyzed using Key Player (e.g., `Alive Combined Network.##h`) into NetDraw, and then load the partition generated by Key Player (e.g. `distvec.##h`) as an attribute file. You can then color the nodes, as illustrated previously, and generate a network map similar to Figure 8.20. In this example, five individuals (colored gray) in the alive combined network were identified using the distance-weighted algorithm, three of whom (Noordin, Akram, and Abdulah Sunata) were also cutpoints. The size of a key player set should, of course, take into account relevant factors, such as time constraints and available resources.

[Key Player] Analyze >KPP-2 Select Nodes to Utilize ># of Nodes Reached Criterion

Analyze>KPP-2 Select Nodes to Utilize>Distance-Weighted Reach Criterion

The diffusion or "reach" algorithms are accessed and estimated in similar ways to the fragmentation algorithms. To run the standard reach algorithm, use the *Analyze>KPP-2 Select Nodes to Utilize># of Nodes Reached Criterion* command; to run the distance-weighted reach algorithm, use the the *Analyze>KPP-2 Select Nodes to Utilize>Distance-Weighted Reach Criterion* command. As with the fragmentation algorithms, both generate partitions that can be used for visualization or inspection. Unfortunately, both are named `reachvec.##h`, which means that the results of one will overwrite the results of the other if you are not careful. The two algorithms also produce "before" and "after" scores that indicate the effective reach of the set.

Table 8.2 presents the results from a key player analysis of the alive combined network using the four key player algorithms. While they produce similar results, the results differ. The two fragmentation algorithms identified four of the same individuals. They only differ in terms

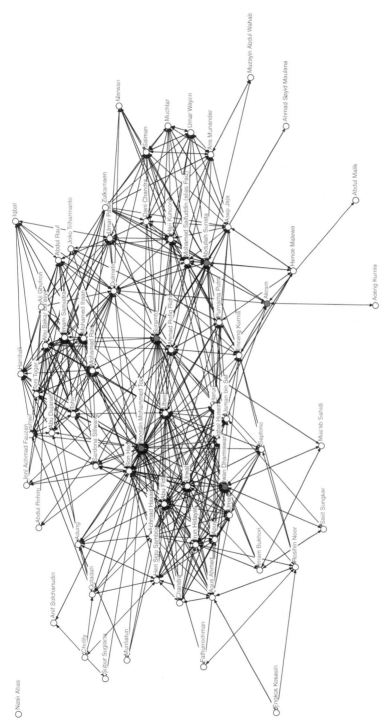

Figure 8.20. Key Players in the Alive Combined Network

275

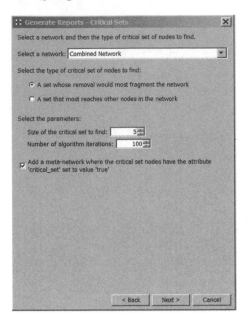

Figure 8.21. ORA Critical Set Dialog Box

of Rosihin Noor and Suramto. There is far less agreement between the two reach algorithms. They only identify two of the same individuals (Noordin Top and Abdullah Sunata) as ideal candidates for the diffusion of misinformation, surveillance, or attempting to turn. This, of course, is not entirely unexpected because they do operate under slightly different assumptions. Thus, analysts would probably want to compare the results of the two algorithms, consider whether path distance should be treated as an important factor, and consult additional relevant information.

Identifying Key Players (Critical Sets) with ORA

[ORA-Main Screen] Analysis >Generate Reports >Locate Key Entities >Critical Sets

We locate key players in ORA using its *Analysis>Generate Reports >Locate Key Entities>Critical Sets* command. The first dialog box that this command calls up (not shown) asks us to indicate which meta-networks we intend to analyze. Here we will use the alive meta-network (Alive Noordin Network.xml). The next dialog box (not shown) asks which networks within each meta-network we intend to analyze. ORA's default settings are typically fine. At the third dialog box (Figure 8.21), however, we will have to change several of ORA's defaults. At the top of the dialog box, we need to indicate which network ("Combined") to use. Then, we have to tell ORA whether we want a set that fragments the network or one that best reaches other actors in the network (recall

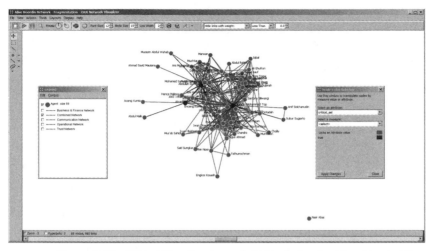

Figure 8.22. ORA Visualization of Critical Set in Combined Alive Network

that ORA does not include distance-weighted algorithms). Next, we have to select the size of the critical set. Finally, we have to choose whether we want ORA to generate a new meta-network that includes a critical set attribute. This is useful for visualization purposes, so we typically will want to select this option as well. Clicking "Next" takes us to the fourth and final dialog box (not shown) where we indicate the type of output we want and where we want any reports to be stored. Clicking "OK" generates a report that contains similar information to the information obtained using Key Player: in particular, the set of critical nodes and before and after fragmentation or reach scores.

The meta-network that includes a critical set attribute that we asked ORA to create should now appear in the Meta-Network Manager. If you visualize this meta-network and adjust the color of the nodes (*Display>Node Appearance>Node Color>Color Nodes by Attribute or Measure*) to reflect whether they are a part of the critical set or not, you should get a network map similar to Figure 8.22. Although the node labels are a little diificult to see, the results are identical to those obtained using Key Player.

[ORA-Visualizer] Display >Node Appearance >Node Color >Color Nodes by Attribute or Measure

8.5   Affiliations and Brokerage

Group affiliation is often an important factor in brokerage processes. For example, in brokering deals in Congress, U.S. senators not only take into account their own interests and desires but also the political party of which they are a part. Although they might want to support a particular

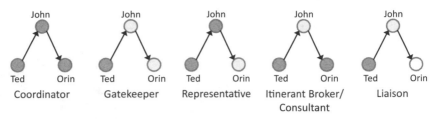

Figure 8.23. Brokerage Roles of "John"

legislative bill, their party membership may constrain what they are able to do and say. Roger Gould and Roberto Gonzalez (Fernandez and Gould 1994; Gould and Fernandez 1989) have attempted to capture this dynamic by identifying five different types of brokerage roles that actors can play based on their group affiliation: (1) coordinator, (2) gatekeeper, (3) representative, (4) itinerant broker/consultant, and (5) liaison (see Figure 8.23 where node color indicates group affiliation).

- *Coordinator* – provides mediation between members of one group where the mediator is also a member of the group
- *Gatekeeper* – provides mediation between two groups where mediator regulates the flow of information or goods to his or her group
- *Representative* – provides mediation between two groups where mediator regulates the flow of information or goods from his or her group
- *Itinerant Broker/Consultant* – provides mediation between members of one group where the mediator is not a member of the group
- *Liaison* – provides mediation between two groups where mediator does not belong to either group

Gould and Fernandez originally conceived of these five types of brokerage roles in terms of directed networks, but tie direction only distinguishes between representative and the gatekeeper brokerage roles. Thus, if we apply their brokerage roles algorithm to undirected networks, each actor identified as a representative will also be a gatekeeper and vice versa. In the following examples, we will return to the alive and free combined network that we analyzed in terms of factions and Newman groups in Chapter 6. If you recall, those two sets of algorithms offered slightly different answers as to which subgroups certain actors belonged, suggesting that they may be in a position of brokerage between such groups. Also, at this writing, only UCINET and Pajek include the Gould and Fernandez algorithm, so we limit our analysis to those two programs.

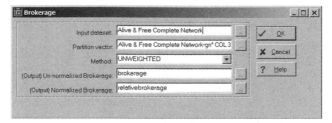

Figure 8.24. UCINET Brokerage Role Dialog Box

Affiliations and Brokerage in UCINET and NetDraw

In UCINET we identify brokerage roles using its *Network>Ego Net-* *works>G&F Brokerage roles* command, which calls up the brokerage dialog box (Figure 8.24).

[UCINET]
Network
>Ego Networks
>G&F
Brokerage roles

As you can see, because this routine needs to know the groups to which actors belong, not only do we need to indicate the network we intend to analyze (Alive & Free Combined Network.##h) but also a partition file that indicates group membership. This partition can be based on predefined groups (e.g., Republican, Democrat) or on groups detected through one or more of the clustering algorithms we examined in previous chapters. Here, I have chosen the three-group (column 3) Girvan-Newman partition that we generated using UCINET in Chapter 6 (Alive & Free Combined Network-gn.##h). Keeping UCINET's defaults and clicking "OK" generates results that are displayed in an output log and saved in two attribute files (brokerage.##h and relative-brokerage.##h). UCINET's output log (a portion of which is presented in Figure 8.25) is extensive. It first lists raw brokerage role scores (i.e., the count of how often each actor "plays" a particular role within the network – note that the Gatekeeper and Representative scores are identical). Next, comes a series of block matrices for each actor, wherein each row/column refers to the various groups in the network, and the numbers in the cells indicate how often each actor plays a brokerage role either between two groups or within a single group. Finally, it provides normalized brokerage scores (i.e., raw brokerage role counts are divided by expected counts – given a random network – based on network size).

Table 8.3 summarizes the results of the Gould and Fernandez brokerage analysis. The Gatekeeper and Representative scores have been combined (not summed) into a single column because (as noted previously) with undirected networks, the scores are identical. The "total" score has been adjusted accordingly as well. Not surprisingly, Noordin is found in the most brokerage roles; in fact, he is the only individual to be located in all four of the types of brokerage roles examined here. Next in terms of total count is Suramto, who has turned up in previous analyses as a potential broker. However, he only functions as a coordinator or gatekeeper but

```
ucinetlog7.txt - Notepad                                        _ □ x

File  Edit  Format  View  Help

GOULD & FERNANDEZ BROKERAGE MEASURES
--------------------------------------------------------------

Input dataset:               Alive & Free Complete Network (E:\Sociology\Social Net
Partition vector:            "Alive & Free Complete Network-gn" COL 3
Method:                      UNWEIGHTED
Normalized Brokerage:        relativebrokerage (E:\Sociology\Social Network Analys
Unnormalized Brokerage:      brokerage (E:\Sociology\Social Network Analysis\Book\[
Warning: Attribute vector has been recoded.

Here is a translation table:

   Old Code    New Code    Frequency
   ========    ========    =========
       1    =>     1           1
       2    =>     2           5
       3    =>     3          10
       4    =>     4           1
       5    =>     5           4
       6    =>     6           1
       7    =>     7           1
       8    =>     8           1

Number of classes: 8

Un-normalized Brokerage Scores

                              1        2        3        4        5        6
                         Coordinat Gatekeepe Represent Consultan  Liaison   Total
                         --------------------------------------------------------
       1    Abdul Malik |    0        0        0        0        0       0 |

       2    Abdul Rohim |    0        0        0        0        0       0 |
   15 Noordin Mohammed Top|  12       19       19        2        8      60 |
   16       Qotadah     |    0        0        0        0        0       0 |
    6       Chandra     |    0        0        0        0        0       0 |
   21     Subur Sugiarto|    0        0        0        0        0       0 |
                         --------------------------------------------------------
    5     Aris Munandar |   10        0        0        0        0      10 |
    7        Dulmatin   |    8        8        8        0        0      24 |
   11        Muchtar    |    0        0        0        0        0       0 |
   10     Hari Kuncoro  |   14        0        0        0        0      14 |
   23       Umar Patek  |    0        2        2        0        0       4 |
   24       Zulkarnaen  |   14        0        0        0        0      14 |
   13 Muzayin Abdul Wahab|   0        0        0        0        0       0 |
    3       Abu Dujanah |    2        4        4        0        0      10 |
```

Figure 8.25. UCINET Brokerage Role Output Log

not as a consultant or liaison. Next comes Dulmatin, whom, you may recall from Chapter 6, we identified along with Umar Patek as a possible broker. Interestingly, what this analysis seems to suggest is that while our "intuition" regarding Dulmatin was correct, it was incorrect regarding Patek. Patek may be important to Noordin's (and others') network in some fashion, but at least in terms of the combined alive and free network, he is not.

Although NetDraw does not include the Gould and Fernandez broker- age role routine, we can still use it to visualize the number of brokerage roles for each actor by varying the size of each node by one (or total) of the brokerage scores. Figure 8.26 does just this where the size of the node indi- cates the Gatekeeper brokerage score. Moreover, the color of the nodes indicates the Girvan-Newman group to which they were assigned and used to calculate the brokerage scores. This network map was created by first loading the combined alive network into NetDraw, and then reading in both the brokerage scores file (brokerage.##h) and the Girvan- Newman partition (Alive & Free Combined Network-gn.##h). Then, the size of the nodes were adjusted using the *Properties>Nodes> Symbols>Size>Attribute-based* command and the color of the nodes was adjusted using the *Properties>Nodes>Symbols>Color>Attribute-based* command. The graph aptly illustrates the results of Table 8.3. Indeed, it amplifies the position of brokerage that Noordin holds between various

[NetDraw]
File>Open
>Uninet data
>Network
File
>Open
>Uninet data
>Attribute data

Properties
>Nodes>
Symbols>
>Color
>Attribute-
based

Table 8.3. *Gould and Fernandez brokerage scores for alive combined network*

	Coordinator	Gatekeeper/ representative	Itinerant broker consultant	Liaison	Total
Abdul Malik	0	0	0	0	0
Abdul Rohim	0	0	0	0	0
Abu Dujanah	2	4	0	0	6
Aceng Kurnia	0	0	0	0	0
Aris Munandar	10	0	0	0	10
Chandra	0	0	0	0	0
Dulmatin	8	8	0	0	16
Enceng Kurnia	0	5	0	2	7
Engkos Kosasih	0	0	0	0	0
Hari Kuncoro	14	0	0	0	14
Muchtar	0	0	0	0	0
Mus'ab Sahidi	0	0	0	0	0
Muzayin Wahab	0	0	0	0	0
Nasir Abas	0	0	0	0	0
Noordin Top	12	19	2	8	41
Qotadah	0	0	0	0	0
Rosihin Noor	4	0	0	0	4
Said Sungkar	0	0	0	0	0
Salman	14	0	0	0	14
Saptono	0	3	0	0	3
Subur Sugiarto	0	0	0	0	0
Suramto	8	11	0	0	19
Umar Patek	0	2	0	0	2
Zulkarnaen	14	0	0	0	14

subgroups in the network (recall that the gatekeeper brokerage role captures an actor's mediation potential between groups). It also highlights that Suramto, Dulmatin, and possibly Enceng Kurnia may be in positions to mediate between groups as well. Of course, this only illustrates the relative potential of actors in terms of gatekeeping; similar network maps can be generated in terms of the other brokerage roles as well.

Affiliations and Brokerage in Pajek

In Pajek the *Operations>Brokerage Roles* command identifies brokerage roles. After opening the alive and free project file (Alive and Free Noordin Network.paj), make sure that the network of interest (e.g., alive and free combined network) is displayed in the first Network drop-down menu and the Girvan-Newman partition is displayed in the first Partition drop-down menu, and then issue the command. This will generate five new partitions, one for each type of brokerage role, all of which

[Pajek] Operations >Brokerage Roles

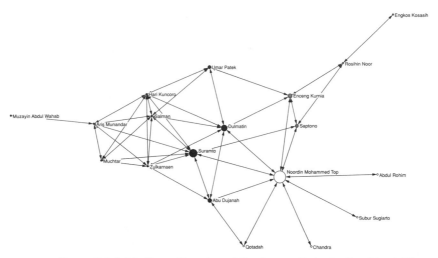

Figure 8.26. NetDraw Drawing of Gatekeeper Roles in Combined Alive Network

are added to the Partition drop-down menu. The class number assigned to an actor in each partition specifies the number of times that actor is found in the corresponding brokerage role.

Info>Partition   We can call up a frequency table for each partition using the *Info >Partition* command, and we can check the individual scores of each *File>Partition* actor using Pajek's *File>Partition>Edit* command. To visualize the *>Edit* network where node size reflects the number of brokerage roles, we need to first convert the brokerage partitions into vectors using the *Partition>Make Vector* command. Then we can visualize the network *Draw>Draw-* similarly to how we did with NetDraw (*Draw>Draw-Partition-Vector*). *Partition-Vector* Specifically, if we highlight the combined alive and free network in the first Network drop-down menu, the Girvan-Newman partition in the first Partition drop-down menu, and a vector generated from the Gatekeeper partition, we will produce a network map similar to Figure 8.27, which, while not identical to Figure 8.26, tells a very similar story.

8.6   Bridges and Network Flow

Perhaps one of the most parsimonious means for detecting bridges within a network is by focusing on the potential flow of resources through a network. Recall from Chapter 6 that one way to identify Newman groups (Girvan-Newman – the approach that UCINET uses) is to first estimate betweenness centrality for each edge/tie (not actor) in the network, remove the tie with the highest betweenness score, recalculate edge

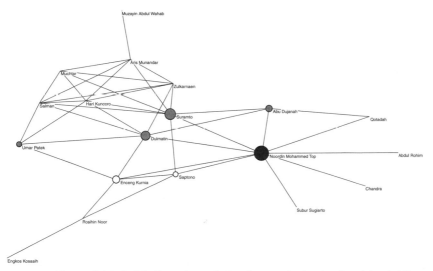

Figure 8.27. Pajek Drawing of Gatekeeper Roles in Combined Alive Network

betweenness centrality, and then iteratively repeat the process until no edges/ties remain. Because edges of high betweenness are assumed to be vital for connecting different parts of the network, it is an efficient method for breaking the network down into large subgroups and then smaller ones. An implicit assumption of this approach is that edges that score high in terms of edge betweenness are likely to span gaps in the social structure, what Ron Burt calls structural holes. In other words, edges that score high in terms of edge betweenness are more likely to be bridges than those that do not.

Edge Betweenness in UCINET and NetDraw

Currently, only UCINET estimates edge betweenness, so we will focus our efforts in UCINET and NetDraw, using the combined alive and free network as an example. Edge betweenness is calculated in UCINET using its *Network>Centrality and Power>Freeman Betweenness>Edge (line) Betweenness* command. Generally, we will want to accept UCINET's defaults and click "OK." The command generates a new network where the cell values are edge betweenness scores. If we examine the network matrix, we can determine which edge has the highest betweenness score.

Unfortunately, while the inspection of a network matrix of edge betweenness scores is feasible with small networks, it becomes increasingly difficult with large networks. An easier way to examine the network is to visualize it in NetDraw. Open your newly generated network

[UCINET] Network >Centrality and Power >Freeman Betweenness >Edge (line) Betweenness

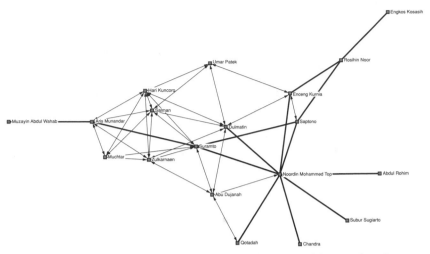

Figure 8.28. Combined Alive Network, Tie-Width Equals Edge Be-tweenness (NetDraw)

[NetDraw]
Properties
>Lines
>Size
>Tie Strength

(probably called "EdgeBetweeness") in NetDraw and vary the size of the ties based on tie strength (*Properties>Lines>Size>Tie Strength*). To see the edges clearly you may need to minimize the size of the labels (or hide them altogether), but you should end up with a network map that looks similar to Figure 8.28. As you can see, some of the ties score higher in terms of edge betweenness than do others. We can probably ignore some because they are ties to individuals with only one tie to the network (known as pendants), but others (e.g., Noordin-Suramto, Suramto-Aris Munandar, Suramto-Saptono) could be of possible interest.

One of the attractions of detecting bridges is that dissolving a tie may, in some cases, be easier to do than removing a particular actor from a network. Why? One reason is that there are always two actors involved in every bridge, and one may be easier to access than the other (e.g., one may be less central than the other or may carry out a role that has higher visibility). Another is that a tie can be dissolved through a misinformation campaign that seeks to create distrust between those on either side of the bridge or through an information operations campaign that attempts to sever the ability of certain pairs of actors to communicate.

8.7   Summary and Conclusion

In this chapter we have examined five approaches for identifying brokers and/or bridges in a network. We began by looking at Burt's (1992a, b) notion of structural holes, which calculates the level of constraint each actor in a network faces. As we saw, it builds on Mark Granovetter's (1973, 1974) notion of weak ties but takes the position that when it comes to identifying brokerage potential, it is not the type of tie that is important but rather the gaps in the social structure. Next we examined how we can use a technique known as bi-component analysis to identify the actors (cutpoints) and bridges (bi-components of size two) within a network whose removal will disconnect it. We then explored Borgatti's (2006) key player algorithms, which identify optimal sets of actors that can be targeted for either fragmenting the network or for diffusing resources through a network. His approach represents an improvement over bi-component analysis because in well-connected networks, cutpoints often do not exist. After this we turned to the Gould and Fernandez algorithms (Fernandez and Gould 1994; Gould and Fernandez 1989) that assume that brokerage is a function of the different groups with which actors are affiliated; thus, not only does this approach require network data, it also requires attribute data indicating the specific groups to which actors belong. Finally, we considered an approach that draws on the notion of betweenness centrality in order to identify ties in a network that are more likely to be functioning as bridges in the network, that is, they are more likely to be the ties through which material and nonmaterial resources flow through a network.

One thing that should be apparent from this chapter's examples is that these algorithms do not always yield the same results. In terms of Noordin's network we identified a number of different individuals (and ties) who may be in a position of brokerage (or a bridge) and therefore warrant closer observation, monitoring, and consideration for the crafting of strategies. However, because the results do vary (and would probably vary even more if we examined all five networks in terms of every possible state of "being" (i.e., alive, alive and free, incarcerated, all). What this highlights is a point that was made in the second chapter: Although social network analysis is a useful tool for the crafting of strategies, a single "magic bullet" algorithm on which we can consistently rely does not exist. Instead, we need to draw on other available information to inform any final decisions that are made.

9

Positions, Roles, and Blockmodels

9.1 Introduction

In Chapter 1, we noted that social network analysts tend to analyze network data in one of two ways: (1) a relational approach or (2) a positional approach (Emirbayer and Goodwin 1994). The former focuses on the direct and indirect ties between actors and seeks to explain behavior and social processes in light of those ties. It highlights the importance of the topography of networks, the centrality of actors, the cohesiveness of subgroups, and the brokers and bridges between such groups. Up to this point, we have essentially focused on the relational approach of social network analysis. In this chapter, we shift gears and explore the positional approach. It differs from the relational approach in that rather than focusing on the ties between actors, it seeks to identify actors who hold similar positions in the social structure. Why are positions seen as important? A position (e.g., student) is typically connected to a particular role or set of roles (e.g., attending class, writing papers, studying for exams) and located within a larger system of positions (e.g., fellow students, professors, staff, administrators). Consequently, some social network theorists argue that actors occupying a particular position/role will be embedded in a similar pattern of ties and exhibit similar types of behavior.

Actors who hold such equivalent positions are said to be structurally equivalent. A set of structurally equivalent actors is referred to as a "block," and the process by which blocks are identified is referred to as blockmodeling (White, Boorman, and Breiger 1976). Be aware that the terminology in this theoretical area can at times be conceptually confusing because the algorithms that analysts have developed to identify structurally equivalent actors vary in their assumptions and names. For example, structural, automorphic, and regular equivalence algorithms all seek to identify actors who occupy similar positions in the social structure, but they differ in their assumptions of what constitutes a set of equivalent actors and as such identify different sets or blocks (we will explore these differences in detail). Once the blocks of a network have been identified, this information can be used in different ways. For example, analysts can simplify (i.e., collapse) a network based on the sets to which each actor belongs (similar to how we simplified networks using role data in Chapter 4) to see if patterns emerge that were not immediately obvious when looking at all of the actors in the network.

The chapter now turns to an overview of structural, automorphic, and regular equivalence, using the Wasserman and Faust network (1994:468) as a working example. This chapter's final section focuses on the techniques of blockmodeling in UCINET, Pajek, and ORA. In this section we only demonstrate structural equivalence algorithms, not because they are necessarily "preferred," but because they are well established and implemented in all three software programs,[1] and how you blockmodel with them is similar to how you blockmodel with automorphic and regular equivalence algorithms.

9.2   Structural Equivalence

Two actors are said to be structurally equivalent when they have exactly the same relationships to all other actors. That is, they must "have identical ties to and from identical other actors" (Wasserman and Faust 1994:468). Another way to think about this is that in order to be structurally equivalent, two actors must be exactly substitutable for one another (Hanneman and Riddle 2005). Because structurally equivalent actors are tied to exactly the same other actors, they score identically in terms of centrality, prestige, and all other social network metrics (Borgatti and Everett 1992:7).[2]

Perhaps the easiest way to get a handle on the notion of structural equivalence is with the hypothetical network displayed in Figure 9.1 (from Wasserman and Faust 1994:468). Assume that the network displays who supervises whom in a company of managers and employees. In terms of this network, some people supervise others, some are supervised by others, and some are both supervisors and supervisees.

In this example only two sets of actors are considered to be structurally equivalent (5 and 6 and 8 and 9). This is because actors 5 and 6 both have

---

[1] Whereas UCINET includes a wide array of equivalence algorithms, Pajek includes algorithms for structural and regular equivalence, and ORA includes only one for structural equivalence (i.e., CONCOR).

[2] The reverse is not true, however. "Actors who are indistinguishable on absolutely all graph-theoretic attributes are not necessarily structurally equivalent" (Borgatti and Everett 1992:7).

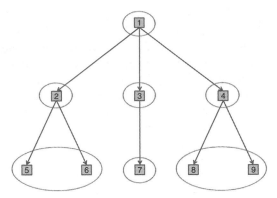

Figure 9.1. Structural Equivalence of Wasserman and Faust Network

ties to actor 2, and actors 8 and 9 both have ties to actor 4. Note that in both sets, the structurally equivalent actors do not have ties to one other. There is no tie between actors 5 and 6, nor is there one between actors 8 and 9. This is important to note because in order for two actors to be structurally equivalent, there does not have to be a tie between them. There can be, but it is not a requirement. What about the remaining actors in the network? They are considered to be in their own equivalence classes (or blocks) because there are no other actors that have exactly the same set of ties that they do. For example, because there is no actor that has exactly the same set of ties as actor 1, it is assigned to its own class, and the same is true of actors 2, 3, 4, and 7. Thus, in the example network there are seven sets of structurally equivalent actors (i.e., classes, blocks).

Structural equivalence is a very restrictive understanding of equivalence. Seldom do we analyze networks in which two or more actors have exactly the same relationships to all other actors; this fact has led some to question the usefulness of the concept. As Wasserman and Faust (1994:468–469) note:

> The fact that structurally equivalent actors must have *identical* ties to and from *identical* other actors is a severe limitation. [For example], two actors can be assigned to the same "manager" position only if they supervise exactly the same employees. Managers from two different companies, or even managers in charge of two different departments, cannot be structurally equivalent. The restriction of identical ties and identical actors, as required by structural equivalence, thus does not provide a general formalization of the theoretical notion of social position. (Borgatti and Everett 1992; Faust 1988)

What this often means in practice is that analysts use some sort of threshold measure to determine who belongs to what equivalence class and what ties exist between equivalence classes (we will see how to do this in Section 9.4).

Moreover, Borgatti and Everett (1992) have noted that structural equivalence is really another form of clustering based on cohesion (as opposed to one based on position), because in order for two actors to be structurally equivalent, they have to have the same ties with themselves, each other, and all other actors, which means that they are always completely contained within the same components of a network. "That is, actors located in different components of a disconnected graph (or in different graphs) can never be structurally equivalent (except isolates). In fact, as a general rule, nodes cannot be structurally equivalent if they are more than two links apart" (Borgatti and Everett 1992:9). Put simply, structural equivalence algorithms identify cohesive subsets rather than "positional" subsets. As a consequence, they and others have argued for more generalized or relaxed definitions of equivalence that they believe possess somewhat more realistic measures of what it means for two actors to be regarded as "equivalent" or "structurally similar" (see, e.g., Borgatti and Everett 1992; Faust 1988; Wasserman and Faust 1994). Automorphic equivalence is one such measure; regular equivalence is another. We consider the former before examining the latter.

9.3   Automorphic Equivalence

With automorphic equivalence, two actors are considered structurally similar if they occupy indistinguishable positions in a network. It is based on the notion of isomorphism, which in graph theory refers to a one-to-one mapping of one set of objects onto another, such that the relationships between the objects are preserved (Borgatti and Everett 1992:11). Isomorphic graphs are identical in terms of all graph theoretic attributes (e.g., density, centralization, number of cliques) and only differ (if at all) in terms of node and edge labels. Whereas the term isomorphism refers to the mapping of one graph onto another graph, automorphism refers to the mapping of a graph onto itself. Actors, then, are considered to be automorphically equivalent with one another if they can be mapped onto one another. For example, two professors would be regarded as automorphically equivalent if they taught the same number of students (although not necessarily the same students) and were supervised by the same number of people (although not necessarily the same people) in identical structural positions.

Consider, once again, the example from Wasserman and Faust (Figure 9.2). In terms of automorphic equivalence, there are five sets or classes of actors. The first thing to note is that actors that are structurally equivalent are also automorphically equivalent (and regularly equivalent).

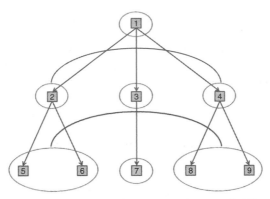

Figure 9.2. Automorphic Equivalence of Wasserman and Faust Network

Actors 2 and 4 are considered automorphically equivalent with one another because although they "supervise" different employees, they supervise the same number of employees. Similarly, actors 5, 6, 8, and 9 are automorphically equivalent because they are supervised by the same number of supervisors even though they are different supervisors. However, actors 2 and 4 are not automorphically equivalent to actor 3 because they "supervise" more employees than does actor 3.

In general then, automorphically equivalent actors have the same indegree and outdegree (if we are examining a directed graph), the same centrality on every possible measure, and so on. But, what about actor 7? Similar to actors 5, 6, 8, and 9, he or she is supervised by the same number of supervisors. The difference is that actors 5 and 6 are colleagues (where "colleague" is defined as someone supervised by the supervisor of oneself) as are actors 8 and 9. Actor 7, however, does not have a colleague, so he or she is sorted into a separate class, at least in terms of a strict or "exact" definition of automorphic equivalence.[3] However, if we are willing to relax the definition somewhat and move to an approximate understanding of automorphic equivalence, then actor 7 positionally looks a lot like actors 5, 6, 8, and 9 in that all five are supervised but they themselves supervise nobody.[4]

Although exact definitions of automorphic equivalence are more common in the literature, UCINET includes three automorphic equivalence algorithms, two of which identify exact automorphic equivalence classes and one that identifies approximate automorphic equivalence classes:

---

[3]   Technically, this means that actor 7 has a different distribution of all types of triads than do actors 5, 6, 8, and 9.

[4]   Thanks are due to Ronald Breiger, who helped immensely in delineating the difference between exact and approximate automorphic equivalence, as well as providing terminology (specifically, "colleagues") that should be intelligible to readers unfamiliar with graph theory.

(1) all permutations, (2) optimization, and (3) equivalence of distances. The first two are "exact" automorphic equivalent algorithms. Of these, the first (*Network>Roles & Positions>Automorphic>All Permutations*) compares every possible swapping of nodes (i.e., all permutations) in its search for automorphisms. When applied to the Wasserman and Faust network, it partitions the actors into same set of classes or blocks illustrated in Figure 9.2. Unfortunately, because it literally examines all possible permutations of a network, it is computationally intense and generally only useful with small networks (unless you are willing to wait a long time for the program to come back with an answer).

[UCINET]
Network
>Roles &
Positions
>Automorphic
>All
Permutations

Thus, with large networks you are often better off using the optimization approach (*Network>Roles & Positions>Exact>Optimization*), which is more efficient. It is also similar to factional analysis, which we explored in Chapter 6.[5] Like factional analysis, with the optimization approach for finding automorphically equivalent actors, analysts indicate the number of blocks or classes into which they want to partition the network. The algorithm then begins by randomly sorting actors into blocks and calculating an initial badness-of-fit measure; it continues to sort actors into blocks until it finds a partition that minimizes the badness of fit score. Like factional analysis, analysts will generally want to examine a range of possible numbers of blocks (unless one has a prior theory about this), to determine what number of blocks provides the best measure of fit. When asked to identify five blocks in the Wasserman and Faust network, this algorithm returns a badness of fit score of 0.00. In other words, there is a perfect fit.

Network
>Roles &
Positions
>Exact
>Optimization

The final algorithm (*Network>Roles & Positions>Automorphic> MaxSim*), unlike the first two, searches for "approximate" automorphic equivalence classes. Using the Euclidean distance between actors, it estimates the degree of automorphic equivalence for each pair of actors. As noted before, Euclidean distance differs from distance in graph theory. In the latter, the distance between two points is measured in terms of the number of lines in the path that connects the two points (i.e., path distance), whereas in the former the distance between two points is the most direct route between them (Scott 2000). The algorithm begins with a (reciprocal of) distance (for binary data) or strength of tie matrix (for valued data), calculates the distance between all pairs of actors, and regards actors that have similar distance profiles as being more automorphically equivalent. For example, Figure 9.3 depicts the output from an "equivalence of distances" (i.e., MaxSim) analysis of the Wasserman and Faust data. A distance matrix appears at the top of the output, whereas a hierarchical clustering graph appears at the bottom. The distance matrix

Network
>Roles &
Positions
>Automorphic
>MaxSim

[5] Recall also that we noted that it is a "special" type of blockmodeling. Structural and regular equivalence optimization algorithms are also available and implemented in UCINET and Pajek.

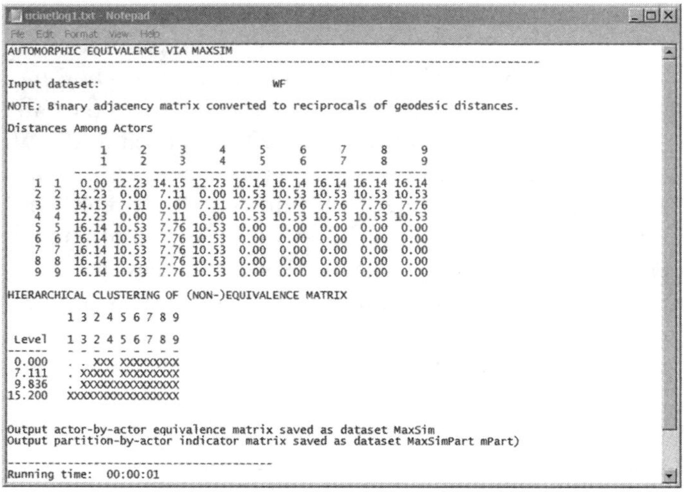

```
AUTOMORPHIC EQUIVALENCE VIA MAXSIM
--------------------------------------------------------------------------------

Input dataset:                          WF

NOTE: Binary adjacency matrix converted to reciprocals of geodesic distances.

Distances Among Actors

              1     2     3     4     5     6     7     8     9
              1     2     3     4     5     6     7     8     9
          ----- ----- ----- ----- ----- ----- ----- ----- -----
   1  1    0.00 12.23 14.15 12.23 16.14 16.14 16.14 16.14 16.14
   2  2   12.23  0.00  7.11  0.00 10.53 10.53 10.53 10.53 10.53
   3  3   14.15  7.11  0.00  7.11  7.76  7.76  7.76  7.76  7.76
   4  4   12.23  0.00  7.11  0.00 10.53 10.53 10.53 10.53 10.53
   5  5   16.14 10.53  7.76 10.53  0.00  0.00  0.00  0.00  0.00
   6  6   16.14 10.53  7.76 10.53  0.00  0.00  0.00  0.00  0.00
   7  7   16.14 10.53  7.76 10.53  0.00  0.00  0.00  0.00  0.00
   8  8   16.14 10.53  7.76 10.53  0.00  0.00  0.00  0.00  0.00
   9  9   16.14 10.53  7.76 10.53  0.00  0.00  0.00  0.00  0.00

HIERARCHICAL CLUSTERING OF (NON-)EQUIVALENCE MATRIX

         1 3 2 4 5 6 7 8 9

 Level   1 3 2 4 5 6 7 8 9
------   - - - - - - - - -
 0.000   . . XXX XXXXXXXXX
 7.111   . XXXXX XXXXXXXXX
 9.836   . XXXXXXXXXXXXXXX
15.200   XXXXXXXXXXXXXXXXX


Output actor-by-actor equivalence matrix saved as dataset MaxSim
Output partition-by-actor indicator matrix saved as dataset MaxSimPart mPart)

----------------------------------------
Running time:  00:00:01
```

Figure 9.3. UCINET MaxSim Output of Wasserman and Faust Network

indicates that the distance between actors 2 and 4 is 0.00, as are the distances between actors 5 through 9. Thus, at a distance level of 0.00 (see the hierarchical clustering matrix in Figure 9.3), actors 2 and 4 are clustered into one equivalence class, actors 5 through 9 are another, and actors 1 and 3 are classes unto themselves.

Actors from different networks could be regarded as automorphically equivalent, although this is technically incorrect because automorphic equivalence is a measure of equivalence *within* a network. When actors from two different networks are regarded as equivalent because they occupy indistinguishable positions (e.g., they supervise and are supervised by the same number of people), this is called isomorphic equivalence. For example, if you regard the network of relations in UCLA's sociology department as distinct from Vanderbilt's, then you would say professors in the two different schools were isomorphically equivalent: They supervised the same number of students, were supervised by the same number of people (e.g., chairs of the department), and (if you are interested in exact automorphic equivalence) have the same number of colleagues. UCINET's automorphic algorithms identify isomorphically equivalent actors as well.

9.4 Regular Equivalence

With regular equivalence, actors do not need to have identical ties to identical other actors nor do they occupy indistinguishable positions in a network. Instead, they must have identical ties to and from regularly

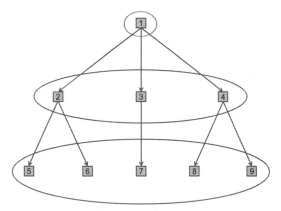

Figure 9.4. Regular Equivalence of Wasserman and Faust Network

equivalent actors (Borgatti and Everett 1988; White and Reitz 1983). Put differently, regularly equivalent actors "do not have to be connected to the same [actors], but they have to be connected to [actors] in the same classes" (de Nooy et al. 2005:280).

> For example, neighborhood bullies occupy the same social position, though in different neighborhoods, because they beat up some kid(s) and are scolded by some irate parent(s), but they do not necessarily beat up the same kid(s) nor are they scolded by the same parent(s). (Wasserman and Faust 1994:474)

In the Wasserman and Faust example (Figure 9.4), there are three classes of regularly equivalent actors: (1) actor 1; (2) actors 2, 3, and 4; and (3) actors 5, 6, 7, 8, and 9.

Actor 1 is in its own class because it is the only actor that has a tie to at least one actor in the second class (all three in this case) and no tie to any actor in the third class. Actors 2 through 4 are regularly equivalent with one another because they each have a tie with at least one member of the first class and one member of the third class. Note that even though actors 2 and 4 have more ties to members of the third class than does actor 3, this does not matter in this case because all that is required is that they have at least one tie to at least one member of the third class. Finally, actors 5 through 9 are regularly equivalent with one another because they have no ties with any actor in the first class and each has a tie with at least one actor in the second class.

Unfortunately, in a given network there can be numerous partitions of actors into classes in order to satisfy the regular equivalence definition. "For example, the partition of actors into structural equivalence classes is a regular equivalence (structurally equivalent actors are also regularly equivalent), and the partition of actors into automorphic (or isomorphic) equivalence classes is also a regular equivalence. But, there may be other regular equivalence partitions in a given network that are neither structural equivalences nor automorphic equivalences" (Wasserman and Faust 1994:475). Consequently, social network analysts typically seek to identify *maximal regular equivalence*, which is the partition of actors that assigns actors into the *fewest number* of equivalence classes. The original regular equivalence algorithm is REGE (accessed by the command *Network>Roles & Positions>Regular>REGE*), which was developed by Douglas White and Karl Reitz (White 1985; White and Reitz 1983). It works best with valued continuous data. For binary and nominal data, the Categorical REGE algorithm (*Network>Roles & Positions>Regular>CATREGE*) is recommended (Borgatti and Everett 1989, 1993). UCINET (and Pajek) also includes a regular equivalence optimization algorithm (*Network>Roles & Positions>Regular>Optimization*) similar to the automorphic optimization algorithm. As before, analysts indicate the number of blocks or classes into which they want the algorithm to partition the network. It then randomly sorts actors into blocks, calculates an initial badness-of-fit measure, and continues to sort until it finds a partition that minimizes the badness-of-fit score. Here again, analysts will generally want to explore a range of possible numbers of blocks in order to determine what number of blocks provides the best measure of fit. Analysts should also be aware that there may be more than one solution; that is, there may be multiple partitions with the same measure of fit. Unfortunately, UCINET only reports one. This is one advantage of Pajek's implementation of regular equivalence optimization algorithm (*Operations>Blockmodeling>Random Start*); it returns all possible solutions, allowing users to visually inspect the various partitions.

Another issue to be aware of is that when analyzing symmetric (i.e., nondirectional) networks without isolates, the maximal regular equivalence is a single class that includes all actors (Borgatti 1988; Doreian 1987; Wasserman and Faust 1994). That is because in symmetric networks with no isolates all actors are tied to some other actor that is also in the equivalence class. This has led analysts to think in terms of "neighborhoods" within networks and developing methods (e.g., ones that take into account path distance) for identifying meaningful classes of regularly equivalent actors (Everett, Boyd, and Borgatti 1990). The categorical REGE algorithm can be used here, as can the "exact" categorical algorithm (*Network>Roles & Positions>Exact>ExCatReg*), but in both cases the "Convert data to geodesic distances" option must be selected.

[UCINET]
*Network
>Roles &
Positions
>Regular
>REGE*

*Network>Roles
& Positions
>Regular
>CATREGE*

*Network
>Roles &
Positions
>Regular
>Optimization*

[Pajek]
*Operations
>Blockmodeling
>Random Start*

*Network
>Roles &
Positions
>Exact
>ExCatReg*

9.5   Blockmodeling in UCINET, Pajek, and ORA

We now turn to an examination of blockmodeling techniques in UCINET, Pajek, and ORA using structural equivalence algorithms. As noted previously, we focus on structural equivalence algorithms, not because they are necessarily "preferred," but because they are well established, implemented in all three software programs, and similar to how automorphic and regular equivalence algorithms are used to blockmodel. Recall that two actors are considered structurally equivalent if they have identical ties with each other and all other actors in the network. Of course, seldom do two actors exhibit the exact pattern of ties, so we generally use a similarity threshold to identify which actors to consider structurally equivalent. Although on the surface this clustering technique may seem straightforward, there are numerous blockmodeling algorithms for identifying structurally equivalent actors. Some are computationally intense, which limits their use to relatively small datasets.

Roles, Positions, and Structural Equivalence in UCINET

For most of this chapter we will use the Noordin Top trust network, but we will begin by examining a relatively small network (also from Wasserman and Faust 1994:364) because it is somewhat easier to illustrate certain blockmodeling features with smaller datasets than with larger ones. In UCINET, locate and display the Wasserman and Faust structural equivalence network (WFSE.##h). It should look similar to Figure 9.5 (a network graph of the dataset appears to the right of the matrix). *[UCINET] Data>Display*

Euclidean distance is a common approach for identifying structurally equivalent actors. Euclidean distance algorithms take network data and calculate a set of points in n-dimensional space, such that the distances between them correspond as closely as possible to the input proximities (Scott 2000:157). UCINET's Euclidean distance structural equivalence algorithm can be accessed with the *Network>Roles & Positions>Structural>Profile* command, which brings up a dialog box similar to the one in Figure 9.6. Accept most of UCINET's default settings, including Euclidean distance default[6] – the one exception being that the "For binary data . . . " option should be set to "Yes," not "No." Also, be sure that the Wasserman and Faust file is indicated as the input dataset (WFSE.##h). Click "OK." UCINET will generate an output report and *Network >Roles & Positions >Structural >Profile*

---

[6] The *Measure of profile similarity/distance* drop-down menu offers an array of methods for estimating structural equivalence, and if you click on UCINET's "Help" button, you will find a brief description of the various methods.

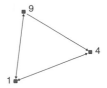

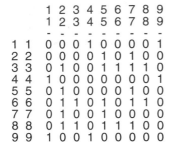

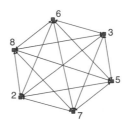

```
    1 2 3 4 5 6 7 8 9
    1 2 3 4 5 6 7 8 9
    - - - - - - - - -
1 1 0 0 0 1 0 0 0 0 1
2 2 0 0 0 0 1 0 1 0 0
3 3 0 1 0 0 1 1 1 1 0
4 4 1 0 0 0 0 0 0 0 1
5 5 0 1 0 0 0 0 1 0 0
6 6 0 1 1 0 1 0 1 1 0
7 7 0 1 0 0 1 0 0 0 0
8 8 0 1 1 0 1 1 1 0 0
9 9 1 0 0 1 0 0 0 0 0
```

Figure 9.5. Wasserman and Faust (1994) Structural Equivalence Network

two new files: a structural equivalence matrix (SE.##h) of Euclidean distances between actors and a structural equivalence partition (SEPart.##h) that assigns each actor to its respective equivalence class.

Data>Display   Figure 9.7 displays the structural equivalence matrix (SE.##h) of Euclidean distances between actors (it is also displayed in the report generated by UCINET). The smaller a number in a particular cell, the more similar those two actors are. A score of 0.00 indicates perfect similarity, which means that the two actors share an identical pattern of ties. Looking at the matrix, you can see that actor 2 is perfectly similar to actors 5 and 7 (0.00) and the same distance away from actors 3 and 8 (16.00) and actors 1, 4, and 9 (26.533).

The next step in the blockmodel process is to permute (i.e., reorder the rows and columns) and partition the original matrix so that actors who are assigned to the same block occupy adjacent rows and columns. To do

Figure 9.6. UCINET Structural Equivalence Profile Similarity Dialog Box

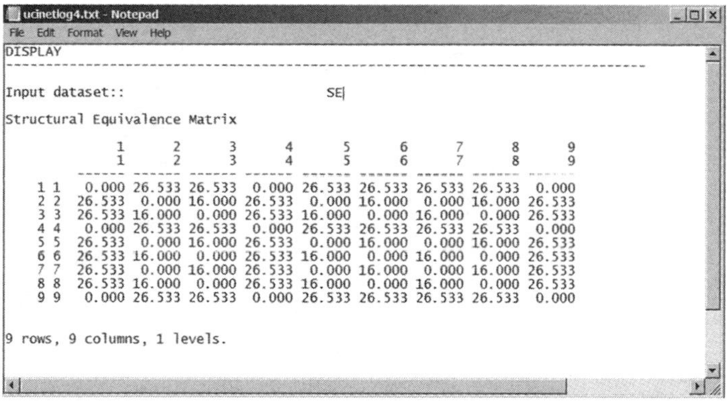

```
ucinetlog4.txt - Notepad
File Edit Format View Help
DISPLAY
------------------------------------------------------------------------------

Input dataset::                          SE

Structural Equivalence Matrix

               1      2      3      4      5      6      7      8      9
               1      2      3      4      5      6      7      8      9
          ------ ------ ------ ------ ------ ------ ------ ------ ------
    1 1    0.000 26.533 26.533  0.000 26.533 26.533 26.533 26.533  0.000
    2 2   26.533  0.000 16.000 26.533  0.000 16.000  0.000 16.000 26.533
    3 3   26.533 16.000  0.000 26.533 16.000  0.000 16.000  0.000 26.533
    4 4    0.000 26.533 26.533  0.000 26.533 26.533 26.533 26.533  0.000
    5 5   26.533  0.000 16.000 26.533  0.000 16.000  0.000 16.000 26.533
    6 6   26.533 16.000  0.000 26.533 16.000  0.000 16.000  0.000 26.533
    7 7   26.533  0.000 16.000 26.533  0.000 16.000  0.000 16.000 26.533
    8 8   26.533 16.000  0.000 26.533 16.000  0.000 16.000  0.000 26.533
    9 9    0.000 26.533 26.533  0.000 26.533 26.533 26.533 26.533  0.000

9 rows, 9 columns, 1 levels.
```

Figure 9.7. UCINET Structural Equivalence Matrix

this we use both the original matrix and the structural equivalence partition file (`SEPart.##h`) generated previously. Let's begin by looking at the partition file using UCINET's display command. It should look similar to the Figure 9.8. Note that the file actually includes three partitions: one at similarity level 0.00 (first column; the highest level of similarity), one at 16.00 (second column), and one at 26.53 (third column; the lowest level of similarity). If we wanted to partition the network in structural equivalence classes at the highest level of similarity between actors, then we would want to use the first partition, and if we wanted to partition the network at the lowest level of similarity, then we would use the third partition.

Note that at the lowest level of similarity, all the actors are assigned to the same equivalence class, so it is of little practical use. If we use the second partition, the actors will be assigned to two classes; if we use the first, they will be assigned to three. Here, we will use the first. To do this we use the *Transform>Block* command. In the resulting dialog box (see *Transform>Block*

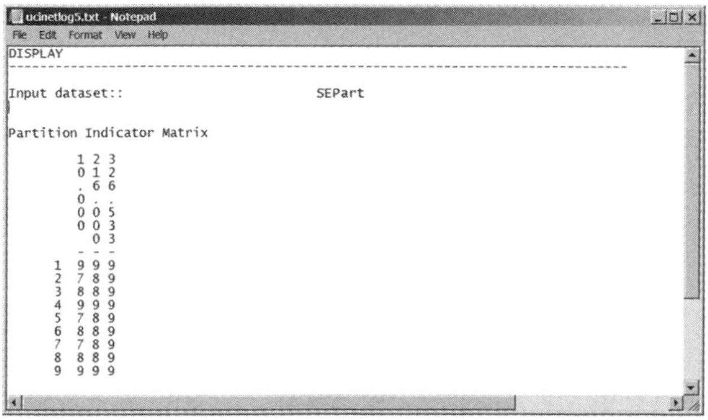

```
ucinetlog5.txt - Notepad
File Edit Format View Help
DISPLAY
------------------------------------------------------------------------------

Input dataset::                          SEPart

Partition Indicator Matrix

         1 2 3
         0 1 2
         . 6 6
         0 . .
         0 0 5
         0 0 3
           0 3
         - - -
     1   9 9 9
     2   7 8 9
     3   8 8 9
     4   9 9 9
     5   7 8 9
     6   8 8 9
     7   7 8 9
     8   8 8 9
     9   9 9 9
```

Figure 9.8. UCINET Structural Equivalence Partition

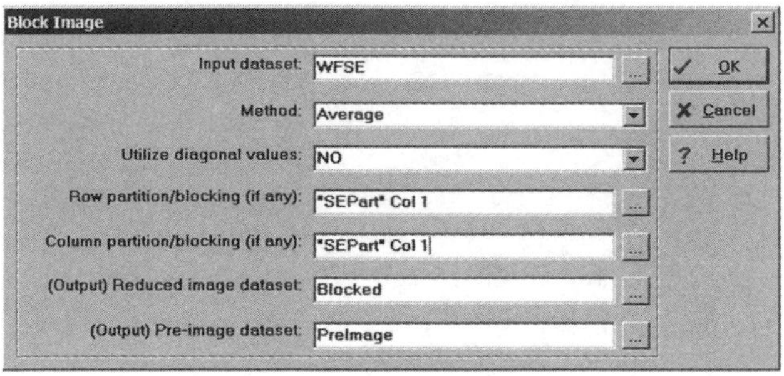

Figure 9.9. UCINET Block Image Dialog Box

Figure 9.9) you need to indicate the input dataset and the row/column partition file. As you can see, I instructed UCINET to use the first partition (column 1) of the "SEPart.##h" partition file.

The resulting output file (see Figure 9.10) provides three pieces of information. First, it tells you to which blocks the actors have been assigned. Next, it provides a permuted and partitioned matrix in which actors in the same equivalence class are grouped together and partitioned from the other classes. As you can see from the figure, actors 5, 2, and 7 have been assigned to the first block or class; 8, 3, and 6 have been assigned to the second block; and 1, 4, and 9 have been assigned to the third block. You can also see that actors within in the first and third blocks send ties only to other actors within their own block, whereas the actors within the second block send ties to each other and members of the first block.

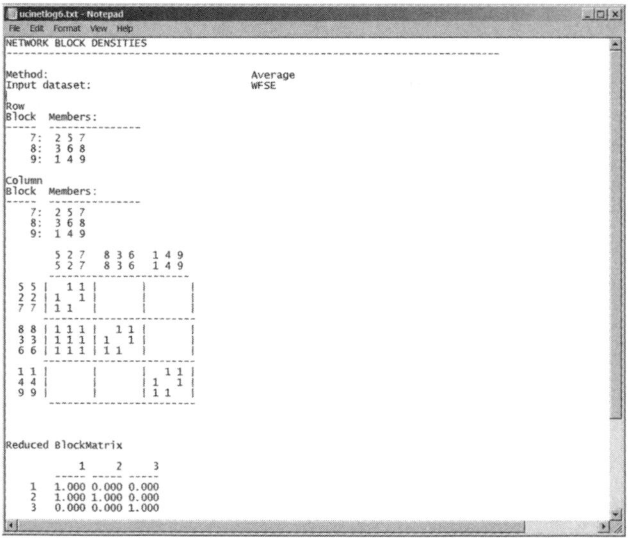
```
ucinetlog6.txt - Notepad
File Edit Format View Help
NETWORK BLOCK DENSITIES
------------------------------------------------------------------------

Method:                                         Average
Input dataset:                                  WFSE

Row
Block  Members:
-----  ---------------
   7:  2 5 7
   8:  3 6 8
   9:  1 4 9

Column
Block  Members:
-----  ---------------
   7:  2 5 7
   8:  3 6 8
   9:  1 4 9

        5 2 7   8 3 6   1 4 9
        5 2 7   8 3 6   1 4 9
       -----------------------
  5 5 |   1 1 |       |       |
  2 2 | 1   1 |       |       |
  7 7 | 1 1   |       |       |
      -------------------------
  8 8 | 1 1 1 |   1 1 |       |
  3 3 | 1 1 1 | 1   1 |       |
  6 6 | 1 1 1 | 1 1   |       |
      -------------------------
  1 1 |       |       |   1 1 |
  4 4 |       |       | 1   1 |
  9 9 |       |       | 1 1   |
       -----------------------


Reduced BlockMatrix

          1     2     3
      ----- ----- -----
   1  1.000 0.000 0.000
   2  1.000 1.000 0.000
   3  0.000 0.000 1.000
```

Figure 9.10. UCINET Permuted and Partitioned Matrix

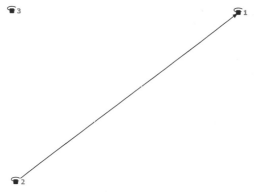

Figure 9.11. Image Matrix Graph (NetDraw)

This pattern of where blocks send ties can be captured in two ways: with an image matrix and a graphical representation of the image matrix. The image matrix itself is the last piece of information that the output file provides. The image matrix collapses each block/class of the permuted matrix into a single cell where the number appearing in the cell indicates the density of ties between the actors of that block. In this case in each of the blocks all possible ties are present, so the density within each block is 1.00. Because all of the actors in the second block (i.e., 8, 3, and 6) have ties to all of the actors in the first block (i.e., 5, 2, and 7), the density of that cell is 1.00 as well. However, because ties are completely absent between the other blocks, their density is 0.00.

The image matrix's corresponding graph (Figure 9.11) captures the relationship between blocks. Although it is quite small here, if you look closely you can see that block 2 is the only block that sends ties to any other block (block 1), whereas all three blocks have reflexive ties to themselves (i.e., block members send ties to other block members).

As suggested previously, the density within and between blocks seldom exactly equals either 1.00 or 0.00 (in other words, actors are seldom perfectly similar or dissimilar), so we generally have to choose some sort of criterion that distinguishes "one-blocks" (sometimes referred to as complete blocks) from "zero-blocks" (aka, null blocks). That is one of the topics we will take up in the next section, in which we examine the Noordin Top network.

Roles, Positions, and Structural Equivalence in UCINET (Noordin)

CONCOR. Here we will use Noordin's alive operational network (`Alive Operational Network.##h`) with the idea that if we can identify actors who are substitutable for one another, we may be able to

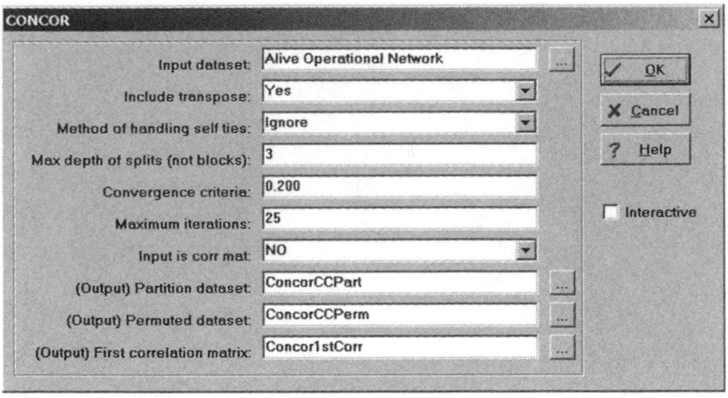

Figure 9.12. UCINET CONCOR Dialog Box

"predict" who might take over for another if the latter is removed from the network. We could examine the network using the Euclidean algorithm that we used previously. However, because the process would be the same, we will instead examine another algorithm: CONCOR, which was one of the earliest approaches to identifying structurally equivalent actors. CONCOR, which stands for "CONvergence of iterated CORrelations," is based on the discovery that repeated calculation of correlations between a matrix's rows (or columns) eventually results in correlation matrix consisting of only +1.00's and −1.00's (Wasserman and Faust 1994:376).[7] It begins by correlating each pair of actors, and then each row of the resulting actor-by-actor correlation matrix is extracted and correlated with each other row. This process is repeated over and over until all of the coefficients approach either +1.00 or −1.00. CONCOR then splits the data into two sets (i.e., the +1.00 set and the −1.00 set). The process is then repeated for each of the sets (or at least those sets with two or more actors) and continues until it runs out of actors to split or arrives at the number of "splits" indicated by analysts at the outset.

The CONCOR command in UCINET is located under the *Network* menu. UCINET now includes two CONCOR algorithms: (1) the standard algorithm where we simply indicate the number of splits we want CONCOR to estimate and (2) an interactive one, which gives us a bit more control over how many and where we want the splits to occur. We will begin with the standard algorithm, which brings up a dialog box that should look similar to Figure 9.12. Note that I have indicated that I want CONCOR to split the data three times, which should give us eight blocks

*Network>Roles
& Position
>Structural
>CONCOR
>Standard*

---

[7]   Recall that correlation coefficients range from −1.00 to 1.00, where −1.00 indicates perfect negative correlation and 1.00 indicates perfect positive correlation. If two actors share an identical pattern of ties (i.e., they are tied to the same actors), their correlation will be 1.00; if two actors have exactly opposite ties to other actors, their correlation will be −1.00; and if two actors ties indicate neither a positive nor a negative association, their correlation will be 0.00.

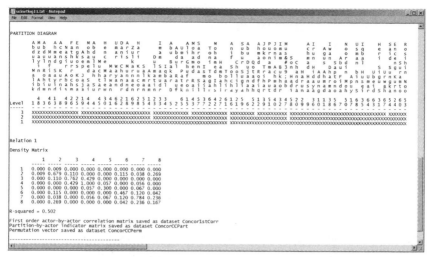

Figure 9.13. UCINET CONCOR Density Matrix

(i.e., 2^3) of structurally equivalent actors (unless after the first or second split, we have a block consisting of only one actor).

UCINET generates a dialog box (not shown – it may be hidden behind the output file) asking you if you want to see a dendogram, which graphically illustrates the splits in the data that have occurred. Click "OK" in order to see this. The output file consists of three panels: the first-order correlation matrix, a partition diagram, and a density matrix. Figure 9.13 displays the last two panels.

The partition diagram indicates where the splits in the data occurred. The bottom row of "x's" (Level 1) indicates the two groups that the first split identified, the second row from the bottom (Level 2) indicates the four groups that the second split identified, and the third row (Level 3) indicates the eight groups that the third split identified. Listed above the rows of x's are the names of the actors, indicating the block to which they have been assigned. As with the profile similarity approach, the density (image) matrix found at the bottom of the output collapses each block/class of the permuted matrix into a single cell where the number appearing in the cell indicates the density of ties between the actors of that block. Note that only one of the densities equals 1.00, so it will not be as straightforward to create an image matrix as it was previously. We take up that question in the next step. Note that UCINET provides a measure of fit (R^2) that compares the partitioned data matrix with an ideal structure matrix (i.e., where cell densities equal block means).[8] In

---

[8] R^2 (aka, the coefficient of determination) estimates the extent to which a model's variables account for the variance in the dependent variable. See Chapter 11.

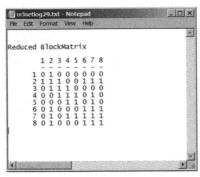

Figure 9.14. Final Image Matrix (Blockmodel), Zero-Block Method (UCINET)

this case, the higher the R^2, the better. UCINET also generates a partition matrix/file that we will use to generate the blockmodel.

How do we identify which blocks to classify as one/complete blocks or zero/null blocks? There are a number of different approaches. The zero-block, or lean fit, approach (Wasserman and Faust 1994:399) only classifies a block as a null block if its density equals 0.00 (i.e., if there is a complete absence of ties) and then classifies the remaining blocks as one (or complete) blocks. If we were to do this with the current network, the final image matrix (i.e., blockmodel) would look like Figure 9.14. What this tells us is, that although most of the blocks share ties with other blocks, the first block does not. It has ties only to the second block. Thus, the gaps between it and all of the other blocks may indicate "holes" in the structure of network that could be exploited. Noordin himself is located in the seventh block, which as we can see from the density matrix in Figure 9.13, is well connected (i.e., its density equals 0.784) and may suggest that if Noordin were to be removed from the network and the network were to reconstitute itself, its future leader would come from this block.

An alternative approach, the one-block approach (Wasserman and Faust 1994:400), only classifies a block as a complete block if a block's density equals 1.00. In the case of the alive operational network, the one-block approach produces a final image matrix (not shown) full of zeros with only one "one-block" (block 4), which in this case (and in most cases) is unhelpful.

Probably the most common approach for distinguishing complete from null blocks is to set a density threshold such that if a particular block's density is greater than or equal to that threshold, it is classified as a complete block, and if it is not, it is classified as a null block (Wasserman and Faust 1994:400–401). The threshold is often set at the density of the overall network (although other densities can be used), which, if you recall

Block Image			✕

Input dataset:	Alive Operational Network	...	✓ OK
Method:	Average	▼	✕ Cancel
Utilize diagonal values:	NO	▼	? Help
Row partition/blocking (if any):	*ConcorCCPart* Col 1	...	
Column partition/blocking (if any):	*ConcorCCPart* Col 1	...	
(Output) Reduced image dataset:	Blocked	...	
(Output) Pre-image dataset:	PreImage	...	

Figure 9.15. UCINET Block Image Dialog Box

from Chapter 5, can be obtained with the *Network>Cohesion> Density>(new) Density Overall* command. The density of the network is 0.1411, so to create a final image matrix using this as a threshold, we turn (once again) to the *Transform>Block* function (Figure 9.15) to first generate an image matrix. As before, we indicate the input dataset and the partition file (here we use column 1 – you may want to inspect the partition file to see why this is so) and click "OK." Once again UCINET's output (not shown) provides a summary of the blocks to which each actor is assigned, the permuted network, and a reduced block matrix (which should look identical to the density matrix in Figure 9.13).

Network >Cohesion> Density>(new) Density Overall

The final step in the process involves dichotomizing the network so that cells with a density of 0.1411 or greater are classified as complete blocks, whereas the rest are classified as zero blocks. We do this with UCINET's *Transform>Dichotomize* command, which brings up the following dialog box (Figure 9.16).

Transform >Dichotomize

Note that I have set the cutoff operator to be "Greater Than or Equal" and the cutoff value at 0.1411. It is also important to indicate that you want the diagonals of the output matrix to follow the dichotomization rule. This is not UCINET's default setting, so you will need to indicate it yourself.

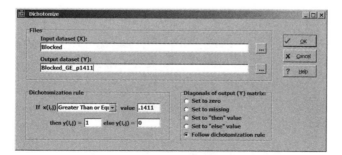

Figure 9.16. UCINET Dichotomize Dialog Box

```
ucinetlog36.txt - Notepad                                          _ □ x
File  Edit  Format  View  Help
DICHOTOMIZE DATASET
------------------------------------------------------------------

Input dataset::                        Blocked
Output dataset::                       Blocked_GE_p1411|
Dichotomization operator::             Greater Than or Equal to
Cutoff value::                         .1411
"Then" value::                         1
"Else" value::                         0
Diagonals option::                     Follow dichotomization rule

Reduced BlockMatrix

        1 2 3 4 5 6 7 8
        - - - - - - - -
  1     0 0 0 0 0 0 0 0
  2     0 1 0 0 0 0 0 1
  3     0 0 1 1 0 0 0 0
  4     0 0 1 1 0 0 0 0
  5     0 0 0 0 1 0 0 0
  6     0 0 0 0 0 1 0 0
  7     0 0 0 0 0 0 1 1
  8     0 1 0 0 0 0 1 1

8 rows, 8 columns, 1 levels.
Number of 1s: 6
Number of cells: 56
Density: 0.107142857142857
```

Figure 9.17. Final Image Matrix, Threshold Method (UCINET)

When you click "OK," UCINET's output will produce a final image matrix that can be analyzed as a matrix (Figure 9.17) or as a network map (Figure 9.18). It now appears that the first, fifth, and sixth blocks are isolated from the rest of the network, whereas the third and fourth blocks and the seventh and eighth blocks are tied with one another, respectively. The eighth block is also connected to the second block, which may place it in a position of brokerage between the seventh and second block, suggesting a possible vulnerability in the network. Analysts may want to consider monitoring this block or explore strategies aimed at isolating it (e.g., through a deception campaign).

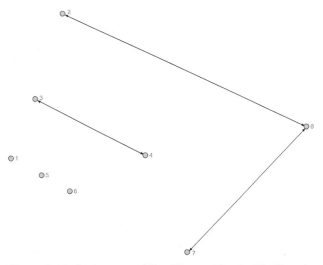

Figure 9.18. Sociogram of Final Image Matrix (NetDraw)

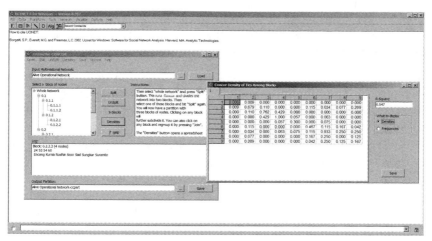

Figure 9.19. UCINET Interactive CONCOR Dialog Box

The interactive CONCOR algorithm provides analysts with a little more flexibility in determining how often and where we want to split the network. You access the interactive dialog box (Figure 9.19) using the *Network>Roles & Positions>Structural>CONCOR>Interactive* command. Once you identify the data you intend to analyze, you first need to click "Load" before you can work with the data. You begin by selecting a block of nodes and clicking "Split." This will split the data in two. From this point, you can choose where you want the splits to occur. In the example in Figure 9.19, the network was initially split using the standard CONCOR algorithm, but then the seventh block (see Figure 9.13) was split. Clicking on "Densities" calls up a window that displays the corresponding density matrix (or frequencies) as well as indicates how well the blocking scheme fits the data. In this case, density of the seventh block has been increased to 0.933 because two actors (Adung and Usman bin Sef) were sorted into a separate block (8); the R^2 has increased as well (0.547). Once we are satisfied with how the network is blocked, we

Network>Roles & Positions >Structural >CONCOR >Interactive

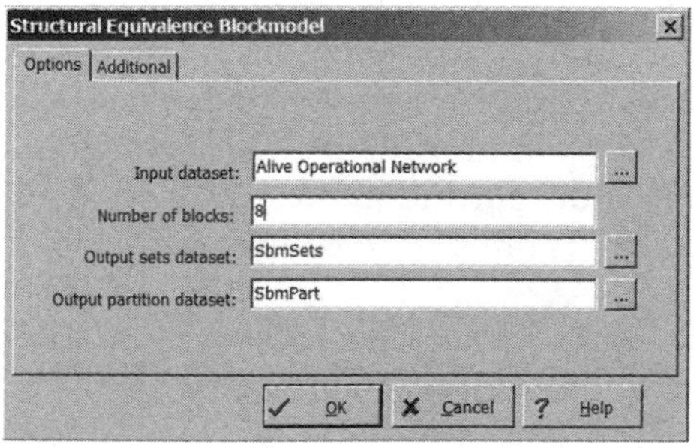

Figure 9.20. UCINET Optimization Structural Equivalence Dialog Box

simply click "Save" (we need to close the density matrix window first), and UCINET generates a partition that we can use to create a final image matrix as we did before.

Network>
Roles &
Positions
>Structural
>Optimization

Optimization. We will consider one final structural equivalence algorithm available in UCINET that is accessed with UCINET's *Network> Roles & Positions>Structural>Optimization* command (Figure 9.20).[9] It permutes the rows and columns of the matrix, trying to find the best fit for the number of blocks the analyst designates at the outset ("8" in this case). Fit is determined by an error score (the lower the better) that compares the final model with a perfect model. Recall that in the case of perfect structural equivalence, in a complete block all possible ties are present, whereas in a null block, no ties are present. Consequently, with this approach an error is considered to occur when a tie is present in a null block or one is missing tie in a complete block (this should sound similar to faction analysis, which as we will see is simply a special form of blockmodeling). The optimization algorithm permutes the rows and columns until it can no longer lower the error score.

When you click "OK," UCINET generates a report (not shown) that indicates the final (and beginning) error score as well as an R^2 fit statistic.[10] As did the reports generated by the other equivalence algorithms, this one also indicates the blocks to which each actor is assigned, it provides a permuted and partitioned (blocked) adjacency matrix, and it displays a density table. In addition, it generates a partition that allows analysts to create a final image matrix (Figure 9.21) using the same steps we used previously. This image matrix tells a slightly different story than the previous one (note that the blocks here, both in content and sequence, do not necessarily correspond to blocks in Figure 9.17 – indeed, in this analysis Noordin is located in the second block, which has a density of 1.00). Here, all the blocks are isolated from one another except blocks 4 and 5.

Because the results obtained by the CONCOR algorithm and those with the optimization algorithm are difficult to compare, how might we choose between the two? We could examine them to see which makes more visual sense. Figure 9.22 is a visualization of the network where the colors of the nodes reflect the blocks identified by the standard (noninteractive) CONCOR algorithm, whereas Figure 9.23 is a visualization of the same network using the optimization partition. Because these networks are displayed here in gray scale, it is difficult to compare the two. It is much

---

[9] Note that this approach provides an option of using either valued or binary data. We will continue to use binary data here so that the results are comparable to the results we got previously.

[10] This feature does not always appear to work; in the previous analysis, UCINET reported an R^2 of 0.00, which is clearly incorrect.

Figure 9.21. Final Image Matrix, Optimization Method (UCINET)

easier to compare them using several different colors. Nevertheless, it does appear that in this case the CONCOR algorithm has done a better job of identifying structurally equivalent actors than has the optimization algorithm.

Roles, Positions, and Structural Equivalence in Pajek The three approaches to structural equivalence illustrated above do not exhaust those that are available in UCINET. Hierarchical clustering is another common approach implemented in UCINET, one that is also implemented in Pajek. Nevertheless, in this chapter we will focus on Pajek's optimization algorithm because it is the one for which Pajek (and its developers) are

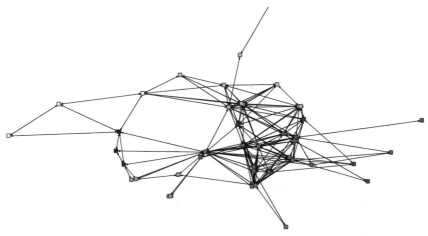

Figure 9.22. Alive Operational Network with CONCOR Partition (NetDraw)

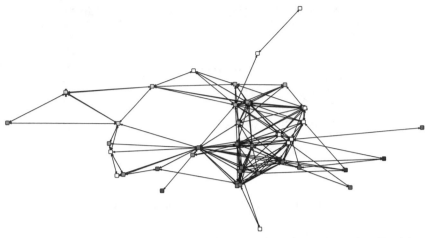

Figure 9.23. Alive Operational Network with Optimization Partition (NetDraw)

best known (Batagelj 1997; Batagelj, Ferligoj and Doreian 1992; de Nooy et al. 2005: 273–291; Doreian, Batagelj and Ferligoj 2005).

[Pajek]
File
>Network
>Read

Begin by loading the trust network file (Alive Operational Network.net) into Pajek using Pajek's *File>Network>Read* command. Next, use Pajek's blockmodeling command (*Operations>Blockmodeling>Random Start*) to call up its blockmodeling dialog box (Figure 9.24). A drop-down menu allows you to indicate whether you want to generate structural or regular equivalence, or define one yourself.[11] You can also indicate how many iterations you want Pajek to perform in its search for the blockmodel partitions (yes, there can be more than one) that minimize the error score as well as how many clusters/blocks you want Pajek to identify. Other options are also available (see the bottom of the dialog box), but in most cases you will want to accept Pajek's defaults.

Operations
>Blockmodeling
>Random Start

Click "Run" and Pajek will generate a report that presents a final image matrix, a final error matrix, and a final error score (Figure 9.25). Note that Pajek's error score is lower than the one found by UCINET. In this case Pajek found only one solution, but if it had found more, it would create a partition for each solution, which means that you can compare them in Pajek's Draw screen (not shown), using Pajek's *Draw>Draw-Partition* command. The solution that Pajek did find differs substantially from any of those found by UCINET and suggests far more interconnection between the various blocks: in particular, blocks 2, 3, and 4.

Draw>Draw-
Partition

[11] Patrick Doreian, Vladimir Batagelj, and Anuska Ferligoj (2005) have developed an approach to blockmodeling known as *generalized blockmodeling*, which allows users to combine a variety of equivalence measures into a single model.

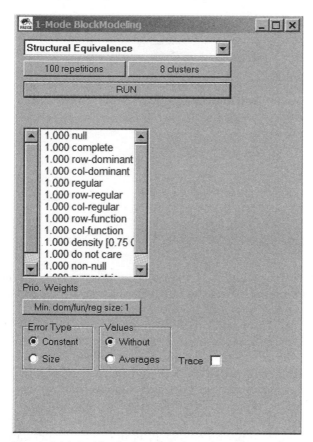

Figure 9.24. Pajek Blockmodeling Dialog Box

Such a conclusion may be misguided, however, because although it is somewhat hard to tell from Figure 9.26, in which the nodes are colored (i.e., gray scale) by the block to which they are assigned, blocks 2, 3, and 4 are relatively small in comparison to the first block. In fact, the fourth block is constituted by a single actor: Noordin Mohammed Top. Perhaps

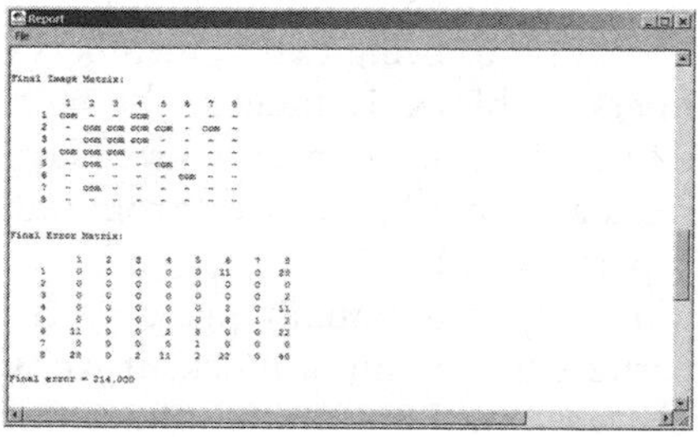

Figure 9.25. Pajek Blockmodeling Report

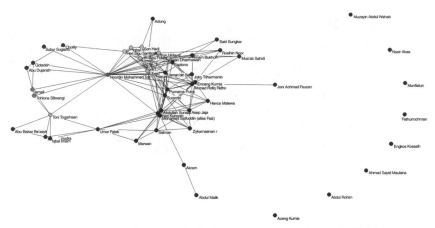

Figure 9.26. Blockmodel of Alive Operational Network (Pajek)

a better way to get a handle on the blocking scheme is to examine the network as a permuted matrix (i.e., a matrix where the rows and columns have been rearranged to reflect the blockmodeling solution).

Partition>Make Permutation

To do this, first ensure that the blockmodel partition found by Pajek is highlighted in the first Partition drop-down menu, and then create a permutation based on that partition, using Pajek's *Partition>Make Permutation* command (or if Pajek found more than one blockmodel solution, ensure that the blockmodel partition you want to use to create the permuted matrix is highlighted in the first Partition drop-down menu).

File>Network >Export Matrix to EPS>Using Permutation

Next, use the *File>Network>Export Matrix to EPS>Using Permutation* command to export the permuted matrix as an EPS file, which can then be displayed similar to Figure 9.27. What this permuted matrix suggests is that perhaps blocks 2, 3, and 4 should be thought of as a single block, and that there are four primary blocks within the network plus a "block" of relatively disconnected actors (blocks 7 and 8). However, blocks 2 and 4 have some unique characteristics, which suggests that we should perhaps treat them separately. Block 2 members (Hambali, Mohamed Ihsan, and Toni Togar), for instance, are connected not only with members of blocks 3 and 4 but also with members of blocks 5 and 7. Block 4 (Noordin) displays a similar pattern. In addition to being tied to members of blocks 2 and 3, he is tied to members of block 1. Indeed, the fact that the Pajek algorithm has identified him as a block unto himself suggests that perhaps he is not easily replaced and that his removal from the network could prove fatal for the group as a whole.

As noted previously, faction analysis is actually just a special type of blockmodel in that it only permits ties within a block. If we wanted to estimate factions within Pajek, we would begin as we did previously, by using Pajek's blockmodel dialog box. This time use the drop-down menu

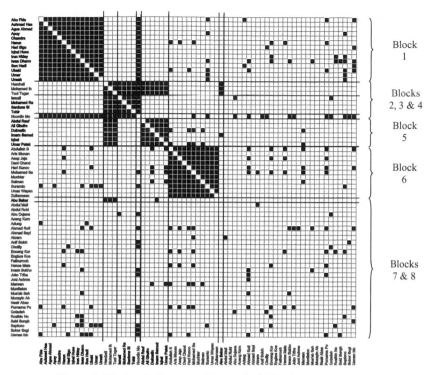

Figure 9.27. Pajek-Generated Permuted Matrix

and select the *User Defined* option. A matrix will appear to the right of the standard options that will allow you to indicate what type of relationship you would like Pajek to estimate within and between blocks (see Figure 9.28). Select each off-diagonal cell and then click on the "0.null" option (circled in Figure 9.28). This will tell Pajek that you want null (i.e., zero) blocks in the off-diagonal cells and complete blocks along the diagonal. Click "Run" and Pajek will conduct a factional analysis that you can visualize in the draw screen.

Roles, Positions, and Structural Equivalence in ORA. In ORA load the alive Noordin meta-network (`Alive Noordin Network.xml`) using either ORA's *File>Open Meta-Network* command or the *Ctrl+O* quick key. There are two ways of identifying structurally equivalent actors in ORA: either from its main screen or its visualizer. Currently, ORA only implements the CONCOR algorithm, which is something of a limitation, but other algorithms will probably be added in the future. To identify structurally equivalent actors from ORA's main screen, we need to use ORA's "Locate SubGroups" report, which can be accessed by

File >Open Meta-Network

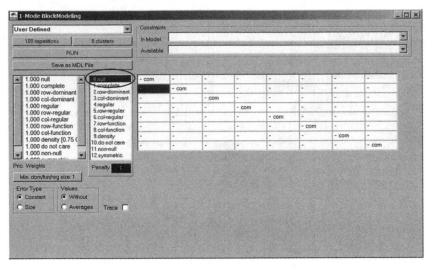

Figure 9.28. Pajek Blockmodeling Dialog Box with User-Defined Option

*Analysis
>Generate
Reports
>Groups
>Locate
SubGroups* ORA's *Analysis>Generate Reports>Groups>Locate SubGroups* command, which calls up the corresponding dialog box (not shown). Click on "Next." At the second dialog box (not shown), indicate which network you want ORA to use for blockmodeling (ORA will use all networks selected to estimate one blockmodel) and click "Next." This will bring up a dialog box similar to one shown in Figure 9.29. Make sure the CONCOR button is chosen and indicate how many levels you want (here, we have selected three). You may remember that ORA allows you to delete isolates prior to identifying subgroups. This can be an attractive option, but for now let's keep our isolates in order to make our results comparable to what we found using UCINET. You may want to come back and rerun the analysis eliminating isolates first. (To do this, simply click on the "Select Network Transformations" tab and then click on the "Remove isolates before clustering" box.) When you click "Next," another dialog box appears (not shown), which asks you what types of output you want. Select all of the options and click "Next." At the next dialog box (not shown), indicate that you want text and HTML output, give your output file a name, click "Finish," and ORA will generate a report for each network that lists each actor by the blocks to which they belong, a hierarchical clustering diagram, a dendogram, a permuted and partitioned matrix, a density table, a reduced block matrix, a graph that corresponds to the density table (and not the reduced block matrix), and a few additional metrics. Note that ORA does not give you a choice in setting your own threshold when it comes to creating the reduced block matrix. It also does not provide you with any measures of fit.

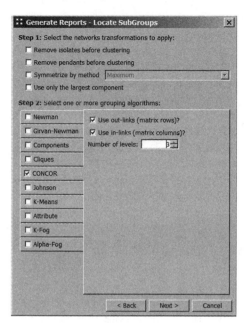

Figure 9.29. ORA's Locate Subgroups Dialog Box with CONCOR Option

To visualize the results generated by CONCOR's algorithm, return to the main screen, and you will note that ORA has created a new meta-network, probably called "Alive Network Groups." Select this and click "Visualize" and you will see a network map that looks something like Figure 9.30. Because it includes both the actors and the CONCOR groups, as well as the ties between actors and actors, the ties between actors and groups, and the ties between groups and groups, this is a relatively unhelpful visualization. However, because ORA allows us to turn objects and ties off and on, we can play with the visualization to make it more intelligible and useful. For example, if you select only the CONCOR groups and the CONCOR blockmodel ties, you will get a graph of the reduced block matrix. If you select the CONCOR groups and the CONCOR block densities ties, then you get the same graph that appeared in the original CONCOR report.

To run the CONCOR algorithm straight from ORA's visualizer screen, first (at ORA's main screen) select the original Noordin Top trust network (not the meta-networks created by ORA). Next, click "Visualize." Then, at the *Visualizer* screen, select ORA's *Display>Node Color>Display Nodes by Concor Grouping* command, indicate the number of splits, click "OK" and ORA will display the network with the nodes colored by the CONCOR groups (Figure 9.31). Note that ORA treats isolates as a separate group (they have been hidden in the graph using ORA's

[ORA-Visualizer] Display >Node Color>Display Nodes by Concor Grouping

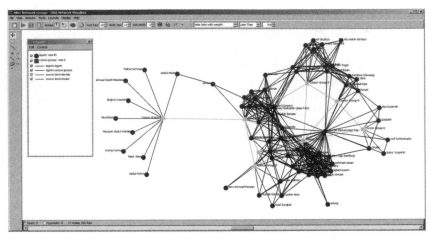

Figure 9.30. ORA Visualization of CONCOR Groups

Actions>Isolates >Hide Isolate Nodes

Actions>Isolates>Hide Isolate Nodes command) and only performs the algorithm on the remaining nodes. Also, note that when you identify the groups from the visualizer, ORA does not provide you with any of the accompanying output that you get when running the algorithm from the main screen. Comparing this blocked network map with the one Figure 9.22 (also based on the CONCOR algorithm) suggests that ORA and UCINET have arrived at similar solutions although one would need to examine the results in detail to know if they are identical.

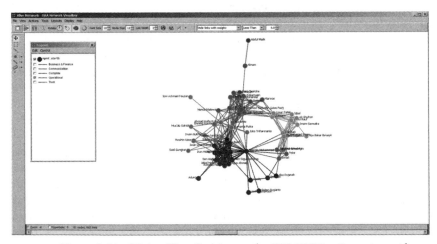

Figure 9.31. ORA Visualization of CONCOR Grouping (from Visualizer)

9.6 Summary and Conclusion

In this chapter we have explored three approaches for identifying actors holding similar positions in a network and sorting them into distinct classes or blocks: structural, automorphic, and regular equivalence.[12] Two actors are said to be structurally equivalent when they have exactly the same relationships to all other actors. Another way to think about it is that, in order to be structurally equivalent, two actors must be exactly substitutable for one another (Hanneman and Riddle 2005). As we saw, structural equivalence is a very restrictive understanding of equivalence. Seldom do two or more actors have exactly the same relationships to all other actors, which is why some have questioned the usefulness of the concept Wasserman and Faust (1994:468–469). What this often means in practice is that analysts use some sort of threshold measure to determine the blocks to which actors belong and the ties that exist between them.

Although structural equivalence is the most widely implemented approach to finding equivalent actors, others have argued on behalf of more generalized or relaxed definitions of equivalence that they believe possess somewhat more realistic measures of what it means for two actors to be regarded as "equivalent" or "structurally similar" (see, e.g., Borgatti and Everett 1992; Faust 1988; Wasserman and Faust 1994). With automorphic equivalence, actors are considered equivalent if they can be mapped onto one another. With regular equivalence, actors are considered to be equivalent if they are connected to actors in the same classes. These three approaches are nested within one another in terms of strictness. That is, structurally equivalent actors are also automorphically and regularly equivalent with one another, and automorphically equivalent actors are also regularly equivalent with one another. The reverse is not true, however. Regular equivalent actors are not necessarily automorphically or structurally equivalent with one another, and automorphically equivalent actors are not necessarily structurally equivalent with one another.

Did we learn anything about Noordin's operational network? Yes, although the results from the various blockmodeling algorithms did not produce identical results, the CONCOR analysis (see Figure 9.18) suggests that there may be a class or block of actors in the network that is in a position of brokerage between other blocks in the network and we may want to monitor this block or craft a deception campaign aimed at isolating or discrediting it. The same analysis also found the block of which Noordin is a highly connected member. As we have noted in

---

[12] One approach to blockmodeling that we did not consider in this chapter was developed by Patrick Doreian, Vladimir Batagelj, and Anuska Ferligoj in what is referred to as *generalized blockmodeling*, which allows analysts to specify a combination of block types in a given network (see de Nooy et al. 2005; Doreian et al. 2005).

previous chapters, actors that are closely tied to a group's leader are unlikely to defect, so this would be a group that we would probably not want to "waste" resources on, in an attempt to reintegrate members through amnesty or deprogramming campaigns. Instead, we should focus our efforts on actors in other blocks, preferably those blocks whose ties with Noordin's block are minimal. The highly connected nature of this block also suggests that if Noordin was removed from the network, future group leaders could emerge from this block. Thus, we probably would want to dedicate some resources to track members of this block. Finally, the optimization approach to Noordin's network uncovered some interesting structural dynamics of the group. We saw that three blocks are highly connected to one another and may be considered a block unto themselves. We also saw, however, that two of these blocks possessed some interesting connections, which indicated that we may want to treat them separately. In particular, we saw that Noordin was identified as block unto himself, suggesting that he may not be easily replaceable and that his isolation could prove fatal to the group. Of course, we only used the structural equivalence algorithms to examine Noordin's alive operational network. We would most likely want to supplement our analysis with an exploration of Noordin's network using both automorphic and regular equivalence algorithms.

Part IV

Social Network Analysis: Advances

10

Dynamic Analyses of Dark Networks

10.1 Introduction

Networks are dynamic. They evolve and change over time as actors enter, leave, and move around. Capturing dynamics such as these and others can be difficult but it is possible. This chapter's purpose is to introduce readers to some of these approaches and demonstrate how to carry out relatively painless but potentially illuminating explorations of dynamic network data. We begin by examining approaches for exploring longitudinal networks both descriptively and statistically, although we do not consider in any great detail highly sophisticated approaches to the analysis of longitudinal network data, such as the actor-based models implemented by *SIENA* software[1] (see, however, Murphy, Everton, and Cunningham 2012). A comprehensive exploration of these models deserves its own book and requires software other than UCINET, Pajek, or ORA. Next we turn to the fusion of social network and geospatial data, which allows analysts to not only geospatially plot social network data but also to calculate geospatially weighted metrics; both features complement existing social network techniques in helpful ways.

10.2 The Longitudinal Analysis of Dark Networks

Historically, longitudinal network data have been difficult to come by and the methods for examining them have been underdeveloped. In recent years, this situation has begun to change. Longitudinal network data and their analyses are becoming more common. Many of these have been largely descriptive in nature, but they are increasingly becoming more sophisticated, employing model-based approaches that seek to identify the underlying mechanisms of network change (Breiger, Carley, and

---

[1] See http://www.stats.ox.ac.uk/~snijders/siena/.

Pattison 2003; de Nooy 2011; Doreian and Stockman 1997; McCulloh and Carley 2011; Snijders 2005; Snijders, Bunt, and Steglich 2010; Steglich, Snijders, and Pearson 2010).

To date, the majority of longitudinal analyses have focused on "bright" or "light" networks. Only a handful of scholars have applied them to dark networks. One example is an analysis of the global Salafi jihad by Xu, Hu, and Chen (2009), which found that it not only evolved into a scale-free network but also appears to have passed through three distinct phases – emerging, maturing, and disintegrating. Another, which builds on the work done by Kossinets and Watts (2006), is the study of a co-offending network (Hu, Kaza, and Chen 2009), which discovered that acquaintances and shared vehicle affiliations served as key facilitators of tie formations, whereas age, race, and gender did not. More recently, McCulloh and Carley (2011) applied social network change detection (SNCD) methods to a number of longitudinal networks, including the Al Qaeda communication network from 1988 to 2004. Their analysis identified events that may have caused sudden changes in the networks they studied, including Al Qaeda.

Unfortunately, few would consider most of these newly developed modeling techniques easy to use; in fact, most of these approaches require specialized software, which is why descriptive approaches are still quite popular and why we feature them here. SNCD is an exception to this general rule. It is relatively easy to use and implemented in ORA, so we will explore it here, as well.

We begin with relatively simple longitudinal network data: the Sampson (1968) monastery data. If you recall, Sampson observed the social interactions of a group of monks and collected several sociometric rankings over a period of time. During his stay, a "crisis in the cloister" developed that resulted in the expulsion of four monks and the departure of several others; in the end, only four remained. Here, we will only focus on the positive measures of liking that Sampson recorded (adapted from de Nooy et al. 2005:93–95). These range from "3" (or "−3"), which indicates the highest or first choice; to "1" (or "−1"), which indicates the last choice; and "0," which indicates no choice. Sampson recorded measures of liking at five different points in time. At time one (T1), the group primarily consisted of novices who soon left to study elsewhere. Time two (T2) captures the period of time shortly after the arrival of several newcomers. Time three (T3) is the period during which one of the newcomers organized a meeting to discuss the monastery's situation. This meeting contributed to the polarization of the community, which ultimately caused the expulsion of four novices, an event that occurred one week after time four (T4), and which led several novices to leave the monastery shortly thereafter. At time five (T5), only seven of the eighteen novices still lived in the monastery.

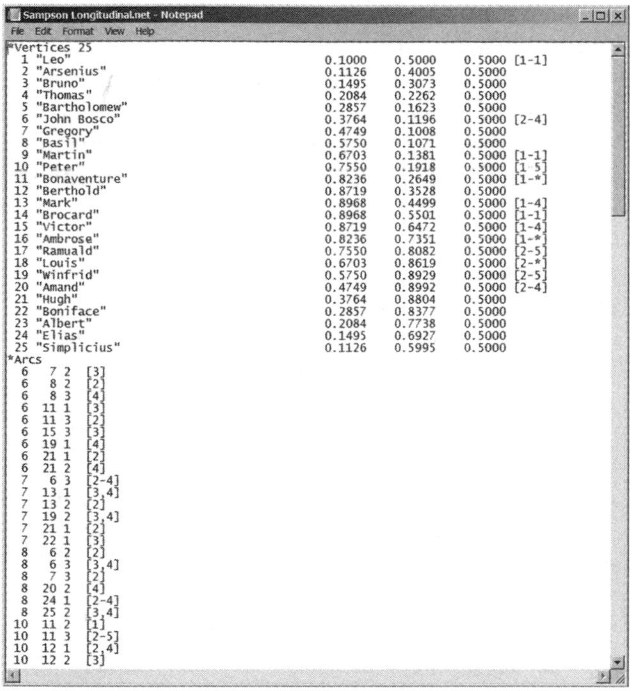


```
*Vertices 25
  1 "Leo"                0.1000   0.5000   0.5000 [1-1]
  2 "Arsenius"           0.1126   0.4005   0.5000
  3 "Bruno"              0.1495   0.3073   0.5000
  4 "Thomas"             0.2084   0.2262   0.5000
  5 "Bartholomew"        0.2857   0.1623   0.5000
  6 "John Bosco"         0.3764   0.1196   0.5000 [2-4]
  7 "Gregory"            0.4749   0.1008   0.5000
  8 "Basil"              0.5750   0.1071   0.5000
  9 "Martin"             0.6703   0.1381   0.5000 [1-1]
 10 "Peter"              0.7550   0.1918   0.5000 [1-5]
 11 "Bonaventure"        0.8236   0.2649   0.5000 [1-*]
 12 "Berthold"           0.8719   0.3528   0.5000
 13 "Mark"               0.8968   0.4499   0.5000 [1-4]
 14 "Brocard"            0.8968   0.5501   0.5000 [1-1]
 15 "Victor"             0.8719   0.6472   0.5000 [1-4]
 16 "Ambrose"            0.8236   0.7351   0.5000 [1-*]
 17 "Ramuald"            0.7550   0.8082   0.5000 [2-5]
 18 "Louis"              0.6703   0.8619   0.5000 [2-*]
 19 "Winfrid"            0.5750   0.8929   0.5000 [2-5]
 20 "Amand"              0.4749   0.8992   0.5000 [2-4]
 21 "Hugh"               0.3764   0.8804   0.5000
 22 "Boniface"           0.2857   0.8377   0.5000
 23 "Albert"             0.2084   0.7738   0.5000
 24 "Elias"              0.1495   0.6927   0.5000
 25 "Simplicius"         0.1126   0.5995   0.5000
*Arcs
  6   7 2  [3]
  6   8 2  [2]
  6   8 3  [4]
  6  11 1  [3]
  6  11 3  [2]
  6  15 3  [3]
  6  19 1  [4]
  6  21 1  [2]
  6  21 2  [4]
  7   6 3  [2-4]
  7  13 1  [3,4]
  7  13 2  [2]
  7  19 2  [3,4]
  7  21 1  [2]
  7  22 1  [3]
  8   6 2  [2]
  8   6 3  [3,4]
  8   7 3  [2]
  8  20 2  [4]
  8  24 1  [2-4]
  8  25 2  [3,4]
 10  11 2  [1]
 10  11 3  [2-5]
 10  12 1  [2,4]
 10  12 2  [3]
```

Figure 10.1. Partial Listing of Sampson.net

Once we are comfortable working with a small dataset, we will move to a larger one (Noordin's alive operational network), examining it first in Pajek and then in ORA (UCINET does not have the capabilities that Pajek and ORA do for generating and examining networks over time).

Longitudinal Networks in Pajek (Sampson Data)

Pajek has implemented helpful functions for analyzing longitudinal network data. Figure 10.1 shows part of the network file `Sampson.net`. In Chapter 4 we noted that Pajek structures network data as edge lists, so here we will focus on the time indicators in square brackets that are added to each actor and arc (or edge).[2]

Note the time code to the right of Leo's name and his associated spatial coordinates (i.e., [1–1]). This indicates that he was at the monastery at time one but left before time two. For time codes associated with actors, Pajek assumes that a time indicator remains valid until it encounters a new one (e.g., John Bosco, who was at the monastery from time two to time four and left before time five). In other words, as the file is currently

[2] These can be entered in various ways: The time codes for the Noordin data were entered by hand after reading the *.net file into a text editor (e.g., Notepad).

coded, not only was Leo at the monastery at time one and left before time two, but the same is also true of Arsenius, Bruno, Thomas, and Bartholomew. Similarly, Gregory and Basil were at the monastery from time two to time four and left before time five, just like John Bosco. Note the "*" included in the time stamp for Bonaventure. This indicates that he was present at time one and stayed beyond time five. In other words, a "*" is synonymous with infinity.

Unlike time records for actors, there must be one for each arc (or edge). In other words, with arcs (and edges) Pajek does not assume that a time indicator remains valid until it encounters a new one. What do these time codes tell us? Well, we can see that at time two, John Bosco (node 6) indicated Gregory (node 7) as his second choice in terms of people whom he liked. Note that he does not choose Gregory at times three or four, however (remember he leaves before time five). Interestingly, Gregory has positive feelings toward Bosco during periods two through three, as indicated by the time record (i.e., [2–4]) to the right of the arc from node 7 to node 6 (note that Bosco is Gregory's first choice in terms of liking in all three periods).

[Pajek] File> Network>Read

Net>Transform >Generate in Time >All Only Different Interval

To see how to generate longitudinal networks in Pajek, first open the Sampson network file (Sampson.net) using Pajek's *File>Network> Read* command. Next, use the *Net>Transform>Generate in Time* command. This calls up a series of dialog boxes that offer several options for generating a series of networks. First, you can choose to generate a network for each period (option *All*), a network only if it differs from the previous one (option *Only Different*), or a slice of the network that spans a specific time interval (*Interval*). The second option is useful if a network does not change much over time. Whichever command you choose, you will next need to specify the first and last time point that you want to analyze, as well as the time interval (step) between successive networks. For this example, choose the *All* option, start at time one, stop at time five, and choose a step value of one (step values must be positive integers). Note that the number of actors changes in the generated networks when actors enter or leave the network. As a result, the partition corresponding to the original longitudinal network may not match the newly generated networks. However, if a corresponding partition appears in the first Partition drop-down menu at the time that you issue the *Generate in Time* command, Pajek automatically creates new partitions for each generated network.

Table 10.1 illustrates how one might compare a network over time. Because the number of choices individuals could make was fixed by Sampson, measures of density and average degree would not tell us too much in this case. However, the network's size and centralization level could capture some of the dynamics occurring in the monastery during Sampson's stay. As you can see, the network grew from thirteen novices at time

Table 10.1. *Comparison of various metrics over time*

	Time period				
	1	2	3	4	5
Size	13.00	18.00	18.00	18.00	7.00
Degree Centralization	14.77	19.48	18.75	9.19	23.33
Closeness Centralization	30.75	41.62	34.68	24.89	60.24

one, to eighteen novices at times two through four, and then dropped to seven novices at time five. The network's centralization measures vary dramatically from one time point to the next. In terms of both degree and closeness centralization, the network became more centralized from time one to time two, became somewhat less so at time three (at the time of the meeting to discuss what was occurring in the monastery – in other words, probably a time of increased polarization), and dropped dramatically at time four (before anyone was kicked out, but when the group was probably the most polarized). At time five the level of centralization had increased, which may reflect the fact that after the mass exodus, only like-minded people remained.

The networks can be visualized over time as illustrated by Figure 10.2. What these visualizations help us see is that it is not until the fourth time period that the network really begins to become divided. This, of course, is captured by the centralization measures in Table 10.1, but visually it is more dramatic. As one might guess, Pajek includes some very nice features for visualizing networks over time. After visualizing the network in the draw screen using the *Draw>Draw-Partition* command, you can switch from one time period to another with the draw screen commands *Previous* and *Next*, as long as the *Network* option is selected in the *Options>Previous/Next>Apply to* submenu. If you are visualizing a partition and/or a vector along with the network, then you can also select the *Partition* and/or *Vector* options in the *Options>Previous/Next>Apply to* submenu. Finally, if you select one of the energy options in the *Options>Previous/Next>Optimize Layouts* submenu, Pajek automatically energizes the network when you move to the next or previous network.

Draw>Draw

[Pajek-Draw Screen]
Previous, Next

Options>Previous/ Next>Apply to>Network

Options> Previous/Next >Optimize Layouts

Longitudinal Networks in Pajek (Noordin Operational Network)

Now let us turn to Noordin's operational network (Noordin Operational Network (Longitudinal).paj) in which time codes have been entered that reflect when members entered and/or left. Of course, when someone enters and leaves a network is a matter of interpretation;

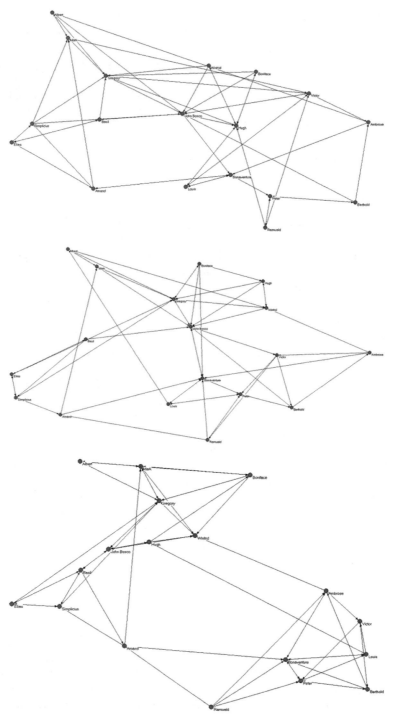

Figure 10.2. Sampson Liking Network at Times 2, 3, and 4 (Pajek)

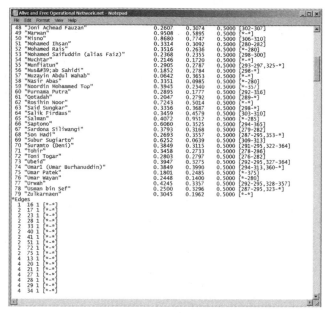

Figure 10.3. Partial Listing of Noordin's Alive and Free Operational Network

consequently, two instances have been created: one where members are considered to have left only if they die or defect (i.e., an alive network) and one where they are considered to have left if they die, are arrested, or defect (i.e., an alive and free network). In both it is assumed that individuals were members of the network unless sources specifically stated that they did not come in contact with the group until a certain time (e.g., when an individual was recruited to be a suicide bomber or provide sanctuary to Noordin).

Figure 10.3 shows a partial listing of the alive and free operational network. It shows the lower half of the list of actors (i.e., vertices) and the upper half of the associated edge list. The actors' time is coded in terms of months with January 1980 equaling time one, but it could have just as easily been coded in terms of years (or some other time period). As you can see, some of the actors are considered to be in the network at all times (i.e., [*-*]). This, of course, is not possible, but without evidence of when they entered or left, they are treated as if they have been members forever. In practical terms, this means that they are treated as members of the network for the duration of whatever period of time is under investigation. Other actors (e.g., Urwah) entered and left the network more than once and are time coded as such (i.e., [292–295, 328–357]). Note also that unlike the time codes assigned to each edge (i.e., tie) in the Sampson data, most are coded as if they have existed forever (i.e., [*-*]). Again, although this is an unreasonable assumption, the practical effect is that the ties are treated as forming once both actors are present in the network and dissolving if either one leaves the network. If you scroll through the network file (e.g., in a text editor), you will note that some of the edges do have specific time records associated with them. Time stamps were only assigned to particular ties if such information could be gleaned from the sources.

*File>Pajek
Project
File>Read*
We will generate the new networks in exactly the same way as we did with the Sampson data. First, load the time-coded Noordin operational network (Noordin Operational Network (Longitudinal).paj) into Pajek. After ensuring that the alive and free operational network is showing in the first Network drop-down menu, use Pajek's

*Net>Transform
>Generate in
Time>All*
Net>Transform>Generate in Time>All command. This time, however, choose 253 (i.e., January 2001) as the first time point and 361 (January 2010) as the last time point with a step of twelve (12). This will generate ten networks, ranging from January 2001 to January 2010. We can

*Options>
Previous/
Next>Apply
to>Network*
visualize these as we did before in Pajek's Draw screen.

We can also examine how the network's topography changes over the ten-year period. To do this, we highlight each network sepa-

*Info>Network
>General*
rately in the first Network drop-down menu, and then issue the *Info>Network>General* command, which produces a report on the density and average degree for each network. Of course, we may not be interested in average degree and density; we may be interested in centralization, clustering, and so on. Each of these measures can be estimated for each network and compared, as well. Although doing this in Pajek is possible, it is much easier in ORA. Before moving to ORA, you will want to save each of the ten newly generated network files (making sure that

*File>Network
>Save*
each is separately showing in the first Network drop-down menu), using Pajek's *File>Network>Save* command.

Longitudinal Networks in ORA (Noordin Operational Network)

Begin by loading the ten time-coded trust network files into ORA, using

*File>Data
Import Wizard*
its *File>Data Import Wizard* command, which brings up the following dialog box (Figure 10.4). Click on "Next" and at the next dialog box, browse for the newly created Pajek network files. When you import a Pajek file containing time records into ORA, ORA attempts to account for the time records and typically creates numerous networks, one for each year represented by the time records. Thus, for January 2003 data, you will want to delete all of the networks except the one ending "−277," and then repeat this for each of the nine remaining years. If ORA consistently read the Pajek data and corresponding time records correctly, then we could simply import the original time-coded data and keep the years that

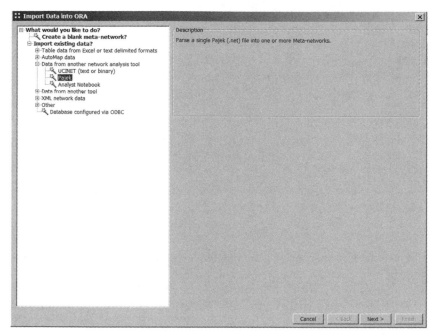

Figure 10.4. ORA's Data Import Wizard (Pajek Option Selected)

we wanted to analyze. Unfortunately, at this writing, the networks do not always "show up" in ORA with the correct number of nodes (although I expect this will eventually be corrected).

An alternative intermediary step is to first import the Pajek networks into UCINET, using UCINET's *Data>Import text file>Pajek* command, which calls up the following dialog box (Figure 10.5). Clicking "OK" creates two sets of files: (1) a UCINET network file and (2) a UCINET coordinate file. The latter file can be used for visualizing networks in NetDraw, but it is the former that interests us here. If we first import all of the Pajek networks into UCINET and then import the resulting UCINET networks into ORA using the same aforementioned commands (except selecting the UCINET option instead of the Pajek option), we will not encounter any time code issues.

UCINET's Data>Import text file>Pajek

ORA File>Data Import Wizard

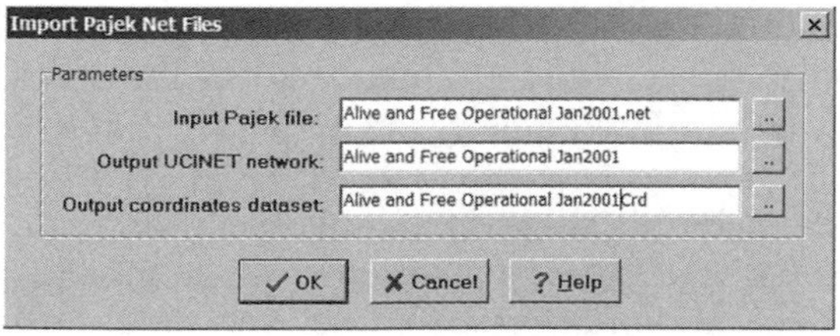

Figure 10.5. UCINET Pajek Import Dialog Box

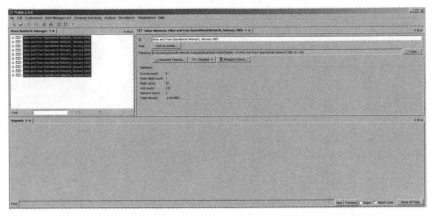

Figure 10.6. ORA's Main Screen with Networks Highlighted

Once the import process is complete, you should have the ten networks loaded into ORA as separate meta-networks. You can obtain topographical metrics for each network following the procedures outlined in Chapter 5, and we can visualize the networks over time by highlighting all ten networks (Figure 10.6) and then selecting the *Visualizations>View Networks Over Time* command. This will produce a dialog box (not shown) that indicates that the networks lack an assigned date. This is not an issue for us here. Click "OK," and ORA will call up its *Visualizer* screen along with a "Networks Over Time" dialog/control box (not shown) that offers options for visualizing the networks as well as "playing" them. If you click "Play," ORA will walk through each of the ten networks (not shown).

Visualizations >View Networks Over Time

Although ORA's capabilities for visualizing longitudinal networks are quite good, here we are going to focus on ORA's capabilities of examining network measures over time. To do this, highlight all ten networks (Figure 10.6) and then select the *Visualizations>View Measures Over Time* command. This will generate a new dialog box (not shown) that asks you what measures you want to view. For now, select ORA's default "All Measures" and click "Compute." This will bring up ORA's "Measures Over Time" function (Figure 10.7), which allows you to select various measures and see (graphically) how they change over time.

Visualizations >View Measures Over Time

Here, fragmentation (top line) and degree centralization (bottom line) have been selected, but as you can see, a number of measures are available for longitudinal analysis. Interestingly, the network became noticeably less fragmented (i.e., more cohesive) between January 2004 and January 2005, which reflects the period of time after the Australian Embassy bombing (July 2004) and before the second Bali bombings (October 2005). After this the network appears to become slowly but increasingly more fragmented, although it may have begun to stabilize in 2007.

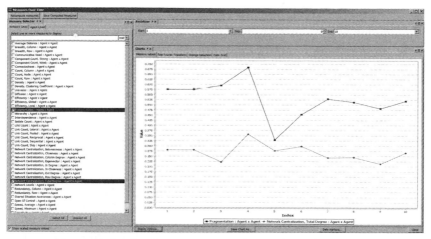

Figure 10.7. Measures over Time of Noordin's Alive and Free Operational Network

In terms of centralization, the network became more centralized between 2003 and 2004 and then slowly returned to its earlier levels. In Chapter 5 we saw that, overall (i.e., not only the alive and free subset), Noordin's operational network was relatively centralized, which suggests that we may want to examine other aspects of the operational network, such as the alive subset. We will do this in conjunction with exploring ORA's change detection functionality.

Before turning to that, however, it is worth noting that if you click on the Source Node Level tab, you will discover that you can see how the position of the actors in the network changes over time as well (e.g., how their degree centrality varies over the period of time under examination). Also, you can save the analysis in various ways by clicking on "Save Chart As ... " found below the chart. If you choose to save it as a *.png or *.jpeg, ORA saves the graph itself; if you choose to save the chart as a *.csv, ORA saves the computed metrics in a format that can be imported into and analyzed in other statistical programs such as Excel, SPSS, Stata, and R.

Social Network Change Detection in ORA (Noordin Operational Network)

Social network change detection (SNCD) is a method that allows for real-time analysis and can alert analysts as to whether and when a sudden change occurs in a network. This, in turn, can help them to identify potential causes for the change and may help prevent unwanted future events (McCulloh and Carley 2011). For example, "terrorist organizations will begin planning their attacks, long before they are actually carried out.

Rapid change detection could alert military intelligence analysts to the shift in planning activities prior to the attack occurring" (McCulloh and Carley 2011:5).

To see how ORA implements SNCD, first read all alive operational networks (these are monthly, not yearly, networks) into ORA using its *File>Open Meta-Network* command.[3] Highlight all 120 networks and select the *Visualizations> View Measures Over Time* command. In the resulting dialog box (not shown), accept ORA's defaults, click "Compute," and ORA's "Measures Over Time" function should be ready for analysis. Building upon and following our previous logic, we analyze both centralization (degree and betweenness) and fragmentation (fragmentation and clustering coefficient) – first descriptively, and then turning to SNCD. In the upper panel of Figure 10.8 the black and gray lines map monthly degree and betweenness centralization, respectively, from 2001 to 2010; in the lower panel, they map monthly fragmentation and clustering coefficient over the same period of time. These graphs indicate that Noordin's alive operational network began to become more centralized (and less fragmented) in 2003 (beginning with time period 24), a process that continued until 2006 (beginning with time period 60). Then, in 2009 when Noordin and a few of the network's key members were killed, the network became significantly less centralized and more fragmented. It was at this time that the network essentially fell apart although remnants did try later to reconstitute the network (International Crisis Group 2010). This is consistent with Bakker, Raab, and Milward's (2011) contention that centralized dark networks tend to be less resilient than decentralized ones, and that they are more likely to collapse if they suffer a shock to the system, much like Noordin's network did. That the network collapsed after the removal of key operatives also appears to lend support for kinetic strategies that remove key members. While this may be true, it is worth noting that initially, Noordin's network was less centralized and may have been able to withstand the removal of key actors. Indeed, it is arguable that the network became more centralized over time because of the kinetic and nonkinetic strategies pursued by Indonesian authorities, suggesting that these earlier strategies are what made Noordin's removal at a later date effective.

To see what SNCD can contribute to this analysis, select the Change Detection tab in the "Measures Over Time" screen, rather than accessing it from ORA's main screen.[4] To simplify our analysis, we will illustrate SNCD using only degree centralization. As with many statistical

---

[3] The January 2001 network is named `Alive Operational Network 2001.01.xml`, the February 2001 is named Alive Operational Network 2001.02.xml, and so on through December 2010 (Alive Operational Network 2010.12.xml).

[4] While SNCD is available from the latter, it is more limited than it is through the "Measures Over Time" screen.

File>Open Meta-Network

Visualizations> View Measures Over Time

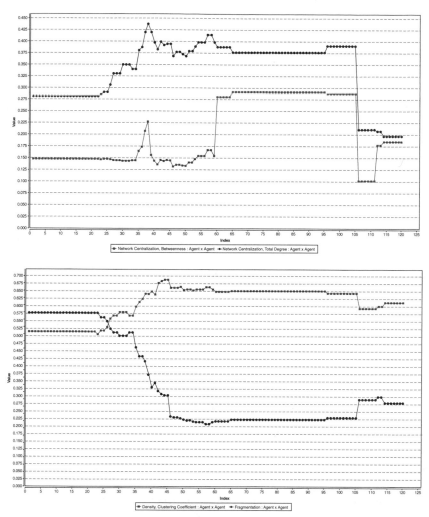

Figure 10.8. Measures over Time of Noordin's Alive Operational Network

approaches, we have to choose between numerous options. We first need to select the process by which to monitor change. One option, the Shewhart x-bar chart method, was originally a quality control technique for monitoring change in a business or industrial process when samples were collected at regular intervals (Shewhart 1927). The cumulative sum (CUSUM) control chart (Page 1961) is generally seen as an improvement over the Shewhart x-bar because of its use of sequential probability ratio testing (McCulloh and Carley 2011:7). The final option, the exponentially weighted moving average (EWMA) control chart (Roberts 1959), has

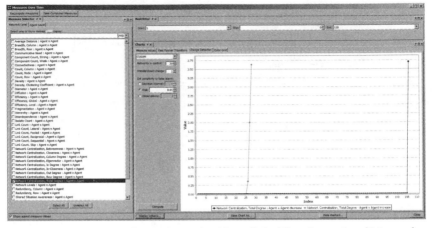

Figure 10.9. Change Detection Noordin's Alive Operational Network

been shown to perform similarly to CUSUM. Here, we follow McCulloh and Carley (2011:7) and use CUSUM, which they recommend for SNCD with longitudinal data. Next, we need to select the number of networks needed in order to form a baseline to which to compare changes. We have selected thirty networks (i.e., a quarter of the total networks), but there is no hard and fast rule. Finally, we have accepted ORA's default risk/decision threshold for a false alarm (i.e., 0.01/3.50) although McCulloh and Carley (2011:15) used 0.017/3.00 in their analysis. This threshold is denoted by the thin, solid line running horizontal across the graph at the 3.50 mark in Figure 10.9. If a change in the network crosses this line, then a significant change is considered to have occurred. Keep in mind that if the threshold is set too high, then analysts may miss an important change in a network under examination. If it is set too low, then analysts may mistake normal change for sudden change and potentially take unnecessary actions. Thus, analysts need to be careful in determining what constitutes a significant change, drawing heavily on experience and being willing to adjust expectations in light of new information.

Looking at Figure 10.9, two significant changes appear to have occurred. One, denoted by the gray (or lighter) line, indicates whether a significant increase has occurred in terms of network centralization; the other, denoted by the black (or darker) line, indicates whether a significant decrease in network centralization occurred. Both cross the decision threshold (i.e., 3.50), indicating that both a significant increase and decrease in degree centralization occurred in the network. When did these occur? Most likely at the point that the lines leave the baseline and begin their climb upward. That the black line begins its climb on September 2009 (the 105th month) is relatively uninteresting because that is when Noordin was killed. However, the fact that the gray line leaves the baseline

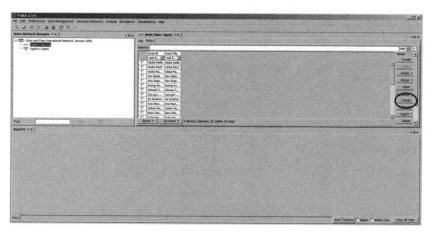

Figure 10.10. Node Class Editor

at February 2003 (the 25th month) is interesting because it occurs at about the time Noordin began to distance himself from Jemaah Islamiyah (JI). Indeed, it occurs only two months after Noordin acquired the explosives left over from the Christmas Eve bombings carried out in 2000 by JI, which implies that the acquisition of the explosives may have been the catalyst for Noordin to strike out on his own (International Crisis Group 2006:3). Thus, the increase in centralization may not have been a response to exogenous pressures, such as the efforts of Indonesian authorities to shut down Noordin's network, but rather to something inherent in the network itself, such as Noordin's leadership style. Of course, it could be the result of both factors.

10.3 Fusing Geospatial and Social Network Data

We now turn to an examination of how ORA fuses geospatial and relational data. We begin by walking through the steps of preparing social network data for fusion with geospatial data, in particular how to enter geospatial coordinates into ORA. Next, we examine how to fuse social network data with corresponding geospatial data in terms of both metrics and visualization.

Preparing Social Network and Geospatial Data in ORA

First begin by loading the January 2001 alive and free operational meta-network (Alive and Free Operational Network January 2001.xml) in ORA using ORA's *File>Open Meta-Network* command. Highlight the agent node class of the meta-network and then click on

[ORA-Main Screen]
File>Open Meta-Network

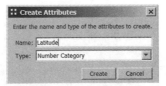

Figure 10.11. Create Attributes Dialog Box

the Editor tab in the Information/Editor panel of ORA's main interface (Figure 10.10).

In ORA we enter geospatial data as actor attributes. ORA allows users to enter geospatial coordinates in a number of different formats: (1) Latitude and Longitude,[5] (2) Military Grid Reference System (MGRS),[6] (3) Universal Transverse Mercator (UTM),[7] and (4) Cartesian.[8] To enter attribute data directly into ORA, click "Create," which is on the right side of the Information/Editor panel (circled in Figure 10.10); this calls up a dialog box (Figure 10.11) where we enter the name of the attribute (e.g., Latitude) as well as attribute type (note that "Number Category" has been selected as the attribute type because geospatial coordinates are nominal, rather than ordered, data).

If we repeat this process for creating longitudinal and MGRS attributes, we should end up with three empty columns in which we can enter geospatial data either by hand or by copying and pasting from a spreadsheet. Included with the data for this chapter is a *.csv file (`LatLonM-GRS2001.csv`) that contains latitude, longitude, and MGRS data that can be copied and pasted into the columns we just created (see Figure 10.12).[9]

Visualizing Social Network and Geospatial Data in ORA

One function implemented in ORA that fuses geospatial and social network data is its ability to visualize social network data geospatially. To *Visualizations>* do this we use ORA's *Visualizations>Geospatial Networks* command, *Geospatial* which calls up a dialog box (not shown), indicating that ORA has not *Networks* detected any location information. Click "OK." This will bring up a dialog box similar to Figure 10.13, which we use to tell ORA where it can find the geospatial information it needs. First, highlight the agent node class in the left-hand portion of the dialog box. Then, click "Add GIS

---

5   See http://en.wikipedia.org/wiki/Lat_lon.
6   See http://en.wikipedia.org/wiki/Military_grid_reference_system.
7   See http://en.wikipedia.org/wiki/Universal_Transverse_Mercator.
8   See http://en.wikipedia.org/wiki/Cartesian_coordinate_system.
9   Although the data are for locations where Noordin network was operative (e.g., Indonesia, Philippines), any correspondence between these and actual locations of members of Noordin's network at a particular time is purely coincidental.

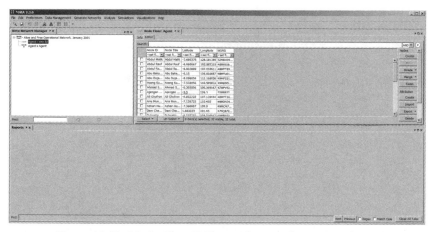

Figure 10.12. Node Class Editor with Latitude, Longitude, and MGRS Attributes

Attribute" toward the bottom of the dialog box. This will bring up a sub-dialog box (also shown in Figure 10.13), which asks you to indicate the type of GIS coordinate system you intend to use; we have chosen MGRS, but we could have just as easily chosen to use latitude and longitude coordinates. Next, select the node attribute where the MGRS coordinate is found, click "Finish," and the subdialog box will disappear. Click "Next" at the bottom of the dialog box, and (not surprisingly) another dialog box will appear where you will want to click "Finish" one more time.

When you do this, ORA's GIS visualizer will appear with the 2001 alive and free operational network mapped geospatially (probably in the lower left of the map). In Figure 10.14 we centered the map by clicking on

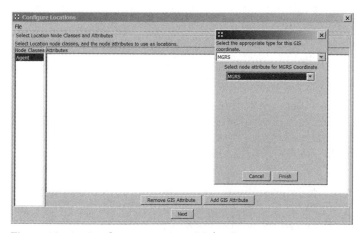

Figure 10.13. Configure Locations Dialog Box

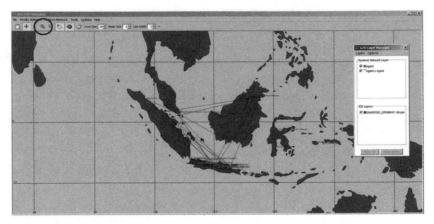

Figure 10.14. ORA's GIS Visualization of Noordin Alive Operational Network

the portion of the map we wanted to center and then zoomed in by first clicking on the "zoom" tool (circled in Figure 10.14) and then clicking on the map.

Although ORA's mapping capabilities are somewhat limited (although you may want to explore ORA's three-dimensional option using the *Options>Use 3D Visualization (NASA WorldWind)* command found in ORA's GIS Visualizer menu), it does allow you to export the network in Google Earth and ArcGIS formats with its *File>Save Map>Save Map to KML* and *File>Save Map>Save Map to SHP* commands, respectively. Picking up on the theme of the previous section, analysts could geospatially map dark networks over time in order to see whether (and how) they vary and what such variances may indicate about the network. An example of this is presented in Figure 10.15, which pictures Noordin's alive and free operational network in 2001, 2004, 2007, and 2010 (the panels run left to right, top to bottom). They indicate that the network was anything but static, and was instead constantly on the move.[10] For example, in 2001 (upper-left panel) the members of Noordin's network were located solely in Indonesia and Malaysia, but by 2004 (upper-right panel) a few members had relocated to the Philippines. In 2007 (lower-left panel) there appears to have been a movement of some members to the island of Java, but in 2010 (lower-right panel), shortly after Noordin's death, the network appears to have dispersed across Indonesia.

File>Save Map>Save Map to KML, Save Map to SHP

[10] A series of networks from 2001–2010 have been created that include geospatial information (e.g., `Alive and Free Operational Network January 2001 (geo).xml`). As previously noted, any correspondence between these and actual locations of members of Noordin's network at a particular time is purely coincidental; thus, the following analysis is purely hypothetical.

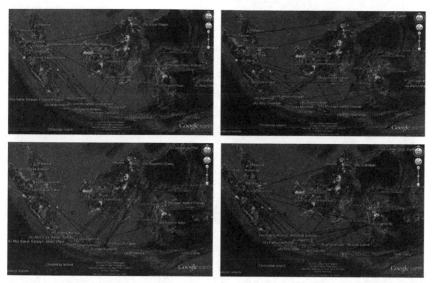

Figure 10.15. Google Earth Maps of Alive and Free Operational Network

The geospatial mapping of social networks suggests something else, as well. In particular, it seems likely that actors who are peripheral to a network in terms of standard measures of centrality may be geospatially located in such a way that they are more central to the network's operations than otherwise believed. Thus, it makes sense to estimate social network metrics that take into account the geospatial location of actors, although given the ease by which persons and resources move through the modern world, they should not be seen as a substitute for, but rather as a compliment to, standard social network metrics. The availability of such metrics is currently limited, but ORA does estimate a few, and it is to that functionality that we now turn.

Geospatially Weighted Social Network Metrics in ORA

When exploring ORA geospatial visualization capabilities, we encountered a dialog box that indicated that it could not detect any location information. That is because we entered the geospatial data as attributes of the actors in the network rather than create a separate location node class. This is fine if all we want to do is visualize social networks geospatially and nothing else. However, if we want to take advantage of ORA's ability to estimate geospatially weighted centrality metrics (Olson and Carley 2009), then we need to create a separate location node class. To do this, right-click on the alive and free operational meta-network

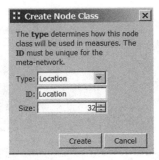

Figure 10.16. ORA's Create Node Class Dialog Box

(`Alive and Free Operational Network January 2001.xml`); this brings up a dialog "bubble" box (not shown) that provides users with several options. Choose the "Add New Node Class" option. This will bring up ORA "Create Node Class" dialog box (Figure 10.16). Using the drop-down menu, select *Location*, and indicate that it should have the same number of nodes (i.e., size) as the number of agents in the network (in this case, thirty-two, but be aware that the size will vary from network to network) because we will assign each actor to a unique location. When done, click "Create."

Next, we need to add an agent-by-location network. Because each agent (actor) will be assigned its own unique location, we need to create a square network (i.e., 32 × 32). To do this, once again right-click on the meta-network, which will call up the dialog bubble box we previously saw. This time, choose the "Add Blank Network" option, which will bring up ORA's "Create Network" dialog box (Figure 10.17). For the source node class, choose *Agent*, for the Target node class, choose *Location* and click "Create."

The next to last step involves assigning actor one to location one, actor two to location two, and so on. We do this by right-clicking on the "Agent by Location" network we just created, which brings up its own dialog "bubble" box (not shown). From the list of options, select "Set

Figure 10.17. ORA's Create Network Dialog Box

Diagonal." The default sets the diagonal to one – that is, True (+1), the option we want – so click "OK." To examine the result, with the agent-by-location network still highlighted in the Meta-Network Manager panel, select the Editor tab found under the Information/Editor panel, which allows you to see the matrix underlying the agent-by-location network (not shown).[11] It is by setting the diagonal to one that we assign each actor to a unique location. The final step involves entering the latitude and longitude coordinates for each actor/location as we did before.[12] Now we are ready to compare standard measures of actor centrality with geospatially weighted ones.

Let's begin by first calculating standard social network analysis metrics for the 2001 alive operational network using ORA's *Analysis>Generate Reports>Locate Key Entities>Standard Network Analysis* command (or use the Generate Reports speed button located on the Editor portion of ORA's main interface). At the first dialog box (not shown) select the network, at the second dialog box (not shown) select only the agent node class for analysis because in this case we are not interested in location metrics, at the third dialog box (not shown) indicate the number of ranked nodes to display (the default is ten), and at the final dialog box (not shown) select the desired output options (e.g., text, HTML, CSV) and click "Finish." As we saw in Chapter 7, this command generates a series of commonly used social network metrics for the trust network. *[Analysis> Generate Reports>Locate Key Entities>Standard Network Analysis]*

Next, analyze the network using ORA's *Analysis>Generate Reports> Geospatial>Geospatial Assessment* command. At the first dialog box (not shown) select the network, at the second dialog box (not shown) accept ORA's defaults because ORA needs the location information in order to estimate the geospatially weighted metrics, at the third dialog box (not shown) indicate that the location node class is the correct one (this option is here just in case there is more than one location node class), and at the final dialog box (not shown) select the desired output options and click "Finish." This report generates a series of distance statistics (e.g., agents closest together, agents farthest apart) as well as betweenness, closeness, and degree centrality metrics weighted by their spatial location. Because we are working with a disconnected graph, we will ignore the closeness scores and focus on the degree and betweenness scores (Table 10.2). *[Analysis> Generate Reports> Geospatial> Geospatial Assessment]*

At first glance the standard metrics output may strike readers as strange because Noordin is not among the top-ranked actors in terms of degree centrality, and he ranks seventh in terms of betweenness centrality. Keep

---

[11] ORA provides two ways of looking at an underlying matrix: Either in "binary view" where relations between objects are simply check marks, or in "numeric view" where you can see the actual cell values.

[12] It is unnecessary to repeat those steps here. However, the following analysis requires latitude and longitude data, rather than MGRS data, so be sure to use the former rather than the latter.

Table 10.2. *Comparison of standard and geospatially weighted centrality metrics*

Standard		Geospatially weighted	
Degree	Betweenness	Degree	Betweenness
Azhari Husin (0.387)	Salman (0.161)	Umar Wayan (0.085)	Salman (0.311)
Hambali (0.323)	Azhari Husin (0.138)	Muchtar (0.083)	Azhari Husin (0.238)
Dulmatin (0.290)	Dulmatin (0.090)	Dani Chandra (0.078)	Dulmatin (0.160)
Umar Patek (0.290)	Umar Patek (0.090)	Hambali (0.074)	Umar Patek (0.160)
Imam Samudra (0.258)	Harun (0.041)	Azhari Husin (0.069)	Hambali (0.058)
Salman (0.258)	Hambali (0.039)	Noordin Top (0.067)	Harun (0.048)
Abdul Rauf (0.226)	Imam Samudra (0.009)	Salman (0.066)	Noordin Top (0.014)
Ali Ghufron (0.226)	Noordin Top (0.009)	Imam Samudra (0.049)	Imam Samudra (0.010)
Iqbal (0.226)		Aris Munandar (0.049)	
6 actors w/same score (0.161)		Zulkarnaen (0.049)	

in mind, however, that this is the network in 2001 when Noordin was still a full and faithful member of Jemaah Islamiyah, so it is not surprising that he does not rank too high. Still, the fact that he was one of eight individuals ranked in terms of betweenness centrality (all the rest had betweenness scores of 0.00) is evidence that Noordin was in a position to form a dark network of his own. Now compare the standard scores with the geospatially weighted ones. Although there is very little difference between the two sets of betweenness scores, the degree centrality scores do differ substantially from one another. Individuals who are not ranked in terms of standard measures of degree centrality are ranked in terms of the geospatially weighted measures (e.g., Umar Wayan, Muchtar, Dani Chandra, and Noordin Top).

All this suggests that analysts will want to want to take such metrics into account (when possible, of course) when crafting strategies. For example, actors who rank lower in terms of geospatially weighted centrality metrics than in terms of standard centrality metrics may indicate that they play roles that, although important, are more peripheral to the network's day-to-day operations (e.g., operating training camps but not participating in actual operations). Moreover, key members who are geospatially removed from the network may be easier to isolate than those who are not (e.g., by disrupting transportation routes or communication links). Of course, we can also estimate these metrics over time, which may help analysts monitor the network to identify emerging leaders and important clusters of actors. Put simply, a close examination of a dark network's geospatial patterns and variance over time can supplement standard forms of analysis. As we noted previously, these should not be seen as a substitute for standard social network analysis but rather as a complement to something that can inform analysts as they attempt to track and disrupt dark networks.

10.4   Summary and Conclusion

In this chapter we have examined two approaches for investigating the dynamic nature of dark networks: the analysis of how networks change and adapt over time and the fusion of geospatial and social network data. With regard to longitudinal networks, we explored both descriptive and statistical detection approaches for studying network change. As noted at this chapter's outset, these are not the only options available to analysts studying longitudinal networks. The actor-based models developed by Tom Snijders and his colleagues (Snijders 2001, 2005; Snijders et al. 2010) model variation in network structure over time, taking into account both processes that are endogenous (i.e., internal) to the network itself as well as factors that are exogenous (i.e., external) to the network, such as actors' attributes (Prell 2011:215). Although promising for the study of dark networks, they have yet to be implemented in UCINET, Pajek, or ORA and are still somewhat difficult for the average analyst to use. The fusion of geospatial and social network data represents an exciting leap forward in the analysis of social networks, allowing analysts to complement traditional social network analysis with geospatially informed ones. On the one hand, the ability to geospatially plot social network data could help analysts detect patterns (both cross-sectionally and longitudinally) that they might have otherwise missed. On the other hand, the availability of geospatially weighted metrics may help in the detection of central and peripheral actors; to be sure, only a few geospatially weighted metrics are currently available, but there is reason to hope that more will be available in the near future.

How have the approaches explored in this chapter improved our understanding of Noordin's network? Our longitudinal analysis of the alive operational network found that it became increasingly more centralized and less fragmented from 2003 to 2006 and then reversed course when Noordin and a few of his close associates were killed in 2009, which corresponded with the essential collapse of the network. This finding is consistent with Bakker et al.'s (2011) that centralized dark networks are less resilient to shocks than are decentralized ones; the authors' work also lent support for the use of kinetic strategies to remove key network members. However, while this conclusion may be warranted, the network only became more centralized over time, and this may have been in response to various strategies used by the Indonesian forces. If this was in fact the case, then when exploring possible strategies disrupting dark networks, analysts may want to consider those that cause networks to become more centralized. For example, sowing distrust may lead a dark network's leaders to become concerned that the security of the network is at risk and cause them to consolidate (i.e., centralize) the network's operations into the hands of a few individuals.

Interestingly, the application of statistical network change detection techniques to the same network indicated that a significant increase in centralization began not long after Noordin acquired explosives left over from the Christmas Eve 2000 bombings, suggesting that the increase in centralization may not have been in response to exogenous factors, such as the efforts of Indonesian authorities, but rather in response to endogenous factors, such as Noordin's leadership style. Of course, the increased centralization of the network could be a result of both internal and external factors. Perhaps just as important, however, this finding highlights the important role that the tracking and seizure of explosives and other weapons may have in the prevention of terrorist attacks such as those carried out by Noordin and other dark networks.

Although the geospatial data used in the examples in this chapter were fictional, they nevertheless point to the potential role that the fusion of geospatial and social network data can play in the disruption of dark networks. For example, apart from the inclusion of geospatial data in the analysis, a network may appear to be relatively static, but once geospatial data are taken into account, analysts make discover that the network is anything but static and is instead constantly on the move. Moreover, the inclusion of geospatial network data highlighted why analysts, when possible, should take geospatially weighted metrics into account when crafting strategies. We saw, for example, how key members who are geospatially removed from the network may be easier to isolate than those who are not. Geospatially weighted metrics should not be seen as being a substitute for standard social network metrics but rather as a complement to them, something that can inform analysts as they attempt to track and disrupt dark networks.

11

Statistical Models for Dark Networks

11.1 Introduction

It is not uncommon when attempting to tease out the causes of a particular outcome that several potential factors are identified, all of which are correlated with the outcome of interest but may not be actual causes. For example, a strong correlation exists between checking into a hospital and subsequently dying. However, few would argue that checking into a hospital typically increases the chance that someone will die. Instead, the correlation between the two events exists because people who are extremely ill and thus have a higher probability of dying are more likely to check into a hospital than are those who are in good health. This correlation is referred to as spurious because it is due to the presence of a third factor, which, in this example, is the state of one's health.

It is also possible for a variable to appear to have either no effect or a negative effect on a particular outcome, when in fact it has a positive one. To illustrate this, consider the following (purely hypothetical) example (adapted from an example presented in Starbird 2006), which cross tabulates whether members of a particular dark network attended college with whether they are a key player (see Chapter 8). If we relied solely on the data presented in Table 11.1, we would probably conclude that attending college reduces the likelihood that a network member will be a key player: 70 percent of members who have not attended college are key players, whereas only 60 percent of those who have attended college are.

Such a conclusion would be wrong, however. Consider the next set of tables, which breaks the data down into whether members are native Indonesians. The first table (11.2a) presents data for those who are native Indonesians, whereas the second (11.2b) presents data for those who are not. Clearly, the story has changed. Now, attending college appears to have a positive effect on whether someone is a key player. Of the native

Table 11.1. *Crosstab of key players and college
education*

Attended college	Key player		
	No	Yes	Total
No	300	700	1,000
	(30%)	(70%)	(100%)
Yes	600	400	1,000
	(60%)	(40%)	(100%)
Total	900	1,100	2,000
	(45%)	(55%)	(100%)

Indonesian members, 100 percent of those who have attended college are
key players, whereas only 82.5 percent of those who have not attended
college are. The same holds true for non-Indonesian members: 25 percent
who have attended college are key players, whereas only 20 percent of
those who have not attended college are. In both cases the difference is not
huge, but attending college still appears to matter. What appears to matter
more, however, is whether a network member is a native Indonesian:

Table 11.2a. *Crosstab of key players and college
education (Indonesians)*

Indonesian attended college	Key player		
	No	Yes	Total
No	140	660	800
	(17.5%)	(82.5%)	(100%)
Yes	0	200	200
	(0.0%)	(100%)	(100%)
Total	140	860	1,000
	(14%)	(86%)	(100%)

Table 11.2b. *Crosstab of key players and college
education (non-Indonesians)*

Non-Indonesian attended college	Key player		
	No	Yes	Total
No	160	40	200
	(80%)	(20%)	(100%)
Yes	600	200	800
	(75%)	(25%)	(100%)
Total	760	240	1,000
	(76%)	(24%)	(100%)

Table 11.3a. *Crosstab of key players and college education (Afghan vet)*

Afghan vet attended college	Key player		
	No	Yes	Total
No	165	370	535
	(30.84%)	(69.16%)	(100%)
Yes	320	235	555
	(57.66%)	(42.34%)	(100%)
Total	485	605	1,090
	(44.50%)	(55.50%)	(100%)

Table 11.3b. *Crosstab of key players and college education (non–Afghan vet)*

Non–Afghan vet attended college	Key player		
	No	Yes	Total
No	135	330	465
	(29.03%)	(70.97%)	(100%)
Yes	280	165	445
	(62.92%)	(37.08%)	(100%)
Total	415	495	910
	(76%)	(24%)	(100%)

86 percent of Indonesian members are key players but only 24 percent of non-Indonesians are. And, because most Indonesian members have not attended college, the aggregated data presented in Table 11.1 are misleading 11.2b.

Finally, consider Tables 11.3a and 11.3b, which break the sample down into whether network members fought in Afghanistan. The first table (11.3a) presents data for those who did, whereas the second (11.3b) presents data for those who did not. In both tables, the effect of a college education appears to be negative. Regardless of whether they are an Afghan veteran, network members appear to be less likely to be key players if they attended college. Specifically, only 42.34 percent of those who fought in Afghanistan and attended college are key players, whereas 69.16 percent of those who fought in Afghanistan but did not attend college are key players. Similarly, only 37.08 percent of those who did not fight in Afghanistan and attended college are key players, whereas 70.97 percent of those who did not fight and did not attend college are key players. Moreover, it appears that being an Afghan veteran matters: 55.5 percent of Afghan veterans are key players, but only 24 percent of non–Afghan veterans are. It is possible that a high percentage of key

Table 11.4. *Regression of key player on variables of interest*

	Model 1	Model 2	Model 3
Attended College	-1.25***	0.90***	0.90***
Indonesian		3.58***	3.59***
Afghan Veteran			0.16
Intercept	0.85	-1.91	-1.99
Pseudo R^2	6.71	31.63	31.69
AIC	2,571.75	1,888.02	1,888.22
BIC	2,582.95	1,904.83	1,910.62

Note: * = $p < .05$; ** = $p < .01$; *** = $p < .001$

players are both Indonesian and Afghan veterans, and this is confounding or hiding the effect of a college education. To see if this were the case, we could cross tabulate the Afghan veteran and Indonesian variables and then parse the data between those who are key players and those who are not, and then between those who attended college and those who did not. As one can see, however, as the number of independent variables increases, the number of potential cross tabulations that are needed to disentangle genuine from spurious effects increases exponentially and becomes impractical. An easier and more practical approach is to use multivariate regression.

Estimating a regression model sounds more daunting than it actually is. That is not to suggest that the math lying behind it is not computationally intense or that it is impossible to make a mistake in interpreting the results. Rather, it is to highlight the fact that standard statistical packages, such as SPSS, Stata, and SAS as well as UCINET and ORA, make estimating such models relatively painless for analysts.[1]

How can regression help us make sense of these tables?[2] Table 11.4 presents the results of a logistic regression model that regresses whether a member is a key player on the three variables previously explored.[3] Model 1 only includes college attendance as a variable and is consistent with the results presented in Table 11.1; it indicates that by itself there is a negative association (note that the coefficient is negative) between attending college and being a key player. Model 2, however, adds the

---

[1] Although Pajek allows users to estimate correlations between variables, it does not currently include the ability to estimate regression models.

[2] The following discussion of multivariate regression does not purport nor is it intended to be exhaustive; it merely seeks to introduce the topic in order to set the stage for the discussion of the regression of social network data. For a helpful introduction to regression, see Hamilton (1992).

[3] A logistic regression was used because the dependent variable is binary (i.e., yes or no); if the dependent variable was continuous, then an ordinary least squares (OLS) model would have been used (Long 1997).

Indonesian variable and two aspects of it are of note. One is that the college coefficient is now positive; the other is that not only is the Indonesian coefficient positive (as expected) but also substantially larger than the effect of having a college education. Finally, Model 3 includes the Afghan veteran variable. Interestingly, the effect of being an Afghan veteran, although positive, is not as large as whether someone has attended college or is a native Indonesian. Moreover, it has very little effect on the overall fit of the model as evidenced by the Pseudo R^2 associated with the model,[4] which only climbs from 31.63 to 31.69. The other two models of fit – the Akaike Information Criterion (AIC) and the Bayesian Information Criterion (BIC) – support this conclusion as well. For both, the lower the number, the better the fit, but as we can see, both actually increase slightly from Model 2 to Model 3, indicating that the third model, which includes an additional variable, actually does a poorer job in explaining whether a member is key player.

This raises the question whether the Afghan variable has a significant effect on whether someone is a key player. Traditionally, social scientists have used measures of statistical significance to help decide whether a variable has a significant effect. Although social network analysts generally use a different approach for estimating measures of statistical significance, it is sufficient to note that social scientists generally consider a variable's effect to be statistically significant if the probability (p-value) that it could have occurred by random chance falls below a particular threshold, typically .05. If the p-value of a particular variable's coefficient falls below .05 ($p < .05$), then the probability that the result could occurred by random chance is less than 5 percent; put differently, the probability that the result represents a genuine association is greater than 95 percent. Similarly, if $p < .01$, then the probability that the result could have occurred by random chance is less than 1 percent, and if $p < .001$, then the probability is less than 0.1 percent. Looking at Table 11.4, we can see that both the college and Indonesian variables are statistically significant at a p-value of less than .01, indicating that there is a strong probability that the positive association between the variables and whether members are key players is genuine.[5] Note, however, that the Afghan variable is not statistically significant; thus, we cannot conclude

---

[4] Pseudo R^2 (and the traditional R^2 – aka the coefficient of determination – used with OLS models) estimates the extent to which a model's variables account for the variance in the dependent variable. Thus, Model 2's pseudo R^2 indicates that the two variables included in the model explain about 32 percent of the variation in whether members are key players, which is not bad, but it means that 68 percent of the variation remains unexplained.

[5] In terms of substantive effect, being Indonesian matters more than attending college, of course. Statistical and substantive significance are consistently conflated with one another. Variables can be statistically significant but have no substantive effect, a fact that gets lost in a lot of research (see McCloskey 1995; Ziliak and McCloskey 2008).

with any confidence that it has a positive effect on whether a member is a key player. Unless there are some unknown variables that we have yet to account for, it appears that the correlation between the two variables is spurious. This is true in spite of the results presented in Tables 11.3a and 11.3b, highlighting one of the dangers of relying solely on cross tabulations and one of the reasons for including multivariate regression in one's analysis.

11.2   Statistical Models for Social Network Data

Regression analysis of social network data differs from standard regression models in two important ways. One difference is that standard statistical models are designed to analyze random samples so that researchers can generalize their results to the population at large. As we saw in the previous section, variables that are statistically significant are seen as being unlikely to have occurred by random chance and thus can be generalized to the population from which the sample was drawn. However, because social network analyses do not typically analyze samples of networks – instead they analyze (at least in theory) complete networks – there is no need to generalize to the population at large. A second difference is that standard statistical models assume that observations are independent of one another, but as we discussed at length in Chapter 1, social network analysis assumes that observations (i.e., actors) are tied to one another (i.e., they are not independent of one another) and that these interdependencies influence behavior.

For these reasons, with social network data we should not use standard approaches for estimating statistical significance. Instead, we should turn to a form a nonparametric estimation known as permutation testing (similar to bootstrapping), which entails the random rearrangement of a network's rows and columns thousands of times in order to calculate a sampling distribution of statistics that can then be compared to the statistics generated by the observed (i.e., actual) network. If the observed statistics differ significantly from the randomly generated ones, we can conclude that the observed statistics could not have occurred by random chance and are "statistically significant."[6]

For example, when calculating the level of correlation between two networks, ORA and UCINET first compute the correlation coefficient between corresponding cells. Then, they randomly permute (i.e., rearrange) the rows and columns (together) of one of the networks and recalculate the correlation. This second step is carried out numerous times in order to compute the proportion of times that a random measure is

---

[6]   This is known as the quadratic assignment procedure or QAP (Krackhardt 1987b).

larger than or equal to the observed measure calculated in the first step. A low proportion (e.g., less than 0.05) suggests that a correlation between networks is unlikely to have occurred by chance and thus is considered statistically significant. UCINET and ORA use a similar approach when regressing a dependent network on a series of independent networks. First, they estimate a standard multivariate regression across the corresponding cells of the dependent and independent networks. Then, they randomly permute the rows and columns of the dependent matrix, recalculate the regression, and store the resultant R^2 and coefficient values. This second step is repeated hundreds or thousands of times in order to compute the proportion of times that the randomly generated statistics are larger than or equal to those generated in the first step, and a low proportion is interpreted to mean that the results could not have occurred by random chance. Finally, the same approach is used when calculating the correlation or regression of attribute data (e.g., centrality and education level – see Chapter 7). In the first step, a correlation or standard multivariate regression is estimated across corresponding values of the dependent and independent attributes; in the second, the elements of the dependent attribute data are randomly permuted numerous times, and the distribution of randomly generated results is compared to the actual results to see whether the latter is likely to have occurred by random chance.

Now let's turn to estimating multivariate regression models in UCINET and ORA. Because we explored how to estimate the correlation between various attributes in Chapter 7, there is no reason to cover that ground again. We will, however, explore how correlations between networks are calculated.

11.3 Statistical Models in UCINET and ORA

Multivariate Regression with UCINET

Regression with Attribute Data. Let's begin by estimating a multivariate regression model using attribute data. For this we use UCINET's *Tools>Testing Hypotheses>Node-Level>Regression* command, which calls up a dialog box similar to Figure 11.1 (which we saw in Chapter 7). In this example, the data file that includes the dependent variable is loaded as the dependent dataset (Alive Operational Network-cent. ##h), and the data file that includes the independent variables is loaded as the independent dataset (Attributes.##h). We also need to indicate the columns in which the attribute data can be found. Here we are regressing normalized degree centrality (column 1) on three independent variables: (1) education level (column 1), which is an ordered variable; (2) Indonesian (column 3), which is a binary variable where "1" indicates

[UCINET] Tools>Testing Hypotheses> Node-Level> Regression

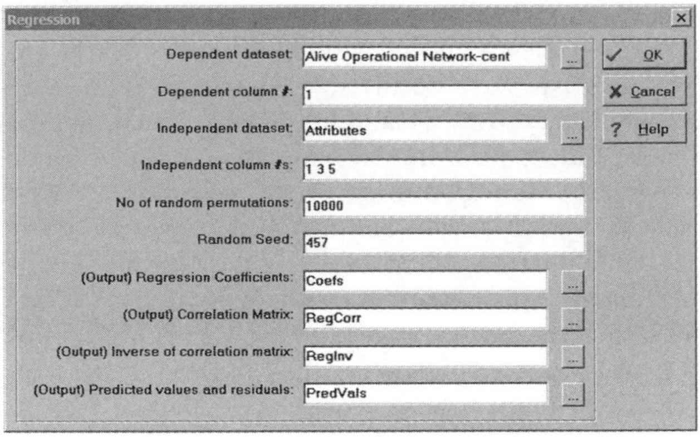

Figure 11.1. UCINET's Attribute Regression Dialog Box

that the actor is Indonesian and "0' indicates that the actor is not; and (3) Afghan veteran (column 5), which is also a binary variable where "1" indicates that the actor is an Afghan veteran and "0' indicates that the actor is not. It is important that the attributes be either ordered or binary. Nominal (i.e., unordered) variables will produce nonsensical results. Indeed, the latter two attribute variables were recoded from the "Nationality" and "Military Training" variables included with the standard attribute data listed in Appendix 1. Note that the default number of random permutations is ten thousand; you can change this, but ten thousand is generally a large enough number to calculate a meaningful distribution of statistical measures.

After the datasets are loaded and the columns containing the dependent and independent variables are indicated (see Figure 11.1), click "OK," and UCINET will generate a multivariate regression report (Figure 11.2). A correlation matrix appears at the top of the report (see Chapter 7 for discussion of correlation coefficients). Below this matrix are the measures of fit. The adjusted R^2, which is generally preferred over the unadjusted R^2 because it takes into account the number of variables included in the model, indicates that the independent variables account for 15.5 percent of the observed variation in the dependent variable (i.e., degree centrality). This is not huge, but given that the *p*-value of the F-statistic (F Value) equals 0.002, we can be reasonably confident that the model has some predictive power. Put differently, there is only a 0.2-percent chance that our independent variables provide no predictive power at all.

The regression coefficients and their associated levels of statistical significance are located at the bottom of the report. Two types of regression coefficients are reported: unstandardized and standardized. Unstandardized coefficients indicate the raw effect that each independent variable

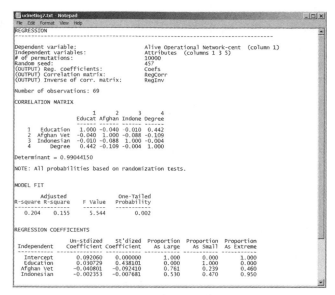

Figure 11.2. UCINET's Attribute Multivariate Regression Output

has on the dependent variable; in this case, the coefficients indicate the estimated amount by which normalized degree centrality changes for a one-unit change in each independent variable. Thus, a one-unit increase in education level leads to a 0.03 increase in normalized degree centrality, whereas being Indonesian or an Afghan veteran leads to decreases in normalized degree centrality of 0.04 and 0.002, respectively. By contrast, standardized coefficients indicate how many standard deviations a dependent variable will change per standard deviation increase in the independent variable. Standardized coefficients are helpful for comparing the effect of each independent variable on the dependent variable when the independent variables have different units of measure. Looking at the output we can see that the effect of education is far greater than that of being an Afghan vet or an Indonesian. Turning to the measures of statistical significance, we can see that UCINET provides three coefficients: the proportion of random trials that yielded a coefficient (1) as large or larger, (2) as small or smaller, and (3) as extreme as the observed value. Generally, the final column is where you will look to determine whether a coefficient should be regarded as statistically significant or not. The results tell us that, whereas we should pay attention to education coefficient, we should not put much stock in the Indonesian or Afghan veteran ones. Put differently, education level appears to have a positive effect on actors' centrality in the network, but being Indonesian or an Afghan veteran do not (i.e., the latter two variables

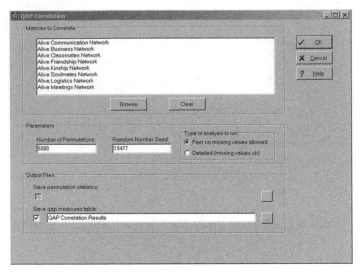

Figure 11.3. UCINET's QAP Correlation Dialog Box

should not be seen as having either a positive or negative effect on actor centrality).

Multivariate Regression with Social Network Data. In the previous section we analyzed attribute data using correlation and regression techniques. The results from these types of analysis answer questions such as, "Are highly educated terrorists more likely to be central players in a terrorist network than are terrorists with very little education?" (The results suggest that they are.) By contrast, when we analyze social network data using correlation and regression methods, we are seeking to answer questions such as, "Are certain types of relationships (e.g., friendship ties) predictive of other types of relationships (e.g., operational ties) than are others?" We'll begin by first estimating the correlation between all of the Noordin alive networks before we regress a particular alive network (operations) on all of the other networks.

Tools>Testing Hypotheses> Dyadic (QAP)>QAP Correlation

To estimate the correlation between networks in UCINET, we use its *Tools>Testing Hypotheses>Dyadic (QAP)>QAP Correlation* command, which brings up a dialog box (Figure 11.3) that asks you to indicate (using the "Browse" button) which networks you want to include. For this exercise, we will examine the correlation between all ten of the alive networks,[7] most of which are visible in Figure 11.3 (note that the default number of permutations is five thousand).

---

[7] Here we have unpacked the trust and operational networks and used the subnetworks contained therein.

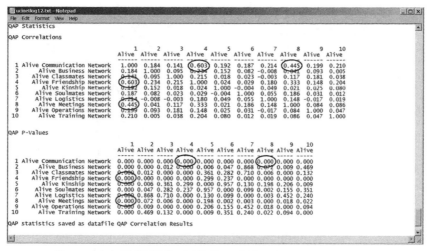

Figure 11.4. UCINET's QAP Correlation Report

Once the files are loaded, click "OK," and UCINET will generate an extensive report, a portion of which is pictured in Figure 11.4. Most of the report contains a separate summary for the correlation between each pair of networks. Each summary reports the observed level of correlation, its associated *p*-value, the average random correlation and its associated standard deviation along with the minimum and maximum correlations, and the proportion of correlations that were larger and smaller than the observed level of correlation. Although the individual summaries are helpful because they provide a lot of useful information, most of the time you will want to scroll down to the bottom of the report where the correlations between the various networks and their associated *p*-values are succinctly summarized in two matrices (Figure 11.4). Looking at the top matrix we can see that there is a high level of correlation between the communication and friendship networks (0.603) and the communication and meetings networks (0.445); looking at the bottom matrix, we can see that both of these correlations are statistically significant ($p < .001$). In fact, the correlations between the communication network and all the other networks are statistically significant. Note also that the values above and below the diagonal are mirror images of each other. Thus, the correlation (and *p*-value) between two networks are actually listed twice, as illustrated by the correlations and *p*-values that are circled in Figure 11.4.

What about the operations network? Although it does not exhibit as high of a correlation with other networks as the communication network does, it does correlate relatively highly (and at statistically significant levels) with the communication (0.199, $p < 0.001$), classmates (0.181,

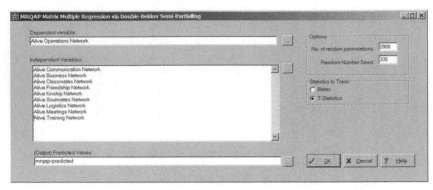

Figure 11.5. UCINET's MRQAP Network Regression Dialog Box

$p < 0.001$), and friendship (0.148, $p < 0.001$) networks. Its correlations with the business (0.093, $p < 0.01$) and meetings (0.084, $p < 0.05$) networks are also statistically significant, but their correlations are not as strong as the other three. Interestingly, there is a negative correlation between the operations and logistics networks, but it is not statistically significant, so we probably do not want to make too much of this, at least not at this point. What is also interesting is that the various networks that we have grouped together as the operational network (i.e., logistics, meetings, operations, and training) do not correlate too highly with one another, except for the meetings and logistics networks (0.148; $p < 0.00$), possibly suggesting that Noordin consciously attempted to keep various aspects of his operational network separate from one another. Whether all these correlations are genuine and whether an association that is not picked up by simply estimating correlations exists between two networks are not questions that quadratic assignment procedure (QAP) correlation can answer. Instead, we need to turn to multivariate regression, which is accessed with the *Tools>Testing Hypotheses>Dyadic (QAP)>QAP Regression>Double-Dekker Semi-Partialling MRQAP* command.[8] This calls up a dialog box (Figure 11.5) where we indicate the dependent (operations) and independent networks we will use in our analysis.

Tools>Testing Hypotheses> Dyadic (QAP)>QAP Regression> Double-Dekker Semi-Partialling MRQAP

It may take UCINET awhile to estimate the model because it recalculates each estimated coefficient numerous times (the default number of permutations equals two thousand). Once it finishes its calculations, it produces a report similar to the one presented in Figure 11.6, which reports the model's R^2, the adjusted R^2, the probability that the observed results could have occurred by chance, and the standardized and

---

[8]   MRQAP stands for Multiple Regression Quadratic Assignment Procedure. The Double-Dekker Semi-Partialling method was developed to adjust for network autocorrelation and mulitcollinearity (Dekker, Krackhardt, and Snijders 2007).

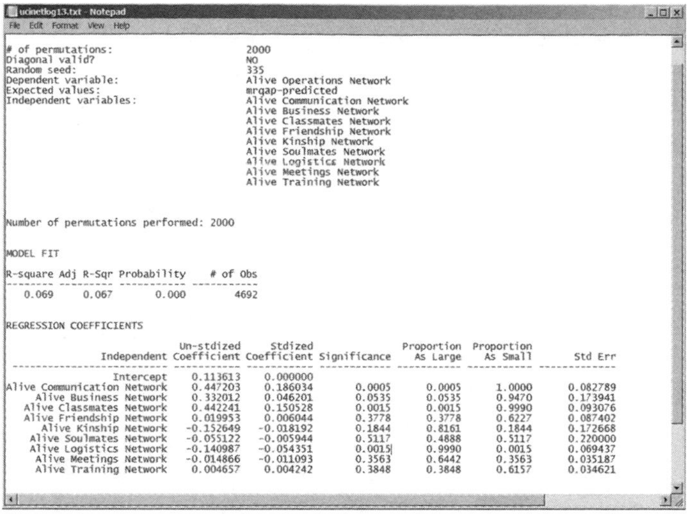

```
ucinetlog13.txt - Notepad
File  Edit  Format  View  Help

# of permutations:                2000
Diagonal valid?                   NO
Random seed:                      335
Dependent variable:               Alive Operations Network
Expected values:                  mrqap-predicted
Independent variables:            Alive Communication Network
                                  Alive Business Network
                                  Alive Classmates Network
                                  Alive Friendship Network
                                  Alive Kinship Network
                                  Alive Soulmates Network
                                  Alive Logistics Network
                                  Alive Meetings Network
                                  Alive Training Network


Number of permutations performed: 2000


MODEL FIT

R-square Adj R-Sqr Probability    # of Obs
-------- --------- ----------- -----------
   0.069     0.067       0.000        4692


REGRESSION COEFFICIENTS

                             Un-stdized      Stdized              Proportion  Proportion
                Independent Coefficient Coefficient Significance   As Large    As Small      Std Err
--------------------------- ----------- ----------- ------------ ----------- ----------- ------------
                  Intercept    0.113613    0.000000
Alive Communication Network    0.447203    0.186034       0.0005      0.0005      1.0000     0.082789
     Alive Business Network    0.332012    0.046201       0.0535      0.0535      0.9470     0.173941
   Alive Classmates Network    0.442241    0.150528       0.0015      0.0015      0.9990     0.093076
   Alive Friendship Network    0.019953    0.006044       0.3778      0.3778      0.6227     0.087402
      Alive Kinship Network   -0.152649   -0.018192       0.1844      0.8161      0.1844     0.172668
    Alive Soulmates Network   -0.055122   -0.005944       0.5117      0.4888      0.5117     0.220000
    Alive Logistics Network   -0.140987   -0.054351       0.0015      0.9990      0.0015     0.069437
     Alive Meetings Network   -0.014866   -0.011093       0.3563      0.6442      0.3563     0.035187
     Alive Training Network    0.004657    0.004242       0.3848      0.3848      0.6157     0.034621
```

Figure 11.6. UCINET's Network Regression Output

unstandardized coefficients along with their associated tests for statistical significance.

In this case the adjusted R^2 is not terribly high (6.7 percent), but because the p-value <0.001, we can conclude with relative confidence that the model does have some explanatory power. Clearly, though, a lot remains unexplained. The coefficients do tell something of an interesting story. Only the communication, classmates, and logistics networks exert a statistically significant effect on the operations network. More precisely, the presence of communication (0.447, $p < 0.001$) and classmate (0.442, $p < 0.01$) ties are positively associated with the presence of operational ties, while the presence of logistic ties (-0.141, $p < 0.01$) is negatively associated with presence of operational ties. Moreover, the standardized coefficients suggest that the effect of communication and classmate ties is about three times that of logistic ties.

What might these results tell us about Noordin's operations? As we noted previously, it appears that he consciously tried to keep his operations as separate from other aspects of his network (in particular, the logistic aspect of the network) as much as possible although he was unable to do so completely. The positive association of the communication with the operations network is not surprising given the important role that communications generally play in most dark network operations. This association suggests that targeting the communication network in some manner (e.g., through information operations or the removal of central players) might be an effective means for disrupting Noordin's operations. The positive association of classmate with operation ties is

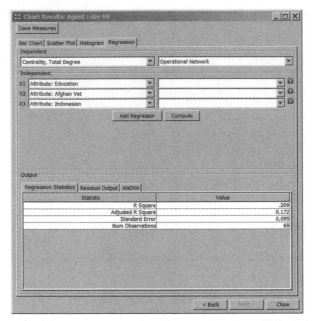

Figure 11.7. ORA's Attribute Regression (Overall Statistics)

perhaps not surprising either, given that we previously saw that class-mate ties were central to Noordin's network. Nevertheless, this positive association once again highlights the important role that school ties have played in Noordin's network and indicates that the construction of alternative schools may provide a viable long-term strategy for disrupting not only Noordin's network but also other dark networks that recruit heavily from extremist schools. The construction of schools might also facilitate the process of reintegrating disaffected individuals back into Indonesian civil society.

Multivariate Regression with ORA

Multivariate Regression with Attribute Data. Let's begin by estimating the same multivariate regression model using attribute data that we previously estimated using UCINET. First, read the alive Noordin meta-network (Alive Network.xml) into ORA using its *File>Open Meta-Network* command. Then, select the *Visualizations>Measure Charts* command (or use the companion speed button). At the first dialog box (not shown) indicate the node class (i.e., agents, organizations, etc.) that you will be using. In this case, there is only one node class, so select it and click "Next." At the next dialog box (Figure 11.7), select the Regression tab, and in the "Dependent" box use the drop-down menu to select the

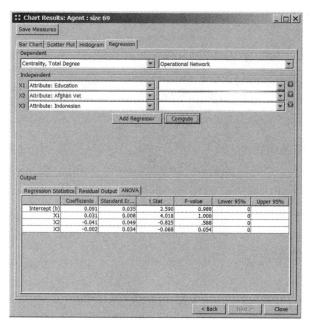

Figure 11.8. ORA's Attribute Regression (Coefficients)

dependent variable *Centrality, Total Degree*. To the right of this box, use the drop-down menu to indicate that you want total degree centrality to be calculated using the operational network. Next, we add our independent variables (i.e., regressors). Click on the "Add Regressor" button and add the three independent: (1) education level, (2) Afghan veteran, and (3) Indonesian. Finally, click "Compute" and the results will appear in the output portion of the dialog box (Figure 11.7). Note that the regression results are separated under three tabs. The first tab ("Regression Statistics") provides the overall results of the model. Comparing ORA's results with those of UCINET's (Figure 11.7) you will note that although they are similar, they are not identical. ORA's R^2 and adjusted R^2 are slightly higher than those estimated by UCINET, which is somewhat disconcerting, especially because an OLS regression estimated using the statistical package Stata confirmed UCINET's results.

Luckily, the coefficients for the independent variables agree with those estimated by UCINET. How do we know with ORA whether a coefficient is statistically significant? We look to the test statistic (t-stat), which indicates the number of standard deviations from the mean of the randomly generated results. If the absolute value of the test statistic is greater than 1.96, then the result is considered to be statistically significant.[9]

---

[9] If the observed results are greater than 1.96 standard deviations from the mean of the randomly generated results, this indicates that it lies beyond the 95th percentile. In other

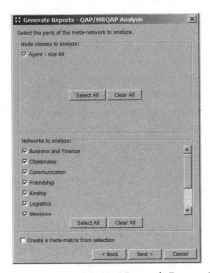

Figure 11.9. ORA's Network Regression Dialog Box

[ORA]
*File>Open
Meta-Network*

*Analysis
>Generate
Reports
>Statistical
Procedures and
Diagnostics
>QAP/MRQAP
Analysis*

Multivariate Regression with Social Network Data. Finally, let us turn to see how to estimate a network regression equation in ORA. Open the alive Noordin meta-network (Alive Noordin Network.xml) in ORA using its *File>Open Meta-Network* command. Next, highlight the meta-network in the Meta-Network Manager and issue ORA's regression command: *Analysis>Generate Reports>Statistical Procedures and Diagnostics>QAP/MRQAP Analysis.* At the first dialog box (not shown) make sure that the meta-network is selected (it should be) and click "Next."

This calls up a dialog box similar to Figure 11.9 where you indicate the networks you want to analyze. In this case we want to analyze all ten, and by default all should be selected. However, it is possible to deselect some of the networks if you do not want to use them in your analysis. Clicking "Next" calls up the next dialog box (Figure 11.10) where, using the drop-down menus as well as the check boxes, we can indicate our dependent and independent networks. Note that the operations network has been identified as the dependent network and that boxes of all of the other networks have been checked to indicate that they are the independent networks. Be careful: The operations network is by default included as one of the independent networks, so make sure that its box is unchecked – see Figure 11.10). Also, the default number of permutations is set at 100, which is a bit small. Increase it to at least 1,000. Click "Next" and at

words, it indicates that there is less than a 5-percent chance that the observed result could have occurred by chance.

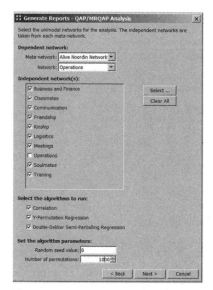

Figure 11.10. ORA's Network Regression Dialog Box

the next dialog box (not shown), provide an output file name and click "Finish."

Like UCINET, it will take ORA more than a few seconds to estimate the coefficients and their associated levels of significance. When it is done, it will produce a report similar to Figure 11.11. As you can see, ORA first reports the correlation between the operations network and all other networks and then the regression results. If you compare these results with those generated by UCINET, you will note that apart from rounding differences the correlation and regression coefficients are essentially the same as is the model R^2.[10] The measures of statistical significance do differ somewhat, but this is most likely due to the fact that we asked ORA to use only 1,000 permutations in its computations of statistical significance whereas in UCINET we used 2,000.[11] The differences do not change the story, however. Classmate and communication ties are positively associated with operation ties, while logistic ties are negatively associated, suggesting that targeting the communication network in some manner might be an effective short-term strategy for disrupting Noordin's operations, whereas building alternative schools might be a viable long-term strategy for either disrupting Noordin's operations or decreasing the likelihood that another dark network like Noordin will emerge in the future.

[10] Note that ORA does not report the unadjusted R^2.
[11] ORA includes both the Dekker semi-partialing method and the Y-permutation method for calculating statistical significance. The latter is the earliest form of MRQAP and is also implemented in UCINET.

Correlation Results

Network	Correlation	Significance	Hamming Distance	Euclidean Distance
Alive Noordin Network : Business and Finance	0.093	0.005	360	40.472
Alive Noordin Network : Classmates	0.181	0.000	476	39.925
Alive Noordin Network : Communication	0.199	0.000	552	39.950
Alive Noordin Network : Friendship	0.148	0.000	452	40.224
Alive Noordin Network : Kinship	0.025	0.192	366	40.768
Alive Noordin Network : Logisitics	-0.017	0.417	402	43.267
Alive Noordin Network : Meetings	0.084	0.020	406	47.497
Alive Noordin Network : Soulmates	0.031	0.169	362	40.719
Alive Noordin Network : Training	0.047	0.087	544	51.923

Regression Results

R-Squared: 0.068985

Variable	Coef	Std.Coef	Sig.Y-Perm	Sig.Dekker
Constant	0.114		0.000	
Alive Noordin Network : Business and Finance	0.332	0.046	0.051	0.044
Alive Noordin Network : Classmates	0.442	0.151	0.000	0.000
Alive Noordin Network : Communication	0.447	0.186	0.000	0.000
Alive Noordin Network : Friendship	0.020	0.006	0.398	0.385
Alive Noordin Network : Kinship	-0.153	-0.018	0.197	0.180
Alive Noordin Network : Logisitics	-0.141	-0.054	0.000	0.001
Alive Noordin Network : Meetings	-0.015	-0.011	0.391	0.380
Alive Noordin Network : Soulmates	-0.055	-0.006	0.437	0.490
Alive Noordin Network : Training	0.005	0.004	0.403	0.411

Figure 11.11. ORA's Network Correlation and Regression Report

11.4   Summary and Conclusion

In this chapter we have examined statistical models for attribute and network data that can help analysts disentangle genuine from spurious effects. As we saw, QAP correlation and multivariate regression models are invaluable to researchers when confronted with the problem of too many variables: that is, when they have identified several factors that could be associated with a particular outcome, it is impossible to distinguish which ones are truly from those that only appear to be. QAP regression is not the only statistical model available for cross-sectional network data. Also available are the p* models (also referred to as exponential random graph models or ERGMs), which differ from the QAP models in that whereas the latter are interested in the relationship between two or more attributes or networks, p* models attempt to draw inferences about the underlying structures of networks (Prell 2011:204). Unfortunately, like the actor-based models, p* models have yet to be implemented in UCINET, Pajek, or ORA (although ORA's Help function indicates that it is scheduled for the near future) and are difficult for the average user to implement in the available software.[12]

How have the approaches explored in this chapter improved our understanding of Noordin's network? The use of statistical models helped us to uncover the evidence that not only does education have a positive effect on the centrality of actors in Noordin's operational network but also ties with classmates are positively associated with operation ties. This is not the first time our analyses have highlighted the importance of schools, classmates, and education, but it does lend additional evidence to the argument that when crafting strategies for Noordin's network or others like it, the central role of education must be taken into account if interventions are to have any long-term effect.

---

[12] Both actor-based and p* models can be implemented in the open-source statistical software, R (R Development Core Team 2011).

Part V

Conclusion

12

The Promise and Limits of Social Network Analysis

12.1 Introduction

We have come a very long way in a relatively short time. Chapter 1 introduced social network analysis's (SNA) basic terms, concepts, and assumptions of social network theories and methods, and Chapter 2 offered a strategic framework into which social network analysis can be embedded for the disruption of dark networks. Chapters 3 and 4 introduced UCINET, NetDraw, Pajek, and ORA and covered the basic skills needed for the collection, manipulation, and visualization of social network data. Chapters 5 through 11 examined some of the more common social network metrics for measuring network topography, detecting cohesive subgroups, finding central and peripheral actors, pinpointing brokers and bridges, locating structurally equivalent actors, analyzing longitudinal and geospatial network data, and disentangling genuine effects from spurious effects.

This final chapter considers the promises and limitations of social network analysis. SNA is not a silver bullet in the fight against terrorist and criminal networks but rather one tool that can be used in conjunction with other tools in the crafting of potential strategies. Moreover, there is also the concern that the theories and methods outlined in this book will be used for ill rather than good. This concern is not limited to SNA but is one that arises whenever knowledge is disseminated in classrooms, through journals, by the creation of software, and so on. Nevertheless, general guidelines do exist as to how such knowledge should be used, which is why this chapter explores the ethics of using SNA for the disruption of dark networks. It considers a variety of ethical traditions before arguing that the just war tradition, which is rooted in the Aristotelian idea that ethics should be guided by the goal of encouraging those practices that allow human beings to flourish, provides helpful guidelines for the proper (and improper) use of social network analysis.

12.2   The Promise and Limits of Social Network Analysis

It is hard to argue with the observation that in recent years SNA has enhanced our understanding of how dark networks are structured and has offered potential strategies for their disruption. We have learned, for example, that the September 11, 2001, terrorist network was relatively decentralized in that its members had few ties to members of other cells (Krebs 2001). Apparently, some did not even know some of the others who were on the same flight as themselves. Despite the network's lack of connectedness, however, a handful of those involved (e.g., Mohamed Atta and Nawaf al-Hazmi) possessed key ties to others that allowed them to control, broker, and facilitate the flow of information and other resources through and across the network (Krebs 2001). The terrorist network that carried out the March 11, 2004, Madrid train bombings displayed similar dynamics (Rodriguez 2005). It was characterized by weak ties (Granovetter 1973) that enabled its cells to maintain operative ties with the larger network while remaining relatively isolated from and unknown to one another. This probably helped the network remain relatively invisible to counterterrorism efforts and provided it with a degree of stability if (and when) group members were captured, as most possessed little or no knowledge of the network's overall structure.

The social network analysis of dark networks took a giant leap forward with Sageman's (2003, 2004) analysis of the global Salafi jihad (GSJ). Not only did it challenge stereotypes that many hold regarding terrorists, but it also found that the GSJ exhibits network dynamics that researchers have discovered about other groups (religious and otherwise). For example, like most social movements (Lofland and Stark 1965; McAdam 1986; Snow, Zurcher, and Ekland-Olson 1980; Stark and Bainbridge 1980), it recruits primarily through social ties – in particular, through kinship and friendship ties (Sageman 2004) – and, as we briefly mentioned in Chapter 1, it displays the characteristics of scale-free networks (Barabási 2002; Barabási and Bonabeau 2003). This led Sageman to argue that the United States should focus its efforts on taking out hubs rather than randomly stopping terrorists at our borders.

Until recently, social network analyses of dark networks has tended to focus on individual-level social networks, in particular, key actors who score high in terms of centrality or whose structural location allows them to broker information and/or resources within the network. However, as we noted in Chapter 2 and elsewhere, while focusing on key individuals may be intuitively appealing and might provide short-term satisfaction, such a focus may at times be misplaced and, in fact, could make disrupting dark networks more difficult than it already is. Indeed, this book's running analysis of the Noordin Top Terrorist network using a range of metrics and focusing on multiple levels has demonstrated that analysts can use SNA to craft a wide variety of strategies for the disruption of dark networks. Most of these strategies are captured in Table 12.1, which not only illustrates the combination of metrics and strategies that have been covered in the previous chapters but also points to numerous combinations that were not explored. In other words, the blank cells in the table should not be interpreted to mean that those particular combinations of metrics and strategies do not exist. Indeed, they almost certainly do. It is just that we did not consider them here. Moreover, one could imagine a three-dimensional version of this table that maps the application of metric and strategic combinations at different levels (i.e., individual, subgroup, institutional), suggesting more than 160 different strategic options for using SNA to disrupt dark networks.

That said, we must keep in mind that SNA is not a silver bullet in the fight against dark networks. To reiterate what we noted in Chapter 2, the generation of strategic options should not be confused with decision making which depends on an array of issues (e.g., knowledge of local context and culture; the assessment of risks, costs, and potential for unintended consequences). SNA can inform decision making, but it should not determine it. A helpful analogy comes from George Crile's book *Charlie Wilson's War* (Crile 2003), which tells the true story of U.S. Congressman Charlie Wilson who, along with CIA operative Gust Avrakotos, helped organize and support the Afghan mujahideen in their fight against the Soviet occupation of Afghanistan. In the book, Crile notes that although Wilson saw supplying the mujahideen with stinger missiles as the key (or silver bullet) for driving out the Soviets, Michael Vickers, a Special Forces and CIA paramilitary operations officer whom Wilson and Avrakotos hired to help oversee the operation, argued that in irregular warfare there is no such thing as a silver bullet. Instead, what matters is getting the mix of weapons right. While supplying the mujahideen with stinger missiles was certainly an important factor in helping them in their struggle against the Soviets, he contended that it was only one tool in the toolbox. Other weapons were needed. Similarly, SNA should be seen as one tool in the toolbox in the fight against dark networks. It must always be used in conjunction with others if the fight is to be successful.

12.3   Disrupting Dark Networks Justly

A review of a few of the social science textbooks sitting on my shelves (e.g, Babbie 1986; Frankfort-Nachmias and Nachmias 1996; Giddens, Duneier, and Appelbaum 2006; Henslin 2007; Israel and Hay 2006; McIntyre 2002; Neuman 1997) found that their discussions of ethics tend to focus on two main areas of interest. The first, the area that

Table 12.1. *Summary of strategies identified for disrupting Noordin's network*

	Kinetic (Targeting)	Nonkinetic				
		Institution-building	PsyOp	Information operations	Rehabilitate, reintegrate	Track, monitor
Topography	Close jihadist schools	Build alternative schools				
Clustering & Cohesion	Remove brokers		Create distrust between subgroups		Rehabilitate noncore members	
Centrality & Power	Remove central members		Deception campaign aimed at central actors	Disrupt communication network	Rehabilitate peripheral members	Monitor central members
Brokers & Bridges	Remove brokers		Discredit brokers; dissolve bridges	Disrupt communication bridges		
Roles & Positions	Remove Noordin		Discredit or isolate block in brokerage position		Target Non-Noordin blocks for ideological reorientation	Monitor actors structurally equivalent to Noordin
Longitudinal Analysis	Remove key actors once network is centralized		Create distrust so that leaders centralize power			
Change Detection	Seize explosives & weapons					Track networks for change Identify emerging leaders
Geospatial & Relational Analysis	Isolate geospatially peripheral members		Isolate geospatially peripheral members			
Multivariate Regression	Disrupt communication network	Build alternative schools		Disrupt communication network	Build alternative schools	

probably attracts the most reflection, is human subjects research, which concerns itself with the need to protect the privacy and rights of the individuals being studied (i.e., the subjects). In this area social scientists appear to exhibit a high degree of consensus about what constitutes the ethical and unethical treatment of individuals, and studies such as Milgram's (1974) Obedience to Authority experiments, Humphreys's (1975) Tearoom Trade study, and Zimbardo's Stanford Prison experiment (Zimbardo 1972, 1973; Zimbardo, Maslasch, and Haney 2000) are held up as examples of research that went awry and violated the rights and dignity of individuals. In terms of human subjects research, SNA raises its own set of issues, such as the impossibility of keeping the identities of subjects confidential when asking questions such as, Whom do you consider a friend? and To whom do you go to for advice? This has been a topic that social network analysts have recently taken up in earnest (see, e.g., Borgatti and Molina 2005; Breiger 2005; Kadushin 2005; Klovdahl 2005; Prell 2011).

A second area, what we might call "professional ethics," focuses on the responsibilities that social scientists have to their colleagues when conducting research (see, e.g., Abbott 1983; Babbie 1986; Neuman 1997). This area concerns itself with the importance of carrying out research as objectively as possible and duly sharing the results of research in a timely manner at professional meetings and in professional journals. Here again, a relatively high degree of consensus appears to exist although perhaps not as high as in the first. Social scientists often disagree about the degree to which research can and should be value free. Nevertheless, most affirm the importance of interpreting data as objectively as possible, although acknowledging that our values and interests may influence the topics we choose to study may lead us to recuse ourselves from considering certain subjects because of an inability to distance ourselves from the topic.

A third area that receives less attention and exhibits far less consensus is what might be called, for lack of a better term, "consumption ethics." This area concerns itself with how the tools, techniques, and theories disseminated in classrooms, at professional meetings, online, and in various publications are consumed and used by others, in particular, whether they are used in ways that prove harmful to innocent individuals.[1] The often unspoken answer is that because we cannot control research once it leaves our hands, we can only hope it will be used for good rather than for ill (Cordoba 2006). To a certain extent this is true. We have little

---

[1] One could argue that this area could be considered an aspect of human subjects research in that both are concerned with preventing harm to innocent individuals. However, this strikes me as a separate area in that although human subjects research is typically concerned with research's direct effects, this area is more concerned with its indirect effects.

control over how technology and power are used. We cannot prevent terrorists or drug cartels (e.g., Al Qaeda, Los Zetas, the FARC), rogue governments (e.g., Nazi Germany, Pinochet's Chile), or even rogue forces within otherwise benign governments from using SNA tools and knowledge to thwart the efforts of authorities that are seeking to disrupt them or to carry out deleterious operations more effectively. As the sociologist (and philosopher) Christian Smith has noted, the technology and power available in the modern world has been and will continue to be used for both good and evil.

> Modernity, it turns out, has multiple faces. On the positive side, the material prosperity of modernity has brought unprecedented capacities for expanding human health, longevity, education, vocational specialization, travel, scientific understanding, and artistic expression... The spread of universal education and global travel has radically expanded the horizons and prospects of the minds and spirits of billions of people... Modern technology greatly reduces multiple forms of drudgery and danger previously required simply to survive... Yet the story is more complicated than that, for modernity also bears its own barbarisms and horrors... What we have learned from these moral extremes is that the astounding increases in human control over the natural world afforded by modern, advanced technologies and organizational systems have amplified not only the potential for moral good but also for shocking evil. (Smith 2010:428, 429, 430)

In spite of the lack of control on how their research is appropriated by the wider world, my sense is that most social scientists consciously or unconsciously set limits as to how far they are willing to let their research be consumed. To take an admittedly farfetched example, I suspect that most, if not all, INSNA (International Network for Social Network Analysis) members would refuse requests from Al Qaeda, Boko Haram (Nossiter 2011), or a local gang to offer classes in SNA so that they can more effectively target key institutions and individuals.[2] A less extreme example are social network analysts who refuse to work in the defense industry or will not accept funding from defense-related agencies because they believe there is no guarantee that any social network data that is collected will be maintained and used in ways that will not harm individuals.

---

[2] Of course, this would not prevent members of such groups from covertly attending social network analysis workshops that are offered internationally on a regular basis. Nevertheless, I think most would agree that there is a difference between knowingly and unknowingly assisting a terrorist network.

Organization research that I have personally conducted has always been as a consultant; this status has granted me access, under varying conditions. But there are conditions upon which I will not compromise: the data are always under my direct control, must be collected under guidelines that I describe, must reside on my computers, as do the names associated with the data. Confidentiality is always guaranteed. The data are never the property of the firm for whom I am a consultant. Names are never associated with network graphs or with network indices and are never revealed to either management or employees. Rather, general patterns are described and used to suggest the way things currently flow and how matters might be changed... Typically, these conditions cannot be met by classified or military research and so I do not do this kind of work. (Kadushin 2005:146)

I am certain Kadushin is not alone in feeling this way. Thus, while some social scientists may give lip service to the "we can only hope that our research will be used for good rather than ill" sentiment, most draw a line between the acceptable and unacceptable dissemination of their research and knowledge. The problem, of course, is that there is little agreement as to where that line should be drawn.

A lack of agreement within the SNA community over where it should be drawn became apparent in 2009 after an advertisement for a postdoctoral position with the Common Operational Research Environment (CORE) Lab at the Naval Postgraduate School was posted on the INSNA listserve (SOCNET). To say that a few members of the SNA community considered the posting inappropriate would be an understatement. One equated it with the "solicitation for people to abet in the murder of innocent civilians" and argued that serious ethical questions are raised "when any *group of killers* seeks to recruit through this listserve for people to help them *target others using SNA techniques*" (emphasis added). Although not everyone shared this gentleman's opinion, it did touch a nerve with many in the SNA community who disapprove of working or consulting for defense-related institutions or conducting research and/or writing software programs using defense-related dollars. Of course, the fact that some social network analysts do accept defense-related dollars indicates that not all social network analysts share this perspective. Indeed, in the debate that followed the initial post, opinions were divided among those who opposed the use of SNA for defense-related purposes, those who supported it, and those who took a more neutral position (Eyre, Johnson, and McCulloh 2010).

While it might surprise some, I am relatively sympathetic to the concerns raised in the debate, not because I necessarily agree with all of the positions argued on behalf of (that would be impossible) or condone the shrillness of some of the posts, but because the debate reflected an intuition among social network analysts that remaining morally neutral as to how SNA theories, tools, and techniques are disseminated and subsequently used by others is neither desirable nor possible. And although it is true that we cannot completely control how SNA (or any form of technology or knowledge) is used by others, we can take some steps that raise the probability that SNA is used justly.

In particular, in what follows, I argue that in the fight against dark networks, SNA should only be used if it helps promote those practices and institutions that increase the likelihood that individuals will be free to live flourishing and dignified lives.[3] In making this argument I briefly consider four ethical traditions that dominate contemporary moral discourse – utilitarianism, Kantian liberalism, libertarianism, and Aristotelianism (i.e., virtue-based, or teleological, ethics) – and conclude that only the last of these offers the resources from which we can derive a sense of what a morally just use of SNA should look like. An obvious objection is that although it is all well and good to talk about notions of "justice" and the promotion of "human dignity," in practice it is much harder to agree as to what such things mean. To a certain extent this is true (see e.g., Sandel 2009), but it is also true that although many of us are loath to admit it, we operate with an intuitive sense of what "the good" consists of and the practices and institutions that promote it.

> So why is murder morally wrong? Because it is the destruction of the personhood of the murdered and the desecration of that of the murderer. Why is stealing morally wrong? Because stealing violates the personhood of the victim as well as that of the thief. Why is lying normally morally wrong? Because it denies what is reality, destroys the trust needed for relations in which persons flourish, and so diminishes the personhood of the lied to and the liar. The same operation can be performed on the many moral goods and bads to which we subscribe. Why are love, justice, kindness, peacefulness, understanding, patience, forgiveness, generosity, equity, faithfulness, and the like moral goods? Because they nurture and protect human personhood. Why are selfishness, injustice, meanness, exploitation, revenge, oppression, hate, exclusion, indifference, and such ills moral bads?

---

[3]   I am aware that one person's dark network is often another's light network, but here I have in mind dark networks, such as Al Qaeda, the FARC, the Los Zetas drug cartel, Boko Haram, etc. – groups that most would agree seek to harm innocent men, women, and children or create levels of societal disruption that prevent ordinary citizens from living lives free of fear. In other words, groups such as these promote practices that do not increase the likelihood that individuals will be free to live flourishing and dignified lives.

Because they frustrate and damage human personhood. (Smith 2010:418–419)

After my review of these four moral traditions, I turn to a brief examination of the just war tradition, which is teleological in its logic, in order to consider how SNA can be used justly in the fight against dark networks. Here I focus on issues such as what constitutes a just war, how it applies to irregular warfare, the judicious use of SNA, noncombatant immunity, and high-value targeting. Along the way I also call on social network analysts to engage in reasoned debate about the ends and purposes of social network analysis, a debate where everyone is welcome at the table and no one is turned away.

Contemporary Moral Discourse

While the four ethical traditions discussed in the following sections do not exhaust all that philosophers have to say about moral reasoning, together they present a useful framework in which to consider ethical disagreements because, as we shall see, they inform many contemporary debates. The following summaries do not attempt to tease out all of the nuances of these respective traditions. Instead, the goal is far more modest. It merely hopes to provide a flavor of these various perspectives and how they inform contemporary moral discourse.

Utilitarian Ethics. Utilitarian ethics, which is associated with philosophers such as Jeremy Bentham (1996 [1789]) and John Stuart Mill (2010 [1863]), argues that when deciding what the right thing to do is, we need to weigh the costs and benefits of various actions, ultimately choosing what is best for the common (i.e., greater) good. The right thing to do, in other words, is to select the option that provides the greatest utility or pleasure for the greatest number of people. While some moral philosophers no longer take this tradition seriously (Wolterstorff 2010:25), it is still a common form of ethical reasoning (Rachels 1999) and regularly makes an appearance in the public square. For example, in the debate over the two-blocks-from-Ground-Zero Islamic Community Center/Mosque, utilitarianism was, for most, the ethical tradition of choice (see, e.g., Friedman 2010; Temple-Raston 2010). And when attempting to dissuade a Florida pastor from burning Qur'ans, General David Petraeus drew on it as well (Nakamura and Hamdard 2010).

More relevant to this book's concern is that the utilitarian calculus often shows up in arguments concerning how wars should be prosecuted. During World War II, for instance, many justified the use of obliteration bombing in utilitarian terms (Allman and Winright 2010:46), and utilitarian reasoning has crept into some versions of just war theorizing.

For example, the U.S. Catholic bishops (National Council of Bishops 1983) argued in their 1983 pastoral letter, *The Challenge of Peace: God's Promise and Our Response*, that in order for a war to be considered just (and thus worth pursuing), the benefits that are expected to accrue must outweigh the costs (i.e., the inherent misery caused by war). Although this approach is intuitively appealing, estimating such a ratio is virtually impossible (Walzer 2004:90) and highlights one of utilitarianism's inherent weakness: namely, the impracticality of translating all moral goods into a common currency such that different choices can be weighed and compared (Sandel 2009).

Of even greater concern to most moral philosophers is how the utilitarian approach does not respect individual rights and liberties. "By caring only about the sum of satisfactions, [utilitarianism] can run roughshod over individual people" (Sandel 2009:37). Two traditions that offer a corrective to utilitarianism's disregard for individual liberty is Kantian liberalism and libertarianism. Both argue that notions of justice should respect individual rights. However, while the latter focuses on the actual choices that people make in a free market, the former focuses on the choices people would make in an original position of (hypothetical) equality (Wolterstorff 2010:25). We consider Kantian liberalism first.

Kantian Liberalism. This ethical tradition, which has its roots in Immanuel Kant (1997 [1785]) and its most influential modern proponent in John Rawls (1971), argues that people possess certain inalienable rights (hence, the greater good does not always trump the interests of individuals). This tradition seeks to locate principles of justice independent of all interest-based perspectives.[4] That is, it seeks to derive principles that rational individuals would arrive at if they set aside their personal moral and religious convictions. Kant, for example, argued on behalf of a universal law, what he called "the categorical imperative," which he believed could bind rational individuals together regardless of their particular ends. Rawls, building on Kant's assumption that universal principles of justice can be arrived at by reason alone, contended that universal principles of justice are those that all individuals would choose if they made their choice from an original position of equality. Thus, for both Kant and Rawls, principles about what is right and just can (and should) be derived independently of (i.e., prior to) particular conceptions of the good.

---

[4] One could subdivide Kantian liberalism into Kantian deontologicalism and Rawlsian social contractarianism (Miller 2011). I choose not to because there is an element of social contractarianism in Kant (1991; Sandel 2009:139), and both authors hold that rational individuals can derive universal principles of justice by reason alone.

Critiques of Kant and Rawls are many and varied, but the one that has probably gained the most purchase is that we are not "free and independent selves, unbound by antecedent moral ties, capable of choosing our ends for ourselves" (Sandel 2005:214); instead, we are moral agents who are constrained and influenced by the communities in which we live and move and have our being (Acts 17:28). Consequently, when it comes to questions of ethics, setting aside one's moral and religious convictions (i.e., particular conceptions of the good) is not always possible, nor is it necessarily desirable (Sandel 1982, 1996, 2009; Smith 2010; Walzer 1983, 2009). Indeed, while the quest for an ethic derived solely through reason alone is a noble goal, it is almost certainly a quixotic one.

> It is tempting to seek a principle or procedure that could justify, once and for all, whatever distribution of income or power or opportunity resulted from it. Such a principle, if we could find it, would enable us to avoid the tumult and contention that arguments about the good life invariably arouse. (Sandel 2009:261)

Thus, to reason about what the right thing to do is, whether as social network analysts or citizens of the various societies of which we a part, we need to recognize the claims that these various communities have upon our moral reasoning. Before turning to how I believe this can be done, however, we need to first consider the libertarian tradition.

Libertarian Ethics. Libertarianism is associated with philosophers such as John Stuart Mill (1989 [1859]),[5] Robert Nozick (1977), Friedrich Hayek (1994 [1944]), and Milton Friedman (1962). It is rooted in the belief of self-possession, and as such argues that each of us has a fundamental right to do whatever we want with the things we own as long as we respect the rights of others to do exactly the same thing. This is why libertarians tend to favor minimal government intervention in the economic and social spheres (Sandel 2009). It is also not unusual for libertarians to embrace an instrumentalist (i.e., rational choice) view of the human person (Becker 1976, 1996; Friedman 1962; Friedman and Friedman 1980), and they often smuggle the utilitarian calculus in through the back door (1989 [1859]), arguing that freedom, especially economic freedom, will, in the long run, benefit society as a whole (Friedman and Friedman 1980:5). Applied to the dissemination of academic research, most libertarians would probably argue that although knowledge can be used in deleterious ways, formally regulating its diffusion is not the

---

[5] Mill's emphasis on individual freedom makes him a favorite among many libertarians as well. How does Mill reconcile the two? He contends that if societies respect the freedom of individuals to do whatever they want, as long as we respect the rights of others to do exactly the same thing, then society as a whole will benefit.

answer. Instead, market forces will help ensure that in the long run the good derived from research will outweigh the bad.

However, available evidence suggests that unfettered markets, whether economic, religious, or academic, do not always benefit the greater good (Titmuss 1971; Zelizer 1978). Moreover, many of the choices we make do not necessarily reflect our preferences as much as they do our needs (Sandel 2005:211) or the constraints placed on us by the networks in which we are embedded (Azarian 2005; Granovetter 1985; Wasserman and Faust 1994).[6]

> Foucault was only the latest in a long line of thinkers – Augustine, Hobbes, and Marx are his most notable predecessors – to remind us that institutionalized networks of giving and receiving are also always structures of unequal distributions of power, structures well-designed both to mask and protect those same distributions. So there are always possibilities and often actualities of victimization and exploitation bound up with participation in such networks. If we are not adequately aware of this, our practical judgments and reasoning will go badly astray. (MacIntyre 1999:101)

Thus, while some may find the libertarian option attractive because of its logical consistency and celebration of individual freedom, it fails to recognize the claims that the communities in which we are embedded influence and constrain the choices we make. Moreover, it naively assumes that unrestrained freedom always leads to a greater good. The ethical tradition we consider next, Aristotelian ethics, does not make such assumptions. It differs from libertarianism in that it openly acknowledges that freedom by itself does not guarantee the creation of the good, whatever that might be. And over against Kantian liberalism, it argues that notions of what is right and just (e.g., When is unfettered freedom appropriate and when is it inappropriate?) cannot be separated from prior notions of what is good. It is to that tradition we now turn.

Aristotelian (Teleological) Ethics. A number of contemporary moral philosophers have criticized freedom-based conceptions of justice, such as libertarianism and Kantian liberalism, for ignoring the claims that communities have on the ethical reasoning of their members (MacIntyre 1984, 1988, 1990; Sandel 1982, 1996; Smith 2010; Taylor 1989; Walzer 1983). This is why some argue for an Aristotelian (i.e., teleological) approach that seeks to link principles of justice with "the moral worth or intrinsic good of the ends they serve" (Sandel 1998:xi). This approach to moral

---

[6] Think of how much more "free" those of us are who have already been granted tenure compared to those of us who have not.

reasoning contends that we need to first consider what we (and others) believe to be the ends and purposes of what we are seeking prior to deriving principles of justice. While this focus on the end, the purpose, or the *telos* as a basis for moral reflection has its roots in the ethics of Aristotle, it includes several modern proponents, such as Alasdair MacIntyre (1984, 1988, 1990, 1999), Michael Sandel (1982, 1996, 2005, 2009), sociologist Christian Smith (2003, 2010), Charles Taylor (1989), and Michael Walzer (1983, 2009), to name a few. These scholars recognize that we cannot know what is right apart from a prior conception of what is good, and that theories of justice that claim otherwise are mistaken.[7]

Many of these scholars also believe that when communities of practice engage in reasoned debates about what is good and just, they are often able to gain insight into the goals and purposes of their communities (Sandel 2009; Taylor 1998). If they are correct, then social network analysts need to attend to the various conceptions of what the purposes and ends of SNA are, if they are to engage in a reasoned debate about acceptable and unacceptable practices. Does this mean that through deliberating about the ends we serve we can resolve all issues that will come before us? Of course not, but as Sandel notes

> A just society can't be achieved simply by maximizing utility or by securing freedom of choice. To achieve a just society we have to reason together about the meaning of the good life, and to create a public culture hospitable to the disagreements that will inevitably arise. (Sandel 2009:261)

Similarly, if social network analysts hope to be a community of practice that responsibly addresses the ethical dilemmas that come before us, at a minimum we need to create and maintain an environment of hospitality where reasoned debate is the norm and not the exception, and where minority and unpopular opinions can be expressed without fear of retribution (e.g., not publishing a particular individual's research simply because of the position he or she takes on various issues).

Returning to the issue at hand, that is, the ethical use of SNA for the disruption of dark networks, we now consider how the just war tradition, which is teleological at its root, can inform the practices of social network analysts involved in the fight against dark networks. As will hopefully become clear, I believe that this fight should only be carried out justly, which raises unique issues for those of us who are attempting to do so.

---

[7] Teleological ethics contains elements of a utilitarian calculus in that as it seeks to identify those practices that promote human flourishing. "It remains distinct from most forms of [utilitarian] ethics, however, insofar as the focus of outcomes is not on events or conditions but rather on the flourishing character of the personhood of personal actors" (Smith 2010:400).

The Just War Tradition

While early formations of the just war tradition predate the Christian Church, it was Christian theologians such as St. Augustine and St. Thomas Aquinas who ultimately provided much of its content. In its infancy, the Christian Church was predominantly pacifist (Yoder 1977, 2009), but as it transformed from a minority religion to the official religion of the land (Stark 1996a), it became impractical for it to remain pacifist. The just war criteria arose, in part, because of this transformation, but the tradition not only sets itself over against pacifism but over against more brutal forms of war as well:

> From the beginning the theory had a critical edge: soldiers (or, at least, their officers) were supposed to refuse to fight in wars of conquest and to oppose or abstain from the standard military practices of rape and pillage after the battle was won. (Walzer 2004:3)

Not much has changed over the centuries. Today, just war theorists still find themselves standing between two sets of theorists: pacifists on the one side, for whom all war is a crime, and realists on the other, "for whom 'all's fair in love and war': *inter arma silent leges* (in time of war, the laws are silent)" (Walzer 2004:ix).

The just war tradition is driven by the vision or goal of a just peace, which is the belief that at war's end, the social, political, economic, and ecological conditions of the offending country should be restored so that its citizens and institutions are able to flourish (*eudaimonia*). That is, they should have the opportunity to live lives that are meaningful and dignified (Allman and Winright 2010). The three sets of criteria of the just war tradition reflect this goal of a just peace (see Appendix 4).[8] The first set (*jus ad bellum* – justice for going to war) places restrictions on the moral ability of authorities to wage war because the horrors that war can unleash are often difficult for a country (and its people) to recover from. The second (*jus in bello* – justice during war) places restraints on how wars can be fought in order to minimize the damage that is done, again reflecting the tradition's concern with war's aftermath. For instance, the criterion of proportionality seeks to ensure that no unnecessary destruction takes place, while the criterion of noncombatant immunity (i.e., civilians can't be deliberately targeted or killed), recognizes that a country's citizens need to be spared as much as possible from the ravages of war if they are to thrive when hostilities cease. Finally, the third (*jus post bellum* – justice

---

[8]   For some years, the tradition identified only two sets of criteria. However, in recent years some theorists (see, e.g., Allman and Winright 2010; Walzer 2004) have begun to argue that there should also be a set of post-war criteria that provide guidelines on what to do after the fighting has stopped.

after war) explicitly concerns itself with the restoration of the country to wholeness, so that its citizens are in a position to live lives that are worth living.

Because the just war tradition developed with conventional warfare in mind, it is legitimate to ask how (and if) it can be applied to the fight against dark networks, a fight that is often fought using unconventional or irregular means. The answer to this concern, I believe, is that it can because the goal of a just peace is one worth fighting for, but only if it is fought for justly. Whether all of the criteria as they now stand (see Appendix 4) can be directly applied to the war against terror is less important than keeping in mind the ultimate goal of the just war tradition – that at war's end, individuals and institutions should be free to thrive.

Fighting Justly with Social Network Analysis

A major focus of those who work with analysts who intend to use SNA to disrupt dark networks should be on lowering the probability that they will use SNA inappropriately and cause innocent civilians to be harmed.[9] The inappropriate use of SNA can be either intentional or unintentional. Some may only see SNA as a tool for the lethal targeting of high value individuals and are little concerned with whether a lack of attention to detail (e.g., the completeness of data, the use of appropriate metrics, the vetting of results with other information) will occasionally lead innocent individuals to get caught in the cross fire. These individuals need to be educated in how such an approach can sometimes cause more harm than good (Roberts and Everton 2011). Others, such as Kadushin, note that because data on dark networks are difficult to collect, they are often incomplete and may inadvertently generate inaccurate findings that lead to the targeting of innocent civilians:

> When the data are used to analyze cut-points in a network such that eliminating a node may break the network apart, inaccuracies can literally be fatal to an "innocent" person. This is not the forum to debate the ethics of counter-terror activities, but few are comfortable with non-judicial killing of people who are not combatants or key terrorists. (Kadushin 2005:148)

Kadushin is almost certainly correct, but as we have repeatedly noted in this book, SNA should inform decision making, not determine it. More-over, if we push his remarks to their logical conclusion, we might be tempted to argue that police departments around the world should be disbanded because their operations sometimes lead to the death or injury of "noncombatants." I suspect, however, that few (if any) social networks

---

[9] Indeed, that is a major motivation behind writing this book.

analysts would advocate the closing of, say, the New York or Los Angeles police departments[10] because such a move would almost certainly lead to an increase, not a decrease, in the harm incurred by innocent civilians. Rather, my sense is that most social scientists expect police women and men to be cautious in their interpretation of information and judicious in their use of force.

The same logic can be applied to the use of SNA in the fight against dark networks. One could credibly argue that by not using SNA in our attempts to disrupt groups such as Los Zetas, the FARC, Jemaah Islamiyah, and Al Qaeda, we actually increase the likelihood that innocent men, women, and children will suffer an injury of some kind. And, of course, we can demand that those who use SNA to disrupt dark networks be held to the same standard as are police forces. Interestingly, in the same paragraph, Kadushin approvingly quotes a post to SOCNET by Elin Waring (2002), who uses social network analysis to study criminal and terrorist networks, suggesting that perhaps he believes that the cautious use of SNA is both possible and desirable:

> I personally think that networks are the way to look at the orga-
> nization of crime, and many SNA tools are helpful for this, but I
> would be very, very cautious. (quoted in Kadushin 2005:148)

In short, then, while we must be cautious in our use of SNA to disrupt dark networks, we should not refrain from doing so because the potential for creating environments where individual lives can flourish outweighs the possibility of creating situations where they cannot. Of course, determining whether a particular strategy will help people live dignified and fulfilling lives is, of course, easier said than done. That does not mean, however, that we should not try.

Another issue, one that Kadushin raises in his quote, is the practice of targeted killing, a practice that the Israelis made famous (Walzer 2009:274) and American presidents apparently have no qualms using (Perez 2010). A common objection to this practice is that it is no different from assassination and thus prohibited by the just war tradition. However, while the tradition prohibits the killing of political leaders, it does not rule out the killing of military personnel or enemy combatants, which terrorists are clearly doing (Walzer 2009:274–275). Moreover, because by definition, targeted killing seeks to avoid the killing of non-combatants, it is almost certainly permitted by the just war tradition. Even pacifists, such as Jim Wallis, leader of the Sojourners' community in

---

[10] Some readers may point to the fact that the majority of police officers in the United Kingdom (UK) do not carry firearms, and this is a primary reason why innocent civilians are less likely to be harmed by gunfire. While it is true that most UK police officers do not carry firearms, some do, and all unarmed officers can call on specialized units that are armed.

Washington, D.C., appear to find this approach more appealing than all-out war. In reflecting upon the killing of Osama bin Laden he remarked

> Indeed, the problem of war is how indiscriminate it is. And it is worth noting that the special forces action that resulted in the death of bin Laden was a very focused effort to bring one perpetrator to justice, rather than just another act of war. We didn't get bin Laden as a casualty of bombing raids or drone attacks on the city that harbored him; instead, this was the result of careful intelligence and a laser-like focus on the man most responsible for 9/11. Some of us believe that should have been the U.S. strategy from the beginning. (Wallis 2011)

It cannot be stressed enough that analysts need to take extra care in making targeting decisions (Walzer 2009:275). This, of course, can be quite difficult, as terrorists often seek to blend in with the crowd, making detection more difficult and the loss of innocent life more likely, which is why just war theorists, such as Michael Walzer, argue that the fight against dark networks should take its lessons from how police forces attempt to avoid the loss of innocent life:

> Here I think we have to adopt standards that are closer to Philadelphia than Afghanistan. In a war zone, collateral damage cannot be avoided; it can only be minimized. The hard question in war is what degree of risk we are willing to accept for our own soldiers in order to reduce the risks we impose on enemy civilians. But when the police are chasing criminals in a zone of peace, we rightly give them no latitude for collateral damage. In the strongest sense, they must intend not to injure civilians – even if that makes their operation more difficult... That seems to me roughly the right rule for people planning targeted killings... They can't avoid imposing some degree of risk on innocent people, and the risks will certainly be greater than those imposed by police in a city at peace, but we must insist on a strenuous effort to minimize the risks. (Walzer 2009:276)

Although it might come as a surprise to some, the U.S. military has adopted counterinsurgency (COIN) standards that are closer to Philadelphia than to Afghanistan.[11] Such standards were highlighted in a National

---

[11] The 2007 counterinsurgency manual (U.S. Army 2007:161) states that "combat, including counterinsurgency and other forms of unconventional warfare, often obligates Soldiers and Marines to accept some risk to minimize harm to noncombatants... In conventional conflicts, balancing competing responsibilities of mission accomplishment with protection of noncombatants is difficult enough. Complex COIN operations place the toughest ethical demands on Soldiers, Marines, and their leaders." Also see Appendix D: Legal Considerations (Section: "The Law of War") of the counterinsurgency manual

Public Radio story (Gjelten 2010) about how SNA has been success-fully used by the U.S. military to target and disrupt IED (i.e., improvised explosive devices) networks in Iraq. The story noted that military lawyers have to approve all targeting operations before they can be carried out, and SNA's mathematical precision provides them greater confidence in making such decisions when compared to relying solely on hunches and intuition. As Major Eugene Vindman, a judge advocate general (JAG) officer, who took an SNA course, noted:

> [We could] maybe do a little bit of analysis on [our] own or ask some intelligent questions of the targeteers to make sure that the target they've identified is not a guy that might have made a wrong phone call to a bad guy but actually has enough links to that bad guy through other activities to actually be a bad guy and therefore be a legal military target. (Gjelten 2010)

Moreover, as we have repeatedly stressed in this book, the lethal targeting of individuals is not the only strategic option and may not be the most desirable one (Schmitt and Perlez 2009). As we have seen, terrorist networks can be remarkably resilient and often recover quite rapidly after a key leader has been eliminated (Bakker, Raab, and Milward 2011; Carley, Lee, and Krackhardt 2002; Carley, Reminga, and Kamneva 2003; Milward and Raab 2006).

Add to this the fact that dark networks often suffer more damage when their members are captured or defect (Popkin 2007, cited in Berman 2009:29) and policies aimed at eliminating the structural conditions that help give rise to and help sustain terrorist groups in the first place (e.g., building alternative schools, improving economic conditions, eliminating ungoverned spaces) can reduce the prevalence of bad dark networks (Borer, Everton, and Nayve 2009; Mortenson and Bryan 2009; Mortenson and Relin 2006; Roberts and Everton 2011), operators should seriously consider the noncoercive strategies outlined in Chapter 2, which, if successful, are highly likely to produce a just peace.

Summary

In this section I have not attempted to elaborate a comprehensive account of what role SNA should play in the just fight against dark networks. Rather, I have attempted to sketch a framework that can serve as a baseline for further moral inquiry into this topic. It is certainly not meant to be seen as the end of the conversation but rather as a beginning. As I

(U.S. Army 2007:229). Of course, just because these standards have been adopted does not guarantee that they will be followed. However, the reverse is also true: Just because a soldier does not follow these standards, does not mean that the Army has not adopted them or is not attempting to enforce them.

noted above, it is incumbent upon all social network analysts – those in academia and those who apply to "real world" problems, for example, dark networks, deliberate questions such as, What are the ends and goals of SNA? What are our ends and goals as social network analysts? and What excellences do we honor within our community?

Does this mean that through deliberation we will resolve all issues that come before us? Of course not. Nevertheless, my sense is that we can reach a rough consensus on a number of issues while hopefully developing a respect for those with whom we disagree about the role that SNA should play in the just fight against dark networks.

12.4   Summary and Conclusion

In this chapter we have considered both the promises and limits of the use of SNA to disrupt dark networks. After summarizing the various combinations of social network metrics and strategic options illustrated in Chapters 5 through 11, I noted that it is better to see SNA as one tool among many that can be used when crafting potential strategies. I then argued, using the just war tradition as an example, that a just peace should be the ultimate goal in any and all attempts to disrupt dark networks, which means that the use of SNA for the crafting of strategies should be guided by a moral framework that seeks to create and sustain societies wherein individuals are free to live flourishing lives. We should settle for nothing less.

Appendix 1

The Noordin Top Terrorist Network

These data were drawn primarily from "Terrorism in Indonesia: Noordin's Networks," a publication of the International Crisis Group (2006) and include relational data on the seventy-nine individuals listed in Appendix C of that publication. The data were initially coded by Naval Postgraduate School students as part of the course Tracking and Disrupting Dark Networks under the direction of Professor Sean Everton, Co-Director of the CORE Lab, and Professor Nancy Roberts. CORE Lab research assistant Daniel Cunningham reviewed and cleaned all coding made by students. Please cite as follows:

Roberts, Nancy and Sean F. Everton. 2011. *Roberts and Everton Terrorist Data: Noordin Top Terrorist Network (Subset)*. [Machine-readable data file].

1. Organizational Affiliation

Definitions of Terrorist/Insurgent and Affiliated Organizations

A terrorist/insurgent organization is defined as an administrative and functional system, whose primary common goal is the operational conduct of terrorist/insurgent activities, consisting of willingly affiliated claimant members. For the purpose of this exercise, factions and off-shoots will be considered separate from their parent organizations in order to prevent coding redundant ties. In other words, the most micro-level affiliations are coded, whereas an individual is coded in the parent organization only if he or she is not listed as being affiliated with a component organization. Terrorist/insurgent affiliated organizations, such MMI and FPI, are also coded in this matrix.

Note that JI Central Command is considered a subcomponent but is not necessarily more or less "micro" than other JI subcomponents such as Mantiqi I or even JI wakalahs. Consequently, an individual affiliated with Mantiqi I and JI Central Command will get a tie in both columns.

List of Terrorist/Insurgent Organizations

1. AMIN (Full name – Angkatan Mujahidin Islam Nusantara – not listed)
2. Abubakar Battalion
3. Al Qaeda (AQ)
4. Cimanggis Group (CG)
5. Darul Islam (DI)
6. Darul Islam Banten Battalion for Region IX (DI)
7. Darul Islam in Maluku (DI)
8. Darul Islam West Java Division (DI)
9. Islamic Defenders Front (FPI)–Pekalongan Branch
10. JI Central Command
11. JI Central Java Wakalah
12. JI East Java Wakalah
13. JI Johor Wakalah
14. JI Mantiqi I
15. JI Mantiqi II
16. JI Mantiqi III
17. JI Wakalah Hudaibiyah
18. Jemaah Islamiyah (JI)
19. KOMPAK Charity
20. KOMPAK Mujahidin
21. KOMPAK-Ambon Office
22. KOMPAK-Solo Office
23. KOMPAK-Waihong
24. Komando Jihad
25. Kumpulan Mujahidin Malaysia (KMM)
26. Laskar Jihad
27. Laskar Jundullah
28. Laskar Khos
29. Majelis Mujahidin Indonesia (MMI)
30. Mujahidin Kayamanya
31. Ring Banten (DI)
32. STAIN Group

Two-mode 79 × 32

2A. Educational Affiliation

Definition of Educational Relations

Educational relations are defined as schools where individuals receive formal education, serve as an employee (teacher, administrative member, etc.), and/or are involved in additional educational or religious instruction at the institution.

List of Schools

1. Adelaide University
2. Airlangga University
3. al-Husein – pesantren (Islamic boarding school), Indramayu, West Java
4. al-Irsyad High School, Pekalongan
5. al-Islam – *pesantren*, Lamongan
6. al-Mutaqien, Indramayu
7. al-Muttaqien, Jepara
8. Bogor Agricultural University
9. Brawijaya University in Malang
10. Darul Fitroh
11. Darusy Syahada – pesantren, Boyolali
12. Gontor
13. Luqmanul Hakeim – pesantren, Johor, Malaysia
14. Miftahul huda – pesantren, Cikampek
15. Pesantren, Isykarima, Solo
16. Pondok Ngruki/al-Mukmin – pesantren, Ngruki, Central Java
17. Reading University, UK
18. Serang Islamic High School
19. STAIN in Solo
20. Sukabumi
21. The Christian University of Malang
22. Universitas anNur/Mahad Aly – pesantren, Solo
23. Universitas Negeri, Malang
24. University of Technology, Malaysia
25. Unknown school in Bangil, East Java

Two-mode matrix, 79 × 25

2B. Classmates/Educational Colleagues

Definition of Classmate Relations

Classmates/educational colleagues are defined as individuals who receive formal education, serve as an employee (teacher, administrative member, etc.), and/or are involved in additional educational or religious instruction simultaneously at the same institution. This relationship is more likely to reflect accurate relationships than the two-mode "Educational Affiliation" matrix because it considers the time in which individuals are present at a school.

Note that the coding on the master sheet will differ from coding based solely on the ICG report. The former used information outside of the

ICG "Noordin's Networks" report for establishing if individuals could be considered classmates/educational colleagues.

One-mode matrix, 79 × 79

3. Communication Ties

Definition of Internal Communication

Internal communication is defined as the relaying of messages between individuals and/or groups inside the network through some sort of medium.

One-mode matrix, 79 × 79

4. Kinship Ties

Definition of Kinship

Kinship is defined as any family connection such as brother, brother-in-law, nephew, and so forth. Kinship will also include current marriages and past marriages due to divorces and/or deaths.

One-mode matrix, 79 × 79

5. Training Events

Definition of Training Relations

Participation in any specifically designated activity that teaches the knowledge, skills, and competencies of terrorism and insurgency. Training does not include participation in a terrorist-sponsored act or mujahideen activity in places such as Afghanistan, Bosnia, Chechnya, or Iraq unless the individuals' presence was to participate in a specifically designated training camp or base in one of these areas.

Note that individuals who participated in the "Australian Embassy Religious Training" and/or the "Training for Bali II in the 'Selera' Restaurant" may reflect redundant ties with the "Operations Network" because some individuals participated in these trainings specific to the Australian Embassy (Sep 2004) and the Bali II (Oct 2005) operations.

List of Training Locations

1. 01–02 Ujunj Kulon Training
2. 03 Mindanao Training
3. 03 Rois Training
4. 99 Mindanao Training
5. Australian Embassy Religious Training
6. Azhari Apprenticeship

7. Jan 04 Bomb Making
8. Jul 04 West Ceram
9. Jun 04 Bomb Making
10. May 04 Training
11. Oct 99 Waimurat, Buru Training
12. Post-Bali Mil Refresh Training
13. Solo course
14. Training for Bali II in "Selera" restaurant
15. 08–01 to 09–01 Training

Two-mode matrix, 79 × 15

6. Business and Finance Affiliation

Definition of Business Relations

Defined as profit and nonprofit organizations that employ people (includes Durassalam Foundation).

Types of Businesses

1. AlBayan Magazine
2. Clothing Business – making and selling clothing
3. CV Courier Business – business that specializes in transfer of information and products
4. DarusSalam Foundation
5. Indonesian Muslim Workers Union
6. Sawt al-Jihad Online Magazine
7. Shock Absorber Repair Shop– the automobile shop that repaired shock absorbers
8. Small Trading Business – exchange of goods
9. Tobacco Business – firm that grows tobacco
10. Used Cloth Business – the collection and sale of used cloth for industrial purposes

Two-mode matrix, 79 × 10

7. Operations

Definition of Operations

Operational relations are defined as individuals who are knowingly in volved in preparing, executing, and/or providing postoperation support. Preparation must directly relate to the operation and can include surveying targets, providing a safe house for preparation, contributing to religious and/or physical training, and participating in a robbery where proceeds fund a subsequent attack. Providing postoperation support, such as hiding fugitives and disposing of explosives, must also be directly related to the operation.

List of Operations

1. Atrium Mall Bombing (Aug 01)
2. Attack on Brimbob Post in West Ceram (May 05; note that Brimbob are paramilitary police and will be listed as such in the document)
3. Australian Embassy Bombings (Sep 04)
4. Bali Bombing I (Oct 02)
5. Bali Bombing II (Oct 05)
6. Bombing Attack on Philippine Ambassador in Jakarta (Aug 00)
7. Christmas Eve Bombings (Dec 00)
8. Marriott Bombings (Aug 03)
9. Mosque Bombing in Yogyakarta (2000)
10. Murder of Palu Prosecutor Fery Silalahi (May 04)
11. Rizal Day Bombing (Dec 00)
12. Robbery of Medan Bank (May 03)
13. Robbery of Mobile Phone Store in Pekalongan (Sep 03)
14. Robbery to Raise Funds for Bali I (Aug 02)

Two-mode matrix 79 × 14

8.   Friendship Ties

Definition of Friendship Relations

Friendship relations are defined as close attachments through affection or esteem between two people. Friendship ties are not defined solely as meetings and/or school ties.

Note that friendship relations can be extremely subjective if they are not explicitly stated in the document. Typically, the implicit relationships are based on consistent and close relationships across time. The relationship between Noordin Top and Azhari Husin, for example, is not explicitly stated as a friendship in the document, but they were close associates for many years.

One-mode matrix, 79 × 79

9A. Religious Affiliation

Definition of Religious Relations

Religious relations are defined as associations with a mosque, church, synagogue, or religious study circle. Religious study circles are only coded if they are separate from other religious entities (e.g., a mosque). We do not include Islamic schools even though we assume that the schools have mosques. Not using the schools prevents duplication of effort with the team constructing the school ties. Additionally, we listed the mosques by the town in which they are located. If there was more than one in a city, we added a numerical identifier plus the name of nearest location.

List of Mosques

1. Banten Mosque
2. Cipayung Mosque Surabaya Mosque I (al-Ikhsan Mosque)
3. Kedire Mosque
4. Pekalongan Pengajian (Religious Study Circle)
5. Solo Mosque (anNur School)
6. Surabaya Mosque I al-Ikhsan
7. Surabaya Mosque II (Airlangga University)
8. Synagogue in Surabaya

Two-mode matrix, 79 × 8

9B. Soulmates

Definition of Soulmate Relations

Soulmate relations are defined as individuals who are affiliated with the same religious institution at the same time. This relationship is more likely to indicate accurate religious ties than the "religious affiliation," because it considers the time frames in which individuals are affiliated with religious institutions.

Note that the coding on the master sheet will differ considerably from coding based solely on the ICG report. The former used information outside of the ICG report for determining time frames in which individuals were affiliated with a religious institution.

One-mode matrix, 79 × 79

10. Logistical Place

Definition of Logistical Relations

Logistical relations are defined as a key place within the archipelago where logistical activity occurred. Logistical activity is defined as providing "safe houses" for meeting/hiding, providing material support in terms of explosives, providing weaponry, or facilitating transportation of personnel or equipment.

List of Places Where Logistical Support Is Given

1. Ambon
2. Anyer

3. Bandung
4. Bengkulu
5. Blitar
6. Boyolali
7. Bukittinggi
8. Buru
9. Cianjur
10. Cotabato
11. Datu Piang
12. Dumai
13. Indramayu
14. Jakarta
15. Kartosura
16. Kuta
17. Malang
18. Medan
19. Mojoagung
20. Mojokerto
21. Palabuhanratu
22. Pasuruan
23. Pekalongan
24. Pekanbaru
25. Poso
26. Sekudai
27. Semarang
28. Solo
29. Surabaya
30. Surakarta
31. Tawau
32. Ungaran
33. Wonosobo
34. Yogyakarta
35. Zamboanga

Two-mode matrix, 79 × 35

11.   Logistical Function

Definition of Logistic Functions

Logistical functions are defined as the support for terrorist/insurgency operations by providing materials, weapons, transportation, and safe houses.

List of Logistic Functions

1. Material
2. Safe houses
3. Transportation
4. Weapons

Two-mode matrix, 79 × 4

12. Meetings

Definition of Meetings

A meeting is a preplanned, coordinated event between two or more individuals. Meetings do not include all styles of communications. Rather, *meeting* refers to a certain location at a certain date with specific individuals. Meetings infer the necessity of a decision, but the data do not specifically identify the decision or meeting subject.

List of Meetings

1. Page 5 ICG. Noordin met the secretary of the central command. 7 June in a hotel
2. Page 5 ICG. After the bombing, talked late into the evening in Bandung in late August
3. Page 6 ICG. At a prearranged spot in the city Mojoagung
4. Page 6 ICG. To discuss electronics training, in Solo, Indonesia, date unknown
5. Page 7 ICG. Meeting in Solo to discuss the protection of Azhari and Noordin
6. Page 8 ICG. Region; Surabaya Location at a house owned by Abu Fida to develop concept for construction of a new Islamic boarding school
7. Page 8 ICG. Noordin met Rois in Ambon or Mindanao
8. Page 8 ICG. Urwha ordered to reestablish contact with Rois and determine his willingness to take part in Jihad
9. Page 8 ICG. Delivery of a letter at a Mosque in Solo
10. Page 10 ICG. June 22nd in Surabaya Discussion of readiness of three suicide bombers by Noordin
11. Page 11 ICG. October 2004 in Pekalongan Central Java, Noordin tasking to lobby for a revolver
12. Page 14 ICG. Lobbying meeting. Loc; Air Kuning May 2001
13. Page 15 ICG. Meeting to request det cord, RP 500K and find possible suicide bombers. Loc; Surabaya

14. Page 15 ICG. Arrangement of lodging for Noordin. Loc; Pekalongan
15. Page 15 ICG. Arrangement for a meeting between Noordin and Sunata. Loc; Pekalongan
16. Page 15 ICG. Discussion for a program of cooperation with KOMPAK. Loc; Pekalongan
17. Page 16 ICG. Set up a meeting between Noordin and Sunata. Loc; Yogyakarta
18. Page 16 ICG. KOMPAK meeting – The big one. Loc; Kartosuro at Joko's House Date Jan 2005
19. Page 17 ICG. Recruitment of university student. Loc; Solo, May 2005
20. Page 18 ICG. Discussion to develop a computer networking cite; Sep. 2005. Loc; Pekalongan

Two-mode matrix 79 × 20

13.   Attribute Data

1) Education Level: highest degree attained, level taught at, studied, participated in, or attended.

0. Unknown
1. Elementary Education
2. Pesantren (Luqmanul Hakiem, Ngruki, al-Husein, Indramayu, Jemaah Islamiyah)
3. State High School
4. Some University (University anNur, Universiti Teknologi Malaysia, Adelaide University, Bogor Agricultural University)
5. B.A./B.S. Designation
6. Some Graduate School
7. M.A.
8. Ph.D. (includes Reading University)

2) Contact with People outside Indonesia: contact with people in different countries outside Indonesia.

1. Unknown
2. Afghanistan
3. Australia
4. Malaysia
5. Pakistan
6. Philippines
7. Singapore

8. Thailand
9. United Kingdom
10. Afghanistan and Malaysia
11. Afghanistan and Pakistan
12. Afghanistan and Philippines
13. Afghanistan, Malaysia, and Philippines
14. Australia and Malaysia
15. Philippines and Malaysia
16. Afghanistan, Pakistan, and Egypt
17. Iraq, Afghanistan, and Pakistan

3) Military Training: the country where an individual received military training and attained veteran status in fighting in known insurgent/conventional wars.

1. Unknown
2. Afghanistan
3. Australia
4. Indonesia
5. Malaysia
6. Philippines
7. Singapore
8. Afghanistan and Indonesia
9. Afghanistan and Philippines
10. Indonesia and Malaysia
11. Indonesia and Philippines
12. Afghanistan and Iraq

4) Nationality of Individual: the country of birth, citizenship, or residence.

1. Afghanistan
2. Australia
3. Indonesia
4. Malaysia
5. Philippines
6. Singapore
7. Saudi Arabia
8. Jordan
9. Egypt

5) Current Status per ICG Article: Defined as the physical condition of the individual.

0. Dead
1. Alive
2. Jail

6) Role (Original): the role an individual assumes in the terrorist/insurgent network.

   0. No info/unclear
   1. Strategist: high-level planner of a terrorist/insurgent network
   2. Bomb maker: individual who constructs bombs
   3. Bomber/fighter: individual who participates in bombing attacks or who is described as a fighter
   4. Trainer/instructor: individual who trains or instructs new members of a terror network
   5. Suicide bomber: individual who plans to or already has performed a suicide attack
   6. Recon and surveillance: individual who engages in the surveillance and recon of targets
   7. Recruiter: individual who engages in identifying and recruiting new members (to include bombers)
   8. Courier/go-between: individual used in communications between members
   9. Propagandist: individual who develops information campaigns
   10. Facilitator: individual who assists in the operation of the network (especially with materials and finances)
   11. Religious leader: individual who provides religious training and support
   12. Commander/tactical leader: individual in charge of operations at the local/tactical level

7) Primary Group Affiliation: the primary group affiliation of each member of the network, generally.

   0. None (Noordin)
   1. Darul Islam (DI)
   2. KOMPAK
   3. Jemaah Islamiyah (JI)
   4. Ring Banten Group (DI)
   5. Al Qaeda

8) Noordin's Network: An individual is considered a member of Noordin's splinter group (Tanzim Qaedat al-Jihad – Organization for the Basis of Jihad), as opposed to simply being linked, if the individual knowingly participated in a Noordin-led operation during any stage, is explicitly stated as a member of Noordin's inner circle, and/or is tied to Noordin through kinship or friendship.

   0. Nonmember
   1. Member

Appendix 2

Glossary of Terms

Actor: An actor can be a person, subgroup, organization, collective, community, nation-state, etc. An actor is sometimes referred to as a node or vertex.

Affiliation Network: An affiliation network is a two-mode network consisting of one set of actors and one set of events.

Arc: An arc is directed tie that connects one actor to another actor.

Attribute: Attributes are nonrelational characteristics of the individual actors in the network. Examples of attributes of individuals include gender, race, ethnicity, years of education, income level, age, region/country of birth. Examples of organizational attributes include total sales, net income, age of the corporation, number of employees/members. Examples of country attributes include GDP per capita, population size, continent.

Automorphic Equivalence: With automorphic equivalence two actors are considered structurally similar if they occupy indistinguishable positions in a network. See *regular* and *structural equivalence*.

Average Degree: Average degree equals the average number of ties among all actors in a network. It is sometimes used as an alternative measure to network density because it is not sensitive to network size.

Average Distance: Average distance refers to the average length of all the shortest paths (i.e., geodesics) between all connected actors in a network and could indicate the speed that information (and other resources) diffuses through a network.

Betweenness Centrality: Betweenness centrality measures the extent to which each actor lies on the shortest path between all other actors in a network.

Bi-Component: Formally, a bi-component is a component without a cut-point. They are the sections of a network where the removal of a single actor does not create a new component.

Blocks, Blockmodeling, and Blockmodels: A set of structurally equivalent actors is referred to as a "block," the process by which blocks are identified is referred to as blockmodeling, with the resulting partition of actors into blocks as a blockmodel.

Bridge: Formally, a tie is said to be a bridge if deleting it would cause the network to disconnect into different components. Less formally, it refers to a tie that bridges a gap in the network.

Brokerage Role: A brokerage role of an actor (e.g., gatekeeper, consultant, representative, itinerant broker, coordinator, liaison) is a function of the combination of a pattern of ties and group affiliation.

Centrality: Centrality measures give a rough indication of the social power of an actor based on their position within the network. A central actor can be seen as someone who has a lot of ties to other actors (*degree centrality*), as someone who is closer (in terms of path distance) to all other actors than others are in the network (*closeness centrality*), as someone who lies on the shortest path (geodesic) between any two actors (*betweenness centrality*) in a network, or as someone who has ties to actors who are highly central (*eigenvector centrality*).

Centralization: Centralization uses the variation in actor centrality within the network to measure the level of centralization. More variation yields higher network centralization scores; less variation yields lower scores. In general, the larger a centralization index is, the more likely it is that a single actor is very central while the other actors are not, so they can be seen as measuring how unequal the distribution of individual actor values are. Centralization scores need to be interpreted in light of the type of centrality (e.g., degree, betweenness, closeness, eigenvector) being estimated.

Clique: A clique is maximal complete subnetwork containing three or more actors.

Closeness Centrality: Closeness centrality captures how close (in terms of shortest path distance – i.e., geodesic distance) each actor is to all other actors in a network.

Clustering Coefficient: The clustering coefficient measures the likelihood that two actors who share a tie with a third actor share a tie between themselves.

Complete Network: A complete network includes not only all relevant actors but also all relevant ties between actors.

Component: A component is a subnetwork in which members are connected to one another (either directly or indirectly) but are not connected with members of other subnetworks. In directed networks, you can identify two types of components: strong and weak. Strong components take into account the direction of ties, whereas weak components do not. In a strong component each pair of actors is connected by a (directed) path and no other actor can be added without destroying its connectedness. By contrast, in a weak component each pair of actors is connected by an undirected path (i.e., a semipath) and no other actor can be added without destroying its connectedness. See *strong component* and *weak component*. See also *bi-component*.

Constraint: Constraint measures the extent to which each actor does not lie in triadic brokerage positions. See *structural hole*.

Coordinator: A coordinator provides mediation between members of one group where the mediator is also a member of the group.

Cutpoint: A cutpoint is an actor whose removal increases the number of weak components in a network. Put differently, it disconnects the network. Also known as cut-vertex, articulation point, and boundary spanner (ORA).

Dark Network: Dark networks are defined as covert (or clandestine) and illegal networks (Milward and Raab 2006; Raab and Milward 2003) and is a term that (can) include terrorist, criminal, and insurgent networks. The term "dark" should not be interpreted normatively. Rather, it is simply a term that seeks to capture the fact that dark networks are those networks that, by definition, try to remain hidden (Tilly 2005).

Degree Centrality: Formally, degree centrality of an actor equals the number of ties incident with it. More simply, it is the count of the number of an actor's ties.

Density: Conceptually, density refers to the degree to which a network is connected. Formally, it is the number of ties in a simple network, expressed as a proportion of the maximum possible number of ties. This formal measure, however, is inversely related to network size (i.e., the larger the network, the lower the density) because the number of possible ties increases exponentially as actors are added to the network, although the number of ties that each actor can maintain tends to be limited. This is why analysts will sometimes turn to other measures, such as average degree, for getting a handle on this dimension of network topography. See *average degree*.

Diameter: The diameter of a network refers to a network's longest geodesic and could be interpreted as how spread out a network is.

Directed Network (Graph): Also known as a digraph (from directed graph), a directed network occurs when one or more ties (arc) are directed from one actor to another.

Directed Tie: A directed tie is commonly known as an arc, which is simply a line that points from one actor to another. See *arc*.

Dyad: A dyad is a type pair of actors with a tie between them.

Dyadic Network: A dyadic network is a type of two-mode network consisting of two sets of actors.

Edge: An edge is an undirected tie that connects one actor to another actor.

Edge Betweenness Centrality: Edge betweenness is similar to (actor) betweenness centrality, except that edge betweenness estimates the betweenness centrality of edges (i.e., ties) in the network, while actor betweenness estimates the betweenness centrality of actors. Like actor betweenness, edge betweenness measures the extent to which each edge in a network lies on the shortest path linking all pairs of actors (i.e., geodesic) in the network.

Eigenvector Centrality: Eigenvector centrality assumes that ties to central actors are more important than ties to peripheral actors and thus weights each actor's summed connections to others by the others' centrality scores. With an undirected network, eigenvector centrality scores are the same as *hubs and authorities scores*.

Faction: A faction is a subnetwork where each actor is tied to all other actors within their own subnetwork but have no ties to actors in other subnetworks.

Fragmentation: Network fragmentation captures the extent to which a network is fragmented. In ORA, fragmentation equals the proportion of all pairs of actors that are not tied with one another. UCINET calculates both this measure of fragmentation and a distance-weighted one that takes into account the shortest path distance between pairs of actors.

Fruchterman Reingold: The Fruchterman Reingold algorithm attempts to simulate a system of mass particles where the vertices simulate mass points repelling each other while the edges simulate springs with attracting forces. It then tries to minimize the "energy" of this physical system. It differs from the Kamada-Kawai algorithm in that it is able to distribute points in both two-dimensional and three-dimensional space. See also *Kamada-Kawai* and *spring-embedded* algorithms.

Gatekeeper: A gatekeeper provides mediation between two groups wherein the mediator regulates the flow of information or goods to his or her group.

Geodesic: A geodesic is the shortest path between two actors. See *path* and *path distance*.

Graph: A graph is a visual model for a social network with ties between pairs of actors (vertices, nodes). A tie can be either present or absent between each pair of actors.

Hubs and Authorities: The hubs and authorities algorithm was initially designed for identifying which web pages functioned as hubs and which ones functioned as authorities, wherein a good hub was defined as one that points to many good authorities, and a good authority is one that is pointed to by many good hubs. Consequently, the algorithm is designed to work with directed networks, but when used with undirected networks, it generates identical scores as *eigenvector centrality*.

Indegree (Outdegree) Centrality: Indegree (outdegree) centrality is the count of direct incoming (outgoing) ties. See *degree centrality*.

Input Domain: Input domain is a measure of prestige that counts all people by whom someone is chosen whether directly or indirectly. Restricted input domain only counts indirect ties at a prespecified maximum distance, which is chosen by the analyst. A restricted input domain of one is the same as *indegree centrality* because it only counts direct ties.

Itinerant Broker/Consultant: An itinerant broker/consultant is a mediator between members of one group where the mediator is not a member of the group.

Kamada-Kawai: The Kamada-Kawai spring-embedded algorithm assumes an attraction between adjacent points (vertices), repulsion between nonadjacent points, and allocates points in two-dimensional space. See also *Fruchterman Reingold* and *spring-embedded* algorithms.

k-Core: Formally, a k-core is a maximal group of actors, all of whom are connected to some number (k) of other group members.

Key Player: There are two types of key player algorithms. One seeks to fragment a network; the other seeks to diffuse information through it. The former identifies the optimal set of actors that either completely disconnects the network or at least fragments it to such an extent that it makes the flow of resources across the network (e.g., communication) more difficult. The latter is designed to find the optimal set of actors that reaches the highest number of other actors.

Liaison: A liason provides mediation between two groups to which the mediator does not belong.

Longitudinal Network: A longitudinal network is network data measured over time.

Loop: A loop is a tie that connects an actor with itself.

Multidimensional Scaling: Multidimensional scaling is a method for locating a social network's actors in k-dimensional space (e.g., 2D, 3D). It is used primarily for visualization purposes. See *Fruchterman Reingold*, *Kamada-Kawai*, and *spring-embedding algorithms*.

Network Size: The size of a network equals the number of actors in the network.

Newman Groups: Newman groups are a series of community-detecting algorithms developed by Mark Newman and his colleagues. Newman groups are defined as having more ties within and fewer ties between groups than would be expected in a random graph of the same size with the same number of ties.

Node: A node is a vertex, an actor.

One-Mode Network: A one-mode network is a network that consists of a single set of actors. See also *two-mode network*.

Outdegree Centrality: See *indegree centrality*.

Partition: A network partition is a discrete classification or clustering of vertices that assigns each vertex to exactly one class or cluster.

Path: A path is a walk (i.e., a sequence of actors and ties) in which no actor and no tie in between the first and last actor of the walk occurs more than once. The one exception is that the first and last actor in a path can be the same actor. See also *trail* and *walk*.

Path Distance (Length): The distance between pairs of actors in a network. The shortest path between a pair of actors is known as the geodesic.

Positional Analysis: Positional analysis differs from the relational approach in that rather than focusing on the ties between actors, it seeks to identify actors who hold similar positions in the social structure. Why are positions seen as important? A position (e.g., student) is typically connected to a particular role or set of roles and located within a larger system of positions, which is why some social network analysts believe that actors occupying a particular position/role will exhibit similar types of behavior.

Proximity Prestige: Proximity prestige is a measure of prestige that for each actor in a network, divides its input domain by the average distance between it and all actors with which it is connected (directly or indirectly).

Regular Equivalence: With regular equivalence actors do not have to have identical ties to identical other actors (i.e., structural equivalence) or occupy indistinguishable positions in a network (automorphic equivalence. Instead, they must have identical ties to and from regularly equivalent actors. See *automorphic* and *structural equivalence*.

Relational Analysis: Relational analysis focuses on the direct and indirect ties between actors and seeks to explain behavior and social processes in light of those ties. It highlights the importance of the topography of networks, the centrality of actors, the cohesiveness of subgroups, and the brokers and bridges between such groups.

Representative: A representative provides mediation between two groups and regulates the flow of information or goods from his or her group.

Social Network: A social network consists of a graph with additional information concerning the graph's vertices and/or lines.

Social Structure: Social structure the enduring patterns of behavior and relationships within social systems (e.g., roles) or the social institutions and norms that have become embedded in social systems in such a way that they shape behavior. Within SNA, social structures are seen in terms of enduring patterns of ties between actors (i.e., social networks).

Spring-Embedded Algorithms: Spring-embedded algorithms are graph-drawing algorithms that treat points (vertices) as pushing and pulling on one another and seek to find an optimum solution where there is a minimum amount of stress on the springs connecting the whole set of points. See also *Fruchterman Reingold* and *Kamada-Kawai*.

Strong Component: In a strong component each pair of actors is connected by a (directed) path and no other actor can be added without destroying its connectedness. See *component* and *weak component*.

Structural Equivalence: Two actors are said to be structurally equivalent when they have exactly the same relationships to all other actors. See also *regular equivalence*.

Structural Hole: A structural hole is a gap in the social structure. See *constraint*.

Tie: A tie is a relation between two actors. A tie can be either directed (arc) or undirected (edge).

Topography: Network topography refers to the overall structure of the network. Commonly used measures include average degree, density, fragmentation, network size, and centralization.

Trail: A trail is a walk where each tie can only be used once. Thus, while all trails are walks, not all walks are trails. See also *walk* and *path*.

Triad: A triad is a set of three actors that may or may not have ties between them.

Two-Mode Network: A two-mode network consists of two sets of actors (i.e., a dyadic network) or one set of actors and one set of events (i.e., an affiliation network). See also *one-mode network*.

Undirected Tie: An undirected tie is a line that connects two actors but does not point from one actor to another. See *edge*.

Vector: A vector is a numerical (continuous) value assigned to each actor in a network.

Walk: A walk is a sequence of actors and ties that begins and ends with actors; it can involve the same actor and the same tie more than once. See also *trail* and *path*.

Weak Component: In a weak component each pair of actors is connected by an undirected path (i.e., a semipath) and no other actor can be added without destroying its connectedness. See *component* and *strong component*.

Appendix 3

Multidimensional Scaling with UCINET

This appendix illustrates how to estimate multidimensional scaling (MDS) coordinates in UCINET, which can then be visualized using NetDraw. The advantage of calculating MDS coordinates in UCINET is that UCINET calculates a stress statistic (while NetDraw currently does not – with one exception). Stress statistics are valuable because they indicate how well the network map fits the data. A stress statistic greater than .20 is generally considered intolerable. Thus, we would not want to rely too heavily on a network map with a high stress statistic. Another advantage of calculating coordinates in UCINET rather than in NetDraw is that with UCINET users can estimate metric and nonmetric MDS models, while NetDraw currently offers only metric MDS. Finally, UCINET can also estimate three-dimensional MDS models, which typically exhibit lower stress levels (i.e., they produce a better fit) than do two-dimensional models. While three-dimensional models cannot be visualized using NetDraw, they can be visualized using Mage, a program that is included as one of UCINET's helper programs.[1] In this appendix we will use a relatively small social network dataset, because it is easier to illustrate these techniques with smaller rather than with larger networks. That said, there is nothing we do in this appendix that you cannot do with larger datasets.

Multidimensional Scaling of Symmetric One-Mode Networks

We will begin with symmetric one-mode networks because it is easier to estimate MDS coordinates for symmetric one-mode networks than

---

[1] Mage was developed as a device to be used in molecular modeling (Richardson and Richardson 1992). For more information, see the article by Freeman, Webster, and Kirke (1998) or http://kinemage.biochem.duke.edu/software/mage.php. Pajek also exports images that can be visualized using Mage. Also, see de Nooy et al. (2011:388–389).

asymmetric ones. For this, we use the marital ties of Padgett's Florentine Families, which we have discussed before. Our first task is to use this network to calculate a set of related coordinates. We consider both metric and nonmetric MDS. We will then read these (and the related network) into NetDraw and Mage.

Metric Multidimensional Scaling

As previously noted, network analysts have long used sociograms to visualize social networks, and in recent years analysts have begun using a series of mathematical techniques to locate the points of a network in such a way that the distances between them are meaningful. MDS is one such technique. It uses the concepts of space and distance to represent a network's internal structure (Wasserman and Faust 1994). The typical input is a symmetric matrix consisting of measures of similarity or dissimilarity between pairs of actors. Output generally consists of a set of estimated distances between pairs of actors that we can represent in one-, two-, three-, or higher-dimensional space (Kruskal and Wish 1978; Wasserman and Faust 1994).

Metric MDS takes a given matrix of proximities that measure the similarities or dissimilarities among a set of actors and calculates a set of points in k-dimensional space, such that the distances between them correspond as closely as possible to the input proximities (Borgatti, Everett, and Freeman 2011).[2] Metric distance differs from distance in graph theory. In graph theory, the distance between two points is measured in terms of the number of lines in the path that connects the two points. In MDS the distance between two points is the most direct route between them. "It is a distance that follows a route 'as the crow flies,' and that may be across 'open space' and need not – indeed, it normally will not – follow a graph theoretical path" (Scott 2000:148–149).

Under UCINET's *Tools* menu, select the *Scaling/Decomposition>* *Metric MDS* command; this should bring up a dialog box similar to (Figure A3.1). There are a number of options available. In general, you will want to accept UCINET's defaults unless you have a good reason not to. Here, I have changed only one default setting: the name of the output dataset in order to make it easier to identify.

Scaling/ Decomposition> Metric MDS

Running this procedure produces both a scatter plot (not shown) and an output file that lists the MDS coordinates and a stress score (Figure A3.2). As you can see, the stress is .30, which tells us that the coordinates do not fit the data relatively well. The coordinates themselves are stored in the file `PadgetMetricMdsCoord2`, which we will use later use to read

---

[2] The Padgett data proximities represent similarities between the families. That is, a "1" in a matrix cell means that the two families represented by that cell share a marital tie.

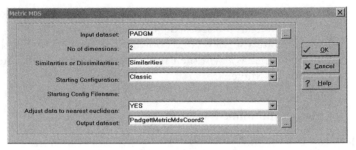

Figure A3.1. UCINET's Metric MDS Dialog Box

into NetDraw. Because the fit is rather poor, let's also estimate a three-dimensional metric MDS model, using the same command, except this time change the "No. of dimensions" option from 2 to 3 (not shown) and the name of the coordinate file that UCINET will generate to Padget-MetricMdsCoord3 (or something similar – just so we do not overwrite the previous coordinate file). When we do this (the dialog box is not shown), we get a better-fitting result (Figure A3.3). The stress level is now below .30 (.195), which means we can be a little more confident with the resulting visualization. Before seeing how to use these two sets of coordinates to visualize the network in NetDraw and Mage, respectively, let's first turn our attention to nonmetric MDS, which is often a better choice when working with binary (i.e., dichotomous) data.

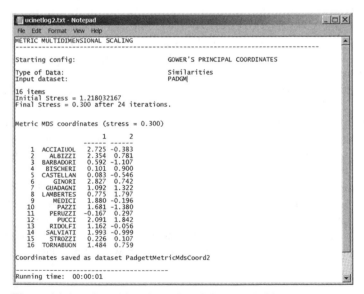

Figure A3.2. UCINET's Metric MDS Output (2-D)

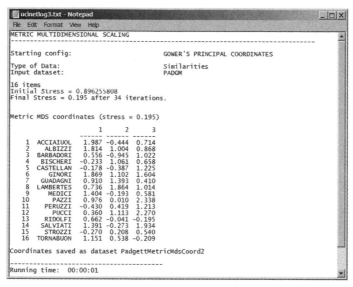

Figure A3.3. UCINET's Metric MDS Output (3-D)

Nonmetric Multidimensional Scaling

There are some limitations to using metric MDS for visualizing social networks. Many relational datasets, such as the Padgett data, are dichotomous (i.e., they simply indicate either the presence or absence of a tie, not its strength). Consequently, UCINET cannot directly use such data to measure proximities. Instead, it first needs to convert it into an alternative (and scaled) metric, such as correlation coefficients, before calculating its metric properties. However, because dichotomous data are not metric (i.e., they only consist of 1's and 0's), it is possible for UCINET to estimate the coordinates incorrectly. Even when the data are valued, metric assumptions may be inappropriate if the data do not represent a definitive scale. For example, a family with four marital ties may not be twice as central a family with only two.

While nonmetric MDS procedures (like metric MDS procedures) use symmetrical adjacency matrices to calculate similarities or dissimilarities between actors, unlike metric MDS, they do not directly convert these values into Euclidean distances. Instead, they consider only rank order. They treat the data, in other words, as ordinal and "seek a solution in which the rank ordering of the distances is the same as the rank ordering of the original values" (Scott 2000:157). Nonmetric MDS is often preferred because it tends to provide a better "goodness-of-fit" (stress) statistic.

To estimate nonmetric MDS coordinates, select the *Nonmetric MDS* option found under the *Tools>Scaling/Decomposition* submenu. This brings up a dialog box similar to the one we used for calculating metric *Tools>Scaling/ Decomposition >Nonmetric MDS*

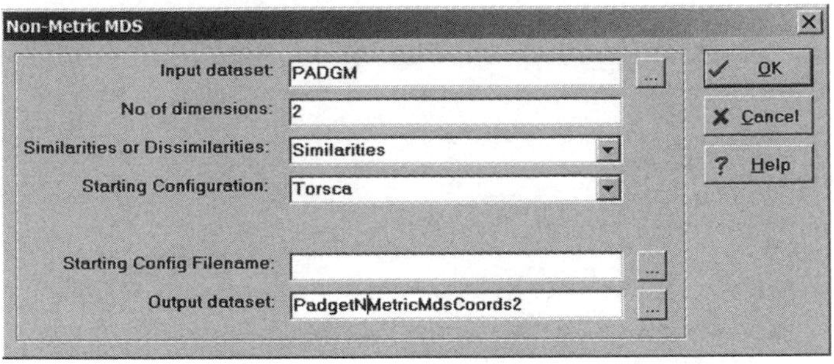

Figure A3.4. UCINET's Nonmetric MDS Scaling Dialog Box

MDS (Figure A3.4). As before, I accepted all of UCINET's defaults except that I changed the name of the output dataset in order to make it easier to identify. Moreover, I estimated both two- and three-dimensional models.

As with metric MDS, this procedure produces scatter plots (not shown), output files (Figures A3.5 and A3.6) that list the MDS coordinates, and a stress score. As you can see, the stress statistic for the two-dimensional model is .02, and the stress statistic for the three-dimensional model is .00, both of which fit the data far better than did the coordinates estimated using metric MDS. Thus, we will use the nonmetric coordinates for visualizing in NetDraw and Mage.

Using UCINET Coordinates with NetDraw and Mage

Using MDS coordinates generated by UCINET to visualize a network in NetDraw is straightforward. First open the Padgett data in NetDraw

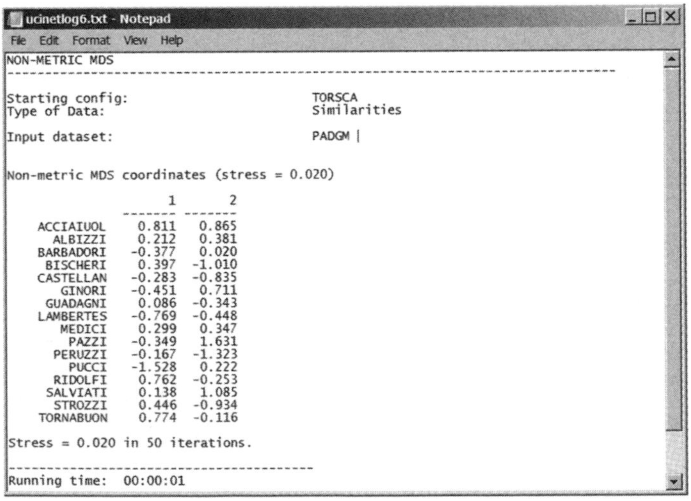
ucinetlog6.txt - Notepad
File Edit Format View Help

```
NON-METRIC MDS
------------------------------------------------------------------------------

Starting config:                               TORSCA
Type of Data:                                  Similarities

Input dataset:                                 PADGM

Non-metric MDS coordinates (stress = 0.020)

                      1       2
                ------- -------
    ACCIAIUOL     0.811   0.865
      ALBIZZI     0.212   0.381
   BARBADORI     -0.377   0.020
    BISCHERI      0.397  -1.010
   CASTELLAN     -0.283  -0.835
      GINORI     -0.451   0.711
    GUADAGNI      0.086  -0.343
   LAMBERTES     -0.769  -0.448
      MEDICI      0.299   0.347
       PAZZI     -0.349   1.631
     PERUZZI     -0.167  -1.323
       PUCCI     -1.528   0.222
     RIDOLFI      0.762  -0.253
    SALVIATI      0.138   1.085
     STROZZI      0.446  -0.934
   TORNABUON      0.774  -0.116

Stress = 0.020 in 50 iterations.

----------------------------------------
Running time:  00:00:01
```

Figure A3.5. UCINET's Nonmetric MDS Output (2-D)

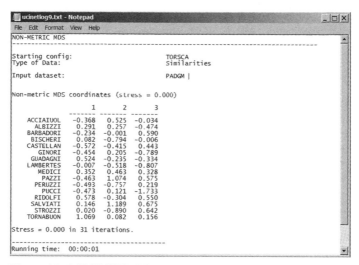

Figure A3.6. UCINET's Nonmetric MDS Output (3-D)

with its *File>Open>Ucinet dataset>Network* command. Next use the *File>Open>Ucinet dataset>Coordinates* command to open the related coordinate file (PadgetNMetricMdsCoords2.##h). NetDraw automatically assigns these coordinates to the respective nodes. You should get a network map similar to the one displayed in Figure A3.7. If you choose a mapping algorithm resident in NetDraw, then in order to recall the coordinates calculated in UCINET, you will need to reissue the *File>Open>Ucinet dataset>Coordinates* command. *[NetDraw] File>Open>Ucinet dataset>Network*

File>Open >Ucinet dataset >Coordinates

To visualize a network with Mage using MDS coordinates generated by UCINET takes a few more steps than it does with NetDraw. We need to first export both the network and coordinate data in a format that Mage can read. To do this, we use UCINET's *Data>Export>Mage* command, which calls up a dialog box similar to Figure A3.8. *[UCINET] Data>Export> Mage*

As you can see, using the radio buttons on the right side of the dialog box, both the network (PADGM.##h) and coordinate data (PadgetN-MetricMdsCoords2.##h) have been loaded into the dialog box. Initially, you will probably want to accept UCINET's default settings. If, later, you want to adjust the size of nodes, the width of ties, and so on, you can play with the various options and see how they alter the resulting sociogram. Clicking "OK" brings up a dialog box (Figure A3.9) that allows you to open the newly formatted network (PADGM.kin) in Mage (Mage can also be accessed with the *Visualize>Mage* command).[3] *Visualize>Mage*

Clicking "OK" opens Mage along with a three-dimensional visualization of the network that appears as an interactive computer display

[3] If the Mage program did not come with UCINET, you can download it at http: //kinemage.biochem.duke.edu/software/mage.php.

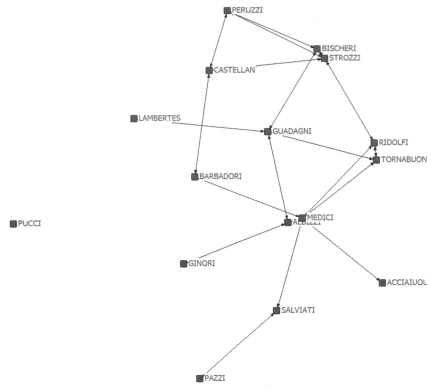

Figure A3.7. Nonmetric MDS Map of Padgett Marriage Network (NetDraw)

(Figure A3.10). Researchers can rotate Mage images, turn parts of the displays on or off, use the mouse to select and identify various points of the network, and animate changes between different arrangements of objects. Here, the background has been changed from black to white and the node

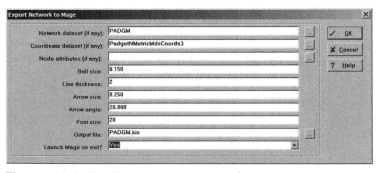

Figure A3.8. UCINET's Export to Mage Dialog Box

Figure A3.9. UCINET's Launch Mage Program Dialog Box

color to gray scale using the using the *Display> White Background* and ~~~Display> White Background~~~ *Display> Gray Scale* commands, respectively.

Mage also allows users to easily change the color of the vertices. For *Display> Gray Scale* example, let's highlight the Medici family because of its centrality. To change the color of the Medici vertex, first select the "Change Color" option under the "Edit" menu. This calls up a new "Changecolor" option along the right hand side of the display (not shown). If you check it and *Edit> Change color* click on the Medici (or any) node, this will bring up a color selection dialog box (not shown). This, in turn, gives you a choice between changing the color of the entire network (list) or a single node (point) in the network. To change the color of the Medici node, select the "Point" option and then the color of your choice. Mage files actually allow for a considerable amount of sophisticated editing. Although that is beyond the scope of this appendix, see Appendix A of *A Guide to the Visually Perplexed* (Everton 2004).

Multidimensional Scaling of Asymmetric One-Mode Networks

Visualizing asymmetric (directed) one-mode networks using UCINET *[UCINET]* is somewhat different because the MDS routines require symmetric

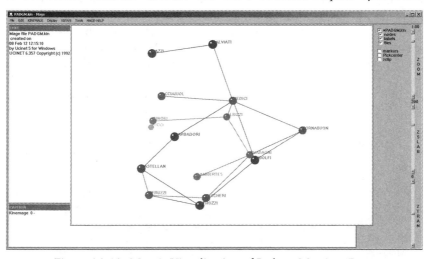

Figure A3.10. Mage's Visualization of Padgett Marriage Data

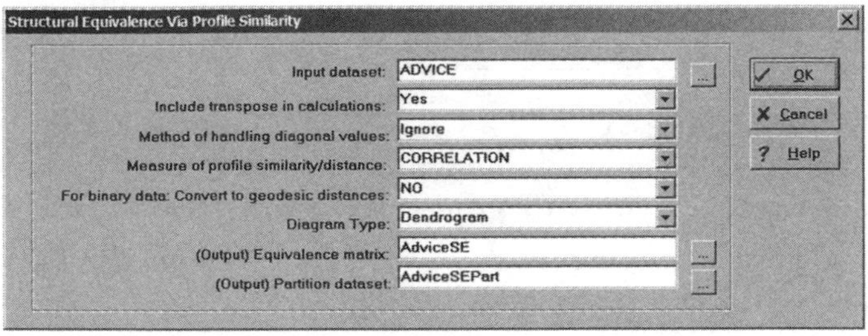

Figure A3.11. UCINET's Structural Equivalence Profile Similarity Dialog Box

matrices.[4] Thus, we need to first calculate an equivalence matrix, based either on the distances (e.g., Euclidean) or the correlations between the nodes of the directed matrix. We then submit this equivalence matrix, which is symmetric, to MDS algorithms. For our purposes here we will use the advice network of Krackhardt's High Tech Managers (1987a), which we have used previously. To calculate an equivalence matrix, under the *Network* menu, choose the *Roles & Positions>Structural>Profile* command. This brings up UCINET's profile similarity dialog box (see Figure A3.11). As is generally the case, accept UCINET's defaults, but change the "Measure of profile similarity/distance" option to "Correlation" because in this case a tie between two individuals indicates similarity.[5] You may also want to change the names of the output files in order to make them easier to identify. This produces both a dendogram (not shown) and a structural equivalence matrix (not shown).

Network>Roles & Positions >Structural >Profile

The next step in the process is to submit the structural equivalence matrix (`AdviceSE.##h`) to the MDS techniques previously discussed (not shown). The stress statistics for the two-dimensional metric and nonmetric MDS were .196 and .129, respectively, while the statistics for the three-dimensional metric and nonmetric MDS were .126 and .088, respectively. This illustrates that nonmetric MDS generally provides a better fit with binary data than metric MDS, and three-dimensional models typically fit the data better than two-dimensional models. Figure A3.12 presents the nonmetric MDS two-dimensional sociogram as

---

[4]　You can submit asymmetric networks to UCINET's *Metric MDS* and *Nonmetric MDS* commands and UCINET will output coordinate files; however, these will most likely be incorrect.

[5]　If we had chosen to calculate the matrix using the Euclidean distance option, then in the resulting matrix the larger the number would indicate the greater the distance of one actor from another. For example, in Figure A3.7 the correlation coefficients along the diagonal are all 1.00 (because each actor is perfectly correlated with itself); if we had chosen the Euclidean distance option, the coefficients along the diagonal would be 0.00. Thus, if we had chosen the Euclidean option, when we instructed UCINET to perform MDS on the structural equivalence matrix, we would need to choose the "Dissimilarities" option rather than the "Similarities" option (see Figure A3.8).

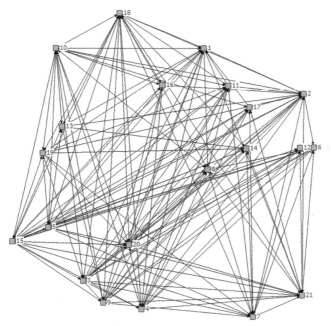

Figure A3.12. NetDraw's Nonmetric MDS Graph of Krackhardt Advice Network (2-D)

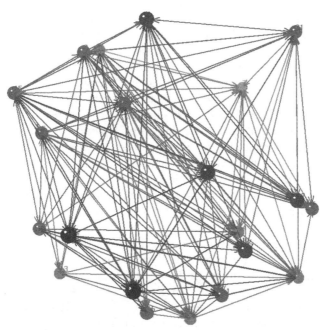

Figure A3.13. Mage's Nonmetric MDS Graph of Krackhardt Advice Network (3-D)

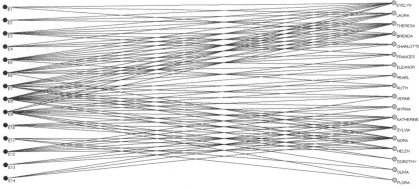

Figure A3.14. Bipartite Graph of Davis's Southern Women

visualized in NetDraw, and Figure A3.13 presents the nonmetric MDS three-dimensional sociogram as visualized in Mage.

Visual Representation of Two-Mode Networks

Two-mode data present additional visualization complexities. To illustrate these, we will use Davis's Southern Club Women (Breiger 1974; Davis et al. 1941), which we examined in Chapter 4. Depending on how we manipulate the data, we can use UCINET to visualize two-mode networks in a variety of ways. We can, of course, convert the data to one-mode (actors or events) data and visualize them using the techniques we discussed. Alternatively, we can visualize the original two-mode network: There are a number of approaches (Borgatti and Everett 1997; Everton 2004). A common approach is to use correspondence analysis, but Borgatti and Everett (1997:247) argue that in correspondence analysis representations of two-mode data that depict the distances between nodes are not Euclidean (i.e., the distances do not necessarily reflect social distance; see, however, Roberts 2000). As such, they recommend that we first convert the two-mode network to a bipartite graph, from which we compute the geodesic distances between all pairs of nodes, which we then submit to MDS techniques (Borgatti and Everett 1997: 249–251).

What is a bipartite graph? "A graph is bipartite if the vertices may be partitioned in exactly two mutually exclusive sets such that there are no ties wholly within either set – i.e., the endpoints of every tie come from different sets" (Borgatti and Everett 1997:247–248). See Figure A3.14. To create a bipartite graph from a two-mode network, we use UCINET's *Transform>Bipartite* command. This brings up a dialog box (Figure A3.15) that requires us to indicate which two-mode network we want to transform. It is important to note that you will want to tell

[UCINET]
Transform
>Bipartite

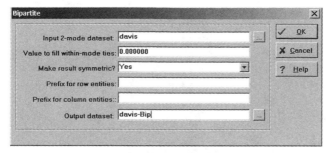

Figure A3.15. UCINET's Bipartite Dialog Box

UCINET to make the resulting graph *symmetric* – this is not UCINET's default option. If you do not change the option to symmetric, you will not be able to calculate the geodesic distance between nodes in the following step. Clicking "OK" will generate a bipartite graph/matrix (not shown) should be a symmetric, one-mode graph with thirty-two rows and columns (eighteen women + fourteen events).

Recall that geodesic distance refers to the length of the shortest path between two nodes. To calculate this in UCINET we use the *Network>Cohesion>Distance* command. In the resulting dialog box (Figure A3.16) indicate that the input dataset is the bipartite network calculated earlier, accept UCINET's defaults, and click "OK." This produces a distance matrix (not shown). If you examine the matrix closely you will note that the geodesic distances between any two women or between any two events is never less than two (Borgatti and Everett 1997:249; Faust 1997). This is because the women are only connected to one another through events and the events are only connected to one another through women, so it always takes at least two steps to get from one woman to another or from one event to another. *[UCINET] Network >Cohesion >Distance*

The next step is submitting this distance matrix to the MDS routines discussed earlier. Nonmetric MDS models yielded the best measures of fit (two-dimensional = .213; three-dimensional = .153) and are displayed in Figures A3.17 and A3.18.

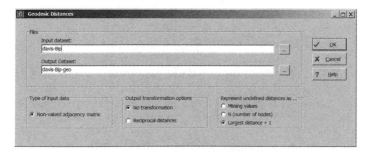

Figure A3.16. UCINET's Geodesic Distance Dialog Box

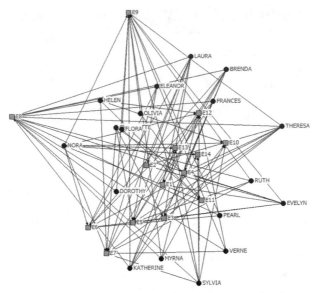

Figure A3.17. NetDraw's Geodesic MDS Graph of Davis's Southern Women (2-D)

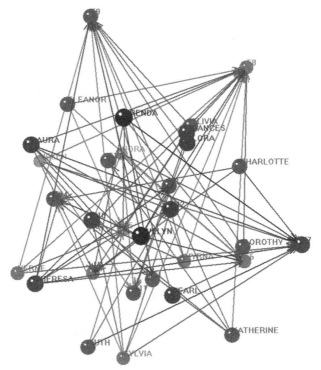

Figure A3.18. Mage's Geodesic MDS Graph of Davis's Southern Women (3-D)

Appendix 4

The Just War Tradition

No single authoritative list of just war criteria exists, and although the following list is "my own," it has been derived and adapted from Allman and Winright (2010), Cole (2002), Walzer (2006), and Yoder (1996).

Jus ad bellum (Justice in Deciding to Go to War)

1. **Just Cause.** This criterion holds that a war may be fought for a justifiable, defensible, and morally necessary cause. To be just, the offense must be actual and verifiable, intentional, and of substantial importance, and it cannot be provoked (i.e., a queen or president can't goad someone into committing an offense so that they can then declare war). Offenses can include aggressive behavior necessitating defense, a threat demanding deterrence, or an injustice demanding reparation (e.g., the Holocaust). It can be committed against a third nation, an ally, or innocent subjects on whose behalf a legitimate authority intervenes. Just war theorists disagree about when intervention on behalf of an oppressed population is legitimate. Walzer (2004, 2006: 67–81) believes that the presumption must be against intervention but acknowledges there are times when the evil being committed is so great (e.g., the Holocaust) that intervention is necessary.

2. **Legitimate Authority.** This criterion asserts that only legitimate authorities may wage war. Examples include individuals who rule through "dynastic dissent" (e.g., kings, queens) and democratically elected officials. An exception to this general rule is officials who have gained their authority through legitimate means but are "bad" rulers (e.g., tyrants); they forfeit their claim to legitimacy. Examples of illegitimate authorities include private citizens who wage wars (e.g., militia groups), bandits and

417

privateers, and those who rebel against one's own sovereign. An exception to this is that rebellion is permitted when sovereigns lose their claim to legitimacy because they are tyrants.

3. **Right Intention.** This criterion states that in order for a war to be just it must be fought with a right intention. The ultimate goal must be the restoration of a just peace. Wars cannot be fought for national honor, aquisition of territory, economic aggrandizement, and so on.

4. **Right Motivation.** A just war must also be fought with the right motivation. There needs to be genuine concern for the victims of the offense as well as love for the enemy, which is why demonstrating mercy after victory is sometimes listed by some as a criterion. Examples of inadmissible motivation include hatred, revenge, cruelty, love of violence, or material gain.

5. **Last Resort.** The just war tradition contends that war must be the last resort, only after everything else has been tried or considered. How one defines "everything else" is somewhat problematic and subject to much debate because there is almost always something else that can be tried. Generally, what theorists have in mind is that the government needs to make a good faith effort to avoid war through negotiation, mediation, arbitration, appeals to international tribunals, cooling off period(s), and formal declaration of war, preceded by a warning and followed by time for the "offending party" to sue for peace. If all of these are sincerely tried (and have failed), then most just war theorists would say that a good faith effort has been made.

6. **Probability of Success.** Finally, in order for a war to be just, success must be probable. If going to war can't fix the problem, then there is no point in going to war. Of course, this is not always straightforward. Sometimes, wars that look easy to win turn out to be much more difficult than anticipated.

Jus in bello (Justice during War)

1. **Proportionality.** Once war begins the punishment must be proportionate to the offense. Thus, the means used must be indispensable and necessary. Any intended destruction inflicted on the enemy must serve the stated ends of the just cause. Nations cannot destroy an enemy battalion simply because they can or because they seek a postwar advantage in further weakening the enemy. In short, unnecessary combat must be avoided even in a just cause.

2. **Dignity of Life.** This criterion is sometimes combined with the criterion of proportionality. It argues that there should be no unnecessary death or wanton destruction because the lasting effect these can have on a country and its citizenry often makes the achievement of a just peace difficult, if not impossible. Examples of behavior that does not respect the dignity of life include the poisoning of wells and rivers, the planting of land mines, and the bombing or profaning of places of worship or sanctuary.

3. **Noncombatant Immunity.** This criterion argues that the means used in war must protect the innocent (noncombatants). Armies must not intentionally or directly kill noncombatants. During a just war, they have an obligation to discriminate combatants from noncombatants and seek to minimize noncombatant death.

Jus post bellum (Justice After War)

1. **Resolution.** This criterion argues that the result of any just war should entail reaching the objectives that served as the (just) cause for going to war in the first place. In other words, the primary parties involved must be held accountable until their mission is accomplished (i.e., blasting away and then letting the offending country pick up the pieces is unacceptable), and they must be prevented from taking advantage of the vanquished country's weakness and seeking additional (and unwarranted) gains.

2. **Reconciliation.** This criterion contends that there cannot be a just peace without reconciliation. However, this call for reconciliation "is not about cheap grace or taking a 'forgive and forget' approach. [Rather] it involves acknowledgment of wrongdoing, admission of responsibility, punishment, forgiveness and perhaps amnesty" (Allman and Winright 2010:14).

3. **Punishment.** This criterion holds that the guilty should be punished for their crimes. It argues that any such punishment should be carried out with transparency and proportionality, and preferably by authorities other than those who led the war, so that the war's victors are not seen as acting as judge, jury, and executioner. In this way, those meting the punishment are seen as legitimate and the punishment is seen as just.

4. **Reconstruction.** This final criterion notes that because a just war's goal involves the restoration of the offending country to wholeness, postwar efforts should involve practical matters such as providing security through policing and the rule of law;

enabling the host government to promote the common good and provide basic services; fostering economic recovery; providing rehabilitation for those victimized by the war (and events that led up to it); and removing unexploded devices, land mines, and munitions to prevent future injuries.

References

Abbott, Andrew. 1983. "Professional Ethics." *American Journal of Sociology* 88(5):855–885.

Abuza, Zachary. 2003. *Militant Islam in Southeast Asia: Crucible of Terror.* Boulder, CO: Lynne Reinner Publishers.

Albert, Reka, Hawoong Jeong, and Albert-László Barabási. 2000. "Error and Attack Tolerance of Complex Networks." *Nature* 406:378–382.

Allman, Mark J., and Tobias L. Winright. 2010. *After the Smoke Clears: The Just War Tradition and Post War Justice.* Maryknoll, NY: Orbis Books.

Anonymous. 2009. "Deception 2.0: Deceiving in the Netwar Age." Unpublished Paper. Task Force Iron, Iraq.

Aristotle. 1998. *The Nichomachean Ethics.* Translated by David Ross, J. L. Ackrill, and J. O. Urmson. Oxford and New York: Oxford University Press.

Arquilla, John. 2008. *Worst Enemy: The Reluctant Transformation of the American Military.* Chicago: Ivan R. Dee.

———. 2009. *Aspects of Netwar & the Conflict with al Qaeda.* Monterey, CA: Information Operations Center, Naval Postgraduate School.

Arquilla, John, and David Ronfeldt. 2001. "The Advent of Netwar (Revisted)." Pp. 1–25 in *Networks and Netwars,* edited by John Arquilla and David Ronfeldt. Santa Monica, CA: RAND.

Arreguin-Toft, Ivan. 2001. "How the Weak Win Wars: A Theory of Asymmetric Conflict." *International Security* 26(1):93–128.

———. 2005. *How the Weak Win Wars: A Theory of Asymmetric Conflict.* Cambridge, UK: Cambridge University Press.

Asal, Victor, and R. Karl Rethemeyer. 2006. "Researching Terrorist Networks." *Journal of Security Education* 1(4):65–74.

Asch, Solomon E. 1955. "Opinions and Social Pressure." *Scientific American* 193:31–35.

Austin, David. 2011. "How Google Finds Your Needle in the Web's Haystack." *Feature Column.* Retrieved from http://www.ams.org/samplings/featurecolumn/fcarc-pagerank.

Azarian, G. Reza. 2005. *The General Sociology of Harrison C. White: Chaos and Order in Networks.* New York: Palgrave Macmillan.

Babbie, Earl. 1986. *The Practice of Social Research*. 4th ed. Belmont, CA: Wadsworth Publishing Co.

Baker, Wayne E., and Robert R. Faulkner. 1993. "The Social-Organization of Conspiracy: Illegal Networks in the Heavy Electrical-Equipment Industry." *American Sociological Review* 58(6):837–860.

Bakker, René M., Jörg Raab, and H. Brinton Milward. 2011. "A Preliminary Theory of Dark Network Resilience." *Journal of Policy Analysis and Management* 31(1):33–62.

Barabási, Albert-László. 2002. *Linked: The New Science of Networks*. Cambridge, MA: Perseus Publishing.

Barabási, Albert-László, and Reka Albert. 1999. "Emergence of Scaling in Random Networks." *Science* 286:509–512.

Barabási, Albert-László, Reka Albert, and Hawoong Jeong. 1999. "Mean-Field Theory for Scale-Free Random Networks." *Physica A* 272:173–187.

Barabási, Albert-László, and Eric Bonabeau. 2003. "Scale-Free Networks." *Scientific American* 288(5):60–69.

Barnes, John A. 1954. "Class and Committee in a Norwegian Island Parish." *Human Relations* 7:39–58.

Batagelj, Vladimir. 1997. "Notes on Blockmodeling." *Social Networks* 19:143–155.

Batagelj, Vladimir, Anuska Ferligoj, and Patrick Doreian. 1992. "Direct and Indirect Methods for Structural Equivalence." *Social Networks* 14:63–90.

Batagelj, Vladimir, and Andrej Mrvar. 2012. *Pajek 2.05*. Lubjlijana, Slovenia: University of Ljubljana.

Bauerlein, Mark. 2004. "Liberal Groupthink Is Anti-intellectual." *The Chronicle of Higher Education* (November 12):B6–B10.

Bavelas, Alex. 1948. "A Mathematical Model for Group Structure." *Human Organizations* 7:16–30.

———. 1950. "Communication Patterns in Task-Oriented Groups." *Journal of the Acoustical Society of America* 22:725–730.

Becker, Gary S. 1976. *The Economic Approach to Human Behavior*. Chicago: University of Chicago Press.

———. 1996. *Accounting for Tastes*. Cambridge, MA: Harvard University Press.

Bentham, Jeremy. 1996 [1789]. *Introduction to the Principles of Morals and Legislation*. J. H. Burns and H. L. A. Hart, eds., Oxford & New York: Oxford University Press.

Berman, Eli. 2009. *Radical, Religious, and Violent: The New Economics of Terrorism*. Cambridge, MA: MIT Press.

Bonacich, Phillip. 1972a. "Factoring and Weighting Approaches to Status Scores and Clique Identification." *Journal of Mathematical Sociology* 2:113–120.

———. 1972b. "A Technique for Analyzing Overlapping Memberships." Pp. 176–85 in *Sociological Methodology*, edited by Herbert Coster. San Francisco: Jossey-Bass.

———. 1987. "Power and Centrality: A Family of Measures." *American Journal of Sociology* 92(5):1170–1182.

Boorman, Scott A., and Harrison C. White. 1976. "Social Structure for Multiple Networks II: Role Structures." *American Journal of Sociology* 81(6):1384–1446.

Borer, Douglas A., Sean F. Everton, and Moises M. Nayve, Jr. 2009. "Global Development and Human (In)security: Understanding the Rise of the Rajah Solaiman Movement and Balik Islam in the Philippines." *Third World Quarterly* 30(1):181–204.

Borgatti, Stephen P. 1988. "A Comment on Doreian's Regular Equivalence in Symmetric Structures." *Social Networks* 10:265–271.

_____. 2002–2005. *NetDraw 2.0.* Harvard, MA: Analytical Technologies.

_____. 2005. "Centrality and Network Flow." *Social Networks* 27(1):55–71.

_____. 2006. "Identifying Sets of Key Players in a Social Network." *Computational, Mathematical and Organizational Theory* 12:21–34.

_____. 2011. *Key Player 1.45.* Lexington, KY: Analytical Technologies.

Borgatti, Stephen P., Kathleen M. Carley, and David Krackhardt. 2006. "On the Robustness of Centrality Measures under Conditions of Imperfect Data." *Social Networks* 28:124–136.

Borgatti, Stephen P., and Martin G. Everett. 1988. "The Class of All Regular Equivalences." *Social Networks* 11:65–89.

_____. 1989. "The Class of All Regular Equivalences: Algebraic Structure and Computation." *Social Networks* 11:65–88.

_____. 1992. "Notions of Position in Social Network Analysis." *Sociological Methodology* 22:1–35.

_____. 1993. "Two Algorithms for Computing Regular Equivalence." *Social Networks* 15:361–376.

_____. 1997. "Network Analysis of 2-Mode Data." *Social Networks* 19:243–269.

_____. 2006. "A Graph-Theoretic Perspective on Centrality." *Social Networks* 28(4):466–484.

Borgatti, Stephen P., Martin G. Everett, and Linton C. Freeman. 2011. *UCINET for Windows: Software for Social Network Analysis.* Lexington, KY: Analytical Technologies.

Borgatti, Stephen P., and Jose-Luis Molina. 2005. "Toward Ethical Guidelines for Network Research in Organizations." *Social Networks* 27:107–117.

Bott, Elizabeth. 1957. *Family and Social Network.* London, England: Tavistock.

Boucek, Christopher. 2008a. "The Sakinah Campaign and Internet Counter-Radicalization in Saudi Arabia." *CTC Sentinel* 1(9):1–4. Retrieved from http://carnegieendowment.org/files/CTCSentinel_Vol1Iss9.pdf.

_____. 2008b. "Saudi Arabia's 'Soft' Counterterrorism Strategy: Prevention, Rehabilitation, and Aftercare." *Carnegie Papers* 97. Retrieved from http://carnegieendowment.org/files/cp97_boucek_saudi_final.pdf.

Brafman, Ori, and Rod A. Beckstrom. 2006. *The Starfish and the Spider: The Unstoppable Power of Leaderless Organizations.* New York: Portfolio.

Brandes, Ulrik, and Thomas Erlebach (Eds.). 2005. *Network Analysis: Methodological Foundations.* Berlin, Germany: Springer.

Brandes, Ulrik, Jörg Raab, and Dorothea Wagner. 2001. "Exploratory Network Visualization." *Journal of Social Structure* 2(1). Retrieved from http://www.cmu.edu/joss/content/articles/volume2/BrandesRaabWagner.html.

Breiger, Ron, Kathleen M. Carley, and Philippa Pattison (Eds.). 2003. *Dynamic Social Network Modeling and Analysis: Workshop Summary and Papers.*

Washington, D.C.: National Academy of Sciences / National Research Council: National Academies Press.

Breiger, Ronald L. 1974. "The Duality of Persons and Groups." *Social Forces* 53:181–190.

———. 1975. "Dual and Multiple Networks of Social Structures: A Study of Affiliation and Interaction." Doctoral Dissertation Thesis, Sociology, Harvard University, Boston.

———. 2005. "Introduction to Special Issue: Ethical Dilemmas in Social Network Research." *Social Networks* 27:89–93.

Breiger, Ronald L., and Philippa E. Pattison. 1986. "Cumulated Social Roles: The Duality of Persons and Their Algebras." *Social Networks* 8:215–256.

Brimley, Shawn, and Vikram Singh. 2008. "Stumbling into the Future? The Indirect Approach and American Strategy." *Orbis* 52(2):312–331.

Buchanan, Mark. 2001. *Ubiquity*. New York: Crown Publishers.

———. 2002. *Nexus: Small Worlds and the Groundbreaking Science of Networks*. New York: W. W. Norton & Company.

Burns, Tom, and G. M. Stalker. 1961. *The Management of Innovation*. London: Tavistock.

Burt, Ronald S. 1984. "Network Items and the General Social Survey." *Social Networks* 6:293–340.

———. 1985. "General Social Survey Network Items." *Connections* 8:119–122.

———. 1987. "Social Contagion and Innovation: Cohesion versus Structural Equivalence." *American Journal of Sociology* 92(6):1287–1335.

———. 1992a. "The Social Structure of Competition." Pp. 57–91 in *Networks and Organizations: Structure, Form and Action*, edited by Nitin Nohria and Robert G. Eccles. Boston: Harvard Business Review Press.

———. 1992b. *Structural Holes: The Social Structure of Competition*. Cambridge, MA: Harvard University Press.

Buskens, Vincent, and Arnout van de Rijt. 2008. "Dynamics of Networks If Everyone Strives for Structural Holes." *American Journal of Sociology* 114(2):371–407.

Carley, Kathleen M. 2001–2011. *Organizational Risk Analyzer (ORA)*. Pittsburgh, PA: Center for Computational Analysis of Social and Organizational Systems (CASOS): Carnegie Mellon University.

———. 2003a. *Destabilizing Terrorist Networks*. Paper presented at the 8th International Command and Control Research and Technology Symposium, National Defense War College, Washington, D.C.

———. 2003b. "Dynamic Network Analysis." Pp. 133–45 in *Dynamic Social Network Modeling and Analysis: Workshop Summary and Papers*, edited by Ron Breiger, Kathleen Carley, and Philippa Pattison. Washington, D.C.: National Academy of Sciences/National Research Council: National Academies Press.

———. 2006. "A Dynamic Network Approach to the Assessment of Terrorist Groups and the Impact of Alternative Courses of Action." *Visualizing Network Information Meeting Proceedings RTO-MP-IST-063*. Retrieved from http://www.vistg.net/documents/IST063_PreProceedings.pdf.

Carley, Kathleen M., Ju-Sung Lee, and David Krackhardt. 2002. "Destabilizing Networks." *Connections* 24(3):79–92.

Carley, Kathleen M., Jeffrey Reminga, and Natasha Kamneva. 2003. *Destabilizing Terrorist Networks*. Paper presented at the 8th International Command and Control Research and Technology Symposium, National Defense War College, Washington, D.C.

Carrington, Peter J. 2011. "Crime and Social Network Analysis." Pp. 236–69 in *The SAGE Handbook of Social Network Analysis*, edited by John Scott and Peter J. Carrington. Los Angeles and London: SAGE Publications, Inc.

Castells, Manuel. 1996. *The Information Age: Economy, Society and Culture, Vol. I: The Rise of the Network Society*. Malden, MA: Blackwell Publishers.

Castilla, Emilio, Hokyu Hwang, Ellen Granovetter, and Mark Granovetter. 2000. "Social Networks in Silicon Valley." Pp. 218–47 in *The Silicon Valley Edge: A Habitat for Innovation and Entrepreneurship*, edited by Chong-Moon Lee, Henry S. Rowen, William F. Miller, and Marguerite Gong Hancock. Stanford, CA: Stanford University Press.

Chaves, Mark. 1997. *Ordaining Women: Culture and Conflict in Religious Organizations*. Cambridge, MA: Harvard University Press.

Christakis, Nicholas, and James Fowler. 2009. *Connected: The Surprising Power of Our Social Networks and How They Shape Our Lives*. London: Little, Brown and Company.

Clauset, Aaron, Mark E. J. Newman, and Cristopher Moore. 2004. "Finding Community Structure in Very Large Networks." *Physical Review E* 70: 066111.

Clayton, Philip, and Paul Davies (Eds.). 2006. *The Re-emergence of Emergence: The Emergentist Hypothesis from Science to Religion*. Oxford and New York: Oxford University Press.

Cohen-Cole, Ethan, and Jason M. Fletcher. 2008. "Detecting Implausible Social Network Effects in Acne, Height, and Headaches: Longitudinal Analysis." *British Medical Journal* 337:a2533. Retrieved from http://www.bmj.com/content/337/bmj.a2533.full.pdf.

Cole, Darrell. 2002. *When God Says War Is Right*. Colorado Springs, CO: Waterbrook Press.

Coleman, James S. 1964. *Introduction to Mathematical Sociology*. New York: Free Press.

Coleman, James S., Elihu Katz, and Herbert Menzel. 1957. "The Diffusion of an Innovation among Physicians." *Sociometry* 20:253–269.

Collins, Randall. 2004. *Interaction Ritual Chains*. Princeton, NJ: Princeton University Press.

Colloton, Patrick T., Benjamin R. Maitre, and Tommy E. Stoner. 2007. "An Adaptive Security Construct: Insurgency in Sudan." Master's Thesis, Department of Defense Analysis, Naval Postgraduate School, Monterey, CA.

Cook, Karen S., and Richard M. Emerson. 1978. "Power, Equity and Commitment in Exchange Networks." *American Sociological Review* 43:712–739.

Cook, Karen S., Richard M. Emerson, Mary R. Gilmore, and Toshio Yamagishi. 1983. "The Distribution of Power in Exchange Networks." *American Journal of Sociology* 89:275–305.

Cook, Karen S., Mary R. Gillmore, and Toshio Yamagishi. 1986. "Point and Line Vulnerability as Bases for Predicting the Distribution of Power in Exchange Networks: Reply to Willer." *American Journal of Sociology* 92(2):445–448.

Cook, Karen S., and J. M. Whitmeyer. 1992. "Two Approaches to Social Structure: Exchange Theory and Network Analysis." *Annual Review of Sociology* 18:109–127.

Cooper, Helene. 2009. "Dreaming of Splitting the Taliban." *The New York Times*. Retrieved from http://www.nytimes.com/2009/03/08/weekinreview/08COOPER.html?_r=.1.

Cordoba, J.-R. 2006. "Using Foucault to Analyse Ethics in the Practice of Problem Structuring Methods." *Journal of the Operational Research Society* 57(9):1027–1034.

Cormen, Thomas H., Charles E. Leiserson, Ronald L. Rivest, and Clifford Stein. 2009. *Introduction to Algorithms*. 3rd ed. Cambridge, MA: MIT Press.

Crile, George. 2003. *Charlie Wilson's War: The Extraordinary Story of the Largest Covert Operation in History*. New York: Atlantic Monthly Press.

Cyram. 2009. *CyramNetminer 3*. Seoul, Korea: Cyram Co., Ltd.

Davis, Allison, Burleigh B. Gardner, and Mary R. Gardner. 1941. *Deep South: A Social-Anthropological Study of Caste and Class*. Chicago: University of Chicago Press.

Davis, James A. 1979. "The Davis/Holland/Leinhardt Studies: An Overview." Pp. 51–62 in *Perspectives on Social Network Research*, edited by Paul W. Holland and Samuel Leinhardt. New York: Academic Press.

de Nooy, Wouter. 2011. "Networks of Action and Events over Time: A Multilevel Discrete-Time Event History Model for Longitudinal Network Data." *Social Networks* 33(1):31–40.

de Nooy, Wouter, Andrej Mrvar, and Vladimir Batagelj. 2005. *Exploratory Social Network Analysis with Pajek*. Cambridge, UK: Cambridge University Press.

———. 2011. *Exploratory Social Network Analysis with Pajek*. Revised and expanded ed. Cambridge, UK: Cambridge University Press.

Degenne, Alain, and Michael Forsé. 1999. *Introducing Social Networks*. Translated by Arthur Borges. Thousand Oaks, CA: SAGE Publications.

Dekker, David, David Krackhardt, and Tom Snijders. 2007. "Sensitivity of MRQAP Tests to Collinearity and Autocorrelation Conditions." *Psychometrika* 72(4):563–581.

DiMaggio, Paul J., and Walter W. Powell. 1983. "The Iron Cage Revisited: Institutional Isomorphism and Collective Rationality in Organizational Fields." *American Sociological Review* 48(2):147–160.

Doreian, Patrick. 1987. "Measuring Regular Equivalence in Symmetric Structures." *Social Networks* 9:89–107.

Doreian, Patrick, Vladimir Batagelj, and Anuska Ferligoj. 2005. *Generalized Blockmodeling*. New York and Cambridge: Cambridge University Press.

Doreian, Patrick, and F. N. Stockman (Eds.). 1997. *Evolution of Social Networks*. Amsterdam: Gordon and Breach Publishers.

Easley, David, and Jon Kleinberg. 2010. *Networks, Crowds, and Markets: Reasoning about a Highly Connected World*. Cambridge and New York: Cambridge University Press.

Emerson, Richard M. 1962. "Power-Dependence Relations." *American Sociological Review* 27(1):31–41.

———. 1972a. "Exchange Theory, Part I: A Psychological Basis for Social Exchange." Pp. 38–57 in *Sociological Theories in Progress*, edited by Joseph Berger, Morris Zelditch, and B. Anderson. Boston: Houghton-Mifflin.

———. 1972b. "Exchange Theory, Part II: Exchange Relations and Network Structures." Pp. 58–87 in *Sociological Theories in Progress*, edited by Joseph Berger, Morris Zelditch, and B. Anderson. Boston: Houghton-Mifflin.

———. 1976. "Social Exchange Theory." Pp. 335–362 in *Annual Review of Sociology*. Palo Alto, CA: Annual Reviews.

Emirbayer, Mustafa, and Jeff Goodwin. 1994. "Network Analysis, Culture, and the Problem of Agency." *American Journal of Sociology* 99(6):1411–1454.

Erickson, Bonnie H. 1981. "Secret Societies and Social Structure." *Social Forces* 60(1):188–210.

———. 2001. "Social Networks." Pp. 314–326 in *Blackwell Companion to Sociology*. Oxford, UK: Blackwell Publishing, Ltd.

Everett, Martin G., and Stephen P. Borgatti. 2005. "Extending Centrality." Pp. 57–76 in *Models and Methods in Social Network Analysis*, edited by Peter J. Carrington, John Scott, and Stanley Wasserman. New York: Cambridge University Press.

Everett, Martin G., John Paul Boyd, and Stephen P. Borgatti. 1990. "Ego-Centered and Local Roles: A Graph Theoretic Approach." *Journal of Mathematical Sociology* 15:163–172.

Everton, Sean F. 2004. *A Guide for the Visually Perplexed: Visually Representing Social Networks*. 4th ed. Stanford, CA: Stanford University.

———. 2007. "To Have and Have Not: IT-Experience, Organizational Status, and Success in the Venture Capital Industry." Doctoral Thesis, Department of Sociology, Stanford University, Stanford, CA.

———. 2012. "Network Topography, Key Players and Terrorist Networks." *Connections* 31(2):1–8.

Everton, Sean F., and Stephen Lieberman. 2009. "Parsimony and the Quantification of Small World Networks." Monterey, CA: Naval Postgraduate School.

Eyre, Keely, Ben Johnson, and Ian McCulloh. 2010. *Ideology, Ethics, Co-authorship Network*. Paper presented at the Sunbelt XXX, the Annual Meeting of the International Network of Social Network Analysts, Riva del Garda, Italy.

Faust, Katherine. 1988. "Comparison of Methods for Positional Analysis: Structural and General Equivalences." *Social Networks* 10:313–341.

———. 1997. "Centrality in Affiliation Networks." *Social Networks* 19:157–191.

Felter, Joseph, and Brian Fishman. 2007. "Al-Qa'ida'sForeign Fighters in Iraq: A First Look at the Sinjar Records." Retrieved from http://www.ctc.usma.edu/posts/al-qaidas-foreign-fighters-in-iraq-a-first-look-at-the-sinjar-records.

Fernandez, Roberto M., and Roger V. Gould. 1994. "A Dilemma of State Power: Brokerage and Influence in the National-Health Policy Domain." *American Journal of Sociology* 99(6):1455–1491.

Fink, Naureen Chowdhury, and Ellie B. Hearne. 2008. "Beyond Terrorism: Deradicalization and Disengagement from Violent Extremism." Retrieved from http://www.ipinst.org/media/pdf/publications/beter.pdf.

Finke, Roger, and Rodney Stark. 2005. *The Churching of America, 1776–2005: Winners and Losers in Our Religious Economy*. 2nd ed. New Brunswick, NJ: Rutgers University Press.

Fischer, Claude S. 2009. "The 2004 GSS Finding of Shrunken Social Networks: An Artifact?" *American Sociological Review* 74:657–669.

Flynn, Michael T., Matt Pottinger, and Paul D. Batchelor. 2010. *Fixing Intel: A Blueprint for Making Intelligence Relevant in Afghanistan*. Washington, D.C.: Center for a New American Security.

Frank, David John, Ann Hironaka, and Evan Schofer. 2000. "The Nation-State and the Natural Environment over the Twentieth Century." *American Sociological Review* 65(1):96–116.

Frankfort-Nachmias, Chava, and David Nachmias. 1996. *Research Methods in the Social Sciences*. New York: St. Martin's Press.

Freeman, Linton C. 1977. "A Set of Measures of Centrality Based on Betweenness." *Sociometry* 40:35–41.

———. 1979. "Centrality in Social Networks I: Conceptual Clarification." *Social Networks* 1:215–239.

———. 1999. "Using Molecular Modeling Software in Social Network Analysis: A Practicum." Unpublished paper. University of California, Irvine.

———. 2000. "Visualizing Social Networks." *Journal of Social Structure* 1(1). Retrieved from http://www.cmu.edu/joss/content/articles/volume1/Freeman .html.

———. 2004. *The Development of Social Network Analysis: A Study in the Sociology of Science*. Vancouver, Canada: Empirical Press.

———. 2005. "Graphic Techniques for Exploring Social Network Data." Pp. 248–269 in *Models and Methods in Social Network Analysis*, edited by Peter J. Carrington, John Scott, and Stanley Wasserman. New York: Cambridge University Press.

———. 2011. "The Development of Social Network Analysis – with an Emphasis on Recent Events." Pp. 26–39 in *The SAGE Handbook of Social Network Analysis*, edited by John Scott and Peter J. Carrington. Los Angeles and London: SAGE Publications, Inc.

Freeman, Linton C., Stephen P. Borgatti, and Douglas R. White. 1991. "Centrality in Valued Graphs: A Measure of Betweenness Based on Network Flow." *Social Networks* 13:141–154.

Freeman, Linton C., Cynthia M. Webster, and Deirdre M. Kirke. 1998. "Exploring Social Structure Using Dynamic Three-Dimensional Color Images." *Social Networks* 20:109–118.

Fridovich, David P., and Fred T. Krawchuck. 2007. "Special Operations Forces: Indirect Approach." *Joint Forces Quarterly* 44(1):24–27.

Friedkin, Noah E. 1981. "The Development of Structure in Random Networks: An Analysis of the Effects of Increasing Network Density on Five Measures of Structure." *Social Networks* 3(1):41–52.

———. 1991. "Theoretical Foundations for Centrality Measures." *American Journal of Sociology* 96(6):1478–1504.

———. 1998. *A Structural Theory of Social Influence*. New York: Cambridge University Press.

Friedman, Milton. 1962. *Capitalism and Freedom*. Chicago: University of Chicago Press.

Friedman, Milton, and Rose D. Friedman. 1980. *Free to Choose: A Personal Statement*. New York: Harcourt Brace Jovanovich.

Friedman, Thomas L. 2010. "Broadway and the Mosque." *The New York Times*. Retrieved from http://www.nytimes.com/2010/08/04/opinion/04friedman.html?_r=1&ref=thomaslfriedman.

Fruchterman, T., and E. Reingold. 1991. "Graph Drawing by Force-Directed Replacement." *Software–Practice and Experience* 21(11):1129–1164.

Galula, David. [1964] 2006. *Counterinsurgency Warfare: Theory and Practice*. Westport, CT: Praeger Security International.

Giddens, Anthony, Mitchell Duneier, and Richard P. Appelbaum. 2006. *Essentials of Sociology*. New York and London: W. W. Norton & Company, Inc.

Girvan, Michelle, and Mark E. J. Newman. 2002. "Community Structure in Social and Biological Networks." *Proceedings of the National Academy of Sciences USA* 99(12):7821–7826.

Gjelten, Tom. 2010. "U.S. 'Connects the Dots' to Catch Roadside Bombers." *Morning Edition*. Retrieved from http://www.npr.org/2010/12/03/131755378/u-s-connects-the-dots-to-catch-roadside-bombers.

Glock, Charles Y. 1964. "The Role of Deprivation in the Origin and Evolution of Religious Groups." Pp. 24–36 in *Religion and Social Conflict*, edited by Robert Lee and Martin E. Marty. New York: Oxford University Press.

Gould, Roger V. 1991. "Multiple Networks and Mobilization in the Paris Commune, 1871." *American Sociological Review* 56:716–729.

———. 1993a. "Collective Action and Network Structure." *American Sociological Review* 58(1):182–196.

———. 1993b. "Trade Cohesion, Class Unity, and Urban Insurrection: Artisanal Activism in the Paris Commune." *American Journal of Sociology* 98(4):721–754.

Gould, Roger V., and Roberto M. Fernandez. 1989. "Structures of Mediation: A Formal Approach to Brokerage in Transaction Networks." *Sociological Methodology* 19:89–126.

Granovetter, Mark. 1973. "The Strength of Weak Ties." *American Journal of Sociology* 73(6):1360–1380.

———. 1974. *Getting a Job*. Cambridge, MA: Harvard University Press.

———. 1979. "The Theory-Gap in Social Network Analysis." Pp. 501–518 in *Perspectives on Social Network Research*, edited by Paul W. Holland and Samuel Leinhardt. New York: Academic Press.

———. 1983. "The Strength of Weak Ties: A Network Theory Revisited." *Sociological Theory* 1:201–233.

———. 1985. "Economic Action and Social Structure: The Problem of Embeddedness." *American Journal of Sociology* 91:481–510.

———. 1992. "Problems of Explanation of Economic Sociology." Pp. 29–56 in *Networks and Organizations: Structure, Form and Action*, edited by Nitin Nohria and Robert G. Eccles. Boston: Harvard Business School Press.

———. 2005. "The Impact of Social Structure on Economic Outcomes." *Journal of Economic Perspectives* 19(1):33–50.

Hamilton, Lawrence C. 1992. *Regression with Graphics: A Second Course in Applied Statistics*. Belmont, CA: Duxbury Press.

———. 1996. *Data Analysis for Social Scientists*. Belmont, CA: Duxbury Press.

Hanneman, Robert A., and Mark Riddle. 2005. "Introduction to Social Network Methods." Retrieved from http://faculty.ucr.edu/~hanneman/nettext/.

———. 2011. "Concepts and Measures for Basic Network Analysis." Pp. 340–369 in *The SAGE Handbook of Social Network Analysis*, edited by John Scott and Peter J. Carrington. Los Angeles and London: SAGE Publications, Inc.

Harary, Frank. 1953. "On the Notion of Balance in a Signed Graph." *Michigan Mathematical Journal* 2:143–146.

———. 1969. *Graph Theory*. Reading: Addison-Wesley.

Harary, Frank, and Robert Zane Norman. 1953. *Graph Theory as a Mathematical Model in Social Science*. Ann Arbor, MI: University of Michigan.

Hayek, Friedrich A. von. 1994 [1944]. *The Road to Serfdom*. Chicago: University of Chicago Press.

Heider, Fritz. 1977. "Attitudes and Cognitive Organization." *Journal of Psychology* 21:107–112.

Henslin, James M. 2007. *Sociology: A Down-to-Earth Approach*. 8th ed. Boston, MA: Allyn and Bacon.

Hoffman, Bruce. 2008. "The Myth of Grass-Roots Terrorism: Why Osama bin Laden Still Matters." *Foreign Affairs* 87(3):133–138.

Høivik, Tord, and Nils Petter Gleditsch. 1975. "Structural Parameters of Graphs: A Theoretical Investigation." Pp. 203–22 in *Quantitative Sociology*, edited by H. M. Blalock. New York: Academic Press.

Holland, Paul W., and Samuel Leinhardt. 1971. "Transitivity of Structural Models of Small Groups." *Comparative Group Studies* 2:107–124.

———. 1972. "Some Evidence on the Transitivity of Positive Interpersonal Sentiment." *American Journal of Sociology* 72:1205–1209.

Homans, George C. 1950. *The Human Group*. New York: Harcourt, Brace & World.

Horgan, John. 2009. *Walking Away from Terrorism: Accounts of Disengagement from Radical and Extremist Movements*. New York: Routledge.

Hu, Daning, Siddharth Kaza, and Hsinchun Chen. 2009. "Identifying Significant Facilitators of Dark Network Evolution." *Journal of the American Society for Information Science and Technology* 60(4):655–665.

Hubbell, Charles H. 1965. "An Input-Output Approach to Clique Identification." *Sociometry* 28(4):377–399.

Huisman, Mark, and Marijtje A. van Duijn. 2005. "Software for Social Network Analysis." Pp. 270–316 in *Models and Methods in Social Network Analysis*, edited by Peter J. Carrington, John Scott, and Stanley Wasserman. Cambridge and New York: Cambridge University Press.

———. 2011. "A Reader's Guide to SNA Software." Pp. 578–600 in *The SAGE Handbook of Social Network Analysis*, edited by John Scott and Peter J. Carrington. Los Angeles and London: SAGE Publications, Inc.

Humphreys, Laud. 1975. *Tearoom Trade: Impersonal Sex in Public Places*. Hawthorne, NY: Adeline.

Iannaccone, Laurence R. 1995. "Risk, Rationality, and Religious Portfolios." *Economic Inquiry* 38(2):285–295.

International Crisis Group. 2006. "Terrorism in Indonesia: Noordin's Networks." Brussels, Belgium: International Crisis Group.

———. 2009a. "The Hotel Bombings." Brussels, Belgium: International Crisis Group.

———. 2009b. "Indonesia: Noordin Top's Support Base." Brussels, Belgium: International Crisis Group.

———. 2010. "Indonesia: Jihadi Surprise in Aceh." Brussels, Belgium: International Crisis Group.

Israel, Mark, and Iain Hay. 2006. *Research Ethics for Social Scientists*. London, UK, and Thousand Oaks, CA: SAGE Publications.

Jackson, Matthew O. 2008. *Social and Economic Networks*. Princeton, NJ: Princeton University Press.

Johnson, Byron R. 2011. *More God, Less Crime: Why Faith Matters and How It Could Matter More*. West Conshohocken, PA: Templeton Press.

Jones, Seth G., and Martin C. Libicki. 2008. *How Terrorist Groups End: Lessons for Countering al Qa'ida*. Santa Monica, CA: RAND Corporation.

Jordan, Javier, Fernando M. Mañas, and Nicola Horsburgh. 2008. "Strengths and Weaknesses of Grassroot Jihadist Networks: The Madrid Bombings." *Studies in Conflict & Terrorism* 31:17–21.

Juergensmeyer, Mark. 2001. *Terror in the Mind of God*. Berkeley, CA: University of California Press.

Kadushin, Charles. 2005. "Who Benefits from Social Network Analysis: Ethics of Social Network Research." *Social Networks* 27:139–153.

———. 2012. *Understanding Social Networks: Theories, Concepts, and Findings*. Oxford and New York: Oxford University Press.

Kamada, T., and S. Kawai. 1989. "An Algorithm for Drawing General Undirected Graphs." *Information Processing Letters* 31:7–15.

Kant, Immanuel. 1991. "On the Relation of Theory to Practice in Political Right." Pp. 73–86 in *Kant's Political Writings*, edited by Hans Reiss. Cambridge: Cambridge University Press.

———. 1997 [1785]. *Groundwork for the Metaphysics of Morals*. Translated by Mary Gregor. Cambridge, UK: Cambridge University Press.

Katz, Leo. 1953. "A New Status Index Derived from Sociometric Data Analysis." *Psychometrika* 18(1):34–43.

Kilcullen, David. 2008. "Political Maneuver in Counterinsurgency: Road-Building in Afghanistan." *Small Wars Journal*.

———. 2009. *The Accidental Guerrilla: Fighting Small Wars in the Midst of a Big One*. Oxford and New York: Oxford University Press.

———. 2010. *Counterinsurgency*. Oxford and New York: Oxford University Press.

Kilduff, Martin, and Wenpin Tsai. 2003. *Social Networks and Organizations*. Thousand Oaks, CA: SAGE Publications.

Kleinberg, Jon. 1999. "Authoritative Sources in a Hyperlinked Environment." *Journal of the ACM* 46(5):604–632.

———. 2000. "The Small World Phenomenon: An Algorithmic Perspective." *Proceedings of the 32nd ACM Symposium on Theory of Computing* 163–170.

Klerks, Peter. 2001. "The Network Paradigm Applied to Criminal Organisations: Theoretical Nitpicking or a Relevant Doctrine for Investigators? Recent Developments in the Netherlands." *Connections* 24(3):53–65.

Klovdahl, Alden S.2005. "Social Network Research and Human Subjects Protection: Towards More Effective Infectious Disease Control." *Social Networks* 27:119–137.

Knoke, David. 1990. *Political Networks: The Structural Perspective*. Cambridge: Cambridge University Press.

Knoke, David, and Edward O. Laumann. 1982. "The Social Structure of National Policy Domains: An Exploration of Some Structural Hypothesis." Pp. 255–270 in *Social Structure and Network Analysis*, edited by Peter V. Marsden and Nan Lin. Beverly Hills, CA: SAGE Publications.

Knoke, David, and Song Yang. 2007. *Social Network Analysis*. 2nd ed. Thousand Oaks, CA: SAGE Publications.

Kontopoulos, Kyriakos M. 1993. *The Logics of Social Structure*. New York: Cambridge University Press.

Koschade, Stuart. 2006. "A Social Network Analysis of Jemaah Islamiyah: The Applications to Counterterrorism and Intelligence." *Studies in Conflict & Terrorism* 29:559–575.

Kossinets, Gueorgi, and Duncan J. Watts. 2006. "Empirical Analysis of an Evolving Social Network." *Science* 311:88–90.

Krackhardt, David. 1987a. "Cognitive Social Structures." *Social Networks* 9:109–134.

———. 1987b. "QAP Partialling as a Test of Spuriousness." *Social Networks* 9:171–186.

———. 1992. "The Strength of Strong Ties: The Importance of Philos in Organizations." Pp. 216–239 in *Networks and Organizations: Structure, Form, and Action*, edited by Nitin Nohria and Robert G. Eccles. Boston: Harvard Business School Press.

———. 1994. "Graph Theoretical Dimensions of Informal Organizations." Pp. 89–111 in *Computational Organization Theory*, edited by Kathleen M. Carley and Michael J. Prietula. Hillsdale, NJ: Lawrence Erlbaum Associates.

Krawchuck, Fred T. ND. "Winning the Global War on Terrorism in the Pacific Region: Special Operations Forces' Indirect Approach to Success." Retrieved from http://igcc3.ucsd.edu/pdf/krawchuk.pdf.

Krebs, Valdis. 2001. "Mapping Networks of Terrorist Cells." *Connections* 24 (3):43–52.

Kruskal, Joseph B., and Myron Wish. 1978. *Multidimensional Scaling*. Newbury Park, CA: SAGE Publications.

Laumann, Edward O., Peter V. Marsden, and David Prensky 1983. "The Boundary-Specification Problem in Network Analysis." Pp. 18–34 in *Applied Network Analysis*, edited by Ronald S. Burt and Michael Minor. Beverly Hills, CA: SAGE Publications.

———. 1989. "The Boundary-Specification Problem in Network Analysis." Pp. 61–87 in *Research Methods in Social Network Analysis*, edited by Linton C. Freeman, Douglas R. White, and A. K. Romney. Beverly Hills, CA: SAGE Publications.

Leavitt, Harold J. 1951. "Some Effects of Communication Patterns on Group Performance." *Journal of Abnormal and Social Psychology* 46:38–50.

Lempert, Robert J., Horacio R. Trujillo, David Aaron, James A. Dewar, Sandra H. Berry, and Steven W. Popper. 2008. "Comparing Alternative U.S. Counter terrorism Strategies: Can Assumption-Based Planning Help Elevate the Debate?" Retrieved from http://www.rand.org/pubs/documented_briefings/2008/RAND_DB548.pdf.

Levitt, Steven D., and Stephen J. Dubner. 2005. *Freakanomics: A Rogue Economist Explores the Hidden Side of Everything.* New York: HarperCollins.

Lewin, Kurt. 1951. *Field Theory in the Social Sciences.* New York: Harper.

Lewis, Ted G. 2009. *Network Science: Theory and Applications.* Hoboken, NJ: John Wiley & Sons, Inc.

Lin, Nan. 1976. *Foundations of Social Research.* New York: McGraw-Hill.

Lofland, John. 1977. "'Becoming a World-Saver' Revisited." *American Behavioral Scientist* 20:805–818.

Lofland, John, and Rodney Stark. 1965. "Becoming a World-Saver: A Theory of Conversion to a Deviant Perspective." *American Sociological Review* 30:862–875.

Long, J. Scott. 1997. *Regression Models for Categorical and Limited Dependent Variables.* Advanced Quantitative Techniques in the Social Sciences Series. Thousand Oaks, CA: SAGE Publications.

Lyons, Russell. 2011. "The Spread of Evidence-Poor Medicine via Flawed Social-Network Analysis." *Statistics, Politics and Policy* 2(1), Article 2: Retrieved from http://www.bepress.com/spp/vol2/iss1/2/.

MacIntyre, Alasdair. 1984. *After Virtue: A Study in Moral Theory.* 2nd ed. Notre Dame, IN: University of Notre Dame Press.

———. 1988. *Whose Justice? Which Rationality?* 2nd ed. Notre Dame, IN: University of Notre Dame Press.

———. 1990. *Three Rival Versions of Moral Enquiry: Encyclopaedia, Genealogy and Tradition.* 2nd ed. Notre Dame, IN: University of Notre Dame Press.

———. 1999. *Rational Dependent Animals: Why Human Beings Need the Virtues.* Chicago: Open Court Publishing Company.

Magouirk, Justin, Scott Atran, and Marc Sageman. 2008. "Connecting Terrorist Networks." *Studies in Conflict & Terrorism* 31:1–16.

Marks, Steven, Thomas Meer, and Matthew Nilson. 2005. "Manhunting: A Methodology for Finding Persons of National Interest." Master of Science Thesis, Defense Analysis Department, Naval Postgraduate School, Monterey, CA.

Marsden, Peter V. 1987. "Core Discussion Networks of Americans." *American Sociological Review* 52(1):122–131.

Maurer, Kevin. 2010. "'Psychological Operations' Are Now 'Military Information Support Operations.'" *Public Intelligence* (July 3). Retrieved from http://publicintelligence.net/psychological-operations-are-now-military-information-support-operations/.

Mayhew, Bruce H. 1980. "Structuralism versus Individualism: Part I, Shadowboxing in the Dark." *Social Forces* 59(2):335–374.

Mayo, Elton. 1933. *The Human Problems of an Industrial Civilization.* Cambridge, MA: Macmillan.

———. 1945. *The Social Problems of an Industrial Civilization.* London: Routledge and Kegan Paul.

McAdam, Doug. 1982. *Political Process and the Development of Black Insurgency, 1930–1970.* Chicago: University of Chicago Press.

———. 1986. "Recruitment to High Risk Activism: The Case of Freedom Summer." *American Journal of Sociology* 92:64–90.

———. 1988a. *Freedom Summer*. New York and Oxford: Oxford University Press.

———. 1988b. "Micromobilization Contexts and Recruitment to Activism." *International Social Movement Research* 1:125–154.

———. 1999. *Political Process and the Development of Black Insurgency, 1930–1970*. 2nd ed. Chicago: University of Chicago Press.

McAdam, Doug, and Ronnelle Paulsen. 1993. "Specifying the Relationship Between Social Ties and Activism." *American Journal of Sociology* 99:640–667.

McAdam, Doug, Sidney Tarrow, and Charles Tilly. 2001. *Dynamics of Contention*. New York and Cambridge: Cambridge University Press.

McCarthy, John D., and Mayer N. Zald. 1977. "Resource Mobilization and Social Movements: A Partial Theory." *American Journal of Sociology* 82(6): 1212–1241.

McCloskey, Deirdre. 1995. "The Insignificance of Statistical Significance." *Scientific American* April:32–33.

McCormick, Gordon. 2005. "The Diamond Insurgent/COIN Model." Unpublished Paper. Department of Defense Analysis, Naval Postgraduate School, Monterrey, CA.

McCulloh, Ian, and Kathleen M. Carley. 2011. "Detecting Change in Longitudinal Social Networks." *Journal of Social Structure* 12(3):1–37. Retrieved from http://www.cmu.edu/joss/content/articles/volume12//McCullohCarley.pdf.

McFarland, Daniel A. 2004. "Resistance as Social Drama: A Study of Change-Oriented Behaviors." *American Journal of Sociology* 109(6):1249–1318.

McGrath, Cathleen, Jim Blythe, and David Krackhardt. 1997. "The Effect of Spatial Arrangements on Judgments and Errors in Interpreting Graphs." *Social Networks* 19:223–242.

McIntyre, Lisa J. 2002. *The Practical Skeptic: Core Concepts in Sociology*. 2nd ed. Boston, MA: McGraw-Hill Higher Education.

McPherson, J. Miller, Lynn Smith-Lovin, and Matthew E. Brashears. 2006. "Social Isolation in America: Changes in Core Discussion Networks over Two Decades." *American Sociological Review* 71(June):353–375.

Metelits, Claire. 2010. *Inside Insurgency: Violence, Civilians, and Revolutionary Group Behavior*. New York and London: New York University Press.

Meyer, John W., John Boli, George M. Thomas, and Francisco O. Ramirez. 1997. "World Society and the Nation-State." *American Journal of Sociology* 103(1):144–181.

Meyer, John W., and Brian Rowan. 1977. "Institutionalized Organizations: Formal Structure as Myth and Ceremony." *American Journal of Sociology* 83(2):340–363.

Milgram, Stanley. 1967. "The Small-World Problem." *Psychology Today* 1(May):61–67.

———. 1974. *Obedience to Authority*. Princeton, NJ: Princeton University Press.

Mill, John Stuart. 1989 [1859]. *On Liberty*. Stefan Collini, ed., Cambridge, UK and New York: Cambridge University Press.

———. 2010 [1863]. *Utilitarianism*. Indianapolis, IN: Hackett Publishing Company, Inc.

Miller, Robert T. 2011. "Waiting for St. Vladimir." *First Things* February:37–43.

Milward, H. Brinton, and Jörg Raab. 2006. "Dark Networks as Organizational Problems: Elements of a Theory." *International Public Management Journal* 9(3):333–360.

Mitchell, J. Clyde (Ed.). 1969. *Social Networks in Urban Situations: Analyses of Personal Relationships in Central African Towns*. Manchester, England: Manchester University Press.

Moody, James. 2001. "Peer Influence Groups: Identifying Dense Clusters in Large Networks." *Social Networks* (23):261–283.

———. 2005. "Fighting a Hydra: A Note on the Network Embeddedness of the War on Terror." *Structure and Dynamics* 1(2). Retrieved from http://escholarship.org/uc/item/7x3881bs.

Moreno, Jacob L. 1953. *Who Shall Survive? Foundations of Sociometry, Group Psychotherapy and Sociodrama*. Beacon, NY: Beacon House.

Moreno, Jacob L., and Helen H. Jennings. 1938. "Statistics of Social Configurations." *Sociometry* 1:342–374.

Mortenson, Greg, and Mike Bryan. 2009. *Stones into Schools: Promoting Peace with Books, Not Bombs, in Afghanistan and Pakistan*. New York: Viking.

Mortenson, Greg, and David Oliver Relin. 2006. *Three Cups of Tea: One Man's Mission to Fight Terrorism and Build Nations . . . One School at a Time*. New York: Viking.

Murphy, Phil, Sean F. Everton, and Daniel Cunningham. 2012. *Casting More Light on Dark Networks*. Paper presented at the Sunbelt XXXII: The Annual Meeting of the International Network for Social Network Analysis, Redondo Beach, CA.

Mydans, Seth. 2008. "Nasir Abbas, Terrorist Defector, Aids Indonesian Police." *International Herald Tribune* (September 12). Retrieved from http://www.iht.com/articles/2008/02/29/asia/profile.php.

Nadel, Siegfried F. 1957. *The Theory of Social Structure*. London: Cohen & West.

Nagl, John A. 2005. *Learning to Eat Soup with a Knife: Counterinsurgency Lessons from Malaya and Vietnam*. Chicago: University of Chicago Press.

Nakamura, David, and Javed Hamdard. 2010. "Petraeus Condemn's Fla. Church's Plan to Burn Koran." *The Washington Post*. Retrieved from http://www.washingtonpost.com/wp-dyn/content/article/2010/09/07/AR2010090701595.html.

National Council of Bishops. 1983. *The Challenge of Peace: God's Promise and Our Response*. Washington, D.C.: United States Catholic Conference.

Neuman, W. Lawrence. 1997. *Social Research Methods: Qualitative and Quantitative Approaches*. 3rd ed. Boston: Allyn and Bacon.

Newman, Mark E. J. 2004. "Detecting Community Structure in Networks." *European Physical Journal* 38(2):321–330.

———. 2006. "Modularity and Community Structure in Networks." *Proceedings of the National Academy of Sciences* 103 (23):8577–8582.

Nohria, Nitin. 1992. "Is the Network Perspective a Useful Way of Studying Organizations?" Pp. 1–22 in *Networks and Organizations: Structure, Form, and Action*, edited by Nitin Nohria and Robert G. Eccles. Boston: Harvard Business School Press.

Nohria, Nitin, and Robert G. Eccles (Eds.). 1992. *Networks and Organizations: Structure, Form, and Action*. Boston: Harvard Business School Press.

Nossiter, Adam. 2011. "Nigerian Group Escalates Violence with Church Attacks." *The New York Times*. Retrieved from http://www.nytimes.com/2011/12/26/world/africa/explosion-rips-through-catholic-church-in-nigeria.html?_r=1&scp=1&sq=nigerian%20churches&st=cse.

Nozick, Robert. 1977. *Anarchy, State, and Utopia*. New York: Basic Books.

Olson, Jamie F., and Kathleen M. Carley. 2009. *Combining Geographic Information and Network Analysis*. Paper presented at the Sunbelt XXIX: The Annual Meeting of the International Network for Social Network Analysis, San Diego, CA.

Onnela, Jukka-Pekka, Jari Saramaki, J. Hyvönen, Gabor Szabo, David Lazer, Kimmo Kaski, J. Kertész, and Barabasi, Albert-Laszlo. 2007. "Structure and Tie Strengths in Mobile Communication Networks." *Proceedings of the National Academy of Sciences of the USA* 104(18):7332–7336.

Osa, Maryjane. 2003. "Networks of Opposition: Linking Organizations through Activists in the Polish People's Republic." Pp. 77–104 in *Social Movements and Networks: Relational Approaches to Collective Action*, edited by Mario Diani and Doug McAdam. New York and Oxford: Oxford University Press.

Padgett, John F., and Christopher K. Ansell. 1993. "Robust Action and the Rise of the Medici, 1400–1434." *American Journal of Sociology* 98:1259–1319.

Page, E. S. 1961. "Cumulative Sum Control Charts." *Technometrics* 3(1):1–9.

Passy, Florence. 2003. "Social Networks Matter. But How?" Pp. 21–48 in *Social Movements and Networks: Relational Approaches to Collective Action*, edited by Mario Diani and Doug McAdam. Oxford and New York: Oxford University Press.

Pedahzur, Ami, and Arie Perliger. 2006. "The Changing Nature of Suicide Attacks: A Social Network Perspective." *Social Forces* 84(4):1987–2008.

Perez, Evan. 2010. "White House Defends Targeted Killing Program." *The Wall Street Journal*. Retrieved from http://online.wsj.com/article/SB10001424052748703793804575512283152390778.html#.

Pescosolido, Bernice A., and Sharon Georgianna. 1989. "Durkheim, Suicide, and Religion: Toward a Network Theory of Suicide." *American Sociological Review* 54(1):33–48.

Peter, Tom A. 2008. "U.S. Begins Hunting Iraq's Bombmakers, Not Just Bombs." *Christian Science Monitor*. Retrieved from http://www.csmonitor.com/2008/0908/p04s01-wome.html.

Podolny, Joel M., and Karen L. Page. 1998. "Network Forms of Organization." *Annual Review of Sociology* 24:57–76.

Popielarz, Pamela A., and J. Miller McPherson. 1995. "On the Edge or in Between: Niche Position, Niche Overlap, and the Duration of Voluntary Association Memberships." *American Journal of Sociology* 101(3):698–720.

Popkin, Samuel L. 2007. *Discussion*. Paper presented at the Terrorist Organizations: Conference Sponsored by the University of California Institute on Global Conflict and Cooperation, La Jolla, CA.

Powell, Walter W. 1985. "Hybrid Organizational Arrangements: New Form or Transitional Development." *California Management Review* 30(1):67–87.

———. 1990. "Neither Market Nor Hierarchy: Network Forms of Organization." Pp. 295–336 in *Research in Organizational Behavior: An Annual Series of Analytical Essays and Critical Reviews*, edited by Barry M. Staw and Larry L. Cummings. Greenwich, CT: JAI Press, Inc.

Powell, Walter W., and Paul J. DiMaggio (Eds.). 1991. *The New Institutionalism in Organizational Analysis*. Chicago and London: University of Chicago Press.

Powell, Walter W., and Laurel Smith-Doerr. 1994. "Networks and Economic Life." Pp. 368–402 in *The Handbook of Economic Sociology*, edited by Neil J. Smelser and Richard Swedberg. Princeton, NJ: Princeton University Press.

Prell, Christina. 2011. *Social Network Analysis: History, Theory & Methodology*. London and Thousand Oaks, CA: SAGE Publications.

R Development Core Team. 2011. "R: A Language and Environment for Statistical Computing." Vienna, Austria: R Foundation for Statistical Computing.

Raab, Jörg, and H. Brinton Milward. 2003. "Dark Networks as Problems." *Journal of Public Administration Research and Theory* 13(4):413–439.

Rabasa, Angel. 2005. "Islamic Education in Southeast Asia." Pp. 97–108 in *Current Trends in Islamist Ideology*, edited by Hillel Fradkin, Husain Haqqani, and Eric Brown. Washington, DC: Hudson Institute.

Rachels, James. 1999. *The Elements of Moral Philosophy*. 3rd ed. New York: McGraw Hill.

Radcliffe-Brown, Alfred R. 1940. "On Social Structure." *Journal of the Rolyal Anthropological Society of Great Britain and Ireland* 70:1–12.

Ramakrishna, Kumar. 2005. "Delegitimizing Global Jihadi Ideology in Southeast Asia." *Contemporary Southeast Asia* 27(3):343–369.

Rapoport, Anatole. 1953a. "Spread of Information through a Population with Socio-structural Bias I: Assumption of Transitivity." *Bulletin of Mathematical Biophysics* 15(4):523–533.

———. 1953b. "Spread of Information through a Population with Socio-structural Bias II: Various Models with Partial Transitivity." *Bulletin of Mathematical Biophysics* 15(4):535–546.

Rapoport, Anatole, and William J. Horvath. 1961. "A Study of a Large Sociogram." *Behavioral Science* 6:279–291.

Rawls, John. 1971. *A Theory of Justice*. Cambridge, MA: Belknap Press of Harvard University Press.

Reed, Brian. 2007. "A Social Network Approach to Understanding an Insurgency." *Parameters* 38:19–30.

Ressler, Steve. 2006. "Social Network Analysis as an Approach to Combat Terrorism: Past, Present, and Future Research." *Homeland Security Affairs* 2(2). Retrieved from http://www.hsaj.org/?article=2.2.8.

Richards, William D., and Andrew J. Seary. 2009. *MultiNet for Windows*. Burnaby, Canada: Simon Fraser University.

Richardson, David C., and Jane S. Richardson. 1992. "The Kinemage: A Tool for Scientific Communication." *Protein Science* 1(1):3–9.

Roberts, John M., Jr. 2000. "Correspondence Analysis of Two-Mode Network Data." *Social Networks* 22:65–72.

Roberts, Nancy, and Sean F. Everton. 2011. "Strategies for Combating Dark Networks." *Journal of Social Structure* 12(2). Retrieved from http://www.cmu.edu/joss/content/articles/volume12//RobertsEverton.pdf.

Roberts, S. W. 1959. "Control Chart Tests Based on Geometric Moving Averages." *Technometrics* 1(3):239–250.

Rodriguez, José A. 2005. "The March 11th Terrorist Network: In Its Weakness Lies Its Strength." *EPP-LEA Working Papers*. Retrieved from http://citeseerx.ist.psu.edu/viewdoc/summary?doi=10.1.1.98.4408.

Roethlisberger, Fritz J., and William J. Dickson. 1939. *Management and the Worker*. Cambridge, MA: Harvard University Press.

Ronfeldt, David, and John Arquilla. 2001. "What Next for Networks and Netwars?" Pp. 311–61 in *Networks and Netwars*, edited by John Arquilla and David Ronfeldt. Santa Monica, CA: RAND.

Rubin, Alissa J. 2011. "Few Taliban Leaders Take Afghan Offer to Switch Sides." *The New York Times*, p. A1.

Sade, Donald Stone. 1989. "Sociometrics of MacacaMulatta III: N-path Centrality in Grooming Networks." *Social Networks* 11(3):273–292.

Safford, Frank, and Marco Palacios. 2002. *Colombia: Fragmented Land, Divided Society*. New York: Oxford University Press.

Sageman, Marc. 2003. "Global Salafi Jihad: Statement to the National Commission on Terrorist Attacks upon the United States." National Commission on Terrorist Attacks upon the United States. Accessed: http://govinfo.library.unt.edu/911/hearings/hearing3/witness_sageman.htm

———. 2004. *Understanding Terror Networks*. Philadelphia: University of Pennsylvania Press.

———. 2008. *Leaderless Jihad: Terror Networks in the Twenty-First Century*. Philadelphia: University of Pennsylvania Press.

Saltzman, Ann L. 2000. "The Role of the Obedience Experiments in Holocaust Studies: The Case for Renewed Visibility." Pp. 125–44 in *Obedience to Authority: Current Perspectives on the Milgram Paradigm*, edited by Thomas Blass. Mahwah, NJ: Lawrence Erlbaum Associates, Publishers.

Sampson, Samuel F. 1968. "A Novitiate in a Period of Change: An Experimental and Case Study of Relationships." Unpublished Doctoral Thesis, Sociology, Cornell University.

Sandel, Michael J. 1982. *Liberalism and the Limits of Justice*. New York: Cambridge University Press.

———. 1996. *Democracy's Discontent*. 2nd ed. Cambridge, MA: Belknap Press of Harvard University Press.

———. 1998. *Liberalism and the Limits of Justice*. 2nd ed. New York: Cambridge University Press.

———. 2005. *Public Philosophy: Essays on Morality in Politics*. Cambridge, MA: Harvard University Press.

———. 2009. *Justice: What's the Right Thing to Do?* New York: Farrar, Straus and Giroux.

Saxenian, AnnaLee. 1994. *Regional Advantage: Culture and Competition in Silicon Valley and Route 128*. Cambridge, MA: Harvard University Press.

———. 1996. "Inside-Out: Regional Networks and Industrial Adaptation in Silicon Valley and Route 128." *Cityscape: A Journal of Policy Development and Research* 2(2):41–60.

Schmitt, Eric, and Jane Perlez. 2009. "Strikes Worsen Qaeda Threat, Pakistan Says." *The New York Times*. Retrieved from http://www.nytimes.com/2009/02/25/world/asia/25drones.html?scp=1&sq=Schmitt%20and%20Perlez,%202009&st=cse.

Scott, John. 2000. *Social Network Analysis: A Handbook*. 2nd ed. Thousand Oaks, CA: SAGE Publications.

———. 2011. "Social Physics and Social Networks." Pp. 55–66 in *The SAGE Handbook of Social Network Analysis*, edited by John Scott and Peter J. Carrington. Los Angeles and London: SAGE Publications.

Scott, John, and Peter J. Carrington (Eds.). 2011. *The SAGE Handbook of Social Network Analysis*. Los Angeles and London: SAGE Publications.

Shewhart, Walter A. 1927. "Quality Control." *Bell Systems Technical Journal* 6(4):722–735.

Simmel, Georg. 1906. "The Sociology of Secrecy and of Secret Societies." *American Journal of Sociology* 11:441–498.

———. 1950a. "The Isolated Individual and the Dyad." Pp. 118–144 in *The Sociology of Georg Simmel*, edited by Kurt H. Wolf. New York: Free Press.

———. 1950b. "The Secret Society." Pp. 345–76 in *The Sociology of Georg Simmel*, edited by Kurt H. Wolf. New York: Free Press.

———. 1950c. "The Triad." Pp. 145–169 in *The Sociology of Georg Simmel*, edited by Kurt H. Wolf. New York: Free Press.

———. [1908, 1922] 1955. *Conflict & the Web of Group-Affiliations*. Translated by Kurt H. Wolff and Reinhard Bendix. New York: Free Press.

———. [1908] 1955. *Conflict & the Web of Group-Affiliations*. Translated by Kurt H. Wolff and Reinhard Bendix. New York: Free Press.

———. [1908] 1971. *On Individuality and Social Forms*. Translated by Donald Levine. Chicago: University of Chicago Press.

Smith, Christian S. 1996. *Resisting Reagan: The U.S. Central America Peace Movement*. Chicago: University of Chicago Press.

———. 2003. *Moral, Believing Animals: Human Personhood and Culture*. New York and Oxford: Oxford University Press.

———. 2010. *What Is a Person? Rethinking Humanity, Social Life, and the Moral Good from the Person Up*. Chicago and London: University of Chicago Press.

Smith, David A., and Douglas R. White. 1992. "Structure and Dynamics of the Global Economy: Network Analysis of International-Trade 1965–1980." *Social Forces* 70(4):857–893.

Snijders, Tom A. B. 1981. "The Degree Variance: An Index of Graph Heterogeneity." *Social Networks* 3:163–174.

———. 2001. "The Statistical Evaluation of Social Network Dynamics." *Sociological Methodology* 31(1):361–395.

———. 2005. "Models for Longitudinal Network Data." Pp. 215–247 in *Models and Methods in Social Network Analysis*, edited by Peter J. Carrington, John Scott, and Stanley Wasserman. New York: Cambridge University Press.

Snijders, Tom A. B., Gerhard G. van de Bunt, and Christian Steglich. 2010. "Introduction to Stochastic Actor-Based Models for Network Dynamics." *Social Networks* 32(1):44–60.

Snow, David A., and Cynthia L. Phillips. 1980. "The Lofland-Stark Conversion Model: A Critical Assessment." *Social Problems* 27:430–447.

Snow, David A., Louis A. Zurcher, and Sheldon Ekland-Olson. 1980. "Social Networks and Social Movements: A Microstructural Approach to Differential Recruitment." *American Sociological Review* 45:787–801.

Sparrow, Malcom K. 1991. "The Application of Network Analysis to Criminal Intelligence: An Assessment of the Prospects." *Social Networks* 13:251–274.

Starbird, Michael. 2006. *Meaning from Data: Statistics Made Clear*. Chantilly, VA: The Teaching Company.

Stark, Rodney. 1987. "How New Religions Succeed: A Theoretical Model." Pp. 11–29 in *The Future of New Religious Movements*, edited by David G. Bromley and Phillip E. Hammond. Macon, GA: Mercer University Press.

———. 1991. "Epidemics, Networks, and the Rise of Christianity." *Semeia* 56:159–175.

———. 1996a. *The Rise of Christianity: A Sociologist Reconsiders History*. Princeton, NJ: Princeton University Press.

———. 1996b. "Why Religious Movements Succeed or Fail: A Revised General Model." *Journal of Contemporary Religion* 11:133–146.

———. 2005. *The Rise of Mormonism*. Edited by Reid L. Nielson. New York: Columbia University Press.

———. 2007. *Sociology*. 10th ed. Belmont, CA: Wadsworth Publishing Company.

Stark, Rodney, and William Sims Bainbridge. 1980. "Networks of Faith: Interpersonal Bonds and Recruitment to Cults and Sects." *American Journal of Sociology* 85(6):1376–1395.

Stark, Rodney, and Roger Finke. 2000. "Catholic Religious Vocations: Decline and Revival." *Review of Religious Research* 42(2):125–145.

Steglich, Christian, Tom A. B. Snijders, and Michael Pearson. 2010. "Dynamic Networks and Behavior: Separating Selection from Influence." *Sociological Methodology* 40:329–393.

Steiny, Donald. 2007. "H. White, Identity and Control (2nd ed.), Cambridge University Press, Cambridge (2008)." *Social Networks* 29(4):609–616.

Stephenson, Karen, and Marvin Zelen. 1989. "Rethinking Centrality: Methods and Examples." *Social Networks* 11(1):1–37.

Strang, David, and Nancy Brandon Tuma. 1993. "Spatial and Temporal Heterogeneity in Diffusion." *American Journal of Sociology* 99(3):614–639.

Sunstein, Cass R. 2003. *Why Societies Need Dissent*. Cambridge, MA: Harvard University Press.

———. 2009. *Going to Extremes: How Like Minds Unite and Divide*. New York and Oxford: Oxford University Press.

Taylor, Charles. 1989. *Sources of the Self: The Making of the Modern Identity*. Cambridge, MA: Harvard University Press.

———. 1998. "Living with Difference." Pp. 212–226 in *Debating Democracy's Discontent*, edited by Anita Allen and Milton C. Regan, Jr. Oxford and New York: Oxford University Press.

Taylor, Michael. 1969. "Influence Structures." *Sociometry* 32(4):490–502.

Temple-Raston, Dina. 2010. "Rancor over Mosque Could Fuel Islamic Extremists." *National Public Radio*. Retrieved from http://www.npr.org/templates/story/story.php?storyId=129387963.

Tilly, Charles. 2004. "Trust and Rule." *Theory and Society* 33:1–30.

———. 2005. *Trust and Rule*. Cambridge and New York: Cambridge University Press.

Titmuss, Richard. 1971. *The Gift Relationship*. New York: Vintage.

Tomaszewski, Irene, and Tecia Webowski. 1999. *Żegota: The Council for Aid to Jews in Occupied Poland, 1942–45*. Rev. ed. Montreal, Canada: Price-Patterson, Ltd.

Travers, Jeffrey, and Stanley Milgram. 1969. "An Experimental Study of the Small World Problem." *Sociometry* 32(4):425–443.

Tsvetovat, Maksim, and Kathleen M. Carley. 2005. "Structural Knowledge and Success of Anti-Terrorist Activity: The Downside of Structural Equivalence." *Journal of Social Structure* 6(2). Retrieved from http://www.cmu.edu/joss/content/articles/volume6/TsvetovatCarley/index.html.

Tucker, David. 2008. "Terrorism, Networks and Strategy: Why the Conventional Wisdom Is Wrong." *Homeland Security Affairs* 4(2):1–18. Retrieved from www.hsaj.org.

———. 2010. "Jihad Dramatically Transformed? Sageman on Jihad and the Internet." *Homeland Security Affairs* 6(1). Retrieved from http://www.hsaj.org/?article=6.1.3.

Turner, Jonathan H. 2006. *Sociology*. Upper Saddle River, NJ: Pearson Prentice Hall.

U.S. Army. 2007. *U.S. Army/Marine Corps Counterinsurgency Field Manual (FM 3-24)*. Old Saybrook, CT: Konecky & Konecky.

U.S. Director of Operations. 2006. "Information Operations: Joint Publication 3–13." Retrieved from http://www.dtic.mil/doctrine/jel/new_pubs/jp3_13.pdf.

U.S. Special Operations Command. 2003. "Doctrine for Joint Psychological Operations: Joint Publication 3–53." Retrieved from http://www.dtic.mil/doctrine/jel/new_pubs/jp3_53.pdf.

Uzzi, Brian. 1996. "The Sources and Consequences of Embeddedness for the Economic Performance of Organizations: The Network Effect." *American Sociological Review* 61(4):674–698.

———. 2008. "A Social Network's Changing Statistical Properties and the Quality of Human Innovation." *Journal of Physics A: Mathematical and Theoretical* 41:1–12.

Uzzi, Brian, and Jarrett Spiro. 2005. "Collaboration and Creativity: The Small World Problem." *American Journal of Sociology* 111(2):447–504.

van der Huist, Renée C. 2011. "Terrorist Networks: The Threat of Connectivity." Pp. 256–270 in *The SAGE Handbook of Social Network Analysis*, edited by John Scott and Peter J. Carrington. Los Angeles and London: SAGE Publications.

van Meter, Karl M. 2001. "Terrorists/Liberators: Researching and Dealing with Adversary Social Networks." *Connections* (3):66–78.

Wallis, Jim 2011. "How Should We Respond to the Death of Osama bin Laden?" *God's Politics*. Retrieved from http://blog.sojo.net/blogs/2011/05/02/how-should-we-respond-death-osama-bin-laden 2011.

Walzer, Michael. 1983. *Spheres of Justice: A Defense of Pluralism and Equality*. New York: Basic Books.

———. 2004. *Arguing about War*. New Haven and London: Yale University Press.

———. 2006. *Just and Unjust Wars: A Moral Argument with Historical Illustrations*. 4th ed. New York: Basic Books.

———. 2009. *Thinking Politically: Essays in Political Theory*. New Haven and London: Yale University Press.

Waring, Elin. 2002. "Conceptualizing Co-offending: A Network Form of Organization." In *Crime and Social Organization: Advances in Criminological Theory*, edited by E. Waring and D. Weisburd. Rutgers, NJ: Transaction Publishers.

Warner, W. Lloyd, and Paul S. Lunt. 1941. *The Social Life of a Modern Community*. New Haven, CT: Yale University Press.

Wasserman, Stanley, and Katherine Faust. 1994. *Social Network Analysis: Methods and Applications*. Cambridge, UK: Cambridge University Press.

Watts, Duncan J. 1999a. "Networks, Dynamics, and the Small-World Phenomenon." *American Journal of Sociology* 105(2):493–527.

———. 1999b. *Small Worlds: The Dynamics of Networks between Order and Randomness*. Princeton, NJ: Princeton University Press.

———. 2003. *Six Degrees: The Science of a Connected Age*. New York: W. W. Norton & Company.

Watts, Duncan J., Peter Sheridan Dodds, and M. E. Newman. 2003. "Identity and Search in Social Networks." *Science* 296:1302–1304.

Watts, Duncan J., and Steven H. Strogatz. 1998. "Collective Dynamics of 'Small World' Networks." *Nature* 393:409–410.

Weeks, Margaret R., Scott Clair, Stephen P. Borgatti, Kim Radda, and Jean J. Schensul. 2002. "Social Networks of Drug Users in High-Risk Sites: Finding the Connections." *AIDS and Behavior* 6(2):193–206.

Weller, Susan C., and A. Kimball Romney. 1990. *Metric Scaling: Correspondence Analysis*. Newbury Park, CA: SAGE Publications.

Wendt, Eric P. 2005. "Strategic Counterinsurgency Modeling." *Special Warfare* September:1–13.

White, Douglas R. 1985. "REGE: A Regular Graph Equivalence Algorithm for Computing Role Distances Prior to Block Modelling." Unpublished paper. University of California, Irvine.

White, Douglas R., and Karl P. Reitz. 1983. "Graph and Semigroup Homomorphisms on Networks of Relations." *Social Networks* 5:193–235.

White, Harrison C. 1992. *Identity and Control: A Structural Theory of Social Action*. Princeton, NJ: Princeton University Press.

———. 2008. *Identity and Control: How Social Formations Emerge*. 2nd ed. Princeton, NJ: Princeton University Press.

White, Harrison C., Scott A. Boorman, and Ronald L. Breiger. 1976. "Social Structure from Multiple Networks I: Blockmodels of Roles and Positions." *American Journal of Sociology* 81:730–780.

Wikipedia. 2007. "Social Structure." Retrieved from http://en.wikipedia.org/wiki/Social_structure.

Wiktorowicz, Quintan. 2004. "Introduction: Islamic Activism and Social Movement Theory." Pp. 1–33 in *Islamic Activism: A Social Movement Theory Approach*, edited by Quintan Wiktorowicz. Bloomington: Indiana University Press.

Wilson, Chris. 2010. "Searching for Saddam: A Five-Part Series on How the U.S. Military Used Social Networking to Capture the Iraqi Dictator." *Slate*. Retrieved from http://www.slate.com/id/2245228/.

Wilson, Gregory. 2006. "Anatomy of a Successful COIN Operation: OEF-Philippines and the Indirect Approach." *Military Review* (November–December):2–12. Retrieved from http://usacac.army.mil/CAC2/Military Review/Archives/English/MilitaryReview_2008CRII0831_art009.pdf.

Wolfe, Alvin W. 1978. "The Rise of Network Thinking in Anthropology." *Social Networks* 1:53–64.

Wolterstorff, Nicholas. 2010. "Duties and Rights: Looking for Help in Understanding Justice." *Books and Culture: A Christian Review* 16(5):25–27.

Xu, Jie, Daning Hu, Hsinchun Chen. 2009. "The Dynamics of Terrorist Networks: Understanding the Survival Mechanisms of Global Salafi Jihad." *Journal of Homland Security and Emergency Management* 6:1–33.

Yasin, Nur Azlin. 2010. "Counter Ideology: Battle for Hearts and Minds in Indonesia." *RSIS Commentaries* 173:1–2. Retrieved from http://www.rsis.edu .sg/publications/Perspective/RSIS1732010.pdf.

Yoder, John Howard. 1977. *The Original Revolution: Essays in Christian Pacifism*. Scottdale, PA: Herald Press.

———. 1996. *When War Is Unjust: Being Honest in Just-War Thinking*. Maryknoll, NY: Orbis Books.

———. 2009. *Christian Attitudes to War, Peace, and Revolution*. Grand Rapids, MI: Brazos Press.

Zelizer, Viviana A. 1978. "Human Values and the Market: The Case of Life Insurance and Death in 19th-Century America." *American Journal of Sociology* 84:591–610.

Ziliak, Stephen T., and Deirdre N. McCloskey. 2008. *The Cult of Statistical Significance*. Ann Arbor: University of Michigan Press.

Zimbardo, Philip G. 1972. "Pathology of Imprisonment." *Society* 9:4–6.

———. 1973. "On the Ethics of Intervention in Human Psychological Research." *Cognition* 2:243–256.

Zimbardo, Philip G., Christina Maslasch, and Craig Haney. 2000. "Reflections on the Stanford Prison Experiment: Genesis, Transformations, Consequences." Pp. 193–237 in *Obedience to Authority: Current Perspectives on the Milgram Paradigm*, edited by Thomas Blass. Mahwah, NJ: Lawrence Erlbaum Associates.

Index

actor, 8
  definition, 397
adjacency matrix, 59, 83, 188, 190, 225, 306, 407
affiliation matrix (or network), 86, 90, 94, 103, 143
affiliation network. *See* two-mode network
  definition, 397
affiliations, xxviii, 14, 42, 94, 105, 277, 320, 385. *See* two-mode network
aggregating social networks
  ORA, 122–123
  Pajek, 117
  UCINET, 112–113
Al Qaeda, xxvi, xxviii, 28, 135, 320, 370, 372, 380
Aquinas, 378
arc, 9, 115, 186, 211, 321, 322
  definition, 397
Aristotelianism, 372, 376–377
Aristotle, 21, 377
Arquilla, J., 37
articulation point, 265. *See* cutpoint
Asch, S., 15
attribute, 14
  definition, 397
Augustine, 378
automorphic equivalence. *See* blockmodels
  definition, 397
average degree, 146
  definition, 397
average distance, 12, 137
  definition, 397
Avrakotos, G., 367
Ayman al-Zawahiri, 17

Bainbridge, W.
  Mormons, 25–26
Baker, W., xxv, xxvi
Bakker, R., 330
Barabási, A.-L., 4, 28
Barnes, J., 3
Batagelj, V., xxxiii, 315
  Pajek, 62–69
Beckstrom, R., xxix, 135
Bentham, J., 373
betweenness centrality. *See* centrality
  definition, 397
bi-component
  definition, 397
bi-component analysis, 253, 264–265
bipartite graph, 414
blockmodels, 13–14
  automorphic equivalence, 289–292
  blockmodeling, 286, 296
  CONCOR, 300–306, 311, 313
  definition, 398
  density threshold, 302
  Euclidean distance, 295–299
  image matrix, 299
  image matrix graph, 299
  isomorphic equivalence, 292
  one-block, 302
  optimization, 306–310
  partition, 291, 293, 296
  partition diagram, 301
  permutation, 291, 310
  regular equivalence, 292–294
  structurally equivalence, 287–289
  structurally equivalent actors, 286

blockmodels (*cont.*)
  Wasserman and Faust network, 288, 289, 293
  Wasserman and Faust structural equivalence network, 295
  zero-block, 302
Boko Haram, 370, 372
Bonacich, P., 206, 208
bootstrapping, 348
Borgatti, S., 4
  average reciprocal distance, 219–220
  centrality measures, development of, 206
  key player, 169, 272–277
  NetDraw, 56–62
  UCINET, 50–55
  visualization of two-mode networks, 414
Bott, E., 3
boundary spanner, 265. *See* cutpoint
boundary specification, xxviii, 39, 76, 77–80
  definitional focus, 78–79
  nominalist, 77–78
  realist, 77
Brafman, O., xxix, 135
Brashears, M., 82
Breiger, R., xxxvi, 3, 290
bridge, 13, 138, 176, 253, 254, 265, 268, 282, 283, 284, 286, 365
  definition, 398
brokerage roles, 278
  definition, 398
brokers, xxviii, xxxi, 13, 176, 198, 205, 253, 280, 286, 365
Burt, R., 283
  structural holes, 253, 254–255

Carley, K.
  ORA, 69
  social network change detection, 28, 320
centrality
  average reciprocal distance, 209, 219–220
  betweenness centrality, 13, 207, 210, 222–225
  betweenness-like measures, 210
  clique count, 238
  closeness centrality, 12, 207, 216–221
  closeness-like measures, 209–210
  definition, 398
  degree centrality, 12, 207, 211–215

degree-like measures, 208–209
  eigenvector centrality, 13, 207, 208
  farness centrality, 216
  flow betweenness centrality, 210
  fragmentation centrality, 210
  geospatially weighted centrality, 337–341
  hubs and authorities, 208, 242, 245
  indegree centrality, 241–242, 244
  influence centrality, 208
  information centrality, 209
  input domain, 245–249
  outdegree centrality, 241
  power (beta) centrality, 208
  proximal betweenness centrality, 210
  proximity prestige, 245–249
  reach (k-path) centrality, 209
  reach centrality, 243
centralization, 11, 152
  definition, 398
Chase, I., 3
clique, 171, 238
  count, 238
  definition, 398
closeness centrality. *See* centrality
  definition, 398
cluster
  Pajek, 63
cluster(s), 12, 138, 140–141, 170, 182, 195–197, 204, 254, 341
clustering coefficient, 148, 149
  definition, 398
cohesive subgroups, 12, 166, 170, 179, 182, 204, 253, 365
collapsing social networks
  NetDraw, 125–126
  ORA, 130–132
  Pajek, 128
combining social networks
  UCINET, 111–113
complete networks, 82
  definition, 398
components
  definition, 398
  strong, 171
  weak, 171
Comte, A., 3
constraint. *See* structural holes
  definition, 398
consumption ethics, 369
conversion, 24–26

coordinator, 278
definition, 399
CORE Lab, xxxv, xxxvi, 371, 385
correlation, 28, 191, 257, 258, 264, 300
of attributes, 228, 230, 236
coefficient, 59, 300, 412
counterinsurgency (COIN), 33, 381
Army and Marine manual, 136, 381
Crile, G.
Charlie Wilson's War, 367
Cunningham, D., xxxvi, 385
cutpoint, 264
definition, 399
cut-vertex, 265. *See* cutpoint

dark network
definition, xxv, 399
data collection, 40
cognitive social structures, 90
diaries, 90
direct observation, 89
experiments, 90
interviews, 89
Lighthouse, xxvii
questionnaires, 87–89
small world research, 90
written records, 90
decentralized networks, xxvi, xxix, 6, 135,
137, 141, 142, 143, 330
Degenne, A., xxxiii
degree centrality. *See* centrality
definition, 399
de Nooy, W., xxxiii
Pajek, 65–69
density, 11, 146
definition, 399
diameter, 12, 137
definition, 399
diffusion, 18, 19, 43, 169, 205, 274, 276,
375
DiMaggio, P., 18
directed network (graph), 171, 172, 184,
186, 208, 233, 235, 239, 243, 278,
290. *See* one-mode networks,
asymmetric
definition, 399
directed tie. *See* arc
definition, 399
Doreian, P., 315
dual networks. *See* two-mode network
Durkheim, E., 3
dyad, 3, 176
definition, 399

dyadic constraint network, 260

Easley, D., xxxiii
edge, 9, 115, 186, 211, 321, 322
definition, 400
edge betweenness
bridges and network flow, 282
definition, 400
Girvan-Newman algorithm, 195
ego networks, 81–82, 254
eigenvector centrality. *See* centrality
definition, 400
emergence, 22–23
Emirbayer, M., 29, 30
equivalence. *See* blockmodels
Erickson, B., 3
secret societies, xxv, xxvi
Everett, M., 4
centrality measures, development of, 206
UCINET, 50–55
visualization of two-mode networks,
414
exchange theory, 4, 206
extracting subnetworks
ORA, 129–130
Pajek, 117, 126–127
UCINET, 122–124

faction
definition, 400
factions, 188–190
Pajek, 310
FARC, 30, 167, 370, 372, 380
Faulkner, R., xxv, xxvi
Faust, K., xxxiii, 27
Ferligoj, A., 315
first-order and second-order effects, 38
Fischer, C., 82
Forsé, M., xxxiii
fragmentation, 12, 137
definition, 400
Freeman, L., 4
betweenness centrality, 222–225
centrality measures, classification of,
207
centrality measures, development of,
206
closeness centrality, 216–219
degree centrality, 211–215
edge betweenness, 283
Mage, 404
UCINET, 49–55
visualization algorithms, 60

Friedkin, N., 166, 206
Friedman, M., 375
Fruchterman Reingold, 67
    definition, 400

gatekeeper, 278
    definition, 400
generalized blockmodeling, 315
geodesic, 10, 12, 137, 144, 195, 209, 210,
    216, 217, 219, 222, 294, 398, 399,
    414, 415
    definition, 400
Georgianna, S., 139
global salafi jihad, xxvi, 11, 17, 90, 136,
    150, 167, 320, 366
Gonzalez, R.
    brokerage roles, 278
Goodwin, J., 29, 30
Gould, R., 30
    brokerage roles, 278
Granovetter, M., 3
    rational action, 30
    social network theory, 14
    strong ties, benefits, 138
    weak ties, strength of, 8, 18–21, 138,
        253, 254
graph
    definition, 400
graph theory, 4, 58, 289, 291, 405

Hanneman, R., 54
Hayek, F., 375
Heider, F., 3
hierarchical clustering, 291, 307
hierarchy, xxvi, 70, 136, 142, 153,
    165
    Pajek, 63, 65, 267, 268
Holland, P., 21
Horvath, W. J., 20
hubs and authorities
    definition, 400
Huisman, M., 49
human subjects research, 369
    social network analysis, 369
Humphreys, L., 369
hypernetworks. *See* two-mode network
hypothesis testing, 38

image matrix. *See* blockmodels
indegree centrality. *See* centrality
    definition, 401
information operations, 35

input domain. *See* centrality
    definition, 401
INSNA (International Network for Social
    Network Analysis), 4, 370
    SOCNET listserve, 371
institution building, 34
interdependence of actors, 15–18
isomorphic graphs, 289
itinerant broker/consultant, 278
    definition, 401

Jemaah Islamiyah, xxx, 34
Just War Tradition, 378–382,
    417–420
    jus ad bellum, 378, 417–418
    jus in bello, 378, 418–419
    jus post bellum, 378, 419–420

Kadushin, C., 371, 380
Kamada-Kawai, 67
    definition, 401
Kant, I., 374
Kantian Liberalism, 372, 374–375
k-core, 182–183
key player, 253, 271–277
    definition, 401
kinetic strategies, 33–34
Kleinberg, J., xxxiii
Knoke, D., xxxiii, 30
Krackhardt, D., 53, 240
Krebs, V., xxvi, 111

law of group polarization, 11
Leinhardt, S., 21
Lewin, K., 3
liaison, 278
    definition, 401
Libertarianism, 372, 375–376
    rational choice, 375
    utilitarian calculus, 375
Lighthouse, xxvii
Lofland, J., 25
longitudinal networks
    definition, 401
    generating, 321–326
    measures over time, 326–329
    social network change detection,
        329–332
Longley, C., xxvii
loop
    definition, 401
Los Zetas, 370, 372, 380

Machiela, C., xxvii
MacIntyre, A., 377
Mage, 409–411
Marx, K., 3
matrix
 for recording social network data, 40
maximal regular equivalence. *See*
 blockmodels, regular equivalence
Mayhew, B., 29
Mayo, E., 3
McAdam, D.
 Freedom Summer, 30
McCulloh, I.
 social network change detection, 28,
 320
McPherson, M., 82
membership networks. *See* two-mode
 network
meta-networks, 69
Meyer, J., 18
Milgram, S.
 Obedience to Authority, 16–17, 369
 small world problem, 90, 140
Mill, J. S., 373, 375
Milward, B., xxv, 330
Mitchell, C., 3
Moody, J., xxxvi
Moonies, 25
Moreno, J., 3, 206
Mormons, 25
Mrvar, A., xxxiii
 Pajek, 62–69
multidimensional scaling, 58, 404
 asymmetric networks, 411–414
 definition, 401
 metric, 405–406
 nonmetric, 59
 two-mode networks, 414
multirelational data, 108
 ORA, 121
 Pajek, 115–117
 UCINET, NetDraw, 108–115

Nadel, S., 3
neighbor, 211, 213, 225, 247, 254
neighborhoods, 294
network
 use of term, 6
network (matrix) transpose, 103
network size, 12, 137
 definition, 401
network topography, 10–12

definition, 403
network visualization, 42
Newman groups, 282
 Clauset, Newman, and Moore, 195–196
 definition, 401
 Girvan-Newman, 195
Newman, M., 194, 401
nonkinetic strategies, 34–37
Nozick, R., 375

one-mode network
 asymmetric, 84–86
 definition, 402
 symmetric, 83–84
Osama bin Laden, 17
 assasination of, 381

p* models (exponential random graph
 models – ERGMs), 360
Pajek project file, 64, 65
parsing social networks
 UCINET, 114–115
partition
 definition, 402
 Key Player, 273, 274
 NetDraw, 198
 Newman groups, 195, 196
 ORA, 129, 130, 201
 Pajek, 62, 64, 65, 69, 128, 232, 233,
 322
 UCINET, 123, 124
path, 10, 171
 definition, 402
path distance, 10
 definition, 402
Pedahzur, A.
 network topography, 136
 suicide attack networks, xxvi
Perliger, A.
 network topography, 136
 suicide attack networks, xxvi
permutation
 Pajek, 63, 64, 65
permutation testing, 348–349
Pescosolido, B., 139
Popkin, S., 36
position. *See* blockmodels
positional analysis. *See* blockmodels
 definition, 402
positive and negative ties
 Pajek, 118–121
Prell, C., xxxiii

prestige, 240
principal components, 60
professional ethics, 369
proximity prestige. *See* centrality
    definition, 402
psychological operations, 35

quadratic assignment procedure (QAP),
    348

R^2 (coefficient of determination), 301, 305,
    306, 347, 350, 355, 357, 359
Raab, J., xxv, xxxvi, 330
Radcliffe-Brown, A., 3
random sample, 348
Rapid Reaction Technology Office
    (RRTO), xxxv
Rapoport, A., 20
Rawls, J., 374
recruitment. *See* conversion
regression
    attribute data, 349–352, 356–357
    MRQAP, 354
    network data, 352–356, 358–359
regular equivalence. *See* blockmodels
    definition, 402
rehabilitation and reintegration, 35–37
relation, 40. *See* ties
relational analysis, 13
    definition, 402
relation name, 121
relation numbers, 117
representative, 278
    definition, 402
restricted input domain. *See* centrality,
    input domain
Riddle, M., 54
Roberts, N., xxxvi
Rodriguez, J.
    Madrid bombings, xxvi, 21
role. *See* blockmodels

Sageman, M., 366
    global salafi jihad, 11, 26
    law of group polarization, 167
    leaderless jihad, 135
    recruitment, 26, 150
    scale-free network, 28, 366
Sampson, S., 320
Sandel, M., 377
scale-free networks, 28, 320, 366
Schwartz, M., 3

Scott, J., xxxiii
Simmel, G., xxv, 3
    secret societies, xxvi
    triad, 254
singular value decomposition, 60
small world problem, 90, 140
small world quotient, 148
Smith, C., 30, 370, 373, 377
Smith-Lovin, L., 82
Snijders, T., 341
Snow, D.
    recruitment, 26
social movements, 4, 366
social network, 9
    definition, 402
social network analysis, 9
    assumptions, 14–15
    as compared to link analysis, 6–7
    as compared to variable-based analysis,
        7
    confirmatory, 38
    exploratory, 38
    journals, 4
social structure, 21–22
    definition, 402
sociogram, 84, 85
Sparrow, M., xxv
Spencer, H., 3
Spiro, J.
    broadway musicals, 140
spring-embedded algorithms, 60
    definition, 403
standard deviation, 152, 153
Starbird, M., 343
Stark, R., 30
    Moonies, 25
    Mormons, 25–26, 142
    new religious movements, 142
statistical significance, 347
    social network data, 348–349
Strogatz, S.
    clustering coefficient, 151
    small world problem, 140
strong components. *See* components
    definition, 403
structural constructionism, 30
structural determinism, 29
structural equivalence. *See* blockmodels
    definition, 403
structural holes, 254–255
    constraint, 255
    definition, 403

dyadic constraint, 257, 260
dyadic constraint network, 260
dyadic redundancy, 257
proportional strength, 260
structural instrumentalism, 29–30
structural location, 24

targeted killing, 380
Taylor, C., 377
ties, 8–9
    definition, 403
    strength of weak ties, 18–21
    weak, Madrid bombing, 21, 366
Tilly, C., 35
tracking and monitoring, 37
trail, 10
    definition, 403
triads, 3
    definition, 403
    Granovetter's forbidden triad, 19–21
    structural holes, 254
Tucker, D., 142
two-mode network, 86–87
    definition, 403

undirected network, 186
undirected network (graph), 146, 172,
        174, 178, 184, 211, 233, 234, 235,
        239, 268, 278. *See* one-mode
        networks, symmetric
undirected tie. *See* edge
    definition, 403
unpacking stacked networks, 109
U.S. Catholic Bishops, 374
Utilitarianism, 372, 373–374
Uzzi, B.
    broadway musicals, 140
    garment industry, 140

valued network, 59, 70, 92, 106, 112, 117,
        122
    centrality measures, 208
    density, 147
    faction error score, 191
van Duijn, M., 49
variance, 152, 153
vector
    definition, 403
    Pajek, 63, 64, 65, 99, 232, 236
    UCINET, 173
vertex. *See* actor
Vickers, M., 367

walk, 10
    definition, 403
Wallis, J., 380
Walzer, M., 377, 381
Warner, W. L., 3
Wasserman and Faust, xxxiii
Wasserman, S., xxxiii, 27
Watts, D., 5
    clustering coefficient, 151
    longitudinal networks, 320
    small world problem, 90, 140
weak components. *See* components
    defintion, 403
Weber, M., 3
Wellman, B., 4
White, H., 3, 69
    structural constructionism, 30
    structural determinism, 29
Wilson, C., 367

Yang, S., xxxiii

Żegota, xxv
Zimbardo, P., 369

Other Books in the Series (*continued from p. iii*)

16. Robert L. Nelson and William P. Bridges, *Legalizing Gender Inequality: Courts, Markets, and Unequal Pay for Women in America*
17. Robert Freeland, *The Struggle for Control of the Modern Corporation: Organizational Change at General Motors, 1924–1970*
18. Yi-min Lin, *Between Politics and Markets: Firms, Competition, and Institutional Change in Post-Mao China*
19. Nan Lin, *Social Capital: A Theory of Social Structure and Action*
20. Christopher Ansell, *Schism and Solidarity in Social Movements: The Politics of Labor in the French Third Republic*
21. Thomas Gold, Doug Guthrie, and David Wank, eds., *Social Connections in China: Institutions, Culture, and the Changing Nature of Guanxi*
22. Roberto Franzosi, *From Words to Numbers*
23. Sean O'Riain, *Politics of High-Tech Growth*
24. James Lincoln and Michael Gerlach, *Japan's Network Economy*
25. Patrick Doreian, Vladimir Batagelj, and Anuška Ferligoj, *Generalized Blockmodeling*
26. Eiko Ikegami, *Bonds of Civility: Aesthetic Networks and Political Origins of Japanese Culture*
27. Wouter de Nooy, Andrej Mrvar, and Vladimir Batagelj, *Exploratory Social Network Analysis with Pajek*
28. Peter Carrington, John Scott, and Stanley Wasserman, *Models and Methods in Social Network Analysis*
29. Robert C. Feenstra and Gary G. Hamilton, *Emergent Economies, Divergent Paths*
30. Martin Kilduff and David Krackhardt, *Interpersonal Networks in Organizations*
31. Ari Adut, *On Scandal: Moral Disturbances in Society, Politics, and Art*
32. Zeev Maoz, *Networks of Nations: The Evolution, Structure, and Impact of International Networks, 1815–2002*
33. Dean Lusher, Johan Koskinen, and Gary Robins, eds., *Exponential Random Graph Models for Social Networks: Theory, Methods, and Applications*